BURNING
THE
REICHSTAG

BURNING
THE
REICHSTAG

An Investigation into
the Third Reich's
Enduring Mystery

BENJAMIN CARTER HETT

OXFORD
UNIVERSITY PRESS

OXFORD
UNIVERSITY PRESS

Oxford University Press is a department of the University of Oxford.
It furthers the University's objective of excellence in research,
scholarship, and education by publishing worldwide.

Oxford   New York
Auckland   Cape Town   Dar es Salaam   Hong Kong   Karachi
Kuala Lumpur   Madrid   Melbourne   Mexico City   Nairobi
New Delhi   Shanghai   Taipei   Toronto

With offices in
Argentina   Austria   Brazil   Chile   Czech Republic   France   Greece
Guatemala   Hungary   Italy   Japan   Poland   Portugal   Singapore
South Korea   Switzerland   Thailand   Turkey   Ukraine   Vietnam

Oxford is a registered trade mark of Oxford University Press
in the UK and certain other countries.

Published in the United States of America by
Oxford University Press
198 Madison Avenue, New York, NY 10016

Library of Congress Cataloging-in-Publication Data
Hett, Benjamin Carter.
Burning the Reichstag : an investigation into the Third Reich's
enduring mystery / Benjamin Carter Hett.
pages cm
Includes bibliographical references and index.
ISBN 978-0-19-932232-9
1. Reichstagsgebäude (Berlin, Germany)—Fire, 1933.
2. Germany—Politics and government—1933–1945. I. Title.
DD256.5.H378   2014
943.086—dc23   2013008386

1 3 5 7 9 8 6 4 2

Printed in the United States of America
on acid-free paper

To Robert Girvan and Dean McNeill: "Best men."

The history we read, though based on facts, is, strictly speaking, not factual at all, but a series of accepted judgments.
        —Geoffrey Barraclough, *History in a Changing World*

CONTENTS
. . . .

Prologue: Berlin, February 27, 1933   3

1. "Satanic Nose": Rudolf Diels   26

2. "SA + Me": Joseph Goebbels   38

3. "What Just Went on Here Is an Absolute Outrage": Rumors   60

4. "Impossible Things": The Investigations   85

5. Brown and Other Books: The Propaganda Battle   122

6. "Stand Up, van der Lubbe!": The Trial   140

7. "This First Crime of the National Socialists": The Fire
at Nuremberg   181

8. "Persil Letters": The *Gestapists'* Tale   215

9. "The Feared One": Fritz Tobias and His "Clients"   248

10. "Snow from Yesterday": Blackmail and the Institute
for Contemporary History   283

Conclusion: Evidence and Self-Evidence   309

Epilogue: Hannover, July 2008   328

Acknowledgments   335
Abbreviations   339
Notes   343
Archival Sources   395
Index   403

BURNING
THE
REICHSTAG

PROLOGUE

BERLIN, FEBRUARY 27, 1933

THE EVENING OF FEBRUARY 27, 1933, was a cold one in Berlin: six degrees below zero centigrade, with a sharp wind out of the east. There had been snow. The streets and sidewalks were icy.

That night twenty-nine-year-old Chief Constable (Oberwachtmeister) Karl Buwert, who had been posted to watch the west and north sides of the Reichstag building from 8:00 to 10:00, was expecting a quiet shift. The weather would keep most people indoors. There was an election on and the Reichstag was not in session; many deputies were away campaigning, and the work of the building's staff slowed down after 9:00. Between the rounds of the lighting man at 8:45 and the Reichstag mailman at 8:50 or 8:55, and the first inspection of the night watchman at 10:00, no one would be moving about inside the building. For this hour or so the Reichstag would be quiet, and, presumably—apart from the porter at the north entrance—empty.[1]

The Reichstag stood at the political and geographic heart of Berlin, a short block north of the Brandenburg Gate and the end of the famous boulevard Unter den Linden. Designed by architect Paul Wallot, it had opened in 1894. In 1916 wartime political pressures compelled an

3

irritated Emperor Wilhelm II to consent to the addition of the words above the main entrance: "To the German People" (*Dem deutschen Volke*). The bronze letters were crafted by the highly respected firm of S.A. Loevy, founded in 1855. The Loevys were Jewish. Later, in 1938, they would secure a commission for work on Hitler's new Reich Chancellery, but in 1939 their firm would be "aryanized," expropriated and sold at a fire-sale price to a non-Jewish businessman. Some members of the family went into exile. Some survived the Nazis by living underground. Some were deported to the death camps and, in the name of the German people, murdered.[2]

In the years of the Weimar Republic (1919–1933), Germany's post–First World War democratic era, the Reichstag became an increasingly busy and crowded place. The deputies and the Reichstag staff amounted to nearly a thousand people, not counting the parties' employees; perhaps fifteen hundred people might be in the building on any given day. One entered the Reichstag through one of five "portals," although the grand Portal I on the west side of the building, facing the Platz der Republik (square of the republic), was only used for ceremonial occasions. By contrast, the deputies' Portal II on the south side facing the Tiergarten resembled a servants' entrance. The same might be said for Portals III and IV on the east and Portal V on the north side, facing a bend in the river Spree.

The Reichstag's ground floor was taken up by kitchens and cleaning rooms, office space for the stenographers and messengers, and even a gymnasium, baths, and a hairdresser. The heart of the building was the main floor, one level up from the street. It was dominated by a long hall (in German: *Wandelhalle*) which, at nearly 320 feet, ran most of the length of the building's west side. Architect Wallot had added the hall to his plans only at the last minute; officials deemed its marble too expensive, and substituted a cheap replacement. At the north end of the hall was a comfortable reading room for the deputies, stocked with four hundred newspapers and periodicals. (In the northeast tower there was also a library with nearly three hundred thousand volumes.) At the south end of the hall was the Reichstag restaurant. Dubbed "Schulze's Caucus" (Fraktion Schulze) after its first proprietor, the restaurant was never much of a success either with its intended clientele, who complained about the quality of the food and the overly formal ambience, or its proprietors, who from Schulze on complained of low attendance. The reporters had their own separate canteen, and members of the public could visit the restaurant only in the company of a deputy.[3]

From the midpoint of the hall, turning toward the east side of the building and passing the equestrian statue of Emperor Wilhelm I, one came to the heart of the Reichstag, the plenary chamber where the deputies met and deliberated. The plenary chamber was a room of nearly seven thousand square feet, originally designed to provide space for 397 deputies. The deputies' seats were arranged in a half-circle, rising up from the front of the room, where there was a large desk for the president of the Reichstag, the speaker's podium, a desk for the stenographers, and seats for members of the Reich cabinet and of the parliament's upper house, the *Bundesrat*, or Federal Council (in Weimar days changed to the *Reichsrat*, or Reich Council). For the sake of better acoustics the chamber was furnished and paneled exclusively with wood. Its placement in the center of the building, with no windows to the outside world, was deliberate: the deputies were to be insulated from any and all disturbances. Fresh air for the chamber was supposed to come from vents in the iron and glass cupola that rose 246 feet above the chamber. A glass ceiling also let in the cupola's light. However, since the circulating air could only reach down to a height of about fifteen feet, the ventilation never did much for the deputies' health and alertness.[4]

In democratic Weimar the number of deputies in each Reichstag depended on voter turnout, and in time the chamber grew crowded with far more deputies than originally planned—466 after the first Reichstag election of 1920, in later years over 600. The 1919 Weimar constitution mandated elections at least every four years, but especially in the crisis-ridden early 1930s they came more frequently. Deputies were elected from ranked party lists in a strictly proportional system, in which every party's share of the popular vote determined its share of deputies. The constitution stipulated that the deputies be paid one-quarter the salary of a Reich cabinet minister, which, as of 1927, meant a deputy received a base salary of 9,000 Reichsmarks per year along with various allowances—roughly corresponding to $25,000 today. Deputies also enjoyed immunity from prosecution, a considerable advantage in a time when many political extremists had scant regard for the law. Although politics in the Weimar Republic were marked by bitter ideological divisions and often violent instability, relations among Reichstag deputies of widely different parties could be surprisingly collegial. Two parliamentarians

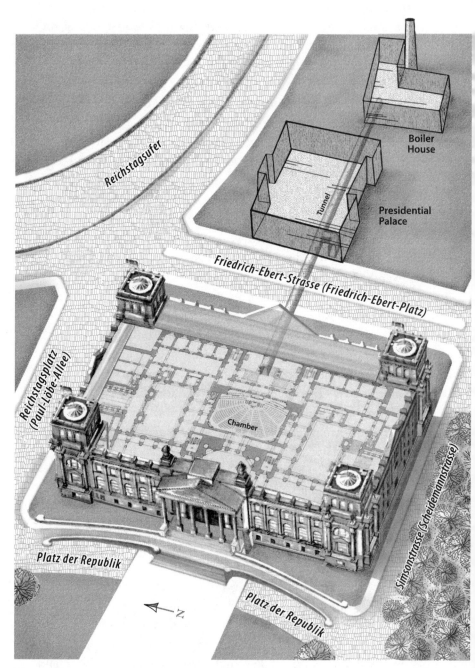

The Reichstag, with the tunnel, Presidential Palace, and boiler house.

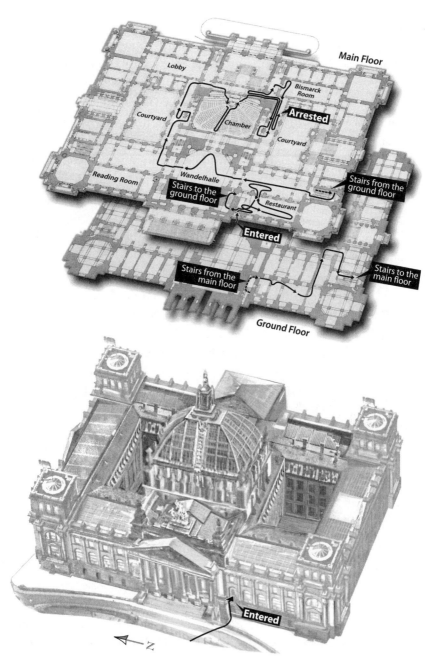

Van der Lubbe's probable path through the building.

with whom we will be concerned in this story—Ernst Oberfohren, who led the caucus of the far-right German National People's Party (DNVP, usually known informally as the German Nationals or simply the Nationalists), and Ernst Torgler, who held the same position with the far-left Communist Party of Germany—were on friendly enough terms to spar while respectfully addressing each other as "Herr Colleague."[5]

What we can know about what happened at the Reichstag on that icy night in February 1933 comes to us through what Chief Constable Buwert and a number of other witnesses remembered. These witnesses, mostly police officers and firefighters, were doing their jobs under sudden, intense pressure. As is often the case during fast-moving and frightening events, the details of timing in their accounts, and of who was where at particular moments, do not all quite fit or match.

At what he recalled as either five or ten minutes past nine, Chief Constable Buwert was standing by the grand steps to Portal I when a "civilian" rushed up to him. "Officer, someone has broken a window pane there!" this civilian exclaimed. "You can see a light there, too," he added.[6]

The "civilian" was probably a twenty-two-year-old theology student named Hans Flöter, who at "9:05 or 9:08"—his recollection—was on his way home from an evening in the State Library a few blocks east on Unter den Linden. As Flöter was crossing the Platz der Republik he heard the sound of breaking glass. He assumed it was merely a careless custodian. A moment later Flöter heard the sound again. He looked up and this time saw a man on a balcony, in the act of breaking a second-floor window. The man, said Flöter, was holding a firebrand. Because of the darkness Flöter could not describe the man at all, other than to note that he was not wearing a hat (though he might have been wearing a cap). Otherwise the whole area around the Reichstag building was empty of people. Flöter went looking for a police officer, found Buwert, and told him excitedly about the break-in. Buwert rushed at once to the spot Flöter had indicated. Flöter, apparently feeling that he had done his duty, continued on his way home.[7]

At almost the same time, twenty-one-year-old Werner Thaler, a typesetter at the Nazi Party paper the *Völkischer Beobachter* (Nationalist observer), was on his way home from work. He had walked along Friedrich-Ebert-Strasse from the Brandenburg Gate to the Reichstag, and crossed the square to the west. It was at that moment, 9:07 or 9:08 he thought, that he too heard the sound of breaking glass. "I saw two men, whom I can't describe, climb in the window that is directly to the right of the main entrance." Later he would become uncertain that there had been two men; perhaps he had seen only one. Like Flöter, Thaler rushed to find a police officer. Like Flöter, he found Buwert.[8]

Buwert and Thaler ran to a spot near the Reichstag's main entrance, underneath the broken window. "We saw that the next window to the right was brightly lit by a fire that was already burning inside the building," said Thaler. Buwert assumed that a door or a curtain inside must be burning. "After about two minutes we both saw the light of two torches in the rooms directly under the broken window," Thaler continued. Thaler thought Buwert seemed stunned, and urged him to shoot at the arsonists. Buwert drew his revolver and fired in the direction of the torches, seemingly without hitting anyone. "After the shot the men must have moved farther inside the building," Thaler recalled later. He also remembered that by this time the first fire engines had arrived, which would make the time about 9:18. Thaler naturally assumed the firefighters could handle the situation, and turned to go home. But as he crossed the Platz der Republik he "turned around one more time and noticed that the cupola of the Reichstag was brightly lit." That could only mean a much larger fire in the plenary chamber at the center of the building. "I ran back to the firemen and told them that the interior of the building was also burning."[9]

Just before Thaler left, probably about 9:17, Buwert saw a uniformed soldier coming toward him. He asked the soldier to go to the police station at the nearby Brandenburg Gate to notify the detachment there of the fire. But Police Lieutenant Emil Lateit, who was in command of the Brandenburg Gate post that night, later testified that it was not this soldier who reported the fire. It was, instead, a young man of about twenty-two, wearing a black coat, a "sport cap," and long sheepskin boots. He delivered his news calmly. This was the first of those puzzling events surrounding the fire which ever since have provided fodder for speculation. In the urgency of the moment Lateit forgot to take down the young man's name. He noted the time, however: it was 9:15. No one has ever been able to determine the young man's identity.[10]

Lateit plunged into action. He took Constables Losigkeit and Graening with him in a police car (later he thought the mysterious young witness had also gone along in the car before disappearing) to the Reichstag. When they reached it, Lateit dictated a note: "9:17. Fire in the Reichstag.

Reinforcements required." Graening rushed the note back to the Brandenburg Gate. Another young police officer, twenty-two-year-old Hermann Poeschel, who like Buwert had been on duty outside the Reichstag, joined Lateit's group.[11]

Lateit and his men now sought to get into the building. They found Portals II and III locked. But the man responsible for the maintenance of the Reichstag, House Inspector Alexander Scranowitz, had heard the sirens and was already at Portal V with a key. These witnesses later had different recollections of exactly how many men were with Lateit by this time, but it was probably Losigkeit, Poeschel, and Scranowitz who followed Lateit into the building through Portal V. It was now 9:20.[12]

They could smell the fires right away. The officers ran from the coat check near the entrance up the stairs to the *Wandelhalle*. Outside the plenary chamber they found some curtains burning, along with the wooden paneling of a storage cupboard for electric cables. Something on the floor was burning as well. Lateit at first took it for a cushion, but it turned out to be a coat.

What these men saw of the fire in the plenary chamber was crucial to the story. At 9:21 or 9:22 Lateit was the first to get a good look at it. He testified later that he saw flames about ten feet wide and much taller coming from the president's desk. There were other flames behind the desk, reaching higher, and forming the pattern of a "burning organ, with the individual flames reaching up like pipes." These flames may have come from the curtains behind the president's desk, although Lateit wasn't certain. He did not notice any other fires in the chamber (although at trial he admitted that he might have seen the drapes on the wall of the stenographers' enclosure burning), nor did he detect any smoke. Poeschel, looking into the chamber from behind Lateit, also described a ten-foot-wide column of fire, but could not say what had been burning. Constable Losigkeit, on the other hand, said he saw flames *behind* but not *on* the president's desk, and others on the stenographers' desk, which stood in a separate enclosure well below. When pressed on the point, though, he admitted that perhaps he might have missed other flames because he had only glanced into the chamber for an instant. Lateit had some experience with major fires. He thought the plenary chamber could still be saved. "Arson! Pistols out!" he ordered. The officers went looking for a culprit.[13]

Perhaps a minute after Lateit, House Inspector Scranowitz looked in the chamber and saw something very different. At what he estimated had been 9:22 or 9:22:30, Scranowitz also saw a fire on the president's desk, and like Lateit, he saw the three curtains behind it burning. But he also claimed that there were flames coming from the cabinet and Reich Council benches, flames in the third and perhaps the second row of the deputies' seats, the speaker's podium, the "table of the house," and "cypress-shaped" flames on the curtains of the stenographers' enclosure. Altogether he thought he saw twenty to twenty-five fires burning in the rows of seats, each one small and producing "cozy, flickering flames."[14]

Constable Poeschel testified that he had looked into the chamber at the same moment as Scranowitz, but saw only the fire on the president's desk. Poeschel's observations squared with Lateit's and, essentially, with Losigkeit's. On the other hand Poeschel was even more uncertain than Losigkeit about what he had seen: "I certainly saw bright flames," he told the magistrate shortly after the fire. "Where the flames might have been, I can't say." Scranowitz claimed with some justice that he knew his building and could read in an instant where exactly the fires were burning.[15]

By this time the fire engines had arrived. The firefighters still believed that they were there to combat a fire in the Reichstag restaurant; when they arrived, the flames from the plenary chamber were not yet visible from outside the building. Company 6 from Linienstrasse, under the command of Senior Fire Chief Emil Puhle, had received the alarm at 9:14 and had reached the Reichstag by 9:18. One minute later Fire Chief Waldemar Klotz's Company 7 from the district of Moabit, northwest of the Reichstag, was on the scene. While Puhle's company began working on getting into the Reichstag restaurant with a ladder, Klotz decided to come at it from inside, through Portal V. As Klotz's firefighters raced up the stairs from Portal V to the main floor, at what was probably 9:22 or 9:23, they met Lateit coming the other way. "Arson!" Lateit yelled to them. "It is burning everywhere." Lateit then ran the short block back to the Brandenburg Gate. The log there recorded his return at 9:25.[16]

Fire Chief Klotz was the next witness to get a good look at the plenary chamber, which, he estimated, he reached at 9:24. He discovered this fire as he raced along the hall toward the restaurant. Scranowitz had not noticed any particular heat coming from the chamber beyond what one might expect from isolated fires, but when Klotz opened the chamber door he was hit by "an absolutely extraordinary heat." And while Scranowitz had not noticed any smoke, Klotz found that now the big room was "thick" with it, so that he could not make out the furnishings or indeed see any flames, although he could see the glow of them coming from one of the balconies. Since in such a large room it would take a long time for flames to consume all the available oxygen and then produce so much smoke, Klotz thought that the fires must have been burning for at least half an hour.[17]

The difference between what Scranowitz saw and felt at 9:22 and what Klotz encountered at 9:24 was the key to a devastating chemical process now underway in the plenary chamber. According to later scientific reconstructions, the fires burning in the chamber were generating gases, which, building up in the enclosed space (the ventilation system had been shut down) quickly began to approach a dangerous mass. At 9:27 it happened: an explosion. Klotz witnessed it. After his first look at the chamber he had gone to bring up a hose. He thought this had taken about two minutes. Just as he got back to the chamber he saw what he called a "burst," and "now the fire visibly spread like lightning across the whole room." The desks, benches, and wood paneling were all ablaze, and the flames were fanned by such powerful drafts that Klotz had to clutch the door tightly to keep from being sucked in.[18]

Meanwhile Puhle's Company 6 had set up a ladder to the window of the Reichstag restaurant. Puhle himself broke one of the windows with an axe and was the first to climb through. A twenty-six-year-old fireman named Fritz Polchow, in his first year with the Fire Department, followed Puhle inside. They found a door and some curtains burning, and a fire-lighter (a common household item in those days, consisting of a ball of sawdust soaked in naphthalene, which one lit with a match to start a fire in a stove or fireplace) that had burned itself out on a table. Putting out these fires went "comparatively quickly," Puhle explained a few weeks later. As this work was underway, Puhle continued, he sent a fireman into the next room to check for other fires. This was Polchow.[19]

Four days after the fire, in a statement to Commissar Bunge of the Berlin police, Polchow said that he had found a staircase behind a counter in this second room. He went down it to a door with a broken window pane, and, as he put it, "ran into police officers coming toward me from below."

Polchow's observation was, after the appearance of the young man who reported the fire to the police at the Brandenburg Gate, the second odd thing to happen that evening. From it arises the question of who exactly these "police officers" were, who were evidently coming from the cellar of the Reichstag. This passage in Polchow's statement is heavily underlined in the prosecutor's copy. The prosecutor, too, must have thought it odd.[20]

Polchow's 1933 account was laconic in the extreme. He elaborated on it in later years. In 1955, by which time he had risen to be second in command of West Berlin's Fire Department, Polchow included his story in a report that the department prepared for Reichstag fire researcher Richard Wolff. In this version, Polchow said he had gone down the stairs looking for a light switch. He had no sooner found one and switched it on than he was confronted by "several pistol barrels that were being held by persons in brand-new police uniforms." Five years after that, in 1960, Polchow added still more detail. "After I had gone down about two to four steps, a light flared up at the bottom end of the staircase," he wrote. There, in a vestibule, were "two or more police officers." Again he noted the new uniforms, and the pistols pointing at him. The officers shone their flashlights in his eyes and called to him "through a broken window" to "turn back immediately." "This is the Fire Department," Polchow answered, but it made no difference to these men. "Turn back or we'll shoot!" Without much choice, Polchow retreated back up the staircase and reported the event, first to an officer named Lutosch, later to Puhle.

In 1960 Polchow explained that when he began telling this story to Commissar Bunge, Bunge suddenly broke off the interview with the words, "That's fine, we already know all the rest." Polchow did not even know if Bunge had recorded the incident in Polchow's transcript.[21]

It will already be clear that in the story of the Reichstag fire, timing is important and minutes count. The timing of Polchow's observation is no exception. In his March 18th statement Puhle said that his company had reached the Reichstag at 9:18, and he thought it had taken about five minutes to get into the restaurant. He had sent Polchow to look around "while" the fires were being doused. This would suggest Polchow was on the stairs at about 9:23 to 9:25. Testifying in October 1933, Puhle said that while his men were working he had gone out into the hallway toward the plenary chamber, and found Klotz bringing up a hose. This would have been between Klotz's first and second views of the chamber, thus between 9:24 and 9:27. Finally, Polchow himself said in 1960 that he thought he had seen the police officers around 9:23. These reports are reasonably consistent, suggesting that Polchow's 1960 estimate was correct, or perhaps a minute or two early.[22]

The difficulty is that at 9:23 or 9:25 there could officially only have been one police officer, Constable Losigkeit, in the Reichstag cellar. House Inspector Scranowitz had sent Losigkeit to the cellar to look for arsonists, because, said Scranowitz, "Some are still running around down there." But Losigkeit never said anything about running into firemen, and there would have been no reason for him not to mention it. Furthermore, he explicitly testified that while he was searching the cellar he was the *only* police officer in the Reichstag. Lateit later brought reinforcements from the Brandenburg Gate to seal off the building, but they could not possibly have been at, let alone inside, the building at 9:23 or 9:25. The mystery of whom exactly Polchow saw, therefore, remains.[23]

Meanwhile, on the main floor, Scranowitz and Poeschel were looking for culprits; the plural is here intentional, as they assumed the fire had to be the work of several men. They hurried out of the plenary chamber into the south hallway, toward the anteroom of the Reich Council offices, known informally as the Bismarck Room. Suddenly a shape detached itself from the shadows along the back wall of the chamber. It was a tall, pale young man, naked to the waist and sweating profusely. Startled, Poeschel ordered him to raise his hands. The man made no effort to flee. In his pockets Poeschel found—or so it was reported at the time—some Communist literature as well as a passport identifying the young man as a Dutch citizen named Marinus van der Lubbe of Leyden. Later Poeschel would testify that van der Lubbe had been carrying only the passport.[24]

House Inspector Scranowitz could hardly contain himself. "Why did you do this?" he bellowed. He later admitted that in his rage he punched van der Lubbe in the ribs.

"Protest! Protest!" was the answer. Whether van der Lubbe was offering a motive for setting fire to the Reichstag or simply complaining about being punched remains unclear.[25]

The director of the Reichstag, Privy Councilor Reinhold Galle, arrived in time to see Poeschel leading the culprit away. Galle glanced up at the clock in the corridor outside the plenary chamber. It read exactly 9:25.[26]

By 9:35 the police had brought the strange young man, now wrapped in a blanket, to the Brandenburg Gate. From there he was taken to the headquarters of the Berlin police at Alexanderplatz—the "Alex," to Berliners—where officers were waiting to interrogate him.[27]

The firefighters attacked the plenary chamber from all sides, running fifteen "B hoses" (75 millimeter) and five "C hoses" (45 millimeter) in from the south, east, north, and west entrances. Some of the water was drawn from a fireboat in the Spree. Once this equipment was in place it took only about seventy-five minutes to get the fire in the chamber under control, and it was completely extinguished by 12:25. By that time, however, the chamber had been totally destroyed, while the glass and iron cupola above it was heavily damaged. Police and firefighters found other fires in the hallways around the chamber, but the damage from them was negligible, as was the damage to the restaurant.[28]

The new leaders of Germany were rushing to the Reichstag even as the firefighters were struggling to save it. Sefton Delmer, Berlin correspondent for the British *Daily Express*, had been tipped off by a source and arrived at the Reichstag by 9:45. Soon after, he saw two familiar black Mercedes arrive, from which emerged Hitler and Nazi Party propaganda director Joseph Goebbels. Hitler, remembering Delmer from an earlier interview, greeted him: "Evening, Herr Delmer." That was Delmer's "ticket of admission." Although British, he had grown up in Germany and spoke fluent German. He was present as the new Prussian Interior Minister Hermann Göring briefed Hitler on the fire.

"Without a doubt this is the work of the Communists, Herr Chancellor," Göring told Hitler. Not yet the sartorially flamboyant figure of later years, Göring was dressed soberly in a homburg and long overcoat; Hitler, too, looked resolutely civilian in a double-breasted raincoat and dark suit. Delmer accompanied Hitler on a tour of the building. At one moment Hitler dropped back to speak to him. "'God grant,' he said, 'that this be the work of the Communists. You are now witnessing the beginning of a great new epoch in German history, Herr Delmer. This fire is just the beginning.'"[29]

TYPICALLY, WORD OF THE FIRE had disturbed Rudolf Diels neither at work nor at home, but rather on a date at the Café Kranzler on Unter den Linden. The thirty-two-year-old Diels had been the commander of Department IA, the political department of the Berlin police, for only a few weeks. The task of Department IA was to defend political stability and domestic security by monitoring and investigating political extremists and the violence or subversion they might commit or plan—much as do organizations like the FBI in the United States or MI5 in Great Britain, or today's Office for Constitutional Protection in Germany itself. Between the Communists and the Nazis of Weimar Berlin, the political police officers had had their hands full.

Diels hurried to the Reichstag, arriving a few minutes before Hitler and Goebbels. Soon, one of Hitler's adjutants summoned him to the "select circle." Diels found Hitler with Goebbels, Göring, and Reich Interior Minister Wilhelm Frick on a balcony overlooking the burning chamber. "Hitler stood leaning his arms on the stone parapet of the balcony and stared silently into the red sea of flames," Diels recalled. "As I entered, Göring came towards me. His voice was heavy with the emotion of the dramatic moment. 'This is the beginning of the Communist revolt; they will start their attack now! Not a moment must be lost!'" Diels could see that Hitler's face was purple with agitation and the heat from the fires. The Führer now launched into one of his trademark rages: "There will be no mercy now. Anyone who stands in our way will be cut down. The German people will not tolerate leniency. Every Communist official will be shot where he is found. The Communist deputies must be hanged this very night. Everybody in league with the Communists must be arrested. There will no longer be any leniency for Social Democrats either.'"

Göring ordered Diels to put the police on "an emergency footing" and insisted that no "Communist and no Social Democratic traitor must be allowed to escape us." By the time Diels returned to the Alex he could already see the results: "astonished arrestees, dragged out of their sleep," were being brought in droves to the Alex's entrance. The arrestees were known opponents of the Nazis, their names and addresses carefully recorded; their number ran into the thousands. But even as the police carried out these official arrests there was a separate, unofficial arrest program. That night Berlin's Nazi stormtroopers, the *Sturmabteilungen* or SA, also went looking for their enemies, mostly Communists. The stormtroopers, Hitler's paramilitary enforcers during his rise to power, had also been making lists, complete with addresses, since at least 1931. They did not bother taking their prisoners to the Alex, however. Instead they dragged them to SA headquarters, empty basements, and abandoned warehouses, for beatings, torture, and in many cases murder. Soon Germans were calling these improvised facilities *wilde Konzentrationslager*, or "wild concentration camps."[30]

How Rudolf Diels's political police officers did their jobs that night and in the following days, and what exactly might have connected their work to the stormtroopers' revenge, would shape the story of the Reichstag fire for decades to come.

An almost metaphysical specialization separated Diels's officers from their colleagues in the criminal sections. In the Berlin police department it was not the "what" of an event that determined which detectives would work on it: political and criminal detectives alike investigated murders, beatings, riots, even arson. It was the "why" that determined jurisdiction. Had a crime been committed out of political motives? Were these motives "left" or "right"? Different officers had different specialties, but all of Diels's detectives were primarily concerned with the "why."

Indeed, in the case of the Reichstag fire, the "what" doesn't tell us anything like the whole story. We, too, are more concerned with the "whys": Why did the Reichstag burn? Why did contemporaries assign powerful meanings to the blaze even as the firemen fought it? Why has its symbolism endured so long and generated so much fury?

GERMANS WHO EXPERIENCED the Reichstag fire as adults remembered it later in strikingly similar ways.

In the early 1930s Walter Kiaulehn was a young reporter for the tabloid *BZ am Mittag* (Berlin newspaper at midday), known especially for his skill and persistence in investigating crime stories. In "exile" in Munich in the 1950s he wrote an elegiac book about his native Berlin, which ended with the Reichstag fire, "the opening act" for all the others. One fire had followed another, said Kiaulehn: "First the Reichstag burned, then the books burned, and soon the synagogues. Then Germany began to burn, England, France and Russia burned, and finally Adolf Hitler burned in his Reich Chancellery. In 1945 Berlin had sunk into rubble and ashes."[31]

At the venerable Heidelberg University, a philosophy student named Hannah Arendt was working on a doctoral dissertation on Augustine's concept of love when news came of the fire. Arendt had already begun to suspect that as a woman and a Jew she had no prospect of a scholarly career in Germany. But she had never much cared for politics. The Reichstag fire changed that. Years later she told an interviewer that the fire "was an immediate shock for me." From that moment, she said, she felt "responsible. That is, I was no longer of the opinion that one can simply be a bystander."[32]

Even closer to the event itself, two men who, in 1933, were themselves political police officers and subordinates of Rudolf Diels, left similar reflections on the meaning of the Reichstag fire. Hans Bernd Gisevius had just turned twenty-nine as he finished his legal training and took a job in Diels's department. He would go on to serve as a diplomat and intelligence officer during the war, become an early opponent of Hitler's rule, and eventually play a role in the famous "Valkyrie" plot to assassinate Hitler in July 1944. In a memoir first published in 1946, but written while the war was still on, he maintained that the burning of the Reichstag was not only the beginning of Hitler's regime, it was the beginning of German complicity. "From then on it went step by step," he wrote, "from deception to credulousness, from self-deception to turning away, and from isolated connivance to 'collective' guilt and atonement." The story of the Reichstag fire was indispensable for "the recognition of how it begins, when an entire people makes itself guilty." The hotheaded vengeance that Hitler's stormtroopers unleashed in the spring of 1933 on anyone who opposed them lead to the "ice-cold terror of the SS state," the systematized mass murder of the last years of the Third Reich. Gisevius believed that a clear historical line ran from what he called the coup d'état of February 27th, 1933, to other notorious events of the Nazi regime: Hitler's purge of his own stormtroopers and conservative opponents in June 1934 (the so-called Night of the Long Knives), the framing and dismissal of two important generals in February 1938, "and from there on inexorably into terror and war." "The Eichmanns," said Gisevius, "only made into a system what these first excesses had alarmingly announced."[33]

In May 1945 Heinrich Schnitzler was a prisoner of war in American custody. Three years older than Gisevius, Schnitzler had been an official in the Berlin political police before 1933. When Diels took over the department, Schnitzler, whose training was as an administrative lawyer, was promoted to chief administrator. He left in 1934, and during the war served with an anti-aircraft unit of the Luftwaffe, the German air force, until his 1945 capture. Like Gisevius, he had gravitated toward the resistance. He kept a diary while a prisoner so that his family could later learn of his experiences. On May 22, 1945, he mused about the Reichstag fire and its "unforeseeable consequences." With it the Nazis had acquired a tool to persecute first the Communists and the Social Democrats, later all the other non-Nazi parties in Germany. In the future, Schnitzler thought, no one would be able to say the words "National Socialism" without conjuring up the "ghastly crimes" the Nazis committed in the concentration camps—and the Reichstag fire had been the "birth hour" of those camps. For Schnitzler as for Gisevius, it had marked the beginning of Hitler's dictatorship, when "law was abandoned" and the regime began to rule "against the German people."[34]

On February 27th, 1933, Adolf Hitler had been in office as Chancellor of the German Reich for only four weeks. He headed nothing more ominous than a shaky coalition government, in which Nazis held only three of thirteen cabinet seats. Two days after his administration took office, Germany's head of state, the venerable Reich President Paul von Hindenburg, dissolved the Reichstag and called elections for Sunday, March 5th. Hitler and the Nazis hoped and expected that the elections would give them a majority independent of their conservative coalition partners, although Hitler had promised, perhaps not very believably, that whatever happened, the electoral outcome would not change the composition of the cabinet.

Then came the Reichstag fire. Hitler and the other Nazi leaders claimed right away that the fire was the signal for a Communist uprising. Only a quick and decisive response could save the country. On the morning of February 28th, Hitler secured Hindenburg's approval for what became known as the Reichstag Fire Decree. This decree put an abrupt end to constitutional rights and the rule of law itself in Germany. About five thousand people whom the Nazis deemed a threat to their rule were arrested. As both Gisevius and Schnitzler recognized, the decree, repeatedly renewed and remaining in force until 1945, was the basic legal warrant for the brutal dictatorship that followed. Ernst Fraenkel, one of the most distinguished writers on law in Nazi Germany, called it the "constitutional charter" of Hitler's Reich.[35]

If the importance of the Reichstag fire is therefore abundantly clear to posterity, its origins are less so. From the very beginning, many people—in Germany as well as abroad—were skeptical of the Nazis' "communist uprising" theory. The timing and the consequences of the fire seemed much too convenient, and the principle of motive—*cui bono*, "who benefits"—suggested the culprits had been the Nazis themselves. Marinus van der Lubbe swore that he had burned the Reichstag on his own. He never deviated from that story. But few found him a very plausible suspect as the initiator of the fire—among other things, he was mostly blind—and so the police, prosecutors, and judges followed the Nazis' directives and set out to prove that van der Lubbe had been the tool of a Communist conspiracy. Non-Nazis, on the other hand, simply reversed the official line and assumed van der Lubbe had been a witting or, possibly, unwitting stooge in a Nazi conspiracy.

Van der Lubbe became the main defendant in the first major political trial of Nazi Germany, which ran from September to December 1933 in a glare of worldwide attention and controversy. Here at least he was not alone. The Nazis had rounded up four other suspects—one German Communist leader and three Bulgarian party activists who had been residing in Berlin undercover—to represent the Communist conspiracy of their propaganda. The evidence against these other defendants could not satisfy even the regime-friendly Reich Supreme Court, and in the end the judges convicted only van der Lubbe. He was executed with what was, even by the standards of the day, great speed, guillotined in the courtyard of the Leipzig prison on January 10, 1934.

For a time after the Second World War, almost everyone, Germans included, accepted that Nazis had planned and carried out the Reichstag fire. Then, starting in the late 1940s, a small group of former Gestapo officers, themselves veterans of the 1933 fire investigation, began to claim that van der Lubbe had actually been telling the truth. They found their most effective spokesman in a member of the Office for Constitutional Protection in the West German federal state of Lower Saxony. His name was Fritz Tobias.

In the winter of 1959–1960, Tobias published a series of articles in the German news magazine the *Spiegel*, making the striking claim that the Nazis had had nothing to do with burning the Reichstag. Marinus van der Lubbe really had been a sole culprit, while Hitler truly believed that the Communists were behind the fire. The need to act, to appear decisive, a need common to all political leaders in all moments of crisis, had driven Hitler to pass the Reichstag Fire Decree. "In a moment of glory for humanity," was Tobias's much-quoted summation, the "civil Reich chancellor" was transformed into the "power-drunk dictator, obsessed with his mission." There was, in short, no careful scheming, no long-range strategy for power, behind the Reichstag fire—or indeed behind Hitler's entire bid for power. It was all a matter of luck, or rather, as Tobias seemed willing to concede, bad luck. His argument, fleshed out with more supporting detail and documentation, was restated in his 1962 book *The Reichstag Fire: Legend and Reality*.[36]

The articles and the book touched off a controversy remarkable for its rancor as well as for its duration. Tobias was breaking a major taboo in acquitting the Nazis of guilt for the fire. His book enraged many people, especially those who had been the Nazis' victims. "It is absolutely incomprehensible to me," Ernst Fraenkel himself wrote Tobias, "how one could spend his short life moving heaven and hell to make innocent lambs out of the rabble of Nazi murderers." Fraenkel remembered that as a lawyer in

Berlin in the 1930s he had defended many people on charges of treachery (*Heimtücke*) because they had dared to insist that the Nazis had burned the Reichstag. Since then he had always reacted "allergically" to arguments such as Tobias's. "My admiration for the men and women who had the courage to voice this claim to the Nazi tyrants is just as great today as it was then," he wrote. He would not be able to look these former clients in the eye if he did not reject Tobias's "false teaching."[37]

It was probably because of reactions like this that Tobias, the amateur historian, saw himself as a persecuted outsider to the historical profession. It didn't help his public image that Germany's neo-Nazis and sympathizers abroad, such as the (later) Holocaust-denying British historian David Irving, rushed to support him. Nonetheless his arguments also gradually gained mainstream support. Influential historians like Hans Mommsen in Germany and A.J.P. Taylor in Britain were early converts. Over time other distinguished historians of Nazi Germany, like Ian Kershaw and Richard J. Evans, came to accept that Tobias was right. Major German media outlets such as the *Spiegel* and the influential weekly newspaper the *Zeit* weighed in furiously on his behalf. It is often noted that the Tobias single-culprit theory now appears in the *Brockhaus* encyclopedia, as sure an indicator as any of its naturalization in the land of settled truth. By the 1970s both the caliber and the conduct of Tobias's opponents were beginning to suffer. They tried repeatedly to bring forward new evidence of Nazi guilt, but this evidence was often tainted by accusations of forgery and misrepresentation. At least some of these accusations turned out to be true. By the end of the 1980s Tobias seemed to have carried the day, although, as we will see, the fight has gone on.

What has generally been missing from the long Reichstag fire debate is the recognition that, like the fire itself, the controversy is also a part of history and needs to be placed into its (several) historical contexts. Arguments and items of evidence that have emerged over time on the question of who actually set fire to the building—to say nothing of the broader implications of the event—cannot be treated in a vacuum. They must be seen in the context of when, how, and by whom they were brought up. For above all what the story of the Reichstag fire tells is how much of what even professional historians take to be settled historical fact is a tale launched, shaped, and reshaped by power and interest.

Most writers on the Reichstag fire have focused either on its importance in leading to the Reichstag Fire Decree, or on the "whodunit" question.

But the fire marked the end of an earlier era as well as the beginning of a new one. It was the climax of a pattern of political violence that had gripped Berlin from 1926, pitting Nazi stormtroopers against the paramilitary auxiliaries of Germany's other political parties: the Communist Red Frontfighters' League or Combat League Against Fascism, the centrist parties' Reich Banner Black-Red-Gold, the Social Democrats' Iron Front, and the Nationalists' Steel Helmet and "Fighting Ring" or "Fighting Squads." The Nazis' Berlin party boss and propagandist Joseph Goebbels had worked out a strategy in which the Nazis gained attention by provoking violence while at the same time posing as its victims. A string of mediagenic sensations preceded the Reichstag fire: a bomb delivered to Goebbels' office, a violent rampage of massed stormtroopers on Berlin's Kurfürstendamm, a nighttime attack on a "cottage colony" inhabited mostly by Communists, the murder of a stormtrooper and a police officer on the torchlit night that Hitler became Germany's chancellor. Historians have recently begun to realize the importance of this steady program of violence in stripping the democratic system of the Weimar Republic of legitimacy and popular support. As the climax of this story, the Reichstag fire was certainly part of the downfall of democracy, but in a different sense than historians have often assumed—one step in a procession rather than a sudden shock.[38]

The Reichstag fire also launched a new phase in the political campaigns of the European 1930s, and hence in the long European civil war between far left and far right. By 1933 many Germans had become convinced that the Nazis were the only possible guarantors of order and stability, even though they were also the Weimar Republic's most violent insurgency. Historians have credited Goebbels with achieving this unlikely persuasive success. But Goebbels' most recent biographer has pointed out that our belief in Goebbels' talents rests largely on his own account. In fact Goebbels was not always the master of deception he wished to be. With the Reichstag fire he suffered a major defeat. Anti-Nazi Germans driven into exile in France and elsewhere, above all the remarkable Communist media entrepreneur Willi Münzenberg, succeeded so brilliantly in fixing the Reichstag fire as the defining symbol of Nazi criminality that the Nazis' image outside of Germany was damaged from the beginning. It never recovered.

Goebbels and other Nazi leaders compounded this damage through their ham-handed staging of the Reichstag fire trial in the autumn of

1933. No doubt to the Nazis' everlasting regret, one of Marinus van der Lubbe's co-defendants was the Bulgarian Comintern official Georgi Dimitrov. An obscure figure in early 1933, marginalized within his own party by factional disputes, the Reichstag fire trial rocketed Dimitrov to political stardom. Fiercely intelligent, flamboyant, utterly fearless, and, as it turned out, a born courtroom advocate, Dimitrov was as fanatical as his accusers, but witty and charismatic in ways they could never dream of matching. By the time his trial was over in December he had succeeded in shredding the Nazis' credibility and establishing himself as the definitive anti-Nazi hero.

Dimitrov's courtroom performance had vitally important consequences. With his newly won stature he was able to play an important role in turning Joseph Stalin and the leadership of the Soviet Union and the Comintern— the "Communist International," the Soviet-lead organization for fostering Communist politics around the world—from their "third period" ideology of unremitting hostility to capitalism *and* social democracy, toward the "Popular Front" era of broad, "anti-fascist" alliances between European Communist parties and other center and left organizations, be they liberal or moderate socialist. This approach proved particularly important in France and Spain, but its influence was soon felt almost everywhere. Stalin made Dimitrov effective head of the Comintern in the spring of 1934. Dimitrov then became the chief spokesman and advocate of the Popular Front, a policy he had always supported.[39]

The reasons for the endurance of the bitter controversy over the Reichstag fire lie in some of the largest themes of German and European history after the Second World War: the memory of the crimes of Nazi Germany, especially of the Holocaust; the fate of efforts to "denazify" Germany; the onset of the Cold War; and, finally, how it came about that Germany gradually made the painful transition to a fully functioning democracy with a respectfully inquisitive attitude to the darker reaches of its own past. The argument over the Reichstag fire cannot be divorced from these broad themes.

For example, the police detectives who investigated the fire in 1933 went on to become cogs in the Nazis' mass-murder machine. After the war these men knew that when the questions about the Reichstag fire came up, other subjects—the Ghetto of Lodz, the deportation of German Jews to death camps in eastern Europe, or the operations of the *Einsatzgruppen* (mobile killing squads) in Poland and the Soviet Union—would not be far behind. Debates about the Reichstag fire from the 1940s to the 1960s were therefore inevitably about these incomparably worse crimes too, sometimes as a kind of code, sometimes as a prologue. As historian Michael Wildt has emphasized, the years immediately after the war were dangerous ones for former Nazi police officials, including those who had been involved in the Reichstag investigation. The 1950s, by contrast, were their "most carefree" time, as Cold War pressures and the consolidation of the new West German state brought an end to the war crimes and denazification trials of the late 1940s. At the end of the 1950s, however, these men found themselves once more in legal jeopardy, particularly from the newly-created "Central Office" for the prosecution of Nazi crimes in Ludwigsburg. This time the threat never entirely receded, and, in Wildt's phrase, these ex-Gestapo men were not to be granted any "peaceful golden years." This pattern graphs perfectly onto the Reichstag fire controversy: the discovery of new evidence, and the development and publication of rival narratives, went through an active phase in the late 1940s, calmed down for most of the 1950s, and returned with new vehemence late in the decade.[40]

The debate over the Reichstag fire in the 1950s and 1960s, mainly because of its embedding in this larger political process, reflected both the state of knowledge at the time and the state of Germans' willingness to deal with it. Fritz Tobias's arguments rested on a belief in the integrity and anti-Nazi stance of the police officers who investigated the fire. In this he was swimming with the current of the time. For years after the Second World War, senior police officers, like senior civil servants throughout the Nazi regime, benefited from the fact that the popular image of a Nazi war criminal was that of a stormtrooper or a concentration camp guard—in other words, a jackbooted thug. The idea of the "desk murderer," the criminal with a tie and a doctorate in law, did not start to catch on until the abduction and trial of Adolf Eichmann in 1961.[41]

Furthermore, the Reichstag fire debate, in which officials who supposedly upheld the law and acted decently were always contrasted with the "real" Nazis who did not, rested on a standard pattern of postwar German defensive argument. Criminal police officers argued that the Gestapo, the Nazis' secret police, had committed all the crimes; early Gestapo leaders like Rudolf Diels argued that *they* had been good, it was the *later* Gestapo under Heinrich Himmler and Reinhard Heydrich that had become Nazified. (Even Heydrich's deputy Werner Best kept up the pattern, arguing that *he* had merely been a conscientious civil servant who had done his best to keep Heydrich on the straight and narrow.) Military officers argued that all crimes had been committed by the SS and not the regular army. And so it went. The trend of recent research has been to explode these distinctions, and to show that soldiers, police officers, judges, officials of the foreign and justice ministries, and many other categories of Germans—public servants and otherwise—were deeply enmeshed in the crimes of the regime. The assumptions that could support Tobias's argument fifty years ago now themselves need to be seen as the product of a particular historical moment.

Above all we must return to the point that Walter Kiaulehn, Hannah Arendt, Hans Bernd Gisevius, and Heinrich Schnitzler saw so clearly: that the fire marked the real beginning of what was arguably the most violently destructive regime in human history. This point was at least partly understood even in 1933, and only became clearer with the years. If the fire was "the birth hour of the concentration camps" and all the other horrors of Nazism, then in a very real sense controlling the narrative of how it happened meant to control the narrative of everything that followed; responsibility for the fire was responsibility for those other fires that Kiaulehn enumerated; to have investigated (or covered for) the culprits of the fire was to have revealed (or concealed) the roots of the Nazi regime. For former police officers, for historians, for citizens generally, the desire to prove who did it and why has always been balanced by a desire to run from the guilt that any connection with the fire implied. The question of "why" put the fire into the hands of Diels's Department IA on that icy February night. As Diels's officers understood, sometimes the "why" questions are the most awkward and painful of all.

1

· · · ·

"SATANIC NOSE"

RUDOLF DIELS

RUDOLF DIELS WAS BORN as few men are to be a secret policeman. He loved nothing more than being elusive. Martha Dodd, the vivacious daughter of American Ambassador William Dodd, who knew Diels well, remembered how he "walked into a room, or rather crept on cat's feet . . . the only man who got by our efficient butler without being announced." She called him "Mephistophelian," an assessment corroborated by an (exiled) journalist who once referred to Diels's "satanic" nose for "future political constellations."[1]

In 1931 Diels was recruited to work in the Prussian Interior Ministry in the belief that he would strengthen the ministry's liberal forces. He came in with a group of young men who would, in various ways, play important roles in the coming decades of German history. Among them was Robert M.W. Kempner, who as a Jewish Social Democrat would be driven into exile by the Nazis but would come back to prosecute them at Nuremberg. There was Hans Globke, who would write the definitive commentary to the Nazis' anti-Semitic Nuremberg Laws of 1935 and then in the 1950s go on to run Konrad Adenauer's Chancellor's Office. And there was Fritz Tejessy, who after the war would head the Office of

Constitutional Protection—the political police—in West Germany's largest state, North Rhine-Westphalia. From this perch Tejessy would pursue his old colleague Rudolf Diels with unrelenting fervor for his participation in the Nazi regime.[2]

In the early 1930s these men still thought they were all on the same side, and Diels formed several habits that would prove to be long-lasting, one of which was the careful cultivation of friends from all backgrounds and political persuasions. With the help of these friends he always got himself out of trouble, no matter how serious, even if toward the end it was only by a hair. Many years later, Diels wrote that "in our barbaric and briskly changing times, one must be careful in the selection of one's enemies."[3]

Diels was careful about little else. He was, by his own admission, an adventurer. When his friend Winfried Martini asked him why he had taken on the job of leading Hitler's Gestapo, Diels replied "it was clear to me that monstrous things were going to happen, and so I wanted, for the sake of a better view, to be in the inner circle." Rudolf Becker, another ministerial colleague, wrote that Diels's foolhardiness got in the way of his desire to use his gifts "for the good and the right." Becker remembered Diels as a dazzling conversationalist, whose love of his own words sometimes got the better of him. Everyone, from the Gestapo officers of the 1930s to the reporters who flocked to him in the 1950s, knew that the more Diels had to drink, the less carefully he spoke, often saying much more than was good for him or anyone else. During the later stages of the war, as the Nazi regime grew ever more repressive, Diels became a dangerous man to be around. One friend remembered how Diels made provocative comments in bars and restaurants: "Sometimes it got embarrassing when the people at a nearby table started paying attention."[4]

Diels thought he could get away with it, and for a long time he did. Amid the repression of Nazi Germany he enjoyed a kind of fool's license, protected by powerful patrons—above all by Hitler's "second man," Hermann Göring. Diels wrote privately after the war that he could have risen to be a minister, like the finance minister and president of the Reich Bank Hjalmar Schacht, because of "Göring's exaggerated esteem for my professional qualities." But instead he used Göring's protection only to save his own skin. Once, when a senior SS officer wondered why the "traitor" Diels had not been "eliminated," the infamous Reinhard

Heydrich responded that the question only proved the officer's naivety—
a reference to Göring's protection. *Why* Göring should have been so keen
to protect Diels is a question to which we will return.[5]

He did not apply his seductive gifts only to his career. Years later a
friend remembered that "Diels was strikingly good looking; he could
hardly save himself from the women." Not that he tried. Diels was tall
and lanky, with thick black hair and penetrating blue eyes, a sardonic
smile always playing around the corners of his mouth, his looks marred
only by the rakish dueling scars he had acquired as a student. He was
charming, worldly, witty, and fiercely intelligent. His second wife Ilse—
who was also Hermann Göring's sister-in-law—wrote in 1945 that with
his intellectual gifts Diels "towered over other men." Leni Riefenstahl,
Hitler's favorite filmmaker, remembered Diels as "an extremely attractive
man" who could have "played the lead in an American western." She
thought that Diels would appeal to many women, and she was right.[6]

It was always women who came up with the most evocative descriptions of Diels. The Countess Ingeborg Kalnoky, who knew Diels in Nuremberg after the war, remembered that his face "was a study in contrasts:
exceedingly pale and deeply lined under the kind of straight bluish-black
hair one connects most often with Latins; eyes that were unexpectedly blue
and whose expression was startlingly frank, mingling vitality and desire."[7]

Sometimes that desire could be a bit of a problem. Diels's career could
have ended abruptly one day in 1931, when a prostitute appeared at the
Interior Ministry holding Diels's Ministry ID card. She said Diels had
beaten her the night before, and accidentally left the card behind. Diels
had earlier told Robert Kempner about the problem, and Kempner saved
his colleague by smoothly buying the card back from the young woman.
Kempner also knew the usefulness of making friends. A few years later
Diels helped Kempner escape the Nazis. This odd relationship endured.
At Nuremberg in 1945 and 1946 Kempner, by then a war crimes prosecutor, sheltered Diels from Allied charges.[8]

The son of prosperous farmers, born near Wiesbaden, in December
1900, Diels received the conventional education for well-off young men
in Imperial Germany. He attended a *Gymnasium*—an academic high
school for the university-bound—in Wiesbaden. He served briefly on the
Western Front at the end of the First World War before going on to university at Giessen and Marburg. He studied medicine for two years before
switching to law, but scientific interests—especially in botany—stayed

with him for the rest of his life. While at Marburg he joined the Corps Rhenania-Strassburg, one of the notorious dueling fraternities common at German universities then, and acquired the obligatory dueling scars on both sides of his face. In the nasty but credible recollection of Hans Bernd Gisevius he earned a reputation that was "not exactly good, but in student terms legendary." Diels held the record for beer consumption and often impressed the other students by biting into the glasses. He also had innumerable romantic affairs.[9]

After university Diels entered the Prussian civil service and worked his way through a string of dreary provincial postings in places like Katzeneln-bogen, Neu-Ruppin, and Peine before being brought to the Prussian Interior Ministry in Berlin in 1931. There he went to work in the political police section, the ministerial analog to Department IA of the Berlin police, with which it worked closely. Diels's job was to draft reports on political "outrages"—riots and other forms of violence carried out by parties or groupings of the extreme left. Diels became an expert on the German Communist Party.[10]

For all of his gifts, the promotions came slowly. After the Nazis had come to power, Diels complained that during the Weimar Republic he had been promoted more slowly to government counselor (*Regierungsrat*) than almost anyone else. His seven years as a junior secretary (*Regierungsas-sessor*) amounted to an "inconceivably long time by today's promotion standards." In 1934 Diels tried to spin this as a sign of his resistance to the democratic system of Weimar. It probably had more to do with his laziness. In the summer of 1932 Diels's immediate superior had complained that Diels's work was "insufficient" and constantly in need of revision, due to his carelessness and lack of interest. Diels preferred to get on in the world in easier ways, like through his marriage to a daughter of the wealthy Mannesmann family, or through making connections with whomever had power or seemed likely soon to get it. His boss at the Interior Ministry in the early 1930s, State Secretary Wilhelm Abegg, applied to Diels a line from the conductor Hans von Bülow: "If he can't play the role, at least he looks the part."[11]

Abegg had his reasons for speaking scathingly of Diels. As state secretary in such an important ministry—in the German system a state secretary is the highest-ranked civil servant in a ministry, reporting directly to the minister—Abegg was a powerful man. But by 1932 Diels's political nose told him that Abegg and the democratic system he represented were on their way out. Germany was coming increasingly under the dominance of a small clique of senior army officers who had the ear of Reich President Paul von Hindenburg. This clique wanted to do away with parliamentary government in Germany and replace it with a military dictatorship. Such a regime could crush the forces of the left, especially Germany's large Social Democratic and Communist Parties, and begin restoring the country's military and diplomatic strength to the great-power status of before the First World War.

The biggest obstacle this clique faced was the federal state of Prussia. Prussia comprised three-fifths of the land and people of Germany. Its government was the anchor of Weimar democracy. Since 1918 Prussia had been governed by a stable coalition of the political parties most committed to democracy—the Social Democrats, the Catholic Center Party, and the left-liberal German Democratic Party (after 1930 the State Party). Prussia's Social Democratic ministers, especially Prime Minister Otto Braun and Interior Minister Carl Severing, were among the most capable of Weimar politicians, and they had at their disposal a major power factor: the well-organized Prussian police, 50,000 strong. Franz von Papen, one of the last chancellors of the Weimar Republic, complained even years later of how frustrating he found the Reich government's complete security dependence on the Prussian government and its police, over which the Reich had no control.[12]

However, in the state elections of April 1932 the Nazi Party's vote in Prussia shot up to 36.3 percent from the meager 1.8 percent it had gained in 1928, and the Braun-Severing administration lost its majority in the Prussian parliament. It limped along as a caretaker government only because, for the moment, the deadlocked parliament could produce no majority for any other administration. At the end of May, politics at the national level, too, took a rightward lurch when President von Hindenburg sacked the comparatively moderate Chancellor Heinrich Brüning and replaced him with the far-right Papen, who was one of the men close to the military clique. Prussia's democrats began to fear that the new chancellor would take advantage of the emergency powers in Germany's constitution to carry out a coup d'état against Prussia. Abegg said later that someone from Papen's immediate circle had warned him directly that such a coup was coming. With the Prussian government gone, the way to an authoritarian regime would be open.

This was where Diels saw his chance. He knew that his boss Abegg was worried about Papen and felt that the Braun-Severing administration

had lost its gumption. Abegg told Diels he thought the Prussian government should convince the Communists to work with the democratic
parties against the Nazis. Diels's ears perked up. He told Abegg he could
arrange a meeting with Communist leaders. Abegg agreed.[13]

On June 4th two Communist leaders, Ernst Torgler and Wilhelm
Kasper, leader of the Communist caucus in the Prussian Parliament, duly
appeared at the Prussian Interior Ministry on Unter den Linden. Abegg
invited Diels to sit in on the meeting, because he wanted a witness to the
conversation.

Abegg reminded Kasper and Torgler of the danger that the national
government would impose a "Reich commissar" on Prussia, with the
excuse that the Prussian government was unable to keep order. He complained that the Social Democratic ministers were sitting on their hands
when action was desperately needed. But the violence that the Communists were stirring up, especially in the industrial Ruhr region, also played
straight into the hands of Papen and the clique, as did the threatening
tone of editorials in the Communist Party's newspaper the *Rote Fahne*
(Red flag). Things would be different if the Communists declared their
commitment to legality. The Nazis had done this, said Abegg, referring
to several famous (if not exactly credible) declarations by Adolf Hitler,
and this seeming commitment to legality had become the Nazis' "strongest weapon."

Torgler asked how the Communists could proclaim their legality in a
way that the public would believe. Laughing, Abegg told him to draft a
secret order and leave it around for the police to find in a search, "like we
do with all your other secrets." Torgler joked that the police would only
find the wrong order. Abegg explained later that the jocular tone of the
conversation was the only way to talk to men who had come up in the
tough world of working-class Berlin politics.[14]

Abegg kept the meeting secret, even from his minister, Carl Severing.
Yet soon the Scherl press empire, owned by the media baron and leader
of the far-right German National People's Party Alfred Hugenberg, had
the story, and on June 26th a Nationalist member of the Prussian parliament accused Abegg of conspiring with the left and trying to do "some
pretty queer business" for the Braun-Severing administration. The source
of the leak, Abegg knew, could only have been Diels. Diels himself, in a
statement later that summer, said that for him the meeting with the
Communists was not a joke at all, but rather an act bordering on treason.

His knowledge of it had brought him into "the most severe conflict of conscience."[15]

In the summer of 1932 Germany was going through the most violent election campaign in its history. On July 17th Communists tangled with Nazis in Altona, a suburb of the city-state of Hamburg on the Prussian side of the border. Fifteen people were killed and another sixty-four hospitalized. On July 20th Chancellor Papen did what informed observers had expected him to do. With a decree formally issued by President Hindenburg under the emergency powers in the German constitution, Papen removed Otto Braun and Carl Severing from office and put himself in place as Reich commissar for Prussia. When the remainder of the Prussian cabinet and Berlin's chief and deputy chief of police refused to go along with him, Papen removed them from office too and put Berlin under martial law (under Lieutenant General Gerd von Rundstedt, later famous as a commander during the war). The decree invoking martial law in Berlin would later have unexpected influence.[16]

Papen claimed that the violence in Altona and elsewhere demonstrated the inability of the Prussian government to keep order. However, the main justification for his coup was Abegg's supposed conspiracy with the Communists. This was what Papen told the country in a radio address on the night of July 20th. Speaking in the declamatory voice of a politician still unfamiliar with the new-fangled radio, Papen said that Prussia's government had lost the strength it needed to fight the Communist party, which was an "enemy of the state." In a passage that clearly drew on a distorted version of Abegg's meeting with Torgler and Kasper, Papen claimed that Prussian leaders had gone as far as offering to help Communists conceal plans for terrorism.[17]

Although both Diels and the new Prussian government denied it—and Diels denied it repeatedly after the war—there is no doubt that Diels was the source of the leak about Abegg's meeting. He was also involved in planning Papen's coup. In the files of Papen's Reich Chancellery are notes of a meeting that took place in Diels's apartment in Berlin on the evening of July 19th between senior officials of the Reich and Prussian governments, including Franz Bracht, the former mayor of Essen who was to become the new Prussian interior minister. Here Diels gave a distorted account of the meeting between Abegg and the Communist leaders, stressing that Abegg was conspiring with Torgler and Kasper to prove the legality of the Communist party through forged documents. After the coup, Diels's co-workers noted that he was instantly on excellent terms with Bracht. Diels even boasted that he had brought down the old government. The Papen-Bracht government slated this young official to be Berlin's deputy chief of police. Resistance in the Interior Ministry forced them to back away from this idea, but Diels did jump the promotion queue to become the youngest-ever Prussian senior government counselor (*Oberregierungsrat*). A few years later, Diels's colleague Heinrich Schnitzler wrote him that Papen's coup was "so far as I can judge it, first and foremost your achievement." Papen himself, in his two postwar memoirs, confirmed that Diels had been the source of the leak about Abegg and the Communists, leading Papen to decide that "one could not let things go on as they were."[18]

IF RUDOLF DIELS HAD PLAYED a key role in this major step on Germany's road to dictatorship, the Papen coup in turn decisively altered his career trajectory. For the next two years Diels would be at the center of every important event in Germany. The coup forged some lasting, if in some cases unlikely, connections among the people involved—Diels, Papen, Schleicher, Torgler, and Hugenberg. It established a pattern for political operations: an ambitious chancellor could strip away constitutional limitations on power by fabricating evidence of a Communist plot.

Even as he enjoyed his promotion, Diels's political nose remained as active as ever. In a biographical note he wrote for his SS file in 1935, Diels recalled that his "authority for fighting Communism" was extended after the coup, and he began dedicating himself "to preparations for the crushing of Communism in Germany, in the closest understanding with the leading men of the Nazi Party." Here he was referring especially to Hermann Göring. Even after the war Diels was honest enough to tell the British that as an anti-Communist he had welcomed the coming of the Nazi regime. Diels developed close ties to the leaders of the Nazis' Berlin stormtroopers. He slipped the Nazis confidential information from the files of the Interior Ministry. In March of 1932 he became a "sponsoring member" of the SA. In the fall of 1933 the former Berlin SA commander, Wolf-Heinrich Count von Helldorff, confirmed that Diels's later administrator Heinrich Schnitzler had come to Helldorff's office in the second half of August 1932 to discuss closer cooperation between the SA leadership and the police for "more effectively combating Marxism." Helldorff had made sure that this connection was maintained after the meeting. In doing this, Schnitzler seems to have been acting in collaboration with Diels, perhaps even on his orders.[19]

In 1968 Fritz Tobias interviewed one of the most infamous SA thugs of early 1930s Berlin, Willi Schmidt, better known by his nickname, Schweinebacke (Bacon Face). Schmidt recalled that Diels and SA *Gruppenführer* Karl Ernst, who succeeded Helldorff as Berlin SA commander in the spring of 1933, were close enough to address each other with the informal *Du*. Once, when Schmidt told Ernst that Diels was a "reactionary," Ernst set him straight. "Listen," said Ernst, "you won't believe it, but Diels was already working with us in 1931." Schmidt gave a similar statement to the Berlin police in 1968.[20]

Yet even as he cultivated Göring and Helldorff and Ernst, Diels kept up his friendly ties to Ernst Torgler and the Communists. After the war, Torgler testified that he had met often with Diels even after the Papen coup, and that he had been able to secure Diels's help in overturning bans on Communist newspapers and freeing arrested party members. Even after the Nazis came to power at the end of January 1933, "negotiations with Herr D. led to the release of Communist election materials," and Torgler gained the impression that Diels was "a thoroughly humane and conciliatory man." Herbert Wehner, later an influential Social Democrat in West Germany, but in the 1930s a Communist Party official, could not persuade Torgler that Diels was not a secret Communist. Wehner tried to convince Torgler that Diels only wanted information, or to lull Torgler and the Communists into complacency. Torgler insisted that Diels wanted to help the Party.[21]

Diels kept his options open even later, when he was working for Hermann Göring as chief of the newly created Gestapo. Diels's ties to the SA did not always please the boss. Göring's press secretary, Martin Sommerfeldt, once watched as an enraged Göring scolded Diels for getting too close to SA commander Ernst Röhm. "Are you conspiring along with him?" Göring wondered. "I'm warning you, Diels, you are trying to bet on two horses!" Diels replied coolly: "The chief of the Secret State Police must bet on all horses, Herr Prime Minister!"[22]

Certainly cultivating Göring and other Nazis in 1931 and 1932 proved to be a wise move for Diels, for the Papen-Bracht government in Prussia would not long enjoy the success of its coup. Just six months later, on January 30, 1933, Adolf Hitler was sworn in as chancellor of the German Reich. At the same time Hermann Göring gained the crucial post of Prussian interior minister and, a few months later, became Prussian prime minister as well.

As Diels told it in 1949, Göring arrived to take charge of the Interior Ministry late on January 30th. Diels was the first person he summoned. "I don't want to have anything to do with the scoundrels around here," Göring told Diels. "Are there any decent men here at all?" Diels admitted that Göring, in his first days at the ministry, "did not allow me to leave his side," and that his ministerial colleagues took this as proof that Diels had been conspiring with Göring. Of course, after the war Diels denied this. Nevertheless, by the middle of February Göring had put the thirty-two-year-old Diels in charge of Department IA at the Alex. Department IA now began to be detached from the rest of the Berlin police and the Prussian administration. It moved into new quarters, first to the Karl Liebknecht House at Bülow Square (today Rosa Luxemburg Square), which had just been confiscated from the Communist Party and renamed the Horst Wessel House for the Nazis' most famous martyr. Then in April it moved again, to what had been an art school in the Prinz-Albrecht-Strasse. Many young Berliners knew the art school for its lively carnival balls—*Dachkahnfeste*, as they were known. Sebastian Haffner remembered the last one, on February 25, 1933: "A teeming crowd, glimpses of silk, naked shoulders and female legs, a crush in which one could hardly move." But this party was broken up by the police, which turned out to be an omen. Soon Berliners would come to dread Prinz Albrecht Strasse 8 for its altogether less innocent crush. With the move the department received a new name, the Office of Secret State Police (*Geheimes Staatspolizeiamt*). The post office supplied the acronym *Gestapa*. This was later modified to *Gestapo*—the now infamous name for what became the Nazis' secret police.[23]

Yet, for all of his worldly success, Diels claimed to be unhappy. One evening in the middle of February 1933 he was at Kempinski's, a toney Berlin café much frequented by senior people from the Interior Ministry. There he ran into his former colleague Robert Kempner, the man who had saved Diels's career by intercepting the prostitute, and who would later protect Diels at Nuremberg. Göring had fired Kempner a few days before. Kempner asked Diels how things were going. "What are you guys doing now? Is there a lot of work?"

"Work and trouble," was Diels's reply. "I have to put lists together."

"What kind of lists?"

"For a certain eventuality."

Kempner understood right away that Diels was talking about arrest lists, lists of political extremists, the "usual suspects" to be rounded up in an emergency. Kempner asked if Diels was referring to the "old" lists that had long lain ready with the Interior Ministry and the police.

"No," said Diels. "Not the old lists." He was making new lists: "The names of old friends of ours are there, too." Kempner understood this point too: the names of democratic politicians, artists, writers, and lawyers were now on the lists along with the Communist leaders.[24]

Later, when he was trying to get himself "denazified," Diels would deny that he had had anything to do with the drafting of new arrest lists. But his own boss had supplied details in the autumn of 1933 in a very public forum—as a witness at the trial of the alleged Reichstag arsonists.

Here Göring explained why, on the night of the fire, he had such exact information on the people to be arrested. In late November 1932 his predecessor as Prussian interior minister, Franz Bracht, had given a secret order to compile lists of home addresses and likely safe houses for anyone who was or who might be suspected of being be an "agitator, troublemaker, and ringleader"—in other words, Communists and other left wing or pacifist figures. After coming into office Göring had not only renewed this secret order, he had sought to confirm and expand the information. He had relieved two men from his ministry of all other duties so that they could concentrate on this assignment. One of these men was Diels.[25]

On February 18th, orders had gone out to all police stations in the state of Prussia to compile lists of leaders and officials of the Communist Party and all related Communist organizations—the paramilitary groups known as the Red Frontfighters' League and the Combat League Against Fascism, as well as the Communists' sports and cultural organizations. The lists were also to include the names of union leaders and officials. In all cases, along with the names, the lists were to provide the addresses of homes and likely hiding places. The completed lists were to be submitted to the Interior Ministry no later than February 26th.[26]

In the early afternoon of Monday, February 27th, Diels sent out an order by radio to all police stations in Prussia. "Communists," said Diels, were "said to be planning attacks on police patrols and the members of national organizations, with a view to disarming them, for the day of the Reichstag elections or a few days before or after." These attacks would be carried out with firearms, knives, and blunt instruments, and in such a way that the attackers could not be identified. Never mind that, as Diels himself wrote after the war, a police raid on the Berlin Communist Party headquarters on February 22nd had turned up "nothing alarming." Diels ordered that "suitable countermeasures" against the Communist threat were to be taken "immediately." Above all, "in necessary cases" Communist functionaries were to be taken into "protective custody."[27]

"Protective custody" was an official euphemism. It was calculated to suggest saving vulnerable people from grave danger. In fact it meant being thrown into prison without charge or trial, and in all likelihood being sent to one of the newly established "concentration camps" to suffer unspeakable beatings and tortures at the hands of the SA.

By shortly after six that evening, all Prussian police stations had received Diels's order. Hours before fire consumed the Reichstag, the police were ready.

2

....

"SA + ME"

JOSEPH GOEBBELS

ONE DAY AROUND 1900, after a long Sunday walk with his family, a small boy in the Rhenish town of Rheydt was afflicted by osteomyelitis—an inflammation of the bone marrow—in his right leg. The infection seemed to revive the pain and paralysis young Paul Joseph Goebbels had already experienced in his foot, but which the family thought he had put behind him. "The next day on the sofa the old pain in my foot came back," he remembered years later. "Cries, incredible pain . . . Long treatment." Doctors at the Bonn university clinic examined his foot and shrugged. For two years the family doctor and a masseur tried to get the foot and leg growing normally again. When he was ten, Joseph went for surgery in nearby München-Gladbach. "Rather a failure," was his later summary. "One of the decisive events of my childhood." He was burdened for life with a club foot.

"Youth from then on rather joyless," wrote the twenty-six-year-old Goebbels. "I had to depend on myself. Could no longer join in the games of the others. Became lonely and eccentric [*eigenbrödlerisch*] . . . My comrades didn't like me. Comrades have never liked me. . . . " In 1919, Goebbels wrote an autobiography couched as a novel in the third person, *Michael*

Voormanns Jugendjahre (The youth of Michael Voormann), in which, he said, "I write my own story with heart and soul . . . without prettying it up, just as I see it." Goebbels wrote that rejection by other children had not only made him lonely, it had embittered him. The very Catholic boy began to quarrel with God. "Why had God made him so that people mocked and ridiculed him?" he wondered. And more fatefully: "Why must he hate, when he wanted to love, when he had to love?"[1]

Compensation for the young Goebbels came in two forms. One was his success in school. His desperate feelings of inferiority drove him to apply his quick mind obsessively to his lessons, even those, like math and physics, in which he felt he had no ability. Little by little he won the respect of his teachers and even his fellow pupils. He earned some additional money for the Goebbels household by tutoring less talented but better-heeled students.[2]

The other compensation lay in his imagination. Goebbels became a voracious reader. This began, by his account, as he lay in hospital after the failed operation. His aunt brought him fairy tales, which he devoured. In books he found "a world of enjoyment." He also began to show a flair for acting and even for producing theatrical performances—a flair which could quickly enough shade into a talent for lying. "Theater, puppet theater," he remembered. "Self-written horror stories [*Schauertragödien*]. Admission 3 pennies . . . " One of Goebbels's biographers writes that the "gulf between bitter reality and the fictitious existence into which he escaped" was the defining quality of his childhood—and, one might add, not just of his childhood.[3]

His club foot kept him out of service in the First World War, a fact that only magnified his feelings of inferiority. Instead he studied: literature and philosophy at the universities of Bonn, Würzburg, Freiburg im Breisgau, and Heidelberg. Very little of the war appears in the pages of his diary: indeed he wrote of his student days in 1918 "I hardly know that there is a war on." The diary reveals an intelligent and ambitious young man, literary, romantic, extremely moody, and—like most young men—with his mind firmly fixed on young women. He wrote a doctoral thesis on the eighteenth-century novelist Wilhelm von Schütz. His doctoral supervisor at Heidelberg, Max von Waldberg, and another professor whom he revered, Friedrich Gundolf, were Jewish.

When Goebbels graduated with his doctorate in 1921 he tried unsuccessfully to make it as a writer and a journalist. He even applied for a job with the *Berliner Tageblatt* (Berlin daily newssheet), the literate, liberal paper owned by the prominent (and Jewish) Mosse family. Resentment over the rejection of this application no doubt colored his later virulent denunciations of the "Jew press" in Berlin. In despair he went to work as a clerk at the Dresdner Bank in Cologne. He read Oswald Spengler's gloomy *The Decline of the West*, which had an "unsettling" and "lasting" impact on him, as did the same writer's *Prussianism and Socialism*. The connection that Goebbels drew between these two qualities became one of the central points of his own ideology. Then he discovered the Nazi Party.[4]

The first mention of the Nazis in his diary comes in a cryptic passage describing his life between January and August 1923, which hints at a melding of ideas and resentments central to Nazi ideology—anti-capitalism and anti-Semitism, with a new suspicion of Gundolf: "The banks and the stock exchanges. Industry and stock market capital. My view is clarified by poverty. Repugnance for the bank and my work. Despairing poems. Jewry. I think about the problem of money . . . Opera. Klemperer as conductor. The Jewish question in the arts. Gundolf. Intellectual insight. Bavaria. Hitler . . . "[5]

Goebbels came into the Nazi Party under the wing of Gregor Strasser, a pharmacist and First World War veteran who was in charge of organizing the Nazis in northern Germany, away from their Bavarian roots. Like Strasser, Goebbels was a revolutionary who, in Spenglerian fashion, placed more emphasis on the "Socialist" than the "National" in the National Socialist German Workers' Party's contradictory name. That Hitler did not share this emphasis was to become Goebbels's constant frustration. His diaries in the early 1930s are peppered with remarks like "The Party must become more Prussian, more active and more socialist," accompanied by complaints that the Munich leadership failed to recognize this.[6]

This was hardly Goebbels's only conflict. In a party dominated by grizzled war veterans, thugs, and adventurers of the stripe of Hermann Göring, Ernst Röhm, and Gregor Strasser, he stood out as the slight young man whose disability had kept him from the trenches. In a party with a great appetite for violence and no use whatsoever for ideas, he was an intellectual who could appreciate—even when he hated—the works of left-wing and Jewish opponents. In 1924, after reading the elegant and savagely sarcastic journalist Maximilian Harden (who had Jewish roots and had changed his name from Isidor Witkowski) Goebbels wrote with grudging admiration that the radical nationalists would have to be "a little livelier, a little more intellectually flexible, to finish off this kind of writer."[7]

It was perhaps Goebbels's sense of physical inferiority, or his memories of childhood rejection, that led him to worship as heroes the young toughs of the SA and eagerly court their affection and approval, a theme that fills the pages of his diary. Had Goebbels not been such a compulsive womanizer one might suspect homoerotic tendencies. In his 1930 eulogy for the Nazi "martyr" Horst Wessel, Goebbels said that Wessel would "remain among us" as he always had been, "with the smile of youth on his red lips." In September 1931 he wrote of a visit to the hostel put up by SA unit Storm 33 in the Berlin neighborhood of Charlottenburg. "Songs, coffee, comradeship. I feel good there . . . " And he went the same night to another SA hostel where he "sang and carried on with the boys. Swell guys! They all love me very much . . ." One day, emerging from a meeting with the establishment conservatives he so disliked, he was met by SA men who saluted him with cries of "Heil!" "Dear boys!" he wrote. "I'd like to hug each one."[8]

Goebbels was a true believer in Hitler and the most extreme of anti-Semites. Diels said that Goebbels had "the capability for a kind of auto-suggestion which led him to believe fanatically what he said and wrote." This is a phenomenon one can observe over and over in the pages of his diary. Even in this private forum, he wrote obvious lies with strident conviction. Yet Goebbels was a political extremist who could step outside of his own fanaticism to observe coolly how his doctrines looked to an opponent. This capacity helped to make him the talented propagandist that he was. One day in 1932 he read a critique of Hitler written by Theodor Heuss, a prominent liberal politician who became the first president of West Germany after the war. "Not at all dumb," he wrote in his diary. "Knows a lot about us. Uses it somewhat meanly. But in any case an impressive critique." He admired American movies, and in the last desperate days of the war sought to make a kind of Nazi *Gone with the Wind* called *Das Leben geht weiter* (Life goes on), which would show the bombed-out cities and the hard lot of German civilians. Goebbels had despaired by then of the mindless optimism of Nazi propaganda, and was looking for something more real, and hence more persuasive. In an irony Goebbels himself could have appreciated, Allied bombers destroyed the Babelsberg film studios where *Das Leben geht weiter* was in production, and the war ended before he could get his film made.[9]

His confidence in his intellectual superiority allowed Goebbels his tolerance for intellectual opponents, and made him want to persuade rather than to compel obedience. In a speech given shortly after the founding of his Ministry of Public Enlightenment and Propaganda in March 1933, Goebbels said "If this government is determined never and under no circumstances to give way, then it has no need of the lifeless power of the bayonet, and in the long run will not be content with 52 percent behind it and with terrorizing the remaining 48 percent, but will see its most immediate task as being to win over that remaining 48 percent." Diels even thought that Goebbels's ambition to exert tyranny imperceptibly through words caused him to despise much of the apparatus of Nazi repression.[10]

Where the confidence failed, so did the tolerance. Anyone, including SA men, who mocked Goebbels's physical limitations or self-dramatizing rhetoric could face his potentially murderous vengeance. This was all the more true for anyone who threatened his position in the Party or his safety. There is plausible evidence that the murders of a police officer, one Constable Josef Zauritz, and a Berlin SA leader, Hans Maikowski, can be traced to such a reaction.

The Nazi regime blamed these killings, which took place during the famous torchlight parade on the evening Hitler became chancellor of Germany, on Communists. But even just a few months later, in the summer of 1933, Diels's Gestapo had evidence that pointed elsewhere. Three stormtroopers told the Gestapo that they had seen an SA man named Alfred Buske shoot both Zauritz and Maikowski. One of these witnesses, Karl Deh, survived to tell the same story to police long after the war. Deh said that at a meeting in late December 1932, SA men had expressed the fear that the Nazi Party, once in power, would push them aside. Goebbels, therefore, had to "disappear before that." Hans Maikowski, who commanded the especially infamous Berlin SA unit Storm 33, declared that he himself would shoot Goebbels "if necessary." Four weeks later, during the torchlight parade, Constable Zauritz was assigned to march with Storm 33. Afterward, as the unit returned to its base "Storm Tavern," Deh stood a few feet away as Buske shot first Zauritz and then Maikowski. "In my opinion," said Deh, "Buske acted on higher orders." He was convinced that Goebbels had learned Maikowski might kill him. Buske had shot Zauritz to eliminate a witness. After these killings, Deh claimed, Buske was promoted, and though unemployed, he always seemed to be in funds.[11]

Evidence that the police gathered at the very start of the investigation is consistent with Deh's story. The doctor who pronounced Zauritz dead noted that he was shot from close range (there was powder in the wound) and by someone standing at the same level, ruling out Buske's story that the shots came from a first- or second-floor window. One witness heard a cry from the street: "A cop has been shot by the Nazis!" Another heard "Stop shooting! You're shooting your own comrade!" Some police officer or prosecutor underlined this part of the statement in red pencil. A third witness claimed actually to have seen two SA men shoot at Zauritz. Nonetheless, the police charged only Communists with the killing—a sign of what was coming in the German justice system.[12]

Goebbels had a relationship with Hitler wholly unlike that of any of the other Nazi leaders. "There was no one but Goebbels" in Hitler's inner circle, Diels wrote, "who could even capture [Hitler's] attention in free, agreeable conversation." The young writer Erich Ebermayer once had a chance to watch this. In February 1933, Hitler still kept his habit of taking afternoon coffee with his entourage at the Kaiserhof Hotel. Ebermayer was a regular at the hotel, and he bribed an elevator attendant to tell him when Hitler arrived for his coffee. Ebermayer noted with surprise that Hitler was quiet and disengaged from the conversation around him, and little interested in the obsequious followers who came to pay their respects. Then Goebbels appeared, "limping more than one would suspect from the news reels," and sat down self-confidently next to Hitler. Hitler immediately became livelier; his stiffness softened. "He relates completely differently to this man than to all the others," Ebermayer noted. Diels thought that Hitler would have been unthinkable without Goebbels. Goebbels was the top man in Hitler's inner circle, "the first interlocutor of the evil demon in Hitler." He "stabilized when Hitler was indecisive, gave his confused plans logical form and his immoderation justification, incitement, and boundlessness."[13]

THE NAZIS CALLED IT "Red Berlin," and indeed since the nineteenth century the city had provided a solid base for Germany's political left: first the liberals, then the Social Democrats, and, by the 1920s, the Communists (the pattern continues: today Berlin is a base for the Greens and the Left Party as well as the long-established Social Democrats). Berlin was one of Germany's leading industrial centers; it was Germany's financial capital, its media capital, and its cultural and intellectual capital as well as its political capital. Since the expulsion of the Huguenots from seventeenth-century France, Berlin had provided a home to migrants from all over Europe. This made Berlin's population, at least by German standards, regionally, ethnically, and religiously diverse. A popular saying had it that "all real Berliners come from Silesia." About 7 percent of Berliners were Jewish, in a country where Jews made up less than 1 percent of the population. Many Berliners proudly claimed Huguenot ancestry (some of them very prominent, like the novelist Theodor Fontane); the many towns and streets around Berlin with "Oranien" (from the Dutch "oranje," or "orange") in their names give witness to the Netherlanders who came to lend their expertise to drainage works. The Nazi Party, as it rose to power, drew support from Protestant rural areas and from regions where the Nazis could play on anti-Prussian and especially anti-Berlin resentments. Berlin itself seemed far from fertile Nazi ground.

So it was an inspired choice when, in 1926, Hitler named Joseph Goebbels *Gauleiter*, or party boss, of Berlin. In a book published in 1932, Goebbels demonstrated his rhetorical and propaganda skills in an appreciation of his post. Berlin, Goebbels conceded, was not Munich, the Nazis' birthplace. Its population was not homogenous, as in other German cities, but a composite of regions, classes, and confessions. Nonetheless, when Nazism arrived in Berlin, Berliners took it up with "the utter vehemence of Prussian toughness and discipline." The Berliner could "devote himself to a cause with the whole passion of his mobile soul, and nowhere is dogged fanaticism, above all in politics, so at home as in Berlin"—which for Goebbels was naturally a compliment. Goebbels thought that Berlin political activists were more brutal than elsewhere. The brilliant, ruthless, fanatical Gauleiter and his adopted city were well matched.[14]

In the autumn of 1930 Hitler made the Gauleiter of Berlin the national director of propaganda for the Nazi Party as well, and Goebbels could dedicate the full force of his agile mind to the promotion of Nazism. The nature of Berlin dictated both the content and the style of his propaganda. "Berlin needs its sensation like a fish needs water," he wrote. "This city lives on it, and all political propaganda that does not recognize that will fail to reach its goal." Red Berlin had hardly greeted the Nazis with open arms. The Party's stormtroopers were soon involved in unremitting and increasingly bloody battles with the paramilitary forces of the other political groupings. In response the Nazis learned how to transmute their experience of violence into effective political propaganda. Nazi propaganda, said Goebbels, "developed organically out of the daily struggle," and over time was systematized "through ever-repeated application." Effective propaganda had to appeal to modern Berlin as it was: to its size and diversity, its toughness, its violence.[15]

Goebbels's business was to lie, but this much was true: he did fabricate a style of political propaganda that grew organically out of the street battles of Berlin in the late 1920s and early 1930s. Goebbels understood that violence got headlines, especially in Berlin, where the national media was concentrated. In his diary he was always happy to record that the "Jew press" had written about another case of Nazi violence: "The main thing is they are talking about us," he liked to say. Key to this strategy was the deployment of the SA.[16]

The Nazi party, from its earliest days as a fringe movement in Munich's beer halls, needed tough young men both to protect its meetings from being broken up by its rivals, and to try to break up those rivals' meetings as well. At first these toughs were known as the "Meeting Police" (*Versammlungs Hauspolizei*); by late 1920 the Nazis had converted them into the "Gymnastics and Sport Section." The evolution of the SA was, however, not just a story internal to the Nazi Party. A bewildering profusion of right-radical militias played a part: in the early and middle 1920s these groups were formed and reformed, banned and formed again. What united them was a burning hatred of Socialists, Communists, Jews, and the Weimar Republic, coupled with an enthusiasm for violence. The personnel moved from one group to another, and among the leading figures in this radical militia scene of the 1920s we can find most of those who would, ten years later, be the leaders of the Berlin SA.[17]

One of the streams that fed the later SA flowed from various militias formed after the First World War by the former naval officer Corvette Captain Hermann Ehrhardt: the *Freikorps* (free corps) known as the Ehrhardt Brigade, and later the "Organization Consul" and the "Viking League." Men of the Organization Consul carried out some of the most notorious assassinations of the Weimar Republic, including the murders of Finance Minister Matthias Erzberger in 1921 and Foreign Minister Walther Rathenau in 1922. In 1921 Ehrhardt agreed with Adolf Hitler that Ehrhardt's organization would work politically for the Nazi Party while remaining militarily under his own command. This, according to historian Peter Longerich, marked the real beginning of what were soon being called the *Sturmabteilungen* (SA) or storm sections. A furious November 1921 brawl in Munich's Hofbräuhaus became this new SA's baptism of fire.[18]

45

There were other paramilitary groups in northern Germany, most of the important ones loosely affiliated in an organization called the *Frontbann*. The Frontbann was founded in the spring of 1924 as a covert means of sustaining the SA when all Nazi organizations were banned in the aftermath of Hitler's failed 1923 Beerhall *Putsch*, or coup. The effective commander of the Frontbann was Ernst Röhm, another war veteran who had fought with a Freikorps unit in Bavaria. One of the Berlin groups affiliated with the Frontbann was the Charlottenburg *Turnerschaft Ulrich von Hutten* (Ulrich von Hutten gymnastics society). Among its members were future Berlin SA leaders Fritz Hahn and Karl Ernst; it later evolved into Hans Maikowski's infamous SA unit Storm 33. Ernst Röhm so impressed the dissolute aristocrat and war veteran Wolf-Heinrich Count von Helldorff that Helldorff left the conservative veterans' organization the *Stahlhelm* (steel helmet) and joined the Frontbann; at the time of the Reichstag fire Helldorff would be the commander of the Berlin SA. At the end of October 1925 the Frontbann was dissolved and in March 1926 the Berlin SA was officially relaunched with Kurt Daluege, despite his nickname "Dummy-Dummy" one of the key early Berlin Nazi leaders, as its commander.[19]

This complex history, in which the SA developed substantially autonomously from the leaders of the Nazi Party, left an important legacy. Relations between the Party and the SA were always tense and competitive. Already in 1924 Hitler had worried about "his" SA being dissolved into the Frontbann, which claimed to be nonpartisan and which Röhm controlled. When Hitler was released from prison at the end of that year he set about recovering his hold on both Party and SA. In February 1925 he declared in the *Völkischer Beobachter* that the SA would have to return to its functions of 1923, which meant "steeling" and "disciplining" Nazi youth for the "idea," rather than actively seeking to overthrow the republic through violence. Röhm, an incurable soldier of fortune, quit and went to join the Bolivian army.[20]

Hitler would later bring Röhm back, but the tensions between Party and SA never went away, and were complicated by ideological as well as tactical differences. The SA was as anticapitalist and antibourgeois as it was anti-Republican and anti-Semitic. SA rhetoric was often hard to distinguish from that of the parties of the left. The Berlin SA's official history characterized the typical Berlin stormtrooper as a "bruiser" (*Rabauke*) with a combination of "hard soldierliness," "stirring revolutionary fire," and "radical socialism." Horst Wessel himself wrote that Nazis from Vienna did not understand his "radical socialist" politics and considered him a "half-Communist." After Hitler had become Germany's dictator, the members of Storm 33 looked back on what they called the "time of struggle" (*Kampfzeit*) and recalled that although they had fought hard against the Communists, they would not forget their struggle against "the thoughtlessness and cowardice of the middle class," which neglected "the economic needs of its national comrades so long as things were going well for itself," which "cravenly left the streets to Marxism," whose lack of political instinct meant that it had "failed even to recognize the danger of the Jews," and all in all was "fundamentally just as hostile to us as was the Red Front." Talk like this could only complicate Hitler's efforts to win over conservative middle-class voters.[21]

Yet it was this SA that Goebbels employed as his main instrument in winning Berlin for the Nazis, in a complicated set of maneuvers that depended for success on ruthless violence coupled with breathtaking mendacity, and a high degree of voter credulity. The result was a string of violent clashes of various kinds—shootings, brawls, ambushes, bombings, and arson attacks, mostly between the SA and the Communist paramilitaries. Goebbels himself, testifying at the Reichstag fire trial in November of 1933, embedded the fire in this longer narrative of political violence. Goebbels's theme here—as it was in his propaganda all the way from 1926 to 1933—was that the Communists committed repeated acts of violence on Nazis, while trying to shift the propagandistic blame onto their opponents.[22]

There was, for instance, the case of Horst Wessel. Wessel, only twenty-two years old in early 1930, was the leader of SA Storm 5 in the rough Berlin neighborhood of Friedrichshain. Despite his youth he had passed through all the typical stations of a Berlin stormtrooper: the Viking League, the *Schwarze Reichswehr* (literally "black army," the underground armed forces that some German officers maintained in the 1920s in defiance of the Treaty of Versailles), and the gymnastics club Olympia, similar to the Turnerschaft Ulrich von Hutten. In Goebbels's account Wessel was a young man who had brought enormous idealism to the Nazi movement, a law student who had gone to live among the workers in the mean streets of Friedrichshain, and recruited them with such success that the Communists assassinated him. The Communists then painted Wessel as a pimp who had been killed by a business rival.

In fact, while it was true enough that Horst Wessel had been killed by a man with Communist ties, Albrecht or "Ali" Höhler, Höhler was more of a pimp and a gangster than a political activist, and Wessel's killing had little to do with politics. It seems to have arisen primarily out of a dispute over rent. At the time of his death, Wessel was mourning the recent death of his brother, and according to one source seemed to be withdrawing from the Nazi movement. He was living with a former (or perhaps still active) prostitute named Erna Jaenichen, with whom he now seemed to spend more evenings than he did with the men of his storm. (Noting this, the men talked of replacing him.) Ali Höhler's lawyer Alfred Apfel claimed later in the 1930s—although unreliably in the view of Wessel's most authoritative biographer—that "I could fill a concentration camp with Nazis if I were ever to reveal the names of the Hitlerites who came to me and thanked me" for having treated Wessel's pimping with discretion.[23]

Wessel's murder roused Goebbels's newspaper, the *Angriff* (Attack), to a demonstration of the Nazi tactic of doublespeak regarding "legality," or whether or not the Party planned to come to power through elections rather than through violence. To its base, especially to the young men of the SA, the Party typically suggested with a wink that the "legality" talk was just a ruse to put the authorities off the scent. At the same time, middle-class nationalist voters could be reassured that maybe the Nazis were not so frightening after all. As Wessel lay dying in the Friedrichshain hospital—he lingered for five weeks after the shooting—the *Angriff* concluded that the only thing to do was to "gather power" in order to "exterminate root and branch" the "noxious Communist brood"—this threat indented and set off in bold type from the rest of the article. Immediately after, in an undertone of regular type, came the almost satirical qualifier: "In the most legal way," followed by "just as one kills off rats or bugs."[24]

This doublespeak worked on its intended targets. A senior Berlin prosecutor advised the Prussian justice minister that this article did not amount to an incitement to or a threat of violence. Rather, it was simply an announcement that if the Nazis came to power they would make vigorous use of their legal remedies against the Communist Party. The minister agreed.[25]

Then there was the SA attack on the Felseneck cottage colony. Like many such poor settlements where, in the trough of the Depression, workers lived in garden sheds that were often no better than paper shacks, Felseneck was a Communist stronghold. One night, said Goebbels, a few

Nazi Party members who lived there had been escorted home by their comrades, so that "they weren't left at the mercy of the Communist rabble." The Communists, he claimed, ambushed them anyway, killing one and injuring several other Nazis.

The evidence gathered in the subsequent police and judicial investigations showed that on the night of January 18, 1932, about 150 SA men had marched far out of their way, allegedly to escort no more than six of their number to the Communist-dominated area around the miserable cottage colony. The SA commander had told his men beforehand that if they saw any Communists they should kill them and get away. The stormtroopers approached the colony in "firing line" after their police escort had mysteriously withdrawn. Fritz Klemke, the young Communist who was killed that night, was someone against whom the SA already had a grudge, and a police officer may have been complicit in his murder. More surprising than Goebbels's spin on this story was that a young Berlin judge named Adolf Arndt, who wrote the trial judgment, accepted it. Arndt was a Social Democrat of partly Jewish background.[26]

There were other events in the violent political history of early 1930s Berlin that involved Goebbels more directly. They showed how his mind worked and who his most important associates were.

On March 14, 1931, the *Angriff* reported an "assassination attempt on Dr. Goebbels." The day before, someone had mailed a bomb to Goebbels's home in the well-to-do suburb of Wilmersdorf. The post office redirected it to the Nazi Party's Berlin headquarters on Hedemannstrasse. An SA man had noticed several thin wires and some gunpowder on the package. Nonetheless he opened it. Inside was a crude bomb made of matches, gunpowder, and firecrackers. Not until the next day did someone from the *Angriff*'s editorial office notify the Berlin police.

"Noteworthy in this connection," ran a police report, was that the police had received a letter dated February 17th, from "Nathan Baruch and Rosa Rosenbaum," asking for Goebbels's private address and declaring that they were "true republicans." A similar letter purported to come from two Communists. The police concluded that the whole thing had been a Nazi publicity stunt. The coverage of the supposed bombing in the *Angriff* amounted legally to a public nuisance. The report closed by asking that the editors of the *Angriff* be prosecuted.[27]

The police continued to investigate. On May 8th, Eduard Weiss, the SA man who had supposedly received the package containing the bomb, gave a statement. Two days before the alleged attack, Goebbels had asked Weiss to open all packages addressed to the Gauleiter. "He justified this by saying that he feared an assassination attempt on his person." Weiss also made several corrections to a statement he had given to the police immediately after the supposed attempt. Among them: in March he had told the police that one of the firecrackers had gone off when he opened the package. In May he amended this to say that Goebbels had ordered him to set the firecracker alight. Indeed, although Goebbels had not been present while the package was being opened, Weiss told the police in May that Goebbels had ordered him to say that Goebbels had been there the whole time. Another employee from Goebbels's office told the police the whole thing was just "advertising for Dr. Goebbels."[28]

The fake assassination attempt unleashed a propaganda battle between the Communists and the Nazis, whose contours foreshadowed what would come two years later, after the Reichstag fire. The Nazis' "Gau leadership" warned Berlin's Nazis to stay calm and disciplined in the face of the Communists' attempt on Goebbels. The Communist *Rote Fahne* mocked Goebbels as a coward; the so-called bomb was nothing more than "a few firecrackers, familiar to every Berlin boy." The highbrow liberal paper the *Vossische Zeitung* (Voss's newspaper), wittier and more detached, headlined the case as "The Little Man's Assassination Attempt." The *Vossische* reprinted correspondence between Goebbels's office and the Berlin police headquarters dating back to the end of January, in which Goebbels repeatedly asked that his address not be publicly divulged, because of the many threats of attack from Communists he had received. "Obviously," said the *Vossische*, "an 'assassination' [was] in preparation."[29]

Although the police documents leave little doubt that Goebbels himself arranged the whole thing, his willingness to deceive extended to the pages of his own diary. "Yesterday morning an assassination attempt with a bomb was made on me," he wrote on March 14th. "Ede Weiss smelled a rat right away and opened carefully. If it had exploded it would definitely have done for my eyes and my face." Goebbels maintained his faith in the tactic. Nearly two months later, Goebbels's office alarmed Berlin's criminal court by sending word that Communists were planning to assassinate Hitler when he appeared to testify at the "Eden Dance Palace" trial of four Berlin stormtroopers. In March 1932, Goebbels warned Chancellor Heinrich Brüning that dissident Nazis were planning an assassination attempt against him.[30]

It was no coincidence that the phony assassination attempt occurred in the run-up to the revolt that Walter Stennes, the SA commander for Berlin and Eastern Germany, tried to lead against Hitler's control of the Nazi Party. Trouble between the Berlin SA and the Party had been brewing since the fall of 1930 when the Party refused to put three stormtroopers on its list of parliamentary candidates. But the real problem was the chronic one of the incompatibility of the goals and temperament of the SA radicals and the calculating Nazi politicians in Munich. The final break came on April 1, 1931, when Hitler sacked Stennes. The Berlin SA leaders declared their solidarity with Stennes, and Stennes led SA units in occupying the Berlin Party offices and those of Goebbels's *Angriff*. Goebbels confided to his diary that the Party was passing through its "most serious crisis" yet.[31]

It was a crisis for him, too: Goebbels was seriously implicated in Stennes's revolt. Department IA believed he had been on Stennes's side, and only jumped back to ostentatious displays of loyalty to Hitler when it became clear that the Stennes revolt would fail. According to police sources, the Munich leadership was well aware of Goebbels's near-betrayal, and his position in the Party had consequently been weakened. Goebbels's most bitter rival within the Nazi Party, Hermann Göring—perhaps because after 1933 the records of Department IA fell into his hands— shared this belief, as did Diels: "Even Goebbels had ridden two horses" during the revolt, Diels wrote after the war. Diels heard this from Stennes himself. In 1933 Stennes wrote a statement for Göring implicating Goebbels in return for being released into exile (he went to China and became an advisor to Chiang Kai-shek; in 1941 he was one of many who vainly warned the Soviet Peoples' Commissariat for Internal Affairs [NKVD] of Hitler's intention to attack the Soviet Union). Stennes also told Hitler's friend and foreign press chief Ernst Hanfstaengl about Goebbels: "Say, Hanfstaengl," said Stennes, pulling Hanfstaengl aside at a meeting and gesturing toward Goebbels, "does Hitler actually know that the initiator of the whole revolt is standing next to him?" Despite Hitler's orders, said Stennes, Goebbels insisted on driving SA men on to "violent demonstrations." Even Goebbels's diary offers corroboration. In February he had written a careful note of a pact with Stennes: "We are entirely at one in the assessment of the political position. . . . We are making an alliance. SA + me. That's power."[32]

In the end, of course, Stennes's revolt failed. Hitler was able to rally most of the SA behind him, although the number of SA men who followed

Stennes out of the Nazi Party was substantial—about one-third of the total Berlin strength. But the bitterness lingered, as did the problem of reconciling the revolutionary violence of the SA with the cool calculation of a political movement trying to win power. When Goebbels sent the pathetic bomb to himself, he must have hoped that with this stunt he could recover the loyalty of the SA and stave off the threat of schism within the Nazi movement, channeling hatred toward the Communists and scoring a propaganda success against them as well. This would prove to be a recurring pattern in Goebbels's tactics.[33]

The idea of using a propaganda action to hold together the fractious Nazis lay behind a much bigger operation that Goebbels carried out in the autumn of 1931. Goebbels had his share of worries that fall about the direction of the Nazi Party. The Nazis were steering toward the Harzburg Front, an alliance with the DNVP, which the radical Goebbels viewed with extreme distaste. "It can't be otherwise," he wrote in his diary on September 16th. "But push for a sole takeover of power by us. Every compromise is repulsive to me." When the Harzburg Front became a reality, Goebbels worried that it was driving the Hitler Youth organization to a crisis: some members were leaving to join the Communists. He responded characteristically. The result was an event whose pattern and subsequent controversy strongly foreshadowed the Reichstag fire.[34]

September 12, 1931, was Rosh Hashanah, the Jewish New Year. That evening, in the affluent heart of west Berlin, where the grand boulevard Kurfürstendamm (or Ku'damm) began its course from Auguste Viktoria Platz to the Grünewald, crowds were on their way to the theaters, movie palaces, and cafes. Meanwhile, around 7:30, masses of stormtroopers (out of uniform) began gathering on the Ku'damm, and at about 8:30, after cries of "Germany awake!" and "Perish Judah!" they started wildly attacking and beating passersby.

The stormtroopers wanted to attack Jews, but could not identify them with any reliability. Victims of savage beatings included a man whom the court later described as "a dark south-German type," and a lawyer who had been a close friend and advocate of the nationalist martyr Leo Schlageter, executed by the French in 1923 and a hero to the Nazis. Other victims included an engineer from India, two Romanians, and an Armenian.

What became known as the "Kurfürstendamm Pogrom" or the "Kurfürstendamm Riot" lasted a little under two hours. Altogether the SA men attacked thirty to forty people. Estimates of the number of stormtroopers involved varied widely. Berlin SA commander Helldorff, who had succeeded Stennes, thought he had seen five hundred to six hundred of his own men, but they had been joined by an equal number from other groups like the *Stahlhelm*. The lawyer Alfred Apfel watched the riot from the balcony of his Ku'damm apartment and took careful notes. With the aid of skills learned during the war, he estimated the size of the mob at twelve hundred to fifteen hundred people.

The police response to a thousand or more marauding Nazis in the center of Berlin was curiously inept. It was nearly 9:00 before they arrived, and it took even longer for seventy riot squad officers from "Inspection West" under the command of Major Walther Wecke to appear and put a final end to the violence. The *Berliner Tageblatt* determined that the regular commander of riot police for that area, one Major Meyer, had reported sick that very day and been replaced by Wecke. There was a rumor that Meyer had been deliberately moved out of the way. These suspicions appear credible in retrospect. By 1932 Walther Wecke was covertly passing information about the police to Nazi leaders. Later that year he joined the Party. He would go on to be one of Göring's police commanders in the early days of the Nazi regime.[35]

Many witnesses observed that the rioters seemed to take their orders from the passengers in two cars that cruised up and down the Ku'damm and the surrounding streets. In one of those cars, an Opel cabriolet, rode Helldorff, along with his deputy, Karl Ernst, and a man who at the time commanded the "Staff Watch" at Berlin SA headquarters, and would go on to spend decades at the center of the Reichstag fire story: Hans Georg Gewehr, better known by his nickname "Heini" or, more colorfully, "Pistol Heini."

Helldorff was born in 1896. He volunteered for military service on the outbreak of war in 1914, and was in combat by his eighteenth birthday in October. He served throughout the war (in the same regiment as future Nazi Foreign Minister Joachim von Ribbentrop), rising to the command of a company and being awarded the Iron Cross 1st and 2nd class as well as the Saxon Order of the White Falcon. Like many veterans he could not adjust to peacetime and joined the famous Lützow Freikorps, which in the "Kapp Putsch" of 1920 played its part in trying to overthrow the new democratic government of Weimar. Helldorff fled to Italy for a time. In 1922, back in Germany, he was investigated for murder, but prosecutors eventually dropped the case. In the mid-1920s Helldorff joined the Nazi

Party and became a Nazi member of the Prussian parliament as well as a leader of the Frontbann.[36]

Karl Ernst had been too young for the war and lacked Helldorff's social pedigree, but his life story also revealed the dislocations which the war had brought to the lives of many young Germans. Ernst was a native Berliner, born in 1904. He had worked for a time as a page and a waiter at the posh Hotel Eden before becoming one of the first recruits to the Frontbann. Ernst's close friendship with the SA commander Ernst Röhm helped assure his rapid rise, as did the fact that Ernst remained loyal to the Party during the Stennes revolt.[37]

On September 18th the prosecutors brought thirty-four defendants, most of them SA men, before the Summary Judgment Court (Schnell Schöffengericht) for Berlin-Charlottenburg. The Nazis deployed their top legal talent: Roland Freisler, who later, as president of the Nazis' People's Supreme Court, would preside over the trials of Sophie and Hans Scholl and most of the men involved in the Valkyrie plot against Hitler—including Helldorff; Hans Frank, Hitler's own lawyer, later head of the General Government of German-occupied Poland; and Alfons Sack, who, like Hans Georg Gewehr, would play an important role in the story of the Reichstag fire. The defendants tried hard to play down the seriousness of the riots. They all claimed it was a matter of pure chance that they had found themselves around the Ku'damm that night. They had known nothing of any plans for violence, and could not even explain what they meant by chanting "Germany awake!" One defendant suggested the words were a "call for peace."[38]

After a five-day trial most of the men, including Gewehr, received light prison sentences. Helldorff and Ernst met the same fate at a later trial. All of them appealed, resulting in a long retrial from December 1931 to February 1932. Nazi propaganda worked hard to shift the blame for the riots. Nazi defendants, lawyers, and press claimed repeatedly that it was Communists who had committed the violence, or at least provoked it with cries of "Germany awake!" One witness said that he thought the SA men "wanted to disguise the demonstration as a Communist one, and only to show their true faces when they were in control of the Kurfürstendamm." A police officer testified that one of the Nazis he arrested was carrying a truncheon with the insignia of the Communist Red Frontfighters' League. The Nazis' legal defenders—once again Freisler, Frank, and Sack—claimed that the police sought to discredit the Nazis by manipulating them into such riots, and that the Prussian Interior Ministry had sent agents into the ranks of the SA with exactly this goal in mind. "It is certain," said Goebbels's *Angriff* in another anticipation of later Reichstag fire arguments, "that the SA leadership was surprised by the incident."[39]

The vital question in all of the Ku'damm riot trials thus became whether or not the SA had planned the violence, and whether Goebbels had been involved in the plans. Ernst and Helldorff testified repeatedly that they had known nothing about the riots until that evening, when they paid a routine inspection visit to an SA base and were told that the storm had gone to the Kurfürstendamm. They rushed after their men, but only to *prevent* violence and send the men home. Helldorff claimed that the presence of so many stormtroopers on the Ku'damm could only be the work of agents provocateurs.[40]

There was sensational evidence to the contrary, implicating Goebbels as well as Helldorff and Ernst. In early November, at Helldorff and Ernst's first trial, the court heard from one Criminal Commissar Wendelin Feistel of Department IA. Feistel testified that in October a middleman had introduced him to an informer with ties to the SA commanders. Feistel would not name the middleman and claimed not to know the name of the informer, on whose reliability he could give no opinion. According to the informer, Goebbels had summoned Helldorff to a meeting three days before the riots, at which he suggested that unemployed SA men be ordered to hold a "demonstration" on the Jewish New Year. The Berlin SA leaders feared that this would leave them open to the criticism that they were using the unemployed as "cannon fodder" and exposing them to arrest. They decided instead to send *all* available SA men to the Ku'damm on Saturday evening. Helldorff would command from his car. The SA leaders had met again after the riot, said the informer, to coordinate their testimony.[41]

This information made Goebbels an indispensable witness. The court summoned him to testify on November 2nd, but the Gauleiter found it prudent to be in Danzig that day, supposedly on a fact-finding mission. At the retrial Goebbels relented—up to a point. He appeared in court on January 23rd. However, since the accusations against him had come from an anonymous informer, he refused to testify. In his diary he recorded his battle with the prosecutor, the experienced specialist in political cases State Advocate Paul Stenig: "Witness in the Helldorff trial. The great sensation! The yellow press lurks. I step forward, make strongest attacks against the police headquarters and refuse to testify on the grounds of decency until the informer is named. And then there is such a clash that it blows up. We [Goebbels and Stenig] scream at each other like the Homeric heroes. Dismissed after strong declaration for the transcript. The SA is beside itself with joy."[42]

When one of the judges warned Goebbels that the court might draw negative conclusions for the defendants from his refusal to testify, Roland Freisler declared "in the name of all the defendants" that Goebbels should keep silent even if his testimony would help the SA men. The judges fined Goebbels five hundred marks for contempt.[43]

On February 9th the court acquitted Ernst, Helldorff, and Gewehr of breach of the peace, although Ernst and Helldorff were given minor fines for yelling anti-Semitic insults. Nineteen of their followers, however, were convicted of breach of the peace, along with the Stahlhelm leader Brandt. The sentences ranged from four to ten months.

The court treated the SA leaders so gently because it was not persuaded that they and Goebbels had planned the riot. The judges found that Goebbels's failure to testify had made it impossible to be certain of his role. Furthermore, they were skeptical of the evidence from Feistel's informer, which was, on the whole, "worthless." No court, it said, could justly rely on the evidence of such a "shadowy figure" (*Dunkelmann*) who might be a self-promoter or even mentally ill, and whose ability to testify accurately the court could therefore not assess.

However admirable as protection of the stormtroopers' civil liberties, the court's findings betrayed at best a breathtaking naivety. Given the tendency of the Nazis and other far-right groups to murder informers—so-called *Fememord* trials resulting from such murders had been a recurring feature of German postwar justice—it is hard to imagine how else the police could have gotten their evidence. The judges showed strong sympathy for Goebbels's motive for refusing to testify, and in fact the judgment was replete with touches of Nazi rhetoric. The Ku'damm, said the court, "especially frequented by Jews," was "a slogan for unsocial pleasure-seeking, for gluttony and the sybaritic life." The key players in the Ku'damm riot—Goebbels, Helldorff, Ernst, and Gewehr—had struck not only at people but at a place with symbolic value for Nazi propaganda, as the judges were quick to appreciate. And they did so while trying to lay blame for their violence at the feet of the Communists. The judges of the Weimar Republic have often been criticized for constituting a right-wing fifth column inside the democratic state. But something more complicated was going on here. The judge who drafted this verdict was the same Adolf Arndt who had written the judgment in the Felseneck case, accepting there too the Nazis' projection of guilt onto their victims. Arndt would appear in the story of the Reichstag fire after the war. His later intervention would reveal the education that came of having become one of those victims.[44]

Goebbels orchestrated the defense down to the selection of the lawyers. "Quarrel over the lawyers for Helldorff," he wrote in his diary in late September. "I'm getting [Hans] Frank to come. At least he'll do it right politically." He also worked behind the scenes to help Helldorff and the other defendants. On September 24th, before Helldorff's first trial began, Goebbels got in touch with members of the Reich cabinet and with Chancellor Heinrich Brüning himself to urge Helldorff's acquittal and the release of the other prisoners. Brüning promised to investigate the matter.[45]

Two days later Brüning even received the Nazis' propagandist. "He was very agreeable," Goebbels recorded, "and accepted my accusations in the cases of Kurfürstendamm and Red Murder in silence." Brüning wrote in his memoirs that he and Goebbels made a deal: Brüning arranged a different judge for Helldorff, while Goebbels ensured that Nazis would not disrupt an upcoming visit by French ministers.[46]

As it turned out, the court was wrong and Feistel's informer, along with liberal and left-wing opinion in Berlin, were right: Goebbels, Helldorff, and Ernst *had* planned the riots. There is conclusive evidence on this point. Even in 1932 a prominent Berlin SA officer had written to Hitler to complain about Helldorff's "shameful" roll in the Ku'damm "affair": "At the giving out of the orders [only] Dr. Goebbels, Ernst, and Helldorff were present and yet the police found out about it." Further confirmation came after the war from none other than Heini Gewehr. In 1960 Gewehr wrote: "Count Helldorff and Karl Ernst had ordered this demonstration and notified the Berlin *Standarten* [SA units]." Later on, Gewehr said, he had been pressured to testify that he, Helldorff, and Ernst had driven to the Ku'damm only to control the violence. "During the trial," he continued, "there were fights between Count Helldorff and me, because I took the view that one should stand up for one's actions."[47]

THE KU'DAMM RIOT was not the first time the Berlin SA unleashed violence aimed at Jews. In October 1930, at the opening of the new Reichstag session, stormtroopers had gone on a rampage around Potsdamer Platz and Leipziger Platz, attacking Jewish-owned shops and business. Goebbels's *Angriff* naturally blamed the whole thing on provocateurs, "Ali Höhler types" in fact, and insisted that the Nazi Party had nothing to do with it. Here again was Goebbels's propaganda of the street.[48]

As late as March 1934 Goebbels and his SA allies from the Ku'damm were still getting up to what Ernst Röhm's biographer Eleanor Hancock has called "political theater." The occasion was the Berlin premier of a British film on the life of Catherine the Great, starring an Austrian actress of Jewish origins named Elisabeth Bergner. Three days before the premier Goebbels complained that his ban on Jewish actors was being flouted and "requested" that German authorities enforce his ban. At the premiere, rioters, among them many SA men, "shouted anti-Semitic slogans, threw eggs at posters in the lobby, and harassed cinema-goers." Ernst gave a speech assuring them the film would be banned. Inside the theater Röhm asked the audience to "remember that Germany was a land of law and order." The next day the film was shut down. By 1934 no such demonstration could have taken place without at least tacit official approval, and Hancock writes that Röhm's part in the affair was likely coordinated with Goebbels and Ernst.[49]

The Ku'damm riot also prefigured the more famous *Kristallnacht* of November 1938, which Goebbels also stage-managed, although by this time Ernst and Röhm had fallen victim to Hitler's murderous calculations. As Saul Friedländer writes, by the autumn of 1938 the idea of a pogrom against German Jews had "been in the air" for some time, perhaps since early 1937. But several factors precipitated it. On November 7th a young Polish Jew whose family had just been deported to Poland from their home in Hannover decided to register a dramatic protest. Herschel Grynszpan, who was living underground in Paris, went to the German embassy there and shot an official named Ernst vom Rath. Rath died two days later. Word of Rath's death reached Hitler and Goebbels at the annual banquet commemorating the Beer Hall Putsch of November 9, 1923. After speaking to Goebbels, Hitler (very unusually) left the banquet and Goebbels gave a speech in his stead, letting the gathering know that the government would not hinder "spontaneous" demonstrations of rage against Jews.[50]

The "spontaneous" demonstrations went ahead. Across Germany 267 synagogues were destroyed by fire and 7,500 businesses were vandalized, mostly by SA men. The shattered windows of those businesses gave the event its name, which means "the night of broken glass." Nazis also murdered nearly a hundred Jews, while several hundred more committed suicide or died as a result of abuse after arrest. Hitler had ordered the arrest of twenty thousand to thirty thousand Jews.

Kristallnacht followed the pattern Goebbels had established with the fake bomb and the Ku'damm riots. In the fall of 1938 Goebbels was again experiencing a career crisis. Hitler had criticized Goebbels's ineffective propaganda during the international crisis that year over the status of the Sudetenland, and Goebbels had further disgraced himself in his master's eyes through his affair with the Czech actress Lida Baarova. Goebbels was, as Saul Friedländer writes, "in need of some major initiative," and now he had one. Nonetheless, although Kristallnacht was Goebbels's operation— Hitler's deputy Rudolf Hess said later that Goebbels was its "originator"— Goebbels had not written about the assassination of Rath in his diary on November 7th or 8th. This "unusual silence," says Friedländer, was "the surest indication of plans that aimed at a 'spontaneous outburst of popular anger.'"[51]

3

....

"WHAT JUST WENT ON HERE IS AN ABSOLUTE OUTRAGE"

RUMORS

AT THE BEGINNING OF JANUARY 1933, many Germans had the impression that the dangerous prospect of a Hitler government—seemingly imminent throughout 1932—had receded. In the most recent Reichstag elections of November 6, 1932, the Nazi vote share had fallen for the first time since 1928. The party was broke, its operatives exhausted and in despair.

It was in this uncertain moment that the brief tenure of Chancellor Franz von Papen came to a sudden end. The calculating General Kurt von Schleicher, who had the ear of President von Hindenburg, had maneuvered Papen into the chancellorship in the summer of 1932. Schleicher was confident that Papen would be a useful tool with which he could bring Nazi support behind a government that would crush Germany's socialists and Communists and put an end to the democratic coalition in Prussia. Schleicher thought that he could buy Hitler's support with a few insubstantial concessions—like ending the ban on the SA that the previous Brüning administration had just introduced—and thus keep Hitler from effective power. After the stunning Nazi victory in the elections of July 1932, however, Hitler would accept nothing less than the chancellorship for himself, and neither Papen nor President Hindenburg was willing to give it to him.

The problem was that the 1932 elections showed that only about 10 percent of Germans supported Papen's government, and Schleicher and the men around him were shrewd enough to know that even a dictatorship needed more popular support than that. An alarming report suggested that the army could not possibly keep order in the event of a civil war between the Communists and the Nazis. Things would be even worse were these groups to join forces against the government, a prospect that did not seem far-fetched after Nazis and Communists collaborated in support of a Berlin transit strike in early November. Schleicher convinced Hindenburg that he had a viable plan to split the Nazis and draw support from the Party's Gregor Strasser wing, politically more left-leaning and tactically more accommodating than Hitler himself, as well as from the trade unions. Hindenburg accepted Schleicher's plan, dismissed Papen, and named Schleicher to the post.

Schleicher's plan failed almost immediately. Hitler succeeded in holding his party together and drove Strasser from his influential position. The unions and the Social Democrats remained unconvinced that any general could have their interests at heart. Meanwhile, Papen, brooding over his fall from power and Schleicher's betrayal, decided the path to revenge lay through assembling an alternate coalition. He would concede the chancellorship to Hitler while keeping what he hoped would be the more important vice-chancellorship for himself, and bringing other right-wing groups like the German Nationals and the Steel Helmet into a "government of national concentration."

Negotiations for such a deal went on in January 1933, while the Nazis were able to camouflage their sharp drop in votes in the November elections with a state election victory in the tiny state of Lippe. The deal almost broke down at the last minute when Hitler insisted that the government must call new elections right away. Nationalist leader Alfred Hugenberg wanted to suspend the Reichstag so that the government could function as a dictatorship, using emergency powers from President Hindenburg, at least until it could calm the economic crisis and restore political stability by outlawing the Communists. In a sign of things to come, Hugenberg grudgingly gave way, and an election was set for Sunday, March 5th. Hitler's new government would enter office facing an immediate election campaign. "It has happened," Goebbels wrote exultantly in his diary. "We are sitting in the Wilhelmstrasse. . . . Like a fairy tale."

Yet to most other observers, especially the Nationalist leaders, little seemed to have changed. "We have hired him," Papen wrote confidently of Hitler. "In a few months we will have pushed him so far into the corner that he will squeak." Decades later it is easy to laugh at his lack of foresight. But in the winter of 1933 there were reasons to believe that Papen was right. After all, Hitler and his two Nazi cabinet colleagues, Minister without Portfolio (and Prussian Interior Minister) Hermann Göring, and Reich Interior Minister Wilhelm Frick, were surrounded and outnumbered by solid establishment figures—Papen, Hugenberg, Papen's Foreign Minister Baron Constantin von Neurath, Defense Minister Werner von Blomberg, to say nothing of the venerable President von Hindenburg. Hitler could not have an audience with Hindenburg without Papen. In a crunch the army would surely stand with its revered old field marshal against Hitler. Anyway, was it not true that the responsibility of power always tamed radicals? That had certainly happened to the Social Democrats after 1918.[1]

"It made little impression on us," wrote Max Fürst years later, "when Hitler came to power in January 1933." Fürst was a young carpenter and furniture maker who had moved to Berlin from Königsberg in 1927. He had spent years as a leader of a left-wing Jewish youth group, and his closest friend (and roommate) was the radical lawyer Hans Litten. "So many, in part dreadful governments, had come and gone. . . . It probably couldn't get any worse than the Papen government." The journalist Sebastian Haffner (at the time a law student) agreed: he, too, thought that Hitler's government would be little different than the preceding Papen and Schleicher administrations.[2]

The life spans of Weimar governments had all been short, and few expected Hitler's to prove the exception. The independent Nationalist politician Gottfried Treviranus wrote years later that everyone he knew expected Hitler to "exhaust himself on the phalanx of Hindenburg, the army, and the constitution." Friedrich Stampfer, editor-in-chief of the Social Democratic paper *Vorwärts* (Forward), asked a foreign correspondent if he seriously believed that "this roaring gorilla can govern," adding that Hitler's government would last no longer than three weeks. Erich Ebermayer, well connected in both literary and political circles, recorded that his mother gave Hitler's government six weeks. But his father, the former chief Reich prosecutor, was more sober. "Even if it only lasts half a year," said Ludwig Ebermayer, "a lot of damage can be done, especially in foreign policy." Then, turning grimmer and more prophetic, the old man added: "But it will last longer. This is no cabinet like any other, one that will just resign someday."[3]

Ludwig Ebermayer had retired in 1926 and in early 1933 he was dying of cancer. Strangely, some of the few active politicians who viewed Hitler's new government with real alarm were among those who were supposed to be Hitler's allies.

NO ONE COULD HAVE CONFUSED Dr. Ernst Oberfohren with a liberal democrat. Oberfohren was the leader of the German National People's Party's Reichstag caucus. A 1931 speech gives a good idea of his political outlook. His party was not in the Reichstag, he said, to "palaver." They were there to declare war on the "system," and on "the bearers of this system." By the "system," of course, he meant the democracy of Weimar Germany.[4]

Nonetheless Oberfohren became an early critic and an early target of the National Socialists, starting with a public war of words with the Nazi leader in Schleswig-Holstein, Hinrich Lohse (later infamous as the Reich commissar, or governor, of German-occupied territories in the Baltic and Belarus regions of the Soviet Union, where he was responsible for widespread atrocities). Lohse attacked Oberfohren as "racially undefined," a freemason, a "political conman." For Oberfohren the Nazis were a southern, Catholic party, unsuitable for a leading role in Lutheran northern Germany, fatally reckless and irresponsible.[5]

When in 1932 the Nazis had come to power in the small northern state of Oldenburg and opened a reign of terror on their political opponents, including the Nationalists, Oberfohren urged the Reich interior minister to use emergency powers to remove Oldenburg Prime Minister Carl Röver from office, just as Papen's government had overturned the Braun-Severing administration in Prussia. Under the headline "Against Every Party-Dictatorship" a German National newspaper quoted Oberfohren as saying "We German Nationals do not one-sidedly reject the idea of a party-state run by Social Democrats, rather [we reject] the idea of a party state altogether." In return, Nazis often disrupted or broke up meetings at which Oberfohren spoke—which at any rate reinforced his point.[6]

When Hitler became chancellor it did not take Oberfohren long to see that the Nazis would rule Germany with the violence and lawlessness they had deployed in Oldenburg, and he began to slip into despair at the lack of resistance. Ernst Torgler later remembered a conversation he had with Oberfohren in the Reichstag on February 6, 1933, the day after the state funeral for the SA leader Hans Maikowski. Maikowski, as we have seen, was shot by one of his own men, possibly on Goebbels's orders, the night Hitler came to power. The Nazis decided to give him the Horst Wessel treatment. That day Torgler noticed Oberfohren's "dreadfully angry expression," but greeted him cheerfully: "Hey, Herr Colleague Oberfohren, I can see the joy in your face at the new governing coalition!" Oberfohren replied gravely: "Oh, you have no idea; what just went on here is an absolute outrage," referring to Maikowski's funeral. Torgler added that he could not repeat publicly the expression that Oberfohren had actually used.

Torgler asked Oberfohren if the new government planned to ban the Communist Party. "Look," Oberfohren replied, "Herr Colleague Torgler, we would be fools" to go along with such a ban. Without the Communists the Nazis would not need the Nationalists to reach a majority in the Reichstag. Then "we would be finished," said Oberfohren. But it was clear that leader Hugenberg did not agree. Oberfohren said that he had warned Hugenberg the Nazis would "devour" the German Nationals, but Hugenberg wouldn't listen. Oberfohren added that he "put nothing at all past the Nazis. I got to know them in Schleswig-Holstein." By another account Oberfohren made the last point even more explicitly: "The Nazis are preparing an important act of provocation," he told Torgler. Again, he had warned Hugenberg, and again Hugenberg would not believe him.[7]

Oberfohren was not the only establishment conservative who did not trust the Nazis and viewed any coalition with them with alarm. His parliamentary colleague Reinhold Quaatz recorded that President Hindenburg (officially non-partisan but close to the German Nationals) complained that Hitler never kept his word, adding "That is really the evil. They are nihilists." In a private conversation in February, Foreign Minister von Neurath, Hindenburg's own choice for that post, complained to the British Ambassador Sir Horace Rumbold that Göring was a "dreadful man" whom Papen could not control. In the dislike that Oberfohren and many of his colleagues felt for the Nazis we can see the roots of what would become the conservative-military resistance to Hitler, culminating in the

Valkyrie plot of July 1944. Many of those resistance figures were prominent German Nationals, notably the former mayor of Leipzig, Carl Goerdeler, and Goerdeler's young protégé Hans Bernd Gisevius.[8]

Even if the German Nationals and the Nazis shared some goals and elements of ideology—extreme nationalism, militarism, and anti-Semitism—they were worlds apart in social composition and style. The Nationalists were devoutly, indeed militantly Protestant, while the leaders of the Nazi Party, as Diels noted, tended to be lapsed Catholics, in whom the apostate's hatred of the church mixed oddly with lingering Catholic influence. The Nationalists were the party of Germany's traditional elites—the aristocracy, the army high command, the senior civil service, and some sections of industry—whereas the Nazis generally came from much lower down in the social hierarchy. Devoted to the idea of an authoritarian political system, the German Nationals had no use whatsoever for the Nazis' contempt for the rule of law, or for the anti-elitism and anticapitalism that often marked Nazi rhetoric.

After the effort to form an alliance at Bad Harzburg in 1931—the Harzburg Front discussed earlier—relations between the two parties had deteriorated steadily. In late 1932 the Nationalists had formed the only basis of support for the Papen administration, and so in the fall election campaign the Nazis aimed their vitriol primarily at the Nationalists. Both parties attacked each other without restraint.

At the outset of the campaign, Goebbels instructed Nazi activists that "the struggle against the Papen Cabinet and the reactionary circles behind it must now begin all along the line." Papen's "regime" was nothing but a "small feudal clique," and the Nazis must fight it without mercy. Papen and Hindenburg had dissolved the Reichstag and called the November election, said a Nazi press release, only because the Nazi-dominated Reichstag elected on July 31st had contained "too few Jews and too many anti-Semites." Goebbels's *Angriff* referred contemptuously to the Nationals' leader Hugenberg as "Hugenzwerg"—meaning "Hugen-dwarf." In an election speech earlier that year, the Oldenburg Nazi Carl Röver denounced the German Nationals as "scoundrels" and "traitors to the people." Violence between the two camps, especially attacks on the other's meetings, was common. In January 1933 SA men murdered a German National official in Pomerania.[9]

The German Nationals pushed back. A Nationalist pamphlet entitled "How the Nazis Govern" exposed the abuses of Nazi rule in the states of

Oldenburg, Braunschweig, and Anhalt. It characterized the Nazis as the party of lies, egoism, and villainy. A similar pamphlet was called "How the Nazis Fight." Its cover showed a clean-cut, uniformed SA man. But crouching behind him was a thug with an insidious, rather sub-mental smile, clutching an anarchist's classic grapefruit-shaped bomb.[10]

Of all the prominent Nazis, the one who felt the German Nationals' dislike and distrust most clearly—and who most defiantly returned it—was Goebbels. Even at Bad Harzburg, Goebbels, who thought the Nationals too bourgeois and too "reactionary," had recorded his particular dislike of Oberfohren, who "pisses and puffs himself up. Oh, what better people are we savages! I have to puke." When the Nazis themselves finally got power, the goal would be to "kick out the reactionaries as fast as possible. We alone will be the lords of Germany . . . "[11]

In a public debate in October 1932 against Oberfohren's friend Otto Schmidt-Hannover, Goebbels again bared the Nazis' teeth. "We are convinced," he said, that only a popular movement that could "deploy the demonstrative weight of fourteen million" would be able to "bring Bolshevism down." Goebbels pointed to the stormtroopers in the audience. "In Berlin," he said, "we have laid twenty-six SA men in the grave." Where, he asked Schmidt, "are your martyrs?"[12]

YET, FOR ALL THE ACTUAL and rhetorical violence of the Nazi party, in his first weeks in office Chancellor Hitler seemed to govern with surprising moderation. The records of his early cabinet meetings reveal a Hitler who rode herd on the authoritarian drive of his German National colleagues, demonstrating the political instincts of a man who led the most popular political party in German history while the German Nationals languished around the 8 percent mark in voter esteem. When Hugenberg urged the outlawing of the Communist Party, Hitler said he thought such a move would be pointless: It was "impossible to outlaw the six million people who stood behind the Communist Party." In another cabinet debate he asked rhetorically if it were "psychologically correct" in the context of the election campaign to minimize the Communist threat by banning the party.

In his public speeches, too, Hitler often struck a conciliatory tone. In his February 1st address to the nation, broadcast over all radio stations, he told Germans that his government's "highest and first task" was the restoration of unity. The government would defend Christianity and the family, while veneration for Germany's past and pride in its traditions would form the foundation of education. This was far from the violent and demagogic tone Hitler had struck since entering politics in 1919. The speech hit its target. Even Erich Ebermayer, far from sympathetic to the Nazis, wondered if "the Chancellor Hitler might think differently than the vote-catcher Hitler did?"[13]

Hitler's seeming moderation did not stem from any lack of readiness to do battle with his political enemies. On February 1st he told his cabinet that the slogan for the coming election campaign would be "Attacking Marxism." In his radio address he ranted about Communist madness attempting to destroy the people. Nothing—not the family, not honor and loyalty, not devotion to the fatherland, not culture and economy, not morality and faith—was safe from this "all-destroying idea." Fourteen years of Marxism, said Hitler, had ruined the country (and here he was certainly stretching the point to suggest that Germany had been ruled by "Marxism" since 1919.) One year of Bolshevism, he continued, would destroy it.

Hitler was, in short, playing a calculated game. Goebbels captured Hitler's tactical thinking in a February 1st diary entry: "Discussed the terror of the reds with Hitler. For now, still no counter measures. First let it flare up."[14]

"First let it flare up" was, in fact, a concise summary of what had for several years been the Nazis' plan for consolidating power. In November 1931 a Nazi official and member of the Hessian state parliament had given the Frankfurt police chief a set of documents laying out contingency plans for a Nazi counter-coup against a Communist uprising. The author of the documents was a young Nazi lawyer named Werner Best, later a senior Gestapo official and deputy of Reinhard Heydrich. Best's drafts, which became known as the "Boxheimer Documents," specified that in the event of a Communist coup the SA would step into the legal vacuum, claiming "the right and the duty to seize and exercise the abandoned authority of the state for the salvation of the people." All orders from SA personnel were to be followed on pain of death, while the SA had the right to pass further emergency decrees as necessary. Field courts were to be established to enforce these decrees; all Germans over the age of sixteen would be subject to compulsory labor, or they would have no right to food. Jews were expressly excluded from both the duty to work and the right to rations.[15]

The revelation of the Boxheimer Documents cast considerable doubt on the Nazis' claims to legality. They responded in a predictable way. The documents, said Goebbels's *Angriff*, were Best's purely private plan for defeating "a hypothetical bloody takeover by the Commies" and restoring legal German state authority. But Communist provocation was never far from Nazi propaganda, and Goebbels's paper also reported that Best was responding to "a plan drafted according to the most precise orders from Moscow for the violent seizure of power in Germany." The Communist document had been obtained by the Nazis' own intelligence service. The Social Democratic authorities in Hesse knew about it, said the *Angriff*, but were covering it up.[16]

The Nazis' private reaction was very different. In March 1932 the local governor in Düsseldorf reported to the Prussian interior minister on an SA circular, signed by Hitler and Ernst Röhm, which said that "the matter in Hesse" had shown that one had to be careful with documents, and that plans for the seizure of power should be drawn up only by the officially designated Nazi authorities. "Obviously after the takeover of power we will settle the scores with our opponents in the most severe way."[17]

Goebbels's diary suggests that for the Nazi leaders the Boxheimer Documents represented a general, not just local, plan for power. In mid-September 1931 (precisely the time that Best was reporting to the Nazis' "Reich Leadership" on the nature of his plan) Goebbels recorded a conversation with Hitler, setting out what seems to be the Berlin counterpart. "SA questions," wrote Goebbels. "What to do when the KPD [Kommunistische Partei Deutschlands, the German Communist Party] strikes. Concrete plan of action. I will be police commissioner for the entire east . . . Helldorff my military leader. We will work well together." In March 1932 the Berlin police confiscated SA mobilization plans, which called for surrounding the capital in the event of an "emergency." As with the Boxheimer Documents, the "emergency" the Nazis had in mind was a coup or counter coup by democratic or left-wing forces. Nazi coup plans were never, therefore, aimed against the state: they were always aimed at the political left on *behalf* of the state. Later, when the Nazis had just come to power and there were rumors that former Chancellor Schleicher might try a military coup against them, Goebbels noted in his diary that Helldorff and Police Major Wecke were collaborating on counter-measures. As Hitler's biographer Joachim Fest points out, that the Nazis would be called in to deliver the state from a Communist threat had been Hitler's governing idea since his ill-fated Munich coup attempt in 1923. It suited his "dramatic as well as his eschatological temperament," even his fixation with Wagnerian themes.[18]

Rudolf Diels had the impression that in early 1933 the Nazi leaders were waiting hopefully for a Communist uprising, "like a tiger that waited for its prey to appear before tearing it to pieces." For Diels's boss Göring, the struggle against Communism had become an all-consuming idea. Göring imagined this struggle taking violent forms: battles at the barricades and bloodily suppressed uprisings. He believed that the Communists would appear voluntarily for this war. At the very least he was certain that once the Nazis outlawed the Communist Party—which both he and Hitler were determined to do—"the enemy would then have to come out of his lair."[19]

Unlike most of the Nazi leaders, Hermann Göring came from a relatively elite social background. His father had been a colonial governor in German South West Africa. Göring himself was a dashing fighter pilot in the First World War, a member of the renowned Richthofen squadron and the last commander of that squadron after Manfred von Richthofen, the "Red Baron," was shot down in 1918. Göring's press secretary at the Prussian Interior Ministry, Martin Sommerfeldt, recalled that Göring was proud of his past and his origins in a "good house."

Göring liked to think of himself as the "right wing" of the Nazi Party, which in this context meant the moderate wing, and many in Germany and abroad did see him this way. Among friends and associates Göring chalked up Nazi lawlessness and radicalism to his bitter rival Goebbels, whom he dubbed "the poison dwarf." Göring had been furious to learn that Goebbels had sided with the Communists in supporting the striking Berlin transit workers in November 1932. He would have liked to "kill the little devil" with his own hands when Goebbels got Hitler to send a telegram supporting the "Potempa murderers," five SA men sentenced to death in 1932 for an especially brutal killing. Goebbels's "National Bolshevism," as Göring saw it, constantly jeopardized negotiations with President Hindenburg for Nazi participation in the government. "Every time I have gotten that hard East Prussian head almost soft," Göring complained, "Jupp [Goebbels's unflattering nickname] clubs me one between the legs."[20]

However, Göring's good old boy persona and seeming moderation were just for show. Sommerfeldt, who admired Göring at first, came to learn how he could "throw off the sheep's clothing" and let out the "raging wolf." Rudolf Diels was not the only one of Göring's associates to liken his cruelty and extravagance to a prince of the Renaissance. And in early 1933 Göring was zealously preparing for his civil war.[21]

As Prussian interior minister, Göring was in command of 50,000 armed police officers, already organized in military fashion. Göring put the police forces of the western Prussian provinces, industrial areas that were Communist bastions, under a special command. To Police Major Walther Wecke—the same man who had suddenly appeared in command of "Inspection West" on the day of the Ku'damm riot—he gave the command of an "especially reliable" squad of police for "motorized deployment" in the capital city. Wecke was constantly by Göring's side.[22]

From the middle of February there came a steady escalation in police measures aimed primarily at the Communists, but also at Social Democrats, liberals, pacifists, left-wing intellectuals, members of human rights organizations, and anyone else likely to be an opponent of the Nazis. On February 14th sixty or seventy Berlin political police officers, led by the Commissars Reinhold Heller and Rudolf Braschwitz, who would figure importantly in the Reichstag fire investigations, searched the Communist Party's offices in the Reichstag. On February 24th the Berlin police closed down the Karl Liebknecht House, the headquarters of the Communist Party, after a search supposedly uncovered leaflets inciting acts of violence and treason. Two weeks later, the building, as we've seen, had been renamed the "Horst Wessel House" and taken over by Diels's Department IA.[23]

Preparations for battle against the Communists were in the works on the legal level as well. Hitler's government revived what it called the "Decree in the Drawer" (*Schubkastenordnung*), left over from the Papen administration and the November transit strike. The draft decree set out penalties—fines or minor jail terms—for anyone who advocated a strike in, went on strike against, locked out workers in, or vandalized an essential service. More ominously, the decree specified that anyone who was suspected of violating its terms could be taken into police custody in the interests of "public security." More ominously still, in a cabinet meeting on November 25th, the then-Reich Interior Minister, Baron Wilhelm von Gayl, argued that stronger provisions had to be added to the decree, including the introduction of "protective custody" (*Schutzhaft*). The cabinet agreed to all this in principle, and work on the draft continued. A few days later came Papen's replacement by Schleicher. Schleicher's short-lived administration did not get around to passing the decree. But the draft sat—literally "in the drawer"—at the Interior Ministry, awaiting its moment.[24]

At a cabinet meeting on February 1st, 1933, Hermann Göring claimed that Communist "acts of terror" were on the increase and that existing legal provisions were inadequate. He said it was time to revive the Decree in the Drawer. The following day, a new draft, now called "Decree for the Protection of the German People" was set before the cabinet. This draft allowed the banning or breaking up of political meetings, political associations, or periodicals, if they posed a danger to "public safety and security." It also contained the former sections on "essential services." But here again, Hitler demonstrated his sense of timing and political calculation. He asked whether it was "psychologically correct" to minimize the Communist danger in the election campaign with the passage of such a decree. Hitler understood that fear of the Communists drove many voters to the Nazis; banning the source of this fear could only hurt his Party. He suggested passing only some sections, and leaving the "essential service" provisions for later.

The cabinet approved a revised draft, and President Hindenburg signed it into law the next day. In addition to the new restrictions on press freedom and political meetings, the decree allowed the police to carry out arrests in the interest of "public security" and hold the prisoners in custody for up to three months. The Social Democrats and Communists began to feel the effects right away. Even before the decree, the Berlin police had banned the Social Democratic paper *Vorwärts*; armed with the new decree they extended the ban. Other newspapers, along with Social Democratic and Communist election rallies, began to be treated in a similar fashion.[25]

The *Berliner Tageblatt* reported on February 23rd that if the trends continued, this election would prove to be the bloodiest yet in Germany. Nazi stormtroopers were now regularly attacking the moderate Catholic Center Party's activists and meetings, along with those of the Communists and Social Democrats. Nazis fired on Catholic demonstrators in Kaiserslautern, while in Krefeld they broke up a meeting and beat the speaker, the former Prussian Prime Minister and Reich Transport and Labor Minister Adam Stegerwald. Göring, following the standard Nazi script, blamed the violence on "provocateurs" from outside the Nazi Party.[26]

On February 17th Göring issued his infamous "Shooting Decree" to all Prussian police officers. The decree said that officers must use their firearms against "enemies of the state." Any officer who failed to do so when he should have would face disciplinary consequences. On February 22nd he went a step further with a decree allowing members of the "National Associations"—this meant the SA, the SS, and the Stahlhelm, the groups responsible for a large share of the violence—to be enrolled as auxiliary police. The text of the decree claimed that increasing "outrages" from left radicals, especially Communists, were an unbearable and constant threat to public security.[27]

It was part of the strange climate in Germany that February that a partially free press could still criticize these measures. The leading Catholic newspaper *Germania*, for instance, noted that it was a "highly dangerous" and "reckless" undertaking to give police authority, including the use of weapons, to young men from an "extraordinarily fanatical political party movement." The *Berliner Tageblatt*, noting the untruth of Nazi claims that past Prussian governments had pressed the Social Democratic Reich Banner into service as auxiliary police, concluded that this "dangerous experiment" was both unnecessary and worrying.[28]

The leading Nazis—apart from Hitler—used their campaign speeches to voice contempt for the very act of voting, challenging their opponents to remove them through civil war. Two Sundays before the election, Wilhelm Frick told an audience in Dresden that this election would be the last. Should Hitler's government somehow fail to win a majority, he said, no other political grouping would win one either, so the government would simply continue as it was. "We are not willing," he said, "to leave the field voluntarily." A few days later, in a speech at the Sports Palace in Berlin, Goebbels told the crowd that National Socialism had burned all its bridges and that there was no way back. He added ominously that the Communists "should not believe that everything will remain as it is today."[29]

Although theoretically the Nazis and the German Nationals were running together for the confirmation of their coalition, in fact there was no let-up in their mutual attacks. There were clear signs that the Nazis did not plan to be burdened with their Nationalist partners any longer than absolutely necessary. On January 30th, as Hitler's coalition was sworn into office, Goebbels wrote that the Nationalist cabinet members were "blemishes" that "must be rubbed out." On February 2nd Hans Frank told Nazi students that the Nazis had no intention of maintaining a coalition as contemplated by the Weimar Constitution (although, as we have seen, Hitler had promised that whatever happened in the election, the cabinet would remain as it was). The Nazis wanted sole power for themselves, said

Frank, to destroy "Asiatic subhumandom" (in other words, Communism). No "liberal sense of law" would keep the Nazis from doing what they needed to do.

American ambassador Frederic M. Sackett—William Dodd's predecessor—reported to the State Department in mid-February on the rising tensions between the Nazis and the Nationalists, and after a press conference for foreign correspondents that the Social Democratic editor Friedrich Stampfer gave on February 23rd, the *Manchester Guardian's* correspondent wrote "one had the curious sensation" that "the time was rapidly approaching when to a large section of the German people the Nationalists would appear as the champions of law and order. Nothing has fostered this feeling more then Herr Göring's famous police circular."[30]

German National newspapers began to criticize, without naming names, those "dumb" enough to imagine that they alone were called upon to save the country. Reinhold Quaatz told a mid-February election rally that the fate of Germany would depend on whether the nationalism or the socialism won out in the National Socialist movement. Quaatz himself had suffered Nazi abuse for his partly Jewish background.[31]

If the Nationals' main worry was their unruly coalition partner, the Nazis were growing increasingly concerned that a Communist uprising was nowhere in sight. Communist resistance to Hitler's new government was doubly hobbled. Joseph Stalin's self-interest put good relations with Hitler ahead of the fortunes of his German followers, at a time when the leader of the Soviet Union was ex officio leader of all the world's Communist parties. Secondly, German Communists were blinded by their own ideology, which saw Hitler's regime as confirmation of the desperate state of capitalism, and so of the excellent prospects for a Communist revolution in the near future. They believed they could sit back and wait for their moment.

Rudolf Diels thought that all Göring's extravagant military preparations were pointless. He knew that the Communists could not possibly launch a successful uprising against the Nazi stormtroopers, especially now that Communists could not count on any help from the police— many of whom were now themselves stormtroopers. But Diels added, "I was never in doubt for a moment that a pretext for outlawing the Communist Party would be found."[32]

Some historians of the Reichstag fire, notably Fritz Tobias and Hans Mommsen, argue that Hitler and other leading Nazis sincerely believed in the specter of an imminent Communist revolt. It was the intensity of their fear and hatred, these writers suggest, that led Hitler and the others to interpret the Reichstag fire immediately as a Communist act; Hitler's rage that night was genuine. Hans Mommsen goes so far as to say that Hitler "lost his nerve" on the night of the fire.[33]

However, this puts too much credence in what Nazis said for propagandistic effect. There were many signs that Hitler and Goebbels understood German Communism was a paper tiger. Hitler, as we have seen, told his cabinet that the Communist threat needed to be *preserved* for the sake of election propaganda. In his diaries Goebbels had surprisingly little to say about the Communists, and what he did write was largely perfunctory. He saved his real invective for the Nationalists. Here as elsewhere his diary was remarkably consistent with his public posture: Even in public, where one would expect him to play up his hatred for the Communists and play down that for the Nationalists, Goebbels could complain of the "giant burden" of fighting a "two-front war" against "the conceit of the Right" and the "class-consciousness of the Left." Joachim Fest notes that it required a lot of effort for the Nazi propaganda to render the Communists that revolutionary threat that the Communists themselves claimed to be. The violence staged by SA men disguised as Communists was supposed to help the illusion along. Certain stereotyped phrases about the (allegedly) shocking discoveries that the police made at the Karl Liebknecht House on February 24th occur so repeatedly in official documents after the Reichstag fire that it is difficult to believe they were more than pre-arranged talking points.[34]

Nazi leaders could not have become paranoid about the Communists from any information Diels's political police gave them. Documents from Britain's MI5 offer unexpected confirmation on this point. In March 1933 Guy Liddell, a senior MI5 officer who spoke fluent German, went to Berlin to strike up a relationship with his German counterparts. Liddell took a dislike to Diels, whom he described as a man with "an unpleasant personality" and "jet black hair, slit eyes and sallow complexion" giving him "a rather Chinese appearance." But Diels was also "extremely polite" and gave orders "that I was to be given every possible facility." Liddell saw documents that had been looted from Communist headquarters by SA men "who just threw [them] into lorries and then dumped them in disorder in some large rooms." Liddell wrote that "all our evidence goes to show that, although the German Communist Party may have contemplated a peaceful street demonstration," Moscow had ordered "no overt act was to be committed which could in any way lead to the wholesale repression of the Party."[35]

One leading Nazi spent much of February in deep frustration. The Third Reich did not seem to begin well for Joseph Goebbels. In early February he felt that he had been pushed aside in the eternal struggle for Hitler's favor. Hitler had promised him a propaganda ministry after the election, but in the meantime had put Bernhard Rust in place as Goebbels's "regent" in the Prussian Ministry of Education and Culture, with many of the duties of a future propaganda minister. To Goebbels this was a betrayal. "I've been left in the lurch," he complained to his diary on February 6th. "Hitler is hardly helping me at all. I have lost my courage." The strength of the German Nationals in the cabinet, those "reactionaries" whom Goebbels so hated, drew his biting sarcasm. "The reactionaries dictate. The Third Reich!" Or—for Goebbels the same thing as dictation by reactionaries— "the Görings rule." And every day Goebbels complained that there was not enough money for the election campaign. In the middle of February he caught a fever and gave himself over to self-pity and to "fantasies."[36]

When Goebbels worried about "reactionary" influence on the Nazi movement or about his own position in the hierarchy, as at the time of the Stennes revolt or Harzburg or Kristallnacht, he invariably turned both to the SA and to a dramatic propaganda stunt. In February of 1933 his hatred for the Nationalists and for Göring, as well as his self-pity and concern for his own position, were running at high levels.

Meanwhile, Chancellor Hitler had been campaigning frenetically. Hitler was his party's most potent election speaker, and since February 1st, when the election campaign officially began, he had spoken somewhere in Germany almost every day. On February 10th he addressed a rally in the huge Berlin Sports Palace. The next day he opened the International Automobile and Motorcycle Exhibition. On February 12th he was in Leipzig for ceremonies commemorating the fiftieth anniversary of the death of Richard Wagner. Back in Berlin on February 14th he spoke before the assembled National Socialist press. On February 15th he was in Stuttgart, on the 16th back in Berlin, on the 17th in Dortmund, on the 18th in Munich, the 19th in Cologne, and on the 20th he returned to Berlin to speak to a group of industrialists. On the 21st he gave interviews to foreign journalists, and on February 22nd, along with attending a cabinet meeting, he issued an order warning his party against provocateurs. Then he was back on the road: On the 24th to an election rally in Munich and on the 25th to Nuremberg.[37]

Hitler returned to Berlin, attending a cabinet meeting again on February 27th. In the late afternoon, the ministers discussed the passage of another decree. This one was introduced to the cabinet by Minister of Justice Franz Gürtner. Gürtner called it the "Decree Against Treason and Treasonous Activities," and he insisted that it must be passed before the March 5th election. The decree set out crushing penalties—death or long penitentiary sentences—for the betrayal of military secrets, for treasonous actions committed for the purpose of rendering the military or the police unable to fulfill their duties, for advocating political strikes, or for publishing materials advocating any such actions. Hitler suggested increasing some of the penalties; Reich Interior Minister Wilhelm Frick proposed renaming the draft the "Decree Against Betrayal of the People." Prussian Finance Minister Johannes Popitz suggested "Decree Against Betrayal of the German People." With this change the cabinet agreed to the decree. President Hindenburg signed it into law the following day.[38]

From Sunday, February 26th, through Tuesday, February 28th, despite the climax of the election campaign, Hitler's speaking calendar was blank. Then a final flurry of appearances would keep him busy from March 1st until the March 5th elections. His long weekend gave him the leisure for a quiet dinner at the home of propaganda director Goebbels on the evening of Monday, the 27th. Goebbels, too, was enjoying an unaccustomed break from his otherwise intense campaign schedule. For the Nazis, who were very conscious of dates and anniversaries, February 27th was a day of some significance: on that day in 1925, at a public meeting in that same Bürgerbräu Keller in Munich from which Hitler had launched his 1923 *Putsch*, Hitler, just released from prison, had ceremonially refounded the Nazi Party. To an overflowing crowd he had explained that Germany had lost the First World War because for long years before the war "the most sacred matters of the whole people had been turned over to parliamentary graft." He also explained the meaning of the Nazi flag and dedicated his party to the "struggle" against Marxism and Jews.[39]

AS THE MONTH OF FEBRUARY went on, the blizzard of special decrees, banned party meetings, and escalating police and SA violence began to alter the mood of relief and surprise at the seeming moderation of Hitler's first days in office.

Even as he puzzled over the restraint of Hitler's first speech as chancellor, Erich Ebermayer noted an undertone. "Somewhat unclear and darkly threatening is his statement about a 'decisive act' that is required to overcome the Communist subversion of Germany. What is that supposed to mean?" A few days later he recorded the dissolution of the Prussian parliament with an emergency decree and the final deposing of the Braun-Severing administration. "That has nothing more to do with law," he wrote. "For the first time Hitler is showing the naked, brutal fist. He is a revolutionary and has never concealed the fact. Now we have the revolution!" Actually, he thought, that wasn't such a bad thing. The more radical the revolution, the shorter its duration.[40]

On February 23rd the Prussian Council of State—the upper house of the Prussian parliament—met to discuss "current constitutional conditions in Prussia." The president of the Council was the veteran mayor of Cologne, Konrad Adenauer, a pillar of the Catholic Center Party (and later postwar West Germany's first chancellor). The Council members understood that they might not have much longer to do their work. Two of the speakers noted that theirs was the last functioning representative institution in Prussia.[41]

Then Ernst Torgler, who alongside his Reichstag duties served as the Communist deputy in the council, rose to speak. Torgler was a tall, good-looking man in his early forties. Despite his party's radicalism, he was an easygoing and collegial parliamentarian, who could turn his charm and good humor on politicians of all parties and had friends in all camps. Torgler had been hearing rumors—they seemed to come from the SA— that the Nazis planned to stage a simulated crime before the election and to blame it on the Communists. With the Nazis putting increasing obstacles in the path of the left-wing and liberal parties, shutting down their papers and breaking up their meetings, Torgler thought that this session of the Council of State might be his last chance to warn Germany's workers.[42]

"We have been told," said Torgler, that "a few days before the election— I don't know: on March 2nd or March 3rd—an assassination attempt will be staged on Herr Adolf Hitler." No harm would come to the Nazi leader. But the attempt would provide an excuse for violent persecution of the Communist Party, just as over fifty years earlier an attempt on the life of Kaiser Wilhelm I had allowed Bismarck to outlaw the Social Democratic Party. If the Communists refused to be provoked into violent actions,

Torgler had been told, the Nazis would do the job themselves. The *Manchester Guardian* reported that the transcripts of Council of State sessions were usually circulated to all members. This last one was not. Later, the Gestapo claimed that Torgler's speech was an effort to deflect attention from his own party's plans to burn the Reichstag.[43]

Other well-informed people were hearing the same kinds of rumors. American Ambassador Sackett reported on February 16th that he had heard Göring might go "to the extent of alleging the existence of emergencies." A few days later the American Consul General in Stuttgart reported that the Nazis' "tenets and methods" would not keep them from intentionally preparing an event that they could exploit to "suppress many forms of liberty granted by the German constitution." The Nazis were said to favor such a move to ensure a successful election outcome.[44]

On February 20th the well-connected Count Harry Kessler recorded in his diary that Wieland Herzfelde, the founder of the Communist publisher Malik Verlag, had told him that the Nazis were planning a staged assassination attempt on Hitler, "which will be the signal for a general bloodbath." Herzfelde might not have been the most credible informant. But two days later Kessler had breakfast with Diels's old boss Wilhelm Abegg. Abegg confirmed the news and also spoke of a coming Nazi bloodbath, but saw hope in the tensions between the Nazis and the Nationalists. The coalition between Papen, Hugenberg, and the Nazis could not last much more than six weeks—until July at the very latest. Papen and Hugenberg were "very worried about the extreme elements," Abegg said, and wanted to get Hindenburg out of Berlin before the election.

Abegg's sources of information had proven accurate in the past. In 1932 Papen's people had warned him of the impending coup. Still, like most Germans, Kessler had trouble believing the worst predictions. A friend with connections to the Nazis warned him on February 23rd to leave Berlin before the election. This friend, the pro-Nazi Austrian writer Karl Anton Rohan, told Kessler that after the election Hitler would crack down on the left and that "in ten years there will be no more Marxists in Germany." Kessler told him politely that he was wrong.[45]

Friedrich Stampfer held a press conference for foreign correspondents on the night of February 23rd. He too mentioned the rumors about a feigned attack on Hitler, as well as another, that SA men would seize Berlin the day after the election. One British reporter commented "extremist exuberance seems to be gathering force, and a provocative incident staged by irresponsible elements might well, it is feared, be the prelude to an outbreak of violence far exceeding last summer's reign of terror."[46]

There was another kind of rumor. We have seen that Robert Kempner claimed Diels tipped him off in the middle of February about the preparation of arrest lists and some of the names on them. Fritz Tobias rejected Kempner's claim outright, arguing in fact that the *absence* of leaks about arrests proved that none were planned; privately he called Kempner a "guy who perjured himself [*meineidiger Bursche*]." But in fact there is evidence of leaks. Kempner claimed that, among others, he warned his friend Kurt Grossmann, a left-leaning newspaper editor and head of the League for Human Rights. Grossmann confirmed this. Very early on the morning of February 28th, as Grossmann wrote later, Kempner called him and warned him to get out of the country. That same day Grossmann fled for Czechoslovakia. Kempner's sources of information were "inexhaustible," Grossman wrote later. "He had the gift of finding out things that remained closed to other people."[47]

Leading German National politicians expected the Nazis to mobilize the SA against the Communists. Reinhold Quaatz had recorded in his diary as early as January 28th a meeting with, among others, Hugenberg, Oberfohren, and Otto Schmidt-Hannover to discuss the state of negotiations with the Nazis. "Nazi[s] want police, then drive the Communists with violence out of the Reichstag and the street," Quaatz noted. In response Hugenberg had suggested "neutralization" of the police, "which Hitler stormily rejected." On February 27th Quaatz wrote that the Nationals' deputy leader Friedrich von Winterfeld was deeply shaken by rumors. "Marching orders for the SA are apparently authentic. (I believe that not only Röhm, but also Göring would have to be involved, if success expected. Not clear whether for or against Hitler)." His lengthy diary entry ended with a terse sentence: "Evening burning of the Reichstag building."[48]

THE REICHSTAG HAD BURNED many times before, at least in the imagination of propagandists and the dreams of activists.

Images of the burning Reichstag cropped up in political propaganda before 1933. Before the Reichstag election of 1930 a Social Democratic pamphlet entitled "Alarm" had featured on its title page an illustration of a Nazi and a Communist each throwing a torch at the building. A pamphlet urging Paul von Hindenburg's re-election as President in 1932 featured an illustration of the Reichstag in flames with the question "It's burning—who will put it out?" Similar propaganda appeared in other countries as well. The German embassy in Paris reported after the Reichstag fire that sometime in late 1931 or 1932 a Danish Communist journal had put an image of the burning Danish parliament on its cover with the headline "This must happen to all bourgeois parliaments." German authorities also thought the burning of the Vienna Palace of Justice in 1927, by a mob protesting the acquittal of right wing defendants, was a precedent for the Reichstag fire.[49]

Two attacks on the Reichstag before 1933 were more than pictorial. In 1921 there was a bomb attack on the Victory Column (Siegessäule) which, in those days, stood directly in front of the Reichstag. The bomb had been wrapped in the pages of a Communist newspaper, perhaps a crude attempt to indicate the authorship of the deed. In any event, the political extremes blamed each other for the bombing. The novelist Joseph Roth delivered one of his mordant columns for the *Neue Berliner Zeitung* on the subject. "A German National thinks a Communist must have done it. A suddenly emerging Communist blames a German National. With this a clash of opinion breaks out, and the whiff of partisan struggle stinks up to the heavens." Leftists at the time, and some historians since, accused the governor of the Prussian province of Saxony of using the attack as a pretext to crack down on Communists. On the other hand, in the fall of 1933 the Gestapo cited this example of the Communists' "gruesome plans" as a precedent for the Reichstag fire. In 1932 reports had reached Berlin's political police that Communists were using the tunnel between the Reichstag president's residence and the Reichstag itself to smuggle explosives into the building. Police searched the Communists' Reichstag offices. They found nothing. Göring, in his then-capacity as president of the Reichstag, was briefed on the case.[50]

In the early morning of Sunday, September 1st, 1929, a bomb exploded in a light shaft on the north side of the Reichstag, near Portal V. The bomb had been equipped with a time delay fuse to make it go off at 4:00 a.m. The explosion could be heard a few miles away in Charlottenburg, although the damage was slight: a few broken windows, no injuries.[51]

It was in fact the fourteenth such bomb attack on public or government buildings since November 1928. The attacks were mostly concentrated in northern Germany—Schleswig-Holstein, Lüneburg, and Oldenburg. On a streetcar mast opposite where the bomb went off someone had left a swastika sticker with the words "Greater Germany Awake!" The blast came during the German Nationals' and the Nazis' campaign for a plebiscite to reject American businessman Owen D. Young's plan for rescheduling Germany's reparations payments. "What would have happened," the Communist *Rote Fahne* wondered with unusual foresight, "if instead of fourteen, only one such attack had taken place, for which the responsibility of the Communist Party could even appear to be proven?" It answered its own question: there would be mass arrests, quick and severe verdicts, and the party would be outlawed.[52]

Berlin's political police investigated energetically, at least judging by the large number of arrests. Rudolf Braschwitz, who would later investigate the Reichstag fire, was one of the officers involved—although curiously no one mentioned this in 1933 or later (except for Braschwitz himself in one of his post-war statements). The police quickly determined that a radical agrarian group based in Schleswig-Holstein, the *Landvolk* (country people), was responsible for all the bombings. The bombers had links to the Organization Consul, which, as we have seen, was a predecessor to the SA. One of the most prominent of the September arrestees was Ernst von Salomon, who had served five years in prison for his part in the Organization Consul's murder of Walther Rathenau. Some witnesses claimed to have seen him carrying a package by the Brandenburg Gate on the night of the Reichstag bombing.[53]

Many of the people arrested were Nazis, among them two editors from the Nazi newspaper in Schleswig-Holstein, and the Hannover Nazi leader Lieutenant Friedrich Wilhelm Heinz, whom the party quickly expelled in an effort at damage control (as a dissident Nazi, he would be arrested on the night of the Reichstag fire). In earlier years Heinz had been charged, though not convicted, in the acid attack on the former Social Democratic Chancellor Philipp Scheidemann, and for the murder of Finance Minister Matthias Erzberger.[54]

The Nazis were clearly worried about the spreading rumors of their involvement in the Reichstag bombing. Hitler himself said that these "ridiculous" and "ineffectual" bombings were only meant "to compromise the National Socialist movement." The Party piously offered a cash reward for anyone who could identify the culprits, and an even higher sum for proof that Prussian authorities themselves had set the bombs—as the Nazis claimed those authorities wanted to create a climate of fear to justify outlawing the Nazi Party. Goebbels himself argued, exactly as liberals and the left would against him after the Reichstag fire, that only the "old

Roman principle *cui bono*" explained the bombs: the beneficiary of the attacks was Foreign Minister Gustav Stresemann, because the "sensational news" of the attacks would "sabotage" the Nazi and Nationalist mobilization against the Young Plan. In the overheated and paranoid atmosphere of Weimar it was not surprising that the Communists suspected the bombings were a government plot against *them*, and that Prussia's reigning Social Democrats were supporting and covering up the guilty Nazis.[55]

Berlin Police Chief Karl Zörgiebel confirmed that a former SA man named Fritz Lessenthin had approached Department IA on July 20th to "connect" the bombings in Schleswig-Holstein with a group called the League of the Friends of Schlageter, which had close ties to the Nazis. Members of the League of the Friends of Schlageter had also discussed bombing "institutions of state importance," although Zörgiebel denied Lessenthin's claim that he had warned the police about the attack on the Reichstag.[56]

The increasing chemical and pyrotechnical sophistication of SA work in the last Weimar years was conspicuous. One of the Nazis arrested in connection with the 1929 Reichstag bomb was a man named Willi Wilske, variously identified as a chemist or a pyrotechnics expert, who had, it was alleged, given bomb-making courses in his Neukölln apartment. According to another report, he told the police that he had met with the bombers only to make plans "for the event of a coup by the left." Otherwise he claimed the profusion of chemicals the police found in his apartment was for making perfume. The police bomb experts did not believe him. By 1932 there were numerous reports of SA attacks on the meetings of political opponents—especially those of the German Nationals—using tear gas. A tear gas attack disrupted a performance of Richard Strauss's opera *Salome* in Wuppertal, and here again the culprits were probably Nazis. An Interior Ministry report from the spring of 1932 anxiously discussed the formation and training of SA "pioneer" squads, which were said to include special "demolition details" (*Sprengtruppen*).[57]

But the Nazis themselves obviously put the greatest importance on the SA's new incendiary skills.

On August 1st, 1932, the night after the Nazis' greatest election success, men of Königsberg's SA Storm 12 committed at least six murders or attempted murders, mostly on local officials and especially Communist politicians, and a dozen arson attacks. The arson attacks were carried out with what the press called "fire bombs." Besides several gas stations, the

Social Democrats' Otto Braun House and the headquarters of the liberal *Königsberger Hartungsche Zeitung* (Königsberg Hartung's newspaper) were also targets. Erich Koch, the Nazi Gauleiter of East Prussia, denied that the Party had anything to do with the attacks, and the Nazis' East Prussian paper dismissed them as a "clever tactic" of the Communists to bring the Nazis into discredit. Nonetheless, in the days that followed a wave of SA violence spread across eastern Germany, through East Prussia and into Silesia. Peter Longerich, the leading historian of the SA, notes that although this violence followed a Nazi electoral triumph, the stormtroopers' feelings were far from triumphant. What happened in Königsberg was not only an "uprising of the SA" directed at left wing and centrist Nazi opponents, but also, indirectly, at the Nazi leadership: it was an expression of impatience and frustration with promises of power that never seemed to materialize, of a desperate desire to force a Nazi consolidation of power through the unleashing of a civil war. Something of this feeling may have accompanied another seeming triumph: the torchlight parade through Berlin on the night of January 30th when Hitler became Chancellor. In a 1936 novel about the SA, a former stormtrooper named Fritz Stelzner wrote that this night's sole purpose was to "ventilate" the need for vengeance. The stormtroopers "had believed in [vengeance] and it was their only hope, when they could hope for nothing more."[58]

At the end of October prosecutors brought members of the Königsberg Storm to trial on the arson charges. The homicide charges took longer to prepare. Rudolf Diels's new boss, Prussian Interior Minister Bracht, considered the case important enough to send Diels himself out from Berlin to investigate it. The Nazi hierarchy also attached unusual importance to the case. Hans Frank, whom Goebbels had praised at the time of the Kurfürstendamm trials for handling political cases correctly, was sent out to defend the men. The stormtroopers refused to testify, and recanted their earlier statements to the police. Nonetheless the court found enough evidence to convict them. The SA men had met that night at the apartment of one of their number, and "there were armed with bottles filled with an explosive." They went out between 5:00 and 6:00 a.m. to carry out their attacks. Their storm leader gave them an order: "At six o'clock it must be burning." The men were also told that "Whatever happens must be kept quiet."[59]

An effort to keep it quiet was probably also behind a break-in at the prosecutor's office during this trial. The authorities believed that thieves were trying to get the documents from the case; a newspaper article about the break-in was headlined "Fear of the Solving of the Case." As the Justice Ministry commented, it was "likely" that the thieves came from the SA.[60]

The SA carried out such operations in Berlin as well. In the 1950s Rudolf Diels gave several reporters information on the Berlin SA's "Arsonists' Commando," designated as the "Unit for Special Missions" (Sondereinheit zur besonderen Verwendung, or ZbV). This unit had used a special self-igniting fluid to spray posters on Berlin's *Litfaßsäulen* or advertising columns, or sometimes streetcars or businesses. Diels said that if reporters wanted more information about the Unit for Special Missions, they would have to talk to Heini Gewehr.[61]

Heini Gewehr, as we have seen, was a childhood friend of Karl Ernst and a prime defendant in the Kurfürstendamm trial. After the war Gewehr himself steadfastly denied any involvement in the Reichstag fire. Yet he left a startling admission about the Unit for Special Missions.

"During my technical training," Gewehr remembered in 1960—he was an engineer—"in chemistry class we were shown how a material in solution remains as a residue after evaporation of the solution." The material in question was phosphorus, which was dissolved and then poured onto a sheet of blotting paper. When the solution evaporated the phosphorus remained, and would catch fire and burn the blotting paper. After joining the SA, Gewehr remembered the demonstration, and the SA used this method in what it called the *Kampfzeit* (time of struggle) to destroy Communist election posters which were out of reach. SA men would pour the solution into bottles or old light bulbs and throw it at the cloth banners. Gewehr claimed that the solution was only weakly combustible. But as with the attacks in Königsberg, the Nazi hierarchy took it very seriously and wanted it kept secret. "This weapon," said Gewehr, "was handled very confidentially and only made known in *Standartenführer* circles," in other words, among SA officers whose rank corresponded to that of a colonel. "In my time it was only rarely used." Later, in court testimony in the early 1960s, he added more details. He had demonstrated the use of the solution to SA commanders, including Count Helldorff, at the urging of Karl Ernst. He had not, he said, himself used the solution "regularly" (*regelrecht*) during the Kampfzeit, at least not during his time at the Staff Watch. But that the solution was used later was, he said, "thoroughly possible."[62]

4

· · · ·

"IMPOSSIBLE THINGS"

THE INVESTIGATIONS

AROUND 11:00 P.M. ON THE EVENING of February 27th, Hermann Göring's press secretary Martin Sommerfeldt was awakened by a telephone call from Göring's private secretary. She told him the Reichstag was burning and that the interior minister expected him there immediately. Sommerfeldt found Göring in the smoke-filled *Wandelhalle*. He seemed calm, and Sommerfeldt thought that although he was shocked by the arson he did not consider it very important. Sommerfeldt got the basic facts from the police and the fire department: the fire had started just after 9:00, one culprit had been arrested, firelighters had been found in the building. Diels told him that the arson was presumably a Communist attack but that the police would not know for sure until they interrogated the suspect.[1]

Sommerfeldt presented a draft communiqué to Göring at about 1:00 a.m. By this time the interior minister was no longer calm. Sommerfeldt later claimed that Göring read the draft and then pounded the desk with his fist and yelled, "This is crap! This is a police report from the Alex, not a political communiqué!" Sommerfeldt's sources had told him they found a hundredweight (just over one hundred pounds) of incendiary material at

85

the Reichstag. "A hundredweight?" Göring bellowed, reaching for a colored pencil. "Ten, a hundred times that!" Sommerfeldt protested that such a figure was impossible. "Nothing is impossible!" Göring shouted. "That wasn't one man, there were ten, twenty men! Man, don't you get it—that was the Commies! It was the signal for a Communist uprising! The beacon! It's happening!"[2]

Sommerfeldt later claimed that he resisted his boss's exaggerations, although such courage is not reflected in documents he composed at the time. Göring dictated a new report on the spot, glancing occasionally at a note on his desk. The Reichstag fire, he said, marked the opening of a Communist uprising. Communist leaders were to be arrested and the Marxist press banned. Göring multiplied the numbers from Sommer-feldt's report, "with a sideways look at me," by a factor of ten.[3]

In the anteroom to Göring's office, Diels, who always behaved, Sommerfeldt observed, with a "smiling lack of respect," asked Sommerfeldt why "the old man" was yelling like that. "Because he is demanding impossible things," Sommerfeldt replied. Only one word in the new communiqué, said Sommerfeldt, was his own: "and." Diels claimed piously in his memoirs that Göring's falsifications had had a shattering effect on "the concept of the state" that he and his officers held dear. In this respect at least Diels's and Sommerfeldt's apologetic postwar accounts corroborate each other. If Göring sincerely believed in a Communist coup attempt, despite the information coming from Diels's police about the Communists' incapacity and unwillingness to do any such thing, why the need to falsify the information at this early stage? The event itself ought to have been enough.[4]

Sommerfeldt soon learned that Goebbels's propaganda office had told the foreign news bureaus of the fire two hours before, while Sommerfeldt was still busy interviewing police and fire fighters. Now he could guess what document Göring had been looking at as he dictated his new communiqué.[5]

At the Alex Sommerfeldt told Arthur Nebe, head of the executive branch of Diels's political police (the branch responsible for arrests and surveillance) Goebbels had put out a communiqué before the Interior Ministry. "Mistake in the staging?" he asked Nebe. Nebe already seemed to share his suspicions, replying, "It certainly happened damned quickly. Maybe something really stinks, but that's a hot potato that we don't want to pick up."[6]

IT WAS THE BERLIN POLICE, especially Diels's officers Helmut Heisig and Walter Zirpins, who had the first chance to investigate the Reichstag fire.

Heisig and Zirpins were strikingly similar in background. Both were from Upper Silesia, Heisig born in 1902 in Ratiborhammer, Zirpins in 1901 in Königshütte. Both had started their police careers in Breslau, Heisig in 1929, Zirpins in 1927, after earning a doctorate in law. In 1931 Heisig was transferred to the Berlin criminal police and it was only after the Nazi seizure of power that he moved to the political police; Zirpins was transferred from Marienburg to the Berlin political police in January 1933. But Heisig had already been working with the Nazis and against Weimar democracy. In August 1932, by his own account, he joined the "National Socialist Police Officers' Working Group," and also began meeting with Count Helldorff and other Berlin SA men to coordinate intelligence for the fight against Communists and Social Democrats—a fight which he himself described as his own "field of work" as of August 1932. After the war, of course, he concealed how closely he had worked with the Nazis.[7]

In 1950 Heisig recalled that when van der Lubbe was brought in, he had burns from the fire, and that he spoke "relatively terrible German." He was, however, lively and revealed an unexpectedly high level of education. In 1961 Zirpins recalled that van der Lubbe could respond to questions "perfectly" in German. "There were no linguistic difficulties." Van der Lubbe wanted the police to believe his story, and took great care that the protocols reflected what he had said. He was both "energetic" and "happy to confess," in stark contrast to his appearance months later at his trial. In 1951 Zirpins had remembered that the first interrogation done in the late night hours had been hard to conduct because the interrogation room was under siege by curious high-level Nazi officials, among them the new Berlin Police Chief Admiral Magnus von Levetzow, Kurt Daluege, and Diels. Nonetheless the detectives managed to "connect" with van der Lubbe, who, said Zirpins, gave a clear account of what he had done and why.[8]

These recollections point to an important contradiction in memories of van der Lubbe. The animated and intelligent van der Lubbe Zirpins and Heisig described is consistent with the young man friends and family in the Netherlands remembered. He stands in striking contrast, as we will see, to the nearly comatose and seemingly mentally handicapped figure van der Lubbe cut at his trial in the autumn. In the autumn van der

Lubbe, even in his few loquacious moments, never demonstrated more than a shaky command of German or the slightest ability to convey ideas clearly. Even in February, however, some witnesses remembered van der Lubbe at the Alex as "stupid" and "silent." An officer named Heyse told Martin Sommerfeldt that van der Lubbe was "as silent as a wall," either "an idiot or one cool customer." This puzzling contradiction is just one element of the larger mystery of Marinus van der Lubbe.[9]

Heisig was the first to question van der Lubbe. The young Dutchman admitted to setting the Reichstag on fire with firelighters and his own clothing. "The first fire went out. Then I lit my shirt on fire and carried it farther . . . I went through five rooms." He insisted that he had acted alone and that burning the Reichstag was his own idea. Asked if he had a "role model" he replied, "No, I do nothing for other people, all for myself . . . No one was for setting the fire." He cheerfully confessed to having set other fires on Saturday, February 25th, at the old Royal Palace, a welfare office in Neukölln, and Berlin's City Hall.

Why had he done it? "The workers should rebel against the state order," explained van der Lubbe, in the kind of language that he seemed to reserve exclusively for the police. "The workers should think that it is a symbol for a common uprising against the state order." He wanted to inspire workers to create their own workers' parliament and their own laws.

Van der Lubbe's indifference to being caught puzzled the police. He had not tried to run, and on a cold winter night had shed and burned most of his clothes. Van der Lubbe told Heisig he hadn't thought he was going to get "pinched." Heisig wondered if in that case van der Lubbe would have turned himself into the police. "Maybe, yes, I don't know."[10]

Later that night Zirpins took over. In the course of long interrogations—Zirpins worked with van der Lubbe for three days—van der Lubbe's life story emerged.

He was born January 13, 1909, in Leyden. His father was a drinker who left the family when Marinus was seven; his mother died five years later. He was raised after that by an older sister and her husband. He apprenticed as a bricklayer because he couldn't think of anything better to do, and became a journeyman—but a serious injury kept him from ever working much at his trade. Already in 1924 he had got some chalk in his left eye, injuring his cornea. Two years later his vision in this eye was down to 30 percent. Then in 1927 some grit got caught in his right eye. In January 1933 he was down to 15 percent vision in the left eye and

20 percent in the right. His peripheral vision was better than straight ahead; to read he had to hold a text directly in front of his eyes; he could recognize people only by voice or if they stood directly in front of him. Since 1928 he had drawn a pension of 6 gulden and 44 cents per week, the equivalent of about 46 euros today, which he supplemented with occasional odd jobs. Probably through a student friend, Piet van Albada, he became acquainted with the "ABCs of Communism" in the latter part of 1928. For a time he had belonged to the Dutch Communist Party, and by late 1928 the Leyden police were already aware of his political activism. They told their German colleagues they thought van der Lubbe was "crazy" (*ein wirrer Kopf*). He left the Communist Party in 1931 in part, he said, because it would not let him go to the Soviet Union.[11]

From the recollections of everyone who knew him, van der Lubbe comes across as something of a holy fool. He was universally well liked, decent, generous, kind, selfless, and unfailingly polite. He intervened when an advocate of Fascism was shouted down speaking to a crowd of workers at the Leyden Grain Exchange. Fascists were workers too, van der Lubbe insisted, and they had the right to express themselves. Workers should speak with each other and listen to each other. He was particularly fond of children. Once he bought some bananas for the young son of a man with whom he was staying, but then he told the boy he had given the bananas away to some children who were even poorer than he was. Another time some schoolboys ran after him as he rode on a farm wagon. Gradually the boys gave up, but one kept running until eventually van der Lubbe hoisted him up to the wagon. "One can meet children through whom one feels that things must be different in the world, and someday will be different," he wrote in his diary. "That lies hidden so to speak even in their eyes." Even in his long, dreadful ordeal as a prisoner of the Nazis, van der Lubbe would remain unfailingly patient and polite with all of the police, judicial, and prison officials with whom he had contact.[12]

He was a young man who yearned to be something that, born in poverty in a time of limited social mobility, he could not be. This yearning strained regularly against reality. He wanted to swim across the English Channel to win some newspaper prize money, and even traveled to Calais for the purpose, but was stopped, apparently, by bad weather. He embarked on extraordinarily adventurous journeys around Europe, walking and hitch-hiking, with little sense of what was involved. In September 1931 he wanted to go to China via Constantinople. From the map he thought he could walk to Constantinople in about three weeks, and then reach China and return inside two or three months. His friend van Albada tried to explain to him the scale of the map, but van der Lubbe could not understand. He set off anyway, and was surprised to encounter snow in Austria. He had thought by going south he would escape the winter. By mid-October he had at any rate reached Yugoslavia, where he gave up and returned home by way of Hungary.

While he was on trial in 1933 his friends published a collection of extracts from van der Lubbe's diaries and letters in an effort to rebut some of the propaganda claims about him. Along with his basic decency, these writings implicitly convey a rather surprising disinterest in politics, which van der Lubbe almost never mentioned. This van der Lubbe had little grasp of political geography—he thought that Zagreb was the capital of Yugoslavia, while Serbia was a separate country—and seemed to believe whatever he heard. Traveling through Croatia he recorded that Serbians were "a completely different people, still half savage, as I have been told here."[13]

In January 1932 he was arrested for breaking a window, not the first of his minor encounters with the law (none of them involving arson, contrary to occasional legends). This did not keep him from another journey. He wanted to see the Soviet Union. But he did not have a visa and he was arrested in April 1932 trying to cross the Polish-Soviet border illegally. He returned to the Netherlands, where he had to serve a three-month sentence for the broken window. He was released in early October. He wanted to set up a facility in Leyden for workers' education, but could not convince welfare authorities to give him the funds for it, even when by November a hunger strike had brought his stocky 5'10" frame down to 151 pounds. When the Nazis came to power in January van der Lubbe decided he had to see events in Germany for himself. He set out again on foot and reached Berlin on February 18th.[14]

What he did for the next ten days is at the heart of the Reichstag fire mystery. If Nazis set fire to the Reichstag, then at some point between February 18th and February 27th SA men or Gestapo officers must somehow have contacted van der Lubbe. That van der Lubbe might, on his own, have decided to break into the Reichstag at just the moment the Nazis were planning to burn it is an unacceptably improbable coincidence (balanced only by the improbable coincidence that on his own he should have broken into the Reichstag at precisely the best moment to avoid all the usual rounds of Reichstag employees). Yet there is no definitive evidence of contacts between van der Lubbe and Nazis before the fire, and it is here that the Tobias/Mommsen single-culprit theory is on its strongest ground. There are, at best, only hints of how such contact might have happened.

We know that from his arrival on February 18th van der Lubbe seemed to drift aimlessly around Berlin, sleeping mostly in homeless shelters in the Alexandrinenstrasse in Kreuzberg or the Fröbelstrasse in Prenzlauer Berg. The most significant interruption came on Wednesday, February 22nd, when he went to the welfare office in the district of Neukölln. Here he got involved in conversations with unemployed workers, some of them Communist activists. These conversations became one of the main links the Nazis drew between van der Lubbe and organized Communism, and for this reason the content of the witness testimony about them is, at best, dubious. But it is clear at least that van der Lubbe was there—and it is clear that two of the "Communists" were in fact Nazi informers.[15]

According to witnesses, van der Lubbe used the welfare office as his soapbox to deliver rabble-rousing speeches to the unemployed workers of Neukölln. He complained, they said, that the Communist Party leadership was "lame" (*flau*). Someone suggested that public buildings be set on fire as a protest. Van der Lubbe agreed: "That's the only way to spark the revolution." Someone else said that the workers should pour gasoline over SA men and light them on fire. Van der Lubbe was transported. "So musht coming!" (*so musch komme*) he cried, in the awkward German he apparently spoke with everyone but the police. How much credibility we can attach to these accounts—which the Nazis extracted from witnesses who were, in some cases, already concentration camp prisoners—is another question altogether.[16]

The night of February 22nd was the only occasion on which van der Lubbe did not sleep in a shelter. Instead a Communist activist named Walter Jahnecke and another man named Kurt Starker took him to Starker's apartment.[17]

Twenty years later East German authorities investigated Jahnecke for having been an informer who betrayed Communists to the Nazis. According to the documents (and we have to be as skeptical of East German legal documents as of Nazi ones) Jahnecke confessed, claiming in defense that he had only exposed people because he thought they were actually Nazi agents. Prosecutors eventually dropped the charges against Jahnecke, but only because his victims had been acquitted, not because these authorities believed him.[18]

Margarete Starker, the wife of Kurt, later maintained that she had never trusted Jahnecke. He always had people around him who "did not correspond to our outlook." Among them was one "Hinz" (actually Hintze) who was, she said, a provocateur. Jahnecke had brought "the provocateur" van der Lubbe to the Starkers, and seemed "very familiar" with the young Dutchman. Starker claimed she had gone through van der Lubbe's pockets, finding a Nazi ID card and food stamps provided by the Nazi Party.[19]

She was at least right that Willi Hintze was a police informer and even an agent provocateur who betrayed some of the Neukölln Communists. Hintze seems to have tried to rouse the other Neukölln Communists, including Jahnecke and Starker, to an attack on the Neukölln welfare office, which then on February 25th became van der Lubbe's first target. The plan was to stage a fight so that the police officers stationed there would take arrestees to the station. Then a squad of eight or ten men under Starker's command, equipped with guns which Hintze said he could acquire, would attack and perhaps even kill the welfare officials. The attack was supposed to take place on February 24th. However, Hintze had tipped off the police and the director of the welfare office and the principals were all arrested that morning. According to Starker, Hintze had also advocated an attack on a local SA tavern. A police report indicated that Hintze was arrested with the others, but was released again when the precinct captain and the director of the welfare office confirmed he was their agent.[20]

The most that can be said is that Jahnecke and Hintze are plausible candidates for having brought van der Lubbe into the orbit of the SA or the Gestapo. It is striking that it was only after these Neukölln encounters, and only after meeting Hintze with his interest in an attack on the Neukölln welfare office, that van der Lubbe began his brief arson campaign with an attack on that very spot. Van der Lubbe was not a pyromaniac and never showed any interest in arson before February 25th. There is also, as the Reich Supreme Court later concluded, virtually no evidence about what he did, where he went or whom he saw on February 23rd and 24th, except that he returned briefly to the Starkers. Magistrate Vogt testified later that van der Lubbe had kept silent under interrogation about his contact with Jahnecke and his stay at Starker's apartment; his desire to cover up these contacts might be significant.[21]

On Saturday, February 25th, van der Lubbe bought four packages of firelighters and, at around 5:00 p.m., lit and tossed one through a back window of the Neukölln welfare office. With typical indifference to results he did not stay to see what happened, but moved right on to the "Red Rathaus," Berlin's city hall. Here he tossed a firelighter in a basement window, which turned out to be an employee's apartment. Again he ran away.[22]

By 8:00 p.m. he had reached the former Royal Palace on Unter den Linden. He climbed up some scaffolding to the roof, lit his two remaining packages of lighters, and tossed them in a top-floor window, again without hanging around to see whether they set anything on fire. His work done for the day, he returned to the Alexandrinenstrasse shelter.[23]

These attempted fires made little impact on Berliners. The papers reported only the fire at the palace, and that not until February 27th, shortly before the Reichstag itself burned. Even the police did not know about all of them before van der Lubbe's confession.[24]

On Sunday, February 26th, van der Lubbe decided to walk from Neukölln to the distant northwestern suburb of Spandau. He could not explain to Zirpins why he had done this, although he suggested that "maybe" it was the first step of his homeward journey. He stayed that night in Hennigsdorf, near Spandau, at a police homeless shelter. Since it makes little sense that van der Lubbe should have walked as far as Hennigsdorf only to turn back for Berlin the next day to burn the Reichstag, advocates of Nazi responsibility for the fire have since 1933 focused more attention on Spandau and Hennigsdorf than Neukölln as the place where the SA or the Gestapo might have gotten to him. Much of the speculation has centered around one Franz Waschitzki (whose name the Reich Supreme Court mistakenly rendered as Waschinski), the man who shared the shelter with van der Lubbe that night. Many unreliable writers have tried to make Waschitzki/Waschinski out to be a Nazi agent. Tobias's spirited demolition of this "legend" is one of the more persuasive elements of his book.[25]

On Monday morning van der Lubbe left the Hennigsdorf shelter at 7:45 and walked back to Berlin. Already by midday, he said, he had thought about setting fire to the Reichstag, and he purchased four more packages of firelighters. The most plausible evidence suggests that van der Lubbe reached the Reichstag around 2:00 p.m., and walked around the building to get a good look at it. Then he walked along the Siegesallee to Potsdamer Platz and east to Alexanderplatz, where he passed the rest of the day. He was waiting, he said, for dark.[26]

Hans Bernd Gisevius noted a problem with this part of van der Lubbe's evidence. In late February it gets dark around 6:00 p.m. in Berlin. Van der Lubbe did not break into the Reichstag until just after 9:00—so between 6:00 and 9:00 he was waiting for more than just dark. "Why in all the world—and where?—did Lubbe wait on that cold winter evening?" Gisevius wondered. Van der Lubbe's description of his movements after 6:00 p.m. could not account for more than perhaps twenty minutes or half an hour. This puzzle was linked, said Gisevius, to a greater one. The evidence of the regular rounds of Reichstag employees—the mailman, the porters, the lighting man—showed that there was a window of opportunity between 9:00 and 10:00 when there would be no one inside the building to disturb an intruder. Van der Lubbe hit this window squarely. Was this only a stroke of luck?[27]

Shortly after 9:00 p.m. van der Lubbe climbed the stairs to Portal I and then clambered up a cornice to a balcony (for van der Lubbe's path through the Reichstag, according to his own account and, in part, physical evidence found by the police, see the map on page 7). He had picked this spot because it was somewhat hidden from sight. "I kicked in the glass of the balcony double door and reached a room," he told the police. He needed ten kicks to get through the window.[28]

This first room was Schulze's Caucus, the Reichstag restaurant. Here van der Lubbe started a fire with one of his packages of firelighters, which he placed under a curtain. "Since the fire did not get going at all, I lit a second piece and put it on the table." He took off his coat and his vest and lit his vest from the "smoldering remnants on the table" in order "to carry the fire farther." He left the restaurant and ran along a corridor until he found paper in one of the offices, and used the third package of firelighters to make what he called "a big fire." He turned around and ran down a flight of stairs to the ground floor, where, he said, he broke into the kitchen by kicking down a door. Here he used the last of his firelighters to set a tablecloth on fire. He set fire to his shirt to light his way, but it quickly burned itself out and he lit a tablecloth instead. It was at this point, as he was running through the kitchen with the burning tablecloth, that he heard a "bang." That was Buwert shooting at what he thought was a man carrying a torch, so we know from the evidence of Buwert and Thaler that this had to be around 9:12 or a little after.[29]

Next van der Lubbe lit some hand towels that he found in the bathrooms and ran back up the stairs. "I took a burning tablecloth with me and came then into a big church"—his description of the plenary chamber.[30]

To understand what really happened that night, the fires van der Lubbe set in the restaurant, on the lower floor, and in the hallways outside the plenary chamber are beside the point. It is what he did in the plenary chamber that matters.

With a bit of burning tablecloth—in some statements he said it was his overcoat or vest—he set fire to one of the curtains that hung at the front of the plenary chamber behind the president's desk. "I tore off a big piece of the burning curtain and ran with it to the other side of the room, where I threw down a part of the curtains." In other words, he ran from the front to the back of the chamber. He claimed that the curtains "burned like thunder" and eventually set fire to the wood. Subsequent tests on the curtains found they did not burn easily.[31]

At this point, by his own account, van der Lubbe was already finished with the plenary chamber. He ran back out into the hallway around the chamber, where with some other bits of burning curtain he set a few more minor fires. He heard voices. "I assumed it was the police, and I waited." He went into the Bismarck Room, an ante room to the offices of the *Reichsrat*, which lay across the hallway from the chamber toward the south-east corner of the building. It was in the hallway by the Bismarck Room, at around 9:25, that Scranowitz and Poeschel arrested him.[32]

He explained his political motives to the police with a clarity and sophistication missing from any of his other statements. The government of "National Concentration" in Germany, van der Lubbe told Zirpins, "created two dangers: first that the workers will be repressed, and second that the national concentration will never allow itself to be pressed by the other states, so that in the end it will come to war." This was why he felt that he, like other workers, had to act. "I chose the Reichstag," he offered, "because that is a central point of the system."

He added, in a passage that in the prosecutor's copy is heavily underlined: "To the question of whether I carried out the deed alone, I declare that such was the case. No one helped me with the deed, and I also did not meet anyone in the whole Reichstag."[33]

Van der Lubbe told this story again and again—later that spring to examining magistrate Paul Vogt, and, in his few lucid moments, at his trial in the autumn. Inevitably there were minor variations from telling to telling, but his account of what he had done in the plenary chamber remained consistent. He had set a curtain on fire by the president's desk, carried a piece of it to the other end of the chamber, turned around and run back through the chamber and out. "Aside from that I did not start any fires in the plenary chamber," as he summed up on one occasion. Sometimes he gave the impression that other fires had arisen spontaneously as he ran by. "I just want to say," he told the magistrate in May, "that it seemed to me that the fires in the chamber burst into flames just like that, as if there was an oven there, but I didn't pay attention."[34]

On March 4th van der Lubbe was brought before a judge for arraignment. Here he was far less articulate than he had been with the police. When the judge asked him if he wanted to say anything about his motives, van der Lubbe replied: "I didn't think about anything at all [*Dabei habe ich gar nichts gedacht*]." The judge formally advised him that he was strongly suspected of committing arson and attempting high treason (in German law high treason is defined simply as an attempt to alter the constitution through violence, and so there is nothing odd about a foreigner being charged with this offense). As a foreigner, and in light of his anticipated heavy sentence, van der Lubbe would be retained in custody. Authority was closing in on the young Dutchman.[35]

HITLER'S CABINET MET AT 11:00 a.m. on the morning of February 28th. It was a transformed chancellor who faced his colleagues. The cautious pragmatism of the first weeks was gone. Now, he said, "the psychologically correct moment for the confrontation had arrived," and it would be "pointless" to wait any longer. After the Reichstag fire he was confident the government would win a majority in the coming elections. Göring told the cabinet that a single person could not possibly have set the fire. It had been carefully prepared at least one hour before it broke out. He estimated that there had been at least six or seven culprits.[36]

Reich Interior Minister Frick presented the cabinet with a new draft decree, formally the "Decree of Reich President von Hindenburg for the Protection of People and State," informally remembered as the "Reichstag Fire Decree." The first paragraph suspended the civil liberties contained in the Weimar Constitution, legalizing the imprisonment without trial of anyone the regime deemed a political threat, and effectively abolishing freedom of speech, of assembly and association, confidentiality of the post and telegraphic communications, and security from warantless searches. The second paragraph gave the Reich government the power to remove any state government from office. This was the foundation of the twelve-year dictatorship to come. It remained in force until Hitler committed suicide in his bunker.[37]

Some historians have argued that the decree was hastily thrown together on the morning of February 28th, and that it represented a radical departure from Weimar emergency laws. But recent research has shown that it was prepared carefully, with an eye to several Weimar precedents and a discriminating sense of what to take from them. Göring himself, as a defendant at Nuremberg, acknowledged that the decree used wording drawn from earlier emergency declarations. One of Diels's officers testified after the war about a high-level meeting at the Alex in mid-February to discuss its terms.[38]

The most important provisions were taken directly from a "sample decree," which the predominantly Social Democratic Bauer government had prepared in the summer of 1919. That arrested persons could be placed in "protective custody"—which, in Hitler's Germany, though not before, meant being sent to a concentration camp—had been a feature of German emergency laws since 1916. But the drafters had followed two 1932 precedents, including that "Greater Berlin Decree" which enforced the Papen Coup of 1932, in stripping "protective custody" prisoners of the Habeas Corpus requirement and other rights that had existed in German law even during the First World War. An emergency law provoked by the crises of 1923 had briefly dispensed with these protections, but protests forced their restoration. It was Papen's 1932 government that abandoned these legal safeguards more definitively. Hitler followed.

On the other hand, the Reichstag Fire Decree did not follow Papen's precedent where it was not appropriate. The Greater Berlin Decree, like most Weimar emergency laws, had called for a military as opposed to a civilian state of emergency, and it had been the army that enforced order in the days after the coup. In February 1933 the civilian version looked more promising to a national government that (as a result of the Papen Coup itself) had Prussia's police force at its disposal, as well as (since February 22nd) the "National Associations" as auxiliary police. On the other hand, the Nazis could not yet be certain of support in the higher reaches of the army. The Reichstag Fire Decree also did not, as the Greater Berlin Decree had done, specify harsher punishments for *Landesverrat*, the second form of treason in German law, which focuses on the betrayal of state secrets. It did not have to. These punishments were already in the decree the cabinet had approved on February 27th. Here again the decree was perfectly tailored to its political and legal context. Such careful drafts-manship was unlikely to have been the product of a rush job in the small hours between the fire and the first cabinet meeting of February 28th.[39]

Millions of Germans—especially among the nationalistic middle classes who formed the main Nazi and German National constituency—greeted without skepticism the official explanation that the fire was a Communist conspiracy. They tended, however, not to leave records of their reaction. One of the few who did was a Hamburg schoolteacher named Luise Solmitz who, despite being married to a Jew, was an enthu-siastic supporter of the new government. On February 28th she noted simply that "the Communists have set fire to the Reichstag," before going on to sing a hymn of praise for Hitler, "whose fame rises to the stars, he is the Savior of an evil, sad German world." The next day, when Göring spoke of the "discoveries" the police had made at Communist Party head-quarters, she noted approvingly that he had spoken "dryly, like an old, grey official, filled with the deepest seriousness." The anti-Nazi Sebastian Haffner wrote later that the Nazis' story had been widely believed. The French ambassador André François-Poncet thought the fire had made the "naive masses in the provinces" both more afraid of the socialist threat and grateful to the Nazis for deliverance from it.[40]

Among non-Nazis, the prevailing reaction was disbelief. The Social Democratic paper *Vorwärts* wrote the next morning, "If it really was arson, then the culprits must be sought in circles which wanted their action to express their hatred for the parliamentary system." This was the last issue of *Vorwärts* until the Nazis were gone.[41]

Erich Ebermayer remembered bringing news of the fire to his father, the former chief Reich prosecutor, whom he found working at his desk. "He is silent for a few seconds, then he says in his purest Bavarian: 'Course, they set the thing on fire themselves!'" Erich brought up the arrest of van der Lubbe—"They couldn't simply invent him?" But "the great criminalist, with fifty years of experience," as he called his father, only smiled.[42]

Annelise Thimme was another child of a well-placed family: her father, Friedrich Thimme, was a prominent historian whom the German govern-ment had commissioned to edit a selection of diplomatic documents to rebut the "War Guilt Clause" of the Treaty of Versailles. She remembered how on the morning after the fire her father "burst out in mocking laughter" at the newspaper report of a "Communist second-storey man" who had set fire to the Reichstag. "He said right away: 'That can only have been Hermann Göring.'" She and her brother gleefully told their schoolmates what their "expert" father had said.[43]

The novelist and physician Alfred Döblin also did not believe for a moment that the Communists were to blame. "You have to ask, *cui bono?*" he wrote later, probably unaware he was echoing Goebbels's reaction to the 1929 Reichstag bombing. Döblin decided he had to leave Germany, and fled in a scene out of a spy movie, giving the slip to a stormtrooper who was watching his door. He remembered standing at the window as his train pulled out of Anhalter station. "I had traveled this way many times before," he said. He loved the lights of Berlin, and "the way it always felt when I came home from somewhere, back to Berlin, and saw them: I breathed deeply, felt good, I was home." Now he turned away from the window and lay down to sleep. "Strange situation; it didn't belong to me anymore."[44]

It was one thing for liberal or left intellectuals to suspect the Nazis. But from the beginning such suspicions reached across the political spectrum, even into the ranks of the Nazi Party itself. The memory of these suspicions would become an important psychological fact later, when controversy over the Reichstag fire returned to postwar Germany. Even someone like Heinz Gräfe—in 1933 a nationalistically inclined law student, later a senior SS officer—could write to his fiancée about the rumors he had heard: "The Reichstag fire was arranged by the Nazis (election propaganda!!), the SA has been mobilized by the thousands in Berlin." Gräfe thought it was a "revolution from the right." Kurt Ludecke had been a Nazi activist from the first hour; at the time of the Reichstag fire he was in the United States running a Nazi press bureau. A few years later he wrote that when he had first heard about the fire, his reaction was "Clever! Well done!" taking for granted that his own Party was responsible. Later, a conversation with his boss, the Nazi propagandist Alfred Rosenberg, made clear to him that Rosenberg shared this assumption.[45]

On March 1st the Nationalist paper the *Deutsche Allgemeine Zeitung* (*DAZ*, German general newspaper) observed that it was incomprehensible that a Communist could be found who was foolish enough to commit the crime. The next day the paper openly criticized Göring for declaring on the night of the fire that van der Lubbe's confession revealed the

"Communist - Social Democratic united front has become a fact." Anyone who was attentive to politics, said the *DAZ*, was more likely to be astonished at the bitterness between the two parties. "But that such a united front . . . should have formed, of all things, for the purpose of the arson of the Reichstag, is extraordinarily unlikely." Generously, even bravely under the circumstances, it added that Social Democratic workers were as shocked as anyone else by the Reichstag arson.[46]

On the same day, under the headline "Lies about the Reichstag Fire," the *DAZ* printed a detailed summary of what foreign papers were saying about the investigations. The paper's ostensible purpose was to criticize baseless foreign accusations of Nazi misconduct. In fact the article read more like the kind of ploy which critics of an authoritarian government use to voice dissent. "Among other things," the *DAZ* reported, "it is claimed that the arrested Dutch Communist is in reality an agent provocateur and was hoodwinked into the arson." Foreign reports found it suspicious that while van der Lubbe had used his jacket and shirt to start fires, he had somehow hung onto his Communist identification papers and passport, and that the police seemed reluctant to publish their evidence or establish a reward for further information. "This very unusual procedure in a great criminal case is evidence that the authorities are thwarting the solving of the crime, in order to misuse a National Socialist provocation as a pretext for the anti-Marxist action."[47]

The paper's skeptical stance reflected real and growing unease among the Nationalists about how the coalition with the Nazis was working out. Already in early March Nationalist supporters were in a state of "deep bewilderment" and letters of complaint were flooding in to Papen's vice chancellor's office and to Hugenberg. The *DAZ's* articles infuriated the Nazis. On March 13th Kurt Daluege, the former Berlin SA leader whom Göring had now installed in the Interior Ministry as overall commander of the police, wrote in indignation to Diels. Daluege referred to quotes from foreign papers about SA atrocities which the *DAZ* had reproduced. Daluege thought the *DAZ* had done this deliberately to "hamper the forward movement of the national revolution." He wanted Diels to forbid German papers to cite any foreign news reports.[48]

AFTER COMPLETING HIS THREE-DAY INTERROGATION of van der Lubbe, Walter Zirpins wrote what he called a "final report" on the case, which he submitted on March 3rd. Those who favor the single culprit theory cite this report as not only the first important statement of it, but as an especially brave intervention by a political police officer under the conditions of the spring of 1933. Fritz Tobias called Zirpins's report "dangerous" (to Zirpins), while describing Zirpins himself an "experienced and especially qualified" officer.[49]

Parts of Zirpins's report seem to support such claims. "The question of whether van der Lubbe carried out the deed alone may without doubt be answered in the affirmative," he wrote. Van der Lubbe had confessed openly, and even before the police took him to the Reichstag he was able to describe where and how he had set the fires in a way that seemed to dovetail fully with the physical evidence gathered at the scene. Furthermore, van der Lubbe had confessed to setting fires at the Neukölln welfare office, the City Hall, and the palace.[50]

But only a few sentences later, Zirpins wrote that "The question of whether especially the extensive fire in the plenary chamber could have arisen so quickly in the manner described" by van der Lubbe should "still be investigated by experts." House Inspector Scranowitz had pointed out the contrast between the fire in the chamber and the others in the restaurant and the kitchen, which were easily extinguished.[51]

Furthermore, Zirpins continued, "the question of whether van der Lubbe was incited to his actions by third parties" was "essentially different." The answer lay in van der Lubbe's political outlook and his "fanatical" will to sacrifice himself. "A guy [Bursche] like this . . . could be only too welcome for the Communist Party," an "excellent tool." "Unambiguous clues" supported this suspicion. Van der Lubbe had persistently sought contact with members of the working class at welfare offices, meetings, and homeless shelters, and opened up political discussions in all such locations. The Communist parliamentary leaders Ernst Torgler and Wilhelm Koennen were probably behind van der Lubbe, as they had met at the Reichstag, as Zirpins put it, "strikingly often" in the days before the fire. Zirpins wrote that witnesses had observed that a suspicious figure left the building very quickly while the fire was in progress; this was likely the principal (Auftraggeber) who had overseen the job. In fact, the police already knew that the one person who definitely left the Reichstag quickly while the fire was in progress was a Nazi Reichstag deputy. But Zirpins was not referring to him.[52]

Zirpins's conclusion was heavily underlined, probably by the Chief Reich Prosecutor, and marked with an "X" in the left margin and another line in the right margin: "Van der Lubbe therefore admits to having worked toward a coup in Germany and with that to having made himself guilty of attempted high treason."[53]

As a witness at the trial that autumn, Zirpins did his level best to back away from the sole-culprit language of his report. Van der Lubbe had given "no answer" to questions about accomplices, said Zirpins, who had touched on this matter only superficially, "because I wanted to leave that for the later investigations." The police had had "a mass of hunches and suspicions" to investigate but no time to follow them up, so Zirpins had no evidence to disprove van der Lubbe's assertions. "I had had only two days," he continued. The Code of Criminal Procedure required that van der Lubbe be arraigned after that.[54]

Zirpins's report, then, linked van der Lubbe to a Communist conspiracy, took seriously witnesses who saw at least one other person hurrying away from the Reichstag, and suggested that the fire in the plenary chamber was qualitatively different from the others and required more evidence from the experts. As a witness Zirpins retreated even further from what his report had said about van der Lubbe as a sole culprit. In 1960, a West German prosecutor, recording a conversation with Fritz Tobias, called Zirpins "one of the originators of the 'fairy tale'" of Communist complicity in the fire. It was Tobias who had given the prosecutor Zirpins's report, and privately Tobias himself wrote that Zirpins's insistence on van der Lubbe's links to the Communists had "given [van der Lubbe] over to the hangman and practically prejudiced the entire case."[55]

However, Tobias's very different *public* presentation of Zirpins's evidence caused the final report to live on in the literature as the first of two *loci classici* for the single-culprit theory. The second came from a press conference that Helmut Heisig gave at the police headquarters in Leyden, Holland, on March 10, 1933.

Tobias gave Heisig an even more glowing character reference than he had Zirpins. According to Tobias, Heisig had been a bright young detective who had impressed Berlin's pre-Nazi Police Chief Grzesinski. Nonetheless Heisig found the early 1930s to be a "bad time" because the worsening political situation obliged him to investigate political extremists. Tobias went so far as to claim that Heisig had "done his duty" and worked diligently *against* the Nazis, scorning to "howl with the brown wolves," even drawing the ire of Hermann Göring in 1932—particularly glaring misrepresentations of the record of an officer who in fact had joined a Nazi organization that year. In Tobias's account, Nazis and Communists alike later cruelly victimized the dutiful Heisig for bravely proclaiming that van der Lubbe had acted alone. The Leyden press conference was the centerpiece of Tobias's argument.[56]

Diels had sent Heisig to the Netherlands to investigate van der Lubbe's background. At this press conference Heisig presented his findings. According to an Amsterdam paper, the *Algemeen Handelsblad*, Heisig said that van der Lubbe had sought contact with Communist and Socialist groups in Berlin. "To what extent," he continued, "these groups influenced the performance of the arson is still not determined. *It has been established with certainty that Lubbe set the fire himself.* . . . The motive of the act was, as van der Lubbe has stated, the promotion of a violent revolution [emphasis added]."[57]

Heisig claimed in his various postwar trials that he had gotten in serious trouble for insisting on van der Lubbe's sole responsibility; the authorities had immediately summoned him home to Germany. Certainly a few days later all German newspapers carried a small item announcing that reports that van der Lubbe had lit the fire in the Reichstag by himself were "not correct."[58]

Most of the evidence, however, shows that Heisig did not in fact tell reporters in Leyden that van der Lubbe had acted alone. An account of his press conference published in the *DAZ* contained wording significantly different from that in the *Algemeen Handelsblad*. (The report came from the *DAZ*'s own correspondent in the Netherlands.) According to this account, Heisig said it was "probable that van der Lubbe had lit the fire himself, *but that the preparatory measures were carried out by accessories* [emphasis added]." Of course the *DAZ* was a right-wing paper generally sympathetic to the government, and in any case subject to German censorship. But other papers in the Netherlands reported it the same way. *Het Vaderland* quoted Heisig as saying "So far as it is currently possible to make a judgment," van der Lubbe "lit the fire, but carried out the preparatory measures with accomplices." The *Nieuwe Rotterdamsche Courant* had identical language. The *Maasbode* offered a variant in which Heisig said "it is in any case clear that [van der Lubbe] did not hatch the plan for the arson alone, but it is not clear whether the accomplices were direct or indirect."

The inference that the *Algemeen Handelsblad* might simply have missed the nuance of what Heisig was saying is strengthened by the fact that its article was in other respects factually sloppy: It called Heisig "Heinrich" rather than "Helmut," and quoted him saying that van der Lubbe had "raced through the Reichstag with gasoline-soaked clothing" and a "torch." Heisig certainly knew that neither allegation was true. Heisig's postwar claim that he was summoned home in disgrace after this press conference is also highly improbable. His investigations in the Netherlands were finished by then, so why would he not return to his work in Berlin? Furthermore, far from being disciplined, he continued to lead the investigations in this very case, before going on to a successful police career in Nazi Germany.[59]

There were good reasons for the ambivalence about accomplices that ran through Zirpins's and Heisig's statements. As the London *Times*' Berlin correspondent Douglas Reed shrewdly guessed, the authorities were probably uncertain how to present the case. "In the early days," Reed wrote, "when the case was still in preparation, the prosecution seemed to have hesitated whether to attribute the fire to one man or several. If one man had done it, and that man were a Communist . . . this would exclude the possibility of Nazi complicity. If several had caused it, this admitted the hypothesis of Communist, but also of Nazi, collaboration." He added, "It was the expert evidence which irrevocably committed the prosecution to the second theory."[60]

Nazi statements from early 1933 give considerable support to Reed's hypothesis. In the *Völkischer Beobachter* on March 1st, Goebbels offered an interpretation that could cover a range of scenarios, writing of "a twenty-four-year-old foreign Communist setting fire to the Reichstag on the instructions of the Russian and German party offices of this world plague." At a press conference on the evening of March 3rd, just after he received Zirpins's report, Rudolf Diels said that van der Lubbe was "*one* of the arsonists in the attack on the Reichstag" [emphasis added]. That the young Dutchman was in contact with the Communist Party of Germany was beyond question, continued Diels, "even according to the investigations done up to this point," though van der Lubbe had followed the Communist Party's guidelines for how workers should conduct themselves with police and had admitted only what could be directly proved against him. "To what extent the investigations thus far have produced well-founded evidence concerning the involvement of other persons cannot be announced in the interest of state security and the ongoing proceedings." A reporter who was at the press conference thought that Diels looked uncomfortable, and gave his statement only "hesitatingly and without confidence."[61]

The ambivalence extended into the indictment. Even here, in the document with which the prosecutors sought the convictions of van der Lubbe's four co-defendants, they left open the question of what those co-defendants might actually have done. How they had specifically been involved in the fire was, said the indictment, irrelevant.[62]

Further support for Reed's inference comes from a memo that Martin Sommerfeldt wrote in October, after the Leipzig trial of van der Lubbe and his co-defendants had been running for a couple of weeks. Even at this stage, Sommerfeldt wrote, only van der Lubbe's conviction could be counted on; the court would likely acquit the other four defendants. Sommerfeldt had gone to Leipzig to give the press a "new line." Reporters should not just report the proceedings "objectively," but rather emphasize that "'Communism' is sitting next to van der Lubbe in the dock," responsible not just for the Reichstag fire, but for all the other attempts at subversion that were subjects of the trial. The press should "gradually" work around to the view that convictions of the other defendants were not important. The point of the trial was "the condemnation of Communism as such."[63]

After the war, as we will see, Heisig and Zirpins urgently needed to sanitize their records under the Nazis. Had they really bravely insisted in 1933 that van der Lubbe was the sole culprit, and had the documents really reflected their steadfastness in the face of political pressure, it would have been a strong point in their favor and they would have stressed it more firmly than they did. Instead, after the war they both tried to distance themselves from the Reichstag fire investigation. Zirpins blamed Heisig for *advocating* the argument that van der Lubbe had *not* been alone. Testifying in 1961, he said that while he did not believe that van der Lubbe had had accomplices, he could not say whether "subjectively" other persons or an organization had been behind him. Zirpins had not been assigned to investigate that question—Heisig had. A year earlier, Zirpins had said that Heisig wanted to "earn his 'spurs'" with the case and "really went hard at it [*recht scharf ins Zeug ging*]." The arrest of other suspects was done at Heisig's instigation. Zirpins even tried to blame Heisig for adding the material about van der Lubbe's Communist connections to the final report. However, when the judge at the 1933 trial asked Heisig whether he had contributed to Zirpins's report, Heisig testified flatly that Zirpins had written the whole thing.[64]

Heisig claimed after the war that he had always believed that van der Lubbe had acted alone. Yet he, too, tried to distance himself from the investigation. He put the blame for the multiple-culprit theory on the Reich Supreme Court and its investigators, and at his denazification trial in 1950 he went so far as to say that interrogating van der Lubbe the first night, and his work in Holland, had been "the full extent" of his involvement in the case—a statement that was clearly false.[65]

The surviving evidence from 1933 shows that not one of these Gestapo officers argued at the time that van der Lubbe had acted alone. In August 1933 Diels complained that the prosecutors had taken too little account of the work of "my officers Dr. Braschwitz and Heisig" and not charged as many people as these officers had wanted, especially the Neukölln Communists with whom van der Lubbe had spoken on February 22nd. In late March Braschwitz sent a letter to every Regional Criminal Police (*Landeskriminalpolizei*) office across the country, saying that reports of Communist subversion plans were important because they showed that the burning of the Reichstag "very plainly was not a matter of a so-called individual act of terror but rather a measure that arose from an obviously prepared political situation through spreading the appropriate messages." A Gestapo memo from September 1933 announced that it was now "fact" that the Reichstag fire was not the "result of a decision by an individual" but rather represented "a new political development, which was planned and prepared by the Communist Party." In 1948 a former Gestapo man named Walter Pohlenz testified that Heisig had ordered his subordinates to ignore any leads pointing to the Nazis and confiscated from them any evidence that did. Pohlenz thought that Helldorff was the ultimate source of this order. In 1956 a former Gestapo officer named Alois Eugen Becker remembered that when he came to work on February 28th he learned from the detectives—by which he must have meant Zirpins and Heisig—that there was no way van der Lubbe had set fire to the building by himself. Such a one-sided investigation had been prefigured in the investigation of the Maikowski and Zauritz shootings on January 30th. In Nazi Germany it became the norm.[66]

A FEW DAYS AFTER THE REICHSTAG FIRE, Rudolf Diels's Department IA opened a new branch, called the Department for Combating Bolshevism, at Bülow Platz (today Rosa Luxemburg Platz). The building had, until recently, been the Communist Party's headquarters, the "Karl Liebknecht House." Now it was the "Horst Wessel House."

At the opening ceremony on March 8th Count Helldorff told an enthusiastic crowd of SA and Stahlhelm men that "for every SA man who is murdered from today on in Berlin or in Brandenburg, three Communists will have to pay with their deaths." This was greeted with thunderous cries of "Heil!" and then the Swastika flag was raised over the building.[67]

Helldorff's tone did not bode well for the quality of police work the building's denizens would produce. That police practices under Hitler were corrupt and barbaric is hardly a news flash. But, as we have seen with Heisig and Zirpins, the integrity of the officers who investigated the Reichstag fire has long been an article of faith for those who believe that van der Lubbe was a sole culprit. Tobias seemed to be speaking at least of Heisig if not others when he referred to officers of the Berlin political police who had been "loyal servants of the Weimar state." Even in 2011 the German journalist and historian Sven Felix Kellerhoff, who has written a book about the fire, determined that all attempts to refute Tobias's conclusions had failed in the face of the "clean [*sauber*]" work of the police investigators, who, four weeks after the Nazis' takeover, "had not yet abandoned their professionalism in favor of partisanship."[68]

Documents from 1933 show that there were two separate teams of police working on the Reichstag case. A team of criminal police officers under Criminal Commissar Bunge investigated "only the technical things," as Bunge himself put it, meaning the physical evidence at the Reichstag (we might call these the questions of "what" happened). Everything else—which meant the "why" along with the "who"—fell into the jurisdiction of Diels's political police. These investigations were headed up by Heisig, with Braschwitz as his deputy. Zirpins carried out only the initial interrogation of van der Lubbe. In March 1933 Braschwitz described his own role as investigating "the culprits and their accessories." These arrangements lasted much longer than a few days or weeks. A Gestapo memo of August 1933, for instance, records that the Reichstag fire file "is currently being worked on by Criminal Commissar Heisig."[69]

After the war, Diels claimed that when he tried to dissuade Göring from prosecuting any suspects other than van der Lubbe, an enraged Göring forbade Diels any further involvement in the investigation, including the exerting of any "influence" on the detectives. Tobias accepted this story and wrote that as early as the beginning of March the investigation was in the hands of the chief Reich prosecutor and the Reich Supreme Court's examining magistrate.[70]

According to the original documents, however, Diels himself not only ordered Heisig to lead the investigation, he specified which officers should assist him and where the teams should work—in the Reichstag itself, with a direct telephone line to police headquarters. That fall, it was Diels's deputy, Hans Volk, who gave German reporters daily briefings on how to report the trial. After the war, Diels's former subordinates treated his command of the investigation as self-evident. Heisig, for instance, wrote Diels in 1948 that he had come to him "repeatedly" either to report or to receive orders. Braschwitz claimed after the war that Diels had recommended him to Göring for investigations of "further culprits" in the fire.[71]

Again the report by British MI5 officer Guy Liddell casts an important light on the investigation. On his visit to Germany in March and April 1933 Liddell met Heisig, who was, he said, in charge of the case against van der Lubbe as well as "other German and Bulgarian Communists accused of complicity in the burning of the Reichstag." When Liddell asked Heisig how it was that the Communists had settled on van der Lubbe as their agent, Heisig seemed "rather embarrassed by the question" but said that "the Communists often publicly got rid of one of their members in order that he might be able to work underground with less risk of detection." From the weakness of Heisig's evidence Liddell decided that "previous conclusions that this incident was a piece of Nazi provocation to provide a pretext for the wholesale suppression of the German Communist Party were amply confirmed."[72]

Diels complained ever more strenuously, both to Chief Reich Prosecutor Werner and to Göring, that the prosecution was not taking enough account of van der Lubbe's ties to the Communist activists in Neukölln. In a letter to Werner, Diels worried that the Communists would "mislead" the public by denying the connections the preliminary investigation had established between van der Lubbe and Berlin Communists. Therefore Diels thought that it was "of the greatest importance" to underscore these connections in the indictment. Several of the Neukölln witnesses should be charged alongside van der Lubbe, even if there was a chance they would be acquitted at trial. Otherwise he thought Communist propaganda would exploit their absence from the case. To Göring, Diels complained that the indictment did not extend to culprits identified in the investigations carried out by Braschwitz and Heisig. It was Werner, not Diels, who politely declined to indict these men, arguing that there was insufficient evidence against them.[73]

As for "the culprits and their accessories" whom Braschwitz and Heisig identified in their "judicious and successful" investigations (as magistrate Vogt put it to Diels), the record reveals efforts to find or manufacture evidence that were completely inept and occasionally comical. The investigations might better have been described as an exercise in rounding up the usual suspects. This is especially true for the arrest of Ernst Torgler.[74]

On the night of the fire a reporter called Torgler to tell him that he was suspected of involvement. More brave than wise, Torgler decided to present himself to the police "to expose this malicious lie before the world." The next morning Torgler appeared at the Alex in the company of lawyer Kurt Rosenfeld. Diels's officers were not sure what to do with a revolutionary desperado who surrendered so obligingly. Eventually the veteran officer Reinhold Heller apologetically informed the Communist leader that he would have to stay there. The government then issued a bulletin denying rumors that Torgler had given himself up.[75]

It was not much different with the Bulgarians. On March 7th one Johann Helmer, a waiter at a restaurant called the Bayernhof, near Potsdamer Platz, told the police about a regular group of customers whom he took to be Polish or Russian. They read nothing but Communist newspapers, and he even thought he had seen them in the company of the young Dutchman on the police posters sometime before Christmas 1932. On March 9th Helmer called again to say that several of the men were in the restaurant. The police descended. They arrested three men who turned out to be Bulgarian Communists: Blagoi Popov, Vasil Tanev, and Georgi Dimitrov. The police took Helmer to identify van der Lubbe in his cell—not in a line up—and Helmer, who strenuously insisted the substantial reward money formed no part of his motivation, said he was certain van der Lubbe was the man he had seen in the restaurant.[76]

Georgi Dimitrov had been a member of the Bulgarian parliament until a 1923 military coup pushed him and many other Communists into violent, though ultimately futile, opposition. He went into exile in Vienna and then Moscow, and was sentenced to death in Bulgaria in absentia. At the end of 1929 he moved to Berlin, where he worked for the Comintern, under a variety of aliases.[77]

This resume made Dimitrov an appealing suspect for the police, and they tried hard to convict him. In a report dated March 16th, a week after Dimitrov's arrest, one Criminal Assistant Kynast told of finding a guidebook called "Berlin in the Pocket" in Dimitrov's apartment. The book consisted of a number of maps. On one, the Reichstag was marked with a cross. Kynast took the book to Rudolf Braschwitz, who "discovered" that the Royal Palace was also so marked, while the Dutch embassy and consulate were underlined. The next day the officers put these items to Dimitrov, who accused them of marking up the guidebook themselves. He refused thereafter to sign any statements.[78]

One of Heisig's main contributions to the trial was to bring forth a witness named Otto Grothe, whose testimony was so unbelievable that the foreign press, Torgler's lawyer Alfons Sack—a Nazi party member whom we have seen in the Kurfürstendamm trial—and ultimately even the judges considered it perjury from a "psychopath." Grothe had been a leader of the Communist Red Frontfighters' League. He claimed that a Communist official from his neighborhood had described to him a meeting on February 23rd at which the Communist leader Ernst Thälmann and other officials had planned the burning of the Reichstag, and that on the afternoon of February 27th the arsonists, including van der Lubbe and the Bulgarians, had all met at the Great Star, the intersection in the middle of the Tiergarten. Torgler and Popov had brought the incendiary material to the Reichstag.[79]

The importance of Grothe's allegations for the prosecution can be gauged from the fact that the indictment devoted a 10-page section to them. On August 15th Magistrate Vogt warned the Gestapo that Grothe's credibility would be essential if his accusations were to stick, and the same day Heisig wrote to his assistant Raben with a plan to buttress it. The police needed to gather information from people who knew Grothe, though naturally not from "arch-Communists" who might not stand up as witnesses themselves. The important thing was that the police should not stress Grothe's more recent activity as a Communist activist. Heisig added that several Communists arrested along with Grothe were strongly suspected of involvement in the fire on the basis of their own statements.[80]

In the Netherlands Heisig had questioned people who knew van der Lubbe and who seemed to say things that were convenient for the German authorities. Van der Lubbe's friend van Albada apparently told Heisig that he thought van der Lubbe had let the Communist Party lure him into "causing trouble," and, further, that van der Lubbe had not really left the Party, but was working for it covertly. Indeed, Heisig testified that Albada had told him van der Lubbe was an "especially suitable object" for carrying out "actions." Van der Lubbe was so "decent" that he would always take the blame on himself. Another friend, Jacobus Vink, said that he had had possession of van der Lubbe's diary, which included addresses for German Communists, until the Dutch Communist Party had collected and destroyed it. Later that year, from London, Vink and Albada vehemently denied these statements and accused Heisig of fabricating them.[81]

Although the police and the prosecutors were willing to put Torgler and the Bulgarians on trial for their lives on the basis of such flimsy or clearly perjured evidence, they were strikingly uninterested in one particularly promising lead, perhaps because it involved a Nazi Reichstag deputy.

At about 9:35 on the night of the fire, a firefighter named Fritz Meusser had seen this deputy run out of Portal V, carrying a large, open briefcase. Meusser heard someone call "Herr Deputy, Herr Deputy!" but the man did not stop. Albert Wendt, the night porter at this entrance— the only one open after 8:00 p.m.—also saw the deputy leave, and insisted that he had not entered the Reichstag at any time after Wendt came on duty at 7:45.[82]

The mysterious deputy was one Herbert Albrecht. Thirty-three at the time but already with an active and adventurous life behind him, Albrecht had volunteered for the last stages of the First World War, and afterward had fought with a Freikorps unit. He had joined the Nazi Party in the early 1920s, long before it had become a major player in German politics, and had worked for the *Völkischer Beobachter* since 1924. His biographical entry in the Handbook of Reichstag deputies proudly listed his service in what he called the "Maikowski Storm," SA Storm 33 based in Charlottenburg, through which a number of important Berlin SA leaders passed.[83]

In late March Albrecht explained to the magistrate—the police had not bothered to take a statement from him—that he had spent the day of the fire sick in bed (he lived in a boarding house on Reichstagsufer, virtually next door to the Reichstag). When the maid told him that Reichstag was burning, he said, he dashed off to save some important papers. The firefighters were already there; the police had checked his Reichstag ID as he came and went. He insisted that the maid and the landlady could confirm his story. But in fact they couldn't. The landlady, Elisabeth Berkemeyer, had seen Albrecht running *from* the Reichstag with documents under his arm, being chased by a police officer, shortly after she learned the Reichstag was burning. She said the maid had told her that Albrecht had been in bed a half hour before the fire. The maid herself, however, one Maria Hessler, "could not say" whether Albrecht had been in his room at that time. There is in fact no record of any witness who saw Albrecht *entering* the Reichstag that evening.[84]

Nonetheless the police—and, later, Fritz Tobias—accepted this alibi at face value, seemingly unconcerned by credible evidence that a zealous SA man had been in the Reichstag as it started to burn, and then had run from it until stopped by police. Tobias went so far as to record that "on the night of the fire criminal police officers were able to confirm Albrecht's statements." The actual statements from Berkemeyer and Hessler amount to nothing like confirmation.[85]

THE REICHSTAG FIRE TRIAL, wrote the Swiss journalist Ferdinand Kugler in the autumn of 1933, had "gained clarity from the experts." He meant the technical experts, and he was right. Starting in the spring of 1933 and continuing to this day, it is these experts—engineers, firefighters, chemists, specialists in thermodynamics—who have provided the most consistent and reliable evidence about the Reichstag fire.[86]

At the end of April the Reich Supreme Court's investigator Magistrate Paul Vogt presided over several experiments in which three experts—the new Berlin fire chief Gustav Wagner, Professor Emil Josse of Berlin's Technical University, and Dr. Franz Ritter from the Berlin-Plötzensee Reich Chemical-Technical Institute—set a number of objects alight to see how they burned. They found that it was all but impossible to get a sample of curtain from the west entrance of the plenary chamber to burn with only a fire lighter. They had even more trouble with seats and desks of the same type and construction as those in the plenary chamber. These, too, would not burn on their own, even after applying a firelighter to them for eighteen minutes. They burned merrily, however, after being dowsed with a half-liter of kerosene.[87]

The Reich Supreme Court commissioned each of these experts to prepare a report on the fire, along with another, a chemist from Halle on the Saale named Wilhelm Schatz. Wagner, Josse, and Schatz also testified at the trial. On the central questions of how the fire in the plenary chamber had started and spread, all of the reports were unanimous. For reasons that aren't clear, the court did not use Ritter's report in the indictment. There seems even to have been a fifth report, written by Dr. Theodor Kristen of the Reich Physics and Technical Institute in Berlin. Like Ritter's report,

Kristen's was not used in court, and the text itself has been lost. Kristen himself, however, told the fire expert Professor Karl Stephan after the war that he had come to the same conclusions as the others.[88]

The Reichstag fire, as Josse explained, posed one basic problem: the witnesses established that the first fires began to burn in the plenary chamber around 9:21, and that the critical point had come at 9:27, when the chamber as a whole had burst into flames. How to explain scientifically the extraordinarily rapid spread of the fire? The experts agreed that at 9:27 there had been either a mild explosion or, perhaps, merely a significant increase in pressure inside the chamber, which had burst the glass ceiling and the glass dust cover and opened the chamber to a rush of air up through the cupola. This rush of air alone, however, could not explain the further spread of the fire. The oxygen would not cause the furnishings and paneling of the chamber to burn unless those fittings, too, had been raised to their ignition temperature by sufficiently hot surrounding fires. The witness testimony showed that the open flames that appeared around 9:21 had quickly gone out and a smoldering fire developed, producing a thick cloud of smoke. This is what Klotz saw at about 9:24.[89]

All the evidence suggests that van der Lubbe could not have reached the chamber before 9:16, and probably not until 9:18. The question, therefore, was how the fire in the chamber could have spread in ten minutes or less to the point that it could either cause an explosion, or generate enough pressure (through gases) to burst the glass ceiling, and furthermore generate enough heat to convert the chamber into what witnesses called a "sea of flames." The experts were unanimous in their conclusion that this could not have happened without the application of some kind of flammable liquid, probably kerosene or heavy gasoline. There were essentially three reasons for this conclusion: the quantity of gas that would be necessary for the explosion or increase in pressure; the condition of the vents in the chamber; and the observations of the witnesses.

Wagner explained that all fires must start with ignition, followed by preheating of the material, which produces "distillation" gases. The ignition must be hot enough to bring the material to a high enough temperature to release the gas, which in turn leads to the chemical reaction we see as fire. For a fire to spread, Wagner continued, there must be other combustible material nearby, and the initial fire must radiate enough heat to bring this surrounding combustible material to its ignition temperature.[90]

The problem was that fire lighters, burning clothes, or burning curtains could never have generated sufficient intensity of heat to raise the oak, pine, beechwood, and leather of the plenary chamber's furnishings to ignition temperature, let alone to burn sufficiently to release enough gas to explain the explosion. These were all materials with high ignition temperatures; so difficult is it to get oak to burn, that doors or stairs made of oak are classed as "fire-inhibiting" under the famous German industrial norms, the DIN. The fire was therefore inexplicable without the use of some kind of accelerant. Only burning gasoline or kerosene could have generated enough explosive gas in the time available.[91]

The condition of the exhaust vents in the chamber also pointed to the use of a flammable liquid. Josse reported that these vents were covered in soot, which could only have accumulated before the bursting of the ceiling, after which the soot would have risen into the cupola. That this soot could have come from burning wood was "out of the question." Schatz agreed, and added that he had also found soot traces around the exits of the stenographers' enclosure, pointing to the use of heavy gasoline.[92]

This hypothesis also fit the observations of those witnesses who had seen the plenary chamber between 9:21 and 9:27. Wagner explained that the fire would have begun with open flames, subsiding into smoke as the flames consumed the oxygen. The second, smoldering phase, would continue to produce gases. It would be short, and after a few minutes the explosion would follow. The earlier witnesses—Lateit and Scranowitz—would not notice waves of heat or a draft, as indeed they had not. But both Wagner and Josse pointed out that by the time Klotz arrived the buildup of uncombusted gas would have created higher pressure, and thus both the outward draft that Klotz felt and the thick smoke that he saw. The flames Lateit and Scranowitz had described were too high and too uniform to have come from burning wood, and Wagner noted that neither of them had heard crackling sounds from the flames, which they would have had the oak itself been burning. What they saw had to have been flames from gasoline or kerosene.[93]

The experts also agreed that the preparation of the fire had probably centered on the stenographers' enclosure. There were both forensic and logical reasons for this. Schatz explained that there was soot in the enclosure's exits, and that a sofa in the enclosure had been completely consumed by fire, which would not have happened had it not been doused with fuel. There were also stairs that led from the enclosure down to the lower floor, from where escape through the tunnel to the president's residence would be easy (the president of the Reichstag, of course, was Göring). Josse agreed. All of the experts speculated that the chamber had been prepared with rags soaked in gasoline placed on the seats, and then connected to the primary fire site with match cord or filmstrips.[94]

Schatz's particular contribution was to suggest that rags soaked with kerosene could also have been set alight with a self-igniting solution of phosphorus in carbon disulfide. Schatz presumably did not know of the Berlin's SA's Unit for Special Missions, the SA's arson attacks in Königsberg, or Heini Gewehr's efforts to train the Berlin SA in the use of just such a solution, but his explanation closely matched Gewehr's account of how such a solution worked. Schatz thought that on the evidence the arsonists had to have had a good knowledge of the Reichstag and be skilled in starting fires. A scientist, a worker in some kinds of factories, a pharmacist, chemist, or student of chemistry would, he said, understand how to produce the self-igniting solution.[95]

At the trial in October Schatz even took the court to the burned out chamber to demonstrate what he suspected had happened. According to reports, Schatz's solution caught fire in six to ten minutes. Recalled to testify on October 31st, Schatz said he had found traces of phosphorus and sulfur in the chamber beneath the tribune and the deputies' seats. He had found no such traces in the restaurant.[96]

The main conclusions of these experts, then, were both clear and unanimous. Wagner was speaking for all when he said, "Since today there is no question of miracles and supernatural phenomena, the course of events cannot have been as van der Lubbe claims." Every theoretical consideration and simple practical experience spoke against the idea that "with the time available, the fire in the plenary chamber could have taken on the extent and unfolded as it was described by the witnesses, unless preceded by a particular preparation of the chamber for the setting of the fire." Van der Lubbe had not had time for such preparation. Therefore "it must be concluded that several persons were required for the preparation of the plenary chamber," and that "these persons required a longer period of time." No one, then or since, has suggested that van der Lubbe brought with him any gasoline or kerosene. The conclusions of the others were all but identical.[97]

When Marinus van der Lubbe was asked about the experiments which suggested he could not have set the fires he claimed, he replied, "I won't give any more statements; the whole thing doesn't interest me anymore and I don't want to have anything more to do with it." Van der Lubbe never left any doubt that he wanted full credit for setting the Reichstag on fire. His petulance in the face of contrary evidence is to this extent understandable. More puzzling is the fact that the very authorities who sought to paint him as a stooge of the Communists seemed to share some of his petulance.[98]

There were, for instance, the expert reports on the fire by Kristen and Ritter that the prosecutors did not use at the trial, although (contrary to Tobias's 1962 assertions) they came to the same conclusions as the others. The man who was Berlin's fire chief on February 27th, Walter Gempp, by his own testimony also submitted a report to Göring, which was in the interior minister's hands by 11:30 on the morning of February 28th. This report, like Kristen's, has disappeared. The inference arises that somebody—the police, the prosecutors, perhaps members of Hitler's cabinet (the expert reports all went to Hitler)—simply did not like or want this conclusion, and kept seeking out other experts in the hope of finding a different one. Then, as the *Times* correspondent Douglas Reed suspected, when the conclusion that van der Lubbe could not have acted alone seemed unavoidable, the authorities made the best of it and prosecuted the case on that theory. But it is easy to see why, faced with propaganda presenting the Reichstag fire as a Nazi plot, the authorities would have preferred the line of Zirpins's report: van der Lubbe had been alone in the Reichstag, but he was there as a representative of a broader Communist conspiracy. We have already seen that the government steered the press toward this theory as it became clear that the trial was going badly for the prosecution.[99]

Remarkably, the authorities did not use at trial important items of physical evidence gathered in the wreckage of the plenary chamber, evidence which pointed to the presence of more than one culprit.

On May 17th one Criminal Secretary Meyer reported that among the debris in the chamber he had found the remains of some cords, and that their presence was explained by the discovery nearby of "the remains of a torch [*Brandfackel*] from which probably a few cords became detached." The accompanying sketch shows that Meyer found these items in the stenographers' enclosure close to the wall of the presidium. The experts, as we have seen, had hypothesized that the arsonists could have used cord to spread the fire from the stenographers' enclosure. But this critical evidence, that by itself seemed to rule out van der Lubbe's single culprit status, was never mentioned again in any of the investigations or hearings.[100]

The story of the nameplates is even stranger. A large cardboard nameplate for each member of the Reichstag was stored in a cupboard outside the plenary chamber. When a deputy was speaking, an attendant would fetch the appropriate nameplate and set it up on the speaker's podium. In the investigatory documents from 1933 there is only one passing reference to these nameplates, similar to the mention of the torch; and van der Lubbe never said anything about them. But references to them began to crop up after the war. The first seems to have been in a long 1949 essay on the Reichstag fire written by Diels's subordinate Heinrich Schnitzler. Schnitzler claimed that van der Lubbe had used these nameplates "to spread the fire in the whole chamber." Twelve years later, Walter Zirpins recalled that van der Lubbe had told him he had "strewn these nameplates around the plenary chamber and they had burned nicely." Zirpins said he himself had seen burned nameplates in the chamber. He did not explain why he did not mention them in his final report.[101]

We could chalk this up to the inconsistencies of memory many years after the fact. But there is no doubt that burned nameplates were found among the debris in the plenary chamber. At least one picture of wreckage in the chamber shows them very clearly. In 2005 a young scientist named Peter Schildhauer from the Fire Laboratory of the Allianz Technology Center (the lab for the Allianz Insurance Company) did some experiments on a surviving piece of one of the original cardboard nameplates. His conclusion was that van der Lubbe would not have been able to get one of these nameplates burning with his fire-lighters or a burning shirt in the time available to him. The fire, according to an Allianz press release, "had to have been well prepared." Only by means of a so-called ignition chain (*Zündkette*), said Schildhauer, echoing the experts of 1933, "could the events be plausibly explained: ignition—accelerant (*Brandverstärker*) like gasoline or kerosene—nameplates—oak chairs." To get the nameplates burning even with a fire lighter (and van der Lubbe insisted repeatedly he had none with him when he reached the chamber) he would have had to arrange the plates like a camp fire, according to Schildhauer. To catch fire, the plates would have to be exposed to flame from the sides or from underneath. But van der Lubbe had had no time to do this. Schildhauer concluded that with the tools and time at his disposal, van der Lubbe "could not have gotten even the heavy oak chairs in the plenary chamber to burn."[102]

Schildhauer noted that the presence of the nameplates in the chamber did not have to mean that they were used to start a fire: accidental effects, such as the actions of the firefighters, could also have spread them around. Since they were stored outside the chamber, however, it is more likely that someone fetched them from their closet and used (or tried to use) them to start the fire, probably with the aid of kerosene or gasoline. Van der Lubbe never mentioned the nameplates in his pre-trial statements, nor in his few lucid moments at trial, and he was not equipped with any flammable liquid. Zirpins wrote nothing about the nameplates in 1933, though he remembered them twenty-eight years later.

IT WOULD BE PERFECTLY REASONABLE to suppose that Nazi authorities pressured the fire experts of 1933 to reach the conclusions that they did. It is therefore important to see what fire experts working since the war, without political pressure, have said about the fire. Schildhauer is not the only one to have weighed in on the question.

In 1970 Professor Karl Stephan and several other scientists from the Institute for Thermodynamics at the Technical University of Berlin reviewed the expert reports from the trial and wrote an assessment of them. Stephan stressed that the period up until the explosion at 9:27 was crucial for understanding the fire as a whole. With the use of thermodynamic models not available in 1933, he calculated that 440 pounds (200 kg) of oak or pine would have had to be burning before the remaining combustible material in the plenary chamber could reach its ignition temperature. His tests confirmed that van der Lubbe could not have managed this in ten minutes with only the use of burning cloth or firelighters, and that the fires that Lateit, Scranowitz, and Klotz witnessed were insufficient to raise the other furnishings to ignition temperature in the time available. Assuming the first fires were started at the president's desk at the front of the chamber, and assuming no use of gasoline or kerosene, it would have taken fifteen and a half minutes for the first rows of seats to reach ignition temperature, thirty-three minutes for the middle rows, and forty-eight and a half minutes for the back rows. Only after at least thirty minutes would the fire have looked like the "sea of flames" that witnesses described after 9:27. Like the experts of 1933, Stephan and his co-authors concluded that the actual development of the fire was only possible with the use of gasoline or kerosene.[103]

Proponents of the single-culprit theory have criticized the scientific experts' findings, those of 1933 and the more recent ones. Tobias devoted a long chapter of his book to "the failure of the experts." His main criticism was that the experts were predisposed to think there had been multiple culprits, and arranged their evidence accordingly. He went on to argue that their analyses of the fire were each different and mutually contradictory. The first point is reasonable enough, but the second is exaggerated: the experts did not disagree on the core matters of the cause and origins of the fire.

The fundamental problem with Tobias's critique, however, was his failure to understand the difference between the period leading up to the bursting of the glass ceiling at 9:27 and the period after. The experts, he said, were wrong to place any faith in the tests they had done on plenary chamber furniture, because the fire had not started from the seats or desks. Van der Lubbe had set the "massive curtains" behind the president's desk on fire; the fire had spread to the paneling and soon there was a hot enough fire to bust the ceiling. The flames now had seventy-five meters more open space and so an "enormous upward pressure with a corresponding draft" could develop. The draft from the burst ceiling then spread the fire through the chamber. This, he argued, was the difference between the fire in the plenary chamber and the others—such as the fire in the restaurant—where there was no glass ceiling to burst. These other fires therefore appeared "a bit pitiful" by contrast.[104]

But this argument is completely beside the point. The question that needs answering is how van der Lubbe (who, as we have seen, probably did not reach the chamber until about 9:16 to 9:18 and left it about two minutes later) could have set a fire that, within about seven to eleven minutes, generated enough heat and gas to cause the explosion and the burst ceiling in the first place. *That* fire had to get going without any draft—and all expert analyses, especially the sophisticated thermodynamic calculations from Stephan's team, show that only flammable liquid could have produced enough gas to explain it. Furthermore, all the draft in the world would not spread a fire through the chamber unless and until the rest of the furnishings and paneling had been heated to their ignition temperature, and there was simply not enough wood burning before 9:27 to do this.[105]

To rebut the contention that some kind of petroleum or self-igniting fluid was necessary to get the fire going, Tobias cited the tests done by the chemist August Brüning, who found no evidence of any such substance. Tobias did not mention that the tests to which he referred came from the Bismarck Room, not the plenary chamber. To get around the inconvenient fact that tests done on the curtains found that they burned only with great difficulty, he argued that the curtains used for the test had come out of storage and still had fire retardant on them, which had worn off the curtains in the plenary chamber. This is plausible, but Tobias introduced no evidence for it, falling into the very trap of unwarranted speculation of which he accused the experts.[106]

Certainly some criticisms of the experts from 1933 are on target. As Hans Mommsen argued, Schatz tried too hard to link evidence to van der Lubbe and Torgler, and came to an odd conclusion, which the court adopted, that van der Lubbe had not been in the plenary chamber at all. However, what could potentially be the strongest argument Mommsen raises in fact only makes clearer the problem that the scientific evidence poses for the single-culprit theory.[107]

The experts' opinions, said Mommsen, rested in large part on House Inspector Scranowitz's observation that, at around 9:23, he saw fifteen to twenty fires burning in the second and third rows of deputies' seats. The other witnesses who saw the plenary chamber in these moments directly contradicted Scranowitz. If Scranowitz's observations were wrong, would not the whole expert analysis collapse?[108]

In fact it would not. As we have seen, the single-culprit theorists already face the problem that there simply wasn't enough wood burning in the plenary chamber before 9:27 to explain the bursting of the ceiling and the sudden massive spread of the fire. If we remove Scranowitz's burning seats, this problem only gets worse. Negating Scranowitz therefore only proves the opposite of what Mommsen is trying to prove, making it even more likely that someone other than van der Lubbe was involved in the fire.[109]

Other attempts to rebut the experts' assessments have only been dilettantish and inept.[110] None of the single-culprit advocates have put forward an expert on fires to rebut the expert consensus. Informed opinion against van der Lubbe's sole responsibility continues to pile up. In a 2001 letter to a *Spiegel* reporter, Albrecht Brömme, at the time Berlin's fire chief, said that the Reichstag fire could have been set by one person only with the use of "liquid or solid" incendiary material. In a 2003 interview he added that the very short time-span of the development of the plenary chamber fire spoke against a single culprit. It is common today, he said, to see huge blazes develop from a single small fire, but the time for a smoldering fire to turn into a large fire lies in the range of "an hour, two hours, and three hours; it never lies in the range of minutes."[111]

In 2007 the German television network ZDF broadcast an investigation of the technical side of the fire on its regular program *Abenteuer Wissen*, or "Knowledge Adventure." The producers asked Dr. Lothar Weber, a professor of chemistry at the University of Bielefeld, to investigate whether the fire in the plenary chamber could have been started with a phosphorus solution in the way Schatz had postulated in 1933. For the cameras, Weber mixed phosphorus in a test tube with a sulfur solution as Schatz had described it. He poured kerosene on some cloth and then the phosphorus solution. Twenty minutes later the cloth had started to burn. "In my opinion," Weber explains, "this is the only way it was at all possible to get the oak seating of the Reichstag to burn."[112]

The Allianz lab recently summed up its position in carefully chosen language: "To get a full fire in the plenary chamber going in about fifteen minutes, according to the few existing objective items of information regarding the available incendiary devices [*Zündhilfsmittel*], the combustible building materials and furnishings present, and the size of the room, for a single culprit with the limitations of Marinus van der Lubbe, without sufficient skills or knowledge of the place, is an enterprise that could scarcely be carried out. On the other hand that does not mean that it is or was technically impossible—at least in terms of the available state of the facts."[113]

There is, therefore, a consensus among the scientific experts who, from 1933 to the present, have examined the Reichstag fire: that Marinus van der Lubbe could have set the devastating fire in the plenary chamber by himself lies somewhere between highly unlikely and impossible to imagine.

But in 1933 this was not the main reason why so many people were skeptical of Nazi accounts.

5

. . . .

BROWN AND OTHER BOOKS

THE PROPAGANDA BATTLE

RIVAL NARRATIVES ABOUT THE REICHSTAG fire snapped into place literally overnight. The regime was first, with Göring's communiqué, issued on the night of the fire. In a national radio address on March 1st the interior minister embellished his communiqué with lurid tales supposedly based on police discoveries: Communist "terror groups" (disguised in SA uniforms) had planned attacks on "transport vehicles, personal cars, warehouses, retail and other stores." Communists had gathered explosives for blowing up bridges, and poison for attacks on SA kitchens, and planned to kidnap the wives and children of leading politicians and police officers. The Reichstag fire was to be "the first great signal" for all this. The evidence accumulated by police showed that at least six to eight persons had been involved in the preparation of the fire, which was part of a "well-prepared plan."[1]

The other side was nearly as fast with its storyline. Before midnight an Austrian reporter named Willi Frischauer, Berlin correspondent for the *Wiener Allgemeine Zeitung* (Vienna general newspaper), had cabled his paper: "There can be little doubt that the fire which is consuming the Reichstag was the work of hirelings of the Hitler Government. It seems that the incendiaries have made their way to the Reichstag through an underground passage which connects the building with the palace of the Reichstag President." The next day the German Foreign Office sent a telegram to its embassies complaining of the "rumors" spread by the left that the Reichstag fire was a job "commissioned by the Reich government." The telegram referred—as official statements would repeatedly—to "overwhelming evidence" that the arson could be traced to the Communists. Yet the government would never disclose this overwhelming evidence.[2]

This failure to disclose came in the face of repeated warnings from Germany's diplomatic posts abroad that something more than mere assertions was needed to make the government's case. A telegram of March 4th from the Paris embassy, for instance, complained, "Simple announcement that government *possesses* overwhelming material does *not* have *reassuring* effect here" [emphasis in original]. Unmoved, Foreign Minister von Neurath responded that the material could not be published while legal proceedings were pending. A memo probably dating from the first days of March held that while some foreign newspapers had wondered whether the fire was not really "the work of an agent provocateur for the government," evidence of van der Lubbe's Communist connections would soon put an end to this "political poison."[3]

It was in these circumstances that Rudolf Diels emerged as the most subtle and clever, but also increasingly the most frustrated, of German Reichstag fire propagandists.

Part of Diels's routine was his skillful courting of the foreign correspondents. He maintained friendly relations with most of them, even those critical of the new regime. He helped them past difficulties with German censorship and with other problems that could arise for journalists in the new state.

One such case involved the American reporter H.R. Knickerbocker, universally known as "Knick," who wrote for the *New York Evening Post* and the *Philadelphia Public Ledger*. Knick was so fearless about exposing Nazi lawlessness that MI5 officer Guy Liddell learned on his visit to Germany that the SA had wanted to arrest him for his "atrocity reports." In May Knick found himself in a scrape with Alfred Rosenberg, the head of the Nazi Party's Foreign Policy Office. Rosenberg had cabled Knick's employers to request that they recall him from Germany, as Knick was sending home "false reports" so filled with "insidious lies" about Hitler's government and conditions in Germany that they were endangering German-American relations. The papers politely refused, replying that they had every confidence in Knickerbocker. In a typical sign of Nazi rivalry, Hitler's friend Ernst "Putzi" Hanfstaengl then arranged the arrest of Rosenberg's assistant Kurt Ludecke, whom Hanfstaengl hated.[4]

When the case had blown over, Knick wrote to his editor, Charles Munro Morrison, "My own small concerns in this country were never so well cared for as now." He told Morrison that Diels himself was watching out for him after the telegram business, even if this put his, Knick's, interests over Rosenberg's. A few months later the Gestapo blocked two of Knick's telegrams, both dealing with SA assaults on American citizens. Diels again intervened and allowed the telegrams to be sent. At the end of October Diels even wrote personally to Knickerbocker to tell him that a prisoner in whom he had taken an interest had been released from a concentration camp. It is a good gauge of Diels's persuasiveness that he could convince the tough and skeptical Knick that this was really all in Knick's own interests.[5]

Yet Diels was seldom happy with the results of his courtship. In late March he took foreign correspondents to visit several celebrity political prisoners, including Communist leader Ernst Thälmann. According to the Associated Press report, Diels told the reporters that Thälmann considered it beneath his dignity as a political prisoner to be held along with criminals. "However," said Diels, "as he has been the leader of the party accused of inciting the Reichstag fire, that cannot be helped." Diels explained that Thälmann was also unhappy with the selection of books, whereupon Thälmann, smiling, handed Diels a book called *Jolly Tales from Swabia*. "We can talk about that afterward," said an embarrassed Diels. The editor of the Communist *Rote Fahne* bravely told the reporters that he had seen prisoners badly beaten by stormtroopers. Again Diels waved the allegation off, saying that this had only happened in the first days of Nazi rule, when people had been taken into protective custody for their own good.[6]

The media landscape of Germany in 1933 was a strange one. After the Reichstag fire the regime speedily "coordinated" the domestic German press so that all German papers, with the occasional exceptions of the *Frankfurter Zeitung* (Frankfurt newspaper) and the *DAZ* were little more than official mouthpieces. Yet the foreign correspondents were still able to operate with considerable, though far from absolute, freedom, so that

Germany did still have something of a free press, albeit only for foreign consumption. American, British, Swiss, French, and other international papers could report on the Reichstag fire and the investigation and trial concerning it, as well as on the brutalities of the SA, the worsening situation for Jews, and the rapid disintegration of political and civil freedoms. Or at least they could to the extent they wanted to. The *Manchester Guardian* was especially fearless and aggressive in its reporting on Nazi Germany. Indeed the *Guardian* emerged from the 1930s with an impressive record: George Orwell, who in *Homage to Catalonia* wrote scathingly about the accuracy of papers of left and right alike, recorded that the *Guardian* was the sole exception; its coverage of the Spanish Civil War left him with "an increased respect for its honesty." The other British "quality" papers, on the other hand, were often reluctant to print what they knew about Nazi Germany, out of political and diplomatic calculation. The *Times* was the worst offender, which was the fault of its editors and not of its correspondents in Germany, Norman Ebbutt and Douglas Reed. Sometimes reporters hesitated to report stories out of well-founded fear of what would happen to their sources or to those already victimized. Louis P. Lochner, head of the Berlin bureau of the Associated Press, decided that his priority was to keep his bureau open so that at least some information from Germany could flow to the United States and elsewhere. This meant that he often kept to himself stories of Nazi atrocities.[7]

Reporters like Knick, and other Americans in Berlin such as the new Ambassador William E. Dodd, who like Knick saw Diels as something of an ally, would have been shocked to learn what Diels really thought of the foreign press. "Immediately after the Reichstag fire," Diels wrote to Goebbels in July, the majority of foreign news outlets had begun a "purposeful and skillful" propaganda campaign to present the fire as a "deceptive maneuver by the leaders of the national movement, especially by Herr Prime Minister Göring," to influence the outcome of the elections and solidify their hold on power (Göring had been named Prussian prime minister in April, while remaining Prussian interior minister). This campaign of lies continued unabated, said Diels, with the result that public opinion abroad took the guilt of the government as a given and even expected the coming trial in Germany to demonstrate this guilt. Blaming the new government for the fire constituted "the mainstay of Jewish-Marxist publicity against the national revolution." A few weeks later, writing to Göring, Diels was even blunter. "The heretofore careful treatment of the foreign correspondents" from newspapers that indulged in such lies and distortions would, he said, have to end.[8]

Diels was therefore exasperated that, despite his efforts, German counter-propaganda had proven a complete failure. He complained that even foreign outlets that might be willing to consider the official German perspective on the fire, either for ideological or "purely journalistic" motives, had not been given the information Diels could have provided "with ease." Bringing van der Lubbe to trial quickly would help, but Diels also had the temerity to urge on Goebbels the need for propaganda that took account of the "sentiments" of people abroad.[9]

Diels bluntly advocated, and the Gestapo carried out, telephone and postal surveillance of the foreign correspondents attending the trial of van der Lubbe and the other Reichstag fire suspects in Leipzig. He even suggested that all reporters be housed in the same hotel to make this easier. The many intercepted letters surviving in the prosecution files speak to the success of these efforts. Diels corresponded with the Czech vice consul about sending an officer to Prague to investigate the activities of German émigrés there, and threatened the British reporter Frederick Voigt even in Paris. The famous American lawyer Arthur Garfield Hays, who traveled to Leipzig to observe the trial, wrote later "I never had any doubt that I was under surveillance and I conducted myself accordingly.[10]

But Diels could not make the Reichstag fire a Nazi propaganda victory. Here the Nazis were resoundingly beaten at their own game.

IN THE COURSE OF 1933 propaganda from outside Germany became the Nazis' main public relations worry, especially in the form of what Arthur Koestler called the most influential political pamphlet since Tom Paine's *Common Sense*, or, as a recent historian put it, "the prism through which most of the world saw Nazism for more than a generation": the *Brown Book on the Reichstag Fire and Hitler-Terror*.[11]

The *Brown Book* was the brainchild of Willi Münzenberg, a highly entrepreneurial and market-savvy Communist press baron. In his time Münzenberg was known as "the Red Hugenberg," the counterpart to the German National leader and his mighty right-wing press and film empire; today we might think of Münzenberg as a Marxist Rupert Murdoch. Before the Nazi takeover Münzenberg had run a media empire that was Communist in editorial sympathy but somewhat independent of the Party itself, which explains why its products were more readable than the turgid official *Rote Fahne*. In addition to daily newspapers like *Berlin am Morgen* (Berlin in the morning) and *Die Welt am Abend* (The world in the evening), Münzenberg put out the magazine the *Arbeiter Illustrierte Zeitung* (Workers' illustrated news), which featured the innovative collages of John Heartfield on its covers and sold nearly a half million copies per issue. He had several book-publishing ventures and distributed Soviet or other Communist films in Germany.[12]

Arthur Koestler remembered him as "a shortish, square, squat, heavy-boned man with powerful shoulders." He was, continued Koestler, "a fiery, demagogical, and irresistible public speaker, and a born leader of men." He had a natural authority that caused Socialist cabinet ministers, cold-eyed bankers, and Austrian dukes to "behave like schoolboys in his presence." Münzenberg was also—and coming from an apostate Communist like Koestler this was saying something—undogmatic and entirely uninterested in the doctrines of the Communist Party. Not surprisingly, the German Communist leaders like Walter Ulbricht and Wilhelm Pieck hated him.[13]

Münzenberg fled Germany after the Reichstag fire and re-established his propaganda empire in Paris. He founded a "Committee for the Victims of Fascism" which featured such non-Communist celebrities as Albert Einstein and Henri Barbusse. Münzenberg's companion Babette Gross wrote that Münzenberg was, if not the inventor, at least the first effective mobilizer of "fellow travelers." After the notorious Goebbels-organized book burnings of the early summer of 1933 Münzenberg started a "German Freedom Library," and a "documentation center" that maintained a morgue of German news clippings and any other information that could be gotten on conditions in Germany. The funds for all this came from the Comintern. Pierre Levi, a publisher of poetry, turned over to Münzenberg his own imprint, Editions du Carrefour, as well as space in his building on the Boulevard St. Germain. By May 15th Münzenberg could write to a friend, "As you know, we are preparing a book on the Hitler government and the Reichstag fire."[14]

The *Brown Book* was largely a cut-and-paste job of newspaper stories from Germany and accounts from victims of Nazi brutality, often smuggled out in bold and enterprising ways. To the extent that it was "written," Otto Katz, an Austrian-Czech Communist intellectual who later came to a bad end in the infamous Slansky show trial of the early 1950s, did the writing. Only a relatively brief portion of the first *Brown Book* actually dealt with the Reichstag fire itself. The rest consisted of an account of the Nazis' rise to power (in typical Communist style, blaming the Social Democrats at every turn), alongside reports of the new concentration camps, the beatings and tortures, and the suppression of all non-Nazi organizations.[15]

For two decades historians generally took the *Brown Book* as a credible source. Starting with Fritz Tobias in the late 1950s, however, they have dismissed it as a "fabrication" or, more colorfully, "a witches' brew of half-truths, forgeries, lies, and innuendo . . . a fraudulent hack job." Applied to the book as a whole, such judgments are not only inaccurate, they represent a failure to grasp the dangers informants ran and the sacrifices they made to get material about conditions in Germany out to where it could be publicized. Perhaps the most dramatic example involved prisoners from the concentration camp at Sonnenburg near Küstrin, where for a time in 1933 the Nazis brutalized such prominent political prisoners as the journalist Carl von Ossietzky and the lawyer Hans Litten. The *Brown Book* contained a special section on Sonnenburg. Much of the information came from a ring of prisoners around the former Communist parliamentarian Erich Steinfurth, who passed information in letters written in invisible ink to his wife Else, who in turn sent them on to Communist officials.[16]

Much of the *Brown Book's* information on Nazi barbarities can be corroborated today. This is true of the information on Sonnenburg. In a section on prisoners murdered at Dachau, the book mentioned Sebastian Nefzger, a Munich school teacher whom guards beat or strangled to death. Camp authorities claimed his death was a suicide. A lawyer named Alfred Strauss was "shot while trying to escape." German documents captured after the war show that these stories were accurate: a brave Bavarian prosecutor tried to bring charges against the notorious Dachau SS guard Johann Kantschuster for Strauss's killing, and even against the Dachau Commandant Hilmar Wäckerle and several other officials for Nefzger's. These investigations, and a few others like them, actually forced Heinrich Himmler—at that time both *Reichsführer SS* (Reich leader of the SS) and Munich police chief—to dismiss Wäckerle.[17]

The Gestapo's own investigations shed light on the German sources for what Münzenberg printed in Paris, and also suggest that much of the information was authentic. The police discovered an office on Unter den Linden that duplicated and forwarded newspaper reports from across Germany. In May 1933 Göring's State Secretary Ludwig Grauert reported that the International Workers' Aid (IAH), part of Münzenberg's organization, had turned itself into an "illegal international news service." Investigations had shown that the IAH used its foreign connections to send atrocity reports to France and Switzerland. Some suspects were in Gestapo custody in Germany.[18]

By November 1933 the Gestapo was afraid that copies of some or even all of the documents from the Reichstag fire trial would be included in the "anticipated supplementary edition of the well-known *Brown Book*." They were right: the second *Brown Book* contained photocopies of the first and last page of the indictment, which the prosecution had tried to keep secret, and included an effective critique of the incoherence and implausibility of the rest of it. "Brave anti-fascists risked their lives to photograph it page by page" and sent it over the border, the second *Brown Book* claimed. This was also true: the "military-political apparatus" of the German Communist Party worked underground in Leipzig, and could count reporters, including the London *Times'* Norman Ebbutt, as well as several of the lawyers, and the defendants Torgler and Dimitrov among its sources. Even the American Consulate helped, allowing the underground activists to store material and hold secret meetings on its premises. Leon Roth was the Communist organizer of these efforts; typically for the politics of the day, he later became a victim of Stalin's purges. The second *Brown Book's* account of the trial suggests that the authors had access to the full official transcript, something which postwar researchers did not until the early 1960s.[19]

Certainly, however, much of the section of the *Brown Book* that dealt with the Reichstag fire was fabricated, and nothing in it can be taken as reliable without corroboration. Münzenberg claimed in the book's preface that "every statement in this book [was] based on documentary material," a claim that was "somewhat misleading," according to Babette Gross. That is putting it mildly. There was little opportunity to try to corroborate the reports that came from Germany, she wrote, and she admitted that the *Brown Book's* account of the fire was later proved wrong in many respects. Where evidence was lacking, Münzenberg and his writers went with hunches. They took it as a given that van der Lubbe could not have done the job himself and that it was the Nazis who benefited from the fire, and then tried to work out how it must have happened. They followed Willi Frischauer in surmising that an SA squad had got into and got out of the Reichstag through the tunnel that connected it with Göring's residence.

Koestler also admitted that the Münzenberg people had had little evidence, and the book was based on "isolated scraps of information, deduction, guesswork, and brazen bluff." "Everything else was a shot in the dark," he wrote. "But it went straight to the target"—even in his mature anti-Communist phase, Koestler claimed that the *Brown Book's* thesis had been right, even if its methods were not. His claim that millions of copies of the *Brown Book* were soon in circulation is certainly exaggerated. A later account suggests a figure in the tens of thousands. Nonetheless it is harder to argue with Koestler's contention that the *Brown Book* "became the bible of the anti-Fascist crusade."[20]

Much of what the *Brown Book* had to say about the fire came in the form of a critique of thirty-one "contradictions" in official statements, most of them really discrepancies between official statements and reasonably ascertainable facts. The account of the fire itself was very brief and largely nonsense, contradicted in many significant respects even by later Münzenberg publications, such as the *Brown Book II* and the *White Book*. The book relied on what would become a cliché of Reichstag fire legends: the tip from an anonymous SA man. Such a man had explained how the Berlin SA had been confined to barracks the night of the fire, and had then been sent out to spread rumors that a Dutch Communist had been arrested, and that Torgler had been the last person out of the Reichstag, before any of this could have been known. The then–Berlin deputy SA leader Karl Ernst had supervised this effort, and thus the *Brown Book* claimed he was only an "initiate," not a direct participant in the arson. Göring had dismissed the Reichstag staff early that day, a canard that would have a particularly long history in this story. The book claimed that van der Lubbe was gay, which explained his link to gay SA commanders like Ernst Röhm; it identified Berlin SA commander Helldorff and the SA men Edmund Heines (by early 1933 Breslau Police Chief) and Paul Schulz as the arsonists. They had waited in the tunnel for a signal that the last deputy had left the Reichstag. Setting up the fire in the plenary chamber had taken them about twenty minutes. They had brought in van der Lubbe and left him there only as a decoy. The idea for the fire had come from Goebbels, its execution overseen by Göring.[21]

The "authentic documents" with which the Münzenberg organization buttressed its case often contradicted one another. Münzenberg's 1935 *White Book* dealt mostly with the June 30, 1934 "Night of the Long Knives," when Hitler broke the SA and murdered its leader Ernst Röhm and many others, including Ernst and Heines. With these men dead, and Helldorff's alibi for the fire bolstered in the trial, the lineup of culprits had changed. The *White Book* featured a "facsimile" of a statement by Karl Ernst, confessing to setting the fire, along with a cover letter from Ernst to Heines. Now the direct participants were Heines, Ernst, Ernst's adjutant Walter von Mohrenschildt, and his fellow SA officers Fiedler and Sander (who the *White Book* claimed also became victims of the June 30 purge, in Fiedler's case erroneously). Like some later writers, the *Brown Book* and *White Book* authors did not care which Nazis had set the fire. For their purposes any Nazi would do.[22]

The *Brown Book* introduced the stories of Berlin Fire Chief Walter Gempp, the psychic Jan Erik Hanussen, and Nationalist politician Ernst Oberfohren, who had all, the *Brown Book* claimed, implicated the Nazis in the fire and had then suffered for it. The Nazis summarily dismissed Gempp from his position and then charged him with fraud (in 1939 he was to die in prison); they murdered Hanussen and drove Oberfohren to suicide (the *Brown Book* claimed the Nazis murdered him as well). Fritz Tobias argued forcefully that the idea that Nazis had taken revenge on these men for Reichstag fire revelations was nothing but Communist falsification. How should we draw the balance?

The weakest of the *Brown Book*'s claims involved Hanussen. Jan Erik Hanussen, the stage name of one Hermann Steinschneider, was a "psychic" well known in Berlin for his séances and performances. Despite his Jewish background he supported the Nazis, and was close to Helldorff and Ernst, lending both men a great deal of money. The *Brown Book* claimed that Hanussen knew of the impending Reichstag fire from Helldorff, and in a bid to enhance his psychic reputation "predicted" it at a February 26th séance, which Helldorff attended. In March, shortly after Ernst took over from Helldorff as Berlin SA commander, Hanussen was murdered. Such a séance certainly took place, and the SA certainly murdered Hanussen, but all of the accounts of the séance that specifically refer to Hanussen's prediction of the fire (other than in the *Brown Book* itself) come from after the war. Moreover, most of the evidence suggests that Helldorff or Ernst ordered Hanussen's murder to get rid of a bothersome creditor. The strongest evidence for a political motive comes from a statement which Rudolf Steinle, one of Hanussen's killers, made in July 1934 in an internal investigation. Steinle claimed Ernst had justified the killing by explaining Hanussen had "the SA in his pocket and Chief of Staff

Röhm in his arse," that Hanussen was in a position "to play the SA against whomever he wants, despite the fact that he is a Jew." Hanussen libeled Röhm and discredited the SA outside Germany in "the most outrageous manner." Two months later Steinle changed his story and said there was "nothing political" about Hanussen's killing—a change that might indicate he was pressured to suppress a real political motive, but which falls short of offering conclusive evidence.[23]

The case grows stronger, however, with Walter Gempp. Gempp had been the Berlin fire chief (*Oberbranddirektor*) since 1923, and was nationally and even internationally respected as a modernizer and a democratizer of the Fire Department. In March 1933, however, the new regime suspended him from duty, at first on the basis that he had allowed the Fire Department to become "contaminated with Communism," a transparently false charge. In April he was investigated for improperly buying a Mercedes as an official car; that case collapsed when it turned out that Gempp's Nazi successor Gustav Wagner used the car too. Finally the Prussian government dismissed Gempp under the Nazis' "Law for the Reform of the Professional Civil Service," on the grounds that his loyalty to the new "National State" was suspect. When the dismissal took effect in February 1934, however, it was ostensibly for a completely different reason. Göring justified it through the Civil Service Law's miscellaneous category, permitting the dismissal of officials for the "consolidation of the public service." By then the general prosecutor at Berlin's Superior Court was investigating Gempp along with many other officials for accepting bribes from a firm called Minimax, which made fire extinguishers. It took five years to resolve this case. In July 1938 the court convicted Gempp of some, though by far not all, of the charges. In May 1939 he died in prison while awaiting an appeal of his conviction. His death was apparently a suicide.[24]

Gempp's problem was that in April 1933 a Strasbourg paper called *La Republique* reported that his suspension followed a meeting the day after the fire in which he had complained that the Fire Department had (deliberately) been given the alarm too late; that when firefighters arrived at the Reichstag they had found about twenty SA men already there; that Göring had forbidden him to order the highest alarm level; and that he, Gempp, had seen enough unused incendiary material in the Reichstag "to fill a truck." The *Brown Book* picked up these allegations.[25]

Tobias portrayed Gempp as nothing but a corrupt official and argued that his prosecution for bribery was legitimate and not politically motivated.

Historian Wolfgang Wippermann, on the other hand, countered that Tobi-as's argument "gives witness to a remarkably uncritical estimation of the role of the justice system in the Third Reich." Gempp was by no means the only civil servant to find himself in this kind of situation: historian Hermann Beck has recently shown that after taking power the Nazis made a "con-certed effort" to use prosecutions for corruption to discredit conservative figures who had become "bothersome and inconvenient." The Reich com-missar for job creation, the mayor of Düsseldorf, and the aristocratic chair of the far-right *Reichslandbund* (Reich Land League) were among the many who shared Gempp's fate. The Nazis hoped such prosecutions would demonstrate that they alone stood for the general interest. To suggest, therefore, that the case against Gempp was not politically motivated would be obtuse even without the dimension of the Reichstag fire. Of course, the categories of corrupt official and anti-Nazi Reichstag fire skeptic are also not mutually exclusive.[26]

There is in fact clear evidence that Gempp suspected the Nazis of in-volvement in the fire, and that they dismissed and prosecuted him for this reason, among others. Gempp thought from the beginning that there had to have been more than one culprit. While still in the burning Reichstag he gave an interview in which he referred to the many different fire sites (*Brandherde*); a torch that had been left on an armchair in one of the hall-ways to set the chair and the adjacent paneling on fire; and signs of kero-sene poured on the carpet of the Bismarck Room. On the plenary chamber itself the newspaper *8 Uhr Abendblatt* (8 o'clock evening news) quoted him saying that "One could observe in various places that probably kerosene had been poured on the floor, presumably from a jerry can. One door had been thoroughly covered in kerosene; from there the burning material flowed on the carpet across half the room."[27]

Gempp's views were generally shared by professional firefighters in the immediate aftermath of the fire, when expressions of opinion still seemed permissible. The day after the fire the *Sächsische Feuerwehrzeitung* (Saxon fire department newspaper) noted daringly that it was clear that the protection of the Reichstag had been inadequate, as it was "incompre-hensible" that "one or more" (*der oder die*) culprits could have laid such an extensive fire in the plenary chamber without anyone noticing, a comment that obviously assumed the fire had required sustained preparation. And an official of the Berlin Fire Department wrote in March that although it was not yet known whether van der Lubbe had had accomplices, nor what means he or they had used, "to judge by the great extent of the fire right from the beginning, it is to be assumed that several culprits were at work." Like Gempp, he referred to a streak of carpet in the Bismarck Room that seemed to have been burned with kerosene.[28]

Gempp seems soon to have become suspicious of the authorities. The day after the fire Göring sent official messages of thanks to the Berlin Fire Department from himself as well as from Hitler. These were printed in the department's bulletin, with a brief introductory statement from Gempp. As printed, Gempp's statement read simply, "I bring the following decrees to the attention of the officers." But a document from the Fire Department's archive shows that Gempp edited a significant line out of this message: as originally scribbled in pencil at the bottom of Göring's letter, Gempp's comment read: "I bring the following decrees, *with recognition {Anerkennung} of the efforts of all involved, which limited the fire to its original source {Herd}*, to the attention of the officers." Gempp then seemed to rethink this and crossed out the italicized lines. This certainly suggests that Gempp was not happy with the response to the fire, as *La Republique* had claimed.[29]

Although Gempp later denied the allegations in the *La Republique* story, the denials were those of a man under considerable pressure from the regime, and he phrased them in a careful way which seemed to permit an opposite interpretation. After the war his widow firmly maintained that Gempp had suspected the Nazis. A June 1933 memo by Martin Sommerfeldt gives a revealing glimpse of the attitude to Gempp in Göring's ministry, and indeed comes close to betraying a link between Gempp's view of the Reichstag fire and his legal problems. On the day after the *Völkischer Beobachter* printed Gempp's "denial" of the *La Republique* story, Sommerfeldt noted that some "politically irreproachable people" in Germany sometimes made "doubtful faces and statements" regarding the case against van der Lubbe, which could not be tolerated. The Gempp case, Sommerfeldt continued, was one such example, which suggests that in the view of Göring's ministry Gempp's statements about the fire were the only problem with this otherwise "politically irreproachable" man.[30]

Ernst Oberfohren, the German National politician with an intense dislike of the Nazis, was perhaps not so politically irreproachable from their perspective. The *Brown Book* claimed that Oberfohren was the author of a memo accusing Goebbels of planning the Reichstag fire in an effort to force the German Nationals to accept the banning of the Communist and Social Democratic Parties. When his memo was handed to foreign reporters and parts of it printed abroad, the Nazis murdered him. The full text of the memo accused an SA squad under the command of Edmund Heines of carrying out the fire, gaining access to the Reichstag through the underground passage. Tobias and many others dismissed Oberfohren's memo as a clumsy Communist forgery that Oberfohren, having died in May 1933, could no longer disclaim. While the "Oberfohren Memo" as printed was in fact a characteristically dubious product of Münzenberg's media factory, a more complex reality lay behind it. Furthermore, as often in the story of the Reichstag fire, the Nazis' cover-up is more revealing than the memo itself.[31]

By the end of March 1933, at the latest, Diels's police had identified Oberfohren as a security threat and had tapped his telephone. Göring testified at the Reichstag fire trial that the tap revealed a conversation between Oberfohren and his secretary, Margarete Fritsch, concerning material that was "incriminating" for "National Socialist leaders." Fritsch said she did not want to give Oberfohren the material, since she had become a Nazi supporter herself, to which he replied "Have you also gone crazy?" On March 26th, political police officers searched Fritsch's apartment and took her to the Alex for interrogation. On the same day they searched Oberfohren's Berlin office and his home in Kiel. But, as Fritsch wrote to Oberfohren a few days later, "the officers said *twice* . . . that they had not found what they were looking for."[32]

The police did find something that was enough to end Oberfohren's career: samples of anonymous letters attacking Nationalist leader Hugenberg, which, evidently, Oberfohren had been sending to prominent people in the Party. At the end of March Oberfohren resigned his position as leader of the German National caucus, gave up his Reichstag seat, and retired to Kiel.[33]

The plot thickened. In early April, before the Oberfohren Memo had become public, Kurt Daluege got hold of a copy. A British reporter, Geoffrey Fraser, had been arrested on April 4th on suspicion of having delivered the memo to the offices of the *Chicago Tribune*. Daluege's note suggested that Fraser be "carefully interrogated" about where the document came from. The *Tribune* itself reported that Fraser was arrested at 3:00 a.m. by the political police and charged with "taking part in the 'anti-German atrocity campaign, spreading false news, and calumniating the government.'"[34]

Daluege's office thought the memo came from the "Otto Strasser circle," in other words from dissident Nazis, although they were not sure if Strasser's people had created the memo or simply obtained a "Communist forgery." Daluege sent the case to Arthur Nebe to investigate. But a handwritten note on Daluege's letter claimed not only that the memo came from the office of Vice Chancellor von Papen, but also that Diels should not learn that they had it, as he had some kind of "connection" to Papen. This was one of the first signs of the split between Daluege and Nebe on the one side and Diels on the other, a split that would become a vital factor in the Reichstag fire investigations and their aftermath.[35]

At the end of April the *Manchester Guardian* reported on the memo. The "Terror" made open mention of it in Germany impossible, but, so the *Guardian* claimed, it represented a serious attempt by someone with contacts to Nationalist members of the cabinet to offer a balanced account of the fire. "In spite of one or two minor inaccuracies" it demonstrated "considerable inside knowledge." The following day the *Guardian* printed a summary of the memo.[36]

The German government responded that the *Guardian* had done nothing more than "openly place itself in the service of Communist propaganda." In denying this the *Guardian* claimed that a copy of the memorandum had passed from a prominent Nationalist politician through someone unconnected to the Communists "into the hands of your correspondent, who was then in Berlin." On August 2nd the *Guardian* reported that the memorandum had been written "at the request of Dr. Oberfohren." But by then Oberfohren was dead. He had been found in his study in Kiel on May 7th, a bullet through his head, apparently a suicide.[37]

"His" memo contained more than "one or two minor inaccuracies." Heines had a solid alibi, placing him in Breslau the night of the fire, and cabinet records show that it was the Nationalists, not the Nazis, who were pressing for the banning of the Communist Party (although Torgler testified that Oberfohren himself had strongly opposed such a ban, if only out of tactical considerations). Many have pointed out that the memo's language does not reflect Oberfohren's high level of education.[38]

In any case, sources like the *Guardian* and the Social Democratic *Neuer Vorwärts* (New forward—the version of the Social Democrats' *Vorwärts*, published after the Reichstag fire by exiles in Prague) had never claimed that Oberfohren actually wrote the memo. The *Guardian*'s cautious phrase (from the experienced Berlin correspondent Frederick Voigt) was only that the memo was "written at the request of Dr. Oberfohren." Voigt was not one to trust Communist propagandists blindly: a few years later he wrote that he had long known that Willi Münzenberg and Otto Katz were "quite unscrupulous." *Neuer Vorwärts* acknowledged that the memo's authorship was mysterious and therefore that its evidentiary value was questionable.[39]

Provenance and authorship are not the same thing, as Daluege's office also clearly realized. Even had the author or authors of the memo come from the Münzenberg organization, they could have based the text on information they had gotten from Oberfohren, or perhaps sent it to him in the belief that he would read it with sympathy. There is evidence that other Communists thought this way. After Oberfohren's death, the police found among his papers a letter from Maria Reese, a Communist Party Reichstag deputy and Ernst Torgler's mistress. She fled Germany after the Reichstag fire, and she sent Oberfohren a letter from Stockholm dated March 15th. "You *know* that we did not set the fire," she wrote. "You *know* that Comrade Torgler is innocent . . . And you remain silent!" That Reese sent this letter to Oberfohren suggests that she knew from Torgler what Oberfohren thought of the Nazis. Other Communists could have possessed the same knowledge.[40]

For there is no doubt that, whoever wrote it, the "Oberfohren" memo set out something approximating Oberfohren's own beliefs. In an interview with a Social Democratic reporter on May 4th (not published until months later), Oberfohren said he had been "advised of the particulars" of the Reichstag fire by someone whom he knew—"unfortunately!"—to be completely reliable. There was "no longer any doubt" that the Nazis "knew about the fire before it happened," and Germany's ministers "allowed it to happen," even celebrated it. When the reporter pushed him for specifics, however, he declined: "Those who know nothing are better off!"[41]

Diels himself believed that Oberfohren might have written the memo. Given that the Gestapo chief had been tapping Oberfohren's phone, this is a telling point. And Oberfohren's friend Otto Schmidt-Hannover wrote in 1955 that he had spoken about the Reichstag fire "many times" with Oberfohren. A few years later Schmidt said that Oberfohren believed that he had "seen through" the Reichstag fire, and "offered criticisms that were as frank as they were incautious."[42]

The evidence that Oberfohren committed suicide is generally persuasive, although Diels wrote in his memoirs that the Kiel police arrested an

SA squad that had murdered Oberfohren on its own initiative. Oberfohren himself told *Neuer Vorwärts* that were it not for his wife, "I would have shot myself long ago."[43]

We are left with the following facts: (1) Oberfohren believed the Nazis had set the fire; (2) the Nazis saw him as a security risk, tapped his phone, and found that he was in possession of compromising material about Nazi leaders; and (3) the Nazis used the anti-Hugenberg letters Oberfohren had circulated to end his political career. The likely inference is that out of fear of what he might say or reveal about the fire, the Nazis were lining up Oberfohren for the Gempp treatment: discrediting rather than killing him. Perhaps they hoped that the exhausted and ill Oberfohren could be driven to suicide. This was what Oberfohren's widow believed. Nazi propaganda exploited Oberfohren's death in much the same way as it did Gempp's: as a fable about the moral exhaustion of the upper-middle classes.[44]

The "Oberfohren Memo" in itself is evidence of nothing. Even had Oberfohren written it, he could not have had direct knowledge of the fire. Still, as so often in this story, it is the Nazi response that is revealing—the wire taps, the searches, the machinations. After Oberfohren's death Frederick Voigt, who was responsible for publishing the memorandum, came in for the same kind of treatment.

Diels wrote to Göring in the late summer of 1933 that the Oberfohren memorandum was an example of the problem of controlling the foreign press. The *Manchester Guardian* had written that there was no other European capital in which the foreign press corps felt as united as it did in Berlin. Diels argued that this feeling of unity explained why the foreign correspondents were reporting "unanimously" that Nazis were behind the Reichstag fire. He concluded that it was time to expel "correspondents of those newspapers who up to now have distinguished themselves as spokesmen for Communist-Jewish agitation propaganda, especially in the case of the Reichstag fire."[45]

The Gestapo's measures against Voigt and the *Guardian* would soon take a stronger form. Voigt was, in the words of the *Guardian's* historian David Ayerst, a man of "immense moral courage" whose "reporting of Nazi excesses" was "not done at second hand." He was friends with many rank-and-file members of the Social Democratic and Communist Parties and, as Hitler's dictatorship took hold, reported what was happening more boldly and bluntly than any other British journalist. It is a tribute to his work that by the end of March German authorities had banned the *Guardian*, and that it was the only paper whose correspondent (by then Robert Dell) was refused admission to the Reichstag fire trial. Berlin became too dangerous for Voigt, so he worked from Paris, arranging for his many German sources to send him information through the French diplomatic pouch. But even in Paris he was in danger. A Gestapo report from September noted that it had been Voigt, "the expelled representative of the *Manchester Guardian*," who had obtained the Oberfohren memorandum. The Gestapo set up a Paris branch. French authorities warned Voigt that the Gestapo would burgle his home and assigned him three bodyguards. If the Gestapo got his documents, Voigt wrote to his editor W.P. Crozier in December 1933, there would be "hundreds of arrests as a result."[46]

The Reichstag fire occurred in a context of a long and violent political struggle in which propagandistic shifting of the blame for violence was inseparable from the violence itself. This was why the rival narratives of the Reichstag fire snapped into place even as firefighters were still trying to douse the blaze, and it is why the *Brown Book* was such a success. This success forced the Nazi regime into a defensive crouch, and it never fully recovered its balance. In the extensive surviving correspondence between Diels's Gestapo, the foreign office, and the propaganda ministry, we can trace the efforts of these authorities to find out who was saying what about them, and observe Diels's constant frustration that the German response was not more aggressive. These efforts and this frustration continued into the autumn, when the trial of van der Lubbe, Torgler, and the Bulgarians would dominate world headlines, and the Nazi regime's efforts to rebut the *Brown Book* would dominate the trial.[47]

6

· · · ·

"STAND UP, VAN DER LUBBE!"

THE TRIAL

THE FOURTH CRIMINAL SENATE of the Reich Supreme Court in Leipzig would be the next authority with a chance to clear up the mystery of the Reichstag fire.

The opening of the trial presented a scene of "no little elegance," in the words of *Times* reporter Douglas Reed, its "sober dignity" all the more striking for its contrast with "the drastic methods of unofficial justice in Germany beyond the courtroom." The German government, as the *Neue Zürcher Zeitung* (New Zurich newspaper) reporter Ernst Lemmer noted, wanted to use the trial to get its own message out to the world. Goebbels's Propaganda Ministry had sent many of its officials to manage the flow of information to the foreign correspondents. There were no fewer than eighty such correspondents in the courtroom, along with forty German colleagues, as van der Lubbe, Torgler, and the three Bulgarians were led in, two policemen to each prisoner. The five judges came next, dressed in the imposing red robes and caps of their office, as were the two prosecutors, Chief Reich Prosecutor Karl Werner and his assistant Felix Parrisius. The presiding judge, Wilhelm Bünger, was, said Reed, a "pickwickian" man of "stern but yet benevolent mien," while the American lawyer and trial observer Arthur Garfield Hays described Parrisius as "the picture of Nazi intolerance." As the judges entered they raised their right arms in the Hitler salute. Everyone in the courtroom except the defendants and the foreign correspondents returned it.[1]

The Reich Supreme Court had been founded in 1879, one of many legal institutions created in the wake of Bismarck's unification of Germany in 1871. The court's judges were divided into senates specializing in either criminal or civil cases; by the 1930s there were nine civil and five criminal senates. Like supreme courts in most countries, the Reich Supreme Court generally heard appeals from the judgments of lower courts, which meant that its hearings were usually matters of arcane legal argument in which the facts had to be taken as the lower court had found them. Cases of high treason, however, were different: Germany's Judicial Code gave the Reich Supreme Court first instance jurisdiction in such cases, which meant that the trials—with all the witnesses and other evidence—were conducted at Leipzig and there was no appeal from the verdict.

The conduct of a German trial could, and often did, look odd to someone familiar with Anglo-American courts. The five judges in their imposing red robes were all entitled to ask questions of the witnesses, although the presiding judge was expected to carry out most of the questioning. The prosecutors and defense lawyers, on the other hand, played only a secondary role in asking questions and bringing out evidence. The defendants also had the right to question witnesses, and in the Reichstag fire trial several of them made extensive use of this right. German law required a defendant in a criminal case to have a lawyer, and the court would provide a "duty defender" (*Pflichtverteidiger*) for a defendant who could not afford his own. In the Reichstag fire case this rule produced some odd results. Van der Lubbe wanted nothing to do with any lawyer; a veteran Reich Supreme Court lawyer named Philipp Seuffert, a DNVP member but sympathetic to the Nazis, was nonetheless assigned to him. German courts could permit foreign lawyers to conduct defenses, and a number of prominent European and American lawyers sought briefs in this case, but the Fourth Senate refused them all. Another veteran lawyer named Paul Teichert was assigned as duty defender to Dimitrov, Tanev, and Popov, but Dimitrov never voiced anything but contempt for Teichert and defended himself with more aplomb than any German lawyer was likely to manage in 1933. Remarkably enough, the seasoned Nazi lawyer Alfons Sack acted for Ernst Torgler—and not as a duty defender, but as Torgler's choice.[2]

Although the trial began and ended in Leipzig, the court actually spent more time at the scene of the crime itself. The proceedings moved to the Reichstag's budget committee room after the first twelve days, the better to question the police and fire department witnesses, Reichstag employees, and prominent government members. For the last month, from November 23rd to the reading of the verdict on December 23rd, the court returned to Leipzig. The nature of the evidence shifted over time. As is typical in a German trial, the focus of the first days was on the questioning of the defendants by the presiding judge. Then the prosecution presented its witnesses. The last segment of the trial featured the prosecution's efforts to link van der Lubbe to a Communist conspiracy by presenting "evidence" of Communist plans for an uprising in February or March of 1933.

Despite the large numbers of lawyers, judges, and defendants, and an army of witnesses, two men dominated the proceedings in different ways and for different reasons: Marinus van der Lubbe and Georgi Dimitrov.

The van der Lubbe who appeared in Leipzig was hardly the energetic young man who had hiked across Europe, roused many rabbles in Leyden, and clambered up the scaffolding of Berlin's Royal Palace to set a fire on its roof. Almost everyone who saw van der Lubbe in court described him the same way. His behavior suggested "a subnormal mentality," said the *Manchester Guardian*, which wondered if he was "a crazy half-wit" or if, as the German press reported, he was merely "simulating imbecility." The Swiss correspondent Ferdinand Kugler wrote that van der Lubbe made an "apathetic, brutish impression." To Martha Dodd, daughter of the U.S. ambassador, van der Lubbe was "[b]ig, bulky, [with] sub-human face and body," "so repulsive and degenerate that I could scarcely bear to look at him." Ernst Fraenkel, who witnessed one day of the proceedings, during which he did nothing but stare at van der Lubbe, recalled later that anyone who saw van der Lubbe would ever after have difficulty believing he could have burned the Reichstag by himself. On all but two of the trial's fifty-seven days van der Lubbe appeared with his head bent down over his chest, often drooling or with his nose running so that his police attendants had continually to wipe his face. He spoke in monosyllables or not at all, and on those two days on which be suddenly became talkative, he spoke an idiosyncratic, guttural mixture of German and Dutch, which few in the courtroom could clearly understand. He struck observers as incapable of action, let alone a coherent thought. President Bünger could extract no clear version of his past life, nor even get him to speak loudly enough to be heard. He repeatedly answered "yes" and then "no" to the same question. At best he answered questions only after a long pause. Sometimes he did not answer at all. Sometimes he giggled.[3]

Many foreign observers at the time, and some later writers, suspected that the authorities kept van der Lubbe drugged. Fritz Tobias on the other hand later argued that the energetic and articulate van der Lubbe of February 27th had fallen victim to a prison psychosis. The Swedish criminologist Harry Söderman examined van der Lubbe and said he found no sign that the prisoner had been drugged, but his examination was purely visual, limited to noting an absence of marks on the arms. After his release in 1934 Georgi Dimitrov told an interviewer from the right-wing French paper *l'Intransigeant* that it was "thoroughly possible" van der Lubbe had been drugged: he was the only one of the prisoners who received separate, specially prepared meals, wrapped in paper with "van der Lubbe" written on the package.[4]

Ernst Lemmer described Georgi Dimitrov as a man in a handsome grey suit who "in a casual pose, with a kind of Balkan *grandezza*, leaned his elbows on the rails, looking younger than his fifty-one years." Douglas Reed wrote that Dimitrov's "remarkable courage and intelligence almost immediately became apparent," and that with his looks he would have made a good film actor. Judging by his performance in the courtroom he would have made a good trial lawyer, too. Even Tobias wrote that "One need be no friend of the Communists"—and no one ever accused Tobias of *that*—to acknowledge, even to admire the conduct of Dimitrov before the Reich Supreme Court."[5]

Dimitrov proved to be the court's and the prosecution's most effective adversary, yet Reed had the impression that by the end of the trial the judges had come to feel a certain "rueful affection" for the man. Dimitrov's witty defiance provided many of the trial's highlights. He told the police that only mindless individuals or Communism's worst enemies could have set fire to the Reichstag, and there was little doubt whom he meant. With typical puckishness, he added, "I am, however, neither mindless nor an enemy of Communism." When Bünger reminded him that Bulgarian authorities had accused him of attempting to blow up a cathedral in Sofia (the allegation was untrue, as even the court finally conceded), Dimitrov dryly replied that ministers said that sort of thing in Germany too. He had a great deal of fun with the Berlin guidebook with maps with which the police sought to link him to van der Lubbe. "I cannot say if this is my map. It is the one laid before me by the police—but I undertake no guarantee for the police." As he said this, Dimitrov made what Reed called an "eloquent gesture" toward the police witness standing before the bench, which produced a roar of laughter from everyone, with the exception of the justices and the impassive van der Lubbe. Ernst Lemmer recorded Bünger's sardonic response: "We can also get by without your guarantee." In any case, after Dimitrov had fired off several more stinging rebukes at the incompetence and dishonesty of the police, the judges expelled him from the courtroom for the first of five times.[6]

THE NEW NAZI REGIME was eager to show the world that Germany remained a country under the independent rule of law. So eager, in fact, that its officials manipulated the trial at every turn.

A few days before the trial began, Helmut Heisig noted that a trusted source had claimed that the bar association had asked Alfons Sack to represent one of the defendants, with the assurance that this defendant "would definitely come away with an acquittal." Sack's client, Ernst Torgler, remembered later that Sack "virtually imposed himself on me" and assured Torgler from the beginning—before examining the evidence—that he would be acquitted. Torgler thought that the SA—"Röhm, Ernst, and Heines"—had "sent" Dr. Sack to him, and that Sack also had the assignment of making sure that traces of "real culprits" would stay hidden. Diels's subordinate Heinrich Schnitzler remembered the same detail after the war, reminding his former boss of the rumors about how "the SA (Ernst) took over the costs of Torgler's defense." The point was important to Tobias. In a 1961 letter he fumed that it was "nonsense" that the SA had paid Torgler's defense costs, adding that if it could be proven they had done so, they might also have set the fire.[7]

Sack's role revealed the regime's tactics. Ernst Lemmer, whom even Tobias considered the most judicious of reporters at the trial, diagnosed the motivation behind Sack's defense strategy for Torgler: Sack, a Nazi handed the defense of Torgler at official urging, sought to "present the heavily compromised van der Lubbe as a sole culprit" and thereby "fight against all rumors of National Socialist involvement." This was naturally also the best way of establishing Torgler's innocence. To underline van der Lubbe's sole guilt, Sack tried repeatedly to find evidence that a strong draft in the plenary chamber could have spread the insignificant fires that were all that van der Lubbe could have set.

Lemmer ultimately concluded that Sack failed to make this case. But Sack's semi-official status in the trial gave his argument importance. Nazi authorities, all too aware of one of the possible alternatives to a solitary van der Lubbe, flirted from the beginning with the idea that he had in fact done it himself. By the second week of the trial, as we have seen, Martin Sommerfeldt was writing that only van der Lubbe's conviction was certain and therefore reporters should stress that "Communism" itself sat in the dock with him. After seeing the weakness of the case against Torgler and the Bulgarians, some elements of the regime—notably those associated with Göring, such as the Gestapo—seemed more than ready to present van der Lubbe as a sole culprit on these modified terms. American lawyer Arthur Garfield Hays even claimed credit for feeding this argument to Sack: Hays told Sack bluntly that the Nazis' tactics were stupid, and that by insisting that van der Lubbe alone could not have set the Reichstag on fire they had invited their opponents to accuse them of a conspiracy. If van der Lubbe had had accomplices at all, it was almost certain that they had been Nazis. Hays sweetened his words slightly by suggesting that it had been reasonable at the beginning to suspect the Communists. But the evidence did not support this suspicion, so why did the government not simply argue that van der Lubbe had had no accomplices? A few days later, Hays wrote, Hitler's friend and court jester Ernst "Putzi" Hanfstaengl had adopted this line, and Hitler himself made a reference to "*an incendiary*" in a speech. The idea was launched, and would eventually become doctrine in the Third Reich: the 1937 official history of the Berlin SA, for instance, recorded that on February 27th "a Dutch Communist set fire to the Reichstag" as "the signal" for a "great armed uprising by the commies." The memory of this strategy would endure into the postwar years, especially among ex-Gestapo men—whose single-culprit theory thus had a very different origin from the self-flattering one they later claimed for it.[8]

Political influence showed itself in other ways as well. Foreign Office records imply Diels knew what the verdict of the trial would be at least five days before it was announced. Leipzig mayor Carl Goerdeler told fellow anti-Nazi Fabian von Schlabrendorff that Judge Bünger complained he had been unable to "collar" the real arsonists. Goerdeler believed the trial caused Bünger a crisis of conscience that ultimately ruined his health. Years later Bünger's widow wrote that he had been under strong political pressure during the trial, always surrounded by police officers. Although he often discussed his cases with her, he never talked about this one.[9]

The evidence that the police and prosecutors presented over the next three months could in no way allay doubts about the trial's fairness. Heisig insisted he was certain van der Lubbe was a Communist, even after Bünger hinted that this could determine whether or not the court sentenced van der Lubbe to death. But when Sack asked him to explain his certainty, Heisig was stumped. Other officers had formed the same impression, was his rather lame explanation, and anyway van der Lubbe had not objected. On another occasion Heisig based his certainty on "the whole manner" in which van der Lubbe said he was "one of those who was not satisfied with the system," and that he was clearly not a supporter of Hitler's government. (Werner, too, seemed to accept that not supporting Hitler's government was enough to establish van der Lubbe as a Communist.) We have seen that Heisig presented questionable statements taken from van der Lubbe's friends Vink and Albada in Leyden, statements that these witnesses later accused Heisig of fabricating. Heisig, however, withdrew nothing. The Dutch witnesses had lied in London, not in Leyden, he said, probably because of Communist intimidation. When Torgler proposed that the court summon them to Germany, Sack tellingly opposed his own client's request.[10]

By contrast, one of the few points on which van der Lubbe was clear and emphatic at the trial was that he was *not* a Communist, nor did he want to "change the form of the state." When he was asked to explain his political views, even in Dutch through the interpreter, he said he could not.[11]

Just like at his press conference in Leyden, Heisig's evidence at trial was a far cry from that brave insistence on van der Lubbe's sole-culprit status with which Tobias and other later writers credited him. On the second day of the trial Sack asked him whether he had interrogated van der Lubbe about accomplices. Heisig gave what the *Guardian* called a "strange reply": Van der Lubbe had not given "sufficient information" in response to these questions, he said—in other words, Heisig regarded van der Lubbe's insistence on his sole guilt as insufficient. A few days later, returning to the same subject, Heisig said that van der Lubbe had "obstinately" maintained he had committed the act alone. Zirpins, as we have seen, also backed away as far as he could from the "single-culprit" language of his March report.[12]

Diels and the Gestapo wanted to emphasize van der Lubbe's ties to the Neukölln Communists, and it had been Kurt Marowsky, one of the most notoriously thuggish of Gestapo officers—even by Gestapo standards— who interrogated the Neukölln witnesses. Neukölln was Marowsky's turf. He knew the local Communists and (perhaps better) the local Nazis, he had his informers, and he knew how to get witnesses to say what he wanted. The informer Jahnecke testified at the trial that it had been Marowsky himself who came to get Jahnecke when Jahnecke failed to answer a summons. Even before the Nazi takeover, Marowsky had regularly treated witnesses to threats, coercion, and bribes; with the arrival of the Nazis his palette had extended to "enhanced interrogations." Marowsky had "always had the suspicion," he told the court, that when van der Lubbe refused to give answers, he wanted to protect someone.[13]

To the puzzlement of most observers in the courtroom, as van der Lubbe slumped double in his seat, drooling and nose running, the police drew a picture of his many remarkable intellectual qualities. Zirpins maintained that he had a "fabulous ability" to come up with dates and remember numbers. "He is so to speak a number genius." He also had a remarkable grasp of and memory for spatial orientation (this of a man who had thought from a map that he could walk to China in a few weeks). He had sketched the scenes of his various fires from memory, and related what he had done precisely, as investigations subsequently confirmed. Zirpins admitted he would not have been able "to reconstruct that as nicely as [van der Lubbe] did."[14]

By contrast, Commissar Bunge, who had tried to lead van der Lubbe through a re-creation of his race through the Reichstag, said that he had to give up the attempt because van der Lubbe became vague and wasn't able to find his way "within the correct time" (which meant within the time van der Lubbe had had at his disposal on the night of February 27th). Many observers thought it improbable that van der Lubbe could have covered all the territory he claimed inside the cavernous Reichstag, which even a veteran deputy once called "a confusing maze of corridors, stairs, and rooms." When Heisig later demonstrated van der Lubbe's path in situ to the court, the *Manchester Guardian*'s correspondent noted dryly, "Everybody was impressed by the enormous amount that van der Lubbe had managed to do in the twelve minutes or so at his disposal."[15]

Observers of the trial, and some participants, were also puzzled by Heisig's and Zirpins's claims that van der Lubbe spoke good German, and that they had been able to understand him without difficulty and without a translator. No such command of the language was evident in the courtroom. Van der Lubbe "could speak very little German," wrote the Swiss journalist Ferdinand Kugler, himself of course a native German speaker. Douglas Reed gave an example of how poorly Lubbe often understood questions, and how materially this could affect his testimony. On one occasion van der Lubbe was asked, "Where did you get the inflammable liquid?" He replied, "I bought it." One of the judges, recalling that van der Lubbe had never claimed to have had a liquid with him, asked that the question be translated. Van der Lubbe then replied, "It wasn't liquid, just packets."[16]

Much of the evidence that the police introduced to implicate van der Lubbe, as well as Torgler and the Bulgarians, was patently ridiculous or fabricated, or both. Dimitrov was able to draw laughter from the court with his mockery of the Berlin guidebook that Braschwitz and his officers had "found." On another occasion Dimitrov claimed that Braschwitz had falsified an interrogation transcript; the transcript did not in fact bear Dimitrov's signature. The testimony of Helmer, the waiter from the Bayernhof Restaurant, was so weak that it provoked the Bulgarians' duty defender, Paul Teichert, to a rare flash of outrage. Teichert complained that the arrest of the Bulgarians had drawn the case into a wrong turn that had invited reproaches of German methods from abroad. Werner angrily retorted, "If people abroad are not satisfied with the way we administer our justice, that is no misfortune for Germany." There were loud cries of "Bravo!" in the courtroom.[17]

Heisig was also responsible for some dishonest or dragooned witnesses. He labored to buttress the credibility of Otto Grothe, whom everyone else in the court, including the judges, had already written off as a perjuring psychopath. Another Heisig witness, a man named Kämpfer, was summoned to court from a concentration camp, where he had made a "full confession" about his ties to Popov. A stormtrooper escorted him into the courtroom, and like other witnesses drawn from concentration camps, he gave his evidence while standing rigidly at attention. Kämpfer said that on the orders of Communist officials, he had let Popov stay in his apartment between May and July and again in November 1932. Tanev had visited Popov in May. Popov, however, claimed to have been in the Soviet

Union at those times, and Tanev had been in Bulgaria. There was credible evidence to support their alibis. Nonetheless, it was with witnesses like Kämpfer and Grothe that Heisig and the prosecution sought to make their case.[18]

NOT ALL OF THE EVIDENCE was falsified or perjured. Most of the witnesses tried to provide honest testimony, and some of what they said pointed toward answers to the mystery of the Reichstag fire.

That Nazi arsonists had been able to enter and leave the Reichstag through the tunnel that connected the cellar of the Reichstag to the president's residence and the boiler house was an idea that, as we have seen, appeared on the night of the fire, and it had been a key element of the *Brown Book*. Several days of testimony in mid-October were devoted to this tunnel, which existed, ironically enough, because Reichstag architect Paul Wallot had wanted to keep the boilers away from the building to protect it against fire. Master machinist Eugen Mutzka, who had been in service at the Reichstag since it opened in 1894, explained that the tunnel was closed off by iron doors in the Reichstag cellar and the boiler house; the locks on the doors could be opened with the Reichstag's master key. It was possible, Mutzka said, that anyone in possession of one of those keys could get through the tunnel to the courtyard of the boiler house, and from there escape over the courtyard wall.[19]

If anyone was going to be in a position to hear activity in the tunnel it would be Paul Adermann, the night porter at the president's residence. Adermann's porter's lodge stood directly over the tunnel, and across the hallway from his lodge was a door to stairs that lead down to it. Adermann insisted that on the night of the fire (he went on duty at 8:00 p.m.) he would certainly have heard anyone moving through the tunnel. He testified that in the weeks before the fire he had heard footsteps on several occasions between 11:00 p.m. and 1:00 a.m. He informed House Inspector Scranowitz and Reichstag Director Galle, who told him he should "watch if anything further happens." Adermann put wood chips on the floor of the tunnel and thin strips of paper across the tunnel doors at night—red strips on the red door and black strips on the black door so that they were inconspicuous. If anyone passed through the tunnel, the wood chips would be disturbed or the paper strips torn. "How often did you find them torn?" Torgler asked. "About six times" was the answer.[20]

As Douglas Reed pointed out, if Adermann had had to check the paper strips, this meant that in fact he could not necessarily hear anyone who passed through it from his post, and it seemed clear that someone besides employees of the Reichstag had a key to the passage. Adermann admitted that he might not have heard trespassers if they wore socks or took care to tread softly and avoid the steel plates on the tunnel floor. In response to a question from Torgler, he admitted—contradicting his initial statement—that it was possible to get into the president's residence, and into the tunnel, through the officials' residence behind it without passing his porter's booth.[21]

On October 17th the court gave the press a tour of the tunnel. Reed, noting that "Göring had expressed the conviction that the incendiaries had escaped through the tunnel," thought that the reporters, having inspected it, "felt the strength of his theory."[22]

Another physical demonstration was designed to test the plausibility of van der Lubbe's account of his actions inside the Reichstag. On the evening of October 12th a police officer re-enacted van der Lubbe's break-in for the court. Van der Lubbe himself refused to demonstrate it.

While Sack kept time with a stopwatch, the officer showed how van der Lubbe had broken into the restaurant, set fire to the curtains by the door to the *Wandelhalle*, crossed back to the window and tried to set fire to curtains there, gone back to the *Wandelhalle*, taken off his jacket and shirt, set fire to his shirt, gone back through the restaurant to a small waiter's room, found a linen cupboard and taken out a table cloth, set fire to the table cloth, run down a flight of stairs, kicked in a window in a door at the bottom of these stairs and climbed through it (without cutting himself—all police witnesses insisted that at his arrest van der Lubbe had had no injuries other than slight burns on his hands), run to the kitchen, broken another window and climbed through it to another small room— the one with a window through which Buwert had fired his shot. The evidence of other witnesses suggested van der Lubbe had had no more than two minutes and five seconds for all of this. As Reed wrote, if van der Lubbe had really done what he claimed, he must have needed much more time than the reconstruction allowed.[23]

The testimony offered by another police officer strengthened doubts that van der Lubbe could really have done everything he claimed. Detective Raben testified about the police efforts to reconstruct van der Lubbe's movements. In demonstrating what he had done, said Raben, van der Lubbe had moved almost at a run and had not stopped at any of the spots where he claimed to have set fires. Raben thought therefore that the time was far too short for van der Lubbe to have lit all the fires. The reconstruction, he added, had been done in broad daylight—not the pitch darkness van der Lubbe had actually faced on February 27th.[24]

Some of the evidence pointed to strange circumstances that the police left unexplored. The most intriguing involved the porter Albert Wendt and the Nazi Reichstag deputy Herbert Albrecht. Wendt was the night porter at Portal V who claimed to have seen Albrecht fleeing as the fire burned. Wendt had been told when he went on duty at 8:00 that only Torgler was still in the building. When Wendt gave this evidence, no one in the courtroom seemed particularly curious who the deputy was. Not until a month after Wendt testified did the court summon Albrecht, who repeated the story he had told the magistrate in March. Detective Bauch gave a summary of the statement of Frau Berkemeyer, Albrecht's landlady, suggesting that she had confirmed Albrecht's story from her own observations, which of course she had not. Reed, for one, thought that Albrecht's evidence had left more questions unanswered than answered.[25]

German courts normally attempt to resolve conflicting testimony by having the witnesses confront one another. Only the irrepressible Dimitrov asked that Wendt be brought back to testify. The court refused to do so. Instead, when the trial was almost over, Chief Prosecutor Werner announced that Wendt had been dismissed for drinking on duty. This could, said Werner, "affect the value of any evidence he had given." The message was clear: Wendt had probably been drinking on February 27th, too. It seemed the Nazis had given Wendt the Gempp treatment.[26]

As we have seen, the evidence given by the expert witnesses Josse, Wagner, and Schatz was the most significant of the trial. Most observers thought that their evidence closed the door on any notion that van der Lubbe had acted alone. One of the most telling reactions came from the *Neue Zürcher Zeitung's* Ernst Lemmer. Among the foreign correspondents, Lemmer was the most skeptical of *Brown Book*-style accounts, and correspondingly the most receptive to Nazi explanations of what had happened. This disposition, plus the deadpan irony of his reports, commended him to Fritz Tobias, who wrote warmly of this "critical and skeptical reporter," and of his paper, "known and respected for its objectivity." But while Tobias gladly quoted Lemmer's characterization of Schatz as a "sneering expert," he said nothing about the effect on Lemmer of the expert testimony. In fact it transformed the tone of Lemmer's reports: the expert reports had "like a searchlight" illuminated the "background [*Zusammenhänge*] of the affair." It was becoming ever clearer, he wrote, that the Reichstag fire had been the work of "cunning political criminals, who simply used the eccentric van der Lubbe as a straw man." After the expert evidence, Lemmer wrote, no one believed Sack's "original theory" of van der Lubbe's sole responsibility.[27]

The reaction to expert testimony in the Nazi press was also revealing. According to the *Völkischer Beobachter*, the experts were "received with skepticism both by the prosecution and the defense." The Nazi paper devoted only a few lines to Schatz's testimony, not mentioning, for instance, Schatz's insistence that the arsonists had to have had technical knowledge and familiarity with the layout of the Reichstag. These reservations were another sign that powerful circles in the regime were swinging back to endorsing van der Lubbe as a lone culprit, only "morally" connected, as the prosecution would seek to prove, to Communism in general. In part this may have been because the evidence, especially Schatz's, suggested culprits who all too closely resembled the Berlin SA's Unit for Special Missions.[28]

IN THE LONG TRIAL—it ran from September to December—a few moments stood out for their inherent drama, or for the sudden light they cast on the fire and its circumstances.

The first of these involved the appearance of Walter Gempp, who, like many witnesses, had been summoned for the sole purpose of rebutting the *Brown Book*. Making light of this fact, Alfons Sack greeted Gempp cheerfully. "I am surprised to find you still alive. Have you any reason to believe that there was any intention to murder you?" Gempp laughed, but Reed wrote that "his mirth somehow did not seem to be the full-throated merriment of a man who has just heard a good joke."[29]

Gempp appeared to deny the claims foreign papers attributed to him, while subtly confirming them. Had a detachment of twenty SA men already been at the Reichstag when the firefighters arrived? No, said Gempp, he had not seen stormtroopers, "at least not in large numbers." Göring had not interfered in his work, and there had been no delay in notifying the fire department. He had not seen "masses" of incendiary material lying about the Reichstag, only a torch found under an armchair in the lobby and traces of gasoline poured on the carpet in the Bismarck Room.[30]

One of the supporting judges, Reich Supreme Court Counselor Hermann Coenders, took up the matter of the gasoline on the carpet. The trail ran from one door to the other, said Gempp; a few stretches of carpet along the trail were "completely burned out." Gempp had bent down to smell the carpet, and believed that it had been gasoline or benzene [*Benzin oder Benzol*], but admitted he was not certain. "But a trail of gasoline or benzene can be distinguished from a trail of water, from extinguishers or something like that, correct?" Coenders asked. Gempp agreed; that the trail was water was "out of the question."[31]

Dr. Brüning had found after chemical tests that this trail did not come from any form of petroleum and his findings must be taken seriously. Schatz had testified to the opposite; his tests on the burned patches of carpet revealed the presence of hydrocarbons. Gempp was a trained engineer with nearly three decades of experience with the fire department, and the question is whether he could really have been in error about the smell of gasoline or the presence of burn marks on the carpet. It seems unlikely that the prosecution pressured Gempp into this testimony. Lateit also testified to seeing a fire on a runner that led from the lobby into the plenary chamber, and described another fire running in a line against the wall, which at first he took for floor lighting. Both of these sound similar to what was in the Bismarck Room, and like fires that would require flammable liquid to set. Werner, however, seemed to want to downplay Gempp's evidence. He asked Gempp whether he had investigated the gasoline stains, which Gempp had not, and he wondered whether the torch under the armchair could not have come from the firemen. Gempp thought that this, too, was "out of the question." A fireman would not have left a torch under something flammable. The *Guardian's* reporter noted that Gempp's evidence about the torch and the gasoline was not mentioned in the German papers he had seen.[32]

House Inspector Scranowitz had in fact testified the day before to seeing this same torch in the armchair. Werner conspicuously didn't like this evidence, asking Scranowitz about this object "which he had referred to as a torch." When Werner also asked him whether it might have been left by a fireman, Scranowitz pointed out that he had been there before the firefighters. This torch, like the remains of the one that the police found in the plenary chamber, was thus a key piece of evidence, as it could not have been left either by van der Lubbe or by the firefighters.[33]

The testimony of Count Helldorff on October 20th also proved unintentionally revealing. Helldorff had been at dinner with his friend and staff leader Achim von Arnim when, he said, he heard fire engines and then received a telephone call about the fire. (Helldorff's inability to give a correct time for these events—his repeatedly changing estimates were all too early—evidently troubled Judge Bünger, who kept trying to resolve the issue.) Helldorff's first reaction to the fire was relaxed. He sent von Arnim to the Reichstag to see if the SA commander was needed there; Helldorff himself went home. Arnim called him around 10:00 to say that his presence at the Reichstag was "unnecessary." But at about 11:00 Helldorff returned to his office in the Hedemannstrasse to meet with his SA subordinates, to whom he gave orders for the arrest of "Communist and SPD functionaries."[34]

In March Helldorff had moved from commanding the Berlin SA to being police chief of Potsdam. Torgler, apparently forgetting that Helldorff had not been a police chief in February, asked whether he had given the arrest orders in his official capacity or as an SA leader. "I gave those orders on my own responsibility," he replied haltingly. "I did not receive instructions from anyone else." As a *Gruppenführer* of the SA, he said, he felt he was justified in arresting enemies of the state, whose guilt for the Reichstag fire was as "plain as day."[35]

It struck most observers as odd that Helldorff should first have been so blasé as to go home, but then call a meeting and order the arrest of Communists and Socialists—on his own initiative and simply on the assumption that they were behind the fire, an assumption that had evidently not come to Helldorff at the restaurant. Dimitrov wondered what evidence Helldorff had for his claim that "criminal elements in the state are generally Marxists." Helldorff replied that on the night of the fire he and the other SA leaders had been of the view that the Reichstag fire was the opening act for "some kind of movement planned by the Communist or Marxist side." It was only because of the quick arrests that this "uprising" did not take place.[36]

Several witnesses said subsequently that Göring had given Helldorff orders for arrests at a meeting at the Interior Ministry. Göring himself, however, confirmed that Helldorff had already given those orders "to his inner circle" before the meeting at the Interior Ministry. Göring maintained that he had only given "state authority" to Helldorff's measures after the fact.[37]

It therefore seemed that two entirely separate mass arrest efforts had been launched that night: a police operation on the orders of Hitler and Göring, and an autonomous SA operation on Helldorff's initiative. The SA's actions recalled the Kurfürstendamm riot, and showed again the continuities between the SA violence of the last years of Weimar and the Reichstag fire. The Berlin SA had been ready for such an operation: it had been making its own arrest lists since 1931.[38]

Göring's appearance at the trial on November 4th stamped an enduring image on the proceedings. A photograph of the fat, uniformed Göring confronting the alert and agile Dimitrov—reworked by the collage artist John Heartfield—became one of the iconic pictures of the trial, especially since Dimitrov succeeded in needling Göring into a humiliating loss of temper.

Martha Dodd, whom Diels invited to court that day, left a vivid account of the interactions between Diels and Göring. Before the day's hearing began, master and servant stood conferring, only a few yards away from her. "I was so fascinated watching these two men that I didn't take my eyes off them until Göring got up to offer his testimony." All the time Göring testified, "Diels was standing behind him, his elbow on the judges' bench, watching every move and listening to every tone and every word coming from his lips." Dodd thought that Diels had had an almost mesmeric influence on his boss. "Göring occasionally would indicate by a change in movement or posture, or tone of voice, in a slight turn of the body toward Diels, how acutely aware he was of his presence." She thought that Diels had probably prepared all of Göring's testimony, a hunch that newly available documents support.[39]

Göring did not so much testify as harangue the court for over three hours. He had had nothing to do with the fire, he said. It had come rather as an inconvenience: "I was like a general who had planned a big attack and who was forced through the action of the enemy to change his plans." He had known that the Communists would act by the election at the very latest, and he wanted to "await this occasion and destroy them at one blow." He regretted that some Communist leaders had "saved themselves from the gallows," as he had intended to destroy them "in such a manner that the entire leadership would have been wiped out through the insurrection." Only public sentiment caused him to move against the Communists immediately after the fire—presumably he had become aware of this public sentiment immediately upon arriving at the burning Reichstag. Like Helldorff and, indeed, like Hitler, Göring had suddenly realized when he arrived at the Reichstag that the Communists were responsible for the fire, and wished only that "the rest of the world had seen that so clearly."[40]

Both Göring and Hitler had also quickly formed the impression that a number of people must have been involved in the arson. Göring's first thought had been to hang van der Lubbe right away; he changed his mind only because he thought he might need van der Lubbe as a witness. The young Dutchman, Göring thought, was a decoy. "When I saw the face of this idiot, everything was clear to me," explained Göring. "The others knew their way around in the Reichstag . . . but that guy there never found the exit." The ones who knew their way around had gotten out through the underground tunnel to Göring's residence.[41]

Martha Dodd remembered how Dimitrov—"a brilliant, attractive, dark man emanating the most amazing vitality and courage," as she described him—watched Göring carefully as he testified, "his face expressing a fiery contempt." Dimitrov pounced as soon as he could. How could Göring have known on the night of the fire that the Communists were to blame, that Nazi Reichstag members claimed to have seen Torgler meeting with van der Lubbe the day before, or that van der Lubbe had been carrying a Party membership book (a claim which by the time of the trial even the authorities admitted was false)?

Göring replied with heavy-handed sarcasm. "In case you were not aware," he said, he was the interior minister. He did not go around checking the pockets of suspects; he relied on the police reports. Sometimes these reports were wrong.

Wasn't it the case, Dimitrov continued, that Göring's statement had given "a definite direction" to the police and judicial investigations and "closed off" the "possibility of finding other paths and the true Reichstag arsonists"?

"I understand what you are driving at," replied Göring. His answer was the same: he was the responsible minister, not a police officer. This was a "political crime," and "in that moment it was clear to me, and it is just as clear to me today, that your Party were the criminals." He added that if the police and magistrates were swayed by the same thinking, "they were only looking in the right direction."

"That is your opinion," said Dimitrov. "My opinion is entirely different."

"But mine is the decisive one."

"I am the defendant, obviously," said Dimitrov, whose wit and nerve never failed.

Dimitrov wanted to know whether Göring was aware that this "criminal" Party ruled over the greatest country in the world, by which he meant Stalin's Soviet Union. Judge Bünger warned Dimitrov against indulging in Communist propaganda, but Dimitrov pressed on with his question, and Göring lost his temper.

"Listen," he said, "I will tell you what the German people know. The German people know that you are conducting yourself here shamelessly, that you have come over here, set the Reichstag on fire, and then still indulge in such insolence with the German people. I didn't come here to let myself be accused by you . . . In my eyes you are a crook who should have been hanged a long time ago."

There were cries of "Bravo" in the gallery.

"Good," said Dimitrov, "I'm satisfied."

Bünger warned him again that if he said another word he would be thrown out.

"I am very satisfied with this statement by Herr Göring."

"I couldn't care less whether you are satisfied or not," said Bünger.

Dimitrov was still trying to ask questions, and Bünger still demanding that he be quiet.

"Are these questions making you nervous, Herr Prime Minister?" Dimitrov asked Göring.

"*You'll be nervous*," Göring yelled, "*when I get you, when you are out of this court, you crook!*"

According to Martha Dodd, Göring was screaming by this point, "hoarse, frightened, his face turning so deep a purple that it seemed the blood would burst forth in a stream; choking, trying to drown out the accusing, brilliant, convicting voice of the other."

Bünger expelled Dimitrov from the courtroom for three days.[42]

In 1933 the world was not accustomed to hearing ministers of major countries sputtering threats like Al Capone. The *Manchester Guardian* commented, "No counsel in a law court worthy of the name would be allowed such license as was given to Herr Göring by the presiding judge." The *News Chronicle* thought that "this threat will be read before a far more powerful court than that of Berlin; it will be read all over the world. And the world, failing an explanation, will draw its own conclusions." The Labour parliamentarian Sir Stafford Cripps wrote to the German ambassador in

London, Leopold von Hoesch, to complain that the British public would be "profoundly disturbed" by Göring's threats, which he hoped would prove a "mis-report." As often in the early days of the Third Reich, this propelled the German Foreign Office into an effort at damage control.[43]

Embroiled as ever in his bitter rivalry with Göring, Goebbels complained to his diary that Göring "only gave a popular lecture on Communism. And then insulted Dimitrov. Not a good production (*Das war keine Regie*)." He noted the "miserable" foreign press reaction. Four days later Goebbels took his turn as a witness. He hoped to "take care of Herr Dimitrov" and was typically confident that "I will really be rolling (*gross in Fahrt*)." Commentators agreed. Dimitrov would "have an opponent worthy of his steel in Dr. Goebbels," the *Guardian* predicted. Reed described the propaganda minister as "A man with a mellow and resonant voice" who knew better than any other National Socialist how to play to an audience.[44]

Like Göring, Goebbels was there chiefly to rebut the *Brown Book*. His main lines of argument were that violence always came from Communists, and that there had been no tension between Nationalists and Nazis in the cabinet. Yet in what seemed like a reversal of his propaganda (calling into question the Tobias/Mommsen argument that the Nazi leaders were obsessed with the Communist menace) Goebbels dismissed fears of a Communist uprising in February, just as he had underplayed them in his diary. Dimitrov asked Goebbels whether the government had mobilized all its armed forces to meet the "armed insurrection" for which the fire was supposed to be the signal. No, said Goebbels, the police and the SA were enough. Dimitrov, said Goebbels, overestimated the danger Communists posed the state if he thought the state would have needed the army as well.[45]

Dimitrov pressed Goebbels about the murders and bomb attacks that Nazis had committed in late 1932 and which Hitler had expressly approved. Although Bünger stepped in to shield Goebbels from answering—"that has nothing to do with this case"—Goebbels demonstratively answered anyway, blaming such attacks on provocateurs from outside the Nazi Party and on disgruntled followers of Walter Stennes. When Dimitrov pressed the point, Goebbels coolly responded. "It seems you want to slander the National Socialist movement. I will answer you with the words of Schopenhauer: Every man deserves to be seen, but not to be spoken with."[46]

Goebbels was usually pleased with himself. "Absolutely great day," he wrote in his diary afterward. "I was in the best form. My examination lasted nearly four hours . . . Dimitrov and Torgler got wretchedly pasted. There is nothing left of them." Moving on to a more important concern: "Press at home and abroad fabulous." And most important: "Above all I got the better of Göring."[47]

WHEN IT CAME TO SOLVING the mystery of the fire, the most important evidence after that of the experts came from van der Lubbe himself. For on two days—November 13th and again on November 23rd—he shook off his stupor and testified, loquaciously if not always coherently. By this point the bar for van der Lubbe's capacity as a witness was not set very high. Reed wrote of the surprise in the gallery when on November 13th van der Lubbe suddenly "held his head up, occasionally looked about him, and audibly answered questions."[48]

What really caught the reporters' attention was van der Lubbe's attempt to explain why, after spending a week in Neukölln, he had suddenly tramped out to Spandau and Hennigsdorf, returning to central Berlin the next day. Bünger asked van der Lubbe where he had been on Sunday, February 26th.

"At the Nazis' (*bei den Nazis*)," came the answer.

"Amid dead silence," the *Guardian* reported, Bünger asked van der Lubbe's interpreter Meyer-Collings whether this was really what van der Lubbe had said. The interpreter confirmed it.

Bünger tried to push further. "With whom, did you say?"

"No one."[49]

It seemed that van der Lubbe had had a conversation with a young man at a Nazi Party rally in Spandau. Only after much effort—van der Lubbe often contradicted himself, and often answered only in monosyllables— could Bünger get van der Lubbe to admit that they had discussed what was said at the Nazi meeting, "the things that [the Nazis] want." Werner wanted to know if they had spoken about the election. The answer was simply "yes."[50]

Reed thought the trail that seemed to open up with van der Lubbe's "with the Nazis'" didn't lead anywhere. Nonetheless the day's evidence provoked a significant reaction from German authorities. The next day the propaganda ministry ordered the German press to limit reports on the trial to sixty lines. Correspondents were to avoid giving detailed descriptions of the defendants or of witnesses. The restrictions would be lifted when the trial reached the stage of closing arguments. "Some surprise was caused by this order," the *Manchester Guardian* reported, right at the moment that there was renewed interest in the trial: most of the witnesses yet to be heard were for the defense, and van der Lubbe had seemed to behave relatively normally. The official explanation was that the German people could not understand why the trial was going on so long, and must be spared this continual exasperation of their feelings.[51]

Ten days later the trial moved back to Leipzig and van der Lubbe again astonished the court with a flood of speech. He gave vent, in what even the official transcript called "a mixture of broken German and Dutch," to frustration about the length of the trial and the lack of result. His remarks indicated how little he understood of what was happening. "We've had the trial in Leipzig," he said, "and then the second time in Berlin, and now for the third time in Leipzig." He regretted that his fellow prisoners were suffering along with him, since they had had nothing to do with the fire. "I am the accused. I want to have twenty years' penal servitude or death, but I cannot stand this trial any longer. What is happening here is a betrayal of humanity, of the police, and of the Communist and Nazi Parties." He complained as well about the "symbolism" of the trial, with which he did not agree. It eventually emerged that by "symbolism" he meant the prosecution's argument that the fire was meant to be the signal for a Communist uprising.[52]

This was one point on which van der Lubbe was uncharacteristically clear. As he had at his arraignment, but apparently not with the police, he firmly denied any political motive for his actions. When Bünger asked him why he had set the Reichstag on fire, he answered "for personal reasons." Bünger insisted that van der Lubbe had acted "with the intention of stirring up the workers." Van der Lubbe replied, "No, I didn't do that." He had decided to burn the Reichstag because he was unhappy with "my personal condition." He did not believe, he said, that burning the Reichstag would help workers.[53]

Of course the most important question was whether he had burned the Reichstag alone. And on November 23rd, while vehemently insisting that he had been alone, his evidence drew a clear picture of the difference between any fire he could have started, and the fire that actually erupted in the plenary chamber after 9:27. As Ernst Lemmer wrote, the evidence demonstrated the "dilettantism" of all of van der Lubbe's attempts at arson—whether at the welfare office, the City Hall, the palace, or in the Reichstag itself. "The main thing," Bünger told van der Lubbe, "is and remains that one cannot assume that you set fire to the Reichstag alone in ten minutes." So long as this matter was not resolved, the trial would have to continue. Bünger reminded van der Lubbe that according to the experts he could not possibly have set the plenary chamber on fire "with a shred of cloth."

"It is not complicated, the fire," replied van der Lubbe. "I set the fire and it spread by itself."[54]

Once again van der Lubbe said he had entered the plenary chamber from behind the president's desk. "Now tell us what you set fire to first in the plenary chamber," asked Bünger.

"The curtain!" said van der Lubbe. "At the front, at the entrance."

Bünger asked him what else he had set fire to, "a table, a chair, or something else?"

"Whatever I found."

"And what was that?"

"A curtain, a drape."

Van der Lubbe said that then he had run to the back of the chamber. What had he done next? "I ran through, ran back to the Bismarck Room."

"Yes, van der Lubbe," said Bünger, "we don't believe you." He explained again that van der Lubbe's story did not match the evidence. Had van der Lubbe set an individual fire on every desk or seat? "You can't tell us that!"

"But I never said that I did that." A moment later, van der Lubbe continued, "I just said what I know, what I set fire to: that is the curtain."

He never claimed to have set fires on the president's desk, in the stenographers' enclosure, on the government benches, deputy seats, or gallery seats, where various witnesses claimed or the forensic evidence established that fires had been set.

"And who set fire to the rest?"

"I can't say at all who set fire to the rest—who is supposed—" here he cut himself off.

Van der Lubbe repeated that he had just run through the chamber once—front to back and back to front and then out to the Bismarck Room. When Bünger asked whether the whole room had then immediately caught fire, van der Lubbe replied, "I have said several times and should have said it before that the fire was able to spread by itself."

Werner asked him whether he had seen other fires in the chamber. After saying that he had seen none besides what he had set himself, he gave another answer: "If I saw several other fires, then the ones on the president's chair, as I came back."[55]

In other words van der Lubbe himself witnessed the early phases of a spreading fire almost certainly set by others. He had expressly said that he *set* no fire on the president's chair. In his confused state, he thought the other fires had spread automatically from the curtains he had lit at the doorways at the front and back of the chamber, or flared up spontaneously from the burning curtain he carried as he ran.

This was Lubbe's longest period of lucidity. After November 23rd, he sank back into his dull lethargy as the trial limped to an end.[56]

GRADUALLY THE MOOD in the courtroom changed. The judges even began to treat Dimitrov indulgently, smiling sometimes as he railed against the prosecution's case. Bünger, said Reed, "became at times almost paternal in his altercations with Dimitrov." Freemasonry sprang up between the various players in the trial, even across party lines. The lawyers, the expert witnesses, the interpreters, and the reporters fraternized and exchanged notes about the case. Only Werner and his assistant Parrisius seemed immune to the thaw, invoking "in grave and ominous words the evidence of witnesses in whom the outside world had little faith."[57]

In the last weeks of the trial, the prosecution attempted to demonstrate the "moral responsibility" of Communism and Communists generally for the Reichstag fire, a tacit admission of the failure to sustain a case against van der Lubbe's fellow defendants, and a way of ensuring that a verdict against van der Lubbe alone would not invalidate the regime's argument that the Communists were behind the fire. The main witness was Diels's subordinate Reinhold Heller, a longtime officer of the political police, whose task was to present evidence of Communist plans for an insurgency in late February 1933. His evidence consisted mainly of police reports and news clippings that he read, according to the *Manchester Guardian*, "in a droning voice often not at all in keeping with their fiery contents." A memo that Diels sent to Göring in April 1934 strengthens the impression that Heller was called in to save a failing case. Diels wrote that with his testimony Heller had performed a valuable service and proven his loyalty to the state.[58]

Although in his closing address Werner dropped the charges against the Bulgarians, he asked for treason convictions against van der Lubbe and Torgler, even though by his own admission the evidence did not show how Torgler had been involved in the fire.[59]

Diels's young subordinate Hans Bernd Gisevius, sent to observe the closing phase of the trial, returned with a scathing memo on Werner's speech. There was no question, Gisevius wrote, that the court was going to acquit Torgler as well as the Bulgarians. The chief prosecutor had not only failed to make his case, he had failed even to "awaken understanding for the indictment." The effects on the foreign press would be especially negative. Gisevius's conclusion seems, given what subsequently happened, particularly significant. The only way something could be retrieved from the situation would be for Sack to give a closing address that went after the chief prosecutor and his arguments. At least this would save face abroad and show that the prosecution's failure was purely the prosecution's own fault.[60]

Sack's closing address became the subject of keen interest at the Gestapo. Ten days before Gisevius's memo, Paul Hinkler, who had temporarily replaced Diels in an internal intrigue, summoned Sack to Berlin with the warning that "it was in his own interest." Hinkler opened the conversation by telling Sack that his life was hanging by a thread. Sack had been too openly critical of Göring and too persistent in his cross-examination of Heller. Sack defended himself indignantly, pointing out that representatives of Göring, Justice Minister Gürtner, and Hans Frank had all approved of his conduct. Hinkler ended the conversation by taking away Sack's notes and tearing them up. He imposed an obligation of silence on Sack with the remark, again, that his life was hanging by a thread. Sack pointed out that Heisig and a junior lawyer had arranged the meeting. Hinkler told Sack to say that the meeting had been about his recent trip to Amsterdam and further steps in the Leipzig trial.

Diels learned of this whole business when he returned to the Gestapo a few days later. In a memo to Göring Diels noted that "Dr. Sack finds himself in a conflict of conscience as a result of this conversation." He had taken on Torgler's defense at the request of the president of the German Bar Association, and thus with the blessing of Justice Minister Gürtner. Diels had the president's letter in front of him. "The letter states that Herr Dr. Sack has been designated to take over the defense of a defendant who would be acquitted."[61]

Diels sent this memo to Göring with a note that Sack had requested a meeting with Göring to receive "guidelines" for his closing address. Diels added: "I ask, if possible, that you receive Sack for a few minutes." Sack's closing address was, therefore, effectively an official Gestapo statement.[62]

Unsurprisingly Sack began with a rebuttal of the *Brown Book* and other propaganda from abroad, and piously stressed his belief in the objectivity of the judges. With this as cover, he launched into a critique of the evidence in the case, blaming both Magistrate Vogt and the police, whose work had been "incomplete" because when the fire broke out "the reconstruction of the police taken over from the old regime had just begun"— a criticism that Sack was careful to legitimize by pointing out that it came from Göring's own testimony. He closed by telegraphing that Göring had consented to Torgler's acquittal. When asked about Torgler's claim of innocence, Göring had responded, "I take note of it; the Supreme Court will decide whether it is true."[63]

A Gestapo officer later recorded that Sack's speech would have been better if his attack on the prosecution have been given adequate official cover. Gisevius, said the officer, "can confirm that it was vainly attempted to get such cover in time." This rather opaque comment gives a sense— along with Diels's confirmation that Sack was promised at the outset his client would be acquitted—of the extent of official manipulation of the trial. By this point, everyone recognized that the trial had been a disaster for the government and was running for cover.[64]

GIVEN THE EVIDENCE the Fourth Senate of the Reich Supreme Court had to work with, its verdict, pronounced December 23rd, could only be flawed. The judgment was an odd mixture of different elements, and it has been the source of controversy ever since.

The court acquitted Dimitrov, Tanev, and Popov, as the prosecution had requested. Contrary to the prosecution argument (but given the evidence about how Sack came to represent Torgler, likely reflecting high-level machinations) the court acquitted Torgler also. To the surprise of no one, the court found van der Lubbe guilty of several counts of treason, "seditious arson," and attempted simple arson, and sentenced him to death.

The testimony of Heisig and Zirpins contributed mightily to the verdict. The court found that Heisig's evidence showed that van der Lubbe's leaving the Communist Party in 1931 had "no influence at all" on his

Communist beliefs; the Leyden police had called van der Lubbe a "rabid Communist." The judges emphasized van der Lubbe's intelligence and his sincere commitment to Marxism, again citing Heisig and Zirpins. The court also took seriously the evidence from the Neukölln Communists, which the thuggish Commissar Marowsky had gathered, to the effect that van der Lubbe had claimed he had been to the USSR, wanted to set off a revolution, was excited about setting public buildings on fire and pouring gasoline over SA men and setting them alight as well—"so musht coming." The court concluded that it must have been in Neukölln that van der Lubbe made contact with his accomplices.[65]

The court had no doubt that van der Lubbe alone was responsible for the fires at the welfare office, the City Hall, and the palace. Certainly he had set some of the fires in the Reichstag. However, whatever he had done there, the judges did not think he was responsible for the fire in the plenary chamber, which was "prepared by another hand" with "large quantities" of kerosene or gasoline and a self-igniting solution, just as Schatz had explained it. At least one and "probably several" accomplices had set this fire. The court did not even believe that van der Lubbe had set foot in the plenary chamber at all.[66]

While the judges accepted the expert evidence, including Schatz's, some of their skepticism of van der Lubbe's claims rested on difficulties of timing. They did not believe—and the evidence had given good grounds for doubt—that van der Lubbe could have done everything he claimed between breaking into the Reichstag restaurant and being fired at by Buwert. It was "indicative" that van der Lubbe had "become uncertain" on this point during one of his interrogations by Magistrate Vogt. The judges also doubted that van der Lubbe had set fire to some curtains in the hallway outside of the plenary chamber, and thought it likely that the arsonists had used up the last of their gasoline or kerosene here and on the carpet of the Bismarck Room.[67]

All of this meant that van der Lubbe had known about his accomplices and acted willingly alongside them. In support of this contention the judges pointed to van der Lubbe's perfectly timed break-in—that hour-long window of opportunity between 9:00 p.m. and 10:00 p.m. with no scheduled rounds of employees inside the Reichstag. Van der Lubbe's role had clearly been to divert attention away from Communist culprits, and in standing by his story he had loyally complied with Communist instructions for legal defenses.[68]

Naturally the court refuted the idea that the accomplices could have been Nazis. It was probably for this reason that it found these accomplices had *not* escaped through the tunnel to Göring's residence. Rather, at least one of them had gotten out through Portal II, the south entrance, shortly after 9:00, and someone else had then locked the door. This finding rested on testimony by a witness named Bogun, which, according to most observers, had been thoroughly undermined at the trial. The allegation that a troop of SA men had used the tunnel to get in and out of the Reichstag was "fully untenable." The court was certain—in light of the political pressure it had no choice but to be certain—that the goal of van der Lubbe's arson had been to spark a Communist uprising.[69]

Along with acquitting Torgler and the Bulgarians, the judges made other findings that, in the context of late 1933, showed integrity, even courage. They did not believe that Dimitrov's Berlin guidebook with its suspicious pencil marks proved anything, although naturally they rejected the idea that the police had supplied the marks. They did not believe a word of the testimony of the waiter Helmer from the Bayernhof restaurant.[70]

However, one issue more than any other has shaped the memory of the verdict. Nothing for which the court convicted van der Lubbe, not even the high treason charges, carried the death penalty on February 27th, 1933. The Reichstag Fire Decree had extended the death penalty to arson and treason. But an ancient and universally honored principle of criminal law—*nulla poena sine lege* (no criminal punishment without a prior law)—meant that a court could not apply criminal punishments retroactively. In violation of this principle, Hitler's government had passed a special law, known informally as "Van der Lubbe's Law" (*Lex van der Lubbe*) on March 29th, extending the death penalty provisions in the Reichstag Fire Decree to crimes committed between January 31st and February 28th, 1933. Seuffert tried to argue that the court could not follow Van der Lubbe's Law. The judges nonetheless ruled that the Enabling Law of March 24th, by which the Reichstag had granted extraordinary powers to Hitler's government for a period of four years, had authorized that government to pass van der Lubbe's Law. In any case the law had not created *new* offenses of arson and treason, only changed the penalties for them, which the court claimed did not violate the principle of *nulla poena*.[71]

Van der Lubbe listened impassively as the judges sentenced him to death, standing as he had throughout the trial, his head hanging down and his mouth open. When the judges had finished "he lowered himself, slowly and clumsily, as ever, into his seat."[72]

The trial had taken a heavy toll on the judges of the Fourth Senate. In early February 1934 Judge Bünger submitted a request for leave. He asked for a longer leave that summer, supplying a doctor's note that stressed his unsteady heartbeat and high blood pressure. Bünger never recovered his health. He retired in April 1936, and died the following March. Even the obituaries in Germany's thoroughly Nazified newspapers said that it was the Reichstag fire trial that had ruined his health.[73]

His supporting judge Hermann Coenders was much blunter. Coenders wrote to the president of the Reich Supreme Court, Erwin Bumke, on December 22nd, just as the trial was ending, to say "I am so physically run down from the Reichstag fire trial that at the moment I am completely unable to work." He asked for a month's leave. The real bombshell came in February. Coenders faced a number of debt and tax issues that were worrying the court's administrators, and he was about to turn sixty. He wanted to take the opportunity to retire, and he submitted a letter of twelve closely typed pages explaining the reasons that had made this decision "easier" for him. He had never wanted to be assigned to the Supreme Court, Coenders complained. He did not like the way it handled cases; the judges were too bound to the documents, while Coenders prided himself on being an investigator who got to the bottom of cases and believed, he said, in an "unpolitical" rule of law. This brought him to the Reichstag fire trial.[74]

The judgment, he said, had been roundly criticized in the National Socialist press as a "miscarriage of justice (*Fehlurteil*)," and, said Coenders, "purely objectively," it was. Yet it was not a miscarriage for which the judges should be blamed. In his view, the verdict had been "a necessary consequence" of the whole proceeding, which had been characterized by "disastrous mistakes" since the beginning of the investigations. Coenders had initially wanted to present this argument in detail in writing, but on further consideration had decided that "a further discussion of the trial at the present time of national upswing is not consistent with the interest of the state," and so he felt it was "a command of duty to stay silent."[75]

Why did Coenders consider the verdict a miscarriage of justice? The Fourth Senate had convicted van der Lubbe, acquitted the other defendants, and found that there had been other culprits, unidentified but certainly Communists. The possible objections to this verdict, therefore, were that (1) the court should have found van der Lubbe had acted alone; (2) the court should have acquitted van der Lubbe; (3) the court should have convicted Torgler and the Bulgarians, or (4) the court should have found that the unidentified co-conspirators were not Communists. The investigation, though not the Fourth Senate, could be criticized for not having produced the real culprits, if indeed there had been other culprits.

Had Coenders believed that van der Lubbe was the sole culprit, he could hardly call a verdict that convicted only van der Lubbe from among five defendants a miscarriage of justice; and since the investigations had from the first moment at least produced van der Lubbe, he would be unlikely to say that the *investigations* had gone wrong from that time. Similarly, had Coenders thought the court should have convicted Torgler and the Bulgarians, why would he criticize the investigations that had brought them to the courtroom? He must, then, have believed that there had been other culprits, whom the police and the magistrate had failed to discover. These culprits might have been Nazis or Communists, of course, or indeed anyone else. The verdict had explicitly said that there had been other, unidentified, Communist culprits, and Coenders thought that verdict was wrong. The only logical inference from Coenders's words, then, was that he thought unidentified persons who were *not* Communists had burned the Reichstag. Little wonder that Coenders expressed the desire to "stay silent" about his opinion "in the interest of the state."

Coenders stood politically far to the right. Observers at the trial noticed he was the only judge to look on approvingly while Göring ranted, and that he was particularly aggressive in questioning Communist witnesses. His personal file is full of intemperate outbursts against Catholics and Jews. On the other hand, he prided himself on his skills as an investigator (he had had particular success prosecuting fraud cases during and after the First World War). At the trial he had effectively shown up a witness who was obviously lying in an effort to link van der Lubbe to the Communists, and it was Coenders who brought out Gempp's evidence that the stains on the carpet of the Bismarck Room had come from gasoline and not water. Coenders had to have been aware, as Bünger was, of Gestapo and other Nazi efforts to manipulate and intimidate the court. It seems, then, that this irascible and highly conservative German judge, after hearing all of the evidence, came to the same conclusion about the fire as had most foreign observers. Only for Coenders this conclusion was much more dangerous.[76]

Cold grandeur: the Reichstag's plenary chamber. (Bundesarchiv)

Looking the part: Rudolf
Diels in 1933. (Bundesarchiv)

The Kurfürstendamm Trial, 1932: Helldorff, right; Ernst, second from right; the lawyer in front with his head down is Roland Freisler. (Landesarchiv Berlin)

DEM DEUTSCHEN VOLKE

The Reichstag burns. (Bundesarchiv)

An alert-looking van der Lubbe poses for the police soon after his arrest, package of firelighters in hand. (Bundesarchiv)

The devastation in the plenary chamber, deputies' nameplates clearly visible. (NARA)

Just an honest cop?
Helmut Heisig in the
1930s. (Bundesarchiv)

Just another honest cop?
Rudolf Braschwitz in the
1930s. (Bundesarchiv)

No longer alert: van der Lubbe as he appeared on almost every day of his trial. (Bundesarchiv)

Dimitrov on trial (standing), typically irritating the judges. Seated, his lawyer Teichert (middle) and van der Lubbe's lawyer Seuffert (left). (Bundesarchiv)

"Limping more than one would expect": Joseph Goebbels arrives to testify at the Reichstag fire trial. (Bundesarchiv)

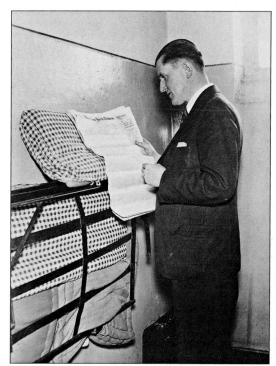

Ernst Torgler reads the *New York Times* in custody: the regime tries to score propaganda points through publicizing such good treatment. (Bundesarchiv)

"Pistol-Heini": Hans-Georg
Gewehr. (Bundesarchiv)

Main architect of one postwar
Reichstag fire narrative: Heinrich
Schnitzler in Luftwaffe uniform.
(Courtesy of Dierk and Klaus-Michael
Schnitzler)

Main architect of the other narrative: Hans Bernd Gisevius testifies at Nuremberg. (Ullstein Bilderdienst/Granger Collection)

Cop-stare: Fritz Tobias in the early 1970s, with his book and his files. (*Der Spiegel*)

FOR MARINUS VAN DER LUBBE the end came quickly. On Tuesday, January 9, 1934, Chief Reich Prosecutor Werner went to visit van der Lubbe in his cell at the Leipzig remand prison. With Werner were the prison director, doctor, and pastor, and van der Lubbe's interpreter.

Werner was there to read two documents to van der Lubbe. The first was the portion of the judgment sentencing the young man to death. The second was a letter from President von Hindenburg rejecting clemency, and thus allowing, in the official euphemism, "justice to take a free course." Werner read these announcements, he said, "slowly and clearly." Van der Lubbe said that he had understood without translation. Hindenburg's decision, Werner continued, meant that the sentence now had to be carried out. The execution would take place the next morning at 7:30. Werner asked van der Lubbe if there was anything he would like.

"I have no more wishes," was the reply.

Werner told van der Lubbe he should "prepare for his last hour." The prison pastor was there to help.

"Thanks for your information," replied van der Lubbe. "I will wait until tomorrow." He did not want to talk to the pastor.[77]

The decision to go ahead with the execution came as a surprise to world opinion, if perhaps not to the prisoner himself. Rumors in Berlin had confidently predicted that Hindenburg would pardon van der Lubbe. Afterward, other rumors claimed that he had done so and that Hitler's government had overruled him. The Dutch government had asked for clemency, but the records of Hitler's Reich Chancellery show that Hitler, Justice Minister Gürtner, and Foreign Minister von Neurath agreed that "an act of mercy for van der Lubbe cannot be supported," and this was the advice that Gürtner presented to Hindenburg. The Dutch had argued, reasonably enough, that executing van der Lubbe would foreclose any chance of finding other culprits. This argument obviously did not interest the Nazi leadership.[78]

At precisely 7:28 a.m. on January 10th, van der Lubbe was led into the courtyard of the Leipzig remand prison. Werner was there again, along with a number of people from the trial, including Parrisius, Bünger, and Seuffert. As the law required, Werner read once again the formal announcement: "The mason Marinus van der Lubbe from Leyden, Holland, has been sentenced . . . to death . . . for high treason in combination with seditious arson and attempted arson. The Herr Reich President made the decision on January 6th of this year not to make any use of his right to grant clemency." And then: "I give the mason Marinus van der Lubbe to the executioner for the execution of the death sentence. Executioner, do your office."

Van der Lubbe, according to the record, "maintained a composed demeanor and made no statement."

Van der Lubbe was to be executed by guillotine. The prison guards handed van der Lubbe over to executioner Alwin Engelhardt's assistant, who led van der Lubbe to the scaffold. The assistant strapped van der Lubbe onto the board, which was "lowered into a level position." Engelhardt released the blade. The whole thing had taken not even a minute. The protocol recorded that van der Lubbe was beheaded at 7:28:55.[79]

So much about the last year of van der Lubbe's life had been bizarre or puzzling that perhaps it was only fitting there should be a bizarre and puzzling epilogue. Van der Lubbe's family wanted to bring his body back to the Netherlands for burial, and indeed on January 10th Werner had told them that the German Code of Criminal Procedure specified that "the body of the executed person is to be turned over to his relatives at their demand for a simple burial without undue ceremony." Then higher powers intervened. In the awkward and embarrassed language of the German Foreign Office's message to the Dutch embassy, "The Reich government does not see itself in the position to give its agreement to the transfer" of van der Lubbe's body to the Netherlands. The provision Werner had cited meant that the burial should be carried out "in the simplest way" at the place of execution. Sending van der Lubbe's body abroad would run counter to the statutory purpose of avoiding "all public sensation." Werner's message to the family, the Foreign Office continued, had merely set out the terms of the statute without expressing his own position.[80]

The German authorities' refusal to turn over the body fueled more rumors. Some speculated that van der Lubbe was not really dead, that the authorities had only announced the execution to satisfy the most impassioned Nazis' lust for vengeance. As a Swedish newspaper reported, there were other and more plausible rumors, especially among lawyers. One of them was that van der Lubbe had been poisoned during the trial. Dutch doctors could have carried out an autopsy and easily confirmed such suspicions. The German historians Bahar and Kugel have argued persuasively in their most recent book on the fire that van der Lubbe's appearance and behavior during the trial were consistent with the symptoms of excessive ingestion of potassium bromide, which, in its trade application

Cabromal, was one of the most common sedatives at the time. Potassium bromide, which tastes like salt, can easily be slipped into food; symptoms of its abuse include mental slowness, loss of memory, apathy, a constantly running nose, and a slumped body posture. We saw that Dimitrov recalled that van der Lubbe, unlike the other prisoners, received special food packets with his name on them. Strikingly, van der Lubbe himself, in his lucid moment on November 23rd, complained repeatedly that he was being overfed: "Food five times a day and six times a day . . . I really can't agree with that." Just after the trial ended, the Amsterdam *Telegraaf* reported on a letter van der Lubbe wrote to his brother-in-law in Leyden, in which he complained, "I am not yet completely all right."[81]

Neuer Vorwärts reported that there was a special section of Leipzig's South Cemetery for bodies that came from the Anatomical Institute, where van der Lubbe's body had lain. But he was buried in another section. On Monday, January 16th, just before the burial, police carefully investigated the cemetery and the area of the grave and then sealed it off. An American reporter who wanted to take pictures was arrested. The grave was guarded day and night, and anyone who asked after its location was to be reported to the police. The *New York Times* also reported that "many secret state police were stationed around the cemetery to keep away the curious" and that van der Lubbe's stepbrother, another relative, and the Dutch consul had each thrown "a handful of earth on the plain black coffin."[82]

THE ACQUITTALS FOR TORGLER and the Bulgarians did not at first make much difference in their lives.

During the trial Göring had threatened Dimitrov, and afterwards Diels tried loyally to help Göring exact his revenge. In 1949 Diels claimed that he learned of the acquittals the day before they were announced, and also heard that Göring wanted to transfer the prisoners from Leipzig—which lay outside of Prussia, and therefore outside of Göring's jurisdiction—to a Prussian concentration camp. Diels immediately worked to countermand these orders, in order, he said, to keep the prisoners safe. He tried to keep them in Leipzig, and when the Leipzig court refused to hold them, Diels claimed that he headed off an attempt by Karl Ernst and the SA to carry out a "thumping"— an SA "thumping" being, in 1933, virtually certain to be fatal.[83]

Contemporary documents, however, tell a different story. Reinhold Heller's minutes of a high-level meeting at the Reich Interior Ministry on

January 4th, 1934, show that everyone present was inclined to let the Bulgarians go abroad at the earliest opportunity—until Diels intervened. Diels argued that Germany would suffer too much propaganda damage from letting Dimitrov agitate from abroad, as other left wing figures, such as Münzenberg and the Czech journalist Egon Erwin Kisch, had done. Instead Dimitrov should be sent to a concentration camp. State Secretary Hans Pfundtner, who was presiding over the meeting, said that Diels's remarks had opened up "whole new points of view." Diels even recruited Heinrich Himmler to support him in these efforts, which Himmler was glad to do. He wrote to "comrade" Diels on January 15th to thank him for his letter and to promise that he would "intervene in the matter 'Dimitrov' in the way Prime Minister Göring and you are doing."[84]

Nonetheless on February 27, 1934—symbolically the anniversary of the fire—Dimitrov, Tanev, and Popov were released on Hitler's orders, and flown to the Soviet Union. Dimitrov recorded a terse account in his diary. He was awakened at 5:30 by Criminal Secretary Raben, one of the investigators of the Reichstag fire. Diels himself accompanied Dimitrov to the airport, telling him "We want good relations with the Soviet Union. If that were not the case, we would not send you to Moscow!" Raben, along with Heller and Marowsky, went with Dimitrov as far as Königsberg. Heller told him on parting "I hope that you will be objective. And not say such dreadful things as others have done." Dimitrov said he hoped to return as a guest of Soviet Germany. Then it was off to Moscow.[85]

We have seen that Dimitrov's career now took a significant upturn. Long an advocate of a broad front strategy to combat Fascism, Dimitrov had been marginalized within the Communist Party for these non-Stalinist views, as they were in the so-called Third Period of Stalinist ideology in the early 1930s. Now, from the spring of 1934, Stalin put Dimitrov, firmly established as an anti-Fascist political star, effectively in charge of the Comintern with the mission of establishing the "Popular Front" strategy across Europe: rather than denouncing Social Democrats as "Social Fascists," allies of Nazis in all but name, Communists would now seek to join in coalitions with Social Democrats and centrist parties. This idea bore its most important fruit in Spain and France in 1936 with the coming into office there of Popular Front governments (leading in turn to the tragedy of the Spanish Civil War).[86]

This is where the Reichstag fire touches one of the broadest and most important currents of twentieth-century history. Many historians have stressed the importance of the Reichstag fire, and especially Münzenberg's exploitation of it, as the beginning of "anti-Fascist" politics. The Popular Fronts were the most important incarnation of this anti-Fascism. Indeed, historians Timothy Snyder and Tony Judt have argued that understanding the Popular Fronts is central to understanding the whole sweep of European politics from the mid 1930s to the mid 1950s. The spirit of the Popular Fronts flowed smoothly into the various wartime resistance movements against Nazi occupation and then cropped up again in coalition governments and political movements in postwar Europe—the early postwar French coalition governments, the "National Front" coalitions of early postwar Eastern Europe, or in such groups as the German Association of Persecutees of the Nazi Regime (*Vereinigung der Verfolgten des Naziregimes*, VVN). Certainly there would have been Popular Fronts without the Reichstag fire. The political configuration of the 1930s—notably the growing German threat to the Soviet Union—would have pushed the Soviets in this direction in any case. But the success of Münzenberg's Reichstag fire propaganda delivered an already-formed constituency, especially in Paris, and a plausible, charismatic leader in the form of Dimitrov. It is probably a belated tribute to the symbolic importance of the Reichstag fire for non-German European leftists that, in the postwar incarnation of the Reichstag fire controversy, a large share of those who argued for Nazi responsibility were survivors or intellectual heirs of the Popular Front and the wartime resistance (especially in the form of Edouard Calic's Luxembourg Committee) and shared its tendency to stark binary argument: Fascist or anti-Fascist, with us or against us.[87]

Sadly, in his later years Dimitrov appeared as a much less sympathetic figure than during his star turn in Leipzig. He spent the war in Moscow, where, like most Moscow Communists, he hung sycophantically on Stalin; he even submitted his diary to Stalin day by day for the dictator's inspection and approval. After the war Dimitrov became the first Communist prime minister of Bulgaria. In this capacity he led the Communist imposition of dictatorial rule, displaying an often shocking ruthlessness. In 1947 he oversaw the show trial and execution of Nikola Petkov, the leader of Bulgaria's Agrarian Union and the Communists' most important and popular opponent. Dimitrov was rougher on his prisoner then the Nazis had been with him; he ignored pleas for clemency for Petkov from— among others—the former French Popular Front Prime Minister Leon Blum, and even from Paul Teichert, Dimitrov's lawyer from Leipzig.

Dimitrov died in Moscow in July 1949, as his country was descending further into late-Stalinist terror.[88]

Ernst Torgler's post-trial fate was considerably less glamorous than Dimitrov's. Despite his acquittal he remained in prison for two more years. In the early phase of the war the Nazis blackmailed him with the safety of his son into drafting sham-Communist propaganda broadcasts to appeal to British workers (in the end his son was killed in action on the Eastern Front, i.e., fighting Communists). The Communist Party expelled Torgler for having defended himself, but not the Party, at his trial. After the war Torgler became a Social Democrat and lived in Hannover, where, always easy going and always credulous, he stayed in touch with Rudolf Diels and befriended Fritz Tobias.[89]

TEN YEARS AFTER THE PUBLICATION of his book on the Reichstag fire, Fritz Tobias wrote privately that he now judged Diels "much more skeptically than just a few years ago." On the one hand, Diels "at times had to live like a predator in the jungle and hold his own," but that sometimes he also had to "go along on the hunt" was "another matter."[90]

Diels claimed in his memoirs that the increasingly and openly murderous quality of Nazi rule placed a major strain on him in late 1933 and early 1934. He began to think about quitting his post after the SA murdered Albrecht Höhler—the killer of Horst Wessel—in the autumn of 1933, and at Nuremberg he said that this killing and that of another prisoner, Adolf Rall, in October, had convinced him to break off contact with Karl Ernst. However, there is credible evidence that Diels was guilty of ordering the murders of the Communists Jonny Scheer, Erich Steinfurth, Rudolf Schwartz, and Eugen Schönhaar at the beginning of February 1934. All of these men were "shot while trying to escape" from Gestapo custody.

After the war both former SA man Willi Schmidt and former Gestapo officer Walter Pohlenz said—separately—that these killings had been carried out by Ernst's stormtroopers on Diels's orders; Schmidt said that without Diels's or Arthur Nebe's help the SA men could never have gotten access to the prisoners. Diels ordered the shootings because these men had killed a former Communist named Kattner, whom the Gestapo had "turned." There was more to this story. Steinfurth and Schwartz had been part of the ring of prisoners at the Sonnenburg concentration camp who smuggled information about camp conditions out to the Münzenberg organization in France; some of this material appeared in the first *Brown Book*. The German embassy in Paris complained that the shootings served as a pretext for renewed demonstrations, strikes, and sabotage on behalf of Dimitrov and imprisoned Communist leader Ernst Thälmann.[91]

As early as September 1933 there were rumors in the exile press that Diels's position as head of the Gestapo was in danger, and that when he was dismissed he would be lucky to survive. Willi Schmidt told Fritz Tobias in the 1960s that Diels had turned to Karl Ernst around this time for help, and Ernst had gladly given it. The friendship of the SA was not necessarily going to help Diels against the SA's bitter rivals in the SS, and in fact SS officers acting for Kurt Daluege searched Diels's apartment and found documents that raised questions in Göring's mind about Diels's loyalty. Warned that the SS was going to arrest him, Diels fled to Czecho-slovakia in the company of Audrey von Klemm, an American woman married to a German-American financier, Karl von Klemm. It was in mid-November that Paul Hinkler replaced Diels as Gestapo chief. Hinkler had been a member of the last Weimar Prussian parliament and police chief of Altona since the Nazi takeover. He also had the distinction, rare among police chiefs before the Nazis, of having been acquitted of a criminal offense by reason of insanity in 1929.[92]

Göring soon changed his mind, however, and after some negotiations with Himmler and the SS, Diels was back in Berlin on December 1st. In a long and uncharacteristically maudlin passage of his memoirs, Diels claimed that he returned out of a selfless commitment to bettering the lot of the wretched prisoners languishing in the concentration camps, when it would have been easier and more comfortable for him to stay in exile. Göring gave him a new title, "Inspector of the Gestapo," and Diels was also named deputy police chief for Berlin. Göring told Diels on his return that the "main culprits" who had framed Diels were Nebe and Gisevius, a point that Ludwig Grauert, Göring's state secretary in the Prussian Interior Ministry, partially corroborated in testimony at Nuremberg: he had, he said, given Gisevius the task of investigating Gestapo abuses, because Grauert did not trust Diels.[93]

Gisevius wrote after the war that he and Nebe had been plying Daluege with revelations about Diels. Gisevius wanted to get rid of Diels because he held Diels responsible for several murders. Nebe went along because, like many old Nazis, he thought Diels was sabotaging the Nazi revolution. According to Gisevius, Diels's return was not the result of

Göring's doubts and the manifest incompetence of Hinkler, as Diels claimed. Rather, Diels had threatened to make "embarrassing revelations." This seems at any rate more plausible than Diels's claim that he returned out of concern for the safety of the Gestapo's prisoners.[94]

Grauert testified at Nuremberg that Diels had been "too young" to hold his own against Karl Ernst (who was four years younger than Diels). In 1962, Grauert told Fritz Tobias that by late 1933 Diels's relationship with Karl Ernst had "taken an untenable form." Grauert and Göring had concluded that it had been asking too much of Diels to stand up to the SA leaders. "Either he had to go along, thus letting himself be corrupted—*this was the impression regarding Diels*—or he would be fought to the knife." Hence the "old fighter" Hinkler was briefly put in charge of the Gestapo. Ambassador Dodd, on the other hand, thought that Diels's sacking was a "ruse"—an attempt to intimidate Diels because of what he knew.[95]

Diels's return to the Gestapo proved to be short-lived. At the beginning of 1934 he seemed to be heading for a nervous, if not also a physical, breakdown. He claimed in his memoirs that in January Göring and Hitler ordered him to prepare the murders of SA leader Ernst Röhm, breakaway Nazi Gregor Strasser, former Chancellor Kurt von Schleicher, and others. These orders threw him into confusion and despair. He told his wife that his Nazi masters were all "murderers." The sarcasm of Gisevius's gloss on this—"Good that he noticed"—hits home. That this was the moment Diels recognized "the worm in the apple," the first time he had been given an order to carry out a murder, is clearly false. Nonetheless, Martha Dodd, who was far from sympathetic to Diels when in 1939 she published a memoir of her time in Berlin, found that in early 1934 he was genuinely nervous and exhausted.[96]

Dodd was twenty-four when she accompanied her family to Berlin. Beautiful, vivacious, and at first fascinated by the Nazi revolution—she alarmed some American diplomats by using the Nazi salute—she began cutting a swathe through Berlin's diplomatic and journalistic society. She was romantically linked with the Hohenzollern Prince Louis Ferdinand, and young aides at the French and Soviet embassies, among others. She had a more complicated relationship with Rudolf Diels.

She wrote about Diels with a mixture of admiration and horror. In a letter to her friend Thornton Wilder in December 1933 she imagined that "when the gravel squeaks under my window at night" it must be the "sinister faced, lovely lipped and gaunt Diels of the Prussian Secret Police" watching outside. In her memoir she wrote that she "was intrigued and fascinated by this human monster of sensitive face and cruel, broken beauty." They went out often, dancing and driving. She never got very far with her German lessons, but Diels spoke fluent English. Their affair— for there seems little doubt that each was one of the other's many conquests—worried the State Department and, at least in retrospect, Dodd herself, because she never wanted to admit to it. When the American author Philip Metcalfe wrote to her in the 1980s asking questions that hinted at the affair, she complained to historian Robert Dallek, who wrote a biography of her father, of Metcalfe's impertinence. And there was certainly little warmth in her comment in a 1975 letter to journalist and Nazi chronicler William Shirer: "Diels is dead, thank God!"[97]

However, in the spring of 1934 she was "seeing a great deal of Rolf Diels," and Diels was not in good shape. Dodd described how he "seemed to cling to me, my brother, and the Embassy," and had fears that his enemies were trying to poison him. The kind of job that Diels did would eventually corrupt a person of even the highest moral character, she thought, and Diels's moral character had not been very high to start with. By that spring Diels was "more neurotic and full of obsessions than anyone I knew in Germany—even those whom he persecuted." He was in constant fear of his life, and the result was melodrama. "One time, when he, my bother, and I went to a restaurant in the country, near Wannsee, he told us dramatically that he anticipated being shot at any moment." When she asked him why he was so afraid, he answered that it was because he knew too much. She took it for granted that one of the things he knew too much about, and that put him in such danger, was the Reichstag fire.[98]

Diels did not imagine the danger. The other predators were in fact circling. Along with Gisevius and Nebe, Göring's police commander Kurt Daluege, Heinrich Himmler, and Reinhard Heydrich were all out for Diels. Daluege in particular, in memo after memo, pointed out what he saw as Diels's disloyalty and unfitness to command the Gestapo. Diels had investigated Hitler himself for perjury in 1931, and had possibly worked with the anti-Hitler journalist Helmut Klotz on Hitler's perjury and to publicize Ernst Röhm's homosexuality. For the SS men these were unforgivable sins. A former secretary at the Gestapo later remembered that after Diels left she constantly had to update his personal file with "news of his further subversive statements." A blunt 1942 letter from

Himmler to Daluege pointed to this long pattern of suspicion and investigation. "Dear Kurt," Himmler wrote, "You told me once that you had various highly incriminating things on Diels from the System Era [Nazi jargon for the Weimar Republic] among your old documents." Himmler wanted to know whether Daluege still had these incriminating things, and if he could send them on. Yet even here, at the highest level of power in the Third Reich, there were signs of fear and paranoia. "I ask you," Himmler wrote, "not to talk to me about this over the telephone, and also not to let anything be sent by teleprinter."[99]

Diels claimed that he asked Göring to be relieved of his post as Gestapo chief. More likely he became a victim of the power struggle that brought Himmler and Heydrich control of the Prussian police along with all the other German police forces. Nonetheless Göring continued to take good care of Diels, naming him local governor of Cologne, then of Hannover, and after 1941 director of shipping for his giant conglomerate, the Hermann Göring Works. Diels divorced his first wife in 1936 and married Ilse Göring, the *Reichsmarschall*'s widowed sister-in-law. He did this, by his own account, reluctantly. Ilse Göring was apparently deeply in love with Diels. He was indifferent to her in every respect save the protection her brother-in-law afforded.[100]

Many well-informed observers continued to believe that Diels was holding onto incriminating information about Nazi leaders, particularly about the Reichstag fire, and that this explained Göring's solicitousness and the slow pace of efforts to arrest a man who, by the early 1940s, was suspected of "anti-State activities." Diels himself admitted possessing such information on a number of occasions, although with Diels one cannot be sure if these were nothing more than boasts made for effect. In 1938 Ulrich von Hassell, who had been ambassador to Italy and was later involved in the July 1944 resistance, wrote in his diary that Ilse Göring told him how Hitler himself did not want to "antagonize" Diels because "he knows too much." Furthermore, the Gestapo accused Diels "of all possible and impossible political and moral failings." What Hassell found especially interesting, and deeply surprising, was that the Gestapo accused Diels of setting fire to the Reichstag.[101]

By his own account, Diels was a fearless critic of the Third Reich and a champion of its victims in the darkest days of the war. There may have been some truth to this, although by 1943 or 1944 a political nose much less sensitive than Diels's could have registered how things were tending. Eventually his self-professed civil courage, or at least his cynicism, caught up with him. Just as in the last days of the Weimar Republic, he was a little too quick to anticipate the change of regime. The Gestapo arrested him in March 1944. By this time there was a limit to how much Göring could or would shield his old protégé. Diels was released after three days, but only pending a trial before the dreaded People's Supreme Court, the den of the infamous Nazi judge Roland Freisler—who was, of course, the former counselor of Helldorff, Ernst and Gewehr.[102]

Diels's hostility to the state had already cost him his position with the Hermann Göring Works in 1943. Göring wanted Diels to report for military duty, but Diels had contracted tuberculosis and went instead to a sanatorium in Lugano, Switzerland. While in Lugano in late 1943 he saw Gisevius, and the two former Gestapo men had a long conversation that would turn out to be crucial in the later story of the Reichstag fire. Gisevius was by this time active in the resistance, and in frequent contact with Allen Dulles of the American OSS. In Lugano, from their later accounts, Gisevius and Diels shared what they knew about the fire. Both of them thought Berlin SA men had set the fire in the plenary chamber. Diels tried to stay in Switzerland, but Swiss authorities forced him to leave in January 1944. The Gestapo added this attempted "desertion" to the indictment for "defeatism." Diels spent some time in another sanatorium in Bühlerhöhe in the Black Forest, and then returned to the farm he had bought (at a suspiciously advantageous price) from the city of Hannover in 1942.[103]

The Gestapo came for him again in October 1944, and Diels languished for months in the cells of his old Prinz-Albrecht-Strasse headquarters. All that Göring would do for him now was to order Ilse to divorce him, because, Göring is supposed to have said, "I don't want any hanged men in the family." Diels's still-loyal first wife, Hildegard, went to see the police officer in charge of Diels's case, to try to find out what was going to happen, and to bring Diels some food. "The officer told me that Diels had been expelled from the SS by Himmler," she said later, "and that he should reckon on a speedy death."[104]

Diels's luck continued to hold, however. In March 1945 the Gestapo released him to an SS Punishment Battalion, with which he was sent to the Western Front near Mainz as an enlisted man. Hildegard was able to visit him at a barracks in Berlin-Steglitz just before Diels's unit moved out. She found him in a state of near collapse. Diels said later that he remained with the unit until it was dissolved, whereupon he surrendered to the Americans. A post-war American intelligence report had it that Diels was admitted to a German army hospital in Wiesbaden in April 1945 with tuberculosis, then transferred to a hospital in Hannover. "On April 10, 1945 he was given a furlough and returned home, where he surrendered to the American troops."[105]

Diels had always been an opportunist: a liberal democrat when men like Wilhelm Abegg controlled the Prussian administration, a conservative of Franz von Papen's stripe when Papen's hour came, and soon enough a Nazi. After the war he would sometimes claim to be a Social Democrat, while keeping up ties to postwar Germany's far right. He was nonetheless, through all of these phases, consistently a nationalist and a virulent anti-Communist, and although his loyalty swung wildly, it always seemed to return to the far right. He equated Dimitrov to Göring in his memoirs, calling them both "magnificent examples of their over-hyped despotisms, the one as worlds away from the principles of morality and the European cultural tradition as the other." But, if he were forced to choose, he would still prefer "the raging fat man." [106]

In the new landscape of postwar Germany, Diels's opportunism and underlying far-right inclinations would play their roles, and both Diels and the story of the Reichstag fire were in for some surprising twists and turns.

7
. . . .

"THIS FIRST CRIME OF THE
NATIONAL SOCIALISTS"

THE FIRE AT NUREMBERG

AFTER THE END OF THE Second World War, Rudolf Diels began two new careers. The first was as a professional witness in the long series of war crimes trials held at Nuremberg between 1945 and 1949. The second was as a defendant in a string of denazification hearings, war crimes prosecutions, ordinary criminal cases, libel trials, and civil service disciplinary proceedings. In both careers the central focus would be on his time as Gestapo chief, and often on the question of what he knew, and what he had done, about the Reichstag fire.

As the end of the Second World War drew near, the United States, Great Britain, France, and the USSR agreed with difficulty on the legal formula for a joint trial of major German war criminals. There were twenty-three defendants (one, Martin Bormann, was missing, presumably killed trying to escape Berlin as the Soviets closed in), among them such major surviving figures as Hermann Göring, Joachim von Ribbentrop, and Albert Speer. The Allies had selected the defendants with an eye not only to their seniority—after the suicides of Hitler, Goebbels, and Himmler, they were generally the most powerful of the surviving Nazis—but also to represent broadly the various bases of Nazi power, in the Party, the civil service, the army, industry, and the press. These men were all charged with crimes against peace (planning a war of aggression), war crimes, and crimes against humanity (the last involved atrocities against civilians, chiefly the Holocaust, as opposed to violations of the laws of war). The defendants were also charged with conspiracy to commit all the above crimes, an unknown concept in European legal systems. In addition to the twenty-three individuals, several Nazi organizations, including the Political Organization of the Party, the SS, SA, Gestapo, and General Staff, were on trial as "criminal organizations." The individuals and the organizations all had defense lawyers who could raise evidence and cross-examine witnesses in the usual way.[1]

In October 1945 two American military policemen brought Diels to the special witness house that the United States Army maintained under the management of the German-Hungarian Countess Ingeborg Kalnoky. Countess Kalnoky was then thirty-six years old and strikingly beautiful. Diels greeted her with a kiss on the hand and gave "his word of honor" that he would not try to escape. Hitler's official photographer, Heinrich Hoffmann, provoked general laughter with his observation that the Americans probably knew Diels might "run away *with* a lady, but never from one." Next to arrive at the witness house was a young woman who had come to see the former Gestapo boss. Broken-hearted at the news that Diels could receive no visitors, she sat on the steps of the house crying, until finally Kalnoky gave her a meal. Then an American officer led her away.[2]

By Christmas 1945 Diels had convinced the authorities to let him pass some of his house arrest at the hunting lodge of the Count and Countess Faber-Castell in Dürrenhembach, south of Nuremberg. Roland von Faber-Castell owned one of the largest pencil-manufacturing companies in Europe. His wife, Nina, was only twenty-eight years old in 1945 but had been a friend of Diels's since the 1930s, when she had been a music student in Berlin.[3]

The countess was also distantly related to a member of the American prosecution team, Drexel Sprecher (the countess was born Nina Sprecher von Bernegg), and the Faber-Castell hunting lodge soon developed into the social center for the Nuremberg trials. Diels was a frequent guest. Nina von Faber-Castell also visited him at the witness house, sometimes staying overnight, and on one occasion leaving behind an expensive negligee. That Diels was having an affair with the countess was soon widely rumored and, apparently, accepted by the count. When Kalnoky asked Diels why he was not concerned about his affair becoming public, Diels only grinned and told her, "that's just my way, the way your aristocratic title is yours." In March 1947 Diels wrote his old Gestapo colleague Heinrich Schnitzler that his time as a witness in Nuremberg had "developed into the most beautiful span of my life" through "another, more soulful event." According to Robert Kempner, Diels was the father of the Countess's first son; Kempner and Drexel Sprecher stood in as godparents.[4]

Kempner had returned to Germany to prosecute Nazis. In the 1930s, a Social Democrat of Jewish background, he had been Diels's colleague at the Prussian Interior Ministry. He was also Diels's protector at Nuremberg. Kempner was a regular visitor to the Faber-Castell hunting lodge. According to a report in the records of the CIA, Kempner, Diels, and the countess were all on such friendly terms that the three of them used the informal "Du" with each other.[5]

But Diels still had plenty to worry about, and in the spring of 1946 his worries were largely personified by his old subordinate, Hans Bernd Gisevius.

NO ONE LIKED HANS BERND GISEVIUS very much. Diels had arranged for him to be sacked from the Gestapo at the end of December 1933, supposedly for "criticizing measures of the Führer and the government," but in fact because he and Arthur Nebe had lost their power struggle with Diels. In October 1933 a warrant for Gisevius's arrest had been issued on the grounds that he was gathering information against the Gestapo. The warrant was rescinded due to outside interference, presumably from Gisevius's patron Ludwig Grauert. Reinhard Heydrich, the fearsome head of the SS's intelligence service, the *Sicherheitsdienst* (Security Service or SD) and later the Reich Security Main Office (RSHA, the institution in which, after 1939, the command of the Gestapo, the criminal police, and the SD was amalgamated), wanted Gisevius removed as the Berlin police chief's deputy for the 1936 Olympics, because Gisevius had created difficulties for the Gestapo until their relationship became the "most unpleasant imaginable."[6]

Yet members of the anti-Nazi resistance did not like him either. He was, in the words of one of his fellow Valkyrie conspirators, "an arrogant intellectual type, without any trace of a soldier's attitude." After the war even the Swiss—who generally avoided anti-German recrimination because of their own complicity—charged him with violating their neutrality by engaging in espionage. They eventually dropped the case.[7]

Gisevius was nakedly ambitious, self-important, and pompous, a blowhard who seized his chance at Nuremberg to engage in moral self-righteousness. The American historian Joseph Persico was on the mark when he wrote that Gisevius's "natural pose was arrogance" and his "native language was sarcasm." At Nuremberg Gisevius delivered his testimony in resonant and ringing tones, sitting ramrod straight, arms stretched out in front of him to embrace the witness box; he did not so much speak as proclaim. The transcript shows that he exasperated the president of the court, Sir Geoffrey Lawrence, who several times had to force him to edit his ponderous speechifying, or stop him from intervening while the lawyers resolved a procedural question. Ernst Torgler wrote his friend Ruth Fischer in 1948 that the best way to get Gisevius to "shut his trap" would be to "tell him what people think of him here." The worst that could be said of Gisevius was that he never abandoned his loyalty to Arthur Nebe, who went on to command an *Einsatzgruppe*, or mobile killing squad, in the Soviet Union during the war. Gisevius claimed that Nebe accepted the responsibility of this command because he knew he could minimize the killings, and because other members of the resistance did not want him to lose his influential position as head of the RKPA. This must rank as the most absurd version ever offered of "fighting the system from within," when one considers that Nebe's Einsatzgruppe B murdered more Jews than any other in the first eight weeks of the German attack, and altogether about 45,000 people from June to November 1941, while Nebe was in command.[8]

Gisevius was no leftist and, at the beginning, no opponent of the Nazis. A member of the German National Party and one of the leaders of its paramilitary organization, the *Deutschnationaler Kampfring* (German National Fighting Ring), he was born in 1904 in Arnsberg, Westphalia, into the kind of upper-middle-class family that had long supplied Germany's senior civil servants. As a student in the early 1930s he was constantly in trouble for speeches abusing Weimar politicians like Chancellor Heinrich Brüning as "rabble" (*Gesocks*). According to Reinhold Quaatz, by late 1932 Gisevius was conspiring against German National leader Alfred Hugenberg, probably out of a desire to push the party rightward, since in June 1933 Gisevius caused a splash by urging the members of the *Kampfring* to go over to the Nazis. That summer he completed his legal training and passed his second state bar exam, qualifying him for a career in the upper reaches of the bureaucracy. He wanted to work for the political police, and that was where he was sent. What he would see there over the next six months would push him into the resistance.[9]

As a diplomat and agent of the *Abwehr* (military intelligence) in Switzerland during the war, Gisevius was in close touch with OSS officer (and later CIA director) Allen Dulles and other American intelligence officials. CIA records confirm that Gisevius passed intelligence of a "very high level" to Dulles, risking his life to supply information "on the anti-Hitler underground movement." Dulles and his circle even nicknamed Gisevius, who stood nearly six and a half feet tall, "Tiny," which Gisevius was pleased to call himself even long after the war. Rumors of his American contacts brought him the attention of the Gestapo. When the July 20th plot against Hitler failed, Gisevius—who had been in Berlin for the attempt—managed to escape to Switzerland only after months hiding in Germany.[10]

In April 1946, the defense lawyers for former Nazi Interior Minister Wilhelm Frick and Reich Bank President Hjalmar Schacht summoned Gisevius to Nuremberg to testify for their clients. Gisevius was given quarters in Countess Kalnoky's witness house. Kalnoky did not yet grasp the depth of the mutual hatred between Gisevius and Diels. She was about to take Gisevius to his room when her housekeeper appeared and innocently asked if Diels was expected for dinner that night. "I noticed that Gisevius gave a start," Kalnoky remembered. "When I looked at him his face was suddenly altered with hate. He almost growled, 'Göring's lackey?'" When Kalnoky responded neutrally that Diels was staying with them, Gisevius asked "Couldn't they find a vacant jail cell for him?" He muttered something about finishing Diels off.[11]

The roots of the Diels-Gisevius feud lay in that murky Gestapo power struggle of 1933. Diels claimed that Gisevius resented him for winning and forcing him out of the Gestapo. He was also convinced that Gisevius had betrayed him to the Gestapo in 1944 after their meeting in Switzerland. Gisevius's hatred for Diels makes the allegation at least plausible, although Diels only seemed to come up with it after he realized that Gisevius's testimony could be dangerous for him; at other times at Nuremberg Diels attributed his arrest to the Nazi Gauleiter Lauterbacher. In no surviving Gestapo record, including those documenting investigations of the Valkyrie plot, is there any reference to Gisevius being a Gestapo informer. He is only mentioned as one of the resistance fighters.[12]

Gisevius wrote a memoir chronicling his experiences, and those of the conservative resistance from the Reichstag fire to the Valkyrie plot, while in Switzerland during the war. Dulles read a draft as early as 1943. The book was published in Switzerland early in 1946 under the title *Bis zum bitteren Ende* (To the Bitter End). Gisevius gave Countess Kalnoky a copy, in case she were "interested in Dr. Diels's career." Kalnoky passed the book on to Diels with a warning that she wanted him to keep out of Gisevius's way. Diels stayed up all night reading it, filling the margins with his notes, especially in the first few chapters. Thus Diels knew what was coming when Gisevius testified at the International Military Tribunal on April 24 and 25, 1946. Part of what came was a solution to the mystery of the Reichstag fire.[13]

DIELS WAS AT THE CENTER of Gisevius's story. Corrupt, unscrupulous, and undisciplined, in Gisevius's telling, Diels had made the early Gestapo little more than a "den of murderers." His ambition and his lack of Nazi background combined to leave no limit to what he would do to earn and stay in Göring's favor. Gisevius, on the other hand, spent his time at the Gestapo looking for evidence that would convince Germans who had not yet been "coordinated" to put an end to Hitler's rule. He found evidence implicating Diels in various crimes, including murder, but he focused on the Reichstag fire. Gisevius's immediate superior Arthur Nebe was a convinced Nazi who thought that Diels was a secret Communist trying to subvert the Nazi revolution. Gathering evidence against Diels, Gisevius and Nebe worked to the same end for different reasons.[14]

There was, for instance, the murder of Albrecht Höhler. As we've seen, Höhler was a small-time hood and Communist tough guy who shot and killed Horst Wessel, the most famous of Nazi martyrs. In 1930 a court sentenced Höhler to six years in a penitentiary. After the Nazis came to power the SA found and killed him. What Gisevius added to the story in 1946 was the detail that Diels had helped the SA by signing an order to bring Höhler to Berlin for Gestapo interrogation. After the interrogation, Diels, along with Karl Ernst and other members of Ernst's staff, took Höhler for a drive east of Berlin. Ostensibly they were returning him to his prison in Wohlau. When one car seemed to break down and the group stopped, Höhler "made the usual attempt to escape." The SA men buried him where they killed him.[15]

When Höhler's body was found only a few weeks later, Diels could not contain his contempt for the "loudmouths" of the SA: "These guys can't even bump someone off properly." He was thinking especially of the "notorious rascal 'Bacon Face'" Schmidt who, ordered to aim precisely, had shot twice to one side. Höhler had been the "only real guy" in the whole story. When the car stopped and the SA men took Höhler into the woods, Diels had asked Höhler what he thought was going to happen next. Höhler smiled and said he imagined he was "going to get pasted."[16]

Gisevius's story about Höhler's murder was only a curtain raiser to another one. Nebe learned from his contacts in the Berlin criminal police of a body found in a field east of Berlin, in a shallow grave and wearing only a shirt; the neck showed signs of strangulation. Through fingerprints the police identified it as Adolf Rall, a petty criminal with a long record. Rall was supposed to be in pre-trial custody at the local court in Neuruppin, a small Brandenburg town northwest of Berlin. He had been ordered to Berlin for interrogation by the Gestapo.[17]

Nebe and Gisevius thought that they might now have something on Diels, so they quietly began investigating. Most of what they learned came from an SA man named Karl Reineking, who had taken a job as a court stenographer. Gisevius first saw Reineking when Reineking began working at the Gestapo in early November 1933, but he did not get to know him well until later—after the Night of the Long Knives had ended the brief flowering of Reineking's career and sharpened his desire for revenge. Reineking came to Gisevius because "he had found out that I was collecting material." Later, according to Gisevius, Reineking was arrested and sent to Dachau. He died soon after, officially a suicide.[18]

Reineking maintained that on October 26, 1933, he had taken down the interrogation of Adolf Rall, a prisoner in the remand cells in Neuruppin, who had asked to "put some vitally important testimony into the hands of the investigating judge." It was at just this time that the newspapers were reporting on the expert evidence establishing that the Reichstag fire could not have been set by one person, and that van der Lubbe's accomplices had used a self-igniting solution. This was exactly what Rall wanted to talk about. He mistakenly assumed that he was safe in the custody of the Justice Department, and that he would be taken straight to Leipzig to testify. Once the papers had splashed his evidence around the world, he would be too conspicuous a target for any Nazi revenge.

Rall had belonged, Gisevius continued, to the Berlin SA Staff Watch and had been involved in the SA's use of a phosphorus solution to set fire to advertising columns bearing Communist posters. At the end of February 1933, Karl Ernst had given Rall and a number of SA men orders to "pull a caper" (*ein Ding drehen*) against the Communists. According to Rall, SA *Sturm-führer* (Storm Leader) Heini Gewehr, a "twenty-five-year-old ne'er do well," was to lead the mission. Gewehr's SA squad got into the Reichstag from Göring's residence, through the underground passage. Everything went smoothly. "For the rest," Gisevius concluded, "see the morning newspapers."[19]

Rall and the others were also told that there would be a "counterpart" to their operation. This was van der Lubbe. How had the SA found him? Gisevius (based on the information of Rall/Reineking) had no light to shed on this critical question. Van der Lubbe was just suddenly, simply, "there." "They got him after the fire in the palace," said Gisevius, "how, I cannot say." One version was that van der Lubbe had been arrested after his first arson attempts and Diels had handed him over to the SA. Gisevius said that Diels had denied this, which, according to Gisevius, could alone be enough "to corroborate the hypothesis." Yet Gisevius did not think this was how it had happened. The other version was that the SA had themselves discovered Lubbe in one of the homeless shelters or at the Neukölln welfare office. Gisevius thought that both versions were "somehow unsatisfactory." He added, though, that although Goebbels had immediately recognized the propagandistic potential of using van der Lubbe to discredit the Communists, this plan went seriously wrong. Lubbe's arrest meant that "the formalities had to be observed; there had to be hearings, investigations, indictments, and ultimately a trial. And the more involved these public activities became, the more the swindle was imperiled."[20]

In Rall's account, Goebbels and not Göring had been the prime mover behind the Reichstag fire. Gisevius and Nebe found this surprising, and had "a hard time convincing ourselves that it was true." As with the naming of Heini Gewehr as a main culprit, here Gisevius's account diverged from the *Brown Book* and other anti-Nazi propaganda of 1933–34, which, although giving Goebbels credit for the idea, had put more emphasis on Göring's role and had never mentioned Gewehr's name. Eleven years after the Reichstag fire, Gisevius had a particular reason to remember Gewehr. His fellow conspirators on the civilian side of the Valkyrie plot had wanted to use Gewehr's evidence about the fire to help persuade the generals that the Nazi regime had been a criminal operation from the beginning. Shortly before the July 1944 attempt to kill Hitler, however, Nebe had been alarmed by a report that Gewehr had been killed in action on the Eastern Front. In the spring of 1946 Gisevius still believed—wrongly, as it turned out—that Gewehr was dead.[21]

Reineking had taken what he learned from Rall's deposition straight to Karl Ernst, who in turn went straight to Diels. Reineking was ordered to "eliminate" the "traitor." Neither Rall's relatives, nor the criminal police, nor the court were ever supposed to learn what had happened to him. The Gestapo story would be that he had escaped without trace. After interrogating him, the Gestapo drove Rall, wearing, so Gisevius had it, only a shirt, out to the countryside. It turned out that Rall was not an easy man to kill: after the officers tried to strangle him he almost escaped, whereupon they shot him. In their panic they buried him so hastily that his body was found the following morning. Reineking became a protégé of Karl Ernst, who took him onto his staff and was even an honored guest at his wedding. Ernst arranged through Diels to get Reineking a job with the Gestapo.[22]

"Was Rall lying?" Gisevius asked rhetorically. "No. Everything that he said is in itself credible." The ultimate proof, said Gisevius, was that Rall's former SA leaders murdered him to cover up his story.[23]

We also have to ask: Was Gisevius lying? Many have thought so. Fritz Tobias called him "a pathological liar, without restraint in his self-idolatry [Vergötzung]," his Nuremberg testimony nothing but "false claims" and "endless fantasizing." Diels complained of the distortions and "fantastical ingredients" of Gisevius's account.[24]

To be skeptical of Gisevius in the late 1940s was reasonable enough. He was, as we have seen, an arrogant self-promoter, and when he wrote his memoirs very little corroborating evidence was available: the people he talked about were mostly dead, their documents not yet discovered. His story contained two important claims that were certainly wrong: Rall could not have participated in the Reichstag fire, as he had been in prison since late 1932; and Heini Gewehr had not been killed in action on the Eastern Front. There were other, more minor errors. In 1933 Rall was in prison in the town of Pritzwalk, not Neuruppin. Reineking, on the other hand, worked at the criminal court in Berlin. Some of the details of Gisevius's story were suspiciously novelistic, such as that he witnessed some crucial events literally by peeking through a keyhole.

At Nuremberg Gisevius was working from memories that by then were over a dozen years old, and it was understandable that a few errors crept into the story, all the more since key elements of it were, by his own account, at least double hearsay: Reineking's version of Rall's words. Still, what is remarkable about the story Gisevius told at Nuremberg is how over time documents and other evidence unavailable (and perhaps unimagined) in 1946 have confirmed its central elements. The story of Rall and Reineking points so squarely to the SA and Gestapo as, respectively, the Reichstag fire culprits and the agents of a cover-up, that its importance is second only to the evidence of the fire experts. Gisevius himself wrote in 1960 that this story was "the special contribution that I believe I have made to the history of the Reichstag fire."[25]

The Rall story did not in fact originate with Gisevius. The émigré newspaper the *Pariser Tageblatt*, founded by the former editor-in-chief of the *Vossische Zeitung*, Georg Bernhard, reported as early as December 1933 on the "elimination" of a "man who knew too much" (*unbequemer Mitwisser*). The paper identified its source as a Berliner whose credibility was "above all doubt." This source reported that at the beginning of November a prisoner in a Berlin jail, identifying himself as SA man Rall of Storm 17, had claimed to have been in the underground tunnel between the Reichstag and the Reichstag president's residence as members of his storm brought in the "explosive fluid" used to burn the Reichstag. The prison director (who, given the context, was probably the source of the story) notified the Gestapo, who brought Rall to the Alex. Prison officials then "heard no more of the case." After a while, when they asked after the whereabouts of Rall's documents, the Gestapo told them that Rall had escaped while being transported back to the prison. The article ended with the bald statement that "about two weeks ago" Rall's body had been found near Strausberg.[26]

Although some of its details of timing are not correct, the gist of this account is consistent both with Gisevius and with information from official documents found only decades later. But much more surprisingly, the first postwar corroboration of Gisevius's story came from none other than Rudolf Diels himself.

IN 1983, RUDOLF DIELS'S LAST MISTRESS, Lisa Breimer, gave Diels's personal papers to the State Archives of Lower Saxony in Hannover. But not directly. The papers first passed through the hands of Fritz Tobias. Tobias had been in touch with Breimer about the papers as early as 1974, but it wasn't until late October 1983 that he and his friend Adolf von Thadden were able to visit Breimer and get a look at them. (Thadden was a founder of the neo-Nazi party the NPD; in opposing the West German government's reparation payments to Israel in the 1950s, he had suggested that Germans had murdered only one million Jews during the war. Tobias's day job was to protect West German democracy against people like him.) By 1983 Breimer was an elderly woman and not well. She was convinced that thieves were trying to steal not only Diels's papers, but also other things that had belonged to him, including a Kandinsky. The police, said Tobias, found no evidence of a break-in or a theft. Certainly it didn't seem that any important papers were missing. Diels's papers were, Tobias recorded, "very extensive. From an examination it appears that there are definitely important and revealing documents that are also not very flattering for Diels." Just to go through these materials, Tobias thought, would take days or weeks. "I took a folder of documents with me," he wrote.[27]

A few weeks later Breimer formally turned the papers over to the state archives. The consignment agreement contained two striking provisions. The first was that the papers would remain closed to the public until January 1, 1994. The second was an exception to the first: Fritz Tobias and Adolf von Thadden could see them any time they wanted.[28]

A researcher who gets the chance to look through the Rudolf Diels papers in Fritz Tobias's personal Reichstag fire archive will quickly begin to wonder about the provenance of some of the documents. Tobias's files contain original letters, signed by Diels, not photocopies. How did he get them? In 1983 he had taken a folder with him. Did all of those documents find their way to the state archives? One letter in Tobias's collection seems especially important.

Diels wrote from Nuremberg on July 22, 1946, three months after Gisevius's testimony. The letter was written in German, but addressed to the British Delegation at the International Military Tribunal. It was headed "Re: Reichstag Fire 1933."

As I have been informed by the defense counsel for the SA, the former SA Leader Heini Gewehr, *who in Gisevius's book* To the Bitter End *is identified as the chief culprit in the burning of the Reichstag and is also held by me to be so*, is presently in an American internment camp.

In the interest of determining the extent of Göring's responsibility, and in light of the considerable interest of the German public in the clearing up of this first crime of the National Socialists, but also because Gisevius brings my name into immediate connection with this event, I ask that Heini Gewehr be interrogated.

The italics indicate the phrases that someone, presumably Tobias, underlined in red pencil. Tobias never cited this document in any of his writings, even the later ones.[29]

Given that Tobias argued for over fifty years that the Nazis had nothing to do with the fire, and particularly that Diels had no inside information and no settled opinion about it, the presence of this letter in Tobias's own collection comes as something of a surprise. Asked in 2010 why he thought Diels had written it, Tobias replied that Diels was only reacting to Gisevius's perjured testimony about the "ringleader of the SA arsonists," and later distanced himself from Gisevius's "endless fantasizing."[30]

Indeed, through the spring and summer of 1946 Diels wrestled with the problem of responding to Gisevius's testimony. The day after Gisevius finished giving his evidence, Diels swore an affidavit. In it he set forth what was to become his standard defense: that under him the Gestapo had fought to restrain Nazi violence and especially to bring SA leaders to trial. The Prussian police had committed "not a single political murder" as long as Diels had been in charge. Whenever Göring or Hitler had given this kind of order, Diels had opposed them. Contradicting his own statements from the 1930s and those of his former subordinates after the war, Diels claimed that his knowledge of the Reichstag fire was "restricted" because Göring had ordered the investigation to be shifted to the Reich Supreme Court at an early stage, and indeed forbidden Diels to work on it thereafter.[31]

But then, in a stream of memos and affidavits in the summer of 1946, Diels confirmed the main elements of Gisevius's story. In early July Diels said that he would not press the court for a correction of Gisevius's statements, "because otherwise I cannot dispute the truthfulness of his testimony. Rather, in essential points it corresponds with mine. I consider his testimony concerning me as the subject of a private quarrel."

In another memo, undated but probably from the same time, Diels wrote, "The depiction of general conditions in Gisevius's book is correct." Gisevius, Diels said, must have heard about the killings of Ali Höhler and Rall directly from Diels himself, "as I never hesitated to describe these two outstanding cases of SA murders." Diels insisted that his prosecution of the cases of Höhler and Rall had earned him the enmity of Karl Ernst. Another version referred to the murder of "a certain Rall," who, because he exposed the Reichstag arsonists, was abducted by the SA. Gisevius repeated only "distorted versions" of these stories "for his own self-glorification." Diels claimed that he had put these and other cases together in a memo for Hitler, which Hitler then took as a pretext for the Night of the Long Knives, an outcome Diels did not want or foresee.[32]

Some of Diels's defenses rose to heights of absurdity. He claimed that there was no connection—organizationally or ideologically—between the Gestapo and the SA. He also managed to claim that his Gestapo colleagues "rejoiced over every emigrant who got safely over the border and did everything to protect the democratic leadership of the past from false arrest."[33]

Diels made other specific allegations about the Reichstag fire at Nuremberg, again largely corroborating what Gisevius had said. These statements, all of them hearsay, have long circulated in literature about the Reichstag fire. In light of the new evidence from Diels's papers, however, and his letter in Tobias's file, they can now carry greater weight.

Diels gave a radio interview on July 15, 1946, in which he was asked about the Reichstag fire. Robert Kempner sent a member of his staff to make a transcript of Diels's remarks. The transcript showed that "In Diels's view the Reichstag was burned by the Berlin SA with the help of Goebbels, and Göring was in agreement with the consequences." Kempner did not remember Diels mentioning other names, but details regarding lower-echelon SA men "did not much interest" the prosecutors at Nuremberg, since their targets were the regime's leading figures.[34]

Diels did mention names when he talked to Adolf Arndt. Arndt was the young Berlin judge who had drafted the verdicts in the Felseneck and Kurfürstendamm cases in the 1930s. In 1946 the Justice Ministry of the newly established state government of Hesse commissioned him to investigate the Reichstag fire. In early May, just a few days after Gisevius's testimony, Arndt obtained special permission from the American military governor General Lucius Clay to question Diels. "Diels left no doubt that he was convinced National Socialists had set the Reichstag on fire," Arndt wrote later. He "decisively" denied his own involvement, and claimed that Hitler had also known nothing of the fire beforehand. Hitler's rage and astonishment at the Reichstag that night had been genuine. Diels told Arndt that SA men under the command of Karl Ernst had done the job. He named Heini Gewehr as one of the perpetrators. The name registered with Arndt, who remembered Gewehr from the Kurfürstendamm trial. Diels also knew by this time that Gewehr was still alive and in an internment camp. He did not say that Gisevius had been the source of his information on the fire, Arndt continued, but rather claimed this as his own knowledge. Diels added that "if he remained alive" he would concern himself with clearing up the fire, "whereby he instinctively grabbed at his throat."[35]

Diels was in fact potentially in danger at Nuremberg, especially from the British. A British memo of May 1946, citing Gisevius's evidence, said that while head of the Gestapo Diels had been "responsible for the grossest of brutalities and barbarisms" and that he should be prosecuted under the Allied Control Council Law 10, which (unlike the Nuremberg tribunal) covered German-on-German crimes committed before 1939. The memo continued that Diels's freedom "would be a menace to the security of the occupation." It is probably no coincidence that Diels sent his letter naming Heini Gewehr as a Reichstag fire culprit to the British. It was the Americans, especially Kempner, who shielded Diels. Gisevius complained to Kempner, "You know how openly [Diels] calls you his great protector every time he is allowed to slander me."[36]

As the gravity of Gisevius's allegations sank in, Diels's tone became angrier. Gisevius hated him, Diels told Kempner, only because Gisevius had not succeeded as a "Gestapist," and had felt free in his book to libel Diels because he assumed Diels was dead. Gisevius had done no more than report "two of my standard stories," distorted to make himself and Nebe look better: the murders of Höhler and Rall. Diels claimed "my conduct in these cases caused the SA," to which Diels attributed all of the guilt, "to attack me as a Communist and to drive me out."[37]

Countess Kalnoky could not help comparing Diels to Gisevius, and to the other resistance fighters (and grieving next of kin) who passed through her witness house. "For all his overriding self-assurance and possible self-aggrandizement," she wrote, "Gisevius had actually fought the regime," which put to shame Diels's claim that he had stayed in government service only to fight the Nazis "from within." Gisevius and his friends had fought the regime from within too, but for them, unlike for Diels, this had been "a front-line position that cost most of them their lives."[38]

Everyone who knew Diels well felt that on some level he understood and even agreed with his kind of criticism, and that in the years after the war he was driven at least in part by a sense of guilt over the part he had played. It was probably for a complex mixture of reasons, then, that Diels was "in a dark mood" after Gisevius's evidence.[39]

GISEVIUS AND DIELS WERE NOT the only people to give information about the Reichstag fire at the Nuremberg trials.

On October 13th, 1945, Robert Kempner got the chance to interrogate Hermann Göring, who had of course fired him from the Prussian Interior Ministry more than a decade earlier. When Göring tried to apologize to Kempner for this, Kempner characteristically thanked him for forcing him to emigrate and thereby saving his life. After that, Kempner later wrote, Göring seemed more relaxed. Indeed, there was an incongruous tone of familiarity between these men. The transcript shows that at one point Kempner referred to Diels simply as "Rolf"; Göring immediately understood whom Kempner meant.

Kempner began by confronting Göring with Diels's allegation that he, Göring, had known that the fire was going to be set off "in some way or another," and that Diels had already prepared the arrest lists. Göring admitted that he had ordered the preparation of arrest lists, but denied that he had known anything about the fire beforehand, let alone that he had planned it. He insisted that the arrests of Communists would have taken place anyway. But Kempner remembered that Göring was rocking back and forth in his chair as he spoke, and that it seemed that Goring "knew more than he was saying."

After a while Göring began to speculate. "If I were to mention any other possibility—" he began, and broke off, saying "but ultimately I still believe it's right that van der Lubbe did all the things in the Reichstag." Kempner asked him to finish his sentence. Göring said that if anyone else had been involved in the Reichstag fire, it would have been someone "who wanted to make difficulties for us."

"Let's talk openly about [Karl] Ernst," prompted Kempner.

"*Jawohl*," said Göring, "that is the man I was thinking of, if anyone else at all had his hand in the game." Diels and his "people" had had nothing to do with the fire, said Göring, but Ernst had been "capable of anything." He had probably thought that if the SA burned the Reichstag and attributed the attack to the Communists, the stormtroopers "could then play a greater role in the government."

Göring's most startling piece of evidence came in an aside. Kempner asked him what Diels had thought of the theory that the SA had burned the Reichstag. Göring replied that Diels had perhaps thought it possible. Kempner pressed the point. Diels, he said, had "reported [to Göring] that the SA was supposed to have set fire to the Reichstag and that the men had repeatedly used your passage." Göring replied that Diels hadn't said that the men had used the passage. What he had said was that "there was testimony in which the SA men had told him about it."[40]

Kempner was not the only person to whom Göring aired his suspicions of Ernst. Otto Meissner, the former state secretary in the Reich president's office, recalled that while he and Göring were interned together Göring had "admitted the possibility that a 'wild commando' from a National Socialist organization"—he suggested Helldorff and Ernst—had planned and set the Reichstag fire and used van der Lubbe "as a tool."[41]

Some years later Göring's former press secretary Martin Sommerfeldt wrote Reichstag fire researcher Richard Wolff that Ernst himself (along with Diels) had told him in 1934 that a squad of SA men had set fire to the Reichstag (although Sommerfeldt stopped short of saying that Ernst had himself confessed to the deed). Ernst was, said Sommerfeldt, "virtually obsessed by a dangerous rage against Goebbels," for whom the fire was a "masterpiece of propaganda."[42]

Göring was of course a liar as well as a mass murderer, and at Nuremberg he had strong motivations to keep lying. Nonetheless, his hesitant accusations of Ernst were plausible, and from his standpoint clever as a fallback position. Should more evidence pointing to the SA's involvement in the fire emerge, Göring could protect himself by arguing Ernst and Helldorff had acted on their own. Indeed later this was exactly what he did. It is striking that Diels must have told Kempner that he had heard SA confessions of setting the fire and passed this on to Göring, and even more striking that Göring confirmed this to Kempner. As Kempner said, Göring probably knew more than he was saying.

Ernst at least possessed the tremendous advantage of being dead, having been shot during the Night of the Long Knives in 1934, apparently while calling out "Heil Hitler." It was different with another witness who emerged at Nuremberg, one who worried Göring far more, and in whom both Diels and Gisevius were deeply interested.

HANS GEORG GEWEHR WAS BORN in Berlin on May 19, 1908. By his own account he joined the youth wing of the DNVP as a schoolboy in 1919. In 1924, like Karl Ernst, he joined the Frontbann. When he turned eighteen in 1926 Gewehr joined both the Nazi Party and the SA. He received the Party member number 36,913 (low enough to be prestigious and coveted after 1933, as it pointed to commitment and sacrifice for the "movement," not just post-1933 opportunism—a number under 100,000 was a qualification for the party's Gold Medal of Honor for "old fighters"). Between 1927 and 1930 he was, he said, politically inactive, while he studied engineering.

Ernst and Gewehr had grown up together in the Berlin neighborhood of Halensee, and perhaps for this reason Ernst appointed Gewehr the leader of his Staff Watch in 1931. The Staff Watch was a small squad with the job of guarding the Party headquarters on Hedemannstrasse. Gewehr served a few weeks in jail after the Kurfürstendamm riots and, as we have seen, claimed that he had a falling-out with Ernst and Helldorff over how to testify about them. He also claimed that while he was in jail, Ernst— who, like many SA leaders, was gay—stole his girlfriend. For a while in the second half of 1932 Gewehr commanded an SA storm in the Berlin district of Wedding, but by his own later admission some combination of Communist pressure and another criminal investigation began to make Berlin too hot for him. Late in the year he left the city.

Early in 1933, so Gewehr's story continued, his (highly implausible) quarrel with Ernst was cleared up. Ernst let Gewehr know that he had separated from the girlfriend, and so "because of the appeal to the greater cause, I drove back to Berlin." Gewehr took over the command of what he called a demoralized and disorganized storm in Berlin-Steglitz. In 1934 Ernst sent him to Rome for two months to train SA men there. "I have always seen this command . . . as amends and as a gesture" in honor of a long friendship, said Gewehr later.[43]

After the war Gewehr gave contradictory versions of where he had been on the night of the Reichstag fire. In a postwar trial he named members of his Steglitz storm as witnesses that he had spent the night at the storm's hostel; later he said that he could not remember if he had been there or at his mother's place in Halensee. He told a journalist in 1960 that he first learned of the Reichstag fire from the rumors that were spreading in Berlin. He got to the site of the fire either by tram or by bus the next morning, and once there couldn't get through the police cordon, although he was wearing his SA uniform. Contradictions aside, it was, as Gisevius pointed out, scarcely credible that on the evening Helldorff was summoning his stormtroopers to arrest thousands of Communists, a key leader like Gewehr would be sleeping *either* at his storm hostel or his mother's apartment.[44]

Gewehr's close ties to Karl Ernst became a grave liability on the Night of the Long Knives. He was arrested and taken eventually to the concentration camp at Lichtenburg in Saxony, which in the summer of 1934 was home to an odd assortment of Communists, dissident Nazis, and SA men. Gewehr claimed that he was not interrogated in the weeks he spent there. But when he was released (in August 1934 Hitler declared an amnesty for political prisoners aimed primarily at SA men like Gewehr) Gewehr was sent back to the Gestapo headquarters in Berlin. There, he said, an SS *Sturmbannführer* asked him who had set fire to the Reichstag. The SS man told Gewehr that he had come especially from Himmler and that Gewehr's transcript would go straight to Himmler the next day. Were this true, it was a sign of how many Nazis suspected Gewehr and his former patron, Ernst, of having set the Reichstag fire. Gewehr himself admitted that after the fire Nazi or SA leaders would sometimes approach him to say "You guys did a great job" or something similar. On another occasion he admitted, "After the Reichstag fire I was occasionally referred to in Party circles, with knowing smiles [*Auguren-Lächeln*], as the technical leader of the Reichstag fire." Nazi party documents confirm that there were rumors in Berlin Nazi circles that Gewehr was initially on the list of those to be shot in the Röhm purge. Gewehr himself said that if Nazis had had reason to suspect him of being "in on" the fire, he would have been killed during the purge.[45]

After the war, Gewehr claimed that by the spring of 1934 his faith in the Nazi Party "had begun to waver," and that the Night of the Long Knives accelerated his disillusionment. At the beginning of 1935 he left the SA and joined the police. Selfless and idealistic as he was, he even rejected the easy path to high office taken by other Nazi "old fighters," and at his own wish joined the police at the lowest rank.[46]

Documents from the 1930s, however, suggest no such disillusionment or reluctance to rise in the Nazi hierarchy. In fact, internal memos show that Gewehr had applied for the Party's Gold Medal of Honor in May of 1934, renewed his application after surviving the Röhm purge, and was still pushing for it in 1936. The Party finally awarded Gewehr the medal in 1937 over the objections of the Berlin office (which were based on "a few events from the year 1934"). Moreover, in September 1934, immediately after his release from Gestapo custody, Gewehr was not too disillusioned to apply for a job commanding an SA training camp. "I don't know if you are aware of my craze for weapons," he wrote, "which is proverbial in Berlin." He applied in 1936 for membership in the SS, noting "I very much miss the comradeship of a political fighting troop."[47]

In 1935 Gewehr was a trainee at a police school in Suhl in Thuringia. A fellow trainee, one Hans-Georg Krüger, heard that from time to time Gewehr dropped "darkly mysterious" hints about the Reichstag fire. One day, wanting to learn more, Krüger made a point of sitting at the same canteen table as Gewehr. Gewehr, who had had a bit to drink, said that "the Reichstag fire had not gone quite like it was in the papers." When the trainees asked for more details, Gewehr grew evasive. Krüger later remembered that although Gewehr had a "certain nimbus" from his long history in the Party, he was not popular among the trainees, who thought him a braggart, and no one took his Reichstag fire story very seriously. Only Gewehr's public court battles in the 1960s caused Krüger to reconsider.[48]

A 1939 police performance review noted that Gewehr's character was not always "steady," and in particular that his off-duty conduct "after the enjoyment of alcoholic beverages" did not always demonstrate "the necessary restraint." That year, after his police unit was sent to newly occupied Bohemia, Gewehr got into trouble repeatedly for drunken and disorderly conduct. In June he was sent back to Berlin and suspended from duty. But on August 31st, as Germany prepared to invade Poland, Gewehr was told that the "gravity of the hour" had saved his career.[49]

Gewehr's position with the Uniformed Police (*Schutzpolizei*, the branch of German police—distinct from both criminal and political police— which handles routine work like walking beats and directing traffic) kept him under the command of Count Helldorff, who had been Berlin's police chief since 1935. In February 1940 Helldorff reported on what Gewehr had gotten up to as a police officer in Poland in the early days of the German occupation. Gewehr had "personally carried out shootings of prisoners," Helldorff wrote. He shot them in the back of the neck and then recorded his "hits" by making notches in the barrel of his pistol. Helldorff believed this was "irreconcilable with an officer's idea of honor."[50]

The commander of the Warsaw Order Police (*Ordnungspolizei*, the organization into which the Uniformed Police was placed in the Third Reich) defended Gewehr on the grounds that the prisoners he had shot were "common," rather than "honorable political criminals." As a later report noted, at least three of them were Jewish and therefore were probably engaged in the kind of black market activity necessary to survive German rule without starving. Gewehr's commander had ordered that his officers should carry out at least one execution themselves so that they understood what ordinary constables had to "go through." Gewehr got off with a reprimand.[51]

Gewehr's brutality may have been too much for Helldorff, but not for Himmler. Since 1936 the SS had repeatedly rejected Gewehr's applications, probably because of the memory of his close ties to Ernst. But the shootings in Poland seemed to cause a change of heart. Gewehr was admitted to the SS in the spring of 1940, with retroactive effect to April 20, 1938 (Hitler's birthday, a traditional day for promotions and appointments in Nazi Germany). He eventually reached the rank of SS-*Sturmbannführer*, equivalent to major.[52]

When he got in trouble again in 1941 for drunken and undisciplined conduct, Gewehr wrote in a long defense, "I joined the police to be a soldier." What he really became was a mass murderer. In the summer of 1943 he was assigned to one of the police battalions under the command of SS-*Obergruppenführer* Erich von dem Bach-Zelewski, who had been given the special task of—ostensibly—combating partisans on the Eastern front. In fact, as historian Omer Bartov has written, for the SS and police units "combating partisans" was a euphemism for committing atrocities against Soviet civilians, especially Jews. As a witness at Nuremberg, Bach-Zalewski himself responded with a simple "yes" to a prosecutor who wondered whether "the struggle against the partisan movement was a pretext for destroying the Slav and Jewish population?" and he explained that the antipartisan operations were a part of the overall plan "to decimate the Slav population by 30 million."

By this point the concepts "Jews" and "partisans" had merged in the Nazi mind, so that, as one German general explained, the natural response to an act of sabotage in a village was to kill all the Jews so that "one can be certain that one has destroyed the perpetrators." Police units were given daily "kill quotas," which they fulfilled by surrounding villages and shooting all the inhabitants, or sometimes burning them in barns or forcing them to walk through minefields. By 1943, with labor an increasing concern in Germany, antipartisan operations evolved into slave-gathering missions in which the police would kill all the women, children, and older people, burn everything standing, and deport the men for slave labor. Timothy Snyder reports that the Germans murdered about 350,000 people as "partisans," of whom at least 90 percent were unarmed—a good indicator that they were in fact purely civilians. We may assume that

Gewehr occupied himself with such activities for much of the war. Records indicate that his unit, Battalion 304, was in action in April 1944 around Lvov and that it was "destroyed" in July. This was consistent with Gisevius's claim that Nebe had heard Gewehr was killed on the Eastern front shortly before the July 20th attempt on Hitler.[53]

In May 1946 Gewehr, very much alive, surfaced in a detention camp, and the news reached Göring's defense team in Nuremberg. Werner Bross, a young lawyer assisting Göring's lead counsel Otto Stahmer, remembered Göring's reaction. To Bross's surprise, the *Reichsmarschall* became agitated. "Even if the SA really set fire to the Reichstag," said Göring, "that still doesn't mean that I knew anything about it. And who is to guarantee that this witness won't buy his own freedom with testimony that incriminates me!" Göring did not want to discuss the matter further.[54]

As we have seen, Diels wanted Gewehr's evidence to probe Göring's responsibility, and presumably to exonerate himself. It is therefore easy to understand why, as Bross records, Göring did not want to call Diels as a witness either, although he told Bross that Diels certainly could give evidence, exculpatory for Göring, about the Reichstag fire. Göring was very nervous that Diels might also testify for Wilhelm Frick. Nonetheless, Göring "strove to demonstrate that he had no interest at all in the Reichstag fire." He told Bross what he had told Kempner: the arrest lists for Communists had been ready for weeks before the fire, and that the Nazis would have found a way to render those people "harmless" one way or another.[55]

DIELS, IN ANY CASE, had his own problems. Gisevius had accused him of involvement in the murders of Ali Höhler and Adolf Rall, as well as of covering up the Reichstag fire. Despite Diels's sometimes vitriolic efforts at defense, evidence to confirm what Gisevius said gradually emerged.

In his official account of Höhler's killing, contained in a report to Göring dating from September 1933, Diels wrote that the Gestapo had brought Höhler to Berlin in August to question him about "new evidence" in the Horst Wessel case. As Gestapo officers were taking Höhler back to the Wohlau penitentiary on September 20th, eight men "dressed as storm-troopers" forced them to stop and took Höhler with them. The Gestapo officers had no choice but to let Höhler go. The Gestapo did not officially know where the alleged SA men had taken Höhler, but, reported Diels, "his death could be assumed with certainty." Diels recommended closing

the investigation, as the killing "was committed for understandable reasons," even though the killers' identities were supposedly unknown.[56]

After the war, Diels told the story differently. He said that he had
himself interrogated Höhler. "You know, Ali," he had told the prisoner,
"things have changed. The National Socialists are in power. They are demanding a new trial in the case against you. What do you think of that?"
Höhler's answer came in the rough dialect of working class Berlin: "I'm
gonna get whacked, dat's official." Of course, this exchange had also been
included in Gisevius's account—except that Diels transposed it to the
scene of an interrogation rather than the moment right before Höhler's
murder. Diels claimed that his Gestapo had heroically refused to surrender Höhler to the SA. The SA abducted him anyway, and shot him "at
dawn in a clearing in the woods east of Berlin." Diels tried to get homicide detectives to investigate, but Roland Freisler intervened to stop him.
Karl Ernst admitted his part in the killing, adding that the orders had
come from the SA commander Ernst Röhm. Röhm in turn said the orders
came from Hitler. Diels confirmed that Gisevius had heard this story from
him. Where Gisevius's account touched on Diels himself, it was "distorted." Otherwise, however, he could not "dispute its truthfulness."[57]

In the years after the war, a number of witnesses claimed that Gisevius's version was closer to the truth than Diels's, and that far from trying
to restrain Ernst and the SA, Diels had gone "along on the hunt." One of
these witnesses was "Bacon Face," the former SA man Willi Schmidt.
Schmidt described himself to police in 1968 as "a well-known SA leader
in Berlin in those days, and in my young years also a daredevil." He maintained that he had started off a convinced National Socialist, but after
events like the Night of the Long Knives he realized "how poorly good
deeds were rewarded." Diels called him "the most eminent killer of the
Berlin SA," and claimed that Karl Ernst had forced him to take Schmidt
into the Gestapo as an officer candidate (*Beamtenanwärter*).[58]

Schmidt said that he met Diels in the spring of 1933 at Ernst's house,
where Ernst asked Diels—in the informal second person, *Du*, used by
close friends—"What do you think of my best storm leader here? He's a
great guy, and he's smart enough too." Diels invited Schmidt to apply for
a Gestapo job. Schmidt found Diels to be a friendly boss, who even paid
for Schmidt's engagement party.[59]

In February 1968, and again a year later, the Berlin police questioned
Schmidt on Höhler's murder. Schmidt told the police that in the middle

of 1933, Ernst informed him that Höhler was in prison in Berlin and that Diels would arrange for Höhler to be "turned over to the SA for liquidation." Schmidt claimed to have seen an order signed by Diels commissioning him and another Gestapo man, Criminal Assistant Walter Pohlenz, to take Höhler from the Alex to the penitentiary in Wohlau. A convoy of cars drove east in the direction of Frankfurt/Oder. Schmidt and Pohlenz were with Höhler. Ernst himself was in another car, accompanied by Diels. When the cars stopped Schmidt saw other prominent SA men, including Horst Wessel's friend Richard Fiedler, and even the "Nazi Prince," Prince August Wilhelm, fourth son of the former Emperor Wilhelm II. Everyone except Höhler and Diels was in SA uniform.[60]

The SA men led Höhler across an open field to the edge of a wood. In his 1969 statement Schmidt said that Ernst and his adjutant Walter von Mohrenschildt startled him by shooting Höhler without warning. The year before he had told the police "Ernst gave the order to shoot, and, as I recall, also Diels." As Höhler lay on the ground, Ernst asked Schmidt if he did not also want to fire a shot. Schmidt did what he was told, but intentionally shot wide. "At this point Höhler was already dead."

When the police asked why he had fired at a dead man, Schmidt replied that he had just been following orders, Ernst's as well as Diels's. That Schmidt fired wide is an important detail: Gisevius used it in his version of Diels's story, and in 1946 Gisevius obviously could not have known of Schmidt's testimony. The detail's appearance in both accounts helps establish their credibility. Other former Gestapo officers, including Pohlenz, corroborated Schmidt's version of Höhler's killing.[61]

The Berlin police believed that Schmidt had not wanted to murder Höhler out of "fanatical" Nazi zeal, but had done what was asked of him "out of blind obedience" to Ernst. A police memo cited a 1937 SA report that Ernst's strong influence led Schmidt to carry out "every order that he received from Ernst without any thought." Since Schmidt was only following orders, the case against him for Höhler's killing was dropped.[62]

At Nuremberg, and later, Diels claimed that his Gestapo had been the first and only effective vehicle of resistance against Nazi barbarism. Central to all of his arguments was the claim that his main opponent had been the SA. Gisevius, as we've seen, told a different story, and here again the evidence that emerged at Nuremberg and after largely corroborates Gisevius's version.[63]

That Diels had close ties to Ernst and the Berlin SA emerged clearly even from his own self-justifying postwar account. There he wrote that as time went by he found himself increasingly allied with the SA against Heinrich Himmler and the SS and their attempt to control the German police. Ernst suggested to Göring that Diels be made an SA *Gruppenführer*. Willi Schmidt recalled that it was to Ernst and the SA that Diels turned in desperation when he became a victim of political machinations in the fall of 1933. Ludwig Grauert, as we have seen, thought that Diels's relationship with Ernst was "untenable" and that Diels was "corrupted" by getting too close to Ernst.[64]

The Höhler case was not the only murder in which Diels's Gestapo seems to have collaborated closely with Ernst's SA. Even the 1937 official history of the Berlin SA refers frequently to the "close cooperation" between the SA and the Gestapo in such matters as the "dissolution" of the German National *Kampfring* or of a "Marxist-Jewish doctors' league." There were also the killings of Jonny Scheer and three other Communists in early 1934. A particularly revealing piece of evidence about Diels involves the murder of an SA man named Helmuth Unger in June 1933. Two other SA men (one of them Bernhard Fischer, later notorious under the modified name of Fischer-Schweder as the main defendant in the Ulm *Einsatzgruppe* trial) brought Unger to an interrogation with Rudolf Braschwitz, and afterward, evidently, took him away and shot him. The SA suspected Unger of having been an informer for the SPD and the political police before 1933. There was also plausible evidence that he had been a lover of Ernst's, and that Ernst wanted him eliminated to cover this up. In July, Unger's father Julius went to see Diels and voiced the suspicion that his son had been shot in the cellars of Gestapo headquarters. Instead of expressing outrage or astonishment that such a thing could happen in his citadel of resistance, Diels replied—so Julius Unger wrote to a prosecutor only a few days later—that if this were true, the grieving father would "simply have to accept it."[65]

In his last days as head of the Gestapo, Diels did what he could to prop up the failing political fortunes of the SA. What seems to be a draft letter from Diels to Göring dated March 1934 complains of measures that had limited the role of the "patriotic associations"—the SA and SS—in such matters as powers of arrest and national defense. These measures were hurting morale, and there were rumors that the government might be taking a line "hostile to the SA." It was therefore necessary to demonstrate the importance of these associations by hiring SA leaders for the Gestapo. The letter asked that Ernst be appointed a special commissioner to the inspector of the Gestapo (Diels, in other words), to advise him and to "support him in the selection of persons for service in the Secret State Police." Around the same time Diels told the American reporter Louis P. Lochner that the virtue of the SA and the SS was that they spread terror, a "wholesome thing."[66]

All of these accounts reveal a consistent story: Diels had gotten too close to the SA, especially to Karl Ernst and his casual murderousness. Even Fritz Tobias came, at least privately, to share this view.

THE TESTIMONY AND MURDER of Adolf Rall, as relayed by Karl Reineking, was the most important element in Gisevius's account of the Reichstag fire. And yet it seemed too sensational to be true, not least because Gisevius spiced it up with improbable, novelistic details. As the distinguished historian Helmut Krausnick wrote in 1960, for a long time Gisevius's story had "been greeted by an understandable skepticism."[67]

Certainly Diels conceded much of Gisevius's story—even that Rall "had to die" because he had supposedly exposed the Reichstag arsonists—with the important qualification that the fire was solely an SA crime that had nothing to do with him. Tobias wrote about the Gisevius/Rall/Reineking story under the heading "Legends, Legends" (and Tobias's article series in the *Spiegel*, which preceded his book, made no mention of Rall). Tobias said that the Gisevius/Rall/Reineking story corresponded "with striking exactitude" to the "rumors and imaginings" about the fire in the heads of Nazi opponents, such as the authors of the *Brown Book*. Rall was nothing more than a typical example of a convict who wanted to enliven his dull prison routine with the excitement of bearing false witness. His evidence was simply an echo of Schatz's testimony of October 23rd about the use of a self-igniting fluid. The Nazis nonetheless felt compelled to kill him because his story would still have undermined their propaganda. Tobias claimed that Reineking's later downfall was due to the hatred that the Nazis' new Prussian Justice Minister Hans Kerrl had borne for him since their days working together in the town of Peine before 1933. He nonetheless conceded that the rapid rise in Reineking's fortunes after October 1933 was a result of his tip about Rall's testimony.[68]

Tobias was forced to this concession because of some important documents that came to light only in the spring of 1960, after his *Spiegel* series had appeared. The documents—from Reineking's SA file—came from the Berlin Document Center, a vast collection of Nazi Party, SA, SS, and police records captured after the war and maintained in Berlin by the Americans until after German reunification. To the surprise of many, the documents showed that in 1946, with minor deviations understandable after thirteen years, Gisevius had reported the story of Reineking's career correctly. The logical inference was that Gisevius's account of Rall's murder might also be correct. Helmut Krausnick, then the director of Munich's Institute for Contemporary History, was so impressed by this discovery that he wrote immediately to a Berlin prosecutor to urge a renewed investigation of Rall's murder.[69]

As part of what turned out to be a broad re-opening of Nazi-era crimes, German prosecutors and police spent much of the 1960s investigating the fates of Rall, Reineking, and Höhler, and the past deeds of former SA men like Gewehr and "Bacon Face" Schmidt—in addition to the question of who had set fire to the Reichstag. Police questioned Karl Reineking's brother Kurt, Schmidt, Gewehr, and many other former SA and Gestapo men.

The second flood of documents came with collapse of the Communist regimes of Central and Eastern Europe between 1989 and 1991, when many previously inaccessible materials became freely available to Western historians. In the 1990s the German researchers Alexander Bahar and Wilfried Kugel discovered documents previously held in East Germany from the original police investigations of Rall's killing in 1933, as well as records of his imprisonment, and Gestapo records about what had happened to him.[70]

These investigations and discoveries corroborated the main points of Gisevius's account of Rall and Reineking, of what they had done, and, to use Diels's phrase, of why they "had to die."

ON NOVEMBER 3, 1933, the *Strausberger Zeitung* (Strausberg newspaper) reported that a "fully undressed" body had been found in the woods by Garzau, near Strausberg, a town about twenty miles east of the center of Berlin.[71]

A forester named Max Kutz had found the body on the morning of November 2nd. Earlier he had seen several cars and some SA men near the clearing where he later found the body, but he had suspected only poaching, not murder. A retired local civil servant named Alfred Paschasius had also seen two unfamiliar cars in the early morning of November 2nd around 6:15. A locksmith named Schüler claimed to have spoken to the SA driver of one of the cars, who told him they were from the Gestapo.[72]

On November 4th, two doctors from Berlin's Institute for Legal and Social Medicine performed an autopsy on the body of what had been a strong and healthy young man. They concluded that his death was caused by a shot through the forehead from close range as well as by "blows with a sharp-edged instrument." The autopsy also revealed "numerous slight bruises and scrapes [Schürfstellen] on the back and limbs." That same day, officers of the police Identification Service had been able to match the fingerprints to a set in their records. The protocol of the autopsy bore the heading "The Investigation of the Death of Adolf Rall."[73]

Rall, born in 1905, was a Nazi mirror image of the Communist Ali Höhler: a small-time hood who by 1932 had gravitated to the SA. In late 1932 he was arrested and charged with four counts of car theft. On April 11, 1933, Berlin's Superior Court convicted Rall on one count and sentenced him to a year in prison (less 111 days for time served). At first he was held pending appeals in Tegel prison in Berlin. On September 6th the authorities moved him to the remand prison in Pritzwalk, a small Brandenburg town seventy-five miles northwest of Berlin. However, on October 20th they moved him back to Tegel following a court ruling that his investigatory custody was over and his sentence had formally begun.[74]

The day after his return to Tegel, Rall submitted a note to the prison authorities:

I have very important information to give in the Reichstag fire trial. Already approximately four weeks ago I wanted to give notice about this, but did not do so because I was moved from one prison to another, and most recently I was ordered to the prison in Pritzwalk. From there I got to Berlin through a complaint. The testimony that I have to give I will give only in court. It is of great importance. I ask therefore to be summoned immediately, since I will soon have served my present sentence.[75]

Rall's testimony was *not*, therefore, a reaction to Schatz's evidence of October 23rd; none of the technical experts had testified by October 21st. If it was true that Rall had wanted to testify "four weeks ago," this would correspond to the opening of the Leipzig trial. Rall's statement attracted swift official attention. On Friday, October 27th, the Gestapo brought him to the Alex. The following Thursday he was dead.[76]

Events in Rall's case kept moving quickly. On November 3rd, the day *before* Rall's body was (officially) identified, police searched Rall's mother's apartment. They told her that Rall had escaped from a prisoner transport and they assumed he was with her. On November 4th, Göring himself ordered a stop to the investigations "against unknown persons for the freeing of a prisoner," which the Berlin prosecutor's office had launched after the discovery of Rall's body. Diels countersigned the order, though in his memoirs he told the story differently, claiming that it was Roland Freisler, at that time state secretary in the Prussian justice ministry, who stayed the Rall case.[77]

Rall's fate remained clouded in obsessive secrecy. Officials at Tegel prison either did not know, or did not want to know, what had happened to him. A note on the prison's letterhead recorded only that on November 2nd Rall had "escaped while being transported back by the Gestapo." The secrecy extended to Rall's next of kin. On August 27, 1934, his mother wrote a letter to the information office of the main criminal court in Berlin-Moabit. Her son, she said, "wouldn't tell me as his mother why he had been arrested. Instead he comforted me that he was innocent and would be freed." She still did not know what kind of sentence he had received or where the authorities had sent him. She mentioned that the police had searched her apartment on November 3rd the previous year. Since then she had heard nothing from or about her son, and was "very worried."[78]

A year later the authorities had still not sent her any information. In July 1935 the minister of justice ordered that Frau Rall be told that she would "receive definitive information shortly." The Gestapo informed the minister that Rall had been transferred to Gestapo custody on November 1, 1933. Rall had "used this opportunity for an escape attempt. In this connection he was shot." The documents, however, show that Rall was transferred to the Gestapo on October 27th, not November 1st. The Gestapo's 1935 letter tried to suggest that Rall never made it to Gestapo custody, but rather was shot on the way there.[79]

Even 1933 newspaper reports, to say nothing of police records, gave the lie to the "shot while trying to escape" story. Had Rall tried to escape, why would the police have buried him in a makeshift grave in Strausberg and search his mother's apartment? Why would they not identify the body until November 4th? And why would they still be so reluctant two years later to tell Frau Rall what had happened? A comparison to documents in similar cases of SA and Gestapo murders from 1933—and they were far from rare—underlines the unusual, indeed breathtaking haste with which Göring and Diels stopped the investigation into Rall's death. Such stays normally came only after months.[80]

No transcript or protocol of any interrogation of Rall seems to have survived. But in April 1938 the director of Tegel Prison wrote to the chief Reich prosecutor in Leipzig. "At the end of October 1933," read the letter, "on the occasion of the trial of van der Luppe [*sic*], who was convicted of arson for the fire in the Reichstag, I sent information [*Mitteilungen*] from prisoner circles here that contained revelations of the prisoner Rall, according to which the National Socialist Party was accused of connections to the arson." It was, said the director, a prisoner named Stelzner who had passed on the information, and Stelzner was subsequently interrogated. A protocol of his interrogation had been sent to the prosecutor in Leipzig. The prison director wanted to know whether Rall's personal documents were also in Leipzig. Handwritten notes at the bottom of his letter indicate that Rall's documents could not be found among the files on van der Lubbe, or indeed anywhere else.[81]

Was Rall's story then only hearsay reported by Stelzner? This is unlikely, as we not only have Rall's October 21st statement that he wanted to testify about the fire, but we know from the documents that he was taken into Gestapo custody, interrogated, and murdered—and of course that the Gestapo searched his mother's apartment, presumably looking for evidence, before Rall's body had been identified. No sign of a Stelzner protocol appears in the surviving prosecutor's files. Those files do contain a note dated August 11, 1934, immediately following Rall's October 21st note that he wanted to testify. "The contents of the dossier regarding the Reichstag fire are without significance for this case," the note reads. Rall, who "allegedly" wanted to "give important testimony in the Reichstag fire trial," later admitted that "his evidence in this matter was a lie and he had only wanted to attain his long-desired freedom again. R. has died in the meantime."

The "dossier" is not in the file. This is perhaps not surprising, given that this is a Nazi record of a Nazi crime. The only place Rall could have "testified" that his evidence was a lie would have been at Gestapo headquarters, probably under what the Nazis, like some later regimes, called "enhanced interrogation." The delicate evasion that Rall had "died in the meantime" also indicates the degree of credibility we should accord this statement.[82]

In 1961 Karl Reineking's brother, Kurt, told police that Karl had claimed he was holding onto "certain documents" about the Reichstag fire trial from his time at the criminal court. Karl said he was keeping them as a defense to "persecution" from Reinhard Heydrich, and that the documents would be published, possibly abroad, if anything ever happened to him. Kurt did not know what these documents said, but he had heard that the police found documents hidden under some coal in the basement of Karl's apartment.[83]

In his 1949 autobiography Diels backed away from his Nuremberg assertions that Nazis had burned the Reichstag. But still he wrote that the SA killed Rall because he had "exposed" the Reichstag arsonists. Willi Schmidt had been one of the murderers. Rall, Diels continued, had indicted himself by saying that he and a few of his cronies had set the Reichstag fire. "He told of a training program, in which he and his accomplices were schooled in the handling of phosphorus incendiaries." Furthermore, according to Diels, the SA men had often tested the phosphorus by throwing it in the corridors and open windows of public buildings. In a later interview Diels explained that in his book he had meant to write that the Nazi *leaders* were not responsible for the fire, but that "wild" SA men could have been, which may perhaps explain why his account of Rall's death remained consistent.[84]

While Diels was strikingly well informed about the contents of Rall's "self-indictment," he gave a mendacious version of the 1933 investigations into Rall's death. When Rall's body was found, the Berlin SA "got wind of the annoying discovery." Karl Ernst hurried to his "friend" Roland Freisler and got a decree instructing the prosecutors and police to drop the investigation. In fact, the documents show, Göring and Diels stopped the investigation into Rall's death. Diels knew perfectly well why Rall "had to die." He knew because, as with Ali Höhler and the Jonny Scheer group, he had given the orders himself.[85]

In October 1957 Diels reverted to his Nuremberg story and told the journalist Friedrich Strindberg that Gisevius's account of Rall and Reineking was "essentially correct," although Gisevius had "erred in many details." At about the same time Diels told another reporter, Harry Schulze-Wilde, about the Rall case and Heini Gewehr's involvement in the Reichstag fire, adding a critique of Gisevius's account. The details

Diels gave about Rall's murder in Schulze-Wilde's report were consistent with the police reports from 1933. "Rall's white shirt, of which Gisevius wrote, Diels explained as 'pure fantasy,'" said Schulze-Wilde. Apparently Diels did not explain *how* he knew it was pure fantasy. "When I asked for details about Rall's death, [Diels] explained this 'professional criminal' did not die from strangling, but from a bullet, and his body had not lain in a field but rather in a forest." But it was true, according to Diels, that Rall had been "bear-like" and not easy to kill. To know this, Diels would either have to have been present at the killing or heard about it from someone who was. Diels also knew that Rall had been in jail at the time of the fire. "Diels's opinion that Rall had not taken part in the arson as such, but rather learned about it through newspaper reports of the Leipzig trial, and thereupon, since he was a member of the Unit for Special Missions and was involved in the major fires, imagined a few things together, was striking to me."[86]

Documents discovered in two different periods, in 1960 and in the 1990s, also tell us a lot about Karl Reineking. Born in 1903, Reineking served with the German army from 1923 until 1931, when he was honorably discharged following an injury. He returned to his hometown of Peine and got a job with the local police. In June 1932 he joined the SA. The following March, as an SA auxiliary policeman, he mistakenly shot and killed another SA man who was disguised in the uniform of the Republican militia, the Reich Banner. This showed Reineking to be "an unreliable SA leader, lacking in conscience," in the words of Peine's SA commander. At the end of June 1933 the SA's internal discipline court expelled him.[87]

Reineking decided to start fresh in the big city. On May 15, 1933, he took up a new job at the criminal court in Berlin, a position he held until October 27th. It was Hans Kerrl, who also came from Peine, who arranged this job for Reineking. Reineking's hopes of advancement were realized when he went to work for the Gestapo on November 1st.[88]

Clearly something dramatic had happened at the end of October. Kurt Reineking told the police that in the fall of 1933 his brother had boasted of being "in very good standing" with Karl Ernst, a surprising claim for a man who had just been expelled from the SA. Yet Ernst himself agreed. On November 4th he sent a letter about Reineking to the "Supreme SA Leadership" in Munich. After noting that Reineking had appealed his expulsion from the SA, Ernst wrote "Today I can inform the Supreme SA

Leadership that Reineking has done the SA an unprecedented service, on which I am prepared to report personally to the Chief of Department II, *Gruppenführer* Schmidt." Ernst also declared that he would be "very pleased" to have Reineking under his command.[89]

Ernst had apparently used his influence with Diels, as he had for other SA men like Willi Schmidt, to land Reineking the job at the Gestapo working under Arthur Nebe. With Ernst's support, Reineking won his appeal against expulsion from the SA and was assigned to Ernst's staff. A photograph shows Ernst and Nebe as witnesses at Reineking's wedding on February 27, 1934—the one-year anniversary of the Reichstag fire, which fell on a Tuesday. The judge who presided over Reineking's appeal of his SA expulsion in December 1933 remembered the following summer that "[d]uring his questioning Reineking insisted vehemently that he had carried out top secret, important commissions for the (former) highest SA leadership and thereby done it unusually great service." Reineking insisted that he should be recognized and re-admitted to the SA for this service, while declaring that "he had to maintain the strictest secrecy regarding the content and the manner of execution of these commissions." He showed the judge a handwritten letter to him from Ernst, which used the informal *Du*.[90]

Documents also show that in 1946 Gisevius had recorded the gist of Reineking's downfall accurately. Karl Ernst's murder in 1934 deprived Reineking of his powerful patron. In late 1935 or early 1936 he was arrested and tried for making "critical remarks" about another former patron, Hans Kerrl. Reineking was sent to the concentration camp at Dachau, and it was from there, in June 1936, that the family learned of his death by "suicide."[91]

We therefore have evidence of the following facts: Rall made a statement in late October 1933 claiming that the Nazi party had, at least, "connections" to the Reichstag fire; on October 27th the Gestapo took custody of Rall from the justice department; on November 2nd Rall was found murdered; on November 3rd, before his body had been formally identified, the Gestapo searched his mother's apartment; on November 4th Göring and Diels halted the investigation; by November 1st Karl Reineking had won a job with the Gestapo, on the recommendation of Karl Ernst, because Reineking had done the Berlin SA an "unprecedented service"; and for nearly two years, the Gestapo refused to notify Rall's family of his death, sticking to the story that Rall had escaped while en route from Tegel to the Gestapo.

Rall could certainly have been lying. Tobias was right to argue that Rall could have become an embarrassment to the SA even had his evidence been false, giving them a motive to kill him anyway. Were this the case, however, there would have been no need to interrogate him so urgently nor to search his mother's apartment. The only reasonable inference therefore is that Rall "had to die" because his testimony was both dangerous to the SA *and* in at least essential points correct.[92]

Other elements of Gisevius's Nuremberg account deserve emphasis. He related many points of detail that subsequent evidence confirmed: that at Ali Höhler's killing, Bacon Face Schmidt fired to one side; that Höhler phlegmatically told Diels he knew he was about to be killed; that Reineking was a court stenographer and SA man who started working for the Gestapo in November 1933, that Karl Ernst was at his wedding, and that Reineking died at Dachau; that Heini Gewehr was twenty-five in 1933, and later served with a police battalion on the Eastern Front; that Rall's body was identified through fingerprints; and that the police planned never to inform Rall's relatives about what had really happened to him. There are also points in which Gisevius's account is *close* to what the documents reveal: that the police found Rall's body fully undressed (in Gisevius's account he was wearing only a shirt); and that the police searched Rall's mother's apartment (Gisevius said it was Rall's *girlfriend's* apartment).

Despite his pomposity and self-importance, Gisevius often displayed considerable integrity and self-restraint when it came to what he could prove and what he could not, even when he urgently needed to prove his case. He admitted that he was far from certain how van der Lubbe had gotten mixed up in the Reichstag fire. During his long legal battle against Gewehr, Gisevius once asked Helmut Krausnick for supporting testimony. Krausnick warned Gisevius that he considered the chapter on the Reichstag fire the weakest part of Gisevius's book. Gisevius replied, "Say that!"[93]

The Nuremberg trials had, therefore, directly and indirectly, generated strong evidence that Nazi stormtroopers had burned the Reichstag in an operation led by Ernst and Gewehr, probably with Göring and Goebbels behind the scenes in some way. This evidence came from two former Gestapo men who were in a position to know—Diels and Gisevius—and who hated each other so bitterly that any point of agreement between them had to be taken seriously. It drew support from Göring's statement to Kempner, particularly with its reference to the SA men who had told Diels about burning the Reichstag, which in turn is consistent with Sommerfeldt's recollection of similar evidence from Ernst; and from Göring's reluctance to summon Gewehr to testify.

The Nuremberg trials came at an unusual historical moment for Germany and the world: it is rare for a regime's documents to fall into the hands of enemies with an interest in exposing the information those documents contain. Nuremberg represented the first opportunity for sustained research, not only in the Third Reich's records but also through interrogations of its surviving leading soldiers and administrators. At the beginning investigators knew very little of how the Third Reich had worked, and knowledge came only slowly: it is startling to learn, for instance, that the records of the Wannsee Conference, a key step on the road to the "Final Solution," emerged only in 1947, after Göring and Joachim von Ribbentrop were sentenced and dead.

This gradual accretion of knowledge, driven by the needs of legal prosecution and defense, also shaped the story of the Reichstag fire. In the late 1940s this story began to change, and the notion that Marinus van der Lubbe had acted alone and the Nazis had had nothing to do with the Reichstag fire gained ground. Once again, Rudolf Diels was at the center of it. Why Diels began to change his story had everything to do with two major developments: the long process of "denazification" in Germany, and the beginnings of the Cold War. The Reichstag fire, which had marked the beginning of Nazi power, continued to burn long after the Nazis' fall.

8

. . . .

"PERSIL LETTERS"

THE *GESTAPISTS'* TALE

IN HIS CLASSIC AND CONTROVERSIAL *The Origins of the Second World War*, the late British historian A.J.P. Taylor decried what he called "Nuremberg history"—by which he meant accounts of Nazi Germany written uncritically from the briefs of Nuremberg prosecutors, based upon the evidence they had gathered, and with the prosecutorial zeal they had brought to their work. The resulting narratives, said Taylor, saw careful planning, premeditation, and high efficiency where really there had been only contingency, improvisation, and chaos. He was, of course, correct. However, there is an opposite and equally unreliable kind of historical writing. We might call it "Persil letter history." It has loomed particularly large in the story of the Reichstag fire.[1]

Persil letters (*Persilscheine*) were a phenomenon of the late 1940s and early 1950s. Named for the most popular brand of laundry detergent in Germany (the name "Persil" came from the two main ingredients, perborate and silicate) they were character references that Germans collected for their "denazification" cases. A good Persil letter could launder a person's brown past and return it to spotless white.

The "denazification" of Germany had been one of the Allies' main goals, announced in proclamations from the major wartime conferences. At the Potsdam Conference of July–August 1945 the United States, Great Britain, and the USSR agreed that the main purposes governing their occupation of Germany would include destroying the National Socialist Party and its affiliated organizations, ensuring "that they are not revived in any form," and preparing for the "eventual reconstruction of German political life on a democratic basis." To this end, war criminals would be punished and all members of the Nazi Party "who have been more than nominal participants in its activities" would be "removed from public and semi-public office, and from positions of responsibility in important private undertakings."[2]

In practice, however, the Allies very quickly found that the goal of removing Nazis from the civil service, the police, courts, schools, and universities clashed head-on with the goal of rebuilding an orderly and peaceful German democracy. To scrutinize the past of every adult German required an unsustainable bureaucratic effort, and no modern society could get by without the officials and professionals who had run the Nazi state. As the Soviet Union began to replace Germany as the Western Allies' main security concern, enlisting Germans on the Western side became a higher priority than prosecuting them. By March 1946 the Americans had handed denazification over to the Germans themselves, while retaining oversight. The procedure the Americans then devised for denazification in their zone in Germany's south and southwest was copied, with minor adaptations, in the French and British zones in the west and northwest as well.[3]

This procedure began with a questionnaire, mandatory for all Germans over the age of eighteen, soon infamous for its 131 questions about the subject's political past. From the questionnaire a prosecutor would decide who was "affected" by the law, and would bring the cases of affected persons before a tribunal of lay judges nominated by the German political parties. These tribunals placed people into one of five categories: Category I for "Main Culprits," II for "Incriminated," III for "Less Incriminated," IV for "Followers," and V for "Exonerated." Category I was intended for such persons as senior officials of the RSHA and all branches of the police, officers of the SS, and all members of the Gestapo. Category II was supposed to be for anyone who had held office in the Nazi Party, anyone who had joined the Party before May 1, 1937, and all members of the SS and Waffen SS. Category V, on the other hand, was for those who "in proportion to their strength" had resisted the regime and thereby suffered disadvantages. The tribunals could hand out penalties, ranging from ten years' hard labor for Category I down to fines for Category IV.[4]

In practice the tribunals proved extraordinarily lenient. Figures for the British zone give the idea: in a total pool of over two million cases, 1.3 percent were placed in Category III, 10.9 percent in IV, and 58.4 percent in V. A further 25.1 percent were judged not affected by the law, which meant the people had not belonged to any Nazi organizations or been active in such groups as the police or SS. The rest of the cases were stayed for one reason or another (the British military government reserved to itself decisions in cases of I and II, but this amounted to a tiny number of people: only ninety, for instance, in the most populous of the new German states, North Rhine-Westphalia). The practice grew even more lenient as successive amnesties covered people born after 1919, or those who had earned only modest amounts of money in Nazi Germany. This leniency has led most historians to class denazification as a resounding failure, or, in the famous coinage of historian Lutz Niethammer, a *Mitläuferfabrik*—a factory that made "followers" out of "main culprits," rehabilitating where it should have punished. But however distasteful the results may look from a moral standpoint, such criticisms are both unhistorical and unrealistic. The paradox of all new regimes is that they are forced to operate with the personnel of the old. This is so even for the most radical and ruthless of them: Lenin's Bolsheviks had to get along with a civil service in which more than half of the officials in central commissariats, and perhaps 90 percent of those in the upper levels of the state bureaucracy generally, had held positions under the czar or the Provisional Government.[5]

Persil letters, then, were one of the main tools by which such large numbers of seemingly incriminated Germans managed to get themselves placed in categories IV or V. One study found that in Bavaria on average every second adult wrote a Persil letter for someone else. The higher the social status of the figure under scrutiny, the more Persil letters he or she was usually able to marshal. We must therefore be skeptical of the information these letters contained. Lutz Niethammer mocked their typical contents: SA men provided mutual assurances that their storm had been nothing but an outdoor club; Gestapo officers vouched for the courtesy of their interrogations; and former Nazi Party members said they had only joined on their bosses' orders.[6]

Rudolf Diels, who both solicited and wrote a large number of Persil letters, was also characteristically sardonic about their accuracy. He remembered how, in 1940, a former colleague with an anti-Nazi political past had come to him to ask for a reference. Diels gladly confirmed the man's "National Socialist outlook," as he had in "a hundred other cases." In 1947 the same man wrote again to ask if Diels would attest that the man had *never* been a serious Nazi and that he was therefore qualified to be "a loyal servant of the new democracy." Once more Diels happily complied.[7]

While the wave of Persil letters crashed over the denazification tribunals, many of the most prominent figures of the Third Reich wrote memoirs, in some cases while awaiting execution at Nuremberg and elsewhere. Foreign Minister Joachim von Ribbentrop, Auschwitz commandant Rudolf Höss, and lawyer (we have seen him representing SA men in the Kurfürstendamm trial and in Königsberg) and governor of Nazi-occupied Poland Hans Frank fell into this category. Books appeared from generals like Erich von Manstein and Heinz Guderian; from senior civil servants like Otto Meißner and Martin Sommerfeldt; from leading politicians like Hjalmar Schacht and Franz von Papen; and, of course, from former Gestapo officers like Diels and Gisevius. Thus a tremendous amount of source material on Nazi Germany was generated by men who knew they might soon be hanged, metaphorically or otherwise, and whose minds were therefore wonderfully concentrated.

The German popular historian Jörg Friedrich has argued that German legal proceedings over Nazi crimes have gone on longer than those in other successor states to authoritarian regimes—as of the writing of this book there are still cases pending. They have also been wider in scope, as much concerned with followers as with leaders, and have taken the forms of civil as well as criminal trials. As a result, litigation has largely shaped the memory of National Socialism, and generated or unearthed the evidence that defines the Third Reich—from Nuremberg to the trial of Adolf Eichmann in 1961 to the trial involving Holocaust denier David Irving, who sued historian Deborah Lipstadt and Penguin Books in 2000, to the trial of John Demjanjuk, who died in March 2012 while appealing his conviction for crimes against humanity as a guard at the Sobibor death camp.[8]

Since Nuremberg, the Reichstag fire, too, has been at the center of many denazification proceedings, criminal and civil trials, generating new evidence, discussion, and revision. The idea that Marinus van der

Lubbe burned the Reichstag on his own—a thesis to which elements of the Nazi regime had resorted during the investigation and trial of 1933—began to be revived by a small group of former Gestapo officers in the late 1940s, above all by Diels and his former subordinates Heinrich Schnitzler, Walter Zirpins, Helmut Heisig, and Rudolf Braschwitz. Not coincidentally, from the 1940s to the early 1960s, these ex-Gestapo men were under almost constant threat of prosecution.

What interest, then, did these former *Gestapisten* have in pushing the single-culprit theory after the war? A case against Rudolf Braschwitz suggests an answer. In 1961 the prosecutor's office in Dortmund investigated Braschwitz for perjury and "the prosecution of an innocent" in the Reichstag fire case. "I have been advised," Braschwitz acknowledged for the record, "that in the present proceeding it is to be investigated whether I incriminated myself in connection with my police work in the solving of the Reichstag arson." He could be found guilty if the evidence showed his investigations had focused on van der Lubbe while ignoring evidence implicating others. Since it would hardly help him to reply that he had worked hard to bring to court unreliable evidence against Dimitrov and the other subsequently-acquitted defendants, the obvious defense for Braschwitz was to insist that no one but van der Lubbe had been guilty.[9]

The justice minister of the state of North Rhine-Westphalia pressed the case against Braschwitz hard, at times against the legal advice of his own prosecutors. The minister argued that Braschwitz should be found guilty of perjury even if his testimony would not have made the difference between van der Lubbe's being found innocent or guilty, but rather only resulted in a harsher sentence. The minister thought the Reich Supreme Court would not have sentenced van der Lubbe to death had he committed the crime along with others—especially if the "others" had been "a group controlled by the National Socialist rulers." Braschwitz was also potentially liable for the prosecution of an innocent person. Although the chief prosecutor argued that van der Lubbe had in any event not been innocent, the minister responded that Braschwitz might have been guilty of prosecuting an "innocent" van der Lubbe even had the young Dutchman only been found "guilty to a much lesser degree than he was charged." In light of van der Lubbe's execution, the minister argued, Braschwitz might even be guilty of homicide.[10]

For Braschwitz, then, the stakes of demonstrating that van der Lubbe had been a sole culprit were very high. This point was equally clear to

Diels, Schnitzler, Heisig, and Zirpins. Even if these men had done plenty of (even) worse things during the Nazi years than send van der Lubbe up the river (and, except for Schnitzler, who had an honorable record after 1934, all of them had) the Reichstag fire could still prove their undoing. There were very good reasons, then, for these former Gestapo men to insist after the war that van der Lubbe had been the only culprit, and that they had done the right thing, even the brave thing, by saying so at the time. Never mind that it wasn't true, and never mind that they hadn't actually said it. They *needed* it to be true, and they *needed* to have said it.

THE TWISTS AND TURNS in Rudolf Diels's story were the most dramatic. In his 1949 memoirs, Diels wrote that until 1945 he had believed that the Nazis had set fire to the Reichstag. Now he "believed this no longer." This statement puzzled the journalist and popular historian Curt Riess, who interviewed Diels extensively a few years later. As the highest police official in the investigations, Riess thought, Diels didn't have to "believe." He could *know*. What he had concluded in 1933 must have been based on some evidence. What evidence could he have seen after 1945 to convince him of the opposite?

Riess put this question directly to Diels. "He was quiet for a long time," wrote Riess. "Then I had an idea. I said to him something to the effect of: 'Did you perhaps write this sentence in your book because you were annoyed at the whole manner in which the trials at Nuremberg were carried out, and especially annoyed at the Americans?'" Diels stood silently for a few moments, then, said Riess, he "suddenly turned and slapped me really hard on the back, and, smiling, said something along the lines of 'There could well be something to that.'"[11]

By the end of 1946 Diels seemed to have recovered from the shock of Gisevius's testimony and was beginning to feel more secure. His Nuremberg testimony, he wrote in 1947, had "found the full acceptance of the British and American and French prosecutors." Robert Kempner in particular had called Diels's evidence "assistance especially deserving of thanks." British War Office documents show that British authorities notified Diels's lawyer at the end of October 1946 that there would be no war-crimes case against Diels and that they no longer considered him a security risk. In February 1947 Diels wrote to Heinrich Schnitzler that "naturally I must let the denazification wave pass over me," but he did not expect it to take him under. British authorities thought that Diels's 1944 arrest and his resignation from state service in 1942 cleared him from suspicion of war crimes.[12]

But between 1947 and 1949, Diels's confidence in his safety began to fade again. His exasperation with the Allied authorities increased. Returning German émigrés—mostly Jews and Communists—with what he saw as their self-righteousness (which really meant their tendency to condemn people like him) could drive him into outbursts of fury. His account of the past, and especially of the Reichstag fire, began to change.

In the spring of 1947, in testimony at the denazification hearing of former Reich Bank President Hjalmar Schacht, Diels denied knowing anything about who had set the Reichstag fire. The prosecutor had summoned Diels specifically to discredit Gisevius's Nuremberg testimony, which had been favorable for Schacht. In this case, then, it was probably Diels's hatred of Gisevius that inspired the change. A year and a half later a letter from Helmut Heisig gave Diels an even stronger motive to rethink his story. Heisig and Walter Zirpins had, of course, been the first police officers to interrogate van der Lubbe. Diels had later sent Heisig to Holland to investigate van der Lubbe's background. Heisig reminded Diels that he had worked on the Reichstag fire case until the end of the trial. Now, wrote Heisig, the prosecutor at the Würzburg denazification tribunal had "found in my person an 'accessory and participant' in the Reichstag fire" and was seeking an indictment. He asked if he could enlist Diels as a defense witness. He added that at the end of March 1948 he had also been arrested in connection with the "evacuation" of Jews from Würzburg. He was writing Diels from the remand prison.[13]

We have seen that Heisig began collaborating with the Nazis and the SA in 1932. He went on to join the Nazi Party in May 1933. Heisig left the Gestapo in 1934, but after several posts with the criminal police in the 1930s he returned at the end of 1940 and was sent to Hohensalza (now Inowrocław, Poland). Two years later the Gestapo made Heisig the Stapo-Leiter, or commander, of its office in Würzburg in Bavaria. In June 1943 the Würzburg Gestapo deported fifty-seven of the last Jews in the region to Auschwitz, and seven more to the Theresienstadt concentration camp near Prague. Prosecutors had what seemed like an overwhelming case that Heisig had organized this deportation. They had found a detailed plan for the deportation, dated June 13, 1943, and "marching orders" for an officer to accompany the victims, dated June 17th. Heisig had signed both documents.[14]

Heisig claimed he had been out of town on the day the deportation took place, and learned of it only when he returned. Confronted with his signature on the documents, he insisted that he had signed them after the fact, which he claimed was a common practice. In a letter to Heinrich Schnitzler he went so far as to say he had merely done his duty as an official and "obviously" had not then known what would happen to the deported Jews. "I am the last person," he declared to the court, "who would not stand to his deed." Historians studying the postwar defenses of Nazi perpetrators have found that it was standard for former heads of Gestapo offices to claim that they did not know that Jews were being deported to death camps on their orders. As for Heisig "obviously" not knowing what would happen to the deportees, a report from Würzburg's own SD office in April 1943 had matter-of-factly explained that some citizens in Würzburg did not believe reports of the Soviet mass murder of Polish officers in the Katyn Forest—because they suspected Germans had dug the mass graves for murdered Jews. In a study of the persecution of Jews in Würzburg, H.G. Adler noted that Heisig's June 13th order called bluntly for the "deportation" (*Abschiebung*) of the Jews, whereas orders for the previous five "transports" had referred euphemistically to "evacuation" (*Evakuierung*).[15]

Heisig's lawyer, Josef Haubach, worked hard on an early version of Persil letter history. Two Würzburg Jews who had somehow managed to survive the attentions of Heisig and the Gestapo—one Dr. Ikenberg and a lawyer named Richard Müller—contributed letters, attesting that Heisig had "in general conducted himself very decently." Müller said that he had not seen Heisig on the day of the deportation. Diels also contributed the letter Heisig had requested, although, while a witness at Nuremberg, Diels had told an interrogator that he considered heads of Gestapo posts like Heisig "hangmen."[16]

At a bail hearing, the court did not believe Heisig's claim that he had signed the documents after the deportation, "as a marching order without signature is pointless." There was no reason why Heisig should have signed this order had he not been directly involved in the deportation. At trial, though, the court found (despite considerable suspicion) that there wasn't enough evidence for Heisig's version of events to be "disproved with certainty."[17]

Heisig had to go through a denazification hearing as well, and here the Reichstag fire emerged as a central issue. The denazification prosecutor initially put Heisig into Category I—the category in which ex-Gestapo officers were supposed to be placed. The indictment alleged that Heisig "was informed of or involved in the Reichstag fire in Berlin." In Heisig's apartment the police found a copy of a Swiss pamphlet alleging that he had planted evidence on van der Lubbe. The indictment argued that "Heisig knew what he was there for": the Gestapo's first duty was the suppression of opposition to the Nazi regime, for which "the main weapon was the concentration camp."[18]

Under interrogation by the denazification prosecutor, Heisig stressed his 1933 press conference in the Netherlands, where, he said, he had told reporters there was no evidence that there had been more than one culprit, demonstrating how crucial this point now was to his defense. He had not known that his statement stood in "the crassest contradiction" to what the "Goebbels press" in Berlin was saying. That was the reason he had been ordered to return directly to Berlin. Naturally he denied planting evidence on van der Lubbe.[19]

Heisig's defense was that the Reich Supreme Court had taken over the entire investigation of the fire, and that even senior police officers were not given the results. He insisted that his opinion, "now as before," was that van der Lubbe "was a loner who had a colossal craving for recognition." As we have seen, the investigation documents contradict Heisig's testimony, showing that he was centrally involved in the fire investigation, not least in bringing forward some of the most dubious witnesses—the waiter Helmer from the Bayernhof restaurant, the "psychopath" Grothe—to testify to the activities of supposed culprits like Torgler and the Bulgarians. In 1950, in his final statement in the case, Heisig stressed his own poverty and illness, and that "as a civil servant and Party member I was nothing other than a follower in the truest sense of the word," or rather, "an un-willing follower." He was able to persuade the prosecutor to drop the charges concerning the deportation of Jews from Würzburg and the Reichstag fire. In the end the denazification tribunal placed Heisig in Category III or "less incriminated." This was the least favorable denazifi-cation outcome for any of the former Gestapo men connected to the Reich-stag fire. Nonetheless, in the autumn of 1954 Heisig was due to resume his career with the criminal police in Wiesbaden when he died suddenly in a freak accident.[20]

Meanwhile, Diels's attitudes to the Allies, German anti-Nazi resistance fighters, and returning émigrés continued to harden as his legal dangers mounted. In early January 1949 authorities in Soviet-controlled East Berlin had issued a warrant for his arrest for the murder of Ali Höhler. The basis for the warrant was the testimony of Walter Pohlenz, the junior Gestapo officer who had himself been involved in Höhler's murder. Pohlenz had also named Karl Ernst and Willi "Bacon Face" Schmidt as suspects, and added for good measure that they and Diels were implicated in the murder of other Communist activists, such as the Jonny Scheer group.[21]

To avoid this prosecution Diels only had to stay out of East Germany. But a potentially more threatening investigation was underway in the west. In 1948 the Bavarian state government commissioned Hans Sachs, a young prosecutor in Nuremberg, to try to bring "the actors of the Third Reich" to justice. Sachs had read Gisevius's memoir and learned that Gisevius accused Diels of at least one murder. "The position and the responsibility that Diels had," Sachs wrote, "especially with the Prussian Gestapo, makes it intolerable to me that he should go about free and unpunished."[22]

A few witnesses told Sachs interesting things. A senior official who had worked under Diels in Cologne reported that in the days before the Night of the Long Knives, Diels—whom, he said, everyone in Cologne called "Borgia"—moved around continuously "like a hunted animal." "This fear was supposed to be due to his participation in the Reichstag fire," Sachs added. At the 1935 Nazi Party rally in Nuremberg, Diels was also supposed to have said things to another official that "necessarily led to the conclusion that Diels himself had been involved in the arson of the Reichstag building." An unnamed female witness told Sachs that Diels had made similar remarks to her at a dance. But of course such hearsay was not going to make for compelling evidence in court, and Sachs was unable to come up with enough evidence for a prosecution.[23]

Diels was far from finished with the justice system, however. The International Military Tribunal at Nuremberg had declared the SS along with the Gestapo and the SD (but *not* the SA) to be "criminal organizations," and under the laws of the occupying powers, anyone who had belonged to these organizations after 1939 had to undergo his own individualized Nuremberg trial. Diels had been an officer in the SS, and so, according to the rules, were the court to find that he had understood the criminal nature of the SS and not left the organization, he could be subject to imprisonment. As with denazification cases he would be cleared if he could prove that he had offered resistance appropriate to his level of influence.[24]

This is what Diels set out to do, armed with a stack of Persil letters from unimpeachable witnesses from the democratic days of Weimar, such as Paul Löbe, Weimar Social Democratic Reichstag president and, even more remarkably, Carl Severing, the Social Democratic Prussian interior minister whom Diels had betrayed in 1932. Even Ernst Torgler, the kind of decent man who is unable to fathom the villainy of others, vowed that Diels was a "thoroughly humane and conciliatory man" whom he could never imagine being guilty of "brutal actions or certainly crimes against humanity." Heinrich Schnitzler held that there had been an "unbridgeable opposition" between Diels's allegiance to the state and the rule of law on the one hand, and the ruthlessness of the Nazi Party, the SA, and the SS on the other. One of Diels's Persil letters came from the Foreign Office official Vicco von Bülow-Schwante, who must have known something about Persil despite himself having had a dubious record in the Third Reich. The author of a large number of Persil letters, von Bülow-Schwante later became a member of the board of the Henkel-Persil Corporation— the maker of Persil detergent.

The letters worked: the prosecutor stayed Diels's case in June 1949. But the "denazification wave" did not fully pass over Diels until the spring of 1952. The Reichstag fire remained one of the main issues in it, along with Diels's conspiracy against the democratic Prussian government in 1932. The prosecutor's draft indictment claimed that given his close work with "leading National Socialists," Göring in particular, it was "not believable" that Diels had not gained a "precise view" of what had happened with the Reichstag fire. He had to have known of the rumors that were circulating before February 27th about a Nazi "provocation" before the election. The prosecutors dropped most of this language from the final version of the indictment, but still referred to the Reichstag fire as one of the Nazi measures that had to have made clear to Diels that National Socialism "was moving increasingly to a basis in violence and illegality."[25]

Diels complained bitterly about the delays in his denazification case, although some of them were his own fault. His case was put on hold, for instance, while the government of North Rhine-Westphalia investigated him for intimidating witnesses and attempting to suborn perjury (the case was dropped after Diels retracted some libelous statements). The delays probably worked to Diels's advantage. As Hitler's war receded and the Cold War advanced, the denazification program began to wind down. In December 1951 the state of Lower Saxony passed a "Law for the Conclusion of Denazification," and the following March Hannover's denazification committee stayed Diels's case, while still placing him in Category V, the one for the exonerated who had resisted Nazi crimes in proportion to their position and influence. And even then Diels was not finished with Reichstag fire litigation. As late as 1959, in a battle with the government of Lower Saxony over Diels's pension, Diels's lawyer felt compelled to suggest that Zirpins and Braschwitz be called to testify that there was no evidence for Diels's involvement in the fire.[26]

Diels's former subordinate Heinrich Schnitzler managed to get through the rest of the Third Reich without participating in any Nazi barbarities. In fact through the twelve years of the Third Reich he was never promoted beyond the rank of government counselor (*Regierungsrat*), which he had held in 1933. In the diary he kept as a prisoner of war in 1945 he wrote that he had faced official allegations that he was "non-Aryan," as well as that he was "politically unreliable" under the terms of the Nazis' civil service law (which is no doubt why archived Gestapo files contain 1933 testimony from Helldorff and others confirming Schnitzler's nationalist and anti-Communist views). Schnitzler had close ties to the group Catholic Action and its Berlin leader Erich Klausener, which would explain the Nazis' suspicion of him; Klausener was one of the victims of the "Night of the Long Knives," and there was evidence at Schnitzler's denazification, plausible given the Klausener connection, that Schnitzler had narrowly escaped the same fate.[27]

Just before the outbreak of the war Schnitzler left the civil service for the Luftwaffe. In January 1943 his commanding officer wrote that Schnitzler had shown himself to be a "cold-blooded and brave officer" under fire. His repeated requests for a transfer to the front were turned down only because his skills as a staff officer made him indispensable behind the lines. Schnitzler got involved with the conservative resistance circle around the former Leipzig Mayor Carl Goerdeler, one of the main figures behind the Valkyrie plot. According to one source, the Goerdeler group had slated Schnitzler for a senior post after a successful coup; when the coup failed Schnitzler avoided arrest only because his contacts either committed suicide or were killed by the Nazis before they could betray him.[28]

Schnitzler therefore managed—although only after a long legal struggle—to get himself denazified into Category V, from which a civil servant had an automatic right to reinstatement at his former level. But in the late 1940s the interior minister in the state of North Rhine-Westphalia was Walter Menzel, the son-in-law of Carl Severing. Menzel bore a grudge against Rudolf Diels and anyone associated with him. He refused to rehire Schnitzler, arguing that Schnitzler's categorization in V was "astonishing" and that his "leading position" in the Gestapo proved his culpability. Schnitzler sued for reinstatement, eventually forcing the government no farther than a settlement in which Schnitzler was reinstated without back pay.[29]

As a non-Nazi and, eventually, a resister, Schnitzler must have hoped for better things after the war, and his bitter resentment of his treatment is understandable. He always had to be wary of enemies eager to highlight the less flattering aspects of his biography. In late 1946 a Communist newspaper pointed out that this former "government counselor at the Gestapo" was now inconspicuously working as an administrator at a seminary. Schnitzler therefore had strong and, again, understandable motives for a public reworking of the past, and over time his account of the Nazi years changed.[30]

In his 1945 prison diary he had written that, although he did not "believe" the Nazis had burned the Reichstag ("the Reichstag was set on fire by the pyromaniac van der Lubbe, without orders"), the fire had been "the birth hour of the concentration camps" and indeed of the Nazi regime generally. As an early and spontaneous expression, offered up before the whole denazification process had begun, we can take this as an authentic reflection of what Schnitzler really thought, and even in hindsight it stands out for its clarity. Nonetheless, as he himself also wryly commented, "to be a martyr is a form of grace, but not a profession." He could not afford to be, and he was not, blind to the connections between versions of the past and well-being in the present.[31]

In his lawsuit against Menzel, the critical issue was what Schnitzler had done after the Reichstag fire. Here he abandoned the idea that Nazi misrule began on the night of the fire. His lawyer, Anton Roesen, argued that the Gestapo that was "so disastrous for Germany" did not develop until Himmler and Heydrich took it over in the spring of 1934—and sacked Schnitzler. "The political police under Diels's leadership cannot possibly be equated with the SS-Gestapo," said Roesen. Diels's Gestapo amounted to the "first and successful attempt to put up state resistance against the National Socialist organizations." Schnitzler had fought against it all—the SA and SS, against the concentration camps and against anything that compromised the rule of law, "in a manner that endangered his life and health." Diels contributed a Persil letter making the same points, and Schnitzler now wrote that "the revolution," the "intoxication of power and blood of a barbarous sub-humanity" had begun not with the Reichstag fire but sixteen months later with the Night of the Long Knives.[32]

NEITHER DIELS NOR SCHNITZLER left the battle to their lawyers. They also took their own arguments public. Between 1947 and 1949, just as they were negotiating the denazification tribunals and trying to restart their careers, Diels and Schnitzler were also at work on memoirs that dealt with the Gestapo of 1933 and, in particular, with the Reichstag fire. They collaborated closely on these works. "It seems to me to be important," Diels wrote to Schnitzler in February of 1947, "to portray our work as a coordinated act of resistance, which at first delayed the move away from the rule of law toward pure terrorism."[33]

Resentment at how they had been treated since the war was a common theme in the letters they wrote one another in this period. Diels wrote viciously about returning émigrés, especially if they were Jewish, as those "who owe their wretched agitator-existence to us." Diels felt he was being hounded by people he had saved from arrest. Drawing on typical Nazi anti-Semitic rhetoric he called Fritz Tejessy, a senior official in North Rhine-Westphalia—whom Diels incorrectly believed to be Jewish, but who was a returned émigré—a "flat-footed thug." "I did not deposit my memoirs in Switzerland to justify myself," Diels wrote piously as early as 1946, but to record the "real events" as a defense against the "disastrous exaggerations of the émigrés." Schnitzler thought that the returning émigrés perspective was "poisoning" German political life.[34]

Diels and Schnitzler shared a particular hatred of Gisevius. Diels tried to downplay his grudge, airily advising Schnitzler for instance to ignore Gisevius's "already discredited" book, but the frequency with which he returned to it belies such easy confidence. Schnitzler called Gisevius "this German National traitor," and wanted to know whether Diels thought he should write an article about the first year of the Gestapo or "a massed attack against Gisevius." A few months later, when Schnitzler heard of an anti-Gisevius article published in the far-right Swiss journal *Neue Politik* (New politics), he sent an approving letter and offered his own article for consideration.[35]

But the main motive for Diels and Schnitzler to write and publish what they did was their legal predicament. In their letters they repeatedly drew connections between favorable publicity and favorable denazification outcomes. When Schnitzler heard about a magazine article praising "our work back then in Berlin—under Diels," he wrote a friend that he needed a copy of it urgently—if necessary "through the application of violence"—given that it touched upon "the Diels complex," the core of his legal appeal. When Diels published his memoirs he sent three copies to Schnitzler with the promise, "If you believe you must give up your own copy as propaganda for the cause, you will obviously receive a replacement." In late 1947 Schnitzler sent a letter to the newspaper the *Welt* to help a friend's legal case. It was only in the "twilight of sensation," Diels wrote Schnitzler, that "the likes of us" could "break through to a platform from which we can defend our skins before the public."[36]

These were not just concerns for Diels and Schnitzler: these men were part of a wide network of former Third Reich officials who stayed in close touch to arrange testimony and coordinate publicity. Most of the other surviving Gestapo men from the Reichstag fire investigations also played a role in the story that Schnitzler and Diels were writing. "Zirpins writes me that he is fundamentally in agreement with my statements," Schnitzler informed Diels in March 1948. The fact that in his writings Schnitzler referred to the Reichstag deputies' nameplates in the plenary chamber, which, as we have seen, was a detail otherwise mentioned only by Zirpins, is a strong hint of how much information Zirpins fed Schnitzler, who had not been involved in the investigations himself. Both Schnitzler and Diels were in touch with Heisig; Schnitzler corresponded with Martin Sommerfeldt. To another former colleague Schnitzler wrote, "it seems to me to be urgently necessary to find a common platform and to mutually coordinate things." He mentioned those with whom he was in contact, along with their denazification status, obviously a central element of their identities: "Rudi Diels, who was denazified in V . . . Maurer, who got IV . . . Kurt Geissler, who is still in a camp."[37]

Like Diels, Schnitzler learned directly from Heisig and Heisig's lawyer Haubach how dangerous the Reichstag fire could still be for these men. Heisig wrote often to Schnitzler, asking for and receiving Schnitzler's help with his denazification and criminal prosecution. At the end of August 1948 Heisig wrote Schnitzler that with "measureless hate and somewhat greater stupidity and arrogance" the prosecutor had alleged that he, Heisig, had been a "conspirator and party" to the Reichstag fire. He asked Schnitzler to contact Haubach.[38]

Schnitzler advised Haubach that because of the "grave" charges Heisig was facing it would be necessary to prepare the trial thoroughly. He gave Haubach Diels's and Zirpins's addresses, stressing that before calling either as a witness he would first have to get their permission to avoid "repercussions" with "disastrous consequences." Schnitzler thought that the Nuremberg judgment had already shown that there was no evidence that the Nazis had burned the Reichstag, but at the very least Heisig's court should give him the chance to raise evidence in his defense. "The difficulty of the task before you," warned Schnitzler, "is that you have the public opinion of the whole world against you." Again the link to publicity emerged: one could only win such a battle by "mobilizing all supporters." Immediately after saying this, Schnitzler asked not to be summoned as a witness.[39]

This was the key point: the right kind of publicity had somehow to be combined with remaining as inconspicuous as possible and avoiding those "repercussions." The radio network Westdeutscher Rundfunk wanted Schnitzler to do a broadcast on the fifteenth anniversary of the fire, to put forward the "sensational" argument that the Nazis had had nothing to do with it. But, Schnitzler complained to Diels, the censors would only permit Schnitzler's involvement if his name, occupation, and title at the time, along with his Party and SA membership were made known right at the start. He had refused. "Pity, it would have been a good opportunity to get a discussion going about the things that are close to our hearts." A month later, Schnitzler asked Diels's opinion about using a pseudonym. Or, Schnitzler wondered, "in light of your book, should we emerge from our reserve? I am not for it, especially since it isn't over 'til it's over [*noch nicht aller Tage Abend ist*]." A few years later, soliciting Schnitzler's testimony for his denazification, Diels promised him that he need not have any worries about possible repercussions: "The public is uninterested."[40]

SCHNITZLER WAS AN ADMINISTRATIVE LAWYER (*Verwaltungsjurist*), not a detective; he had not investigated the Reichstag fire himself, and he admitted he had little idea of what the detectives had done. His prison diary is a document extraordinarily free of resentments and bitterness given the conditions under which it was written, and reveals Schnitzler to have been a thoughtful and cultivated man whose anti-Nazi sympathies were genuine. In this diary he wrote that he "believed" rather than that he "knew" that van der Lubbe had acted alone. In 1947 he wrote, "No one has yet succeeded in solving" the Reichstag fire mystery, and in his letter to Josef Haubach he said only that the Nuremberg court had thought the issue couldn't be resolved one way or the other. But by 1949 his view had hardened; indeed, his sons strongly insist that he was "absolutely convinced" that van der Lubbe had acted alone.[41]

In January of that year *Neue Politik* began running an article in several parts entitled "Another View of the Reichstag Fire." The author was identified only as "a German police specialist," who had worked in the political police under Carl Severing.[42]

In fact the author was Schnitzler. The article appeared in *Neue Politik* through the intervention of Diels and Countess Faber-Castell. The editor of the journal was a Zürich lawyer named Wilhelm Frick (not to be confused with the Nazi interior minister of the same name), who also ran the publishing house Interverlag. Later in 1949 Frick would publish the first edition of Diels's memoir, and in his legal capacity he represented Diels in a number of libel cases in Switzerland. In the 1930s Frick had been the German general consul in Zürich, and a leading figure in the *Eidgenössische Front*, a Swiss pro-Nazi organization. Bahar and Kugel write that Allied authorities banned *Neue Politik* in Germany in 1948 because of its Nazi content, although it is worth noting that the same authorities also prevented the publication of Gisevius's *Bitter End* in Germany simply because Gisevius had once been with the Gestapo.[43]

Indeed, Schnitzler, whose biography was similar to Gisevius's in important ways—both were highly conservative Gestapo officials who were forced out before the Gestapo was taken over by Himmler and Heydrich and who then gravitated to the Valkyrie resistance—now took up a position as Gisevius's mirror image. If Gisevius was the founder of the postwar narrative of Nazi guilt for the Reichstag fire, Schnitzler more than anyone else was the originator of the postwar version of van der Lubbe as sole culprit. All of the essential elements of what would, a decade

and more later, become the Tobias/Mommsen interpretation of the Reichstag fire, feature in Schnitzler's article. Hitler and his new government
were genuinely paranoid about the Communists; and after January 30,
1933, they waited anxiously for the Communists to make good on their
revolutionary slogans and call for a general strike and a "violent uprising."
Meanwhile, the political police, under its new head Rudolf Diels, went on
working as it had under the Social Democratic minister Severing (Schnitzler's account, like later ones, glossed over the fact that it was Diels's
betrayal regarding that secret meeting with Torgler and Kasper that
threw Severing and most other democratic Prussian officials out of office).
The violence of the election campaign in February and March 1933 and
the steadily escalating repression of Nazi opponents were also absent
from this account—though not, as we have seen, from Schnitzler's 1945
prison diary.

At every stage of the case, Schnitzler claimed, the political police had
done their best to resist the demands of the Nazi leaders and uphold the
rule of law. Orders for arrests of Communists on the night of the fire were
the least they could do without "arousing the impression of immediate
disobedience." The police did not even work from arrest lists compiled
either during the Severing era or during the first weeks of the Nazi takeover. They had to spend hours looking up names and addresses in their
archive before the first arrests could begin. The SA and SS were not
involved in any of the arrests in Berlin. It was a purely police matter. The
"decent treatment" that the police accorded van der Lubbe quickly
brought him to trust his interrogators and he confessed to everything,
while demonstrating a firm command of the German language. (His later
silence at trial was a product of his dismay at being shoved out of the
limelight at his own trial in favor of people he did not know.)

Like Diels, Heisig, and Zirpins, Schnitzler distanced himself from the
investigation, which he had only heard about from Diels and the officers
involved (which however in his case, unlike the others', was entirely believable). But Schnitzler claimed that these officers had insisted that
indicting Torgler, Dimitrov, Popov, and Tanev could not be "justified."
Orders from the very top forced them to do it anyway; the later acquittals
vindicated their first instincts. Neither the National Socialists nor the
Communists succeeded in proving the other's guilt because in the end it
was "the deed of an individual." Marinus van der Lubbe "was the culprit
and he was the only culprit." This had been the finding of the "professional

criminalists" who had gone soberly about the task of finding the truth. Then, however, certain "political circles" got involved. "No use could be made of a sole culprit, so van der Lubbe *must* have had accomplices." Schnitzler also blamed the expert witnesses for testifying to the presence of inflammable liquids, which they had done only to "attract attention and win their spurs." Here, then, an enduring interpretation of the Reichstag fire was set: conscientious police work had been undone by politicians and experts; there was no question of the police themselves having framed suspects, fabricated evidence, or suborned perjury to cover for the real perpetrators. The detectives had believed all along and had bravely tried to convince their masters that van der Lubbe had been a sole culprit.

In light of the allegations that Heisig was facing just as Schnitzler was writing his articles for *Neue Politik*, this argument seems little more than a defensive vindication of this small group of former Gestapo officers. Given Schnitzler's own need to rehabilitate Diels's Gestapo to get through his denazification and be reinstated in the civil service, the advantages of claiming that there was "still not a single National Socialist" in the political police of 1933, that Göring himself had complained that the police were still "contaminated with Marxists," and that Diels was the "most hated man" in the SA, SS, and the Nazi Party, who himself had had "no idea" who was behind the fire, were obvious. Yet Schnitzler's role in the Reichstag fire debate is complex, and should not simply be condemned. Schnitzler was a decent man forced to live a good part of his adult life in an indecent time. If he did not respond to this challenge like a martyr—a grace, as he wrote, not a profession—he did so with more resolution than most. In the circle of Diels's former officers Schnitzler was, by far, the least exposed to legal danger after 1945. His diary shows that he genuinely believed van der Lubbe had acted alone, and that he, like Diels, had a shrewd eye for the significance of political developments in the 1930s. The likely inference is that Heisig, Diels, and Zirpins fed him misinformation, in the hope of benefiting from his integrity and relatively good record—an inference strengthened by the fact that Schnitzler was the first to mention publicly the deputies' nameplates in the plenary chamber, a detail which seems to have come from Zirpins.[44]

How Diels and Schnitzler thought about the timing of publication also revealed their instrumental use of the past. Diels wrote Countess Faber-Castell early in 1948 that a "flanking supplement" like Schnitzler's article would increase the effect of his own book. Schnitzler adopted the idea, writing to Diels that if his piece was to play the "flanking role" for Diels's book that they intended, "we must discuss the plan in detail and coordinate it with your book." Extracts from Diels's book began appearing in the May 12, 1949 edition of the weekly newsmagazine the *Spiegel*.[45]

The first page of the first installment featured a prominent sidebar headed "Guiding Principles," which made the motives behind Diels's argument amply clear. "The depictions of the Third Reich that have appeared so far," he wrote, referring presumably to memoirs like Gisevius's, presented neither "pauses nor accelerations" in the way that events had unfolded. The authors ignored the part that "anti-revolutionary"—meaning non-Nazi, establishment conservative—forces had played. According to Diels, the "first great push" toward revolution did not come until the "Bartholomew's night" of the Night of the Long Knives, which "was not an end, but a beginning." It was only after this that murder became a matter of state policy. Diels thought that the first year of Hitler's rule was the only moment in which it had been possible to avoid "catastrophe." After that, any and all resistance was futile.[46]

After some introductory character sketches of Göring and Goebbels, which revealed Diels's gifts as a writer and a sharp-eyed observer, came his new version of the Reichstag fire. Diels described how his subordinate, whom he called "Schneider"—he carefully protected Schnitzler's anonymity, just as Tobias would a decade later—had interrupted Diels on his date at the Café Kranzler to tell him that the Reichstag was burning. When they arrived at the Reichstag van der Lubbe was already being interrogated. The Dutchman's "forthright confession" led Diels to conclude that van der Lubbe hadn't needed any help: "Why shouldn't one match suffice to set the flammable cold grandeur of the plenary hall . . . in flames?" Diels knew his readers would expect him to identify Nazis as the arsonists, and he apologized for not doing so. After the fire, he wrote, and up until 1945, he had in fact believed the Nazis had done it. "Today I do not believe it any longer."[47]

Again he told of the brave and conscientious Gestapo, fighting the violence and lawlessness of the Nazi leaders and the SA. Diels said that he had tried to talk Göring out of prosecuting Torgler and the Bulgarians. Göring's reaction was to have "a raving fit," and to tell Diels in no uncertain terms that he and Hitler both believed that Communism needed "to be struck a blow."[48]

We've seen that the investigation documents from 1933 directly contradict the idea that Diels resisted Nazi demands to prosecute more

Communists. According to those documents, Diels tried to drive prosecutions of other defendants forward, and complained when Werner would not follow his lead. The *Spiegel* articles also gave a misleading account of Diels's role in Dimitrov's post-trial fate, and repeated his insistence that Göring had kept him away from the investigation. Diels had, he claimed, written to the International Military Tribunal at Nuremberg in 1946 to say that "the German people had a right to demand that the court solve the Reichstag fire." But of course Diels had done more than suggest an investigation; in 1946, as we have seen, he had written that he believed that Heini Gewehr had been the main culprit and that Allied authorities should interrogate him. Nearly three years later Diels no longer wished to push this particular theory. The denazification process, and probably the fate of Heisig in particular, had shown him how dangerous the fire could still be. The idea of van der Lubbe as a sole culprit, with which the Nazis had flirted as the 1933 trial turned sour, now offered a safer path: as in 1933, it could again exonerate men like Diels who had once done the Nazis' will.[49]

TO UNDERSTAND THE MOOD of the West Germany that was emerging in 1949, it helps to know that one of the first bills taken up by its new parliament, the Bundestag, was an amnesty for Nazi crimes: in the biting words of historian Norbert Frei, "the new democracy found nothing more pressing than making things easier for an army of minor and not all that minor Nazi criminals."[50]

West German opinion surveys of the late 1940s and early 1950s fill out the picture. In one case 57 percent of respondents agreed with the proposition that "National Socialism was a good idea that was badly carried out," and 72 percent were willing to say at least something positive about Hitler, with 10 percent agreeing he was "the greatest statesman of this century." On the other hand, former resistance fighters and returning émigrés, even such prominent ones as Marlene Dietrich or the future West Berlin mayor and federal chancellor Willy Brandt, were widely resented, sometimes hated. In a June 1951 survey 30 percent of respondents thought the men of the Valkyrie plot should be "judged negatively"; three years later 24 percent thought surviving resistance fighters should be barred from high office in the West German government.[51]

When it became clear that the Cold War would make impossible any agreement between the Western Allies and the Soviet Union on the shape of a united Germany, France, Britain, and the United States agreed to create a new state from their respective occupation zones. The constitution of the new Federal Republic of Germany was ready in May 1949, and that summer a bitterly contested election—some historians have called it "the last Weimar election" for its ideological extremes—produced a parliament with a Weimar-ish array of eleven parties, ranging from the Communists on the far left to the German Party and the German Conservative Party on the nationalist right. By 31 percent to 29.2 percent the new center-right Christian Democratic Union (with its Bavarian sister party the Christian Social Union) narrowly edged out the venerable Social Democratic Party to form the largest caucus and, with two smaller right wing parties, formed a coalition which (by one parliamentary vote) put the seventy-three-year-old former mayor of Cologne, Konrad Adenauer, into office as West Germany's first chancellor. The new country's capital was in the modest college town of Bonn on the Rhine; the first chancellor's office was in a natural history museum, where visitors reached the mighty Adenauer by ducking under a stuffed giraffe. With little alternative, in October of that year the Soviets responded by creating the German Democratic Republic—East Germany—from their occupation zone.[52]

The economic and political success of the Federal Republic, especially since the dramatic events of 1989–90, has caused us to forget that most West Germans experienced the late 1940s and 1950s as a time of deep insecurity. Fear of political instability reached across the ideological spectrum. Eugen Kogon, a Christian-socialist opponent of the Nazis who had survived six years in the Buchenwald concentration camp, became known after the war as a scholar and editor of the high-brow liberal periodical the *Frankfurter Hefte*. In 1954 Kogon wrote a despairing editorial, "Almost with our Backs to the Wall," complaining about the large numbers of former Nazi civil servants, teachers, prosecutors, and judges who were finding work again. He feared they heralded a full return of Nazi power, and that it might already be necessary to retreat to the "resistance bunker of the spirit."[53]

Yet from near the other end of the political spectrum, Rudolf Diels agreed with Kogon. Just two months after Kogon's editorial Diels complained in a letter about the "united scoundrelhood" that was calling him "a top Nazi" when really he worried only that the Nazis would make a come-back. At the same time, he feared that some day "the Ivans," in other words the Soviets, would "cash in this whole chattering democracy."

Diels thought the only thing to do was to go abroad to escape Nazis and Communists alike. Paraguay was a possibility. He wasn't alone in his frustrations. Heinrich Schnitzler complained how unfair it was to be a public servant when "every ten to twelve years" public servants could count on becoming the "victims" of a political reversal. In his Christmas address to the nation in 1958, Chancellor Adenauer lamented that most living Germans had never known "peace, freedom, and security, a life free from anxiety." In 1959 Otto Schmidt-Hannover, the former DNVP Reichstag caucus leader and friend of Ernst Oberfohren, wrote that Germans were living in a time of crisis, in the "haze of coming atomic catastrophes."[54]

If these dangers—the return of the Nazis, invasion or subversion by Communists, decennial regime change, nuclear war—really lurked everywhere, then the only sensible course was to act as Diels advised: tailor the past to fit the present, and ride out the wave. When he wrote "in our barbaric and briskly changing times, one must be careful in the selection of one's enemies," he was referring not to 1933 but to 1954. Germans of Diels's generation had seen three regime changes in their adult lives; little wonder that many expected a fourth to come soon. The calming effects of the postwar "economic miracle," to say nothing of the dramatic end of the Cold War in 1989–1990, were beyond the horizon, and few Germans in the 1950s could imagine so rosy a future.[55]

The new West Germany was a country in which over six million people had been members of the Nazi Party, while millions more had been a part of organizations affiliated with the Nazis, or had served in one of the police forces of the Third Reich. Of course a large share of adult men had served in the armed forces. Perhaps seven million Germans had lost their lives in the war; inhabitants of most cities had been bombed, and thousands had lost their homes; around thirteen million ethnic Germans from western Poland, Czechoslovakia, Hungary, and Yugoslavia had been forcibly expelled from their homes and arrived as refugees on what was still German territory—mostly in Bavaria and Schleswig-Holstein. The last phase of the war had been undeniably terrible for Germans. Many more were killed in the last ten months than in the preceding fifty-nine; in just the last ninety-eight days 1.4 million German soldiers were killed in action, while on average in 1945 more than a thousand German civilians were killed every day in bombing raids. In the last year of the war, the failing Nazi regime had subtly publicized its massive crimes, thus implicating the general population in them, as a means of heightening fear of allied vengeance were Germany to be defeated. After 1945 Germans who had been victims of the Nazis—primarily Jews, Communists, and other political opponents—were mostly dead, in exile, or (especially in the case of surviving Communists) in East Germany. People who had kept their heads down and tried to get along had always been more numerous, and were only more so at the end of the war.[56]

The reaction of the West German population both to the horrors of war and the guilt of peacetime was therefore the same: most people tried simply to get by and to shelter themselves in a careful, fearful conformity. Probably no election slogan has ever captured the mood of a country like the one on which Adenauer was resoundingly re-elected in 1957: "No Experiments." There was a further, less obvious, corollary of this careful mood, and of the relative numbers of former Nazis and former victims. Historians are often puzzled by the generosity of surviving Jews and anti-Nazis in giving Persil letters to their oppressors—something we have seen here with the letters that Severing and Löbe wrote for Diels and that Ikenberg and Müller wrote for Heisig. But seen in context this is hardly a surprise. As Diels understood, one could never be sure that today's de-nazification defendant might not return as tomorrow's Gauleiter. Go along to get along was the motto; those who nonetheless persisted with incriminating testimony against ex-Nazis had to reckon with shrill accusations that they were nothing but informers or denouncers, and would face exclusion from "respectable" society.[57]

It was in this resentful and uncertain country that the new magazine the *Spiegel* rose to become the most important news outlet, and the already long-running controversy over the Reichstag fire began to take on a new shape.

In late 1946 Rudolf Augstein was a twenty-three-year-old former artillery officer and war correspondent. Since the Allies forbade many older and more experienced journalists from working if they had been too deeply involved in Goebbels's propaganda machine, Augstein easily found a job in Hannover working for a new magazine called *Diese Woche* (This week), which the British military government sponsored. *Diese Woche* immediately demonstrated a good understanding of democracy by fiercely criticizing the occupation authorities who paid for it, and the irritated British cut it loose. In January 1947 the staff started putting out the magazine as the *Spiegel*, with Rudolf Augstein as editor in chief. The *Spiegel* went on to become the most influential news outlet in postwar Germany. Augstein led it until his death in 2002.[58]

The early *Spiegel* was a youthful magazine in all respects. Most of the reporters and editors were too young to have had much memory of the Weimar Republic. They had been stamped by the Nazi regime, especially by time spent in the Hitler Youth and the armed forces, and by the experiences of war, defeat, and occupation. They wrote in a sarcastic "barracks tone," with ample use of military jargon and an obvious familiarity with military subjects. The age of the staff had important consequences for the new magazine's political tone. One of the British officers who stood as its godfather had to explain to Augstein what a labor union was. The *Spiegel* was, in the words of Augstein biographer Peter Merseburger, "rebellious and irreverent," critical of the occupying Allies and of their denazification policies, and of the new Adenauer administration and its focus on integration into the Western military and economic alliances. It was fiercely nationalistic and often anti-Semitic in tone. It voiced "the attitudes, resentments, and prejudices of the defeated or occupied" against what they saw as "victor's justice," the condemnation of German soldiers as war criminals, or the "democratic parties as stooges of the allies."[59]

The *Spiegel*'s nationalistic stance has earned much criticism from left-leaning commentators and historians, who point to the prevalence of former Nazis, including men who had participated in mass shootings and other crimes, among its early reporters and editors. More sympathetic critics argue that it is unrealistic and ahistorical to expect that in postwar Germany the *Spiegel* could have done anything but reflect the prejudices that it did.[60]

Only a few installments of Diels's memoirs had appeared in the magazine when Lower Saxony's press council objected that Diels could not write for the press until his denazification case was resolved. Authorities worried that the series might inspire "Nazi feelings" in its readers, and it could influence Diels's pending hearing (which was no doubt Diels's intention). Augstein responded with typical lack of deference. To suggest the articles could influence the denazification tribunal was an "overestimation of the influence and significance of the *Spiegel*," he wrote. Readers' letters were running strongly against Diels, and the few Nazis who wrote in were more angered by his "betrayal" in expressing anti-Nazis views than they were inspired by his advocacy. The council did not buy the argument, and ordered the magazine to stop the series after the eighth installment or risk losing its license to publish. The *Spiegel* had planned to run twenty installments.[61]

Diels strongly influenced the young Augstein and his magazine in its early years. He admired its independent stance, even as he masked his admiration in condescension to Augstein himself. Augstein, a believer in the "great man" theory of history, was fascinated by anyone who had been close to the Third Reich's center of power. He adopted as his own Diels's new argument that the Night of the Long Knives rather than the Reichstag fire had marked the real beginning of the Third Reich. Augstein's brother Josef was Diels's lawyer through many of his post-war legal battles, including his denazification.[62]

Augstein himself was too independent and skeptical to share all of Diels's ideological fixations, such as his sympathy for West German politicians who were former or neo-Nazis. Yet Augstein employed people like Horst Mahnke, who during the war had been an SS officer and had spent some time with an *Einsatzgruppe*. Mahnke's record was so bad that even the CIA, never notably squeamish about working with ex-Nazis, would not intervene in 1956 to help him visit the United States with a delegation of *Spiegel* staffers, due to what it delicately called his "radical" background. Mahnke's work at the *Spiegel* began in 1950 with an offensively anti-Semitic series on the black market in coffee. He went on to be head of the international section, and was then Bonn correspondent before leaving in 1959 for the Springer weekly *Kristall*. Yet looking back from the 1990s, Augstein insisted that anyone who had lived through the 1950s, "when high- and highest-level Nazis received high- and highest level posts," could not reproach the *Spiegel* for employing people like Mahnke.[63]

The mood of post-war West Germany shaped the emerging narrative of the Reichstag fire in complex ways. On the one hand, there was the reaction that Hans Bernd Gisevius got from the time of Nuremberg on. This "German National traitor," as Schnitzler called him, was a particular target of vitriol for his work with American intelligence during the war and his testimony after it. "'Collaborators' are always in a difficult position," as Gisevius himself wrote with rueful realism in a 1946 letter to Allen Dulles. He thought he would have to lie low for years. Rudolf Pechel, editor of the conservative journal the *Deutsche Rundschau* (German review), wrote in the late 1940s that Gisevius was "possessed by an unbridled craving for recognition," and was none too choosy about his methods of advancement. In 1960 Rudolf Augstein devoted several closely printed pages in the *Spiegel* to a jeremiad against Gisevius, whom he denounced as "the Karl May of the Reichstag Fire"—comparing Gisevius to the hugely popular turn-of-the-century German writer who never visited the American West in which his stories were set. Augstein, like Diels and others who spread the myth of a law-abiding Gestapo of 1933 staffed by principled democrats, nonetheless criticized Gisevius for volunteering to join this "particularly unlovely authority." In 1957 the *Spiegel* reported that Gisevius's advocacy of American military withdrawal from Germany was straining U.S.-German relations. The article gleefully quoted Chancellor Adenauer himself, who said that he would never trust a former Gestapo man like Gisevius.[64]

Augstein's magazine, however, was pleased to trust a good number of former Gestapo men, starting with Diels and continuing with Walter Zirpins, the police officer who had interrogated van der Lubbe.

EVEN IF WALTER ZIRPINS'S CAREER with Diels's political police had been brief, he did not emerge from the war with a record that seemed likely to serve him well in the postwar world.

In early May 1933 Kurt Daluege's office accused him of using a Jewish "agent." Zirpins's immediate superior defended him on the grounds that the person in question was in fact not an agent, "just a good informer." Diels fired him anyway, noting on May 23rd, "On my orders Zirpins is, as of today, no longer active in the Secret State Police."[65]

After the war Zirpins claimed repeatedly that he and Diels had disagreed about the Reichstag fire case. Zirpins, so he said, had fearlessly advocated the view that van der Lubbe was a sole culprit. The more opportunistic Diels had sought to prove the case against other Communist suspects. Diels "finally told me he could not overdraw his credit on my account," Zirpins said in 1951, and this was why Diels had agreed to Zirpins's "transfer." In the 1950s, when it was expedient to deny having wanted to be in the Gestapo, Zirpins claimed that this "transfer" had come "at my own wish," although the contemporary record clearly shows otherwise.[66]

Zirpins spent most of the 1930s as an instructor at the Berlin Police Institute in Charlottenburg. Eventually he found his way to Reinhard Heydrich's Reich Security Main Office (RSHA). In the spring of 1940 Zirpins was sent to command the criminal police in Litzmannstadt, the city formerly known as Lodz in the country formerly known as Poland. "Litzmannstadt" was in what the German now called the "Gau Wartheland," territory of the former Poland that was annexed to Germany and was to be

"Germanized" in an enormous ethnic cleansing operation. The Nazis sent around twenty thousand ethnic Germans to live there, while deporting tens of thousands of Jews and Poles to the General Government, the non-annexed segment of German-occupied Poland. But in April 1940 the Nazis also sealed 162,000 Jews into the newly created Lodz Ghetto. On April 30th an order of the Lodz police chief forbade inhabitants of the Ghetto to leave it, and on May 10th another order authorized police officers to shoot any Ghetto inhabitant trying to escape.[67]

"Not just its economic life, but the city's whole existence was con-trolled by the Jews," one Nazi observer wrote of Lodz before the building of the Ghetto—"which was reflected to an appalling degree on the streets." A look at the residential areas in the north of the city, where the Jews tended to live and which later became the site of the Ghetto, demon-strated their "complete lack of will to contribute to building up the city." The houses were dilapidated and "covered, like their owners, in filth, bugs and other vermin." The stench, said the observer, was overwhelming and "presses one's lungs." The creation of the Ghetto was primarily a public-health measure, to keep the city free from the epidemics of cholera, typhus, and dysentery, which the Jews' unsanitary conditions had caused. But the Ghetto also served the "Germanization" of the city, and "through the formation of the Ghetto the mobilization of Jewry for work that serves the community has been achieved." The author of this report, entitled "The Ghetto in Litzmannstadt from a Criminalistic Perspective," from a journal edited by Reinhard Heydrich, was the police commander, SS-*Sturmbannführer* Walter Zirpins.[68]

The Nazis had needed brutal violence to force the Jews of Lodz into the ghetto, resulting in the deaths of hundreds (Zirpins wrote that the Jews' willingness to contravene police regulations proved how little they cared about the authorities' orders). Once in the ghetto its inhabitants suffered from extreme overcrowding, disease, and malnutrition. Condi-tions grew increasingly desperate; according to the Nazis' own figures, 43,441 people died in the ghetto between 1940 and 1944, *not* counting those whom the Nazis deported to the death camps; figures collected by the Ghetto's (Jewish) internal management showed that in the seven-month stretch from June 16, 1940 to January 31 1941, and thus while Zirpins was in charge of the Lodz criminal police, there were 7,383 deaths (Zirpins wrote that "the Jews in the Ghetto are naturally not subject to especially opulent living conditions").[69]

The job of the criminal police in Lodz was to enforce this regime of imprisonment, slave labor, expropriation, and slow starvation. Contemporary records, and even his own article, show that Zirpins was directly involved in the least savory tasks and was willing to explain them with the most offensive Nazi anti-Semitic rhetoric. He described the Jews as "uniformly flatfooted kaftan-wearers." The Ghetto amounted to a "herding together of criminals, racketeers, usurers, and swindlers." The innately Jewish quality of deceitfulness made Jews well suited to be informers; even the stereotype of Jews as secretly powerful string pullers made an appearance in Zirpins's writing. "The Jews have fine schnozzes for finding out when two authorities or officials do not get along particularly well," he wrote. They were good at stirring up trouble. Nonetheless, although Ghetto police work was demanding, Zirpins concluded by saying that because of its novelty, it was "above all professionally rewarding," even "satisfying."[70]

After 1945 Zirpins tried to deny or at least minimize the worst aspects of his wartime record. Seeking reinstatement in the civil service in 1947 he claimed that he had never become a Nazi Party member; that he was given an SS rank only as an arbitrary official measure in 1939; and that he had never belonged to the SD. Actually, he had applied for Party membership but was turned down because of a hold on new admissions; he applied to join the SS in 1937; and he belonged to the SD. Nonetheless, the tribunal judging his record with the SS placed him among the "good Germans" of Category V.[71]

Still, Zirpins had problems returning to police work. After two years' internment by the British, he made his living in the late 1940s in Hamburg first as a chemical salesman and then as an accountant and expert on white-collar crime, appearing frequently as a witness in the Hamburg courts. In 1947 he applied to lead the State Police Office in Hannover. British authorities told him flatly that there was "no possibility" of his employment with the police in their zone. Zirpins later claimed that he withdrew his candidacy because "the time appeared not yet ripe, although as a non–Party member I could certainly have carried the day." At the end of 1950 the State Criminal Office of Lower Saxony wanted to hire him to teach—of all things—a course on the investigation of arson. But the Interior Ministry objected.[72]

This was where publicity could play a role. In March 1951 the *Spiegel* ran an article on West Germany's emerging Federal Criminal Police

Office (BKA), meant to be the West German analog of the old Reich Criminal Police Office (or RKPA, which, under Arthur Nebe, had formed Office V of the RSHA alongside the Gestapo and the SD). The author was one Bernhard Wehner, a former police official who had joined the SA and the Nazi Party in 1931, but emerged after the war as one of the inventors and popularizers of the idea that the German criminal police had always been both highly professional and entirely apolitical (read: non-Nazi). In 1949 Wehner had published a long series of articles in the *Spiegel* making exactly this point. Nazi Germany's RKPA had been "unparalleled" (*einmalig*), Wehner wrote. But now, because of the denazification process, "the elite of proven German criminalists are on welfare or live from temporary allowances (*Wartegeld*)." One of Wehner's star examples was Walter Zirpins, a "non-Party member" from the Charlottenburg Police Institute, whom the Nazis had retained only because of the "special capabilities" he had demonstrated in Weimar days. In 1939 Zirpins had become an SS-*Hauptsturmführer* "honoris causa." Otherwise his bio read: "Last leader of the Hamburg Kripo [the common German acronym for the criminal police], instructor in criminology and criminalistics at Prague University, consultant for Kripo training, editor of textbooks, member of the IKPK [the forerunner of Interpol]. Today an expert on economic criminality." There was no mention of Lodz.[73]

Yet the BKA still would not take Zirpins, despite the fact that almost half of its senior officers had themselves been involved in Nazi crimes. Finally, in October 1951 the Interior Ministry of Lower Saxony offered Zirpins the directorship of its criminal police. Earlier Zirpins had refused an offer of the same job at a lower pay grade, because, as he put it, "regrettably, the state has most emphatically taught me that one acts suicidally when one acts out of mere idealism." The "bitter times since 1945"—the years before that were apparently just fine—"force me only to [help] where this does not come too much at my cost."[74]

After taking the job in Lower Saxony Zirpins scored an immediate public triumph when an investigation under his leadership caught a man named Erich von Halacz, who had set off bombs in several north German towns. West German Federal President Theodor Heuss and the federal and Lower Saxon interior ministers sent their formal congratulations. Zirpins himself wrote about the case for the *Spiegel*, under the triumphant title "We Got Halacz." Zirpins struck a tone remarkably similar to Schnitzler's pieces on the Reichstag fire two years earlier, even in some cases using

the same phrases: like Schnitzler, Zirpins wrote of long-suffering but dedicated police officers, whose efficiency was constantly challenged by irresponsible public opinion and treacherous political currents. For eight days
during the investigation Zirpins had slept by the phone on an old army
cot; in four days he had managed only eight hours of sleep. "It was no
different for my staff."

These heroic police officers had to contend with a rumor that the bomb
attacks were politically motivated. "The right accused the left and the left
the right," said Zirpins. He found himself, he said, fleeing from reporters
and shunning publicity. "From my presence the press would presumably
have jumped to speculations that I would have gladly avoided." What
sort of speculations? Some articles mentioned, he said, "that I had earlier
been involved in solving the Reichstag fire." Zirpins maintained that his
interest in that fire had been purely "criminalistic," and he wanted to
declare "officially" that "the Reichstag arsonist van der Lubbe was just as
much a single culprit as von Halacz." How did Zirpins know? Halacz,
like van der Lubbe, had confessed. "There were no political accomplices."
He added: "I was glad about that."[75]

Even Zirpins's old colleague and advocate Bernhard Wehner thought
it had been a bad idea for Zirpins to say that Halacz had been a sole
culprit just like van der Lubbe. "I would either not have mentioned it,"
Wehner wrote at the time to Fritz Tobias, or would not "have just glossed
over the historical fact that the Reichstag fire probably was a bit different"
than Halacz's crimes.[76]

Wehner's view proved prescient. Shortly afterward a commentator on
Bavarian State Radio complained that Zirpins, who had been responsible
for hushing up a Nazi crime in 1933, was at it again. Outraged, Zirpins
wrote demanding a retraction—and at the same time sought to distance
himself from the investigation of the Reichstag fire. "I only carried out
the first interrogation of van der Lubbe, and after the conclusion of this
purely criminalistic task, my work was already over after three days." He
hadn't belonged to the commission Göring set up to investigate, and had
had nothing whatever to do with the political investigation that followed.
Zirpins forwarded a copy of this letter to Fritz Tobias.[77]

Just as senior officials were congratulating Zirpins for the arrest of
Halacz, they discovered his articles on the Lodz Ghetto. The Lower Saxon
cabinet considered firing Zirpins, but decided not to in light of "miti-
gating circumstances," which the surviving documents do not illuminate.

For Zirpins this was a powerful reminder, and not the last, of how dangerous his past could be. There are also hints that this controversy brought Zirpins and Fritz Tobias together, and that Tobias may have intervened quietly in the Interior Ministry to help save Zirpins's job. In 1960 Tobias wrote to Zirpins of "my basic attitude to you, which you should especially have gotten to know in certain critical times." Another letter a month later warned Zirpins of some coming bad publicity, "which for you—and also a little for me and others in looking back at the year 1952—is connected with the word 'Litzmannstadt.'"[78]

Zirpins learned to keep quiet about the Reichstag fire. A few years later, when Reichstag fire researcher Richard Wolff wrote to him for information on the case, Zirpins replied, "In view of the political experiences I have had in the van der Lubbe case, I regret that I must refrain from giving any statement." Zirpins was still trying to maintain this silence in late 1957 when reporters provoked a conflict between Zirpins's desire to stay silent and his strategy of shifting the blame for the politicization of the Reichstag fire case onto Diels.[79]

In November 1957, a friend told Diels that Zirpins was saying in interviews that at key moments Zirpins had objected to the conduct of the Reichstag fire investigations, and Diels had responded "please think of my career." Diels's resultant rage provoked him to a candid statement about what motivated his accounts of the early Gestapo. "Since 1945," he wrote Zirpins, "I have taken every opportunity to stand up for the colleagues who worked under me in 1933," and offered confirmation for all who asked that they had worked for the Gestapo only "under 'compulsion,'" a line of defense in the denazification tribunals. "In no single case have I incriminated a former official or even named him as a witness, when it was a matter of exculpation of my person against various, mostly foolish, accusations." Zirpins was the only one, said Diels, who had not responded loyally.

An emollient reply from Zirpins resolved this collegial quarrel. But it revealed that after more than a decade of denazification and rehabilitation, the Reichstag fire could still frighten these ex-Gestapo men. Diels wrote that he had neither "a well-founded knowledge nor a strong opinion" about the Reichstag fire, contrary to the "foolish idea" that he was "always forced to hear from journalists and historians" that he was the "only living person" who had "seen the 'background.'" He wanted to ask the Reich (*sic*) minister of the interior to commission an investigation of the case.

But "I would also thereby avoid naming any names," he added—which he seemed to mean as comfort to the publicity-shy Zirpins. Zirpins excused his earlier remarks by explaining that Diels's friend had threatened him with revelations of "certain events in the Warsaw Ghetto or Lodz." "You will understand," said Zirpins, "that such a situation could only outrage me to the greatest extent."

Diels had also written: "I fear in any case that the methods of a Herr Tobias, who by all accounts approaches the interpretation of the documentary material, which is certainly available to him as an official, with monomaniacal self-satisfaction, will only hurt the elucidation of the case."[80]

This was a note of something new. Fritz Tobias had served on a denazification tribunal in Hannover in the late 1940s; upon entering the Lower Saxon Interior Ministry he became a patron of such former Nazi police officers as Wehner and Zirpins—although, he said, Diels "kept out of my way." In the mid-1950s he entered the story of the Reichstag fire, and would dominate it for nearly six decades.

9

. . . .

"THE FEARED ONE"

FRITZ TOBIAS AND HIS "CLIENTS"

THERE WAS SOMETHING VERY AMERICAN about Fritz Tobias. He was self-made and self-reliant, regarding authority with suspicion and treating received wisdom with disdain. In the United States men like Tobias tinker with inventions in the garage, or fill web pages with arcana about the Kennedy assassination (actually a major preoccupation for him as well) or UFOs or climate change (in which Tobias did not believe). As a German of the wartime generation he became obsessed with the Reichstag fire. And he came to haunt it, no less than Diels, Goring, Gisevius, or the cipher at its core, Marinus van der Lubbe. For more than a half-century Tobias's account of the fire has been the dominant narrative.[1]

Fritz Tobias was born in Berlin in 1912. His father, Martin, was a porcelain painter. Tobias's mother died in early 1919 and Martin came back from the First World War suffering the effects of wounds. The older brothers left the house as soon as they could, leaving Fritz as the target of his father's ambitions. On Sundays Martin Tobias would drag him along to Berlin museums and art galleries, awakening Fritz's interest in science, art, and history. He became "an insatiable bookworm" who did well enough in school to be admitted to a *Gymnasium*, an academic high school for the university-bound, through a special program for the gifted off-spring of poorer families. In 1926, however, Martin Tobias moved to Hannover to take a job helping to found a new union. There Fritz was put into a vocational high school (*Oberrealschule*) rather than a *Gymnasium*, and was glad to leave school at his first opportunity for an apprenticeship in a Social Democratic bookstore.[2]

That was where he was working on April 1, 1933, when an SS squad seized the bookstore. The SS men fired through the windows and lined the staff up against the wall. "We didn't know what was going to happen," said Tobias later with some considerable understatement. The Nazis closed down the bookstore and Tobias was out of a job. He went to a business college and learned typing and shorthand, skills that, as it turned out, would serve him well in myriad ways. He worked in a lawyer's office in Hannover until the outbreak of the Second World War (the lawyer, he said, was a very decent man, proving in reverse the adage that a good lawyer must necessarily be a bad person).

At the start of the war Tobias was drafted into the army. Here, too, he did clerical jobs, in the Netherlands, Russia, and finally Italy, where he ended up as a prisoner of the Americans after being seriously wounded. He was treated in an American hospital and given blood transfusions. "Maybe I have black blood now," he said in a 2009 interview. In the army he was promoted rapidly, although he never asked for any such thing. "If all German soldiers had been as efficient as I was," he said in the same interview, "we would have won the war."

After the war he ran into Otto Brenner, one of the most important of German labor leaders, for many years the chairman of the huge union IG Metall. Brenner had been a customer in Tobias's bookstore before 1933 and remembered him with respect. Brenner brought Tobias into the Head Denazification Committee for Hannover, where he eventually became the deputy chair. This job would have involved Tobias in the denazification of important people in Hannover, including Diels, or at least allowed him to get information about their cases—which would turn out to be very important in Tobias's later role as a historical researcher.

Again, Tobias's superiors kept promoting him. He rose to be a division leader (*Abteilungsleiter*) in the Lower Saxon Ministry for Denazification. His supervisor asked him if he wanted to rise to the next rank and become a government counselor (*Regierungsrat*), which might be called the lowest rank of the senior positions in a German ministry. Tobias says he was not enthusiastic about this prospect, and looked into the question of what kind of pension a government counselor got. When he learned the answer he signed on, and eventually he rose to the very senior position of ministerial counselor (*Ministerialrat*) in the Office for Constitutional Protection.[3]

His was, by any measure, a post-war German success story. Even by the early 1950s Tobias had become an influential figure in Hannover. One of the old Nazis whose denazification case Tobias handled was Bernhard Wehner, the man who wrote about police issues for the *Spiegel*. "Who would have thought," Wehner wrote to Tobias in early 1951, "that I would exchange such lines with the 'Feared One' from Hannover's Ministry of the Interior."[4]

Wehner and Walter Zirpins, the two most important post-war promoters of a sanitized version of the history of the German criminal police, also became Tobias's protégés in the early 1950s, in Wehner's case even as Tobias worked on his denazification. Tobias seemed to have had a special soft spot for former Nazi policemen, and played a critical role in helping them return to their careers after the lean years of detention and denazification. In return, it seems, he adopted their view of recent history.[5]

After the war Bernhard Wehner was investigated, though never prosecuted, for war crimes. He had joined both the Nazi Party and the SA in 1931 and the SS in 1940. In a letter to Tobias of July 21, 1951, Wehner remembered how seven years earlier he had stood in front of the "genius of the thousand-year Reich"—Hitler—to report on Count Claus von Stauffenberg's assassination attempt the day before. Wehner wondered what would have happened to him after the war if he had had to identify a still-living Stauffenberg as the would-be assassin. "Perhaps it is not always a misfortune to come too late."

All of this information on Wehner comes from Tobias's own file, and none of it suggests that Wehner was anything other than a convinced Nazi who would gladly have sent Stauffenberg to the gallows. Indeed, in one installment of his *Spiegel* series on the criminal police, Wehner relayed how Hitler had asked him if it were not a miracle that he had survived Stauffenberg's attack. Wehner obliged: "Yes, my Führer, it is a miracle." Yet, seven years later, Tobias tried to arrange a police job for Wehner in Lower Saxony, and when that did not work out, used connections to win him an appointment as chief of the criminal police in Dortmund (where Wehner became, among other things, the boss of Reichstag fire detective

Rudolf Braschwitz). Wehner recalled the "decency and humanity" Tobias had shown him. "My family and I owe our livelihood mostly to you."[6]

In 1950 the *Spiegel* commissioned Wehner to investigate allegations of corruption in the police department of the Lower Saxon Interior Ministry. Wehner's research, although never actually published in the *Spiegel*, provided evidence for the prosecution and dismissal of the head of the criminal police department, whose replacement was none other than Walter Zirpins. Tobias seems to have lurked in the background of all of this, pulling strings. Wehner kept him fully informed about the investigation, and there were rumors later that Tobias's intrigues got Zirpins his job. When Zirpins scored his triumph in the Halacz investigation, Wehner wrote Tobias "Dear God how I envied Zirpins . . . Without the '45 collapse that would have been *ipso facto* my job."[7]

Why exactly Tobias, who was nominally a Social Democrat, developed such a protective fondness for Nazi police officers remains unclear. That it proved crucial for the Reichstag fire controversy, however, is certain. Still, Tobias might not have emerged as the central player in the Reichstag fire controversy had it not been for a chain of events beginning with efforts to re-open the Reichstag fire trial in 1955.

IN 1954, A LAWYER NAMED ARTHUR BRANDT decided to return to Berlin. Brandt had begun practicing law there in 1921 and was involved in some of the most famous trials of Weimar Berlin, including the so-called Cheka trial of a number of Communist agents in which Paul Vogt, later the examining magistrate in the Reichstag fire trial, did the judicial investigations. Like most left-leaning and Jewish lawyers, Brandt was in mortal danger when the Nazis came to power. He fled to Switzerland the day after the Reichstag fire, found his way to America, became an American citizen, and qualified for the bars of New York and Massachusetts (after an interval producing figure-skating performances and getting his daughters to appear in films with skating legend and movie star Sonja Henie).[8]

Brandt returned to Berlin with the intention of specializing in restitution cases for victims of Nazism. One of his first cases came from Johannes Marcus van der Lubbe, Marinus's older brother, who asked Brandt to take up Marinus's rehabilitation. In 1951 the government of West Berlin had passed a law, known as the WGG, for "Restitution for National Socialist injustice." The WGG allowed victims (or their survivors) to apply to overturn judicial verdicts that had been based on laws serving the "strengthening of National Socialism" or "National Socialist ideas," or on "racial, religious, or political grounds." The point was that only the actions of the Nazi *court* mattered, not those of the prisoner. Even a guilty prisoner was entitled to restitution and rehabilitation if the verdict had been a "Nazi" one in the ways the law specified.[9]

Marinus van der Lubbe, executed in a highly political trial on the basis of a Nazi law passed retroactively against him, should have fitted these terms perfectly. The law did not require evidence of his innocence, in other words evidence that someone else had burned the Reichstag. As Brandt argued in one of his briefs to the court, there could hardly be any doubt that the judgment condemning van der Lubbe to death had "served the strengthening of National Socialism" and that it was reached on "political grounds."[10]

But West Berlin courts of the 1950s sometimes interpreted the law in surprising ways, demonstrating just how hard it was for victims of Nazism to get their claims recognized in postwar Germany. The Berlin Court of Appeals ruled in 1956, for example, that the heavy tax imposed on Jews who left Germany after 1933 was not one of those laws which "strengthened National Socialism," nor was it a product of Nazi ideology. Similarly, the "pulpit paragraph," under which the regime could punish dissident clergymen, did not amount to Nazi injustice because such provisions had existed in German law before the Nazis. The same point applied to Nazi persecution of gay men.[11]

When Brandt submitted his petition to overturn the Reich Supreme Court verdict at the end of September 1955, the press took immediate notice. Brandt's petition set off a chain of actions and reactions that amounted to a rebirth of controversy over the Reichstag fire. Most of the important subsequent events in the controversy were direct or indirect products of Brandt's case.[12]

First came Cold War paranoia. Two days after Brandt had submitted his petition, the West German embassy in the Hague cabled the Foreign Office in Bonn to inform officials that from a newspaper interview with J.M. van der Lubbe it seemed that the initiative for the retrial application came from an "unnamed mysterious go-between, who will also take on costs." This mysterious go-between had apparently contacted J.M. van der Lubbe six weeks earlier. However, the embassy thought that Brandt's preparations for the trial had already been going on for a year, and reported that J.M. van der Lubbe had emphatically denied that Communists were behind the retrial application—exactly what the embassy meant to imply by "unnamed mysterious go-between."[13]

Although Brandt only needed to show that the Reich Supreme Court had condemned van der Lubbe for purely political reasons or on the basis of Nazi laws, as lawyers often do he "argued in the alternative": the Nazis had also executed van der Lubbe, Brandt claimed, for a crime he had not actually committed. With this argument Brandt began to be drawn into the search for answers to the Reichstag fire mystery.[14]

Brandt claimed he was approached by a young man who declared himself a former stormtrooper. This man told him that van der Lubbe had been nothing but a stooge of the SA; the witness himself had brought van der Lubbe into the already-burning Reichstag through a side-entrance. Although Brandt recorded the man's evidence in a notarized statement, he felt he could not use it for the litigation, as the former SA man was convinced that he would be killed were Brandt to make his name public. Nonetheless Brandt used the man's information in his arguments to the court, without naming the source.[15]

"I heard it from an SA man" had been the classic trope of unreliable Reichstag fire stories from the *Brown Book* on. Such a man probably approached Brandt and probably made a statement along the lines that Brandt claimed. Brandt's reputation for integrity was such (he was "a man of honor," as Berlin lawyer and historian of the bar Gerhard Jungfer put it to me) that he deserves the benefit of the doubt. Furthermore, in the 1990s Brandt's daughter Helga still remembered being with her father when he met the putative SA man. Gisevius claimed to have heard a tape recording of the man's statement.[16]

But of course this does not mean the statement was true. Because of Brandt's discretion we do not know who the SA man was. He could have been lying for any number of reasons. There is no trace of the notarized statement today, and the Local Court (*Amtsgericht*) in Bremerhaven, where the statement was apparently taken and where it would then have to be archived, informed me that it could not be located without knowing its number. There are also factual reasons to be skeptical. Van der Lubbe could not have been smuggled into the Reichstag when the building was already visibly burning; by that time Scranowitz and Poeschel had already arrested him.[17]

Nonetheless Brandt believed the story, and it inspired him to keep going for more than a decade with van der Lubbe's case. The application under Berlin's WGG moved forward slowly (the prosecutor complained that this was because Brandt had spent too much time in America and kept trying to get an oral hearing, instead of relying on documents in the German manner). But the case also began to acquire its own momentum. Neither Brandt nor the prosecutor seemed able to resist the lure of re-opening the question of who set the fire. Both made an effort to iden- tify witnesses and take statements from them.[18]

Many witnesses were still alive. Magistrate Paul Vogt, Brandt's old adversary from Weimar days, gave a statement insisting that Hitler's regime had not tried to influence his investigations and that the case had unfolded entirely in accordance with the law. An administrative judge named Alois Eugen Becker came forward after he saw an article in the newspaper the *Frankfurter Rundschau* (Frankfurt review) in which people who might have been expected to have information about the fire denied all knowledge. Becker had been a political police official in 1933 under Diels. He testified that in mid-February a meeting took place at which the terms of the future Reichstag Fire Decree were discussed. Beyond that he knew little that was concrete, though he did say that there had been rumors around the Gestapo headquarters in Berlin concerning Nazi in- volvement in the fire, and that the detectives working on the case had told him that van der Lubbe could not have done it alone. Becker reported that Diels's remarks the morning after the fire had been "as usual somewhat cynical, without being in any way definite."[19]

The most important witness was Diels himself, who gave a deposition in early 1957. By this point Diels had brought evasion to a high art. "I cannot testify here to more on the case of van der Lubbe than I explained in my book," he said. He did not deny Becker's evidence, claiming only that he could barely remember Becker. He repeated his claim that his knowledge of the case was limited because Göring had cut him out of the investigation.

He continued with a virtuoso display of sinuous negation. "I have ab- solutely considered the idea that the SA could have set fire on the Reich- stag not to be impossible," he said. "On the other hand, I was then, and am now, of the view that the assumption that van der Lubbe absolutely could not have set fire to the Reichstag alone is erroneous." Van der Lubbe had been "a pathological arsonist" who was "well supplied with incen- diary materials." After speaking with van der Lubbe, Diels had become convinced that the suspect had set the fire alone. "That on the other hand later I did not close my mind to the rumors about the involvement of the SA had nothing to do with this, my original opinion." He did not elaborate. It was a skillful performance, creating the impression that he himself was not directly involved and could treat the whole subject with intellectual detachment.[20]

Brandt used the press to bring the Reichstag fire back into the court of public opinion. Apparently at Brandt's urging, in late 1957 the journalist Curt Riess wrote a series of articles on the fire for the magazine *Stern*. Similar series ran in other illustrated weeklies. Riess's series (written under the pseudonym Peter Brandes, which means roughly "Peter of the fire") was based on what information was available in 1957, which was in fact very little. His account was indebted to such dubious sources as the *Brown Book*, the *White Book*, and Diels's memoirs, alongside contemporary newspaper accounts. Nonetheless Riess also interviewed people who might have had information on the fire. And back around came Diels. What Diels told Riess—as well as what he said to two other reporters at approximately the same time—constituted the most valuable part of these articles, although it would still be a few years before full details of what Diels had said, and *that* he had said it, became public. Riess accepted Diels's version of how he and other "brave police officers" had fought against the violence of the SA. Goebbels had been the main inspiration for the fire. Karl Ernst had been in charge of the operation, and in turn Ernst had delegated its execution to Heini Gewehr.[21]

In May 1958 the Berlin Superior Court dismissed Brandt's case on a technicality: he and J.M. van der Lubbe had missed the deadline for filing the claim. In 1965, however, a change in the laws allowed Brandt and van der Lubbe to revive the case and bring it once again before the Berlin Superior Court. This time the prosecution sided with Brandt. The court was not so easily won over, however, and the result was the kind of verdict that leaves nonlawyers scratching their heads. On April 21, 1967, the Superior Court acquitted van der Lubbe of attempted high treason and seditious arson, but substituted a verdict of conviction for arson endangering life. Thirty-three years after his execution, the court converted van der Lubbe's death sentence to eight years in a penitentiary.[22]

After this Robert Kempner took over the case from Brandt. Kempner made determined efforts, lasting into the early 1980s, to get a German court to overturn the conviction completely. These efforts succeeded briefly in the Berlin Superior Court in December 1980. But in 1981 the

Court of Appeals overturned this decision, again on technical grounds, and thereafter the case bogged down in the issue of exactly which court had jurisdiction, without producing any important new evidence.[23]

After almost thirty years of renewed litigation, decades after the original crime, the legal result for the van der Lubbe family had been underwhelming. But the effects on the emerging Reichstag fire controversy were considerable.

FRITZ TOBIAS'S HISTORICAL GRAND THEORY was that most things happen by mistake or by accident, and he applied the same reasoning to his own life as well, as did others: Rudolf Augstein described him as "the amateur researcher who set out to prove the guilt of the Nazi leaders" only to come up with proof of "their noninvolvement."[24]

Documents from the *Spiegel*'s archives show that Tobias was in touch with the magazine as early as March 1956, though the negotiations for commissioning articles based upon his research did not get serious until November 1957. The timing is not a coincidence, for this was precisely when the weeklies *Stern* and *Weltbild* were running their series on the Reichstag fire, at Arthur Brandt's urging and to support his case on behalf of the van der Lubbe family. Tobias himself said in 2008 that the *Spiegel* had become interested in his work, after rejecting it a few years before, only following the appearance of the other series.[25]

Testifying in 1961, Tobias claimed that his research into the fire was finished by 1957, and that State Advocate Dobbert, the Berlin prosecutor who was Brandt's opponent in the van der Lubbe case, put him in touch with the *Spiegel*. In a short bio written around the same time, Tobias said that Dobbert had referred the *Spiegel*'s Berlin correspondent to "the Reichstag fire specialist in Hannover." Dobbert, like Brandt, knew how to use the press to advance his case, and Tobias was his chosen instrument. In early 1958 Tobias and the *Spiegel* agreed that Tobias's materials would appear in the magazine as a series. Tobias kept Dobbert informed of how the work was progressing. In mid-1958 he promised Dobbert that he would "very much enjoy" the series, for both professional and nonprofessional reasons. Dobbert helped Tobias in turn by sending him microfilm rolls of original documents in the possession of the Berlin prosecutor's office, which were then unavailable to the public.[26]

The *Spiegel*'s editors felt that Tobias's writing needed some punching up to be print-ready. They assigned one Dr. Paul Karl Schmidt, a journalist and popular history writer, to be his ghostwriter. Schmidt wrote under various pseudonyms, of which the best-known was Paul Carell (under which name his book *Hitler Moves East* was also published in English). He worked slowly on the project through 1958, delaying the planned appearance of the story. But his involvement in the project raised more serious issues as well.[27]

Schmidt was yet another *Spiegel* writer with a troubling record from the Nazi years. He had been the press secretary in Joachim von Ribbentrop's Foreign Office. In May 1944, when the Nazis were about to deport Jews from Budapest to the death camps, Schmidt sent a memo to a senior Foreign Office official warning that this "planned action" would attract considerable attention abroad. "The opponents will cry out and speak of persecution (*Menschenjagd*)" in order to use such "atrocity stories" to "try to whip up their own feelings and also those of neutral countries." To prevent this, Schmidt proposed that explosives be planted and then discovered in the buildings of Jewish societies and synagogues, and that evidence be fabricated that they were trying to undermine the Hungarian currency. "The cornerstone of such an action," wrote Schmidt, "has to be a particularly crass case, on which one can then hang the great crackdown." As Bahar and Kugel have written, it is a particularly piquant irony that the *Spiegel* should have assigned the polishing and recasting of Tobias's prose to a man who had advocated the creation of false pretexts for Nazi crimes. Historian Christina von Hodenberg has written that Schmidt was a central figure in a network of journalists who were former members of the Foreign Ministry's propaganda office, and who after the war brought a distinctly far-right—even "under-cover Nazi"—tone to much of the West German press.[28]

Tobias said that he met Schmidt at the *Spiegel* offices in early 1957. "I did not work with him more closely," he testified in 1961. "He simply produced a compressed version of my manuscript." By 1961 Tobias had good reason to distance himself from Schmidt, and he maintained he had not known Schmidt earlier and had had nothing to do with the *Spiegel* retaining him to work on the manuscript. "I did not know at the time," Tobias's testimony continued, "that Dr. Schmidt was supposed to have been . . . an especially fanatical and dangerous National Socialist."[29]

Actually, Tobias may have known Schmidt much earlier. He told a former *Spiegel* reporter in 1996 that he had referred Schmidt to the *Spiegel* in the first place. Schmidt's role as ghostwriter had been a term of the contract between Tobias and the *Spiegel*, which also suggests that Tobias may have had some influence in Schmidt's selection. In April 1958, just after this collaboration began, Tobias wrote, "Schmidt was a good Nazi and an especially dangerous one, because he was certainly capable and useful," making almost exactly the point that, under oath three years later, he denied ever having known. Tobias had made his own enquiries about Schmidt. In his papers there is a copy of Schmidt's 1944 memo about the Hungarian Jews, although it is not clear when he acquired it.[30]

In 1958 Tobias showed no sign of concern about Schmidt's past. When a Social Democratic friend warned him about Schmidt's record, Tobias wondered if his friend wanted "to exclude them all," adding all that mattered was "how [Schmidt] writes today." And there he defended Schmidt's practice of writing about German war experiences with words like "heroic," and saw nothing wrong with a Schmidt article that equated the Nuremberg prosecutions both to Stalin's show trials and to the Reichstag fire proceedings. Tobias himself later wrote that in Nuremberg Hermann Göring "imitated with astonishing success" the starring courtroom role that Dimitrov had played thirteen years earlier. By 1969, though, Tobias was taking a different tone, complaining to Rudolf Augstein of "my permanent 'incrimination' through the person of your former employee Dr. P.K. Schmidt."[31]

The delays in publishing Tobias's *Spiegel* series, especially through 1958, were a source of constant frustration for Tobias. In the spring of 1959, however, the pace picked up. The *Spiegel* took Schmidt off the project and reassigned it to Gunther Zacharias, who worked faster. The articles began appearing in October. It may be that Tobias's relationship with his police protégés—or, as he called them, his "clients"—contributed to a greater sense of urgency.

IN 1958, IN THE SOUTH GERMAN CITY of Ulm, a major prosecution of members of an *Einsatzgruppe* for mass shootings in Lithuania in 1941 developed almost accidentally out of a routine civil action launched by the former SS-*Oberführer* Bernhard Fischer-Schweder. The prosecutor in the case against Fischer-Schweder was a man named Erwin Schüle, who, with the aid of captured Nazi records gathered in the American-run Berlin Document Center, was able to reconstruct the crimes with a high degree of precision, and secure long prison sentences again the main defendants. The Ulm trial suggested just how many Nazi crimes remained undiscovered and unavenged long after the war, and how extensively police and judicial authorities sheltered incriminated colleagues from prosecution. Schüle grew deeply worried about the rule of law in West Germany. On May 8, 1960, the limitation period for prosecuting all Nazi crimes short of first-degree murder (thus including second-degree murder and manslaughter) would run out. In the face of an East German propaganda campaign exposing ex-Nazis in West German justice, it became politically essential to speed up the pace of investigations.[32]

The result, in the fall of 1958, was the creation of a new authority with a cumbersome name: the Central Office of the State Justice Ministries for the Investigation of National Socialist Crimes (*Zentralstelle der Landesjustizverwaltungen zur Aufklärung nationalsozialistischer Verbrechen*). The Central Office was based in Ludwigsburg, a suburb of Stuttgart. Erwin Schüle became its first director.

West German society was changing at the end of the 1950s, and the earlier reluctance to deal with Nazi crimes was beginning to diminish. In part this was a reaction to the increasingly apparent stabilization of the Federal Republic: it was becoming clear that Bonn was not Weimar, and with the threat of Nazi resurgence beginning to fade, justice was becoming a more affordable luxury. The knowledge and stimulus to thought which the Ulm trial provided was also a factor, especially as other sensational Nazi trials followed: the Eichmann trial in 1961 and, between 1963 and 1965, a massive trial in Frankfurt of personnel from Auschwitz. One historian has written that the Auschwitz trial marked the end of a period in which the interests of Nazi criminals greatly determined the politics of the Federal Republic. In 2008 the Institute for Contemporary History in Munich reported that between 1945 and 1958 West German authorities had investigated 52,083 persons for Nazi crimes, while for the period 1959 to 2005 the number was 120,211. In fact almost half of all convictions of Nazi criminals in West Germany between 1946 and 1965 came in the first half of the 1960s, while for most of the 1950s the number of investigations had dropped to almost nil. The renewed prosecutorial energy of the late 1950s was in every way distinct from the denazification of a decade and more earlier. No occupier mandated this new wave (West Germany had become fully sovereign in 1955); Ludwigsburg's cases were criminal investigations traditional in form and potential consequences, rather than, like denazification, an administrative purge with pedagogic elements.[33]

West German police forces were very aware that a conspicuous number of Ludwigsburg investigations involved their own officers, many of whom were in prominent positions. Recent research on the fates of Gestapo officers after 1945 has highlighted that the year 1959 marked a real caesura in their lives, as Ludwigsburg rushed to launch investigations before the May 1960 deadline. Paul Dickopf, who became president of the Federal Criminal Police Office (BKA) in 1965 but had long before been its "grey eminence," complained to American intelligence officers in the summer of 1960 that the Central Office had become known among his colleagues as the "Office for the Prosecution of Police Officers." The police, he said, felt powerless to fight back because Ludwigsburg's purpose was "praiseworthy." Yet the prosecutions were hampering operations and recruitment for the BKA. Dickopf worried that weakening the BKA would make West Germany "a push-over for Eastern intelligence services" and thus "a weak link and danger point in the whole Western defense system." The CIA officer who recorded these comments (which were obviously shrewdly pitched for American ears) noted that Dickopf's position and obvious sincerity made them "worth attention." Dickopf was a friend of Walter Zirpins.[34]

Like his former Gestapo colleagues Zirpins and Heisig, Rudolf Braschwitz had had a hard time in the years just after the war. He had been held in American custody until February 1947, when he was turned over to Czech authorities, in whose hands he spent over a year. While in Czech custody he wrote a short account of his life. He had joined the criminal police in 1923. From 1928 to 1933 he had been with the Berlin political police, where he had organized Foreign Minister Gustav Stresemann's bodyguard and—this seems to be the only official document in which he ever mentioned this—investigated "bomb attacks by radical right organizations," including, as we have seen, the 1929 attack on the Reichstag. After 1933 he had worked mostly for the vice squad. From September 1942 to April 1944 he had been, he said, with the criminal police in Stettin and then spent a few months in Prague. He finished out the war in Salzburg.[35]

After the Czechs let him go things began to look up for Braschwitz. He was denazified in 1950, receiving, like Zirpins and Diels, Category V status. In October 1954 he started working for the criminal police in Dortmund, eventually rising to be deputy chief (under Tobias's protégé Bernhard Wehner). Starting in 1956, however, at first as a result of pressure from a public sector union, Braschwitz fell under virtually constant investigation. Claims he had made in his Nazi-era *curricula vitae*, such as that he had carried out "special commissions" for Göring, came back to haunt him. When asked what sort of "special commissions" he had performed, Braschwitz replied that this had been "in connection with the Reichstag fire." About a week after the fire Göring had "expressed the idea that the fire could not have been laid by van der Lubbe alone. My commission was to investigate further culprits." During these investigations, he added, he had been unaware of "suspicion" that SA members may have been involved.[36]

In 1959 a former Communist youth activist accused Braschwitz of savagely beating and torturing him at Gestapo headquarters in 1933. The investigation of this case—which was ultimately stayed—metastasized into an investigation of Braschwitz's other activities with the Gestapo. Braschwitz was accused of covering up for those who were guilty of the Reichstag fire, and thereby exposing the innocent to prosecution. A prosecutor wrote that authorities would investigate whether Braschwitz had committed perjury by denying National Socialist involvement in the fire at the 1933 trial, and even if he had been involved in any way in the murder of Ernst Oberfohren. It was in this context that Braschwitz gave the statement we saw earlier in which he acknowledged the legal jeopardy he could face for his part in the Reichstag fire investigation.[37]

Braschwitz had claimed that in 1943 he was with the police in Stettin, but it came out that in fact Arthur Nebe had sent him to the Security Police and Security Service in German-occupied Kiev, Ukraine. "I had the express commission to bring pure criminal police work to bear in Ukraine through appropriate organizational measures," said Braschwitz, when forced to explain this embarrassing posting. Translated, this meant that he had been involved in the "anti-partisan" campaign—"as dirty a war as has ever been fought," in the words of one recent historian of the SS. Evidence emerged that Braschwitz had belonged to the "inner staff" of Erich von dem Bach-Zelewski, the commander of anti-partisan operations in the Soviet Union. A fellow defendant characterized Braschwitz's work there as consisting of "determining the enemy position, interrogating prisoners, and gathering all intelligence that could in any way yield useful information about the enemy." Prosecutors suspected that Braschwitz had been involved in mass shootings of Jews, but they were unable to come up with specific evidence against him.[38]

None of these cases resulted in a trial, let alone a conviction. But from 1956 to 1963, when the last of the investigations was stayed, Braschwitz was constantly under investigation, and by the end he was well past his retirement date. Like many ex-Nazis, his travails never moved him to remorse, only to self-pity: he complained of the "heavy psychological burden" of these investigations, one shared by other policemen who were only "trying to put their whole strength" at the disposal of the "democratic system."[39]

As with Zirpins, these cases affected Braschwitz's willingness to talk openly about the Reichstag fire. Throughout these investigations Braschwitz maintained that van der Lubbe had been the sole culprit, but earlier he had taken a different line. In the early 1960s Gisevius told his lawyers that Braschwitz could testify that Reinhold Heller and Heisig had controlled the 1933 investigation, and that it was well known in the Gestapo at the time that it was "suicidal" to get too interested in this case; that one day in 1938 Arthur Nebe had told Braschwitz that Heller had owed his promotion to his part in covering up the true nature of the fire; and that Braschwitz had "his own ideas" about who was behind it, about which he would testify in court though he would not talk to reporters. The basis of all this must have been conversations that Gisevius had had with Braschwitz (or perhaps with Nebe), and it is unlikely that Gisevius would want his lawyers to summon Braschwitz unless he thought Braschwitz's evidence would support his case. According to reporter Harry Schulze-Wilde's report of his 1957 interview with Diels, Diels also seemed to expect Braschwitz to speak about the fire along the lines Gisevius set out. Diels telephoned Braschwitz during this interview and seemed to be surprised by the conversation, afterwards advising Schulze-Wilde it would be better to stay out of Braschwitz's (and Schnitzler's) way.[40]

The *Spiegel* and Fritz Tobias came to Braschwitz's assistance, as they had earlier for Wehner and Zirpins (by 1959 Wehner could help himself: when a journalist called attention to his SS record, Wehner, as head of the Düsseldorf criminal police, leaked a hint that the police knew of the journalist's criminal activities). In October 1959 the *Spiegel* dismissed the union's allegations against Braschwitz as nothing more than the product of an inter-union dispute. Just how helpful Tobias's Reichstag fire research could be to Braschwitz emerged from a note Tobias sent to his collaborator, *Spiegel* reporter Gunther Zacharias. A prosecutor from Dortmund had been to see him, said Tobias, about the charges that Braschwitz had "persecuted innocents" in the Reichstag fire case. The prosecutor complained that he had ordered the article series directly from the *Spiegel* in 1959 but not received it. Tobias wondered if Zacharias could look into the matter.[41]

Braschwitz was not the only officer from the Reichstag fire investigation who had to fear the new Central Office. In the spring of 1960, after two private complaints, prosecutors in Hannover began investigating Walter Zirpins over his role in policing the Lodz Ghetto.[42]

The investigation made clear not only how barbaric the conditions at Lodz had been, but also how vital a role Zirpins's criminal police had played in sustaining them. The prosecutor found that Zirpins could not have genuinely believed that the ordinances he enforced were serving a legitimate policing purpose "if the ghettoization itself had recognizably breached inviolable principles of justice and humanity." Astonishingly, however, the prosecutor concluded that such a breach could not "be proven with certainty," at least "for the period of the defendant's activity in Lodz." He therefore stayed the case.[43]

Zirpins had already learned that when the subject of Lodz came up, the Reichstag fire would not be far behind, and vice versa. Fritz Tobias wrote to Paul Karl Schmidt that when he had found Zirpins's final report on the fire among the papers of Torgler's lawyer Alfons Sack, Zirpins had "urged me not to mention his name at all." Zirpins at first tried to insist that the report was a forgery. Eventually Zirpins conceded that this was an absurd claim. "Typical case of repressed past!" said Tobias. As the tempo of investigations over Lodz and the Reichstag fire accelerated after 1960, Zirpins grew reluctant so say anything at all about the fire. Testifying in 1961, Zirpins downplayed his influence on the case while also distancing himself from the sole-culprit theory. He did not believe van der Lubbe had helpers, but could not say whether or not "accessories or an organization" had been behind van der Lubbe "from a subjective standpoint." It had not been his job to investigate such questions and he had not in any case had enough time; unlike Heisig, he had not been ordered to investigate van der Lubbe's political connections. "My conclusion regarding the sole guilt of van der Lubbe rested at the time on the gist of my interrogation along with the confirmation at the scene, but without any consideration of an investigation of clues."[44]

It was in this context, or rather contexts, that Fritz Tobias's series on the Reichstag fire began appearing in the pages of the *Spiegel* on October

21, 1959: a time in which ex-Nazis, especially police officers, and espe-cially those police officers who were already Tobias's protégés, were coming under renewed threat in a rapidly changing moral and legal cli-mate. In late 1958, as delays by Paul Karl Schmidt held up publication of the *Spiegel* series, Tobias complained to Rudolf Augstein that "those of my clients" from whom he had received "material and information" were growing impatient. It is hard to imagine that these "clients" might have been persons other than the police officers who benefited from Tobias's work. The changing climate of the late 1950s was about to collide with the enduring symbolism of the Reichstag fire.[45]

FRITZ FOBIAS'S ARTICLES APPEARED under the title "Stand Up, van der Lubbe!" which had been one of Judge Wilhelm Bünger's frequent exhor-tations to the principal defendant.

The series channeled the case that the ex-Gestapo men had been making since their denazification days, above all in Schnitzler's articles and Diels's memoirs. Tobias's story was a simple one: van der Lubbe had burned the Reichstag all by himself. To make this case, Tobias portrayed Diels's Gestapo exactly as Diels had, and maintained that in 1933 both Zirpins and Heisig had argued bravely that van der Lubbe was the sole culprit. The most important evidence for this was Zirpins's final report and Heisig's Leyden press conference. Just as Heisig had done in his des-perate 1948 defense and Schnitzler in his articles, Tobias argued that most of the investigations after early March 1933 (and all of the mistakes) had been made by Magistrate Vogt and the expert witnesses, not by the police. Most of what had been said about the fire after Heisig's and Zirpins's work was merely willful distortion—whether by Nazis trying to implicate Communists or the reverse. As Schnitzler and Diels had also argued, Tobias claimed that it was Hitler's and Göring's paranoid fantasies that led them to claim immediately—and honestly believe—that the fire was a Communist plot.

The first installment was more than sufficient to give Tobias's account of what had actually happened at the Reichstag. The remaining ten in-stallments, running into January 1960, were attacks on what Tobias called the "legends" of the Reichstag fire. His book, published just over two years after the end of the *Spiegel* series, maintained the same propor-tions: most of its (considerable) length amounted to exercises in legend debunking (the English translation, published in 1963 in the UK and

1964 in the United States, was only about half the length of the German original and omitted vital elements of Tobias's argument). From the remove of over fifty years, however, it is not hard to see the limitations in this debunking.

For one thing, Tobias was utterly unskeptical of Nazi sources. He quoted statements from Goebbels and Göring uncritically, and took many facts straight from reports in Nazi newspapers. Diels, "the former Assessor Dr. Schneider" (Tobias, like Diels, protected Schnitzler's anonymity), and Göring's State Secretary Ludwig Grauert all "confirm today that Hitler and his closer entourage seemed firmly convinced of the guilt of the Communists on the night of the fire." In any case, had the Nazis wanted to influence the course of the investigation and cover up their guilt they would have had to begin with Helmut Heisig. Such a thing was apparently unthinkable, since for Tobias Heisig was far from being "a confidant of the Nazis," but rather someone they regarded with keen suspicion. Tobias did not report that Heisig had been conspiring with the Nazis against the Weimar Republic since August 1932, and said nothing of the deportations of Jews from Würzburg in 1943, although he certainly knew about them. In his book he cited a letter Heisig wrote to Diels in October 1948 (Tobias had a copy in his own archive) that mentioned this accusation.

Tobias also reported that Heisig agreed with Zirpins that van der Lubbe had set all the fires at the Reichstag (as well as the earlier ones at the welfare office, City Hall, and palace) all by himself. In fact, as we have seen, neither of them took that position in 1933; the documents show that Heisig was particularly aggressive in rounding up evidence to link van der Lubbe with "Communists," and by the time of Tobias's articles, Zirpins was actually blaming Heisig for the multiple-culprit theory. In Tobias's account these officers were convinced of van der Lubbe's sole guilt in part because he explained his path through the Reichstag so consistently, and because the later police searches of the Reichstag itself came up with no evidence pointing to other culprits. Of course, Heisig himself had testified in 1933 that "various contradictions" had emerged in van der Lubbe's story, "which will probably be a subject of further proceedings." Just as Schnitzler had done, Tobias contrasted the work of these conscientious Gestapo officers with the spurious evidence and "unscrupulous" experts that brought Torgler and the Bulgarians to trial and heavily influenced the court's findings.[46]

To be sure, assuming one knew nothing of the facts, Tobias's conclusions sounded entirely plausible. This helps to explain their enduring appeal. Thoughtful readers will almost always respond sympathetically to the debunking of a conspiracy theory, the demonstration that what seemed to be conspiratorial malevolence was in fact merely the product of blind chance and human blunders. Tobias was certainly right that much of what had been written about the Reichstag fire before 1959 had been fabricated, embroidered for propaganda or sensation, or sloppily researched. We could place the Münzenberg publications, Richard Wolff's long article from 1956, and the bulk of the illustrated magazine features in this category. Before Tobias, even professional historians had generally taken sources like Münzenberg's *Brown Book* seriously. Tobias laid into them all with brio and took apart such legends as that van der Lubbe's homosexuality had brought him to the attention of the SA, or that he had met his accomplice "Paul Waschinsky" in Hennigsdorf; that Karl Ernst had written a "confession" just before his murder; or that the Fire Department had deliberately been notified too late.[47]

But Tobias also demonstrably created some legends of his own. In some cases he may not have understood the issue at stake: as we have seen, he did not seem to understand that the key to the spread of the fire in the plenary chamber was the period up to 9:27, before drafts through the cupola could have had any effect. In other cases, like most historians, he fell prey to relatively minor and no doubt inadvertent factual errors. It was not true, even in 1959, that "almost everything" that had been "deployed as an argument for the guilt of the Nazis" came from the Münzenberg publications. Gisevius's account had nothing to do with the *Brown Books*, nor did Diels's statements pointing to Ernst and Gewehr. Tobias dismissed the Oberfohren Memorandum as a Communist forgery, supporting this in part with the claim that none of the former officials of the Third Reich, including Diels, had dealt with the Oberfohren case in their memoirs. In fact Diels had written that Oberfohren was murdered by an SA squad. Tobias also noted that Gisevius did not mention Oberfohren, which was true, while elsewhere Tobias sought to discredit the former "youth leader of the German Nationals" with the argument that Gisevius had simply copied from the *Brown Book*, which emphasized Oberfohren's story.[48]

In other places, however, it is difficult to escape the conclusion that Tobias deliberately falsified the record as he found it. We have seen how selectively, and misleadingly, he related Heisig's record. There are many other, even starker examples. In building up Zirpins as a witness for the single-culprit theory, Tobias misrepresented his testimony. He quoted Zirpins testifying in 1933 that van der Lubbe's "method was the same with all the fires," as van der Lubbe had explained in his statement. "I assume," Zirpins continued—"it is clear to me—he did it himself." Tobias neglected to mention that here Zirpins was expressly referring only to the fires at the welfare office, City Hall, and the palace, and not to the Reichstag.[49]

Another example involved the case of the mysterious young man who appeared at the Brandenburg Gate at 9:15, told the police there was a fire at the Reichstag, and then vanished. In a 1956 letter to the Munich Institute of Contemporary History, Hans Flöter, the student who was one of the first witnesses of the fire, recalled that he had met a young man named "Neumann" at the trial in October 1933. Neumann, said Flöter, claimed to be this mysterious witness. Neumann had apparently explained that the summons had reached him too late, which was why he never testified. Yet somehow he was there with the other witnesses, which Flöter understandably found "very unclear." The other thing that Flöter remembered was that Neumann was a Nazi who worked at the *Völkischer Beobachter* and was presumably a stormtrooper, as he told Flöter he had been given "strict instructions" not to appear in uniform at the trial.[50]

Fritz Tobias made very selective use of Flöter's letter in his 1962 book. He deployed Flöter's recollection of "Neumann" to demolish the idea that there had been anything suspicious about this young man, since writers who believed the Nazis had burned the Reichstag presented him as a Nazi who was somehow involved in the plot. From the information in Flöter's letter Tobias reported only that Flöter had met Neumann at the trial and that Neumann said he was summoned too late to testify; he did not mention that Neumann was a Nazi. Tobias added that the only reason Neumann did not testify was that he had no useful information to contribute, something Flöter had not said. Then Tobias supplied Neumann with a motivation and a back story. Neumann had stood next to Constable Buwert and Thaler watching the fire burn in the Reichstag restaurant; it was Neumann, not the passing soldier, whom Buwert had told to report the fire to the Brandenburg Gate. Neumann went home "in the consciousness of having honestly contributed his part to fighting the fire." When he realized from the news reports that some considered his role in the fire suspicious, he reported to the police, who referred him to the chief Reich prosecutor. The prosecutor determined that Neumann's evidence was immaterial. It was only his conversation with Flöter that had "transmitted his role as reserve witness to posterity."[51]

All of this was cut from whole cloth. We know only that the mysterious young man appeared at the Brandenburg Gate at 9:15, made his report, and vanished. There was no "Neumann." Flöter himself admitted this in 1962, when he realized that he had confused "Neumann" with Werner Thaler, the typesetter at the *Völkischer Beobachter*—it was Thaler with whom Flöter had chatted at the trial. None of the relevant witnesses—Flöter, Thaler, Buwert—remembered seeing a man of Neumann's description as the Reichstag began to burn. In statements from February 28 and March 22, 1933, Thaler clearly remembered finding Buwert and seeing the soldier; Buwert "may" have been already in the company of a "civilian," which at that moment was likely Flöter. For his part, Buwert remembered only one civilian who accompanied him to the window; when this civilian saw through the windows what seemed to be an arsonist carrying a torch, he urged Buwert to shoot. This civilian was certainly Thaler. Flöter did not see anyone else besides Buwert.[52]

Tobias's account of Buwert's actions was sourced to an "oral report of the now–Police Inspector Buwert, Berlin." This suggests that Tobias interviewed Buwert in the late 1950s or early 1960s; perhaps Buwert told Tobias something about the mysterious young man then. But in 1933, when the memory was fresh, he said clearly that there had only been Thaler. Still unexplained in any case was Tobias's selective use of Flöter's letter and his fabrication of Neumann's motives and experiences with the Authorities. Testifying at the trial in 1933 Police Lieutenant Lateit noted that in highly publicized cases, if a witness's information were mislaid, that witness would usually report later to fill in the gaps. But in this case the mysterious witness had never come forward—evidence which also points up the imaginary quality of the back story Tobias created for Neumann. Remarkably, in the 1980s Tobias went so far as to claim that he had tried to convince Flöter *in 1957* that Flöter had confused Neumann with Thaler, and that Flöter refused to concede this point. This poses the question of why Tobias would still use Flöter's recollection of Neumann five years later in his book, a question which Tobias neither raised nor answered.[53]

In places, Tobias's book was more nuanced than the *Spiegel* articles. The book was more frank about the nature of Zirpins's final report, although

Tobias still claimed it as evidence for Zirpins's sincere belief in a single culprit. The articles had hardly dealt with Gisevius's account and made no mention of the Rall/Reineking story. In between the series and the book the Berlin Document Center material on Reineking had come to light, adding considerable support to Gisevius's account. Accordingly Tobias devoted a substantial section of his book to attacking Gisevius and rebutting the Rall story. Tobias criticized Gisevius for not knowing that there had been a number of false confessions to the Reichstag fire—but of course the SA had only murdered Rall and not the others, which tells us something about what the stormtroopers thought. He claimed that Rall (whom he called "Hans," not "Adolf," while mocking other writers for getting the name wrong) had only asked to testify on October 27th, after reading news reports of chemist Wilhelm Schatz's testimony about a self-igniting fluid. But the newly available documents show that Rall asked to testify on October 21st, before the expert witnesses had been heard at all.[54]

Tobias's book also contained elements of interpretation that had not been part of the *Spiegel* articles. Probably the most quoted line of the book is his conclusion on the significance of the fire, contained in the Afterword: "In a moment of glory for humanity, in the blazing symbol of the defeated Weimar State, the dictator Adolf Hitler, intoxicated with power and obsessed with his mission, emerged from out of the civil Reich chancellor." The Nazi seizure of power was therefore not, as generally believed, the work of "cunningly planning political demons." "We must," said Tobias, "come to terms with the disturbing fact that blind chance, an error, unleashed a revolution." By asking his readers to accept this, Tobias was effectively erasing from the historical record the Nazis' lust for power and the ruthlessness with which they sought it—the violence, aggression, and racial vitriol that, as most historians have demonstrated, lay at the heart of their program. This is what historians call a "Cleopatra's Nose" argument, one that, in the words of Tony Judt, "takes the last move in a sequence, correctly observes that it might have been very different, and then deduces either that all the other moves could also have been different or else that they don't count." It is as much a sign of Tobias's limitations as a historian as of his apologetic intentions. Revealingly, the English translation completely omitted this "Afterword."[55]

THAT TOBIAS NOT ONLY BENT THE RECORD, but bent it knowingly, emerged from his dealings with witnesses as well as from the text itself.

His handling of his "client" Zirpins provides one such example. Tobias knew that Zirpins was responsible for writing in his final report that van der Lubbe had been an "accessory" to a Communist crime. Tobias believed this language had handed van der Lubbe "over to the hangman," but, as he wrote *Spiegel* journalist Zacharias, "this historical role [of Zirpins] doesn't need to be emphasized." He told Schmidt in 1958 that on "collegial grounds" he did not want to illustrate Zirpins's "chain of mischief."[56]

When a witness who was not a client dared to put forward an inconvenient fact, Tobias would not hesitate to browbeat him. He did not, for instance, like Fritz Polchow's recollection of seeing gun-wielding policemen in the cellar of the Reichstag. This recollection, as we have seen, resurfaced in a 1955 Berlin Fire Department report on the Reichstag fire. Tobias wrote to Emil Puhle, who had commanded Polchow's company, to tell Puhle what to say in response. "Naturally there is a laughably simple explanation," said Tobias, for this "murder mystery." The "excited" fireman who was looking for "arsonists" saw what he expected to see: "Suspicious individuals!" After effectively telling Puhle what to say, Tobias generously concluded, "I am very eager for your opinion!" Puhle responded as desired, adding that he had never heard the story about police and guns.[57]

Tobias was even willing to strong-arm Zirpins when it suited him. Zirpins was reluctant to give Tobias an interview and asked Tobias not to publish his name, a request Tobias said he would respect "for collegial reasons" though he hoped that Zirpins would reconsider. A few years later Tobias tried again. "The thing would be easier," he wrote Zirpins, "without a prior conversation with you." Tobias insisted he wanted to talk to Zirpins only out of sympathy for Zirpins's position, as Zirpins should already have learned "in certain critical times." Zirpins denied that he was responsible for the "accessory" language in the final report, blaming those parts on Heisig instead. This raised a problem, since Heisig's sincere commitment to the single-culprit theory was central to Tobias's argument. Tobias responded that he could not accept Zirpins's account, and continued in a more threatening tone, warning Zirpins of a soon-to-be-published article in the magazine *Revue*. It was in this letter that Tobias, as we have seen, reminded Zirpins of the possibility of bad publicity, which for both of them was connected with the year 1952 and the city of "Litzmannstadt" (Lodz). Tobias said again that on "purely collegial grounds" he wanted to give Zirpins a chance to discuss matters objectively. "I am only the reporter," said Tobias; "the world will judge."[58]

Years later, Tobias explained that he had been "tough but fair with Zirpins." But in this correspondence he seemed to be threatening Zirpins with revealing some of the nastier elements of his past in order to get him to talk about the Reichstag fire in a way that fit Tobias's preconceptions. It is important to note that in 1960 Zirpins's record in Lodz, even that he had been there at all, was not yet publicly known.[59]

Nonetheless Tobias depicted Zirpins as a conscientious, indeed courageous, officer, the kind of man whose word one should believe. Tobias knew enough about Zirpins's past to wonder if this was really so, but he didn't admit to any doubts. Zirpins was "just in the criminal police" in Lodz, Tobias explained in 2009, as if policing the Lodz Ghetto were the same thing as policing his quiet Hannover suburb. Tobias portrayed Heisig in even more glowing terms, despite his knowledge of the deportations of Jews to Auschwitz and Theresienstadt for which Heisig was responsible. He also obviously knew that Zirpins blamed Heisig for insisting there had been other culprits in the Reichstag fire.[60]

What is most intriguing about the Tobias/Zirpins correspondence is the hints it contains about their past connections: "Certain critical times," "the year 1952," "Litzmannstadt." As we have seen, the government of Lower Saxony had almost fired Zirpins 1952 when officials there learned of his articles about the Lodz Ghetto. Tobias's words imply that he had helped save Zirpins's career. There is an even murkier story. A journalist named Heinrich L. Bode claimed in 1960 that Zirpins owed his appointment to Tobias's intrigues. This would seem nothing more than a nasty rumor, were it not at least partially corroborated by Tobias's own correspondence and his dealings with Bernhard Wehner. There is no doubt that Tobias played a central role in getting Zirpins's predecessor fired and thus opening up the job for Zirpins. In 1960 it seemed Tobias was looking to call in some favors.[61]

By the late 1950s, Tobias's bullying manner was already well known among surviving Reichstag fire insiders. Diels complained to Zirpins about the "monomaniacal self-satisfaction" with which Tobias went about his work. By October 1958 senior officials in the West German Federal Justice Ministry were worried about what Tobias was up to. He had gone so far as to bring a prosecutor with him to interrogate Magistrate Vogt. Tobias dismissed Vogt's refusal to answer questions as "arrogance, self-aggrandizement, and divisiveness"—and here we must remember that in researching the fire, Tobias was, in theory at any rate, nothing more than a private citizen, although (as we shall see) he could use his position with the Constitutional Protection to significant threatening effect. When a Justice Ministry official warned Tobias against rendering "a distorted and tendentious picture" of the Reichstag fire, Tobias simply replied that he was "the recognized world expert" on the subject.[62]

What drove Tobias? It is an article of faith among his opponents that he was a closet Nazi; indeed, they speculate that his war record was as suspect as Heisig's or Zirpins's or Braschwitz's—that he served in the *Geheime Feldpolizei* (GFP), the military equivalent of the Gestapo. If this were true it would perhaps explain his otherwise puzzling sympathy for his "clients." No publicly accessible military service records corroborate the allegation, and Tobias himself refused to release the confidential records that could have refuted it, a refusal which the authority holding these records upheld as late as the end of 2012. In old age, however, Tobias admitted that in the Netherlands he had carried out "military police duties," including pursuing deserters; he had even "had to read denunciations from Dutch citizens against one another," which, though Tobias did not say so, could have involved exposing Jews to deportation. While carrying out such tasks Tobias admitted he had worn the insignia of the GFP. But he still denied actually belonging to it.[63]

Tobias was also willing to say things that did not exactly enhance his anti-Nazi credibility. Hitler was "in some ways a genius," he said, but one who was "systematically conned" by the army, even by Gisevius, who, Tobias claimed, duped the Führer into the Night of the Long Knives by feeding him false information about SA commander Ernst Röhm (a particularly glaring overestimation of the influence of a very junior official whom Diels fired from the Gestapo at the end of 1933). Viktor Lutze, Röhm's successor, was a "decent man" and a "real idealist." Foreign Minister Joachim von Ribbentrop was nothing worse than a smooth and well-traveled man whom the Ministry's civil servants sabotaged. Even Tobias's champion, *Spiegel* editor-in-chief Rudolf Augstein, wrote that Tobias's "political theses" (like the "moment of glory for humanity" line in the "Afterword") were "nonsense" (*Unfug*), and he was keen to point out that the *Spiegel* had not printed them. (In the same letter Augstein rather surprisingly wrote that the only possible valid objection to Tobias's argument was that one man alone could not have set the fire, about which "I personally have no opinion.")[64]

Tobias's attitudes amounted more to naiveté about individual Nazis and their movement than support of them. Ironically, he therefore let himself be used by unscrupulous figures of the far-right in much the same way as had van der Lubbe. As he grew older he seemed to become less careful about his affiliations. He was on friendly terms with the Holocaust denier David Irving, even contributing an essay to a 1998 Festschrift for Irving. In 2010 Irving, who is legally barred from entering Germany, sneaked into the country to visit Tobias in Hannover, posting an account of the visit and two photos on his blog. (Tobias did not agree with Irving in important ways: Irving recorded that Tobias "still thinks I am wrong about Adolf Hitler's partial ignorance on what Heinrich Himmler was up to.") In May 2011, the far-right German publisher Grabert-Verlag put out a new edition of Tobias's Reichstag fire book. Grabert's offerings otherwise run to reprinted Nazi-era soft porn and "revisionist" tracts claiming that Germany lost the Second World War only because of "betrayal" from within.[65]

Identifying Tobias's naiveté, however, neither ends the inquiry nor excuses his conclusions. His naiveté rested on blindness to the real nature and consequences of the Nazi regime. This is what allowed Tobias to take seriously the self-serving statements of people like Hermann Göring or his Gestapo subordinates, to ignore or downplay the wartime records of men like Zirpins, Braschwitz, and Heisig (at least when not exploiting those records to extract testimony from these "clients"), and to treat so insouciantly the extent to which Nazi aggression and murderousness shaped the Party's drive to power as well as its practices once it got there.[66]

There was, therefore, a political agenda behind Tobias's writings, one that was both nationalistic and self-justifying. If it was really only chance that turned Hitler into a dictator and sparked his "revolution," then no blame could attach to Germans (individually or collectively) for putting Hitler in office, perhaps not even to Hitler himself, that "genius" who was constantly the victim of intrigue and bad advice. In a late 1960s letter to Braschwitz, Tobias supplied a revealing caricature of his opponents' views: they wanted, he said, to blame Nazis, and hence Germans, for the fire, not "a foreigner" like van der Lubbe. The implication is that Tobias himself *did* want the dictatorship to have been brought on by the acts of a foreigner. In 1960 he complained to Helmut Krausnick that historians were "hopelessly blocked" from understanding the whole Nazi seizure of power because they misunderstood the Reichstag fire. Only Tobias's new interpretation could supply "the preconditions for a rational assessment" of

Germany's "unmastered past"—another sign of the historical and symbolic importance of his subject.[67]

Mastering the past was not Tobias's only motivation for writing about the Reichstag fire. It was, as we have seen, no coincidence that the single-culprit theory revived amid the war crimes and denazification proceedings of the late 1940s. It was no more a coincidence that these were also the birth years of the Cold War. The debate over the Reichstag fire moved to its climax in the most tense years of that struggle, coinciding precisely with the severe east-west crisis over the status of Berlin between 1958 and 1961 which culminated in the building of the Wall. We cannot fully understand Tobias's role in the Reichstag fire controversy if we do not keep firmly in mind that he was, by profession, an officer of one of West Germany's domestic intelligence services.

RUDOLF DIELS HAD BEEN THE FIRST CHIEF of the Gestapo, Schnitzler and Gisevius his subordinates. Gisevius had gone on during the war to work for the Abwehr, the main German military intelligence service, and to pass information to Allen Dulles and the Office of Strategic Services (OSS). Fritz Tobias was a senior official of the Constitutional Protection in Lower Saxony, and (by his own account at least) worked for the British Secret Intelligence Service (SIS) after the war. The most important figures in the Reichstag fire debate therefore all had something to do with intelligence; Diels, Schnitzler, and Gisevius all aspired to return to intelligence work after the war. This striking fact has received little attention from researchers. But it is difficult to imagine that men like this would not weigh the consequences of their writings about the fire for their intelligence ambitions, and there is evidence that they did so. Above all, Tobias's intelligence role and his connections to the others form an important, if murky, part of the Reichstag fire story.

The onset of the Cold War came as a triple blessing to the ex-Gestapo men. First, the Allies increasingly came to conclude that if the real enemy was the Soviet Union, and the key strategic priority was the defense of western Europe from both Soviet invasion and domestic Communist subversion, then they urgently needed German officials, officers, and policemen for that defense. Denazification was a luxury they could no longer afford, and denazification programs grew more lenient with time until they were wound up altogether after 1950. Secondly, men like Diels and Schnitzler could exploit their records of battling Communists under the

Nazis to prove to the "self-righteous" Allies that the ex-*Gestapisten* had been right all along about the real political threat. One recent historian of West Germany has stressed that anti-Communism was the key vehicle for integrating ex-Nazi officials into the new democracy (as indeed it had earlier been the key vehicle for integrating right-wing non-Nazis like Diels and Schnitzler into the Nazi system): in the 1950s a public official could not openly avow Nazi positions, but there was no limit on anti-Communism. Third, the worsening Cold War stimulated the re-creation of a German security state, especially after the North Korean invasion of South Korea in June 1950. In that year the Allies approved the federal police force, the BKA, and a federal domestic security service, the Federal Office for Constitutional Protection (BfV). There were analogous branches of the Office for Constitutional Protection in the West German federal states and in West Berlin, which was technically not part of the Federal Republic as Berlin lay under the joint management of the four wartime allies. The Americans also sponsored a new foreign intelligence service under the former Nazi general Reinhard Gehlen. These developments offered old Nazis the prospect of new jobs.[68]

Hannover in the 1950s was a particular stronghold of West Germany's unrepentant Nazis, and Diels, who returned there after his time in Nuremberg, was close to many of the most prominent figures. He turned these ties to advantage by acting as an informer for the British and Americans, and for the West German security services as they developed. The American CIC (military counter-intelligence) hired him in 1948 to provide information on "KP [Communist Party] Matters." For his services Diels received a "salary" of twelve cartons of cigarettes per month, supplemented occasionally by ration cards and cans of Crisco—an eloquent comment on the real sources of value in postwar Germany.[69]

The first leader of the Federal Office for Constitutional Protection was Otto John, whom Diels had known since before the Nazis. For a few years Diels cultivated John, or perhaps vice versa. According to an American report, John visited Diels every four weeks to get his advice. In 1953, when British authorities arrested a number of Nazi activists from the so-called Naumann Circle, Diels sent John a typically cynical letter, eloquently revealing his attitude both to the new West German state and to his own past: "You must now be rather burdened with work," he wrote, as "bannings, house-searches, indictments, and arrests" were going on *"urbi et orbi* like in the good old days."[70]

Schnitzler knew what Diels was up to and wanted to join in. As early as March 1948 he was already wondering how he might use his knowledge of Communists from his days in the political police to find employment in one of the new agencies. "Can't I capitalize on this material?" he asked. Schnitzler knew that some kind of intelligence organization was being formed "in a legendary castle near Frankfurt." He wanted Diels's help. "Can't one discuss these things with the relevant gentlemen? You certainly have first-class connections in this regard."[71]

It seems that until Otto John got the Constitutional Protection job in late 1950, Diels had been angling to head the agency. Thomas Polgar, at the time a young CIA officer in Germany closely involved in the oversight of the Constitutional Protection, says that Diels was never considered for the job. Indeed he was "lucky not to be prosecuted." But at the time many high-profile former Nazis were landing senior positions in the West German government, and in fact Hubert Schrübbers, who led the Constitutional Protection from 1955 to 1972, was eventually forced to resign over revelations of his Nazi past. Diels could, and clearly did, entertain hopes. A 1949 CIC report claimed that "Diels is anxious to head the new *Geheimpolizei* [secret police] of the Bundesrepublik [Federal Republic]." Diels, continued the report, was a friend of Chancellor Adenauer, whom Diels had helped in the Nazi years. The CIC thought that Diels was a strong contender for the job "since he is politically clever." A September 1950 report had it that Diels had been in touch with a senior official who wanted Diels to meet with Adenauer and President Theodor Heuss to talk about heading the Constitutional Protection. Diels's friend Alfred Martin told the CIC that Diels had been "secretly proposed as chief of the security police."[72]

The 1949 CIC report also claimed that Diels saw Gisevius as his rival for the job. On the face of it, Gisevius might have been a more plausible candidate. He had good connections with important figures in American intelligence, such as Allen Dulles and William "Wild Bill" Donovan. "Gisevius has applied for the job as head of the Secret Police of the Bonn Government and is held in some favor by the Americans and British," the report continued. Gisevius's problems lay more with the Germans. Thomas Polgar remembers that Gisevius was "absolutely hated" by German traditionalists, for having been a "traitor" during the war and a key witness in several postwar trials of senior Nazi officials. Yet like Diels, Gisevius was also "tainted by earlier associations with Nazi security services."[73]

In July 1954 Constitutional Protection chief Otto John appeared to defect to East Berlin. Whether in fact the Soviets kidnapped him, as he claimed after returning to West Germany in late 1955, remains unclear. Diels's reaction to John's disappearance was fierce and public. "Persons who commit treason will always be unreliable," he told an American intelligence agent, playing on John's involvement in the Valkyrie resistance. Diels jeopardized his pension by writing a scathing pamphlet, *The John Case: Background and Lessons*, in which his far-right political sympathies re-emerged, after a period in which his legal problems had forced him at least to try to sound democratic in public. Diels vented his contempt for the Allies, the Nuremberg proceedings, even the most conspicuous victims of the Nazis: the Communists, who "were compensated with outrageous sums of money" because "Hitler got in the way of their civil war plans," and (presumably referring to Holocaust survivors and refugees) the "whole armies of black gypsies, who were showered with hecatombs of money."[74]

For this pamphlet Diels was subjected to harsh criticism in the Bundestag, and since he was technically still a civil servant, a disciplinary hearing from the government of Lower Saxony, which (as always) he managed to scrape through without serious penalty. He returned to another kind of old habit: "As a consequence of that publicity," said a 1954 CIC report, "Diels stored all his files and personal papers at an undisclosed hiding place."[75]

It was in this milieu of past and present intelligence officers, with their mix of Cold War concerns and resentments from the recent past, that Tobias was operating as an official of Lower Saxony's Office for Constitutional Protection. There are hints that Tobias's work on the Reichstag fire might have been at least in part the product of an official commission. These hints are supported by Tobias's having lied under oath about some of his intelligence background, and having kept quiet for many years about another element of it.

Gisevius and his lawyers suspected that the vitriol in Tobias's writing might stem from an official, if covert, assignment to attack advocates of Nazi responsibility for the fire like Gisevius himself. Tobias gave some revealing nonanswers to their questions. "I have never taken advantage of my official position as a member of the Office for Constitutional Protection to acquire material in an illegal manner," he testified in 1961. But when asked if he had acquired documents *legally* through the Constitutional

Protection, Tobias declined to answer, citing the preservation of official secrets. Had he gathered information on Gisevius himself through the office? Again, he denied having done so illegally. When asked whether he had gathered information about Gisevius in the course of an official investigation, he replied again, "I decline to answer with reference to my duty to maintain official secrets." He did, however, admit that in working on the Reichstag fire he had gathered whatever material he could about those who had written about it. There is in fact no doubt that he used his position to collect documents relevant to the Reichstag fire that were only available to government officials. A look through the publicly accessible van der Lubbe files at the Berlin Landesarchiv, the archives of the city of Berlin, to say nothing of Tobias's own document collection, quickly confirms this practice. He either had official authorization to do this or he made illegal use of his position with the Lower Saxon Constitutional Protection. There isn't a third possibility.[76]

There is also no doubt that Gisevius was a target of the German security services. In the early 1950s he lived in the United States, and therefore fell into the jurisdiction of the Federal Bureau of Investigation. In 1953 the Bureau became concerned that Gisevius might be a "subversive" when an informant (who had to be German and might have come from one of the German constitutional protection offices) warned that Gisevius was connected to Otto John. Remarkably, even in 1953, before John's disappearance, the Bureau was worried that "any information obtained by the subject [Gisevius] will find its way to Dr. Otto John," and, through him, to the Soviet Union. The Bureau's sources also reported that Gisevius had connections to the writer and editor Eugen Kogon, the pastor Martin Niemöller, and other advocates of West German military neutrality in the Cold War. This was a policy that ran directly counter to the goals of the Adenauer administration as well as to those of the Truman and Eisenhower administrations; West German military strength was essential if NATO countries were to mount any credible deterrent against a possible Soviet attack.

It is unlikely that the FBI could have harbored these fears or obtained this information without the aid of German intelligence services. Every mention of the specific source of the information that Gisevius would pass information to Otto John is blacked out in the publicly available copies, but, along with the "several sources" who in 1950 doubted whether "Gisevius would be found acceptable [as head of the Constitutional Protection] even by the Allies at the present time [and that] Adenauer's reaction to a possible nomination of Gisevius was 'Only over my dead body,'" he was probably a German official. Chancellor Adenauer himself called Martin Niemöller an "enemy of the state" whose opposition to German rearmament amounted to "treason"; Adenauer's Interior Minister Gustav Heinemann left the cabinet because of his dispute with Adenauer on this issue, and because of his close ties to Niemöller; and Gisevius was if anything closer to Heinemann than to Niemöller. One FBI report had it that Gisevius's reputation among pro-American, pro-Adenauer Germans was "very bad." Even after Otto John won the Constitutional Protection position, there were reports in the German press, monitored by American intelligence, that Gisevius was in line for a similar job in Bonn. The FBI report continued that if he got it, it would "create adverse feeling against the United States."[77]

Tobias betrayed the same kind of hatred for Gisevius that Diels and Schnitzler had felt, and expressed it even more intemperately. In a lecture in Göttingen early in 1961 he spoke of a legendary Central American king who was merciful in all respects save one: he executed historians who wrote untruthfully. Tobias said he regretted that the Federal Republic had no such law. Asked about this lecture later while testifying, Tobias said bluntly that had Gisevius lived in Central America, he "would have been in danger of being punished." He approvingly repeated criticisms of Gisevius from people with obvious biases, like Diels, and even Manfred Roeder, a vicious Nazi military judge who had investigated resistance figures like the theologian Dietrich Bonhoeffer and the Canaris-Oster circle of which Gisevius himself was a part. Tobias wrote to Helmut Krausnick that one had to hear Roeder himself speak in order to understand Gisevius's "evil role." Even for Tobias this is an extreme example of preferring the word of a serious Nazi to that of a resistance fighter. Tobias misrepresented and misstated facts regarding Gisevius's involvement with the Reichstag fire investigation and trial, his testimony at Nuremberg, and the notion that he had remained a Gestapo agent until the end of the war.[78]

Tobias claimed, under oath, that he had only been working for the Lower Saxon Constitutional Protection since July 1959. Newly available documents, however, reveal that Tobias was working there at least by the summer of 1954. Although it may be true, as Rudolf Augstein and others wrote, that a change of administration led to Tobias's being transferred to another department in the mid-1950s, a 1958 memo drafted by an official of the West German Justice Ministry records that Tobias "must at some point have been occupied with work for the Constitutional Protection in Lower Saxony . . . *In this period he claims he intended to seek out the truth regarding the circumstances of the Reichstag fire trial* (emphasis added)." Although Tobias claimed several times that he had completed his research on the Reichstag fire by 1957, his correspondence with Zirpins and others shows that he went on working right up to the publication of his book in 1962, and indeed beyond—he never stopped interviewing people and gathering documents on the subject.[79]

Tobias had therefore not only researched the Reichstag fire while working for the Constitutional Protection, he later covered this fact up. As so often in this story, the cover-up is significant. There is another intriguing fact about Tobias's intelligence connections. In an interview in the autumn of 1996, he told a former *Spiegel* reporter, Peter-Ferdinand Koch, that he had worked for the British SIS after the war. His job was to be a "scout," which involved interrogating former Gestapo officers to identify those who might be useful for British intelligence. He would have had ready access to such people from his work for the Hannover denazification committee. Tobias also told Koch that he had referred both Diels and Paul Karl Schmidt to the *Spiegel* as potential authors. This might be what Tobias meant when he told Augstein in 1958, "I expressed my sympathy and trust to you ten years ago." Tobias's work for the British may also be reflected in the 1958 federal Justice Ministry memo noted above, which recorded that Tobias had worked for the Constitutional Protection and that "he *also* spoke occasionally of intelligence work" [emphasis added]. Were the story about his working with the SIS true, it would be another indication of how deeply Tobias involved himself in the postwar careers of these ex-Nazis, and of how much he tried to cover up those ties later on.[80]

Lower Saxony was perhaps the German state in which senior officials made the greatest efforts to shelter former Nazi police officers from investigation by the Ludwigsburg Central Office. In one case, a former Gestapo officer from Tilsit who was being investigated for murder (and after the war worked for North Rhine-Westphalia's Constitutional Protection) was shielded from arrest by Lower Saxon colleagues. In 1961 a remarkable member of the Ludwigsburg Central Office, the prosecutor Barbara Just-Dahlmann, made a sensational speech alleging that just this sort of police interference was seriously hampering the prosecution of war criminals. The Central Office could not just send its investigation documents to any police authority in West Germany, she said, because it couldn't be sure that the documents wouldn't fall into the hands of an officer under investigation. One of the strongest reactions to her speech came from the interior minister of Lower Saxony, Otto Bennemann, who insisted that the police in Lower Saxony had made extraordinary efforts to keep their ranks clear of Nazi criminals and that many of his officers had been persecuted in the Third Reich. Historian Annette Weinke argues that this was willful blindness on Bennemann's part, and she suggests that Bennemann criticized Just-Dahlmann strongly in order to cause trouble for her. Bennemann was Fritz Tobias's boss, and his aggressive willingness to defend his own people raises an important issue. Weinke suggests that one of the motives for Bennemann's words was to defend Walter Zirpins, whose Lodz case was by then prominent in the news. What else might Bennemann or other authorities have been willing to do to defend their officers? We have seen that Tobias was probably referring to officers like Zirpins when he mentioned his "clients," and his book can be read as a vindication of them—even if at times Tobias seemed to be vindicating Zirpins against the latter's own will. The prime minister of Lower Saxony in these critical years, from 1946 to 1955 and from 1959 to 1961, was the Social Democrat Hinrich Wilhelm Kopf. During the Nazi period Kopf was deeply involved in, and profited mightily from, the "aryanization" of Jewish homes and business in Germany and Poland; in 1948 he had been forced to defend himself against accusations about his wartime conduct which the Polish government passed to the British.[81]

As a senior official of the Lower Saxon Constitutional Protection, Tobias could also be useful to the *Spiegel* in many ways. In 1959 the magazine was involved in a legal conflict with the Constitutional Protection after reporting that officials of both the federal and the Lower Saxon offices had attempted to abduct and deport two people suspected of being Czech agents. The *Spiegel* couldn't sustain the allegation and had to back down. Tobias was able to play a "balancing" role, as he put it in a meeting with Augstein and *Spiegel* managing editor Hans Detlev Becker. Tobias reported with satisfaction that Augstein and Becker were prepared in the future "to engage in appropriate considerations for a kind of collaboration [*Zusammenarbeit*] or understanding" with the Constitutional Protection. Tobias's notes indicate that he mediated not just between the *Spiegel* and the Lower Saxon office, but with the highest levels of the federal office as well.[82]

Tobias kept a large picture of van der Lubbe on the door of his study. "Everything I have done," he said in 2008, "I have done for that poor boy." He meant that he had tried to restore van der Lubbe's dignity as a young man who made his own decisions, to rescue him from the enormous condescension of historians.[83]

This may be so. But Tobias also had other motives, and his work had other beneficiaries.

10

····

"SNOW FROM YESTERDAY"

BLACKMAIL AND THE INSTITUTE FOR CONTEMPORARY HISTORY

HANS MOMMSEN CAME FROM A DYNASTY of German historians. His great-grandfather was Theodor Mommsen, a historian of Rome and one of the leading figures of German intellectual life in the late nineteenth century. His father, Wilhelm, was a professor of history in Marburg, where Hans Mommsen was born in 1930. His late twin brother Wolfgang was likewise a distinguished historian. An uncle was director of the German Federal Archives after the Second World War.

In the 1950s Mommsen studied history at the University of Tübingen under Hans Rothfels, a towering figure in the postwar German historical profession, not least because of his unassailable moral position as a victim of Nazi persecution. Mommsen earned his doctorate in 1959 and went on to hold positions as what Germans call an *Assistent*—roughly comparable to an assistant professor in North America—at Tübingen and Heidelberg, before landing a professorship of his own at the Ruhr University in Bochum in 1969. Mommsen became in time one of the most important and influential of postwar German historians. Before that, he was, for about eighteen months in 1960 and 1961, a researcher at the Institut für Zeitgeschichte—the Institute for Contemporary History—in Munich.

In those days the Institute was the best address for research on German twentieth-century history. In the early 1960s its director was Helmut Krausnick, "a brilliant historian" in Mommsen's words, who nonetheless struggled for recognition among his peers because of his conservative politics. The editor of the Institute's journal, the *Vierteljahrshefte für Zeitgeschichte* (Quarterly journal for contemporary history, or *VfZ*) was Mommsen's teacher Hans Rothfels. Among Mommsen's younger colleagues were such figures as Martin Broszat and Hermann Graml, historians who, like Mommsen himself, would dominate German historical research for decades.

Mommsen was once, as he remembered, "close friends" with Graml. By 2010, however, the friendship was effectively over. These eminent historians had had a falling out over a "memo to file" (*Aktennotiz*), or, as Mommsen put it, "the memo to file that wasn't," the memo that was nothing but "snow from yesterday."[1]

THE INSTITUTE FOR CONTEMPORARY HISTORY was established in the late 1940s to promote serious historical research to "re-educate" Germans about the horrors of Nazism. This was not always a popular mission, and battles over how much enlightenment was a good idea raged not just between the Institute and certain segments of German society, but within the Institute itself. The Institute was and is a public body. It was therefore often subject to fierce public criticism; its director and its board often had to strike a delicate balance between enlightenment and survival. On the other hand, the mostly young scholars who worked there were highly idealistic. Hermann Graml wrote years later that they had all believed that enlightenment based on solid scholarship on the Third Reich was essential to liberate Germans from National Socialist delusions (*Irrlichten*). They went at this task with "missionary zeal."[2]

The Reichstag fire was one of the subjects proposed at the Institute's founding for its research attention, and given the "missionary zeal" of its young scholars, it was all but inevitable that the Institute would oppose the single-culprit theory. It supported a long report on the fire by Richard Wolff, published in 1956 in the newspaper *Parlament* (put out by the West German governmental department responsible for "political education"), which argued the case for Nazi culpability and was very critical of Diels's post-1949 disavowal of Nazi responsibility. And the Institute supported

Hans Bernd Gisevius in the earlier phases of his many trials in the 1960s against Hans Georg Gewehr and Fritz Tobias (see below). Graml wrote a positive evaluation of Gisevius's *To the Bitter End* for a lawsuit between Gisevius and Tobias in 1962, which also contained a highly critical assessment of Tobias's conclusions—with fateful consequences, as we will see. In 1960 the Institute commissioned a rebuttal of Tobias's arguments, and Director Krausnick recommended renewed investigation of the murder of Adolf Rall on the basis of citations from Gisevius. At a meeting of the Institute's academic council in 1962, several members noted that the Institute was expected to take a position on "particular falsifications of the facts of contemporary history" in "controversial publications," such as those by the American journalist William Shirer, the Nazi apologist David Hoggan—and Fritz Tobias.[3]

Knowledge of the Institute's attitude toward the Reichstag fire made Tobias suspicious from the beginning. In 1957 he asked the Institute to let him see the documents underpinning Wolff's article, especially the Berlin Fire Department report that claimed that Fritz Polchow had found himself threatened by gun-wielding policemen. The Institute agreed. Then Tobias himself pointed out that Wolff had promised the Fire Department he would keep the report confidential. The Institute responded by telling Tobias he would need the Fire Department's permission to see the report. This infuriated Tobias. The Institute then relented and sent him the report anyway.[4]

Three years later, in 1960, Gisevius published a series of articles in the weekly newspaper the *Zeit* in response to Tobias's *Spiegel* series. Here Gisevius acknowledged receiving materials from the Institute. Tobias wrote in rage to Krausnick, claiming that the Institute had not made a single document from Wolff's papers available to him. When Krausnick reminded Tobias of the facts, Tobias replied that he found it hard to understand why Krausnick hesitated to "face the unpalatable truth." That "unpalatable truth" involved "significant corrections" to history of the Third Reich's first phase, corrections that, Tobias warned Krausnick, "were coming."[5]

Tobias's conduct over the Fire Department report inspires skepticism about his ability to tell a story accurately, even where he himself was directly involved. There was, however, a more troubling story about his relations with the Institute.

IN EARLY 1962, GISEVIUS SUED TOBIAS over some of the more outrageous claims in his book. Gisevius's lawyers commissioned Hermann Graml to write an evaluation of Gisevius's *To the Bitter End*. Graml's report enraged Tobias. Tobias, in Krausnick's words, believed himself "in all controversial questions to be in possession of the absolute 'truth' ['*der Wahrheit*' *schlechthin*]," and for him there could never be any question of reasoned debate. For Tobias the world was divided into those who were with him and those who were against him. He was both able and willing to use his powers as an official of the Constitutional Protection to force people from the latter into the former category.[6]

In the extensive correspondence between Krausnick and Tobias one finds occasional ominous tones. In the summer of 1963, for example, Tobias wanted to offer Krausnick "an occasion to reconsider" his position. Complaining that the director had always favored Gisevius's account of the fire, Tobias wrote that years ago he had predicted that one day Krausnick would regret this "one-sidedness." "I am prepared to let bygones be bygones. It is up to you alone to determine how the future unfolds." Tobias had been patient with Krausnick, he said, but in this matter—a "confrontation between a complex of lies and legends" and "the truth"— there could be no more compromise. The director replied dryly that from Tobias's tone he, Krausnick, were he to remain unrepentant, could well imagine "'how the future will unfold.'" Mild irony was lost on Tobias. "It truly would have been better had you spared yourself the trouble of writing this letter," he replied. He warned that Krausnick had maneuvered himself into a "fatal situation."[7]

Behind Tobias's mob-boss language lay the fact that Krausnick had been a member of the Nazi Party between 1932 and 1934. Like much of the information Tobias deployed, this was a fact not publicly known in 1962. As an official of the Constitutional Protection, Tobias was able to uncover it—and he was willing to use it.

Graml's report was the catalyst. In May 1962, soon after Gisevius had introduced it into his lawsuit, Tobias sent a copy to his *Spiegel* collaborator Gunther Zacharias, with the recommendation that the "Institute for the Falsification of History" would be a good subject for a *Spiegel* investigation. Tobias immediately began looking for dirt on Graml. However, Graml, born in 1928, was too young to have done anything very troubling during the Third Reich.[8]

Tobias therefore focused on Krausnick. As an official, Tobias enjoyed an advantage that most journalists and historians did not: that of access to the Nazi Party files stored at the American-run Berlin Document Center. In late July he wrote Zacharias, "I have the documents that explain the panicky reluctance of the director to make himself conspicuous by shedding all too much light on the matter." These documents showed that Krausnick was "an Old Fighter"—"a brown goat who has been made the gardener in the meager fields of the Hitler Reich!" Gisevius might accuse Tobias of being a neo-Nazi, but, Tobias gloated, "Krausnick trembles that his brown past will come out."[9]

Tobias suspected Krausnick especially feared his "brown past" would come out were he to endorse Tobias's theory—because then the political left, and the East German government, would make Krausnick a particular target of scrutiny. Better, then, to go along with Gisevius and Wolff and stay inconspicuous. "He is not free in his decisions," as Tobias put it. Tobias was only willing to do without the scandal that would follow exposing Krausnick's past for reasons of "higher state-political interests," as such a scandal might supply a propaganda victory for East Germany.[10]

As it turned out, though, Tobias wasn't willing to do without the scandal for long. In the fall of 1962 he made Krausnick an offer the director couldn't refuse. Gisevius had known what was coming and warned Krausnick. The Institute's archivist, Anton Hoch, wrote in reply to Gisevius that "It is certainly very interesting for me to hear what possibilities one has—for private purposes!—as a member of the Constitutional Protection." In October Tobias reported happily to Zacharias that the Institute had run up the white flag. "Dr. Krausnick flew back from southern Italy and is negotiating through one of my acquaintances. They will no longer support Gisevius." "I only hope," he added with false piety, "that this praiseworthy decision does not come too late." He would have preferred it, he said, if the historians from Munich had "given in voluntarily to my line," rather than being forced "violently" to do so by Tobias's "mobilizing public opinion." But in any case, he concluded, the Institute's capitulation meant that "the main battle is won."[11]

The incident understandably left Krausnick bitter and frustrated. Hans Mommsen had earlier accused Krausnick of "prejudice" against Tobias. In late 1963 Krausnick replied to Mommsen with an indignant catalogue of Tobias's actions, which, even "for a person without prejudice" would eventually "start to smell." Tobias was close to people like Hans-Georg Gewehr and Kurt Ziesel, a far-right novelist and journalist who had subjected Krausnick and the Institute to scathing criticism. Despite his status as an official of the Constitutional Protection, Tobias had given an interview to the *Soldatenzeitung* (Soldier's newspaper), a far-right paper that greeted Tobias's book with enthusiasm. Tobias had accused Institute historian Martin Broszat of "deliberate deception" for Broszat's neutral 1960 article on the Reichstag fire controversy, an accusation that outraged Krausnick. And, of course, Tobias had blatantly abused his official opportunities to obtain materials about Institute members "for purely private reasons." Krausnick called Tobias's testimony from the Gewehr litigation on this point an "indirect confession." Someone from the Constitutional Protection had appeared at the office of the Göttingen historian Karl Otmar von Aretin to threaten him in the event he did not adopt Tobias's views ("ask Herr von Aretin himself about it!"). Now, said Krausnick, out of pure revenge for Graml's report, Tobias "was about to 'use' my party membership."[12]

The matter with Karl Otmar von Aretin had to do with a documentary film on the Nazi seizure of power that Aretin had put together for the Bavarian government in 1958. A thirty-second segment of the film presented Gisevius's account of the Reichstag fire. "At the time I was enormously proud of this film," said Aretin years later. When Aretin moved to Göttingen to take up a position there—a move that brought him to the state of Lower Saxony, in other words into Tobias's jurisdiction—"it was brought to my attention" that Tobias had argued for van der Lubbe's sole guilt and that "I should correct this passage."

Aretin refused to do so, and "Suddenly strange things happened." The Lower Saxon Constitutional Protection investigated him and anyone with whom he associated. One day "a gentleman" from the Constitutional Protection appeared in his office and told him he should cut the Reichstag fire passage out of his film. Aretin refused. The Constitutional Protection man threatened him that such obstinacy could cost him his academic career, "should Herr Tobias, who was very annoyed, make it known how I was conducting myself in this matter. It proved that I would not take new scholarly discoveries seriously." Aretin, with aristocratic self-confidence, showed the man the door: "I would not let myself be blackmailed." Tobias left Aretin in peace, but Tobias's opponents now began beating a path to Aretin's door. "I came to the conclusion that not only Tobias and his friends, but also his opponents were crazy." Aretin's story, like the German sources in Gisevius's FBI file and Tobias's willingness to use Krausnick's past against him, suggests how deeply involved the Constitutional Protection was in the Reichstag fire controversy.[13]

Krausnick's Nazi Party membership, however short-lived, was without question a black mark on his record. Nonetheless, if joining the party in 1932 spoke to genuine commitment rather than opportunism, leaving it in 1934 took some courage. In contrast to Tobias's witnesses, friends, and allies—Zirpins, Braschwitz, Heisig, Gewehr, and Schmidt—Krausnick was not guilty of any crimes during the Third Reich. After the war, he was in the forefront of those who tried to bring Germans face to face with their past, at a time when this was a far from safe or popular activity. This work earned him the sustained enmity of the far right. Krausnick's own research focused on the very darkest chapters of National Socialism, especially in his study of the *Einsatzgruppen*, which Hitler's biographer Ian Kershaw has called "groundbreaking."[14]

However, in the face of Tobias's threats, Krausnick and the Institute changed their position on the Reichstag fire. One product of this change was that "memo to file" that became such a sore point for Hans Mommsen.

IN EARLY 1960, IN THE WAKE of Tobias's *Spiegel* series, the Institute for Contemporary History commissioned a schoolteacher from Baden-Württemberg, Hans Schneider, to write a rebuttal. Schneider, born in 1907, had studied history and philology at the universities of Tübingen, Munich, and Berlin, and in the 1930s became a teacher at a *Gymnasium*. In 1934 he joined the Nazi Party, in which he became the "culture leader" of the Party chapter in Baiersbronn in the Black Forest. After imprisonment in 1945 and 1946 for his Party membership, he returned to teaching at the *Gymnasium* in Freudenstadt, also in the Black Forest. In 1960 he joined the Social Democratic Party.[15]

Schneider impressed both Krausnick and Hans Rothfels, the editor of the Institute's *Quarterly*, with a draft critique of Tobias's articles. The Institute was under pressure, particularly from schools and public officials, to come up with a response to Tobias, but could not spare any of its own staff from other projects. Krausnick suggested Schneider undertake a study of the state of research on the Reichstag fire that would reveal "the line between what has really been proven and not proven." The *Quarterly* would then publish the results with an introduction from Rothfels.[16]

However, the Institute soon began having second thoughts about Schneider. In the fall of 1960 Krausnick was already describing Schneider with reserve as an "apparently qualified outsider," and complaining that hiring him was only an unsatisfactory "expedient," since "hopes connected with freelancers have seldom been fulfilled." In July 1961 Schneider came to the Institute for a meeting with Krausnick, Broszat, Graml, and Hoch. They discussed whether Schneider should write a "questioning," a "strong critique," or a "refutation" (*Infragestelling, Erschütterung, Widerlegung*) of Tobias's Reichstag fire case. The representatives of the Institute decided unanimously that "for tactical reasons a questioning or a strong critique would thoroughly suffice." A refutation would require positive proof of the actual culprits, which the state of the sources did not permit. They agreed that Schneider would deliver his manuscript between November 15 and December 1, 1961.[17]

Teaching duties and ill health kept Schneider from finishing his project. Meanwhile external pressure on the Institute mounted. In 1962 the same Paul Karl Schmidt who had worked with Tobias on the *Spiegel* series published (under the pseudonym Jürgen Westerhoff) a glowing review of Tobias's book in the magazine *Kristall*, which was edited by the former SS *Einsatzgruppe* member and former *Spiegel* staffer Horst Mahnke, the one whom the CIA had thought too "radical" to visit the United States. The review amounted to an attack on the Institute, and on Krausnick personally; it was one volley in a larger far right campaign to try to stop or deter the critical scholarship the Institute carried out. Krausnick, said "Westerhoff," had promised a "serious debate" with Tobias, but the best he could do was to use Gisevius and Wolff as sources, the one discredited by litigation against Gewehr, the other by Tobias. The Institute had not assigned any of its most distinguished members to study this "hotly contested piece of our contemporary history." Instead it had done no more than commission "a school teacher from the Black Forest."[18]

Helmut Krausnick was a fine historian. But no less than Diels, Schnitzler, Zirpins, Heisig, and Braschwitz, he was a pragmatist, one whose Institute depended on public funding—in other words, on the good will of politicians, and hence indirectly on public opinion. Public relations and those urgent questions from schools and public officials, as well as considerations of the "tactics" of a proper response to Tobias's thesis, had driven him to commission an institutional reply to Tobias in the first place. By the summer of 1962 the public relations shoe was on the other foot. Krausnick had had enough of the fight, and of Schneider.

In July 1962 Krausnick wrote Rothfels that they could not be certain what would come of Schneider's work, but that "one must most definitely reckon that nothing will come of a refutation of Tobias." Hans Mommsen, he said, could step in and write an evaluation of Tobias's work instead. In September, as we have seen, Krausnick learned that Tobias would reveal his Nazi Party membership if the Institute did not change its line. In what could hardly be coincidental timing, by late October the Institute had decided to cancel Schneider's project. Krausnick asked Schneider to come to Munich for a meeting. In three discussions, which took place on November 9th and 10th, Krausnick explained that he wanted to find a way out of the "situation" that would satisfy all parties. The manuscript that Schneider had now submitted to the Institute was far longer than the agreement had called for. Furthermore, after a "thorough examination" of Schneider's text, a conclusive result, one that would "constitute a refutation of Tobias's thesis," could not be expected. Never mind that a refutation of Tobias was precisely what the Institute had *not* asked for the previous year. Since "we *publicly* announced a statement *of the Institute for Contemporary History* in the Reichstag fire case," Krausnick explained to Schneider, "we are not in a position to publish a *result* that we cannot stand behind" (emphasis in original).

Krausnick said that he considered it necessary to ask one of the Institute's staff to step in, and he asked Schneider to hand over his manuscript and all the research materials that he had gathered. Schneider apparently accepted that the copyright in his material belonged to the Institute, and that the Institute could forbid him to publish it elsewhere. Krausnick had prepared a draft agreement in these terms; the Institute would pay Schneider 2,000 DM for the work he had done and, when it had prepared its own statement on the Reichstag fire, would give him the opportunity to comment on it before publication.[19]

Then Schneider began to have doubts. He insisted on his right to use his research materials for his own publication. The possibility of an agreement broke down and the Institute decided to try a heavier-handed approach. Sometime in November 1962 Krausnick sent Mommsen to meet with the Institute's lawyer, Dr. Ludwig Delp, who had particular expertise in matters of copyright, and who in fact had already advised the Institute on another case in which, for political reasons, the Institute wanted to stop an author from publishing. Mommsen recorded the results of this meeting in that memo to file, or that "memo to file that wasn't," as he later described it.[20]

According to the memo, Delp explained that simply because the Institute had commissioned Schneider to research the Reichstag fire, copyright in Schneider's work did not automatically pass to the Institute.

Furthermore, the conditions for a unilateral cancellation of the contract by the Institute were "unfavorable." Neither Schneider's delays nor the length of the manuscript could justify it. Nor could the "tendency and thesis" of Schneider's work, not only because this was the sort of risk publishers normally ran, but also because the work "had at first received the express support of the Institute." In short, the Institute had to allow Schneider to publish his analysis elsewhere, so long as he did not try to suggest that the Institute stood behind his work.

For the Institute this was unacceptably bad news. "The Institute has an interest," Mommsen wrote, "in preventing the publication of Herr Schneider's manuscript," most importantly because its appearance would be "undesirable" for "general political reasons." Schneider had to be stopped, and therefore it might be "advisable," Mommsen continued, to stop him "by means of pressure from the ministry in Stuttgart"—in other words, Schneider's employer. It was unclear whether Schneider would agree to this, and so the negotiations would have to be undertaken carefully. Legally the Institute had no claim on the copyright in Schneider's work or in the content of materials that it had provided to him. "But," Mommsen continued, "in the negotiations with him it is advisable to use this argument, which for lack of legal advice Herr Schneider obviously takes seriously, to bring him to a settlement." If that failed, perhaps an offer of 5,000 or 6,000 DM might do the trick.[21]

Only an enormous amount of pressure could have driven honorable men like Krausnick and Mommsen to work behind the scenes to threaten Schneider's job, take advantage of his legal ignorance to bully him into caving, or bribe him into not publishing his work. What had put the Institute into such a panic? In light of all the circumstances—the public attacks to which the Institute was subjected from Tobias and his allies, the ever-present concern about its public funding, and Tobias's blackmailing of Krausnick—the answer seems to lie in those "general political reasons" that Mommsen said made publication of Schneider's work "undesirable." This is certainly what Schneider thought. He wrote that the Institute had bowed to outside pressure—in other words, to fear of "Tobias, Augstein, and company."[22]

On November 30th Krausnick wrote to Schneider to tell him that were he to quote or even refer to source material the Institute had supplied him, he would be engaging in "open conflict with the Institute" for which there would be "consequences." Krausnick hoped that Schneider would understand that it was in his own "best interests" if the Institute "relieved" him of a work that offered no prospect of success, and could seriously damage his health. "We would also not be able to take responsibility for this before your school authority," Krausnick added ominously.[23]

The Institute succeeded in preventing Schneider from publishing his work in his lifetime. His manuscript was finally published only in 2004, ten years after his death. The story of the Institute's handling of Schneider did not become publicly known until 2000, when a Reichstag fire researcher named Hersch Fischler published an account of the critical documents—Mommsen's memo and Krausnick's bullying of Schneider—in the newspaper the *Tageszeitung* (Daily newspaper).[24]

At first Mommsen responded that Fischler's claims were untrue. He had, he said, drafted his memo only *after* Krausnick's letter to Schneider, and so it was effectively irrelevant. This claim makes little sense. Mommsen's memo refers to Krausnick's meetings with Schneider on November 9th and 10th, and recommends precisely the course of action that Krausnick took at the end of the month. The only logical explanation is that Krausnick had asked Mommsen to get Delp's advice on how to handle the situation before writing to Schneider. The memo had to have been drafted sometime between the meeting and Krausnick's letter.[25]

Indeed, in a 2003 film interview, Mommsen took a different tack. He claimed that canceling the deal with Schneider had really been Krausnick's doing. In the film Mommsen grows visibly angry. When asked about his line that publication of Schneider's research was undesirable for "general political reasons," Mommsen gestures furiously while retorting that, in order to libel him, the interviewer has "taken this one-half sentence in an unofficial memo [*Protokoll*]" with "nothing more behind it than that" and for which he was "the only witness." When the interviewer says she wants to understand what "general political reasons" could mean, Mommsen interrupts her by saying "there is nothing to understand," and then, as the interviewer finishes her question, yells, "I don't know!" He wrote the sentence forty years ago, he says. "What do you still want to use it for today?"[26]

In July 2001 the Institute officially responded. Mommsen's statement that the publication of Schneider's manuscript was "undesirable" for "general political reasons," and his suggestion that Schneider be pressured through the Stuttgart ministry to abandon the project, were, from an academic viewpoint "completely unacceptable," although Schneider's manuscript was in

fact not "ready for publication (*publikationsreif*)." The Institute's then-director
Horst Möller criticized Krausnick in the documentary film. The suppression
of Schneider's draft was, he said, "absolutely impossible" for an academic.
"Scholarship *must* be free, it must incidentally be free even in error, and therefore one cannot exert pressure through an employer. 'General political reasons,' whatever they might be, cannot play any role in the evaluation of a
scholarly manuscript."[27]

More recently Mommsen has argued that Schneider's manuscript simply wasn't publishable: too long for the *Quarterly*, too short for a book,
more footnotes than text. Schneider criticized Tobias without putting forward any evidence of who actually set the fire (which, however, was exactly
what Schneider and Krausnick had agreed to). He added that Krausnick
managed the whole situation with Schneider "terribly."[28]

Indeed, as Horst Möller's comments implicitly acknowledge, the responsibility for what happened with Schneider really did lie with Krausnick and Delp and not Mommsen. Krausnick was the boss; Mommsen's
memo seemed only to record Delp's advice, as Krausnick had likely
instructed Mommsen to do. Mommsen was a vulnerable young scholar
without stable employment. Just as the Institute was pushing Schneider off
the Reichstag fire case and handing it over to Mommsen, Mommsen was
deeply angry about something else. In July 1963 Krausnick informed him
that the federal government office that handled political education (then
called the *Bundeszentrale für Heimatdienst*) did not want to publish the manuscript about the persecution of Jews in the Third Reich on which Mommsen had spent most of his time as an employee of the Institute. The
Bundeszentrale had advanced money for the project, and so Mommsen
would have to buy it back before it could be published elsewhere. Mommsen complained that Krausnick had strung him along on the project and
then "torpedoed" it.[29]

If Krausnick bore the responsibility for the treatment of Schneider, one
can nonetheless understand and even sympathize with the reasons why he
did what he did, even apart from the blackmail to which Tobias subjected
him. The Reichstag fire was far from the only case in which Krausnick
took careful account of the forces arrayed for and against a particular historical interpretation. His job was to be a kind of politician of history, and
he always worked in accordance with Bismarck's maxim that politics was
the art of the possible. In the 1950s and early 1960s his Institute was, in
the words of historian Wolfgang Benz, an "outsiders' guild" dependent on

governmental goodwill. From 1960 the federal government had three seats on the Institute's board. The states of Bavaria, Hesse, and Baden-Württemberg had one each, and there were two more for the other states collectively. These governments therefore had a direct impact on the nature of the Institute's research.[30]

In 1959, for instance, the historian Eberhard Jäckel and a former general were working on a project for the Institute about German relations with Vichy France. The Federal Defense Ministry would not let them see some critical sources because it was "at the moment undesirable for foreign policy reasons to work on such a subject." The Institute's academic council and board acknowledged that foreign policy considerations needed to be kept in mind when planning the timing of publications. There were other examples. At a meeting in 1960 a senior federal official urged the Institute to publish research that would help rebut East German allegations about the Nazi pasts of important West German officials, among them Hans Globke, the lawyer who had drafted the official commentary to the Nazis' Nuremberg racial laws and since 1953 had been the state secretary in Adenauer's Chancellor's Office. A few years later a senior official complained to Krausnick about a recent article on the Valkyrie conspiracy in the *Quarterly*. "All articles about the 20th of July," he wrote, "must take very careful consideration of what great significance the events then have today for domestic political controversies." The official was annoyed that the article discussed the conspirators' plans to make Martin Niemöller, a friend of Gisevius and fellow advocate of German neutrality, head of state after the overthrow of Hitler.[31]

The general unwillingness of 1950s West German society to dwell on its responsibility for the victims of Nazism also affected the Institute's practice. Most German scholars at the time held to a code of rigorous objectivity by which they viewed research by émigrés and victims of Nazism with suspicion, on the grounds that the latter were "emotional" rather than objective (a disposition that often crops up in the Reichstag fire debate: in 1986 the political scientist Eckhard Jesse patronizingly dismissed the anti-Tobias views of Robert Kempner and Golo Mann because, since the fire had directly or indirectly forced them to emigrate, their position on it could only be "emotional," lacking the objectivity of a "scientist"). "It is generally clear," the *Stuttgarter Zeitung* (Stuttgart newspaper) wrote in 1950, that "one cannot measure recent German history with the standards of the denazification tribunals (*Spruchkammern*)"—another way to express what we have called "Nuremberg history." A historian named H.G. Adler, himself a survivor of Theresienstadt and Auschwitz, had support from the Institute for a project on the deportation of Jews from Germany. But by 1961 he was complaining bitterly about a country and a government that would not allow a Jew to see documents pertaining to Jews from the Second World War. A Jew "remains a Jew and should recognize that he is not to get mixed up in any matters of old Nazis and their patrons." He felt there was a general attitude in Germany that very obvious criminals—"concentration camp and Gestapo functionaries"— could be sacrificed, but so-called "honorable" officials were at all costs "to be spared possible troubles." Even Hans Rothfels, whom the Nazis had driven from his academic chair and his country for not being "Aryan," argued it was not the Institute's job to "wallow in guilt."[32]

Just to what extent "general political reasons" affected Krausnick's assessment of the Reichstag fire controversy came out in one of his exasperated letters to Mommsen. Mommsen and Tobias had criticized Krausnick for saying only that "Tobias's thesis was not to be refuted," rather than that it was correct. Krausnick explained that he felt no desire "for the sake of Herr Tobias's lovely eyes" to expose the Institute to the suspicion among "those whose judgment matters to us" that it had "gone and joined the whitewashers." He was concerned, in other words, that the nationalist politics behind Tobias's thesis could also hurt the Institute's reputation with the center and left.[33]

In the early 1960s the Institute faced a sustained attack from the far right. Tobias, despite being an avowed Social Democrat, was a central player in this attack, but far from the only one—although most of the other fierce critics were in some way linked to Tobias. This was one of the ways in which, through some combination of naivety and obsession with sustaining his own argument, Tobias let himself be used by partisans of the extreme right. His ally Kurt Ziesel laid into Krausnick and the Institute in a 1963 book, *Der deutsche Selbstmord* (The German suicide). On the Reichstag fire controversy, said Ziesel, the Institute had done nothing more than help Gisevius to spread "Communist legends." Neither Krausnick nor Gisevius possessed the courage to "confess their error," and merely attempted to create doubts about the truth that Tobias had discovered. As Krausnick had suspected he would, and despite the Institute's change of face, Ziesel used Tobias's information to "out" Krausnick, calling him in essence a well-connected Nazi historian whose work had drawn the approval of leading regime figures. There can be little doubt that Ziesel coordinated this attack with Tobias. Apart from the information about Krausnick's Party membership, Ziesel also cited a letter Tobias had written to the editor in chief of the *Zeit*. Both must have come from Tobias.[34]

Ziesel, it later turned out, was one of the many journalists and pundits who worked covertly for General Reinhard Gehlen's Federal Intelligence Service (*Bundesnachrichtendienst*, BND), to circulate opinions that the conservative-nationalist BND found useful. Ziesel had been on the staff of the *Völkischer Beobachter* in the 1930s, and after 1939 served as a war correspondent. After the war he chaired a far-right organization called the Germany Foundation and edited the Foundation's journal, the Germany Magazine. The Munich Court of Appeals deemed the Germany Foundation "antidemocratic."[35]

Ziesel compared Krausnick's opposition to Tobias to his fierce criticisms of the arguments of David Hoggan, an American historian who went from arguing that a British conspiracy forced Germany into the Second World War to denying the Holocaust. Krausnick had accused Hoggan of manufacturing evidence, and wrote, "rarely have so many inane and unwarranted theses, allegations, and 'conclusions' . . . been crammed into a volume written under the guise of history." For Ziesel there was "no doubt" that Hitler had started the war "carelessly," but there was "also no doubt that he was often, in a virtually criminal way, provoked to it." Ziesel therefore supported Tobias with the same enthusiasm and for the same reasons that he supported a Holocaust-denying neo-Nazi. This was not, of course, Tobias's fault. But it is important to understand that his argument went with the grain of such far-right positions, and was therefore eagerly used by people like Ziesel at a time when such figures seemed to be gaining political ground.[36]

The Institute's academic council increasingly worried about public attacks from the likes of Tobias, Ziesel, and Paul Karl Schmidt. In the summer of 1963, Hans Rothfels told a council meeting that "The Institute finds itself in a new situation as a result of a certain shift in public opinion." He pointed to the "highly questionable apologetics" that were accompanying the defamatory attacks made by the far right on the Institute and "all of us." A year later Krausnick noted that it "hardly needed to be mentioned" that the Institute had been subjected to defamatory attacks in far-right periodicals and letters.[37]

It was also in this context, therefore, that Hans Mommsen's definitive article on the Reichstag fire appeared in the *Quarterly* in the autumn of 1964. With all of the prestige of the Institute and of Mommsen himself behind it, this article all but settled the Reichstag fire debate: henceforth, most historians would believe Tobias's account of the Reichstag fire, at least as filtered through Mommsen, and they would feel little need to look behind it.

For Mommsen the Reichstag fire controversy was more a generational and methodological than an ideological question. The generation that experienced Nazi Germany as adults—and that wrote the first historical accounts of it—was stuck in "Hitler-centric" explanations of the Third Reich, in other words those that stressed the centrality of Hitler's ideas and will in the unfolding of Nazism. Historians call these kinds of explanations "intentionalist."[38]

Mommsen made his name as perhaps the most prominent among the historians who challenged the intentionalist view. Historians like Mommsen are called "functionalists" or "structuralists." They argue that the development of Nazi Germany was beyond the control or plans of any one person, even Hitler. Instead it was the product of impersonal forces: economic patterns, competing bureaucratic agencies and factions of the Nazi movement, grass-roots pressure, and (occasionally) resistance. Little that happened in Nazi Germany was specifically planned; some things were the products of chance. For Mommsen, not only was the Reichstag fire controversy really one between intentionalists and functionalists, it provided an important "opening" for the functionalists' arguments.[39]

Very few historical works are not in need of revision and correction fifty years after their date of publication. This is all the more true the more recent the events narrated, and the more recently significant new sources have become available to researchers. It is therefore hardly a criticism of Mommsen's article to note that many of its arguments can no longer be maintained. He took over from Tobias the core notion that Diels, Heisig, Zirpins, and Braschwitz were non-Nazis who had carried out honest investigations in 1933 and told the truth about them both at the time and after the war. As with Tobias, this argument depended on believing what these men said when they were in considerable legal jeopardy: for instance, to support the proposition that Diels, Reinhold Heller and Braschwitz tried to convince Göring that van der Lubbe had acted alone, Mommsen cited only Diels's 1949 memoir and, even more remarkably, a 1961 letter from Braschwitz to a prosecutor—when of course Braschwitz was under investigation for his role in convicting van der Lubbe. In any case, as we have seen, the investigation documents which became available in the 1990s overwhelmingly contradict this picture of courageous officers telling truth to power and insisting on van der Lubbe's sole culprit status. Mommsen also accepted that the report of the fire expert Dr. Franz Ritter contradicted those of Josse, Wagner, and Schatz, and this was why it was not used at the trial. This was an easy argument to make when the report was not available, but we now know it is not true: Ritter reached the same conclusions about van der Lubbe as a sole culprit as did his colleagues. Mommsen wrote not only that Schnitzler and Diels drafted their 1949 accounts of the fire without consulting each other (Diels, said Mommsen, relying on Diels's own account, only became aware of Schnitzler's writing when it was already being printed), but that Schnitzler took some of his information from Heisig "who had no reason at all for an apologetic position." Again, none of this can be maintained today.[40]

Yet Mommsen's article, in comparison to Tobias's work, was both more methodologically sophisticated, and more obviously indebted to a methodological (as opposed to a political) agenda. Mommsen avoided two of Tobias's significant failings: he was bluntly critical of Tobias's famous finding that only the blind chance of the fire had converted Hitler into a dictator; and he did not repeat Tobias's explanation of how fire could have spread through the plenary chamber, which rested on a failure to understand how such a conflagration works. Instead, Mommsen limited himself to the critique of the expert witnesses that we saw in chapter 4, without in fact putting forward any positive explanation for the spread of the fire.[41]

Mommsen suggested that his writing amounted to a "sober" attempt to demonstrate what could be empirically known about the fire, resorting to "hypotheses" only where necessary to "make evident the connections between clearly determined facts." In fact, given the paucity of reliable sources with which he could work, his long article is better read as a brilliantly constructed series of hypotheses connecting a relatively small number of unarguable facts. In part, the lasting value of his article rests on the imaginative and analytical flair with which he connected these facts. But we could go further and say that much of what Mommsen wrote retains its full force today. His discussion of the political effects of the fire, and especially of its failure as propaganda for the Nazis, is a model of thorough, thoughtful, and solidly researched historical explication. Also of enduring interest is his discussion of the reasons why the Nazis did not want to bring in the army to defend against a supposed Communist coup attempt. The Nazis were fighting in two directions, against the Nationalists as well as the Communists, and they recognized that the army represented the Nationalists' best hope of turning back the Nazis' consolidation of power. This remains a crucial insight.[42]

It is only when we understand the decisive importance of the Institute's judgments in early postwar Germany that we can fully understand the impact of Mommsen's article. In the 1950s and 1960s the Institute was widely seen not only as an important research center, but as the final adjudicator of historical truth about the era of Nazism. This was why people wrote to Krausnick seeking the Institute's definitive opinion on Tobias's writings, and why in turn he felt pressured to respond. Indeed, in its first two decades, the bulk of the Institute's work did not consist of purely academic research at all, but rather of the preparation of expert reports for prosecutions and other court cases involving ex-Nazis. In the mid-1950s the Institute was preparing about 150 such reports every year; the founding of the Ludwigsburg Central Office caused a jump to 246 in the course of 1958; by 1966 the number had risen to 600 per year. The Institute eventually published two volumes of these reports (from which Graml's report on Gisevius and Tobias is conspicuously absent), not counting the lengthy analyses that four of its scholars prepared for the Frankfurt Auschwitz trials of the mid-1960s, which appeared separately.[43]

This is not to underrate the quality of what Mommsen wrote. On the contrary: By the standards by which historians judge these things— thoroughness of research and range of sources, clarity of argument and analysis—Mommsen's article remains far and away the best writing on the Reichstag fire. He spoke not only with his own (considerable) authority, but with the weight of Krausnick's Institute and Rothfels's journal behind him. It is above all for this reason that the great majority of professional historians have come to accept the single-culprit theory of the Reichstag fire.

TOBIAS HAD CELEBRATED THE SURRENDER of the Institute for Contemporary History with the remark, "they will no longer support Gisevius." He was referring to the litigation between Gisevius and Hans Georg Gewehr. His remark fell between a trial verdict of February 1962 and an appeal decision that would follow the next year. As Tobias enthusiastically supported Gewehr, helping him with information and advice, the litigation became something of a proxy battle between the Institute and Tobias—until the Institute bowed out after Tobias's successful blackmailing of Krausnick. It was the last of the many legal battles that brought to light important new evidence about the Reichstag fire.

Gewehr vs. Gisevius was also part of the pattern of actions and responses that had driven the Reichstag fire controversy forward since 1955, when Arthur Brandt's re-opening of the van der Lubbe case had led to the appearance of Richard Wolff's *Parlament* article and the popular magazine series by Riess, Strindberg, and Schulze-Wilde. State Prosecutor Dobbert in turn played midwife to Tobias's article in the *Spiegel*. Gisevius's lawsuit against Tobias's book led to Graml's expert report, which brought Tobias's vengeance on Krausnick and the Institute. The last steps also came from Gisevius's response to Tobias.

"Reichstagsbrand im Zerrspiegel" was the title of a series of articles that Gisevius published in March 1960 in the *Zeit*. The title was a pun meaning roughly "the Reichstag fire in a distorting mirror," the "mirror" of course a reference to the *Spiegel*, which in German means "mirror." The first three installments, and the opening section of the fourth, offered a critique of Tobias's articles. However, it was the rest of the fourth article that proved to be important and, for Gisevius, fateful. Here, once again, he accused Gewehr of having burned the Reichstag.[44]

We have seen the consequences of these articles in stimulating the search for documents, which led to the discovery of Karl Reineking's SA file corroborating Gisevius's 1946 story of what happened to Adolf Rall. Another consequence was that prosecutors in Düsseldorf began investigating Gewehr for involvement in the Reichstag fire. Gisevius also intended his accusation to force Gewehr either to "admit his culpability through further silence" or be forced into suing Gisevius for libel. If Gewehr took the second course he would have to bring forward evidence; "his mere insistence on innocence will not do." And from his evidence would come, thought Gisevius, "highly interesting follow-up questions." If Gewehr denied everything, why had he kept silent for fourteen years in the face of Gisevius's allegations? On the other hand, if he at least partly conceded connivance—"then the inflammatory [*eifernd*] Tobias thesis of van der Lubbe as the sole culprit collapses." Gisevius's plan succeeded, up to a point. Gewehr did launch a libel lawsuit against Gisevius. The litigation would drag on for the rest of the decade.[45]

Its most important effect was that it brought to light considerable new evidence. Surprisingly little documentary evidence on the Reichstag fire was available to researchers at the beginning of the 1960s, a point that we need to remember when reading both Tobias and Mommsen. Only in early 1962 was the full stenographic record of the Leipzig trial found (only seven of the fifty-seven days of the transcript had been available for Tobias's book). Most of the other documents from the 1933 investigation and trial were in the Soviet Union and hence inaccessible. Even the Reich Supreme Court's official reasons for judgment did not come to light until the litigation of the 1960s. Gisevius had written his book and his articles without any documents that could prove his "statements about the existence—and the liquidation—of that justice employee Reineking," and of course it was his 1960 articles that stimulated the discovery of at least some of these. Others remained locked away until after the end of the Cold War.[46]

In the first round of *Gewehr vs. Gisevius*, Gewehr sued to compel Gisevius to retract what he had written. Gewehr's lawyer was Anton Roesen, who a decade earlier had acted for Heinrich Schnitzler. Through Roesen, Gewehr made what were, under the circumstances, some rather surprising concessions. He accepted that Diels had told Arndt and Kempner at Nuremberg that Gewehr was among the Reichstag fire culprits, arguing only that Diels's 1949 book, with its endorsement of the single-culprit theory, superseded any earlier statements. (Of course, by this logic Diels's 1957 statements, and his 1956 interview in the *Frankfurter Rundschau*, in which he said that the Reichstag could have been burned by a "wild" SA squad, superseded his book.) In October 1933 Rall, Roesen argued, had "remembered, from his guest role with the SA, attempts . . . to burn posters on the advertising columns with phosphorus, and he may also have thought of the plaintiff"—Gewehr—"who had earlier been well-known in the Berlin SA as the leader of Karl Ernst's Staff Watch, and of whom he [Rall] perhaps also knew that in *Standartenführer* circles [Gewehr] had advocated the use of this 'weapon.'" This was at any rate a confirmation from Gewehr that Rall really had been a Berlin SA man with experience setting fires, a fact that appears in no surviving SA documents.[47]

The case also brought forward new witnesses. The journalist Harry Schulze-Wilde had met Diels for the first time at the home of the Faber-Castells in the summer of 1947. There, Schulze-Wilde claimed in 1961, Diels told him that at the Gestapo all of the officers had been convinced that the Nazis were behind the fire. "Only it had never been talked about. It had simply been presumed." Diels also said, "you must ask Heini Gewehr," and explained that Gewehr was one of the people who as early as 1932 had belonged to an "arsonists' commando," designated as the "Unit for Special Missions." This unit, according to Schulze-Wilde's paraphrase of Diels, "had, for instance, sprayed *Litfaßsäulen* [advertising columns on Berlin's streets], street cars, and bank premises with a particular fluid that ignited after a certain time." Gewehr, said Diels, was the only member of the unit who survived the Night of the Long Knives.[48]

Schulze-Wilde interviewed Diels about the fire on two later occasions as well, in 1952 and in 1957, and found that Diels told essentially the same story, especially as it concerned Gewehr. In the 1957 interview, for instance, Schulze-Wilde testified that it had been "beyond all debate" for Diels that Heini Gewehr was one of the culprits. Diels had also "said a few things about the mixture of the chemical solution."[49]

In late 1957 Diels also gave interviews about the fire to two other journalists. One was Friedrich Strindberg, adoptive son of August Strindberg, an aggressive reporter who during the Second World War had been one of the first to gather detailed information about the death camps. In 1957 Strindberg was the editor-in-chief of the weeklies *Quick* and *Welt-bild*. He interviewed Diels over the course of an evening in his own apartment in Munich in "October or early November" 1957, followed by an afternoon at Lake Starnberg and another evening at Diels's hotel. As he did so often, Diels began by telling Strindberg that he could say nothing "from his own knowledge" about Nazi guilt for the Reichstag fire. However, after talking about other things, Diels himself seemed to want to return to the question of the fire. Both Strindberg and his wife had the impression that "Diels was depressed by an old guilt."

Diels told Strindberg about his meeting with Gisevius in Lugano, confirming "the truth of the Gisevius report," including the stories of Rall and Reineking. Gisevius's written account was mistaken in many details, said Diels, "but the essential elements are correct." Then, over several hours, Diels retreated bit by bit from his claim of knowing nothing about the Nazis and the Reichstag fire. He continued to insist that he had not known about the fire in advance. But from several events he had formed the conclusion that the Nazis had done it.

Rall, said Diels, had testified that the Reichstag had been burned with the same chemical solution that SA men had used in 1932 to set fire to advertising columns and streetcars. Diels also confirmed that it had been Reineking who conveyed the gist of Rall's testimony to Karl Ernst. Naturally, Diels denied that the Gestapo had been responsible for Rall's murder. But "the most important lead" that Diels gave Strindberg was Heini Gewehr. Diels insisted "repeatedly" that Gewehr was "the only surviving witness of the arson"; in fact, in language very similar to his 1946 letter to the British delegation at Nuremberg, Diels told Strindberg that "If you get this Heini Gewehr to talk, then you will know the truth about the Reichstag fire." Through a series of "crazy chances" Gewehr had survived the Röhm purge, in which all of the other Reichstag arsonists had been "liquidated." Diels knew as well that during the Second World War Gewehr had been a senior police officer, and that in 1957 Gewehr lived "somewhere in the Rhineland."

Strindberg was so struck by Diels's statements about Gewehr that he retained a former police officer, Criminal Commissar Rudolf Lissigkeit, to seek out Gewehr in Düsseldorf, but without much result. Gewehr denied any involvement in the Reichstag fire. Strindberg submitted a transcript of Lissigkeit's interview to the court. Uninformative in itself, it is at least confirmation that Diels really had given Strindberg Gewehr's name. Strindberg also sent a man named Hans Rechenberg, a former assistant to Göring, to question Gewehr. Perhaps because of Rechenberg's credibility in Gewehr's eyes, he got somewhat more out of the old stormtrooper, though again no decisive confessions.[50]

By 1961 Diels himself could no longer add his eloquent but maddening voice to the dispute. In 1957, just as the information he had given Schulze-Wilde, Strindberg, and Curt Riess about Gewehr appeared in print, Diels died suddenly, a few weeks short of his fifty-seventh birthday. Indeed, the mention of Gewehr in Riess's *Stern* magazine story appeared opposite an inset announcement that "A few days ago the former first chief of the Gestapo, Rudolf Diels, died as the result of a hunting accident." Diels, the note continued, had played a definitive role in the report, although the report did not expressly link the naming of Gewehr to Diels—this point did not become public until 1961.[51]

Diels had always lived dangerously, and he certainly had his share of enemies, even after the war. A 1950 American intelligence report had claimed that Fritz Dorls, one of the leaders of a neo-Nazi party called the Socialist Reich Party (SRP), tried to recruit Diels and grew angry when Diels declined. The report said that Dorls had "reminded Diels that as the former chief of the Gestapo he has many enemies and he therefore should join Dorls's party for protection." Diels replied, "God would decide when he was to die."

God evidently decided it would be in a hunting accident. In the 1980s Diels's (and Tobias's) friend Adolf von Thadden gave Tobias the story of what had happened; Thadden had evidently heard it from Lisa Breimer. Diels and Breimer had driven out to a lake for a picnic. Diels first went off by himself to shoot a duck. As he was getting the shotgun out of his car the trigger caught and Diels shot himself in the abdomen. Breimer heard the shot, ran to find him, and drove him to the hospital, but the doctors quickly determined, according to Thadden, that "there was nothing to be done." Diels phlegmatically summoned the local town mayor and made a will, leaving his money to Breimer. He went as he might have wished, with the stoicism he had admired in Ali Höhler. He asked for a cigarette and to be left alone to die. Ten minutes later he was dead.[52]

In the spring of 1960, Gewehr himself gave an interview to Kraus-nick and Hermann Graml at the Institute for Contemporary History. Graml reported on the conversation in a letter to Hans Schneider. Schnei-der had asked for notes or a tape of the interview. Graml declined, as Gewehr had insisted on confidentiality. He added that "the conversation with Gewehr produced or promised for the future practically nothing at all that could further the investigation of the Reichstag fire." Gewehr had insisted that he not only had nothing to do with the Reichstag fire, but also that he knew nothing more about it than anyone else who was alive at the time. Graml added, however, that "for the remarkable fact that already in 1933/34 Berlin Party, SA, and SS circles connected him with the fire, he offered explanations that sounded in fact halfway plau-sible, without, admittedly, being fully convincing." Graml felt that there remained a few gaps and contradictions that were too large to rule Gewehr out as a culprit, yet also not large enough to force him "to show his colors." However inconclusive the interview may have been, Gewehr himself, through his lawyer, strenuously insisted on keeping the notes of the interview confidential. The Institute reports that these notes have subsequently been lost.[53]

We do, however, have a few hints as to their contents. Krausnick wrote to Mommsen in 1963 that Gewehr's "memo" (this probably refers to Gewehr's 1960 letter to Tobias's *Spiegel* collaborator Gunther Zacharias) was "somewhat more carefully written" than his oral statements at the

Institute. Krausnick went on to note that in the litigation against Gisevius, Gewehr probably had "good reasons" for keeping quiet about the fact
that as a prisoner after the 1934 SA purge, he was immediately interrogated about his knowledge of the Reichstag fire, and was asked about it
again in 1937 by Himmler himself. Gewehr, Krausnick continued, "had
the firm impression that he was intended to be shot on June 30, 1934,
although until shortly before that he had been abroad." These facts, which
Gewehr had evidently shared with Krausnick and Graml, suggested to
them both that "the corresponding suspicions of Gewehr can by no means
be chalked up only to the nonsense of Gisevius or to his carelessness, but
rather existed first in the most important party circles," which remained
uncertain even up until 1945 that the Reichstag arsonists had not come
"from their own ranks."[54]

In a letter to Krausnick a few months before, Tobias complained that
Krausnick had betrayed the contents of Gewehr's interview "more or less
correctly" to Gisevius. This fact emerged, said Tobias, from the request of
one of Gisevius's lawyers to question Krausnick in court about Gewehr's
admission that he had "given many courses of instruction [on setting fires
with the phosphorus solution] at a point near in time to the arson."[55]

This new evidence was also applied to the criminal investigation of
Gewehr himself. Yet in the end the prosecutor stayed the case. The evidence was entirely hearsay, whether from Rall/Reineking/Gisevius or
Diels/Schulze-Wilde/Strindberg. "The possibility cannot be excluded,"
the prosecutor wrote, that "Diels held the accused to have been involved
purely on the basis of suspicion." It was no longer possible to tell what
facts or evidence might have underpinned this suspicion.[56]

This was an appropriate conclusion in a criminal investigation in which
a man's liberty was at stake, and appropriate in light of the evidence available in 1960. For a historical investigation in the early twenty-first century
the position is entirely different. As we have seen, documents from Diels's
papers and from Tobias's private archive, all unavailable to most previous
researchers, make clear not only how close Diels was to Karl Ernst, but also
how deeply involved he was in the Berlin SA's crimes. These facts stand in
dramatic contrast to the way Diels liked to present himself—as the fearless
opponent of SA violence—and Diels's self-presentation was widely believed
in the 1950s and 1960s. But we can now say that when Diels pointed to
Karl Ernst and Heini Gewehr as the culprits in the Reichstag fire, he did
so on the basis of intimate knowledge of their operations.

At first, Gisevius did not fare well in court against Gewehr. In February 1962 the 6th Civil Chamber of the Düsseldorf Superior Court ruled that Gisevius had to refrain in the future from claiming that Gewehr had played a role in the Reichstag fire, retract the claims he had already made, and pay all the costs of the litigation. As we have seen with Brandt's van der Lubbe case, it was generally difficult for victims and opponents of Nazism to find justice in West German courts in the years after the war, not least because most of the judges remained very much products of Hitler's Germany in training and outlook. In *Gewehr vs. Gisevius* the very language of the judgment gave this away: without irony or apology the court referred to Nazis as "party comrades" and the Weimar Republic as "the system era," which was Nazi jargon. It praised the "political zeal" of the young stormtrooper Gewehr and thought that his account of his own life was given in a "remarkably open, candid, and confident manner." This open, candid, and confident account had not, of course, included anything about Gewehr's activities as a mass murderer in Poland or the Soviet Union. Whether a court that spoke so unselfconsciously of "party comrades" and the "system era" would have cared is, in any case, debatable.[57]

Gisevius was determined to appeal, even in the face of pessimistic advice from his lawyers. "Believe me," he urged them, "this Reichstag fire story is about something fundamental, which goes deep into the problem of research into contemporary history." He was right, and in fact the Düsseldorf Court of Appeals agreed with him and partially reversed the lower court's verdict.[58]

The Court of Appeals accepted a number of Gisevius's central claims as proven, including that Rall had accused SA men of involvement in the fire; that the SA had murdered him; and that Schulze-Wilde and Strindberg had given an accurate précis of Diels's outlook. The court considered it proven that Rall had mentioned the name "Heini Gewehr," noting that it was "not obvious how the defendant could already have come up with this name in Nuremberg, although he had never known the plaintiff personally," and that the evidence of Schulze-Wilde, Arndt, and Strindberg "testified unanimously that Diels expressly named the plaintiff to them as one of the culprits." That Strindberg had sent Lissigkeit to interview Gewehr was further corroboration; indeed, "If Rall really accused the SA of complicity in his confession, he would have had to name names to make this confession credible."

The court also found that the circumstances of the fire "do not speak in general unambiguously for van der Lubbe's sole guilt." It struck the court as unlikely that van der Lubbe could on his own have picked the precise moment to enter the Reichstag at which there were no regular rounds of employees, or that he had had enough time to set all the fires he claimed. On the other hand, it was not proven that Rall's accusation of Gewehr was *true*. The evidence against Gewehr was only hearsay. Therefore, Gisevius could no more prove Gewehr had been a culprit than Gewehr could prove his innocence. The court ruled that Gisevius could not continue to allege Gewehr's involvement, but neither could he be obliged to retract what he had written, because "no one can be compelled to retract a fact that is possibly correct."[59]

This was an impressive judgment, intelligent and even-handed, "not only excellent judicial work," as Gisevius's lawyer wrote, "but also a not inconsiderable success of our joint efforts in the Court of Appeals." It is important to note this character of the judgment, since writers on the Reichstag fire are prone to the incorrect assertion that Gisevius's "questionable" evidence was "refuted" by the outcome.[60]

The West German Supreme Court denied Gisevius's further appeal in January 1966, but without addressing the evidence, which could not be the subject of an appeal at that level. This meant that the Court of Appeals' resolution of the case was confirmed. Gisevius was not finished with Gewehr, however. On the strength of the earlier judgments, Gewehr launched yet another suit, this time against the editor in chief and publisher of the *Zeit* and against Gisevius personally for monetary compensation for the damage to his health and reputation. In 1969, after a long series of hearings and appeals, the Superior Court in Düsseldorf ordered the publisher to pay Gewehr 30,000 DM, and Gisevius to pay 26,307 DM—although Gewehr had to pay eight-ninths of the costs of the proceedings. These hearings, unlike the earlier ones, brought forth no new evidence about the Reichstag fire, although they did considerable damage to Gisevius's finances. He died, a ruined man, in 1974.[61]

By then the Tobias/Mommsen single-culprit theory was becoming generally accepted among historians, and the central figures of the Reichstag fire controversy, those who knew something about the fire from personal experience, were passing from the scene—Heisig in 1954, Diels of course in 1957, Schnitzler in 1962, Gisevius in 1974, and finally Gewehr and Zirpins in 1976. The nature of the controversy changed. Whatever it might have lost by the 1970s in its ability to produce new evidence it made up for in nastiness and pointless dishonesty.

CONCLUSION

EVIDENCE AND SELF-EVIDENCE

THROUGH ALL THE TRIALS, revelations, and recantations, one element of the Reichstag fire controversy remained constant: arguments about it were never just about the fire, perhaps never really about the fire at all. They were about nationalism and collective guilt, the memory of Nazism and the Holocaust, and the main currents of European politics in mid-century. Even after the 1960s they generally continued to pit outsiders to German society, some of them victims of the Nazi period, against insiders, comfortable and wishing to remain so.

The catalytic figure in the arguments of the 1970s and 1980s was Edouard Calic. Calic was, in the words of his most effective German critic, an "Italian citizen of Croatian origin" (a clear assignment of outsider status) and "like millions" a victim of the "chaotic times of the first half of this century." Calic was born in 1910 in a Croatia that still belonged to the Austro-Hungarian Empire. He became (and thereafter remained) an Italian citizen when his native Istria was taken over by Italy after the First World War, but to escape Mussolini his family moved to the newly created Yugoslavia. In the early 1940s Calic was a doctoral student at Berlin University and a correspondent for a Zagreb newspaper when he was arrested and spent three years in the Sachsenhausen concentration camp north of Berlin.[1]

After the war Calic returned to journalism, living mostly in Paris and Berlin. He became well known in the late 1960s for a number of books on the Nazi period, especially one called *Hitler Unmasked*, which purported to present transcripts of interviews that Richard Breiting, editor of the *Leipziger Neueste Nachrichten* (Leipzig latest news), conducted with Hitler in 1931. Calic developed a particular interest in the Reichstag fire, and in 1968 became one of the founders of the International Committee for Scholarly Research on the Causes and Consequences of the Second World War, more commonly known as the Luxembourg Committee. For an initial public symposium in April 1969, Calic, who like his forerunner Willi Münzenberg possessed a talent for recruiting eminent persons to his cause, arranged for West German Foreign Minister (and soon to be Chancellor) Willy Brandt, former French Culture Minister André Malraux, and Pierre Grégoire, speaker of the Luxembourg parliament, to serve as honorary presidents of the committee. A number of distinguished scholars and political figures filled out the committee's academic council. Here is an important continuity: the Luxembourg Committee, in its style, composition, personnel, and ideological commitments, breathed the spirit of the Popular Front. This was anti-Fascism reconstituted for the late 1960s, the era of the Prague Spring and student demonstrations across the Western (and Eastern) world. It followed that, for the Luxembourg Committee, Fritz Tobias, the virulently anti-Communist Constitutional Protection man who made the ex-Gestapo officers' theory of the Reichstag fire the dominant narrative, was the Fascist. In fact Tobias shared the Luxembourg Committee's basic and binary assumptions about the politics of the issue, and seemed perfectly willing to play his assigned role. He was capable of criticizing one of his opponents of the 1960s for having "carried on in a dreadfully anti-Fascist manner."[2]

Tobias at first responded to Calic and to some of Calic's witnesses just as he had to Krausnick and Aretin. In 1968 a former SA man named Franz Knospe was ready to come forward to back Calic. Tobias seems to have used a combination of "Bacon Face" Schmidt (with whom Tobias had become friendly) and his own Constitutional Protection authority to intimidate Knospe, and then in turn deployed Knospe to intimidate Calic. A flurry of allegations and police investigations followed, with little result. In any case it soon became clear to Tobias that against Calic more conventional tactics would suffice: some of the materials Calic put forward were no more authentic than parts of Münzenberg's *Brown Books* and *White Book*.[3]

In 1972 the Luxembourg Committee published, under the nominal editorship of the distinguished Swiss historian Walther Hofer, the first volume of a "Scholarly Documentation" concerning the Reichstag fire, which aimed squarely at countering Tobias's sole-culprit argument. Most of the volume was taken up with excerpts from the reports of the technical experts of 1933. The one really new and important item was Professor Stephan's thermodynamic analysis of the course of the fire, proving beyond almost all doubt that accelerants van der Lubbe could not have possessed had spread the fire in the plenary chamber. There were also a number of statements from firefighters who had been at the burning Reichstag, taken between 1960 and 1971, all responding to Tobias and especially to the way Tobias had manipulated Emil Puhle into contradicting Fritz Polchow's memory of armed police officers lurking in the Reichstag cellar.[4]

One could of course debate the probative value of this material. The firefighters' statements especially, gathered as they were around thirty years after the event and in an effort to rebut Tobias, might have been shaped by the same kinds of manipulation that Tobias employed with Puhle. Still, there is an obvious difference between documents that honestly record possibly inaccurate facts, and documents that are forged. It was with the second volume of this "documentation," published in 1978, that Calic's Luxembourg Committee got into the second, more serious kind of trouble.

The 1978 volume contained transcriptions of what seemed to be a number of documents pointing to Nazi responsibility for the fire. Some purported to come from one Eugen von Kessel, a Gestapo officer who was murdered on June 30, 1934, as well as from von Kessel's brother Hans. Eugen von Kessel, so the documents suggested, had learned from such sources as Reinhold Heller, Ernst Oberfohren, and Richard Breiting of the involvement of key figures like Diels and Reinhard Heydrich in the fire. Other statements by people such as the Weimar Social Democratic Reichstag president Paul Löbe, and more letters supposedly from Breiting himself, were to bolster the case.[5]

In September and October 1979, the journalist Karl-Heinz Janßen, a friend and ally of Tobias, laid into Calic in a series of articles for the *Zeit* entitled "Geschichte aus der Dunkelkammer" (History from the darkroom). In Janßen's articles—as always in this controversy—it was clear that anger and frustration on subjects far removed from the Reichstag fire, and of a very different order, lurked below the surface. It probably wasn't a coincidence that earlier the same year the broadcast in West Germany of the American television miniseries *Holocaust*, filmed in part in West Berlin and starring Meryl Streep, had provoked an unprecedented degree of German self-scrutiny and self-criticism, but also an angry backlash that the series represented an American "expropriation" of German history. Janßen's articles took a sneering tone toward victims of Nazism and betrayed an obvious exasperation with West German rituals of guilt over the Nazi era, breathing the kinds of resentment that Diels and others had expressed in the 1940s and 1950s. It was only because of the "guilt complex toward victims of Hitler's rule" that contemporaries of the Third Reich carried with them that Calic could count on "preferential treatment." A "magic word" gave Calic access to high-level officials and scholars—"victim of National Socialism." Calic himself (whom Janßen repeatedly referred to as "the Italo-Croat Calic") was a "shady character" (*zwielichtige Figur*) whose influence on politicians, journalists, and scholars was one of the "most astonishing chapters of postwar German history." (By revealing contrast, Janßen described Melita Wiedemann, a former reporter for Goebbels's *Angriff* and later a Tobias ally, as an "eternal idealist.") Janßen sneered at Calic and his colleague Pierre Grégoire for considering themselves, as former concentration camp prisoners, more credible historical witnesses than those who had served the Third Reich. As self-evident as it might seem to many that a victim of Nazi persecution would generally be more believable on the subject of Nazi crimes than a former perpetrator, and as gratuitously nasty as Janßen's remarks were, his attitude was consistent with the skepticism of victim narratives very common in postwar German historical research. Just a few years later, in a famous exchange of letters with the distinguished Holocaust scholar Saul Friedländer, Martin Broszat could complain that "German historians more focused on rational understanding" faced the "problem" of dealing with a "contrary form of memory among those who were persecuted and harmed by the Nazi regime," which "functions to coarsen historical recollection." Yet in the 1950s Broszat had worked on a large study of postwar German expellees from east-central Europe based on survivor testimony; he called this evidence of (non-Jewish German) memory a "true representation of the reality of what happened."[6]

However distasteful their tone, Janßen's pieces were clever, devastating, and, in their way, amusing. His critique covered both Calic's *Hitler Unmasked* and the documents in the 1978 Luxembourg Committee volume. *Hitler Unmasked* was, Janßen demonstrated, full of anachronisms and mistakes. The transcripts presented a Hitler who in 1931 was somehow already knowledgeable about a number of German and foreign statesmen who became important only later—Roosevelt, Churchill, Leon Blum, Franz von Papen. Janßen poked fun at the inept and conspicuously Croatian-sounding German that Hitler seemed to speak in these interviews. Hitler used many expressions common in Serbo-Croatian but unknown in German: *Diskretionsrecht* ("right of discretion"), which does not exist in German though it does in Serbo-Croatian; and "house of crystal" rather than "house of glass." In German one would not idiomatically say that a building was *verbrannt* ("burned"), yet documents in the Hofer volume cite Theodor Wolff, a master of German style, saying just that. Rudolf Hess spoke of *Undisziplin* ("indiscipline") when in German one would say *Disziplinlosigkeit*. In Serbo-Croatian the appropriate word is closer to *Undisziplin*. Janßen gleefully offered many similar examples.[7]

Calic took Janßen and the *Zeit* to court for libel over these articles, without success. The Berlin Superior Court gave judgment in November 1982, dismissing Calic's suit and obliging him to pay the costs. The essence of the court's reasoning was that Janßen's articles, however polemical, involved expressions of opinion permissible in the public realm. The court did not rule on whether or not Calic had put false documents before the public. This judgment was confirmed on appeal in February 1984.[8]

Two years later, a collection of essays edited by Uwe Backes, with contributions from Tobias, Mommsen, and a number of their allies, completed the destruction of Calic. Janßen contributed a piece and repeated his critique of the documents' authenticity, while other writers pointed out their numerous inaccuracies, contradictions, and anachronisms. The response of the Luxembourg Committee could, in the words of one of the most balanced and neutral accounts of the controversy, only lead "to irritation even for well-meaning observers." The committee's obvious response would have been to submit the original documents to a neutral party for an opinion on their authenticity. Walther Hofer rejected this as unreasonable. Nonetheless, as criticism mounted, the committee declared its willingness to submit the documents to an examination by the West German Federal Archives in Koblenz. It then emerged that not a single one existed in its original form; all were copies. Swiss historian Christoph Graf, another of the committee's leading figures, explained that one had to assume the originals no longer existed. The Federal Archives refused to carry out any examination on this basis.[9]

Hofer then submitted some of the documents (now with, in one case, an original) to the Zürich Kanton Police for an opinion on their authenticity. Methodological criticisms of this examination seem beside the point when one learns that the examination turned up another anachronism in the supposed notes of Eugen von Kessel. Although Kessel was murdered in the Röhm purge of June 30, 1934, "his" notes bore a watermark from 1935. Hofer and Graf now claimed that the document was a summary of Kessel's notes made after his death. They had not said this before.[10]

In short, no one should be willing any longer to place any faith in the "Breiting" or "Kessel" documents. Even Calic, in a 1979 interview with the *Zeit*, backed away from them, claiming that he had warned Hofer against including them in the 1978 volume. The documents proved nothing, he had protested; what did it matter what Breiting noted down in 1933? It is, of course, entirely possible that someone other than Calic actually forged the documents, and that he was a victim rather than a perpetrator of a hoax. Since the forged documents ostensibly came from private sources in East Germany, Hersch Fischler has suggested that East German authorities might have fed then to Calic. This is plausible, but there is no evidence for it in the files of the East German *Stasi*; those files do record, on the other hand, that the *Stasi* tried and failed to recruit Calic as an "unofficial collaborator" in 1971, and that the Stasi intercepted and copied documents being sent to Hofer from Breiting's heirs in Leipzig. Janßen's thorough demonstration of the Serbo-Croatian tendencies in the language of the documents at any rate points a large finger in the direction of Calic as the author of the forged documents.[11]

The scandals over these forgeries obscured two other developments in the Reichstag fire controversy. One recent historian, while accepting that Calic's documents were forged, also noted that the first Luxembourg Committee volume had delivered a fully persuasive critique of Tobias's single-culprit theory. The same might in fact have been said of Hans Schneider's doomed project for the Institute for Contemporary History, but that text remained unavailable to readers until 2004. Furthermore, in the 1980s, some of the documents from the Leipzig trial were beginning to be published in East Germany. Janßen, Mommsen, and other authors whose criticisms of Calic were so devastating focused only on the forgeries and took no notice of the Luxembourg Committee's critique of Tobias, nor of the newly emerging documents. In other words, Tobias's single-culprit theory had been quietly rebutted by the end of the 1980s, but with all the noise surrounding Calic—and the understandable exasperation with his forgeries—professional historians did not register this fact at all.[12]

WE CAN STILL SEE THE EFFECTS. Today the overwhelming consensus among historians who specialize in Nazi Germany remains that Marinus van der Lubbe burned the Reichstag all by himself. There are several reasons why this is so.

First, even professional historians cannot conduct their own primary and archival research on a broad range of subjects. On most matters they must rely on the work of others. Among established historians of Nazi Germany (leaving aside Walther Hofer and Christoph Graf, with their problematic connection to Calic) only Hans Mommsen has spent time looking at the primary sources for the Reichstag fire, and even he seems generally to have relied on Tobias's own collection of documents. Mommsen's brief was in any case to give a scholarly opinion of Tobias's work on behalf of the Institute, rather than to conduct his own study from the bottom up, a point that is often forgotten.

A small group of Tobias opponents—today including Hersch Fischler, Alexander Bahar, and Wilfried Kugel—have done sustained archival work on the subject (without, certainly, coming to the same conclusions—Fischler believes the German Nationals were also behind the fire, and has engaged in fierce polemics against Bahar and Kugel). The broader community of mainstream historians, however, has either ignored or rejected their findings. To explain this, Fischler, Bahar, and Kugel themselves cite the concentration of academic and media power arrayed against them (Hans Mommsen, the *Spiegel*, the *Zeit*). There is much to this; but it must also be said that they often do not help themselves by giving weight to dubious sources, pushing irrelevant or unpersuasive arguments, or occasionally straying into the territory of fringe conspiracy theorists (Shell Oil was behind the Reichstag fire!) The Reichstag fire has always attracted this kind of speculation, and likely it always will: google the words "Reichstag fire" and you will find countless web sites accusing the administration of George W. Bush of arranging the attacks of September 11, 2001, to secure passage of the Patriot Act. Such derailments in more recent Reichstag fire research are all the more regrettable as they can distract from the often extraordinary thoroughness and resourcefulness of the archival detective work.[13]

Nonetheless, the most important factor behind acceptance of the single-culprit theory is the way historians make judgments about subjects on which they have not themselves done in-depth research in primary sources. What virtually all historians know about the Reichstag fire is that (1) Tobias's book was endorsed by Mommsen and thus, effectively, by the prestigious Institute for Contemporary History, and (2) Calic injected a series of forged documents into the debate. On the basis of these facts it seems easy to conclude who is right and who is wrong, and for historians whose research does not focus on the fire, this is enough. The rancor and bitterness of the Reichstag fire debate has also made it appear an unappealing and unprofitable field for two generations of historians, especially in Germany.

We can see how this process works when we look at recent, widely admired works of scholarship on Nazi Germany. In his celebrated biography of Hitler, Ian Kershaw writes that Tobias's book, "supported by the scholarly analysis of Hans Mommsen," is "compelling." Most of the citations in Kershaw's account of the fire, however, are to Mommsen or to the Backes essay collection, even where the real source of the information lies elsewhere. For instance, when Kershaw writes that "The first members of the police to interrogate van der Lubbe . . . had no doubt that he had set the fire to the building alone," he cites Mommsen, although of course the information really comes from Heisig, Zirpins, and Schnitzler as channeled by Tobias—and is in any case incorrect. Where Kershaw does cite Tobias directly, he cites the full, though politically problematic German edition; many English-language historians are content to cite the truncated and sanitized English translation. Kershaw's tone is even-handed and he at least accurately recapitulates the facts as Tobias and Mommsen gave them. In other cases, it seems even distinguished historians decide that, since the question is settled, they do not need to read the literature on the fire carefully or restate and cite it accurately. This carelessness has also played its part in keeping the Tobias thesis in place.[14]

THE NOTION THAT VAN DER LUBBE was the sole culprit in the Reichstag fire first arose (apart from in the unclear mind of van der Lubbe himself) as a fall-back position devised by elements of the Nazi regime as it became clear that the Reichstag fire trial was going badly and they were losing the propaganda battle to Münzenberg. Heinrich Schnitzler, who sincerely believed in the single-culprit theory, confided it to his diary in 1945, but as a public argument it was revived a few years later as part of a legal defense and rehabilitation strategy for some of Schnitzler's ex-Gestapo colleagues. These officers had brought van der Lubbe to the guillotine, and Torgler and the Bulgarians within a hair of it, through an investigation relying on both faked evidence and absurdly improbable witness testimony. They went on to commit serious crimes in connection with the Nazi Holocaust.

Fritz Tobias, who emerged in the 1950s as an unlikely champion and protector of these officers and many others like them, built their defense up into his sensational *Spiegel* series and his 1962 book. Looking back with the perspective of a half century and with the evidence now available, it is beyond question that Tobias misrepresented evidence that spoke against his thesis, quoted both credulously and selectively from Nazi sources, and presented his Gestapo "clients" as trustworthy while suppressing much of what he knew about their subversion of the Weimar Republic and their involvement in major Nazi crimes. Furthermore, Tobias made full use of his position as a senior officer of the Constitutional Protection to bully and even blackmail opponents into giving up the debate. His crowning achievement was to convert the Institute for Contemporary History—whose prestige and influence in its special subject is unrivalled—to grudging acceptance of his view through threatening its director, Helmut Krausnick, with revelations of his Nazi past. To this day Mommsen's influential article on the fire has largely settled the matter for professional historians. Yet it was a more or less direct consequence of Tobias's campaign against Krausnick and his Institute (for which, of course, Mommsen himself should not be blamed).

The misrepresentations and distortions of truth in Tobias's writing bear comparison to that other notorious denier of Nazi blame, Tobias's friend David Irving. If denying that the Nazis burned the Reichstag carries nothing like the moral and historical stakes of denying the Holocaust— and certainly it does not—Tobias's position of worldly power enabled him to conduct his debate much more malevolently, and much more successfully, than Irving has conducted his. And if Tobias's account falls away, then so does Mommsen's, since insofar as Mommsen dealt with responsibility for the fire, he was writing a commentary on and an assessment of Tobias. This leaves Mommsen's account of the politics around the fire, much of which remains compelling.

We must, then, go back to the evidence and start again, and in this book I have tried to suggest what such a revised account of the Reichstag fire might look like. Disproving one thing does not prove another. As Hermann Graml wrote in a typically thoughtful and judicious short essay on the Reichstag fire controversy, scientific details on the course of the fire do not prove that the SA set it, any more than do the facts of the politically driven police and judicial investigations of 1933. Nonetheless this revision must begin with the statements of the fire experts, undisputed by people with relevant professional knowledge, who from 1933 to today have held that it is somewhere between highly unlikely and impossible that van der Lubbe alone could have set the fire that destroyed the plenary chamber with the time and tools available to him. We have seen that van der Lubbe himself was utterly unable to come up with a convincing explanation of how he could have done so, and indeed his testimony of November 23, 1933, showed that he was dimly aware that fires he had not started were springing to life around him as he left the plenary chamber. That van der Lubbe was not a sole culprit is a conclusion, I have argued, on which the evidence permits us a high degree of certainty.

Of course this conclusion does nothing to identify van der Lubbe's fellow culprits. For this we have to fall back on the fallible and often untrustworthy accounts of people who were "there." We cannot, therefore, have the same level of certainty on this question that we can have about the fact that van der Lubbe was not alone. Nonetheless, it is impressive that Hans Bernd Gisevius supplied an account of the fire at Nuremberg, without access to any documents, which his bitter enemy Rudolf Diels repeatedly corroborated, and which since Nuremberg has been substantially supported by the discovery of documents whose very existence Gisevius probably could not have suspected in 1946. The statements of Gisevius and Diels, especially Diels's letter to the British delegation at the International Military Tribunal in Tobias's own papers, and all the documents that show that the SA murdered Adolf Rall because it feared his revelations, suggest that the culprits probably—though only probably—were that team of SA men that had already acted in other

Goebbels propaganda stunts—Helldorff, Ernst, and above all Gewehr. This is not to say that Helldorff and Ernst were themselves present at the scene; they had alibis and clearly were not. But Gewehr, the SA's recognized expert in the deployment of phosphorus for political arson, was never able to give a consistent and plausible account of where he had been that night. Even many of his SA comrades assumed he had been the culprit, and he seems to have bragged about it to fellow police trainees after having had (as often) too much to drink. The SA was making increased use of such phosphorus solutions in the second half of 1932, most strikingly in Königsberg, while at the same time going to considerable length to keep this "weapon" secret. That the Nazis would offer some kind of "provocation" in the days before the election was very widely rumored in informed political circles in Berlin.

Van der Lubbe's fellow culprits probably escaped through the tunnel to Göring's residence and the boiler house; even the physical relationship of the tunnel and the stenographers' enclosure supports this hypothesis. There are other possibilities, however. The Nazi deputy and SA man Herbert Albrecht fled from the building through Portal V, in a manner that was at the very least suspicious, and the police could not subsequently confirm his alibi although they claimed they could. Other items of evidence found in the Reichstag suggested a culprit's escape, especially a never-explained broken pane of glass on the east side of the building. Commissar Bunge thought a culprit could have escaped through it even after the police had cordoned off the building, as with huge fires the cordon "is never what in the interest of such a case would have been desirable."[15]

Then there is the question of how far up the Nazi chain of command we can locate plans or orders for the Reichstag fire. Here the evidence permits only a still more tentative conclusion than it does for the involvement of the SA. The fire seems, however, entirely consistent with the pattern of operations that Goebbels established in Berlin after his arrival in 1926; the comparison with the Kurfürstendamm riot of 1931 is especially illuminating, not least in the involvement of Helldorff, Ernst, and Gewehr as well as in its selection of a symbolic location for an SA attack with the goals of holding together the fractious Nazi constituency and preserving Goebbels's own position in a difficult time. Goebbels was also prone to these kinds of operations when he worried that the Nazis were being too accommodating to the German Nationals, and abandoning the radicalism Goebbels favored. Martin Sommerfeldt's account of the speed with which the propaganda ministry responded to the fire, although it must be read skeptically—like all documents from former Nazi officials—also points to Goebbels. The Boxheimer documents described a Nazi scenario for seizing power similar in key respects to what Nazis alleged was happening—a Communist coup—in February 1933. Hermann Göring would probably have had to have been involved in any Nazi attack on the Reichstag, especially if the arsonists escaped through the tunnel. Certainly as interior minister he had control of what was, by any standards, a corrupt police investigation. It is possible, though unlikely, that the SA carried out the attack on the Reichstag entirely on its own initiative, with no orders from higher up, as Göring suggested at Nuremberg. As for Hitler, apart from the somewhat suspicious gap in his speaking schedule from February 26th to 28th, there is no evidence, not even indirect evidence, that he knew of, let alone ordered, the Reichstag fire.

As a number of authors have pointed out, any claim that Goebbels was involved in the Reichstag fire must confront the entry in his diary (only discovered in the 1990s) for April 9, 1941. There Goebbels recorded a conversation with Hitler the day before, in which they had discussed the assassination attempt on Hitler made by Georg Elser in 1939 at the Bürgerbräu beer hall in Munich. "Other conspirators [Hintermänner] still not yet found," Goebbels noted. "Culprit persists in silence. Führer thinks Otto Strasser." This led to a discussion of the Reichstag fire. "For the Reichstag fire his guess is Torgler as initiator. I think that's out of the question. He is much too bourgeois for that. For our police and justice system and their instinct for investigations [Spürsinn] the Führer has no courteous respect."[16]

Hermann Graml writes that this passage shows that neither Hitler nor Goebbels thought that Nazis had burned the Reichstag, let alone that they had ordered it. But we have already seen that Goebbels lied regularly in his diary: about the bomb he sent to himself, about the Kurfürstendamm riot, and about his own role in Kristallnacht (on the latter, Saul Friedländer wrote that the "silence in Goebbels's diary between November 7 and 9, 1938, is the surest indication of plans that aimed at a 'spontaneous outburst of popular anger,' which was to take place without any sign of Hitler's involvement"). Goebbels meant his diaries for publication, or at least as the basis for future publications, which would not encourage honesty about his own misdeeds. Why, then, from 1941 on, did he openly admit in his diary to knowledge of the murder of Jews, when he would not admit to these lesser crimes? This is certainly a serious question. One answer is that what Goebbels wrote in his diary was always consistent with the story he gave out publicly. He had publicly as well as privately denied involvement in the Reichstag fire, as he denied involvement in planning the bomb, the Kurfürstendamm riot, or Kristallnacht. But he spoke both frankly and publicly about the Holocaust. In November 1941, as *Einsatzgruppen* were murdering Soviet Jews in the hundreds of thousands, he wrote in his magazine *Das Reich* that "the fate befalling the Jews is harsh, but more than deserved. Pity or regret is completely out of place in this case." Jews had "miscalculated" in "triggering" the war and "world Jewry" was "now gradually being engulfed by the same extermination process that it had intended for us . . . it undergoes destruction according to its own law: 'An eye for an eye, a tooth for a tooth.'" Such examples could be multiplied many times over. We might add that the investigators for whom Hitler had so little respect never even tried to find more Reichstag fire perpetrators after December 1933, which seems to be a kind of quiet confession.[17]

The other problem is van der Lubbe. If van der Lubbe had fellow culprits, why did he never betray them? And why would the Nazis pick him? It is virtually certain that if Nazis burned the Reichstag, they had to have at least maneuvered him into the building. It is possible that poor van der Lubbe did not fully grasp that others were at work, and genuinely believed he was solely responsible for the fires (his testimony on November 23rd, even in the passage in which he acknowledged that he had seen fires he had not set springing up in the plenary chamber, points to this). He may have been determined to cover for the person or persons who arranged for him to break in to the Reichstag. His brother Cornelis said in March 1933 that Marinus was "capable of taking the guilt on himself, and if he is one of the culprits, he will never betray his fellows." Perhaps the drugs that, it seems more likely than not, the Nazis gave him during the trial, and which would explain his addled and apathetic appearance, were expected to keep him quiet. In the end, however, we have very little evidence of what van der Lubbe did with his time in the critical days before the fire, and none that firmly connects him to any known Nazis, aside from vague hints of what he did in Neukölln with people who, like Jahnecke and Hintze, were Nazi informers. For the SA or the Gestapo to trust this young man—mostly blind, a stranger to Berlin, possessing a very imperfect grasp of German—with such an important role seems to fly in the face of all reason. Death has long since taken anyone who knew or might have known the facts; this part of the mystery seems destined to stay with us.[18]

That the single-culprit theory established itself in Germany after the war was a product of Tobias's determination and methods, but also of a particular constellation of political pressure and the state of knowledge of Nazi crimes in the 1950s and 1960s. We are only now beginning to discover the full extent to which self-justifying accounts of the Nazi past—"Persil letter" history—shaped historians' understanding of the Third Reich for decades. A recent book on the German Foreign Office under the Nazis makes clear how much this institution was implicated in the Holocaust, and the extent to which its officials managed to obscure this truth after the war, through legal and media campaigns strikingly similar to those of Diels, Heisig, Braschwitz, Zirpins, and Schnitzler. Historian Ulrich Herbert, author of a 1996 biography of Reinhard Heydrich's deputy Werner Best, showed how deeply Best influenced the writing of history. Best himself bragged that Hans Buchheim from the Institute for Contemporary History had based his writings on "long conversations between us." Best industriously organized a system of "witness agreements and exculpatory testimony," which also sounds similar to what Diels and his colleagues managed in the late 1940s. Michael Wildt's work on the Reich Security Main Office also demonstrates how self-justifying testimony regarding this organization at Nuremberg shaped the historical record for years afterward. Only in relatively recent years have we come to understand the full involvement of the German army and German police formations in genocidal operations on the Eastern front. Recent research has also shown how successfully former police and Gestapo officers were able to manipulate the media and legal climate in postwar West Germany to cover their own records and shelter themselves from prosecution. The result of all this research has been to collapse the distinction on which Tobias and his "clients" rested in putting forward their arguments: that between conscientious, "unpolitical" police officers and civil servants on the one hand, and ideologically driven Nazis on the other. This was, we now know, a distinction without a difference.[19]

The debate over the Reichstag fire is, therefore, a period piece, reflecting the state of knowledge of about 1958 or, at best, 1964. In recent years, younger German historians have been producing promising research that casts new light on the problem, sometimes indirectly (from time to time younger historians have told me privately that they are suspicious of the single-culprit theory, but that in the very small world of German academia they would fear for their careers if they were to say so publicly). There has been much recent research on the media environment of the 1950s and 1960s, with considerable criticism of the *Spiegel* and its ex-Nazi journalists. Some of this literature, like two recent biographies of *Spiegel* journalist Paul Karl Schmidt, argues explicitly that in covering up Nazi involvement in the Reichstag fire, Schmidt (and Tobias) were following the ideological line of Schmidt's infamous memo about covering up the deportation of Hungarian Jews. From another angle, Thomas Raithel and Irene Strenge have cast doubt on Mommsen's argument that the Reichstag Fire Decree was a spontaneous response to the fire itself; Raithel and Strenge show how much careful drafting and consideration of precedent went into it. Such a case reinforces the evidence from witnesses like Alois Eugen Becker, who recalled meetings before the fire for the purpose of drafting the decree, which in turn suggests that Göring's Interior Ministry and Diels's police had at least a good idea of what was coming. In 2010 a young historian named Marcus Giebeler published a dispassionate history of the controversy over the fire. Giebeler did not do archival research for his study, but his reading of the secondary literature brought him to the conclusion that the single-culprit theory has been refuted and that its defenders are fighting a rear-guard action. Bahar, Kugel, and Fischler have not, he says, as of yet established their counter-theses, although he finds that the theory of Nazi responsibility, though not definitively proven, is nonetheless "probable."[20]

Why does it matter? Proof of Nazi responsibility for the fire would, in Graml's sharp formulation, establish nothing more than that the Nazis "did not shrink from the crime of arson" in pursuing their political goals, while proof that they had nothing to do with it could hardly mitigate their guilt for more drastic crimes. This is true, but it misses the point on a number of levels. To understand what makes the Reichstag fire, in which no one died, comparable to those other crimes we have to return to the fire as symbol, as the foundation of the narrative of Nazism, as the "birth-hour of the concentration camps."

I have tried to show here that when we set the Reichstag fire in its context of late-Weimar political violence, we understand it differently: it forms part of the process in which the democracy of Weimar was steadily delegitimized by the escalating violence on the streets of Berlin and other cities. The postwar context is, if anything, even more important for understanding the issue. Not everyone is as dispassionate as Professor Graml: arguments over the Reichstag fire have always been deployed in much larger controversies, from Münzenberg on. Tobias's arguments were enthusiastically taken up by a postwar German right that welcomed a chance to say that allegations of a Nazi crime were lies. More or less unrepentant ex-Nazis like Paul Karl Schmidt and Kurt Ziesel used this argument as a stick to beat the Institute for Contemporary History, and they themselves linked Tobias's thesis to far-right positions (like David Hoggan's) on responsibility for war and genocide. Janßen's demolition of Calic breathed a barely suppressed rage at constant reassertions of German guilt for the Holocaust, while Calic's Luxembourg Committee was a left-leaning propaganda exercise on the model of Münzenberg's various ventures. When so many people have invested such importance in a question, historians must follow, or they will fail to understand an important dimension of their subject. We come back to a point we have seen before: ultimately, to control the narrative of the fire is to control the narrative of Nazism itself. Hence the fire's enormous symbolic as well as practical importance. This point was crystal clear to Tobias, who stressed how his work would refashion reigning interpretations of Nazism, as it was to Münzenberg, to Schmidt and Ziesel, to Calic, to Ernst Fraenkel, and to countless others.[21]

There is a still more fundamental point. Normally historians reach a consensus about what has or has not happened in the past through open debate and reasoned argument based on the presentation of verifiable evidence. At least this is what they think they do. In the case of the Reichstag fire, though, we will go very wrong if we assume that the process leading to a consensus had much to do with a dispassionate search for truth. In this case, the story started as the desperate defense strategy of war criminals. It was adopted and channeled by a shadowy intelligence officer with seemingly dubious motives and connections, and who then used blackmail to compel a prestigious Institute to accept it. Helmut Krausnick and his Institute, vulnerable and buffeted by competing currents of public opinion, decided that in this case the game wasn't worth the candle, and that if they were not prudent the fire would consume them as well. Such was the enduring power of the Reichstag fire, thirty years and more after it consumed the plenary chamber.

The story, of course, had started with lies—Nazi as well as Communist— and continued with them as far as the efforts of Calic. What Zirpins,

Heisig, Braschwitz, and Gewehr deserved was the serious attention of the justice system followed by punishment consistent with the appalling scale of their crimes. What they got instead was Tobias's zealous advocacy, based to a considerable extent on lies. Timothy Snyder has recently commented that "you can't extricate truth from authority when you don't really believe in truth," and furthermore that "fact used as propaganda is all but impossible to disentangle from the politics of its original transmission." He made the latter point in the context of the Katyn massacre, the murder of thousands of Polish officers by the Soviet NKVD which, as we have seen, was also a subject that interested Tobias. The victims' bodies were discovered by the Germans, and so the murders "were politics before they were history." Exactly the same problems have shaped the Reichstag fire debate. The story has been serially entangled in various kinds of authority—political, legal, and cultural—and various interpretations of it or items of evidence have inevitably born the taint of their origins. Too many people, furthermore, have seen only the fire's instrumental uses, and worried little about the truth.[22]

It seems likely that the drift of historical research will continue to move away from Tobias, especially now that he is not here to compel obedience: Fritz Tobias passed away, age ninety-eight, on January 1, 2011. He had fallen twice in December, the second time injuring a rib. He refused to go to a hospital, instead taking to his bed over Christmas with a prescription for painkillers. A friend said that he had very much wanted to outlive his slightly younger rival Walther Hofer (who made it to June 1, 2013). "But his body just wouldn't go along anymore."[23]

IN 1933 THE NAZIS REPAIRED the major structural damage from the Reichstag fire. They cleared the wreckage, sold more than 150 tons of iron from the cupola as scrap, and installed 2,250 new panes of glass. After 1935 they used the building as an exhibition hall for such productions as "Bolshevism Unmasked" in 1937 and "The Eternal Jew" in 1938 and 1939. Hitler planned to rebuild Berlin as "Germania" after victory in the Second World War. According to the plans, the bend in the river Spree by the Reichstag would be dominated by a massive stone "Hall of the People" which, at a height of 951 feet, would rise higher than the observation decks of the TV Tower in today's Berlin, or a little below the 1,046 feet of the Chrysler Building in New York. Hitler's architect Albert Speer wanted to tear down the Reichstag for this monstrosity, but Hitler preferred to save the old parliament, if perhaps only to provide a measure for the scale of the new hall.[24]

As the war turned grimmer for Germany after 1943, the Reichstag's windows were bricked up and it was converted into a maternity clinic and a factory for radio tubes. Perhaps it was a legacy of Münzenberg's propaganda that the Soviets saw the building as the ultimate symbol of Nazism, and it was the Reichstag's fate to become the site of the last battle for Berlin in 1945. Soviet forces opened their attack by firing 1,400 shells at the building; the subsequent hand-to-hand fighting—the Reichstag was defended by a scratch force of SS men and Hitler Youth—was fierce and bloody. The photograph of Soviet soldiers unfurling the hammer-and-sickle flag atop the Reichstag is one of the iconic images of the Second World War, indeed of the twentieth century, even though looted wristwatches visible on the arm of one of the soldiers had to be airbrushed out.[25]

After the war the Reichstag seemed fated to remain without a role. As Berlin and Germany became divided, the Reichstag fell just inside West Berlin, but there was never any question of moving the West German Bundestag from its base in Bonn to West Berlin, which did not legally belong to the Federal Republic. Repairs moved very slowly. In 1954 the remnants of the cupola were blown out with thermite. In 1960 the West German government decided to restore the Reichstag to serve a "parliamentary function," although no one was very sure what that might be. Architect Paul Baumgarten won a competition for the redesign. His plenary chamber was more than twice the size of Wallot's original, but until the 1990s the only function the Reichstag served was as museum space for an exhibit called "Questions on German History." Then the opening of the Berlin Wall and the Bundestag's (very close) 1991 vote to return the capital to Berlin rescued the Reichstag from irrelevance.[26]

In 1995 the artists Christo and Jeanne-Claude produced their "Wrapped Reichstag (Project for Berlin)." For two weeks in June and July they wrapped the Reichstag in 1,076,390 square feet of thick, woven polypropylene fabric with an aluminum surface, and 9.7 miles of blue polypropylene rope. The artists had been lobbying to carry out this project for nearly twenty-five years (Christo comes originally from Bulgaria and was very familiar with the story of Dimitrov); when it finally happened it came as a prologue to extensive renovations of the Reichstag to make the old building once again suitable for service as Germany's parliament. The British architect Sir Norman Foster designed a new glass cupola. The asbestos that Baumgarten's remodeling had introduced into the plenary chamber—no doubt this seemed a good idea at the time, in this of all places—had to be removed again.[27]

The symbolism of the wrapped Reichstag could be taken different ways. The jury that selected the architects for the remodeling of the building thought that the wrapping would give the Reichstag a "new dimension," indeed it would allow the building to become the symbol of a new and open Germany. On the other hand, perhaps inevitably, some were uncomfortable with what seemed a sanitizing, a literal covering-up, of less savory elements of the recent German past. In the end, the festive atmosphere that surrounded the wrapped Reichstag, and the building's service since 1999 as the re-created home of German democracy, lend force to the more optimistic assessment.[28]

On January 10, 2008, seventy-four years to the day after Marinus van der Lubbe's execution in Leipzig, Germany's chief federal prosecutor Monika Harms announced that her office had quashed his convictions for both attempted high treason and arson. Authority for this decision came from a 1998 law for the "Overturning of Unjust National Socialist Judicial Decisions in the Administration of Criminal Justice." Under this law, verdicts that violated elementary ideas of justice for the purpose of upholding the National Socialist regime on "political, military, racist, religious, or world-view" grounds were to be reversed. Van der Lubbe had been executed on the basis of both the Reichstag Fire Decree, which specified the death penalty for the offenses for which he was convicted, and, as we have seen, "Van der Lubbe's Law," which had applied these penalties to him retroactively. Both were "specifically National Socialist" and therefore unjust provisions. The law did not require any factual consideration of his guilt or innocence, nor did Harms carry one out.[29]

Legally, at least, this is where the story of the Reichstag fire ends. Arthur Brandt had asked a court in the 1950s to come to just such a conclusion, and it had refused to do so, as had the court that in 1967 absurdly converted van der Lubbe's death sentence into prison time. In 2008, though, it seemed self-evident to Germany's top prosecutor that van der Lubbe had been convicted under laws in themselves so unjust that they vitiated the result, whatever the state of the evidence. That this was self-evident to a senior prosecutor is a sign of how far the debate, and Germany itself, have come.

EPILOGUE

HANNOVER, JULY 2008

"ARE YOU SURE YOU WANT TO take this subject on? Do you know what happens to people who write about the Reichstag fire?"[1]

When I met him in the summer of 2008, Herr Ministerial Counselor (ret.) Fritz Tobias was ninety-five years old, a slight, wiry man with the remorseless, unblinking glare that lawyers I know call a "cop stare." Although he had lived in Hannover since well before the Second World War, he still spoke with traces of the hard-boiled accent of his native Berlin. He liked to insist on the point. Berliners are known for their tough humor; this humor is what kept him going, he said.

I was at the beginning of my research on the Reichstag fire controversy. I had fallen into this project more or less accidentally. Earlier I had written a book on the Weimar-era German trial lawyer Hans Litten, who was one of thousands arrested the night of the fire. I tried to find out something about these arrests—what kind of documents might remain, especially concerning how someone might have ended up with his name on the arrest lists. I quickly learned that these lists, their timing, even their very existence, formed one of the sites of contention in the Reichstag fire controversy. I had not before paid much attention to this question. I assumed that the prevailing opinion—van der Lubbe did it alone—was correct. The vehemence of the controversy baffled me. Why, after all, could one care very much who burned the Reichstag? The Nazis had done one or two worse things. A public building, even a large and symbolically freighted public building, did not seem very important next to Auschwitz, Treblinka, Babi Yar, Leningrad, and Stalingrad. But when an issue puzzles a researcher, perhaps that is a sign that something else, something more interesting, is going on below the surface. I began to grow curious about the fire. At about this time my friend, the Berlin lawyer Gerhard Jungfer, mentioned to me that he had been involved in the last effort to re-open the Reichstag fire trial; he had an extensive file on the case. Would I like to read it? I would and did, and was surprised at how much evidence lawyers like Arthur Brandt, Robert Kempner, and Gerhard and his colleagues had raised, evidence that pointed to the Nazis as culprits. I read Tobias's book and most of the other literature about the fire.

I learned that Tobias was still alive. I thought it would be a good idea to talk to anyone I could who had been involved in the debates, on whatever side they might be. I found Tobias's address (a confusing one to a non-German—*In den Sieben Stücken*—"in the seven pieces"? Really?) and wrote asking if I could visit him. I did not expect an answer. I remember telling the postal clerk when I mailed the letter that this was probably a stamp wasted. At least I would know I had tried. Then to my surprise Tobias wrote back within days, inviting me to see him in Hannover. I really only had one thing to ask him: Why? What was this whole thing about?

His answer was brisk and clear. "You think the Communists are gone? They're not gone. Their state is gone, but they're not." The Reichstag fire controversy was all about the Communists. The acquittals of Torgler, Dimitrov, Popov, and Tanev had given Stalin and his followers an enduring propaganda weapon. The acquittals proved that the charges against them were nothing but Fascist propaganda. They used this outcome to argue that every *other* allegation of a Communist crime was nothing but Fascist propaganda. Tobias told me that before he became interested in the Reichstag fire, he thought he might research the massacre in the Katyn Forest—a mass murder of Polish officers carried out by the Soviets in 1940 and blamed on the Nazis. There was clearly a pattern to his preoccupations.

Communism did not, however, exhaust Tobias's explanations for the controversy. He defined himself in purely Enlightenment terms: He had no need of religion, he said, he was interested only in science, in rationality, in facts. Sounding a little like Mr. Gradgrind, he insisted that what distinguished him from his opponents was that "I have facts! Facts!" Whereas—a point he repeated frequently—they had only lies, forgeries, and legends. "My enemies," he said—for him they were never merely opponents—"are all fanatics." Virtually in the same breath, and with cop stare firmly in place, he went on to denounce these "enemies" as "fools, Communists, and criminals." It was not clear if those were three separate categories.

He did not see much rationality anywhere else—not in ordinary people, not in leaders, not in history. He believed that most things in history happened by accident or blunder. Perhaps this explains why some of his most enthusiastic early champions were British historians like A.J.P. Taylor, who held much the same view. There is a kind of historical pattern, he said: In a crisis, the leader is called upon to make a decision, which, time and time again, he does on the basis of fears, preconceptions, and pressures to act. Having acted, the leader must stick to his course, however foolish it may begin to appear. This, for Tobias, was the story of the Reichstag fire: Hitler had been trapped by his spontaneous and sincere accusation of the Communists. He could not back away from it without looking weak, something Hitler could never permit himself. Tobias thought it was the same with the Night of the Long Knives, in which only Gisevius's machinations convinced Hitler that Ernst Röhm and the SA were plotting against him. Having denounced Röhm as a traitor, Hitler again could not back down. Tobias applied the same reasoning to the Cuban Missile Crisis and the attacks of September 11, 2001. I was unable to convince him that the Kennedy of the Cuban crisis would have responded differently to September 11th than did George W. Bush.

His opinion of general public intelligence was no higher. As we spoke he gestured around his office, toward his extensive library and his vast collection of files, and wondered rhetorically why he went on trying to enlighten people. "I could just relax here," he says, "read my books, have a nice time." His belief in the general incompetence of human beings extended to such issues as global warming: he was a convinced "climate change skeptic," on the basis that we insignificant and inept human beings could never have such an influence on the planet.

Accusations that he had Nazi sympathies clearly infuriated him even more than the submental criminality of his "enemies." "I was fully unincriminated," he said. He used the evocative German word *unbelastet*, literally "unburdened." What about the accusations from some quarters that he worked for the Geheime Feldpolizei, the "Secret Field Police," the Nazi military police? "As if that were the same thing as being with the Gestapo," he replied. Libel can be prosecuted as a criminal offense in Germany, but the prosecutor's office, Tobias said, would not touch this one. "Why not?" I asked. "If it is untrue, then it is libel." "It's *mudslinging*," he said (*Verleumdung*). He waved a hand and looked away. "This is what I have to put up with all the time." Why wouldn't he consent to the release of his military records, which would end the matter? "Why should I have to go through this, to prove it every time?" he asked in return.

Later in the conversation he rolled back his sleeves and gestured to scars from an American shelling in Italy at the end of the war. "I suffered under the Nazis," he said.

Tobias lived in a comfortable suburban bungalow. Its most notable features were its wild but beautiful back garden—and his private archive.

This archive is legendary among Reichstag fire researchers. Hans Mommsen cited some of his findings to the "Tobias Archive," but writers who disagreed with Tobias were unable to gain access to it. Various German public archives, including the large Federal Archives, were interested in acquiring it, but Tobias was reluctant to give it up, even in his will. He had invested enormous time and money in chasing down the documents, he told me. Why should his enemies profit from his labor? "I should just burn it all," he growled. The cop stare intensified.[2]

Nonetheless Tobias was proud to show me around five or six rooms of his house filled with documents, carefully organized in binders in the German fashion, neatly labeled and installed in floor-to-ceiling bookcases. By no means did these files pertain only to the Reichstag fire. He had binders on many other subjects in German history and about politics in all regions of the world, especially those burdened with terrorism or civil war. Many of the files covered the assassination of John F. Kennedy— naturally, Tobias thought Lee Harvey Oswald acted alone. Ever the good political policeman, he had files on his opponents as well, newspaper clippings and other information, none of it flattering. Visiting Tobias again a year later, I noted with some trepidation that one of his files was about me.

On the Reichstag fire itself, Tobias's document collection was over-whelming. Some of these binders held the source material for his *Spiegel* articles and his book. But he had gone on researching the fire ever since, for half a century, writing to people who might have information, inter-viewing witnesses, arranging (as we have seen) the placing of Rudolf Diels's papers in the State Archives of Lower Saxony, contributing articles to newspapers and magazines and zealously clipping out others, often enough launching or intervening in the rancorous litigation of which the participants in this debate have been so fond.

When I met Tobias I had as yet no very fully formed view on his con-troversy. This is what I had told him in my letter; I wanted simply to hear and understand his side. But it never seemed to occur to Tobias that I might not fully agree with him, not then in 2008, not when I visited him a year later, not in the correspondence we exchanged until his death. Not even my increasingly skeptical questions ("Why do you think Diels accused Heini Gewehr? Why did he agree with Gisevius?") seemed to trigger any doubt. Probably the extraordinary rancor of the Reichstag fire controversy in Germany had conditioned Tobias to hear respectful courtesy as agreement. In any event neither of us was very interested in my view. I wanted to know what he thought; he wanted to tell me. "Ask me any question and I'll make a speech," he said, and making speeches was mostly what he did. I had the feeling he had made the same speeches many times before.

This perhaps explains why, toward evening on that July day, he offered me material from his files. I could take a binder or two back to my hotel, read them, make copies if I like. What would I like? I had not expected or asked for such a generous offer, but I knew my answer. Without hesita-tion I asked for his files on Rudolf Diels.

This appeared to be the wrong thing to say. Tobias froze. The Diels documents had nothing to do with the Reichstag fire, he said. The cop stare returned. Why was I so interested in Diels? I explained that I thought Diels was both fascinating and important. Surprising me again, he walked to one section of his shelves, studied the binders for a few moments, and then selected and gave me two of them.

That night, reading through the files in a Hannover hotel room, I came across Diels's July 1946 letter to the British delegation at Nurem-berg, with its accusation that Heini Gewehr had burned the Reichstag in "this first crime of the National Socialists." I felt pieces moving around in my mind. This was an original, with Diels's inimitable signature at the bottom, and red pencil underlining that looked like it was from Tobias himself. Where had Tobias found this document? How long had he had it? Why had he never mentioned it? Why had he always insisted that Diels knew nothing about the fire? By the time I returned the binders to Tobias the next day my views were already changing.

ACKNOWLEDGMENTS

. . . .

After he read the acknowledgments section of one of my earlier books, the late Herr Ministerialrat Fritz Tobias wrote me that he thought I had a decent capacity for gratitude. The normal rule, he said, was that doing someone a favor just makes you one more enemy. I am under no illusions that he would have liked the book that resulted from my study of his fire and his controversy, and I am reasonably sure he would have changed his mind about my gratitude could he have read it. But though it might have surprised him, in fact I remain extremely grateful for the courtesy he showed me on the two occasions I visited him in Hannover, and for his surprising generosity in letting me see and even copy his files on Rudolf Diels. He was, whatever else, a pioneer in the literature of Germany's contemporary history, and any book on the Reichstag fire has to take him seriously.

Herr Professor Hans Mommsen was also extremely friendly and courteous, and patient with my questions, when I visited him in 2010. Heinrich Schnitzler's sons Herr Dierk and Herr Klaus-Michael Schnitzler went well out of their way to meet me in Bonn in 2012 to allow me to see their father's papers, and gave permission for me to use the picture of their father that appears in this book. My dear friend Gerhard Jungfer let me work through his huge file of documents on the Reichstag fire case and told me about his involvement in the last (unsuccessful) effort to re-open the trial in the early 1990s. I must also extend my deep thanks to Professor Karl Otmar von Aretin, Dr. Alexander Bahar, Professor Christoph Graf, Herr Hersch Fischler, Herr Markus Henneke, Herr Peter-Ferdinand Koch, Herr Günter Strumpf, and Dr. Friedrich Winterhager, who were generous with time, correspondence, and materials. I spoke to Mr. Thomas Polgar and Mr. Peter Sichel, both retired from the CIA, about another project, but their comments about people like Kempner, Diels, Gisevius, and the general atmosphere of early postwar Germany were both fascinating and unexpectedly helpful for this one.

Professor Karl Stephan and Dr. Peter Schildhauer, whose work has contributed so much to understanding the technical side of this story, answered my poor historian's questions about the mysteries of fire, and very kindly took the time to read the relevant draft sections of this book. Professor Lothar Weber kindly answered my questions about phosphorus.

Funding for a good number of journeys to distant archives, and for a two-year sabbatical from my teaching duties from 2009–2011 during which time I did most of the heavy lifting for this book, came from a range of sources: fellowships from the John Simon Guggenheim Foundation and the American Council of Learned Societies, the PSC-CUNY research grants program, and the Hunter College Presidential Travel Grants and Sabbatical Leave and Scholar Incentive Program. Hunter College President Jennifer Raab, Provost Vita Rabinowitz, and history department chairs Barbara Welter and Rick Belsky were all incredibly helpful in making these arrangements possible. Deep thanks to all.

I owe a very great debt to the staffs of the twenty-five archives in four countries I visited in working on this project. In particular I would like to thank Frau Bianca Welzing-Bräutigam of the Landesarchiv Berlin, who has been a remarkable source of help and advice for every one of my research projects since my graduate student days, and Frau Jenny Gohr of what is now the Jahn-Behörde for the records of the East German *Stasi* (the BStU). Frau Gohr's kindness and helpfulness (special thanks for those coffee breaks) stand in particularly pleasant contrast to the grim purpose of the records she oversees. I would also like to thank Herr Dr. Klaus Lankheit of the *Institut für Zeitgeschichte* and Herr Heinz Egleder, archivist of the *Spiegel*, in whose office I was able to spend three pleasant and fascinating days (and also got to see the inside of the *Spiegel's* famous, rather psychedelic canteen). Most of this book was written in the congenial surroundings of the Wertheim Study at the New York Public Library, for which special thanks to the Wertheim Study's overseer, Jay Barksdale—I know I am not the only New York-area writer who is grateful for the grace with which Jay creates the perfect place to write.

Two gifted young scholars helped me with some of the research: Paul Moore with materials from the British National Archives and the archives of the *Guardian*, and my own doctoral advisee, Irit Bloch, with many of the German newspapers and the Knickerbocker papers. Two other outstanding graduate students, Chelsea Schields and Ky Woltering, actually volunteered to read the manuscript and provided me with some very helpful comments. Chelsea also helped me locate some Dutch sources and helped with the Dutch translations. In recording my gratitude to young scholars who have not yet reached the land of tenure, I would also like to stress that they bear no blame for the wayward ideas I express here.

Several colleagues and friends read some or all of the manuscript and were extremely generous in providing comments: Christoph Kimmich, Daniel Siemens, Nik Wachsmann, and Robert Girvan—Rob, reprising his extremely helpful role from my last book, demonstrating that no good deed goes unpunished.

Of course, after all the generous help I have received from the people who read and commented on the manuscript, all errors remain my own responsibility.

For my agent, Scott Mendel, and my indefatigable editor at Oxford University Press, Tim Bent, this book has been a bit of an odyssey, and I owe them huge thanks for their patience and perseverance. Tim suggested this topic to me when I had the vague idea of writing something about Rudolf Diels and has stuck with it through thick and thin. The conventions of publishing often do not give editors sufficient formal credit, but after all the energy he has put into helping me clarify the theme and narrative of this project, this is Tim's book too. Oxford University Press is in fact a delightfully professional organization for a writer to work with, and thanks are due as well to production editor Joellyn Ausanka and to assistant editor Keely Latcham for their skills, not to mention their patience and good humor.

Once again my lovely wife Corinna has had to put up with my extended physical absences on research trips and occasional mental absences at home while in the throes of writing. After three books she knows the ropes; she has borne it all with good humor, and I cannot thank her enough.

This book is dedicated to two of my oldest friends, Robert Girvan (who of course also read the manuscript) and Dean McNeill. For thirty years (can it be?), simply by being who they are and living with courage, honesty, and decency, Rob and Dean have taught me a lot without ever trying to do so. This dedication is my very humble and inadequate thanks.

New York
June 2013

ABBREVIATIONS

. . . .

BA-BL   Bundesarchiv Berlin Lichterfelde (Federal Archives Berlin Lichterfelde)

BA-K   Bundesarchiv Koblenz (Federal Archives Koblenz)

BA-L   Bundesarchiv Ludwigsburg (Federal Archives Ludwigsburg)

BL   Butler Library, Columbia University

BNA   British National Archives

BSM   Bayerisches Staatsarchiv München (Bavarian State Archives Munich)

BSN   Bayerisches Staatsarchiv Nürnberg (Bavarian State Archives Nuremberg)

BStU   Der Bundesbeauftragte für die Unterlagen des Staatssicherheitsdienstes der ehemaligen Deutschen Demokratischen Republik (The Federal Commissioner for the documents of the State Security Service of the former German Democratic Republic, the Stasi Archive)

BSW   Bayerisches Staatsarchiv Würzburg (Bavarian State Archives Würzburg)

BFA   Berliner Feuerwehr Archiv (Berlin Fire Department Archive)

BDC   Berlin Document Center

DNVP   Deutschnationale Volkspartei (German National People's Party)

ETH	Zeitgeschichtliches Archiv, Eidgenössische Technische Hochschule (Contemporary History Archive, Federal Institute of Technology)
FRUS	Foreign Relations of the United States
GStA	Geheimes Staatsarchiv Preußischer Kulturbesitz (Secret State Archives of Prussian Cultural Collections)
IfZ	Institut für Zeitgeschichte (Institute for Contemporary History)
IWM	Imperial War Museum
JA	Jungfer Archive
LAB	Landesarchiv Berlin (Archives of the City of Berlin)
LNRW-D	Landesarchiv Nordrhein-Westfalen, Abteilung Rheinland, Hauptstaatsarchiv Düsseldorf (State Archive of North Rhine-Westphalia, Rhineland Section, Main State Archive Düsseldorf)
LNRW-M	Landesarchiv Nordrhein-Westfalen, Abteilung Westfalen, Münster (State Archives of North Rhine-Westphalia, Westphalia Section, Münster)
LOC	Library of Congress
LSH	Landesarchiv Schleswig-Holstein (State Archives of Schleswig-Holstein)
MGA	Manchester Guardian Archive
NARA	National Archives and Records Administration
NHH	Niedersächsisches Hauptstaatsarchiv Hannover (Lower Saxon Main State Archive Hannover)
NJW	*Neue Juristische Wochenschrift* (New Legal Weekly)
NL	Nachlass (personal papers)
PA-AA	Politisches Archiv des Auswärtigen Amts (Political Archives of the German Foreign Office)
SA	Sturmabteilungen (Storm Sections—Stormtroopers or "Brownshirts")
SpA	*Spiegel* Archive
TA	Tobias Archive

TBJG   Tagebücher des Joseph Goebbels (the diaries of Joseph Goebbels)

USHMM   United States Holocaust Memorial Museum

VfZ   *Vierteljahrshefte für Zeitgeschichte* (Quarterly journal for contemporary history)

VT   Verhandlungstag (Day of proceedings), the individual volumes of the transcript of the Reichstag fire trial. These 57 volumes can now be found in the BA-BL R. 3003/245-301; full copies are also in the library of the IfZ, and some days are in the BStU.

NOTES

· · · ·

PROLOGUE

1. Josse, Report, May 15, 1933, BA-BL R. 3003/56; Buwert Statement, February 28, 1933, BA-BL R. 3003/1, Bl. 6–7.

2. Helmuth F. Braun and Michael Doormann, *"Dem Deutschen Volke": Die Geschichte der Berliner Bronzgießerei Loevy* (Cologne: Dumont Literatur & Kunst Verlag, 2003), 14–45.

3. Michael Cullen, *Der Reichstag: Parlament, Symbol, Denkmal* (Berlin: Be.Bra. Verlag, 1999), 186–200; Thomas Mergel, *Parlamentarische Kultur in der Weimarer Republik: Politische Kommunikation, symbolische Politik und Öffentlichkeit im Reichstag* (Düsseldorf: Droste Verlag, 2002), 83 ff.

4. Cullen, *Reichstag*, 186–200; Mergel, *Parlamentarische Kultur*, 83 ff.

5. Mergel, *Parlamentarische Kultur*, 81; on Oberfohren and Torgler, see Chapter 3.

6. Buwert Statement, February 28, 1933, BA-BL R. 3003/1, Bl. 6–7.

7. Flöter Statement, February 28, 1933, BA-BL R. 3003/1, Bl. 20.

8. Thaler Statement, February 28, 1933, BA-BL R. 3003/1, Bl. 17; Thaler Statement, March 22, 1933, BA-BL R. 3003/2, Bl. 176–79.

9. Thaler Statement, February 28, 1933, BA-BL R. 3003/1, Bl. 17.

10. Lateit Statement, February 28, 1933, BA-BL R. 3003/1, Bl. 8; Lateit Statement, March 14, 1933, BA-BL R. 3003/2, Bl. 12–25; 14 VT 23.

11. Poeschel Statement, March 17, 1933, BA-BL R. 3003/2, Bl. 53–55.

12. Lateit Statement, February 28, 1933, BA-BL R. 3003/1, Bl. 8; Lateit Statement, March 14, 1933, BA-BL R. 3003/2, Bl. 12–25; Losigkeit Statement, March 14, 1933, ibid., Bl. 25–28; Poeschel Statement, February 28, 1933, BA-BL R. 3003/1, Bl. 11; Poeschel Statement, March 17, 1933, BA-BL R. 3003/2, Bl. 53–55; 15 VT 53; Scranowitz Statement, March 16, 1933, BA-BL R. 3003/2, Bl. 44–49.

13. Lateit Statement, March 14, 1933, BA-BL R. 3003/2, Bl. 12–25; Losigkeit Statement, March 14, 1933, BA-BL R. 3003/2, Bl. 25–28; 14 VT 44; 15 VT 31, 54, 56–57.

14. Scranowitz Statement, March 16, 1933, BA-BL R. 3003/2, Bl. 44–49; Josse Report, May 15, 1933, BA-BL R. 3003/56; 16 VT.

15. Poeschel Statement, March 17, 1933, BA-BL R. 3003/2, Bl. 53–55; 16 VT. At trial Poeschel said he got a look at the chamber from two different angles, the first time over Lateit's shoulder and the second time over Scranowitz's: 15 VT 59–60, 61.

16. Alfons Sack, *Der Reichstagsbrand Prozess* (Berlin: Ullstein, 1934), 17–18.

17. Klotz Statement, March 15, 1933, BA-BL R. 3003/2, Bl. 33–37; Josse Report, May 15, 1933, BA-BL R. 3003/56; 16 VT 55 ff.

18. Klotz Statement, March 3, 1933, BA-BL R. 3003/53, Bl. 17; Josse Report, May 15, 1933, BA-BL R. 3003/56.

19. Polchow Statement, March 3, 1933, BA-BL R. 3003/53, Bl. 15–16; Puhle Statement, March 1, 1933, Ibid., Bl. 14–15; Puhle Statement, March 18, 1933, BA-BL R. 3003/2, Bl. 41–43.

20. Polchow Statement, March 3, 1933, BA-BL R. 3003/53, Bl. 15.

21. Polchow Statement, March 3, 1933, BA-BL R. 3003/53, Bl. 15; Feuerwehrbericht, October 11, 1955, IfZ ZS/A 7 Bd. 2; Polchow Statement, July 14, 1960, in Walther Hofer, et al., eds. *Der Reichstagsbrand: Eine wissenschaftliche Dokumentation*, Bd. 1 (Berlin: arani Verlag, 1972), 230–33.

22. 16 VT 155–60.

23. 15 VT 45.

24. "The Reichstag Fire Trial," *Manchester Guardian*, October 14, 1933.

25. Scranowitz's evidence 15 VT 173; Hans Schneider, *Neues vom Reichstagsbrand? Eine Dokumentation: Ein Versäumnis der deutschen Geschichtsschreibung* (Berlin: Berliner Wissenschafts-Verlag, 2004), 64. Scranowitz's own testimony leaves the impression that van der Lubbe was protesting being punched.

26. Bericht, March 7, 1933, BA-BL R. 3003/2, Bl. 89 ff.

27. Lateit Statement, March 14, 1933, BA-BL R. 3003/2, Bl. 23–24.

28. Foth, "Feuer im Reichstag," *Preussische Feuerwehr Zeitung*, March 1933, BFA; "Riesenbrand im Reichstag," *Vorwärts*, February 28, 1933, morning.

29. Sefton Delmer, *Trail Sinister: An Autobiography* (London: Secker and Warburg, 1961), 185–89.

30. Rudolf Diels, *Lucifer Ante Portas: Zwischen Severing und Heydrich* (Zürich: Interverlag A.G., 1949), 144, translation from J. Noakes and G. Pridham, *Nazism 1919–1945: A Documentary Reader*, vol. 1, *The Rise to Power, 1919–1945* (Exeter: University of Exeter Press, 1998), 140–41; Martin Schuster, *Die SA in der nationalsozialistischen "Machtergreifung" in Berlin und Brandenburg 1926–1934* (Berlin: Ph.D. dissertation, 2005), 231.

31. Walther Kiaulehn, *Berlin: Schicksal einer Weltstadt* (Munich: C.H. Beck, 1997), 567.

32. Hannah Arendt, "'What Remains? The Language Remains': A Conversation with Gunter Gaus," in Arendt, *Essays in Understanding, 1930–1954: Uncollected and Unpublished Works*, ed. Jerome Kohn (New York: Harcourt Brace, 1994), 5.

33. Hans Bernd Gisevius, *Bis zum bitteren Ende* (Zürich: Fretz & Wasmuth Verlag, 1946), 113; *Bis zum bitteren Ende: Vom Reichstagsbrand bis zum 20. Juli 1944* (Hamburg: Rütten & Loenig Verlag, 1960), 71–72, 94; Gisevius to Oberloskamp, November 12, 1969, ETH NL Gisevius 16.4.

34. Heinrich Schnitzler, *Prisoner of War Nr. 3404933*, NL Schnitzler I, 26–27.

35. Ernst Fraenkel, *The Dual State: A Contribution to the Theory of Dictatorship* (New York: Oxford University Press, 1941), 3.

36. Fritz Tobias, *Der Reichstagsbrand: Legende und Wirklichkeit* (Rastatt: G. Grote'sche Verlagsbuchhandlung, 1962), 592.

37. Fraenkel to Tobias, August 14, 1971, BA-K N 1274/65a NL Fraenkel.

38. On violence and legitimacy, see Pamela Swett, *Neighbors and Enemies: The Culture of Radicalism in Berlin, 1929–1933* (Cambridge: Cambridge University Press, 2004).

39. Longerich, *Goebbels*, 15. Ivo Banac, "Introduction," in Banac, ed., *The Diary of Georgi Dimitrov 1933–1949* (New Haven, CT: Yale University Press, 2003), xxvi–xxviii; Alexander Dallin and F. I. Firstov, *Dimitrov and Stalin 1934–1943: Letters from the Soviet Archives* (New Haven and London: Yale University Press, 2000), 6.

40. Michael Wildt, *Generation des Unbedingten: Das Führungskorps des Reichssicherheits-hauptamtes* (Hamburg: Hamburger Edition, 2003), 839–45.

41. Wildt, *Generation des Unbedingten*, 16.

1: "SATANIC NOSE"

1. Martha Dodd, *Through Embassy Eyes* (New York: Harcourt, Brace & Company, 1939), 52; Diels to Müller-Meiningen, n.d., 1954, NHH VVP 46, NL Diels, Bd. 15.

2. Robert M. W. Kempner, *Ankläger einer Epoche: Lebenserinnerungen* (Frankfurt/Main: Verlag Ullstein, 1983), 112.

3. Rudolf Diels, *Der Fall Otto John: Hintergründe und Lehren* (Göttingen: Göttinger Verlagsanstalt, 1954), 15.

4. Martini to Tobias, March 18, 1975, TA; Becker to Sachs, October 10, 1948, Gustav Schlotterer Statement, December 1, 1947, BA-K Z/42/IV/1960, Bl. 13, Bl. 95.

5. Diels to Schnitzler, March 26, 1947, NL Schnitzler II; Bach-Zelewski Statement, June 17, 1947, BA-K Z/42/IV/1960, Bl. 64–65.

6. Martini to Tobias, March 18, 1975, TA; Ilse Diels Statement, August, 1945, BA-K Z/42/IV/1960, Bl. 146; Leni Riefenstahl, *Leni Riefenstahl: A Memoir* (New York: St. Martin's Press, 1993).

7. Ingeborg Kalnoky, *The Guest House: A Nuremberg Memoir* (Indianapolis: Bobbs-Merrill, 1974), 64.

8. Kempner, *Ankläger*, 111–12.

9. Gisevius, *Bis zum bitteren Ende* (1960), 99.

10. Gisevius, *Bis zum bitteren Ende* (1960), 99; Diels Interrogation, February 19, 1949, BA-K Z/42/IV/1960, Bl. 32–33; questionnaire, August 10, 1949, NHH NDS 171 Hannover Nr. 28640, Bl. 1.

11. Diels to Hess, June 12, 1934, NHH VVP 46 NL Diels, Bd. 10; Severing to Staatsanwalt Bielefeld, August 13, 1948, BA-K Z/42/IV/1960, Bl. 490; Abegg to Staatsanwalt Bielefeld, October 6, 1948, ibid., Bl. 10–11.

12. Franz von Papen, *Der Wahrheit eine Gasse* (Munich: Paul List Verlag, 1952), 214.

13. Wilhelm Abegg to Staatsanwalt Bielefeld, October 6, 1948, BA-K Z/42/IV/1960, Bl. 10–11.

14. Severing to Staatsanwalt Bielefeld, August 13, 1948, BA-K Z/42/IV/1960, Bl. 490–97; Abegg to Severing, August 4, 1932, IfZ F 48.

15. Abegg to Staatsanwalt Bielefeld, October 6, 1948, BA-K Z/42/IV/1960, Bl. 10–11; Severing to Staatsanwalt Bielefeld, August 13, 1948, ibid., Bl. 490–97; Karl-Heinz Minuth, *Das Kabinett von Papen: 1. Juni bis 3. Dezember 1932* (Boppard am Rhein: Harald Boldt Verlag, 1989), Bd. 1 191 n. 3; Anlageheft zu der Erwiderung der Reichsregierung, August 25, 1932 BA-K Z/42/IV/1960, Bl. 489.

16. Bericht des Regierungspräsidenten in Schleswig, July 19, 1932, in Minuth, *Kabinett von Papen*, Bd. 1 248–56; Papen, *Wahrheit*, 216–18.

17. Abegg to Staatsanwalt Bielefeld, October 6, 1948, BA-K Z/42/IV/1960 10–11; Franz von Papen, Radio Address, July 20, 1933, Deutsches Historisches Museum/ Deutsches Rundfunkarchiv, *Stimmen des 20. Jahrhunderts: Preußen in Weimar*, audio compact disc, 2001.

18. Vermerk, July 25, 1932, in Minuth, *Kabinett von Papen*, Bd. 1 246–47; Anklage, November 1, 1950, Tejessy an den öffentlichen Kläger, December 8, 1949, LNRW-D Rep. 372/278, Bl. 4–5, Bl. 29; Abegg to Severing, August 4, 1932, IfZ F 48; Schnitzler to Diels, December 2, 1936, NHH VVP 46 NL Diels, Bd. 10; Papen, *Wahrheit*, 215; Franz von Papen, *Vom Scheitern einer Demokratie 1930–1933* (Mainz: v. Hase & Koehler Verlag, 1968), 233.

19. "Subject Rudolf Diels," December 17, 1945, A.E.E. Reade, Group Captain, BNA WO 309/294; Rudolf Diels, Lebenslauf, September 2, 1935, NARA BDC Roll Number A 3343 SSO-149, 1255–56; Helldorff to Schnitzler, October 27, 1933, GStA Rep. 90 P Nr. 4, Bl. 162; Schnitzler Äußerung, August 2, 1932, GStA Rep. 90 P Nr. 4, Bl. 169; Schnitzler to Diels, December 2, 1936, NHH VVP 46 NL

Diels, Bd. 10. There is some confusion about the spelling of Helldorff's name—it is often given as Heldorf—but the most thorough study finds that there should be two *f*s: Ted Harrison, "'Alter Kämpfer' im Widerstand. Graf Helldorff, die NS-Bewegung und die Opposition gegen Hitler," *VfZ* 45 (3) 1997: 385–424.

20. "Besprechung mit Willi Schmidt/Schweinebacke am 27.7.68 in Hannover," TA; Schmidt Statement, February 18, 1968, LAB B Rep 058/2271 Bd. 3.

21. Ernst Torgler Statement, March 20, 1949, TA; "Herbert Wehner, Notizen, May 23, 1946," ibid.

22. Martin H. Sommerfeldt, *Ich war dabei: Die Verschwörung der Dämonen, 1933–1939* (Darmstadt: Drei Quellen Verlag, 1949), 57.

23. Diels, *Lucifer*, 127; Haffner, *Defying Hitler: A Memoir* (New York: Farrar, Straus and Giroux, 2002), 112.

24. Kempner, *Ankläger*, 110–11.

25. 31 VT 82-83.

26. "Polizeiführer-West," February 18, 1933, in Hofer, *Reichstagsbrand*, 488.

27. Diels, "Funkspruch," February 27, 1933, 14:59, BA-BL R. 3003/202; Diels, *Lucifer*, 139.

2: "SA + ME"

1. Goebbels, "Erinnerungsblätter," TBJG *Sämtliche Fragmente*, Bd. 1 27.6.1924–31.12.1930 (Munich: K.G. Saur, 1987), 14; Joseph Goebbels, *Michael Voormanns Jugendjahre*, quoted in Reuth, *Goebbels*, 16, 19. München-Gladbach is now Mönchengladbach.

2. Reuth, *Goebbels*, 17, 27.

3. Goebbels, "Erinnerungsblätter," 3; Reuth, *Goebbels*, 21.

4. Goebbels, "Erinnerungsblätter," 4, 8, 23–26.

5. Ibid., 23–26.

6. TBJG Vol. 1 27.6.1924–31.12.1930 (Munich: K.G. Saur, 1987), 30; TBJG Part I Vol. 2/I (Munich: K.G. Saur, 2005), 394.

7. TBJG vol. 1, 30–31.

8. TBJG Part I Vol. 2/II (Munich: K.G. Saur, 2004), 104; Goebbels in Herbert Michaelis et al., eds., *Ursachen und Folgen vom deutschen Zusammenbruch 1918 und 1945*, Bd. 7, *Die Weimarer Republik: Vom Kellogg-Pakt zur Weltwirtschaftskrise 1928–1930* (Berlin: Dokumenten-Verlag Dr. Herbert Wendler & Vo., 1962), 371; TBJG Part I Vol. 2/II, 122.

9. Diels, *Lucifer*, 84; TBJG Part I Vol. 2/II, 203; *Das Leben geht weiter: Der Letzte Propagandafilm des Dritten Reichs*, documentary film, dir. Mark Cairns, Polar Film + Medien GmbH, 2003.

10. Goebbels, speech, in J. Noakes and G. Pridham, *Nazism 1919–1945: A Documentary Reader* (Exeter: University of Exeter Press, 1984), 187; Diels, *Lucifer*, 85–86.

11. Aktenvermerk, March 18, 1943, Deh, Vernehmung, LAB B Rep. 058/6394, Bl. 40–41, Bl. 76–93.

12. Bericht, January 30, 1933, LAB A Rep 358–01/7085, Bl. 5; Marie Marunge Statement, January 31, 1933, ibid., Bl. 32; Emil Kleinke Statement, January 31, 1933, ibid., Bl. 32; Hermann Hahn Statement, January 31, 1933, ibid., Bl. 36; generally LAB A Rep 358–01/7085–7096.

13. Diels, *Lucifer*, 59, 88, 90; Erich Ebermayer, *Denn heute gehört uns Deutschland . . . Persönliches und politisches Tagebuch: Von der Machtergreifung bis zum 31. Dezember 1935* (Hamburg: Paul Zsolnay Verlag, 1959), 29.

14. Joseph Goebbels, *Kampf um Berlin: Der Anfang* (Munich: Zentralverlag der NSDAP Frz. Eher Nachf., 1932), 11–12, 27–28.

15. Goebbels, *Kampf*, 28, 17, 21, 43.

16. Daniel Siemens, "'Prügelpropaganda': Die SA und die nationalsozialistische Mythos vom 'Kampf um Berlin,'" in Michael Wildt and Christoph Kreuzmüller, eds., *Berlin 1933–1945* (Munich: Siedler Verlag, 2012) 37; Bernhard Sauer, "Goebbels 'Rabauken.' Zur Geschichte der SA in Berlin-Brandenburg," *Berlin in Geschichte und Gegenwart: Jahrbuch des Landesarchivs Berlin* (Berlin, 2006), 113.

17. Peter Longerich, *Geschichte der SA* (Munich: C.H. Beck, 2003), 23.

18. Longerich, *Geschichte der SA*, 26.

19. Sauer, "Goebbels Rabauken," 107–11; Daniel Siemens, *Horst Wessel: Tod und Verklärung eines Nationalsozialisten* (Munich: Siedler Verlag, 2009) 52–57.

20. Longerich, *Geschichte der SA*, 47–49; Schuster, *SA*, 32.

21. J.K. von Engelbrechten, *Eine Braune Armee entsteht: Die Geschichte der Berlin-Brandenburg SA* (Munich-Berlin: Verlag Franz Eher Nachf., 1937), Vorwort; *Storm 33: Hans Maikowski, Geschrieben von Kameraden des Toten*, 1. Auflage (Berlin-Schöneberg: NS Druck und Verlag, 1933), 2.

22. 34 VT 15–23.

23. Alfred Apfel, *Behind the Scenes of German Justice: Reminiscences of a German Barrister 1882–1933* (London: John Lane, 1935), 164; Daniel Siemens, *Horst Wessel: Tod und Verklärung eines Nationalsozialisten* (Munich: Siedler Verlag, 2009), 96–98.

24. "Kampf um Berlin," *Angriff*, January 23, 1930.

25. Sethe to PJM, February 6, 1930, PJM to Sethe, February 20, 1930, LAB A Rep. 358-01/695, Bl. 2, 3.

26. "Rote Laubenkolonien," *Rote Fahne*, January 29, 1932; "Bei den Siedlern," *Welt am Abend*, January 20, 1932; Judgment, December 22, 1932, BA-BL R. 22/66804; Villwock Statement, February 3, 1932, LAB A Rep 358-01/37, 422; Hett, *Crossing Hitler*, 137–38, 150; "Der Dreh der Journaille," *Angriff*, January 20, 1932; "Die Nazis sind Schuld," *Angriff*, January 21, 1932.

27. Polizeipräsident, March 27, 1931, LAB A Rep 358/509 Film A 573.

28. Weiss Statement, May 8, 1931, ibid.; Francke Statement, May 13, 1931, ibid.

29. "Attentat auf Dr. Goebbels," *Angriff,* March 14, 1931; "Sprengladung im Postpaket," *Angriff,* March 14, 1931; "Dem Feigling Goebbels gewidmet," *Rote Fahne,* March 19, 1931; "Das Attentat des kleinen Mannes," *Vossische Zeitung,* March 15, 1931, LAB A Rep 358/509 Film A 573; *Vossische Zeitung,* March 17, 1931, ibid.

30. TBJG Part I Vol. 2/I, 363; Hett, *Crossing Hitler,* 65–66; Brüning to Schmidt-Hannover, October 20, 1948, BA-Koblenz, N 1211/2 NL Schmidt-Hannover, Bl. 257; "Goebbels 'Attentatsgerücht' eine Denunziation? *12 Uhr Blatt,* March 13, 1932, BA R. 8034 III 152, Bl. 160.

31. Conti to OSAF, September 8, 1930, in Hans-Adolf Jacobsen and Werner Jochmann, eds., *Ausgewählte Dokumente zur Geschichte des Nationalsozialismus 1933–1945,* Bd. II (Bielefeld: Verlag Neue Gesellschaft GmbH, 1961); Reuth, *Goebbels,* 141; "Die Stennes Revolte," IfZ MA 747; Goschler, *Reden, Schriften, Anordnungen,* 248 n. 2; Ian Kershaw, *Hitler 1889–1936: Hubris* (New York: W.W. Norton, 1999), 172–73, 346–49; TBJG Part I Vol. 2/I, 376.

32. "Die Stennes Revolte" IfZ MA 747; Diels, *Lucifer,* 185, 107; Reuth, *Goebbels,* 191; Ernst Hanfstaengl, *Zwischen Weißem und Braunem Haus: Memoiren eines politischen Außenseiters* (Munich: R. Piper & Co. Verlag, 1970), 226–27; TBJG Part I Vol. 2/I, 350; Christopher Andrew, *The Mitrokhin Archive: The KGB in Europe and the West* (London: Allen Lane, 1999), 124.

33. Siemens, "Prügelpropaganda," 39; Kershaw, *Hitler 1889–1936,* 350; Reuth, *Goebbels,* 189–90.

34. TBJG Part I Vol. 2/II, 100, 132.

35. Judgment, LAB A Rep 358/20, Bd. 4, 5–7, 9, 12–18, 22–28, 34–36, 38–39, 41–42, 54; "Die Ausschreitungen im Westen," *Berliner Tageblatt,* September 14, 1931, evening; His-huey Liang, *Die Berliner Polizei in der Weimarer Republik* (Berlin: de Gruyter, 1977), 191–92.

36. *Weltwoche,* September 15, 1944, ETH NL Gisevius, 10 Correspondence, Helldorff; Harrison, "'Alter kämpfer,'" 387.

37. "Charakteristik des Grafen von Helldorff," September 18, 1931, NARA BDC NSDAP Hauptarchiv, Film 146 frames 1724–30, frame 1732 ff; "Ein Jahr Karl Ernst," *Der Montag,* March 16, 1934, BA R. 8034 III 113, Bl. 6.

38. "Die Kurfürstendamm-Rowdies," *Berliner Tageblatt,* September 18, 1931, evening.

39. "Verantwortlichkeit der 'Führer,'" *Berliner Tageblatt,* September 23, 1931, evening; "Helldorff 6 Monate Gefängnis," *Berliner Tageblatt,* November 8, 1931, morning; "Die Kurfürstendamm-Rowdies," *Berliner Tageblatt,* September 18, 1931, evening; "Die Zeugen vom Kurfürstendamm," *Berliner Tageblatt,* September 19, 1931, evening; "Die harmlosen Automobilisten," *Berliner Tageblatt,* October 27, 1931 evening; "'Wir haben gelacht,'" *Berliner Tageblatt,* November 2,

1931, evening; "Helldorff hat es gewusst!" *Berliner Tageblatt*, November 7, 1931, morning; "Goebbels und Helldorff," *Vorwärts*, November 3, 1931; "Gedanken zum Kurfürstendamm-Prozess," *Angriff*, January 2, 1932; "Herr Minister, warum klagen Sie nicht?" *Völkischer Beobachter*, January 5, 1932; "Schluß der Verteidiger-Plädoyers" *Angriff*, February 8, 1932.

40. "Der Prozess wegen der S-A Krawalle," *Berliner Tageblatt*, September 23, 1931, morning.

41. "Besprechung Goebbels-Helldorff?" *Berliner Tageblatt*, November 3, 1931, morning; "Goebbels und Helldorff," *Vorwärts*, November 3, 1931; Judgment, February 9, 1932, LAB A Rep 358/20 *Kurfürstendamm Krawalle*, Bd. 4, 98.

42. "Wir haben gelacht," *Berliner Tageblatt*, November 2, 1931, evening; TBJG Part I Vol. 2/II, 202.

43. "Dr. Goebbels gegen die Denunzianten," *Angriff*, January 24, 1932; "Der Spitzel wird nicht genannt," *Angriff*, January 27, 1932; Dieter Gosewinkel, *Adolf Arndt: Die Wiederbegründung des Rechtsstaats aus dem Geist der Sozialdemokratie (1945–1961)* (Bonn: Verlag J.H.W. Dietz Nachf. GmbH, 1991), 46.

44. Judgment, LAB A Rep 358/20, Bd. 4, 51–52, 146, 148, 98–100; Gosewinkel, *Arndt*, 46–48, 73. As an SPD parliamentarian in 1949 Arndt would say that "otherwise than in the Weimar Republic" the courts should be willing to "punish all attacks on democracy's free order with the entire force of the law." Frei, *Adenauer's Germany*, 22.

45. TBJG Part I Band 2/II, 108.

46. Ibid., 109, 112; Harrison, "'Alter Kämpfer,'" 392.

47. Schuster, *SA*, 158 note 177; Gewehr to Zacharias, March 27, 1960, IfZ ID 103–60.

48. "Lockspitzel verursachen Straßenkrawalle," *Angriff*, October 16, 1930.

49. Eleanor Hancock, *Ernst Röhm: Hitler's SA Chief of Staff* (New York: Palgrave Macmillan, 2008), 146–47.

50. Saul Friedländer, *Nazi Germany and the Jews*, vol. 1, *The Years of Persecution* (New York: Harper Collins, 1997), 266–68, 270–74.

51. Ibid., 271–72; Richard J. Evans, *Lying about Hitler: History, Holocaust and the David Irving Trial* (New York: Basic Books, 2002), 61.

3: "WHAT JUST WENT ON HERE IS AN ABSOLUTE OUTRAGE"

1. TBJG Part I Vol. 2/III (Munich: K.G. Saur, 2006), 120; Joachim Fest, *Hitler: Eine Biographie* (Berlin: Ullstein Taschenbuch, 1998), 528.

2. Max Fürst, *Gefilte Fisch und wie es weiterging* (Munich: Deutscher Taschenbuch Verlag, 2004), 658–59; Haffner, *Defying Hitler*, 107.

3. Gottfried Reinhold Treviranus, *Das Ende von Weimar: Heinrich Brüning und seine Zeit* (Düsseldorf: Econ-Verlag, 1968), 366; Ebermayer, *Denn heute*, 13.

4. Ernst Oberfohren in Herbert Michaelis et al., eds., *Ursachen und Folgen vom deutschen Zusammenbruch 1918 und 1945*, Bd. 8, *Die Weimarer Republik. Das Ende des parlamentarischen Systems* (Berlin: Dokumenten-Verlag Dr. Herbert Wendler & Co., 1963), 316.

5. Hinrich Lohse, "Abermals in eigener Sache," *Schleswig-Holsteinische Tageszeitung*, March 8, 1929, "Und Wieder die Welle Dr. Oberfohren," *Schleswig-Holsteinische Tageszeitung*, December 29, 1929, BA-BL R. 8034 III 336, Bl. 25, Bl. 35; Peter Wulf, "Ernst Oberfohren und die DNVP am Ende der Weimarer Republik," in Erich Hoffmann and Peter Wulf, eds., *"Wir bauen das Reich." Aufstieg und erste Herrschaftsjahre des Nationalsozialismus in Schleswig-Holstein* (Neumünster: Karl Wachholtz Verlag, 1983), 165–187, 175.

6. "Gegen jede Parteidiktatur," *Deutsche Tageszeitung*, July 30, 1932, BA-BL R. 8034 III 336, Bl. 6; Wulf, "Oberfohren," 177.

7. 31 VT 139–40, 142; "The Reichstag Fire Trial," *Manchester Guardian*, November 6, 1933.

8. *Die Deutschnationalen und die Zerstörung der Weimarer Republik. Aus dem Tagebuch von Reinhold Quaatz 1928–1933*, ed. Hermann Weiß und Paul Hoser (Munich: R. Oldenbourg Verlag, 1989), 225; Jeremy Noakes, ed., *British Documents on Foreign Affairs*, Part II Series F vol. 44, *Germany 1933* (Ann Arbor: University Publications of America, 1993), 70; Fest, *Hitler*, 991.

9. Wilhelm Kube, "Volkswahlen gegen Herrn v. Papen," BA-BL R. 8034 II 9030, Bl. 5a; "Abrechnung mit den Hugenzwergen," *Angriff*, September 20, 1932, ibid., Bl. 8; Goebbels in J. Noakes and G. Pridham, *Nazism*, vol. 1, 106; Röver in *Wie die Nazi regieren*, BA-K ZSg.1-44/7; "Nationale Bundesgenossen," *Vorwärts*, January 12, 1933, BA-BL R. 8034 II 9030, Bl. 167.

10. *Wie die Nazi regieren*, 22; *Wie die Nazi kämpfen*, BA-BL R. 8034 II 9030, Bl. 140.

11. TBJG Part I Vol. 2/II, 122–23.

12. "Versammlung," BA-BL R. 8005 Bd. 60.

13. Karl-Heinz Minuth, ed., *Die Regierung Hitler. Teil 1: 1933/34, Band 1, 30. Januar bis 31. August 1933* (Boppard am Rhein: Harald Boldt Verlag, 1983), 2, 29; Domarus, *Hitler*, 192–93; Ebermayer, *Denn heute*, 17.

14. Minuth, *Regierung Hitler*, 9; Domarus, *Hitler*, 192; Diels, *Lucifer*, 126, 130–31; TBJG Part I Vol. 2/III, 121.

15. "Aktenvermerk" in Gerhard Schultz, ed., *Staat und NSDAP 1930–1932: Quellen zur Ära Brüning* (Düsseldorf: Droste Verlag, 1977), 229; text of the Boxheimer Documents in Herbert Michaelis et al., eds., *Ursachen und Folgen vom deutschen Zusammenbruch 1918 und 1945*, Bd. 7, *Die Weimarer Republik: Vom Kellogg-Pakt*

zur Weltwirtschaftskrise 1928–1930 (Berlin: Dokumenten-Verlag Dr. Herbert Wendler & Co., 1962), 377–79.

16. "Was blieb von der Hessenhetze?" *Angriff*, December 15, 1931.

17. Reg. Präs to IM, March 7, 1932, GStA Rep. 77/4043/311, Bl. 31.

18. Ulrich Herbert, *Best: Biographische Studien über Radikalismus, Weltanschauung und Vernunft, 1903–1989* (Bonn: Verlag J.H.W. Dietz Nachfolger, 1996), 113; TBJG Part I Vol. 2/II, 100; TBJG Part I Vol. 2/III, 119; Schuster, *SA*, 222–25; Fest, *Hitler*, 455.

19. Diels, *Lucifer*, 131.

20. Sommerfeldt, *Ich war dabei*, 15–18, 23, 34.

21. Ibid., 15.

22. Diels, *Lucifer*, 131, 133.

23. *DAZ*, February 15, 1933; "Polizei Erneut im Reichstag," *Volkswille*, February 16, 1933, TA; 22 VT 133–34; "Liebknecht Haus geschlossen," *Berliner Tageblatt*, February 25, 1933, morning.

24. Minuth, *Kabinett von Papen*, Band 2, 1009–12, 1013–22.

25. Minuth, *Regierung Hitler*, 9, 28–30, 83 and 83 note 49; RGBl 1933 I, 35–40.

26. "Gegen Wahlterror" and "Gleichheit vor dem Gesetz," *Berliner Tageblatt*, February 23, 1933, morning.

27. "Hilfspolizei," *Berliner Tageblatt*, February 25, 1933, morning; Thomas Friedrich, *Die Missbrauchte Hauptstadt: Hitler und Berlin* (Berlin: Propyläen Verlag, 2007), 431.

28. "Hilfspolizei," *Berliner Tageblatt*, February 25, 1933, evening.

29. "Der 5. März," *Berliner Tageblatt*, February 20, 1933, evening; "Goebbels über die Zukunft," *Berliner Tageblatt*, February 25, 1933, evening.

30. TBJG Part I Vol. 2/III, 120; "Frank II gegen Hugenberg," *Vorwärts*, February 3, 1933, BA-BL R. 8034 II 9030, Bl. 171; "Workers' Resistance to Nazi Regime," *Manchester Guardian*, February 24, 1933; Sackett to Secretary of State, February 13, 1933, *FRUS 1933* vol. 2, 188–90.

31. "Maulwurfskrieg!" *Vorwärts*, February 7, 1933, BA-BL R. 8034 II 9030, Bl. 171; "Quaatz über die Koalition mit Hitler," *Hamburger Abendblatt*, February 16, 1933, ibid., Bl. 173; "Abrechnung mit den Hugenzwergen," *Angriff*, September 20, 1932, ibid., Bl. 8.

32. Diels, *Lucifer*, 131.

33. Hans Mommsen, "Der Reichstagsbrand und seine politische Folgen," *VfZ* 12 (1964): 365.

34. Hermann Beck, *The Fateful Alliance: German Conservatives and Nazis in 1933. The Machtergreifung in a New Light* (New York and Oxford: Berghahn Books, 2008), 165; for the stereotyped phrases see documents in PA-AA R. 98417, *Reichstagsbrandstiftung*.

35. Guy Liddell, "The Liquidation of Communism, Left Wing Socialism and Pacifism in Germany," BNA KV 4/111.

36. TBJG Part I Vol. 2/III, 121–22, 125–26, 134; Reuth, *Goebbels*, 189–90 and 647 note 105.

37. Domarus, *Hitler*, 203–15.

38. Minuth, *Regierung Hitler*, 123–24.

39. Domarus, *Hitler*, 215–16; Clemens Vollnhals, ed., *Hitler: Reden, Schriften, Anordnungen. Februar 1925 bis Januar 1933*, Band I: *Die Widergründung der NSDAP Februar 1925–Juni 1926* (Munich: K.G. Saur, 1992), 14–28.

40. Erich Ebermayer, *Denn heute*, 17, 20.

41. *Preußischer Staatsrat*, 5. Sitzung am 23. Februar 1933, 71–72, 84, 89.

42. Ernst Torgler, "Der Reichstagsbrand und was nachher geschah," *Die Zeit*, October 21, 1948.

43. *Preußischer Staatsrat*, 5. Sitzung am 23. Februar 1933, 103–4; "Before the Reichstag Fire. Torgler's Warning to Prussian State Council," *Manchester Guardian*, August 28, 1933 (This translation is a modified version of the *Guardian*'s); Reinhold Heller, "Bericht," November 10, 1933, BA-BL R. 3003/191, Bl. 94.

44. Sackett to Secretary of State, February 16, 1933, *FRUS* 1933 vol. 2, 191; Consul General to Secretary of State, February 21, 1933, *FRUS* 1933 vol. 2, 193–98.

45. Abegg to Staatsanwalt Bielefeld, October 6, 1948, BA-Koblenz Z/42/IV/1960, 10–11; Harry Graf Kessler, *Tagebücher 1918 bis 1937*, ed. Wolfgang Pfeiffer-Belli (Frankfurt: Insel Verlag, 1996), 750–52.

46. "Workers' Resistance to Nazi Regime," *Manchester Guardian*, February 24, 1933; Reed, *Burning*, 295. Neither Reed nor the *Guardian* identified Stampfer as the "leading socialist" who spoke at the press conference, but the *New York Times* did: "Vorwaerts Defies Hitlerite Regime," *New York Times*, February 24, 1933.

47. Tobias, *Reichstagsbrand*, 257–58; Tobias, Interview with the Author, Hannover, July 20, 2008; Kempner, *Ankläger*, 110; Kurt R. Grossmann, *Ossietzky: Ein deutscher Patriot* (Munich: Kindler Verlag, 1963), 357, 153.

48. Quaatz, *Tagebuch*, 228, 236–37.

49. Hofer, *Reichstagsbrand*, 467; Vermerk, BA R. 3003/199, Bl. 44; "Denkschrift über die kommunistischen Umsturzbestrebungen in Deutschland," no date, PA des AA R. 98307.

50. Joseph Roth, "Rundgang um die Siegessäule," in *Joseph Roth in Berlin: Ein Lesebuch für Spaziergänger* (Cologne: Kiepenheuer & Witsch, 1999), 218 (Originally appeared in the *Neue Berliner Zeitung*, March 15, 1921); Werner T. Angress, *Stillborn Revolution: The Communist Bid for Power in Germany 1921–1923* (Princeton: Princeton University Press, 1963), 165–67; Reinhold Heller, "Bericht," November 10, 1933, BA-BL R. 3003/191, Bl. 93; Anonymous (Heinrich Schnitzler), "Der

Reichstagsbrand in anderer Sicht," *Neue Politik*, 2. Januar Heft 1949, IfZ ZS/A-7; Tobias, *Reichstagsbrand*, 111.

51. "Bombenanschlag auf das Reichstags-Gebäude," *Berliner Tageblatt*, September 2, 1929, evening.

52. "Hitler Attentäter unbehelligt," *Rote Fahne*, September 3, 1929.

53. "Ernst von Salomon erkannt," *Berliner Tageblatt*, September 27, 1929, evening.

54. "Der Consul verhöhnt Windisch," *Rote Fahne*, September 13, 1929; "Neue Spur in der Bombenaffäre," *Berliner Tageblatt*, September 27, 1929, evening; "Ernst von Salomon erkannt," *Berliner Tageblatt*, September 27, 1929, evening; Susanne Meinl and Dieter Krüger, "Friedrich Wilhelm Heinz: Vom Freikorpskämpfer zum Leiter des Nachrichtendienstes im Bundeskanzleramt," *VfZ* 24 (1994): 39–70, 44.

55. "Flugpost," *Angriff*, September 9, 1929; "Warum die Republik Bombenhetze betreibt," *Angriff*, September 16, 1929; Joseph Goebbels, "Politisches Tagebuch," *Angriff*, September 23, 1929; "IA will keine Bombenattentäter finden," *Rote Fahne*, September 3, 1929.

56. "Reichstagsattentat ein Lockspitzelmanöver der IA," *Rote Fahne*, October 25, 1933; "Zörgiebel der Mitwisserschaft überführt," *Rote Fahne*, October 27, 1933; "Zörgiebel verklagt die 'Rote Fahne,'" *Rote Fahne*, October 29, 1929; "Zörgiebel Meineidig?" *Rote Fahne*, October 31, 1929.

57. "Reichstagsattentat ein Lockspitzelmanöver der IA," *Rote Fahne*, October 25, 1933; "Die Vernehmungen," *Berliner Tageblatt*, September 12, 1929, evening; "Die Berliner Vernehmungen," *Berliner Tageblatt*, September 13, 1929, evening; "Deutschnationale Scheiben zerkrachen," *Vorwärts*, September 20, 1932, and "Krawalle in einer DNVP-Versammlung," *Berliner Volks-Zeitung*, September 28, 1932, in BA R. 8034 II 9030, *Reichslandbund Pressearchiv, Nationalsozialisten u. Deutschnationale Volkspartei*, Bl. 9, 17; "Tränengas im Theater," *Welt am Abend*, October 22, 1932; Reg. Präs. to IM, March 7, 1932, in GStA Rep. 77/4043/311, Bl. 31.

58. Longerich, *Geschichte der SA*, 157–59, 165; Fritz Stelzner, *Schicksal SA* (Munich: F. Eher Nachf., 1936), 157.

59. "Planmäßiger Mord in Königsberg," "Erklärung der Gauleitung der NSDAP," *Königsberger Hartungsche Zeitung*, August 1, 1932, morning; "Mordterror Auch in Marienburg," *Königsberger Hartungsche Zeitung*, August 2, 1932, evening; "Die Brandstifter SA Leute," *Königsberger Hartungsche Zeitung*, August 5, 1932, evening; "Um 6 Uhr muß es brennen," *Welt am Abend*, November 1, 1932.

60. "Angst vor der Aufklärung," *Vossische Zeitung*, November 1, 1932; OSTA LG to GSTA OLG, November 2, 1932, JM to GStA, November 8, 1932, GStA 84a/53565.

61. Schulze-Wilde to Amtsgericht München, July 28, 1961, TA; Friedrich Strindberg, Statement, November 15, 1960, LNRW-D Rep. 372/990, Bl. 111.

62. Gewehr to Zacharias, March 27, 1960, IfZ ID 103–60; Gewehr Testimony, June 7, 1963, ETH NL Gisevius 17.1.

4: "IMPOSSIBLE THINGS"

1. Sommerfeldt, *Ich war dabei*, 25–26. Sommerfeldt's account of a calm Göring at the Reichstag obviously conflicts with Diels's. Fallible memory may be at issue (Diels for instance recorded that Helldorff was at the Reichstag, which was incorrect). Or possibly Sommerfeldt presented his old boss in a somewhat more sympathetic light, either out of residual loyalty, or as indirect self-protection.
2. Ibid., 26–27.
3. Ibid.
4. Ibid., 27–28; Diels, *Lucifer*, 88.
5. Sommerfeldt, *Ich war dabei*, 28.
6. Ibid., 29.
7. Helmut Heisig, Interrogation, August 17, 1948, BSM, Spruchkammer Akten Karton 666, Bl. 43; Heisig, c.v., BA-BL BDC RS Film C 198 Heisig; Heisig, Reference for Schnitzler, October 26, 1933, BA-BL ZA VI/372 Akte 7.
8. Heisig, Denazification Hearing Protocol, February 7, 1950, BSM, Spruchkammer Akten Karton 666, Bl. 75, 75a; Zirpins Examination, July 6, 1961, in LNRW-D Rep. 372/992, Bl. 35; Zirpins, "Befragungsprotokoll zum Reichstagsbrand," December 26, 1951, IfZ ZS 199 1; Heisig testimony, 6 VT 31.
9. Sommerfeldt, *Ich war dabei*, 28–29.
10. "Gespräch" BA-BL R. 3003/5, Bl. 46 ff, Bl. 47. For their most recent book, Alexander Bahar and Wilfried Kugel had a transcription prepared of the stenogram underlying this document, and found several corruptions in the typed version of the text. Perhaps the most significant is that in the stenogram van der Lubbe refers to walking through the district of Wedding on February 20; this reference is missing completely from the typed text. SA Storm 17, which several contemporary sources connected to the fire, was based in Wedding. Bahar and Kugel, *Der Reichstagsbrand: Geschichte einer Provokation* (Cologne: Papyrossa Verlag, 2013), 107–8.
11. "Gespräch" BA-BL R. 3003/5, Bl. 46 ff, Bl. 46 ff, Bl. 47; van der Lubbe Statement, March 2, 1933, BA-BL R. 3003/1, Bl. 65; Leyden Police Report, March 2, 1933, BA-BL R. 3003/2 Bl. 125–26; van der Lubbe Statement, February 28, 1933, in BA-BL R. 3003/1, Bl. 58; Martin Schouten, *Marinus van der Lubbe. Eine Biographie* (Frankfurt: Verlag Neue Kritik, 1999), 15–21, 52; currency conversion Internationaal Instituut voor Sociale Geschiedenis calculator, http://www.iisg.nl/hpw/calculate-nl.php, visited November 6, 2012.

12. Schouten, *van der Lubbe*, 41, 48; *Das Rotbuch: Marinus van der Lubbe und der Reichstagsbrand* (Hamburg: Edition Nautilus, 2013), 124.

13. *Rotbuch*, 121.

14. Schouten, *van der Lubbe*, 37–49; van der Lubbe Statement, February 28, 1933, BA-BL R. 3003/1, Bl. 58.

15. Van der Lubbe Statement, February 28, 1933, BA-BL R. 3003/1, Bl. 58.

16. Panknin Statement, March 29, 1933, BA-BL R. 3003/5, Bl. 61–62; 6 VT 64.

17. 4 VT.

18. Tarkowski Statements, February 19 and March 11, 1953, BStU MfS Ast Ic 41/53, Bl. 7, Bl. 42; Böhr Statement, March 12, 1953, ibid., Bl. 44–45; Jahnecke Statements, March 12, 1953, and July 30, 1953, ibid., Bl. 46–47, 86–88, 91; Schlussbericht, September 11, 1953, ibid., Bl. 135.

19. Margarete Starker, Statement, September 9, 1953, ibid., Bl. 129–32.

20. Bericht, March 30, 1933, 211; Revier Neukölln to Untersuchungsrichter beim Reichsgericht, April 1, 1933; Hintze Statement, April 3, 1933; Starker Statement, April 11, 1933, BA-BL R. 3003/152, Bl. 75, Bl. 76, Bl. 78–80, Bl. 110–13.

21. Judgment December 23, 1933, in Dieter Deiseroth, ed., *Der Reichstagsbrand und der Prozess vor dem Reichsgericht* (Berlin: Verlagsgesellschaft Tischler, 2006), 225ff, 238; 6 VT 143.

22. Van der Lubbe Statement, February 28, 1933, BA-BL R. 3003/1, Bl. 59–60.

23. Ibid., Bl. 59.

24. "Brandstiftung im Berliner Schloß?" *DAZ*, February 28, 1933; Walter Zirpins, *Schlußbericht*, March 3, 1933, BA R. 3003/1, Bl. 67–78.

25. Van der Lubbe Statement, February 28, 1933, BA-BL R. 3003/1, Bl. 59; Report, November 3, 1933, BA-BL R. 3003/112, Bl. 175–76; Tobias, *Reichstagsbrand*, 552–68; Bahar and Kugel, *Reichstagsbrand: Provocation*, 228.

26. Judgment in Deiseroth, *Reichstagsbrand*, 242; van der Lubbe Statement, February 28, 1933, BA-BL R. 3003/1, Bl. 59.

27. Hans Bernd Gisevius, "Reichstagsbrand im Zerrspiegel," *Die Zeit*, March 11, 1960.

28. Van der Lubbe Statement, March 1, 1933, BA-BL R. 3003/1, Bl. 61.

29. Ibid., Bl. 61–62.

30. Van der Lubbe Statement, February 28, 1933, BA-BL R. 3003/1, Bl. 60. In his statement on March 1 he corrected the order of steps in the restaurant but not in a way that seems to make any difference: van der Lubbe Statement, March 1, 1933, BA-BL R. 3003/1, Bl. 61.

31. Van der Lubbe Statement, March 1, 1933, BA-BL R. 3003/1, Bl. 61–62.

32. Ibid., Bl. 62.

33. Van der Lubbe Statement, March 2, 1933, BA-BL R. 3003/1, Bl. 63–64.

34. Van der Lubbe Statement, April 8, 1933, BA-BL R. 3003/6, Bl. 74; van der Lubbe Statement, May 10, 1933, ibid., Bl. 166, 169.

35. Van der Lubbe Statement, March 4, 1933, BA-BL R. 3003/1, Bl. 84.

36. Minuth, *Regierung Hitler*, 128–29.

37. In Minuth, *Regierung Hitler*, 130; Cabinet Meeting, 4:15 p.m., February 28, 1933, in ibid., 132–33. Text of the Decree in Ernst Rudolf Huber, ed., *Dokumente zur deutschen Verfassungsgeschichte*, 3rd ed., Bd. 4 (Stuttgart: Verlag W. Kohlhammer GmbH, 1991), 663–64; translation of the Decree from Noakes and Pridham, *Nazism*, 142.

38. Mommsen, "Reichstagsbrand," 398–99; Thomas Raithel and Irene Strenge, "Die Reichstagsbrandverordnung. Grundlegung der Diktatur mit den Instrumenten des Weimarer Ausnahmezustands," *VfZ* vol. 48 (2000): 422–23, 434–35, 438, 440, 444; Kempner, *Kreuzverhör*, 47; Dr. Alois Eugen Becker Statement, December 5, 1956, LAB B Rep 058/1293, Bl. 69–70.

39. Mommsen, "Reichstagsbrand," 398–99; Raithel and Strenge, "Die Reichstagsbrandverordnung," 422–23, 434–35, 438, 440, 444.

40. Luise Solmitz in Werner Jochmann, *Nationalsozialismus und Revolution. Ursprung und Geschichte der NSDAP in Hamburg 1922–1933. Dokumente* (Frankfurt: Europäische Verlagsanstalt, 1963), 426–27; Haffner, *Defying Hitler*, 120; Beck, *Fateful Alliance*, 119.

41. "Riesenbrand im Reichstag," *Vorwärts*, February 28, 1933, morning.

42. Ebermayer, *Denn heute*, 32.

43. Annelise Thimme, "Geprägt von der Geschichte. Eine Aussenseiterin," in Hartmut Lehmann and Otto Gerhard Oexle, eds., *Erinnerungsstücke: Wege in die Vergangenheit* (Vienna: Böhlau Verlag, 1997), 163–64.

44. Alfred Döblin, *Abschied und Wiederkehr*, in *Zwei Seelen in einer Brust* (Munich: DTV, 1993), 265 ff.

45. Wildt, *Generation der Unbedingten*, 153; Kurt G.W. Ludecke, *I Knew Hitler: The Story of a Nazi who Escaped the Blood Purge* (New York: Charles Scribner's Sons, 1937), 569, 580.

46. "Die politische Folgen," *DAZ*, March 1, 1933; "Unsere Meinung," *DAZ*, March 2, 1933.

47. "Lügen über den Reichstagsbrand," *DAZ*, March 2, 1933, PA des AA R. 98417; "Unsere Meinung," *DAZ*, March 12, 1933.

48. Daluege to Diels, March 13, 1933, BDC PK Akten Diels, film 301, frame 1330; Beck, *Fateful Alliance*, 123–24.

49. Tobias, *Reichstagsbrand*, 76, 82–83.

50. Zirpins, Abschlußbericht, March 3, 1933, BA-BL R. 3003/1, Bl. 67 ff, Bl. 73.

51. Ibid.

52. Ibid., Bl. 74–77.

53. Ibid., Bl. 72–75.

54. 6 VT 62.

55. Aktenvermerk, LNRW-D Rep. 372/990, Bl. 85–86; Tobias, "Anmerkungen zum Hefter 11," SpA Tobias Papers, Bd. 8 "Zacharias."

56. Fritz Tobias, "Stehen Sie auf, van der Lubbe!" *Der Spiegel*, October 21, 1959; Tobias, *Reichstagsbrand*, 10–11, 87–89.

57. "Brandstichting in Het Rijksdaggebouw," *Algemeen Handelsblad*, March 11, 1933, evening.

58. "Die Untersuchung gegen Lubbe," *DAZ*, March 15, 1933.

59. "Van der Lubbe hat das Feuer im Reichstag allein angezündet. Die Vorbereitungen von Helfershelfern getroffen," *DAZ*, March 14, 1933; "van der Lubbe had geen Medebrandstichters," *Het Vaderland*, March 11, 1933; Justizpressestelle to RGR Vogt, March 15, 1933, BA-BL R. 3003/2, Bl. 88; "Brandstichting in Het Rijksdaggebouw," *Algemeen Handelsblad*, March 11, 1933, evening.

60. Douglas Reed, *The Burning of the Reichstag* (London: Victor Gollancz Ltd, 1934), 299.

61. Joseph Goebbels, "Das Fanal!" *Völkischer Beobachter*, March 1, 1933; "20 000 Mark Belohnung für die Aufklärung des Reichstagsbrandes," *DAZ*, March 5, 1933; Gestapo summary of evidence from "Philipsborn," September 16, 1933, BA-BL R. 3003/201, Bl. 172.

62. Sack, *Reichstagsbrand*, 108.

63. Sommerfeldt Memo, October 6 1933, BA-BL R. 3003/199, Bl 70–71.

64. Zirpins Testimony July 6, 1961, LNRW-D Rep. 372/992, Bl. 34, 37; Zirpins Examination, January 4, 1960, LNRW-D Rep. 372/990, Bl. 81; 2 VT, 72; Zirpins to Tobias, IfZ ZS A7/7.

65. Heisig, Denazification Hearing Protocol, February 7, 1950, BSM, Spruchkammer Akten Karton 666, Bl. 75a.

66. Diels to Göring, August 11, 1933, BA-BL R. 3003/199, Bl. 127; Braschwitz to all Landeskriminalpolizeistellen, March 27, 1933, BA-BL R. 3003/3, Bl. 212; Memo, September 25, 1933, BA-BL R. 3003/156, Bl. 13; Becker Statement, December 5, 1956, JA; Abschrift, November 27, 1948, BStU MfS ASt 35 Js 164/48 GA, Bd. 1, Bl. 24–25. As evidence from an East German investigation, this information must be treated with skepticism.

67. "Übernahme des Karl-Liebknecht-Hauses durch den Staat," [name of paper illegible], March 9, 1933, BA R. 8034 III 187.

68. Tobias, *Reichstagsbrand*, 10; Sven Felix Kellerhoff, "Der Mann, der den Reichstagsbrand aufklärte," *Welt Online*, January 5, 2011.

69. 27 VT 82-83; Braschwitz to Untersuchungsrichter, March 11, 1933, BA-BL R. 3003/109, Bl. 107; Verfügung, August 18, 1933, BA-BL R. 3003/156, Bl. 11.

70. Diels, *Lucifer*, 149; Tobias, *Reichstagsbrand*, 307–8.

71. Vermerk, March 3, 1933, Vermerk, March 4, 1933, BA-BL R. 3003/109, Bl. 259, Bl. 260; Sommerfeldt Report, October 6, 1933, BA-BL R. 3003/199, Bl.

73; Heisig to Diels, October 12, 1948, TA; Braschwitz Stellungnahme, January 13, 1959, in LNRW-W, Personalakten Nr. 2688, Bd. 1, Bl. 13.

72. Guy Liddell, "The Liquidation of Communism, Left Wing Socialism and Pacifism in Germany," BNA KV 4/111.

73. Diels to ORA July 14, 1933, BA-BL R. 3003/9, Bl. 376–77; Diels to Göring, August 11, 1933, BA-BL R. 3003/199, Bl. 124; Werner to Diels, July 20, 1933, BA-BL R. 3003/9, Bl. 379.

74. Vogt to Diels, August 15, 1933, BA-BL R. 3003/139, Bl. 129.

75. Ernst Torgler, "Der Reichstagsbrand und was nachher geschah," *Die Zeit*, October 21, 1948.

76. Helmer Statement, March 7, 1933, Statement, March 9, 1933, BA-BL R. 3003/35, Bl. 1, Bl. 7–9.

77. Reed, *Burning*, 51–52, 70; Judgment, December 23, 1933, in Deiseroth, *Reichstagsbrand*, 232–33.

78. Kynast Report, March 16, 1933, BA-BL R. 3003/35, Bl. 41–43; Dimitrov Statement, March 17, 1933, Statement, March 18, 1933, BA-BL R. 3003/35, Bl. 49, Bl. 50.

79. Reed, *Burning*, 260–61; Judgment, December 23, 1933, in Deiseroth, *Reichstagsbrand*, 280; Grothe Statement, July 22, 1933, BA-BL R. 3003/139, Bl. 132 ff.

80. Vogt to Reichstagsbrandkommission, August 15, 1933, BA-BL R. 3003/139, Bl. 130; Heisig to Raben, August 15 1933, BA-BL R.3003/139, Bl. 134; Abschrift, April 10, 1933, BA-BL R. 3003/139, Bl. 125.

81. Heisig Report, March 9, 1933, BA-BL R. 3003/2, Bl. 142; 2 VT 40–41; Vink Statement, March 10, 1933, BA-BL R. 3003/2, Bl. 145; Reed, *Burning*, 178–79.

82. Meusser Statement, March 18, 1933, BA-BL R. 3003/2, Bl. 62; Wendt Statement, March 20, 1933, BA-BL R. 3003/3, Bl. 74–75.

83. Reichstagshandbuch 1933, 87 (http://daten.digitale-sammlungen.de/~db/ bsb00000008/images/index.html?id=00000008&fip=xseayaeayaqrsewqea yaewqfsdreayaxdsydeaya&no=&seite=88); Reed, *Burning*, 253–54; Tobias, *Reichstagsbrand*, 294.

84. Albrecht Statement, March 24, 1933, BA-BL R. 3003/2, Bl. 150–51; Elisabeth Berkemeyer Statement, February 27, 1933, Maria Hessler Statement, October 26, 1933, BA-BL R. 3003/110, Bl. 7–9.

85. Tobias, *Reichstagsbrand*, 295.

86. Ferdinand Kugler, *Das Geheimnis des Reichstagsbrandes* (Amsterdam: Van Munster's Verlag, 1936), 111.

87. Protocoll April 25, BA-BL R. 3003/5, Bl. 162–63; Protocoll April 27, 1933, in BA-BL R. 3003/55, Bl. 162–70.

88. Professor Karl Stephan, e-mail to the Author, April 15, 2011.

89. 22 VT 31 ff.

90. 22 VT 175.

91. Wagner Gutachten, May 22, 1933, in BA-BL R. 43 II/294, Bl. 139; 22 VT 181; Schatz Gutachten, June 26, 1933, BA-BL R. 3003/56, Bl. 27 ff, Bl. 33.

92. 22 VT; Schatz Gutachten, Bl. 32–33.

93. Wagner Gutachten, Bl. 131, 135; Schatz Gutachten, Bl. 36; Josse Gutachten, May 15, 1933, BA-BL R 43 II/294, Bl. 243; 22 VT 181–82.

94. Franz Ritter, "Über den Brand im Reichstag," June 9, 1933, BA-BL R. 3003/56, Bl. 21–23; Schatz Gutachten, Bl. 34–35; Josse Gutachten, Bl. 269; Wagner Gutachten, Bl. 155–57.

95. Reed, *Burning*, 186; "Van der Lubbe Not Alone," *Manchester Guardian*, October 24, 1933; 22 VT 218–20, 252; Schatz Gutachten, Bl. 41.

96. Reed, *Burning*, 187, 215.

97. 22 VT 184.

98. Vogt Vermerk, April 26, 1933, BA-BL R. 3003/5, Bl. 154.

99. 16 VT 151, 161.

100. Report, May 17, 1933, BA-BL R. 3003/56, Bl. 9.

101. Schnitzler, "Reichstagsbrand"; Zirpins Testimony, July 6, 1961, LNRW-D Rep. 372/992, Bl. 36, 39–40.

102. Allianz Zentrum für Technik Press Release, February 25, 2005, at http://www.allianz.com/de/presse/news/unternehmensnews/geschichte/news11.html, accessed June 28, 2009; Dr. Peter Schildhauer, e-mail to the Author, September 4, 2012.

103. "Expertise des Instituts für Thermodynamik der Technischen Universität Berlin vom 17. February 1970," in Hofer, *Reichstagsbrand*, 97–115, 100–109, 112; Professor Karl Stephan, e-mail to the Author, April 15, 2011.

104. "Stehen Sie auf, van der Lubbe!" *Der Spiegel*, December 2, 1959; Tobias, *Reichstagsbrand*, 450, 452.

105. "Stehen Sie auf, van der Lubbe!" *Der Spiegel*, December 2, 1959.

106. Ibid.

107. Mommsen, "Reichstagsbrand," 372–82.

108. Ibid., 373–74.

109. Professor Karl Stephan, e-mail to the Author, April 15, 2011.

110. See Alfred Berndt, "Zur Entstehung des Reichstagsbrands. Eine Untersuchung über den Zeitablauf," *VfZ* 23 (1975): 77–90. Berndt tried to suggest that van der Lubbe had in fact had more time, beginning with breaking into the Reichstag at 8:59 rather than 9:05 to 9:10. As Karl Stephan pointed out in a devastating rebuttal (Karl Stephan, "Brandentstehung und Brandablauf," in Hofer, *Reichstagsbrand*, 130–40, originally 1978), Berndt's argument rested not only on attributing incredible "slow-wittedness, indecision and torpor" to all

the relevant witnesses, police and firefighters, and virtual "genius" to van der Lubbe, he assumed that all the witnesses who gave time estimates of what they saw or heard were substantially wrong in the same direction, a kind of collective hysteria. Among many other problems, Berndt's effort to find enough time for van der Lubbe in the plenary chamber raises the question of who set all the other fires, or who or what Buwert fired at seven and a half to eight minutes after van der Lubbe broke into the Reichstag. Tellingly, single-culprit advocates have quietly let Berndt's argument lie. Sven Kellerhoff's recent argument that the phenomenon of "backdraft" explains "all known details" of the fire is even less persuasive. "Backdraft" occurs in cases of fires in closed rooms; when the oxygen is consumed the raised temperatures cause pyrolysis, the decomposition of compounds through heat. Unoxidized and thus combustible gases rise and collect under the ceiling. The pressure in the room drops. If oxygen then enters the room, it can mix with the gases within seconds and lead to a disastrous explosion. The theory here is that it was Klotz who brought backdraft disaster to the plenary chamber by opening the door to bring in a hose. But as Peter Schildhauer explained, backdraft "presupposes a fire that has already become very large, which first of all can generate such great heat that correspondingly great quantities of pyrolysis gases arise, and secondly consumes the available oxygen so rapidly, that the flames are extinguished again. . . . A backdraft occurs therefore only in a later phase of a fire and not already at the ignition. Therefore the appearance of a backdraft only says something about the size of the fire and the ventilation situation, but not anything about the source of ignition and the initial fire." In the case of the Reichstag, the burning of the curtains, which was all that van der Lubbe claimed to have set on fire, "would not suffice for this." (Schildhauer, Comment on Kellerhoff, February 12, 2008, on file with the Author). According to Karl Stephan, Kellerhoff's argument "proves the opposite" of what he wants to prove, because a backdraft would be most likely with the use of kerosene. Otherwise the wood would form pyrolysis gases too slowly. (Stephan, Comment on Kellerhoff, February 8, 2008, on file with the Author). Kellerhoff claimed that "backdraft" had "not yet been researched" in 1933, and thus his explanation was a breakthrough unavailable then, but he is wrong about this as well. Stephan says that the phenomenon of "backdraft" was "certainly known to the experts in 1933," it was just that, the use of English being less common then, it was known as *Rauchgasexplosion* (Karl Stephan, e-mail to the Author, April 15, 2011). Indeed, anyone who takes the trouble to read the trial transcript, which presumably Kellerhoff did not, will find that in fact Wagner discussed the possibility of a *Rauchgasexplosion* and rejected its application to the Reichstag fire for exactly the same reason as did Schildhauer (VT 22 176). In 2002 Kellerhoff had apparently been certain that another phenomenon, "flashover," explained the fire; he seems to have quietly dropped that one, and advisedly so, as experts like Stephan found flashover no more compelling an explanation than backdraft. See Bahar and Kugel, *Reichstagsbrand: Provokation*, 291–94.

111. Albrecht Brömme to Klaus Wiegrefe, March 26, 2001, BFA; Interview in Tina Mendelssohn and Gerhard Brack, *Neues vom Reichstagsbrand*, documentary film, 2003, YouTube, accessed April 13, 2011.

112. "Reichstagsbrand mit Kohlenanzünder?" http://abenteuerwissen.zdf.de/ZDFde/ inhalt/26/0,1872,5565338,00.html, accessed February 10, 2012; Professor Lothar Weber, e-mail to the Author, February 7, 2012.

113. Dr. Jürgen Lieske, Allianz Global Corporate & Specialty AG, e-mail to Dr. Alexander Bahar, February 14, 2008, copy on file with the Author.

5: BROWN AND OTHER BOOKS

1. Göring, Speech of March 1st, PA des AA R. 98307.

2. Willi Frischauer, *The Rise and Fall of Hermann Goering* (Boston: Houghton Mifflin Company, 1951), 4; "Telegram to European Missions," February 28, 1933, PA des AA R. 98417.

3. Paris Embassy to AA, March 4, 1933, PA des AA R. 98417; Neurath to all Missions, March 6, 1933, PA des AA R 98304; Memo, no date, PA des AA R. 98417.

4. Guy Liddell, "The Liquidation of Communism, Left Wing Socialism and Pacifism in Germany," BNA KV 4/111; *Philadelphia Public Ledger* to Knickerbocker, May 8, 1933, Morrison to Knickerbocker, June 1, 1933, Huburtus Renfro Knickerbocker Papers, Columbia University; Philip Metcalfe, *1933* (Sag Harbor, N.Y.: The Permanent Press, 1988), 127.

5. Knickerbocker to Messersmith, August 7, 1933, Messersmith to Knicker-bocker, August 11, 1933, Diels to Knickerbocker, October 31, 1933, Knicker-bocker to Morrison, May 15, 1933, Huburtus Renfro Knickerbocker Papers, Columbia University.

6. "Arrested Reds Unhurt in German Cells," *Chicago Daily Tribune*, March 26, 1933.

7. David Ayerst, *Guardian: Biography of a Newspaper* (London: Collins, 1971), 507; George Orwell, *Homage to Catalonia* (San Diego: Harcourt Brace, 1980), 65; Elizabeth Wiskemann, *The Europe I Saw* (New York: St. Martin's Press, 1968), 19–20; Metcalfe, *1933*, 115.

8. Diels to Goebbels, July 11, 1933, BA-BL R. 3003/201, Bl. 214; Diels to Göring, August 30, 1933, GStA Rep. 90 P/68/3, 150–52.

9. Diels to Goebbels, July 11, 1933, BA-BL R. 3003/201, Bl. 214.

10. Diels to Göring, September 22, 1933, BA-BL R. 3003/199, Bl. 65; Diels to Gestapa Saxony, September ibid., Bl. 77; intercepted letters BA-BL R. 3003/195; Diels to Vice Consul Renet, July 13, 1933, BStU MfS HA IX/11 ZR 881 A6, Bl. 45; Arthur Garfield Hays, *City Lawyer: The Autobiography of a Law Practice* (New York: Simon and Schuster, 1942), 364.

11. Arthur Koestler, *The Invisible Writing: Being the Second Volume of Arrow in the Blue: An Autobiography* (New York: Macmillan, 1954), 199; Anson Rabinbach, "Staging Antifascism: The Brown Book of the Reichstag Fire and Hitler Terror," *New German Critique* 103 vol. 35 No. 1: Spring 2008, 99.

12. Rabinbach, "Staging," 100; Babette Gross, *Willi Münzenberg: A Political Biography* (East Lansing: Michigan State University Press, 1974), 211–12.

13. Koestler, *Invisible*, 205–6.

14. Gross, *Münzenberg*, 216, 242–43.

15. *Braunbuch über Reichstagsbrand und Hitlerterror*, facsimile of the original 1933 edition (Frankfurt/Main: Röderberg Verlag GmbH, 1978).

16. McMeekin, *Red Millionare*, 265; Else Steinfurth Statements, January 15–16, 1934, BA-BL NJ 14220 Bd. 1, Bl. 4–8; Rudolf Schwarz Statement, January 9, 1934, ibid., Bl. 21–22.

17. STA LG München II to the GSTA, June 1 1933, in NARA RG 238, Prosecution Exhibits, T 988 Roll 17, frames 091930, 091954–55; Goeschel and Wachsmann, *Nazi Concentration Camps*, 5–6.

18. Grauert to AA, May 19, 1933, PA des AA R. 98424.

19. Notes, November 6, 1933, BA-BL R. 3003/201, Bl. 24; *Braunbuch II*, 67, 69; Roths's handwritten notes, 1936, BStU MfS HA IX/11 SV 1/81 Bd. 35, Bl. 2–3.

20. Gross, *Münzenberg*, 247–48; Koestler, *Invisible*, 199; McMeekin, *Red Millionaire*, 266.

21. *Braunbuch*, 106–29.

22. *Weissbuch über die Erschiessungen des 30. Juni* (Paris: Editions du Carrefour, 1935), 107.

23. *Hanussen Zeitung*, March 8, 1933, cited in Tobias to Water Görlitz, April 17, 1972, TA; *Munich Abendzeitung* October 5/6 1955 quoted in Alexander Bahar and Wilfried Kugel, *Der Reichstagsbrand: Wie Geschichte gemacht wird* (Berlin: Quintessenz Verlag, 2001), 646–47; Riess to GSTA Berlin, January 15, 1967, LAB B Rep. 058/6398, Bl. 53; Steinle to Gestapa, July 25, 1934, NARA RG 242 BDC Microfilm SA Collections P-Akten Rudolf Steinle; Steinle Statement, September 18, 1934, NARA BDC P-Akten Wilhelm Ohst.

24. "Wieder eine Auslandshetze entlarvt!," *Völkischer Beobachter*, June 11/12, 1933; Wolfgang Wippermann, "Oberbranddirektor Walter Gempp: Widerstandskämpfer oder Krimineller? Kein Beitrag zur Reichstagsbrandkontroverse," in Wolfgang Ribbe (ed.) *Berlin Forschungen III* (Berlin: Colloquium Verlag, 1988), 214,

220–23, 228; GSTA LG Berlin to Geheimes Staatspolizeiamt, September 14, 1933, BA-BL R. 3003/132, Bl. 165–66.

25. Wippermann, "Gempp," 207–9.

26. Wippermann, "Gempp," 228; Beck, *Fateful Alliance*, 127–28, 277.

27. "Hörbericht aus dem verwüsteten Plenarsaal," *Völkischer Beobachter*, March 1, 1933; "Reichstag 15. Alarm!" *8 Uhr-Abendblatt*, February 28, 1933.

28. "Reichstagsgebäude in Flammen—Alarmstufe 15," *Sächsische Feuerwehrzeitung*, February 28, 1933, Oberbaurat Foth, "Feuer im Reichstag," *Preussische Feuerwehr Zeitung*, March 1933, BFA.

29. Göring to Oberbürgermeister, February 28, 1933, Gempp's handwritten notes March 5, 1933, printed text March 9, 1933, BFA.

30. Milly Gempp to the *Der Spiegel*, December 26, 1959, BFA; Sommerfeldt to Grauert, June 12, 1933, BA-BL R. 3003/214, Bl. 6–7.

31. *Braunbuch*, 77–80, 88; Tobias, *Reichstagsbrand*, 644–56, 171–204.

32. Margarete Fritsch to Diels, March 30, 1933, BA-K N 1211/76, NL-Schmidt; Fritsch to Oberfohren, April 5, 1933, LSH Abt. 309 Nr. 22766, 167; 31 VT.

33. "Herr Oberfohren und seine Sekretärin," *Kieler Volkskampf*, April 7, 1933, BA-K N 1211/76, NL Schmidt; typed letter copies ibid.; Wulf, "Ernst Oberfohren," 184.

34. "US Protests Nazi Charge of 'Lie Factory,'" *Chicago Tribune*, April 5, 1933.

35. Sonderabteilung Daluege to the Police President, May 13 1933, Sonderabteilung Daluege, Notiz, May 15, 1933, BA-BL Film 14719. I am grateful to Dr. Alexander Bahar for a copy of this document.

36. "The Reichstag Fire," *Manchester Guardian*, April 26, 1933.

37. "The Reichstag Fire," *Manchester Guardian*, August 15, 1933; "The Reichstag Fire," *Manchester Guardian*, August 2, 1933.

38. Sack, *Reichstagsbrand*, 117.

39. Voigt to Crozier, August 24, 1936, quoted in Ayerst, *Guardian*, 518; "Hugenberg muss aussagen!" *Neuer Vorwärts*, October 29, 1933.

40. Reese to Oberfohren, March 15, 1933, LSH Abt. 309 Nr. 22766, Bl. 159.

41. "Hugenberg muss aussagen!" *Neuer Vorwärts*, October 29, 1933.

42. Diels to Werner, September 20, 1933, BA-BL R. 3003/132, Bl. 161; Schmidt-Hannover to Wolff, October 4, 1955, IfZ ZS/A 7 Bd. 2; Otto Schmidt-Hannover, *Umdenken oder Anarchie. Männer—Schicksale—Lehren* (Göttingen: Göttinger Verlagsanhalt, 1959), 349–50.

43. Sprenger Report, May 7, 1933, Theile Statement, May 8, 1933, LSH Abt. 309 Nr. 22766, Bl. 150–51, Bl. 148; Ida Oberfohren to Dr. A. Ritthaler, June 1, 1955, IfZ ZS/A 7 Bd. 1; Diels, *Lucifer*, 221; "Hugenberg muss aussagen!" *Neuer Vorwärts*, October 29, 1933.

44. Ida Oberfohren to Dr. A. Ritthaler, June 1, 1955, IfZ ZS/A 7 Bd. 1; Beck, *Fateful Alliance*, 168–69, 228.

45. Diels to Göring, August 30, 1933, GStA Rep. 90 P/68/3, 150–52.

46. "Bericht Reise 16.-19.9.33" BA-BL R. 3003/201, Bl. 31–34; Ayerst, *Guardian*, 510, 513, 514; Voigt to Crozier, December 18, 1933, quoted in Ayerst, *Guardian*, 515.

47. See for instance Diels to Goebbels, July 11, 1933, BA-BL R. 3003/201, Bl. 214; Bülow-Schwante, Memo, August 18, 1933, Diels to AA, August 22, 1933, Bülow-Schwante to Diels, August 28, 1933, Bülow-Schwante to Propaganda Ministry, August 31, 1933, Bülow-Schwante to Gürtner, September 6, 1933, PA des AA R. 98417.

6: "STAND UP, VAN DER LUBBE!"

1. *Neue Zürcher Zeitung*, September 21, 1933, evening; Reed, *Burning*, 38, 40–42; Hays, *City Lawyer*, 352.

2. On German legal procedure see Hett, *Death in the Tiergarten*, 18–31; on the lawyers Arthur Garfield Hays, *City Lawyer: The Autobiography of a Law Practice* (New York: Simon and Schuster, 1942), 339–88.

3. "First Day of the Reichstag Fire Trial," *Manchester Guardian*, September 22, 1933; "The Reichstag Fire Trial," *Manchester Guardian*, September 23, 1933; Kugler, *Geheimnis*, 26; Dodd, *Embassy Eyes*, 58; Fraenkel to Tobias, August 14, 1971, BA-K N 1274/65a NL Fraenkel; Reed, *Burning*, 43.

4. 6 VT 12; Georgi Dimitrov, *Reichstagsbrandprozess* (Berlin: Dietz Verlag, 1953), 214.

5. *Neue Zürcher Zeitung*, September 24, 1933, 2nd Sunday Edition; Tobias, *Reichstagsbrand*, 359.

6. Dimitrov Statement, March 20, 1933, BA-BL R. 3003/35, Bl. 129–30; Reed, *Burning*, 51, 53, 98; "Der Prozess in Leipzig," *Neue Zürcher Zeitung*, October 6, 1933, evening; "Dimitroff Forcibly Removed From Court," *Manchester Guardian*, October 7, 1933.

7. Heisig to Schneppel, September 18, 1933, BA-BL R. 3003/109, Bl. 24; Torgler statement April 15–17 1945, TA; Schnitzler to Diels, undated notes, NL Schnitzler II; Tobias to Roesen, August 23, 1961, TA.

8. *Neue Zürcher Zeitung*, October 18, morning; Hays, *City Lawyer*, 377–78; J.K. von Engelbrechten, *Eine Braune Armee entsteht: Die Geschichte der Berlin-Brandenburg SA* (Munich-Berlin: Verlag Franz Eher Nachf., 1937), 267.

9. Note, December 18, 1933, PA des AA R. 98417; Fabian von Schlabrendorff, *Offiziere Gegen Hitler* (Frankfurt/Main: Fischer Bücherei, 1960), 25; Doris Bünger to Calic, September 12, 1966, in Uwe Backes et al., eds., *Reichstagsbrand: Aufklärung einer historischen Legende* (Munich: R. Piper, 1986), 293–94. Although Calic probably forged many documents, including part of this letter, his strongest opponents present this passage in their own book as authentic.

10. 2 VT 61–75; 6 VT 32–33; 21 VT 232–35, 238; Reed, *Burning*, 179.

11. 1 VT 76, 261–70, 71.

12. Heisig's words: "Bei dieser Frage gab er keine genügenden Auskünfte," 2 VT 73; 6 VT 36; Zirpins 6 VT 42–63.

13. 6 VT 63–134. On Marowsky's conduct see 8 VT 82, Hett, *Crossing Hitler*, 119–20, 181.

14. 6 VT 55.

15. 27 VT 81; "The Reichstag Trial," *Manchester Guardian*, October 23, 1933; Mergel, *Parlamentarische Kultur*, 88.

16. Kugler, *Geheimnis*, 31; Reed, *Burning*, 180.

17. 11 VT, in H. Bernard et al., eds., *Der Reichstagsbrandprozess und Georgi Dimitrov: Dokumente*, Bd. 2 (East Berlin: Dietz Verlag, 1989), 179–80; Reed, *Burning*, 241.

18. Reed, *Burning*, 256–57.

19. Eugen Mutzka, Protocol, April 12, 1933, BA-BL R. 3003/5, Bl. 87–88; Reed, *Burning*, 149.

20. Reed, *Burning*, 154; 19 VT, 53/58–140, 143.

21. Reed, *Burning*, 154; 19 VT 57.

22. Reed, *Burning*, 162.

23. Reed, *Burning*, 127.

24. Reed, *Burning*, 169.

25. "The Reichstag Fire Trial," *Manchester Guardian*, October 14, 1933; 15 VT 101–43; Reed, *Burning*, 132, 255; 37 VT 121–51.

26. Reed, *Burning*, 254–55, 310–11; Bahar and Kugel, *Reichstagsbrand*, 246.

27. Tobias, *Reichstagsbrand*, 301, 429; *Neue Zürcher Zeitung*, October 24, 1933, morning, and December 6, 1933, morning.

28. "Comedy in Reichstag Trial," *Manchester Guardian*, October 25, 1933; *Völkischer Beobachter*, October 25, 1933.

29. Reed, *Burning*, 139.

30. 16 VT 146–173/180.

31. 16 VT 155–56.

32. 22 VT 215; 14 VT 33; 16 VT 157–58; "Reichstag Fire Trial," *Manchester Guardian*, October 16, 1933.

33. 15 VT 179–81, BA-BL R. 3003/259.

34. "Surprising Evidence at the Reichstag Trial," *Manchester Guardian*, October 21, 1933; 20 VT 34–36.

35. "Surprising Evidence at the Reichstag Trial," *Manchester Guardian*, October 21, 1933; 20 VT 43–45.

36. "Surprising Evidence at the Reichstag Trial," *Manchester Guardian*, October 21, 1933; 20 VT 45–46.

37. 31 VT 121–22.

38. Schuster, *SA*, 231.
39. Dodd, *Embassy Eyes*, 61; Grauert to Göring, November 2, 1933, BA-BL R. 3003/204, Bl. 255.
40. 31 VT 94.
41. 31 VT 103.
42. 31 VT 121–34; Dodd, *Embassy Eyes*, 60.
43. "Göring's Wild Outburst at Reichstag Trial," *Manchester Guardian*, November 6, 1933; Cripps to Hoesch, November 5, 1933; Bülow-Schwante to Neurath, November 6, 1933; Bülow-Schwante to Embassy, November 21, 1933, PA des AA, R. 98417.
44. TBJG 1933, 306–9; "Reichstag Defence Counsel in Angry Scene," *Manchester Guardian*, November 8, 1933; Reed, *Burning*, 243.
45. Reed, *Burning*, 244–45; 34 VT 55.
46. 34 VT 81.
47. TBJG 1933, 310.
48. Reed, *Burning*, 251; "Dutchman Startles the Court," *Manchester Guardian*, November 14, 1933.
49. 37 VT 171–72; "Dutchman Startles the Court," *Manchester Guardian*, November 14, 1933.
50. 37 VT 172–92.
51. Reed, *Burning*, 250; "'Exasperating' Fire Trial," *Manchester Guardian*, November 15, 1933.
52. "Van der Lubbe Speaks Out," *Manchester Guardian*, November 24, 1933; 42 VT 47–75/80.
53. 42 VT 142.
54. *Neue Zürcher Zeitung*, October 23, 1933, morning; 42 VT 154–64.
55. 42 VT 164–71.
56. Reed, *Burning*, 271.
57. Ibid., 255.
58. "The Reichstag Trial," *Manchester Guardian*, November 28, 1933; Diels to Göring, April 16, 1934, GStA Rep. 90 P/5, Bl. 127.
59. Sack, *Reichstagsbrand*, 190.
60. Gisevius Report, December 14, 1933, BA-BL R. 3003/200, Bl. 45–46.
61. Diels Memo, December 9, 1933, BA-BL R. 3003/200, Bl. 66–70.
62. Diels to Göring, December 11, 1933, BA-BL R. 3003/200, Bl. 72.
63. 56 VT; Reed, *Burning*, 324–25.
64. Schneppel to Nebe, January 13, 1934, BA-BL R. 3003/200, Bl. 6–8.
65. Judgment, December 23, 1933, in Deiseroth, *Reichstagsbrand*, 230, 237, 301, 315–16.
66. Ibid., 239–41, 245, 259–60.

67. Ibid., 257, 259.

68. Ibid., 263.

69. Ibid., 262, 298–99; "Reichstag Fire Trial," *Manchester Guardian*, October 19, 1933.

70. Judgment December 23, 1933, in Deiseroth, *Reichstagsbrand*, 285–86, 289.

71. Ibid., 320–21.

72. Reed, *Burning*, 330.

73. Bünger to Bumke, February 2, 1934; Dr. Med. Bruno Gittner Zeugnis, June 1, 1934; Justice Min. to Pres. Reichsgericht February 21, 1936; *Leipziger Tageszeitung*, March 22, 1937, BA-BL. R. 3002/PA/112, Bl. 40, 44, 75, 91.

74. Coenders to Bumke, December 22, 1933; Coenders to Bumke, February 17, 1933, BA-BL. R.3002/PA/128, Bl. 46, 50–58.

75. Coenders to Bumke, February 17, 1933; ibid., Bl. 50–58.

76. On Coenders in the trial see Tobias, *Reichstagsbrand*, 404; 16 VT; *Manchester Guardian*, November 9; *Manchester Guardian*, November 16.

77. ORA Werner Protocol, January 9, 1934, BA-BL R. 3003/68, Bl. 28.

78. "Commutation Seen for van der Lubbe," *New York Times*, January 6, 1934; "Lubbe trotz Begnadigung geköpft," *Neuer Vorwärts*, January 21, 1934; Vermerk, January 8, 1934, BA-BL R 43 II/294, Bl. 439.

79. Agreement, January 9, 1934, BA-BL R. 3003/68, Bl. 22.; "Protokoll über den Vollzug der Todesstrafe an dem Maurer Marinus van der Lubbe," January 10, 1934; ibid., Bl. 29.

80. AA to Royal Dutch Embassy, January 13, 1934; *Socialdemokraten* January 14, 1934, *Socialdemokraten* January 15, 1934; ibid., Bl. 49–51, Bl. 56–58.

81. *Socialdemokraten*, January 15, 1934; ibid., Bl. 58; Bahar and Kugel, *Reichstagsbrand: Provocation*, 244–45; *Telegraaf* quoted in *Neue Zürcher Zeitung*, December 23, 1933, morning.

82. *Neuer Vorwärts*, January 28, 1934; "Van der Lubbe Buried as Guards Stand By," *New York Times*, January 16, 1934.

83. Diels, *Lucifer*, 264–65.

84. "Ergebnis der Besprechung vom 4. Januar 1934," TA; Himmler to Diels, January 15, 1934, IfZ ZS/A 7, Bd. 1.

85. Ivo Banac, ed., *The Diary of Georgi Dimitrov 1933–1949* (New Haven and London: Yale University Press, 2003), 7–8.

86. Diels, *Lucifer*, 267–69. Diels seems to have been playing a double game: William E. Dodd, *Ambassador Dodd's Diary, 1933–1938* (New York: Harcourt, Brace & Company, 1941), 65, 67.

87. Rabinbach "Staging Antifascism," 97–126; Tony Judt and Timothy Snyder, *Thinking the Twentieth Century* (New York: Penguin Press, 2012), ch.6; on the Luxembourg Committee see Conclusion.

88. R.J. Crampton, *Bulgaria* (Oxford: Oxford University Press, 2007), 323, 336.

89. Norbert Podewin and Lutz Heuer, *Ernst Torgler: Ein Leben im Schatten des Reichstagsbrandes* (Berlin: Trafo Verlag Dr. Wolfgang Weist, 2006), 150–70.

90. Tobias to H.D. Röhrs, March 27, 1972, TA.

91. Diels, *Lucifer*, 223; Rudolf Diels, undated affidavit (probably Nuremberg, 1946), NHH VVP 46 NL Diels, Bd. 21; Willi Schmidt, interview with Tobias, July 27, 1968, TA; Krim-Insp. A.K. Berlin, November 27, 1948, OSTA an den GSTA LG Berlin, December 12, 1949, BStU MfS ASt 35 Js 164/48 GA Bd. 1, Bl. 24–25, 27; Volksgerichtshof Judgment, May 4, 1935, BA-BL NJ 14220 Bd. 1, Bl. 433–34; Botschaft to AA, February 5, 1933, PA des AA R 99493.

92. "Der Chef der braunen Tscheka in Schutzhaft-Gefahr?" *Frei-Saar Chronik*, September 3, 1933, PA des AA R. 98428; Tobias interview with Willi Schmidt, Hannover, July 27, 1968, TA; Diels, *Lucifer*, 234, 237; Sauer, "Goebbels 'Rabauken.'"

93. Diels, *Lucifer*, 238–39, 246–49; Grauert Interrogations, December 5, 1946, January 15, 1947, BSN Rep 502 KV-Anklage Interrogations G 73.

94. Gisevius, *To the Bitter End*, 51–52.

95. Grauert Interrogation, January 15, 1947, BSN Rep 502 KV-Anklage Interrogations G 73; "Besprechung mit St. Sekr. Grauert am 13.10.1962," TA; Dodd, *Diary*, 65, 67.

96. Diels, *Lucifer*, 278–81.

97. Metcalfe, *1933*, 201; Dodd, *Embassy Eyes*, 53; Dodd to Metcalfe, August 10, 1982, LOC, Martha Dodd Papers, container 7; Dodd to Dallek, October 31, 1985, LOC, Martha Dodd Papers, container 4; Dodd to Shirer, November 14, 1975, LOC, Martha Dodd Papers, Container 9.

98. Dodd, *Embassy Eyes*, 52–53, 56, 134–35.

99. Klaus Wallbaum, *Der Überläufer: Rudolf Diels (1900–1957). Der Erste Gestapo-Chef des Hitler Regimes* (Frankfurt/Main: Peter Lang, 2010), 77–80; Schneider to Spruchgericht Bielefeld, March 23, 1949, NL Schnitzler I; Himmler to Daluege, July 13, 1942, BA-BL NS 19/2470.

100. Diels, *Lucifer*, 283; Ingeborg Kalnoky, *The Guest House: A Nuremberg Memoir* (Indianapolis/New York: Bobbs-Merrill, 1974), 72–73.

101. Ulrich von Hassell, diary entry for June 15, 1938, IfZ ZS/A 7 Bd. 1.

102. Bülow-Schwante Statement, June 21, 1947, BA-K Z/42/IV/1960, Bl. 57; Diemers Statement, September 2, 1947, NHH VVP 46 NL Diels, Bd. 27.

103. Diels Deposition, February 19, 1949, BA-K Z/42/IV/1960, Bl. 33; CIC Personality Report, Rudolf Diels, July 5, 1950, NARA CIC D001018, Diels, Rudolf.

104. Diels Deposition, February 19, 1949, BA-K Z/42/IV/1960, Bl. 33; Ernst August Prinz von Hannover, Affidavit, April 25, 1949, NHH NDS 171 Hannover Nr. 28640; letter of five participants, July 22, 1946, BA-K Z/42/IV/1960, Bl. 89; Hildegard Diels-Mannesmann, Affidavit, no date, ibid., Bl. 77–78.

105. Diels Deposition, February 19, 1949, BA-K Z/42/IV/1960, Bl. 33; Hildegard Diels-Mannesmann, Affidavit, no date, ibid., Bl. 78; CIC Personality Report, Rudolf Diels, July 5, 1950, NARA CIC D001018, Diels, Rudolf.

106. Diels, *Lucifer*, 263.

7: "THIS FIRST CRIME OF THE NATIONAL SOCIALISTS"

1. Telford Taylor, *The Anatomy of the Nuremberg Trials* (New York: Alfred A. Knopf, 1992), 25–26.

2. Christiane Kohl, *Das Zeugenhaus: Nürnberg 1945: Als Täter und Opfer unter einem Dach zusammentrafen* (Munich: Wilhelm Goldmann Verlag, 2006), 43–44; Kalnoky, *Guest House*, 65–67, 74–76.

3. Kohl, *Zeugenhaus*, 86.

4. Diels to Bogs, August 22, 1949, JA; Kohl, *Zeugenhaus*, 134–35, 158; Diels to Schnitzler, March 26, 1947, NL Schnitzler II; Kempner to Margot (?), November 19, 1982, USHMM RG-71.002.01, Box 140; Sprecher to Kempner, August 13, 1983, USHHM RG-71.004.01, Box 239.

5. NARA RG 263 (CIA) Personal Files, Second Release, Diels, Rudolf, RC Box No 25 Location RC 230/86/22/04.

6. Prussian MP to Prussian IM, December 15, 1933, GStA Rep. 90 P/8/1, Bl. 4; Maisch Report, October 21, 1954, NARA RG 65 FBI, Box 16 Folder 62–85289, Sec 2, 1 of 1; Gisevius, *Bitteren Ende*, (1946), 72–73; Heydrich to Helldorff, February 17, 1936, IfZ ED 82.

7. Joachim Fest, *Staatsstreich: Der lange Weg zum 20. Juli* (Munich: btb-Verlag, 2004), 85; Memo, October 4, 1954, Washington Field to Director, FBI, NARA RG 65, Box 16 Folder 62–85289, Sec 1, 1 of 2; the memo is quoting the Kaltenbrunner Reports, see *Spiegelbild einer Verschwörung*, 479; Maisch Report, October 21, 1954, NARA RG 65, Box 16 Folder 62–85289, Sec 2, 1 of 1; C. Gisiger, "Ein sensationeller Prozess? Das militärgerichtliche Strafverfahren gegen Eduard von der Heydt, Hans Bernd Gisevius und Josef Steegman vor dem Divisionsgericht 6 (1946–1948)," Historisches Seminar University Zurich, October 2005; "Einstellung eines militärgerichtichen Verfahrens," unidentified newspaper clipping, USHMM RG-71.005.01, Box 264.

8. Joseph E. Persico, *Nuremberg: Infamy on Trial* (New York: Viking, 1994), 325; film clips at http://resources.ushmm.org/film/search/index.php, visited February 10, 2009; Nuremberg *Proceedings*, vol. 12, 175; Torgler to Fischer, February 27, 1948, TA; Hans Bernd Gisevius, *Wo ist Nebe? Erinnerungen an Hitlers Reichskriminaldirektor* (Zürich: Droemersche Verlagsanstalt, 1966), 240 ff; Timothy Snyder, *Bloodlands: Europe Between Hitler and Stalin* (New York: Basic Books, 2012), 205; Peter Klein, ed., *Die Einsatzgruppen in der besetzten Sowjetunion 1941/42. Die Tätigkeits- und Lageberichte des Chefs der Sicherheitspolizei und des SD* (Berlin: Edition Hentrich, 1997), 62–63.

9. Gisevius's intemperate speechifying BA-BL R. 3001/57358; his anti-Hugenberg conspiracy, Beck, *Fateful Alliance*, 281.

10. Memo from SAC, WFO to Director FBI, October 21, 1954, quoting letter of Assistant Director CIA to Department of State, March 25, 1948, NARA RG 65 FBI, Box 16 Folder 62-85289, Sec 2, 1 of 1; Gisevius, *Bittern Ende* (1946), Bd. 2; Gisevius to Dulles, undated, August 1955, Mudd Manuscript Library, Princeton, Allen Dulles Papers, Box 29 Folder 2 "Gisevius"; Wätjen to Dulles, January 21, 1946, Mudd Manuscript Library, Princeton, Allen Dulles Papers, Box 57 Folder 1 "Wätjen."

11. Kalnoky, *Guest House*, 178–80.

12. Diels to Kempner, July 20, 1946, TA; also on the Lugano meeting Torgler to Fischer, February 27, 1949, TA; RA Oberloskamp, Schriftsatz, August 28, 1961, ETH NL Gisevius 16.21; Diels, "Zum 'Bittern Ende' des Hans Bernd Gisevius; Ein Vorspiel,'" *Deutsche Rundschau*, vol. 71 Heft 8, August 1948, ETH NL Gisevius 10; Diels, Affidavit, undated, BSN Rep 502 Englische Dokumente D 15–22; Hermann Graml, "Gutachten," May 3, 1962, ETH NL Gisevius, 15.15; Peter, *Spiegelbild*.

13. Dulles to Gisevius, Feb 5, 1946, ETH NL Gisevius, 10 Correspondence, Dulles, Allen; Dulles, "Introduction," in Gisevius, *Bitter End* (1947), xiii; Kalnoky, *Guest House*, 182–85.

14. Gisevius, *Bitter End* (1947), 40–42. In this section, for translation convenience, citations come where possible from the 1947 English edition of the book; where relevant passages from the 1946 German original were cut from the translation, however, citations are to the German edition.

15. Gisevius, *Bitter End* (1947), 61; Gisevius Statement, May 23, 1960, LNRW-D Rep. 372/990, 12–13.

16. Gisevius, *Bittern Ende* (1946), 82–83.

17. Gisevius, *Bitter End* (1947), 61–63.

18. Gisevius, *Bittern Ende* (1946), 87–88, 94.

19. Gisevius, *Bitter End* (1947), 67–72.

20. Gisevius, *Bitter End* (1947), 70, 77–80.

21. Gisevius, *Bitter End* (1947), 74; Gisevius, "Reichstagsbrand im Zerrspiegel," *Die Zeit*, March 25, 1960.

22. Gisevius, *Bittern Ende* (1946), 89–92; Gisevius, *Bitter End* (1947), 64.

23. Gisevius, *Bittern Ende* (1946), 102.

24. Tobias to the Author, March 3, 2010; Diels, *Lucifer*, 221.

25. Gisevius, "Reichstagsbrand im Zerrspiegel," *Die Zeit*, March 18, 1960.

26. "Ein unbequemer Mitwisser beseitigt," *Pariser Tageblatt*, December 12, 1933.

27. Vermerk, July 29, 1974, TA; Tobias to Martini, March 6, 1984, TA; Vermerk, October 28, 1983, TA. On Thadden see Robert G. Moeller, *War Stories: The Search for a Usable Past in the Federal Republic of Germany* (Berkeley: University of California Press, 2003), 27.

28. Dr. Christine van den Heuvel, note in the catalogue, November 7, 1984, Niedersächsisches Landesarchiv Hauptstaatsarchiv Hannover.

29. Diels to the British Delegation, IMT, July 22, 1946, TA. A comparison of other Diels letters that can be found in different places—for instance his letter to Kempner from August 6, 1946, of which Tobias has one signed copy and another is in Kempner's papers—shows that Diels was in the habit of keeping a signed letter copy for his own files.

30. Tobias to the Author, March 3, 2010.

31. Diels Affidavit, April 26, 1946, NHH VVP 46 NL Diels, Bd. 21; Diels, Memo, no date, in NHH VVP 46 NL Diels, Bd. 22.

32. Diels Statement, July 2, 1946, Memo, no date, NHH VVP 46 NL Diels, Bd. 21.

33. Diels Affidavit, July 3, 1946, NHH VVP 46 NL Diels, Bd. 22.

34. Kempner to Amtsgericht Frankfurt, October 15, 1961, LNRW-D Rep. 372/992, Bl. 70; Kempner to Kriminalkommissar Boixen, January 3, 1961, LNRW-D Rep. 372/990, Bl. 144.

35. Arndt to *Die Zeit*, April 14, 1960, LNRW-D Rep. 372/990, Bl. 200; Arndt Deposition, June 9, 1961, LNRW-D Rep. 372/992, Bl. 15–16. Arndt said that he questioned Diels the day that Walther Funk testified about the Reichsbank's holdings of gold taken from concentration camp prisoners. Funk testified May 6th about the gold.

36. BAOR/15228/10/JAG "Dr. Rudolf Diels," May 4, 1946, BNA WO 309/294 "Interrogation of Dr. Rudolf Diels, Regierungspräsident of Cologne 1934–1936 and Hannover 1936–1940"; CC for Germany, to Col. Phillimore, November 30, 1945, BNA WO 309/768; Phillimore to BOAR, December 7, 1945, in ibid; Gisevius to Kempner, October 1, 1948, USHMM Archive Robert M.W. Kempner Collection RG-71.004.03 Box 241, Folder Gisevius 1948–1960.

37. Diels to Kempner, August 6, 1946, Diels to Kempner, April 17, 1946, TA.

38. Kalnoky, *Guest House*, 187–88.

39. Ibid., 186.

40. Robert M.W. Kempner, *Das Dritte Reich im Keuzverhör: Aus den unveröffentlichten Vernehmungsprotokollen des Anklägers in den Nürnberger Prozessen* (Munich: F.A. Herbig, 2005), 29–31, 34, 42–43, 46.

41. Otto Meissner, *Staatssekretär Unter Ebert—Hindenburg—Hitler: Der Schicksalweg des deutschen Volkes von 1918–1945, wie ich ihn erlebte* (Hamburg: Hoffmann und Campe Verlag, 1959), 283.

42. Sommerfeldt to Wolff, September 23, 1955, IfZ ZS/A 7 Bd. 1.

43. Gewehr to SS Oberabschnitt Ost, January 11, 1936, IfZ Fa 74; Gewehr to Zacharias, March 27, 1960, IfZ ID 103–60.

44. Sitzung June 7, 1963, ETH NL Gisevius 17.10; Gewehr to Zacharias, March 27, 1960, IfZ ID 103–60; Gisevius, "Zur Vernehmung Gewehr," ETH NL Gisevius 16.26.

45. Reichsschatzmeister Munich to Gauleitung Gross-Berlin, June 7, 1934, NARA BDC Microfilm PK D044 Hans Georg Gewehr; Gewehr to SS Oberabschnitt Ost, January 11, 1936, IfZ Fa 74; Judgment, February 20, 1962, ETH NL Gisevius 16.24; Gewehr to Zacharias, March 27, 1960, IfZ ID 103–60; Vermerk, Berlin, January 25, 1937, NARA BDC Microfilm PK D044 Hans Georg Gewehr; Einstellung 8 Js 3483/60, Oberstaatsanwalt Düsseldorf, n.d., IfZ ZS/A 7 Bd. 6; Gauschatzmeister to Reichsschatzmeister, December 1, 1936, IfZ Fa 74.

46. Gewehr to Zacharias, March 27, 1960, IfZ ID 103–60.

47. Gewehr to Wehmann, September 3, 1934, BA-BL ZM 772 Akte 16; Helldorff to Frick, March 23, 1936, BA-BL ZB 1049 Akte 8, Bl. 2; Vermerk, Berlin, January 25 1937, NARA BDC Microfilm, PK D044 Hans Georg Gewehr; Gewehr to SS Oberabschnitt Ost, January 11, 1936, IfZ Fa 74.

48. Krüger to 6. Zivilkammer, January 6, 1961, ETH NL Gisevius IV 17.9; Sitzung June 7, 1963, ETH NL Gisevius IV 17.10.

49. Kommando der Schutzpolizei Beurteilung, August 1, 1939, BA-BL ZB 1049 Akte 8, Bl. 29; Vermerk, June 26, 1939, ibid., Bl. 18; Reichsführer SS August 31, 1939, ibid., Bl. 21.

50. Helldorff, January 25, 1940, ibid., Bl. 31.

51. Vermerk, April 16, 1940, Kommandeur der Ordnungspolizei to Befehlshaber der Ordnungspolizei March 1, 1940, Stellungnahme, April 16, 1940, ibid., Bl. 36–38, 45, 47.

52. Memo, February 7, 1940, ibid., Bl. 27.

53. Gewehr to Reichsführer SS, August 25, 1941, Chef des Kommandoamtes to von dem Bach, July 21, 1943, Reichsführer SS July 27, 1943, Higher SS and Police Commander for Russia South and Ukraine to Chief of Bandenkampfverbände, September 20, 1943, BA-BL ZB 1049 Akte 8; Nuremberg *Proceedings* vol. 4,

481, 483; Omer Bartov, *The Eastern Front, 1941–1945, German Troops, and the Barbarization of Warfare,* 2nd edition (New York: Palgrave, 2001), 120, 125; Snyder, *Bloodlands,* 234–50; H.-J. Neufeldt, J. Huck, G. Tessin, *Zur Geschichte der Ordnungspolizei.* Schriften des Bundesarchivs (Koblenz, 1957), 91.

54. Werner Bross, *Gespräche mit Hermann Göring während des Nürnberger Prozesses* (Flensburg and Hamburg: Verlagshaus Christian Wolff, 1950), 196.

55. Bross, *Gespräche,* 129.

56. Diels to Göring, September 23, 1933, LAB B Rep 058/2271, Bd. 2, Bl. 51–53.

57. Diels, *Lucifer,* 222–23; Diels Statement, July 2, 1946, NHH VVP 46 NL Diels, Bd. 21; Diels Memo, no date, ibid.

58. Schmidt Statement, February 8, 1968, LAB B Rep 058/2271, Bd. 2, Bl.104, Bl. 108; Alfred Martin, Statement, February 19, 1962, ibid., Bd. 1, Bl. 162; Diels, *Lucifer,* 180.

59. Tobias Interview with Schmidt, July 27, 1968, TA.

60. Schmidt Statement, February 8, 1968, LAB B Rep 058/2271, Bd. 2, Bl.105–8; Schmidt Statement, February 26, 1969, LAB B Rep 058/2271, Bd. 4, Bl. 104–9.

61. Schmidt Statement, February 8, 1968, LAB B Rep 058/2271, Bd. 2, Bl. 107; Jaager Statement, August 15, 1963, ibid., Bl. 34; Sanders Statement, June 6, 1969, LAB B Rep 058/2271, Bd. 4, Bl. 191–92; Pohlenz Statement, August 30, 1968, LAB B Rep 058/2271, Bd. 3, Bl. 68–69.

62. GSTA Kammergericht, December 20, 1968, LAB B Rep 058/2271, Bd. 4, Bl. 33–34; Vermerk (n.d.; presumably October 1969), ibid., Bl. 227–31.

63. Diels, *Lucifer,* 258–61; Diels Affidavit, July 3, 1946, NHH VVP 46 NL Diels, Bd. 22.

64. Diels, *Lucifer,* 232–36; "Besprechung mit St. Sekr. Grauert am 13.10.1962," TA.

65. Unger Anklage, July 26, 1933, LAB B Rep 058/10792, Bl. 161.

66. Draft "Dem Herrn Ministerpräsidenten," March 13, 1934, GStA Rep. 90 P/5, Bl. 205; Draft to Gruppenführer Karl Ernst, March 1934, GStA Rep. 90 P/5; Louis P. Lochner, *What about Germany?* (New York: Dodd, Mead & Company, 1942), 50.

67. Krausnick to GSTA Landgericht Berlin, May 5, 1960, LAB B Rep 058/6401, Bl. 2.

68. Diels, *Lucifer,* 221; Tobias, *Reichstagsbrand,* 534, 544–45.

69. Krausnick to GSTA Landgericht Berlin, May 5, 1960, LAB B Rep 058/6401, Bl. 1–2.

70. Bahar and Kugel, *Reichstagsbrand,* 29.

71. "Eine Leiche gefunden im Walde vom Garzau," *Strausberger Zeitung,* November 3, 1933, GStA Rep. 84a/53362, Bl. IA.

72. Kutz Statement, November 3, 1933, GStA Rep. 84a/53361, Bl. 26–30; Paschasius Statement, November 3, 1933, ibid., Bl. 31–33.

73. Report of Autopsy, November 4, 1933, ibid., Bl. 20–23; Erkennungsdienst Report, November 4, 1933, ibid., Bl. 6.

74. Seiffert Statement, November 16, 1933, LAB A Rep. 358-01/8300, Bl. 1; Anklage, January 19, 1933, LAB A Rep. 358-01/8300; Note, August 10, 1933, ibid.; Strafgefängnis Tegel, October 9, 1933, Ruling of the 20th Strafkammer, October 17, 1933, Gerichtsgefängnis Pritzwalk, October 20, 1933, Strafgefängnis Tegel, October 21, 1933, LAB A Rep. 358-01/8299, Bl. 271, Bl. 272, Bl. 274, Bl. 277.

75. Rall Statement, October 21, 1933, BA-BL R. 3003 Bd. 112, Bl. 126–27.

76. Strafgefängnis Tegel to Amtsgericht Dresden, November 11, 1933, Geheimes Staatspolizeiamt, November 30, 1933, LAB A Rep. 358-01/8299, Bl. 282 ff.

77. Marie Rall to Auskunftstelle, August 27, 1934, GStA Rep. 84a/53360, Bl. 35; Göring, order of November 4, 1933, ibid., Bl. 54; Diels, *Lucifer*, 214.

78. Strafgefängnis Tegel, LAB A Rep. 358-01/8300; Marie Rall to Auskunftstelle, August 27 1934, GStA Rep. 84a/53360, Bl. 35.

79. Vermerk, July 8, 1935, GStA Rep. 84a/53360, Bl. 43–44; Schmidt Statement, February 26, 1969, LAB B Rep 058/2271, Bd. 4, Bl. 104–9; Gestapa to JM, August 2 1935, GStA Rep. 84a/53360, Bl. 45.

80. GSTA LG to PJM, September 14, 1933, GStA Rep. 84a/53355, Bl. 15; Göring to Hitler, September 26, 1934, GStA Rep. 84a/53359, Bl. 11; GSTA LG to PJM, April 17, 1934, GStA Rep. 84a/53357, Bl. 25.

81. Director, Strafgefängnis Tegel, to ORA Leipzig, April 22, 1938, BA-BL R. 3003/56.

82. Vermerk, August 11, 1934, BA-BL R. 3003 Bd. 112, Bl. 128. The Nazi euphemism for torture was *verschärftes Verhör*.

83. LKP Nebenstelle Peine, Report, May 10, 1961, LAB B Rep. 058/2271, Bd. 1, Bl. 77–78.

84. Diels, *Lucifer*, 147, 221–22; "Die Wissenden schweigen," *Frankfurter Rundschau*, February 26, 1956.

85. Diels, *Lucifer*, 213–14.

86. Einstellung, 1960, IfZ ZS/A 7 Bd. 6, Bl. 8; Schulze-Wilde to Amtsgericht München, July 28, 1961, TA; Schulze-Wilde to Curt Riess, February 1, 1961, BA-K N 1385 NL Riess Bd. 72.

87. Dienstleistung Zeugnis, April 28, 1934, NARA BDC RG 242 SA Collections P-Akten, D 281 Reineking; Beschluss, January 9, 1935, ibid; Einstellung, 1960, IfZ ZS/A 7 Bd. 6.

88. Reineking's Lebenslauf, January 16, 1935, BA-BL ZA II 10156, Bl. 36–37. See also Kurt Reineking, Statement to LKP Nebenstelle Peine, January 14, 1961, LAB B Rep. 058/2271, Bd. 1, Bl. 56; Einstellung, 1960 IfZ ZS/A 7 Bd. 6.

89. Ernst to Oberste SA Führung, November 4, 1933, NARA BDC RG 242 SA Collections P-Akten, D 281 Reineking.

90. Kerrl to Himmler, July 19, 1934, NARA BDC RG 242 SA Collections P-Akten, D 281 Reineking; Kurt Reineking Statement, January 14, 1961, LAB B Rep. 058/2271, Bd. 1, Bl. 56; Karl Reineking's Lebenslauf, January 16, 1935, BA-BL ZA II 10156, Bl. 36–37; Amtsgerichtsrat Schomerus to Kerrl, July 17, 1934, LAB B Rep. 058/2271, Bd. 1.

91. Reineking Statement, January 14, 1961; Karl Reineking's Death Certificate, June 2, 1936, LAB B Rep. 058/2271, Bd. 1, Bl. 5657.

92. Gisevius, *Bis zum bitteren Ende*, 64.

93. Krausnick to Tobias, September 6, 1968, IfZ ID 103/153.

8: "PERSIL LETTERS"

1. A.J.P. Taylor, *The Origins of the Second World War* (Harmondsworth, Middlesex: Penguin Books Ltd., 1984), 36–37.

2. Potsdam Conference, Protocol of Proceedings, August 1, 1945, http://avalon .law.yale.edu/20th_century/decade17.asp, accessed January 4, 2013.

3. Eckart Conze, *Die Suche nach Sicherheit. Eine Geschichte der Bundesrepublik Deutschland von 1949 bis in die Gegenwart* (Munich: Siedler Verlag, 2009), 31; the most authoritative study of denazification remains Lutz Niethammer, *Entnazifizierung in Bayern: Säuberung und Rehabilitierung unter amerikanischer Besatzung* (Frankfurt/Main: S. Fischer Verlag, 1972).

4. Clemens Vollnhals, *Entnazifizierung: Politische Säuberung und Rehabilitierung in den vier Besatzungszonen 1945–1949* (Munich: DTV, 1991), 16–20.

5. Niethammer, *Entnazifizierung*; Vollnhals, *Entnazifizierung*, 33; Richard Pipes, *A Concise History of the Russian Revolution* (New York: Vintage, 1996), 368. For one of the few contrary views on denazification: Konrad Jarausch, *After Hitler: Recivilizing Germans, 1945–1995* (New York: Oxford University Press, 2008).

6. Niethammer, *Entnazifizierung*, 613, 615.

7. Diels, *Fall John*, 47–48.

8. Jörg Friedrich, *Die kalte Amnestie: NS-Täter in der Bundesrepublik* (Berlin: List Taschenbuch, 2007), vi–vii.

9. Braschwitz Deposition, April 5, 1961, LNRW-D Rep. 372/991, Bl. 75.

10. JM NRW to GSTA Hamm, August 23, 1960, LNRW-D Rep. 372/993, Bl. 44–45. The sections of the criminal code which Braschwitz had potentially violated were §§ 154 and 344.

11. Diels, *Lucifer*, 147; Riess testimony, June 12, 1961, LNRW-D Rep. 372/992, Bl. 22.

12. Diels to Dreier, October 9, 1947, in NHH NDS 171 Hannover Nr. 28640, Bl. 33; A.E.E. Reade to Kubuschok, October 30, 1946, BNA WO 309/294; Diels to Schnitzler, February 18, 1947, NL Schnitzler II.

13. *Schaffhauser Bauer*, April 15, 1947, ETH NL Gisevius 8.1.15.1 Reichstagsbrand; "Zum 'Bittern Ende' des Hans Bernd Gisevius. Ein Vorspiel," *Deutsche Rundschau*, 71. Jahrgang, Heft 8, August 1948, ETH NL Gisevius, 10 Correspondence, Diels, Rudolf; Heisig to Diels, October 12, 1948, TA.

14. Tobias, *Reichstagsbrand*, 90–91; Heisig Statement, March 30, 1948, BSW Staatsanwaltschaft Würzburg 407, Bd. 2, Bl. 147; Anklage, August 25, 1948, BSW Staatsanwaltschaft Würzburg 407, Bd. 3, Bl. 362, 365; "Schlußbericht," November 27, 1947, BSW Staatsanwaltschaft Würzburg 407, Bd. 1, Bl. 48.

15. Heisig to Schnitzler, May 2, 1949, NL Schnitzler I; Heisig Statement, March 30, 1948, Heisig Statement, April 12, 1948, BSW Staatsanwaltschaft Würzburg 407, Bd. 2, Bl. 147, Bl. 151; Jan Kiepe, "Zwischen Ahndungsbemühung und-behinderung; Das gesellschaftliche und rechtspolitische Umfeld bei Ermittlungen gegen ehemaligen Gestapo-Mitarbeiter," in Mallmann, *Die Gestapo nach 1945*, 177; Kershaw, *Hitler, Germans, and the Final Solution*, 202; Adler, *Der verwaltete Mensch*, 370.

16. Haubach, October 1, 1948, BSW Staatsanwaltschaft Würzburg 407, Bd. 4, Bl. 439; Diels Interrogation, October 17, 1946, BSN Rep 502 KV-Anklage Interrogations D 33 Rudolf Diels.

17. Beschluß, November 2, 1948, BSW Staatsanwaltschaft Würzburg 407, Bd. 4, Bl. 490; Beschluß, November 26, 1948, ibid., Bl. 509; Protocoll, April 1, 1949, Judgment, April 30, 1949, BSW Staatsanwaltschaft Würzburg 407, Bd. 5, Bl. 580, Bl. 652.

18. Klageschrift, June 17, 1948, BSM Spruchkammer Akten Karton 666, Bl. 42.

19. Heisig Vernehmungsniederschrift, August 17, 1948, BSM Spruchkammer Akten Karton 666, Bl. 43.

20. Protocol, February 7, 1950, BSL, Spruchkammer Akten Karton 666, Bl. 75a, Bl. 75c; Anna Luise Heisig to Schnitzler, February 11, 1956, NL Schnitzler I.

21. "Betr: Heute durchgeführte informatorische Befragung des hier einsitzenden Walter Pohlenz," November 27, 1948, OSTA LG Postsdam to GSTA LG Berlin, December 12, 1949, Haftbefehl, January 5, 1949, BStU MfS ASt 35 Js 164/48 GA Bd. 1, Bl. 25, 27, 36.

22. Sachs to Abegg, September 25, 1948, BSN KV-Anklage Organization G 250.

23. Sachs to Gantt, August 5, 1948, Sachs to Gisevius, August 12, 1948, Sachs to Abegg, September 25, 1948, Staatsarchiv Nürnberg KV-Anklage Organization G 250.

24. See e.g. *Die Spruchgerichte; Herausgegeben vom Generalinspekteur für die Spruchgerichte in der Britischen Zone*, 2. Jahrg/Nr 3 März 1948, 81–82; Heiner Wember, *Umerziehung im Lager: Internierung und Bestrafung von Nationalsozialisten in der britischen Besatzungszone Deutschlands* (Essen: Klartext Verlag, 1991).

25. Heinrich Schnitzler Statement, September 7, 1946, BA-K Z/42/IV/1960, Bl. 60; Ernst Torgler Statement, March 20 1949, Vicco von Bülow-Schwante

Statement, June 21, 1947, BA-K Z/42/IV/1960, Bl. 57, Bl. 172; Einstellung, June 24, 1949, in NHH VVP 46, NL Diels, Bd. 16. On Bülow-Schwante see Eckart Conze et al., *Das Amt und die Vergangenheit: Deutsche Diplomaten im Dritten Reich und in der Bundesrepublik* (Munich: Karl Blessing Verlag, 2010). Entwurf der Anklageschrift NHH NDS 171 Hannover Nr. 28640, Bl. 44–46; Anklage, November 1, 1950, LNRW-D Rep. 372/278, Bl. 29.

26. LNRW-D 372/278; Entnaz. Hauptausschuss der Stadt Hannover, Entscheidung, March 31, 1952, Verfügung, April 3, 1952, in NHH NDS 171 Hannover Nr. 28640, Bl. 312, 317; Notes of a conversation with Diels, October 3, 1954, Schulz-Koffka to the court, February 4, 1954, Schulz-Koffka to the court, March 19, 1959, TA.

27. Schnitzler, diary entry for May 22, 1945, *Prisoner of War Nr. 3404933*, NL Schnitzler I; Geissler Affidavit, January 7, 1948, LNRW-D NW 1023/1865.

28. Schmidt to Verbandspräsident, January 1943, NL Schnitzler I; Fischer-Fürwentsches, Persil letter for Schnitzler, June 7, 1946, NL Schnitzler I (The writer was Schnitzler's brother in law, which of course affects the weight to be given to this).

29. Anton Roesen Begründing, April 10, 1948, LNRW-D NW 1023/1865; Entscheidung, June 10, 1948, LNRW-D NW 1037/5655; Siemsen to Land-gericht Düsseldorf, September 22, 1948, LNRW-D NW.Pe Nr. 118; Vermerk, June 7, 1949, in ibid.

30. *Volksstimme*, November 7, 1946, NL Schnitzler I.

31. Schnitzler, diary entry May 22, 1945, *Prisoner of War Nr. 3404933*, NL Schnitzler I; Schnitzler to "Herrn Ministerialrat," May 10, 1948, NL Schnitzler I.

32. Roesen to LG Düsseldorf, September 30, 1948, LNRW-D NW.Pe Nr. 118; Roesen Begründing, April 10, 1948, LNRW-D NW 1023/1865; Diels Statement, ibid; Schnitzler to Johannes Maassen, July 3, 1949, NL Schnitzler II.

33. Diels to Schnitzler, February 18, 1947, NL Schnitzler II.

34. Diels to Schnitzler, November 24, 1950, Diels to Schnitzler, November 20, 1946, NL Schnitzler I; Schnitzler to Maassen, July 3, 1949, NL Schnitzler II.

35. Diels to Schnitzler, February 18, 1947, Schnitzler to Diels, June 17, 1948, Schnitzler to Diels, March 20, 1948, NL Schnitzler II; Schnitzler to *Neue Politik*, May 5, 1948, NL Schnitzler I.

36. Schnitzler to "Willy," March 19, 1948, Diels to Schnitzler, May 30, 1949, Unidentified writer to Schnitzler, December 18, 1947, NL Schnitzler I.

37. Schnitzler to Diels, March 20, 1948, NL Schnitzler II; Sommerfeldt to Schnitzler, December 26, 1952, NL Schnitzler I; Schnitzler to Janich, March 3, 1948, NL Schnitzler II.

38. Heisig to Schnitzler, August 31, 1948, NL Schnitzler I.

39. Schnitzler to Haubach, September 19, 1948, NL Schnitzler I.

40. Schnitzler to Diels, February 29, 1948, Schnitzler to Diels, March 20, 1948, NL Schnitzler II; Diels to Schnitzler, no date, NL Schnitzler I.

41. Schnitzler to Kogon, November 24, 1947, Schnitzler to Anna Luise Heisig, February 15, 1956, NL Schnitzler I; Klaus-Michael Schnitzler, e-mail to the Author, October 16, 2012.

42. Anonymous (Heinrich Schnitzler), "Der Reichstagsbrand in anderer Sicht," *Neue Politik*, 2. Januar Heft ff 1949, in IfZ ZS/A-7 Bd. 8.

43. Bahar and Kugel, *Reichstagsbrand*, 830 note 19; Diels to Gräfin Nina Faber-Castell, February 23, 1948, in NL Schnitzler II; Intelligence Section to Book Censorship Section, BAOR, January 13, 1949, BA-BL BDC RK Certificates, Film C 55, Gisevius.

44. Schnitzler, "Der Reichstagsbrand in anderer Sicht."

45. Diels to Nina Faber-Castell, February 23, 1948; Schnitzler to Diels, February 29, 1948, NL Schnitzler II.

46. Rudolf Diels, "Leitsätze," *Der Spiegel*, May 12, 1949.

47. Rudolf Diels, "Die Nacht der langen Messer," *Der Spiegel*, May 19, 1949; Rudolf Diels, "Die Nacht der langen Messer," *Der Spiegel*, June 2, 1949; Rudolf Diels, "Die Nacht der langen Messer," *Der Spiegel*, June 9, 1949.

48. Rudolf Diels, "Die Nacht der langen Messer," *Der Spiegel*, June 9, 1949.

49. Rudolf Diels, "Die Nacht der langen Messer," *Der Spiegel*, May 19, 1949; Rudolf Diels, "Die Nacht der langen Messer," *Der Spiegel*, June 9, 1949.

50. Norbert Frei, *Adenauer's Germany and the Nazi Past: The Politics of Amnesty and Integration* (New York: Columbia University Press, 2002), 13.

51. Elisabeth Noelle and Erich Peter Neumann, *Jahrbuch der öffentlichen Meinung 1947–1955*, 2nd Edition (Allensbach am Bodensee, Verlag für Demoskopie, 1956), 133–39; Riess to Augstein, May 7, 1965, BA-K N 1385, NL Riess Bd. 74.

52. Conze, *Suche*, 110–20.

53. Eugen Kogon, "Beinahe mit dem Rücken an der Wand," *Frankfruter Hefte*, vol. 9 no. 9, September 1954: 641–45.

54. Diels to Preusser, November 25, 1954, NHH VVP 46 NL Diels, Bd. 15; Schnitzler, diary entry for June 26, 1945, *Prisoner of War Nr. 3404933*, NL Schnitzler I; Conze, *Suche*, 16; Schmidt-Hannover, *Umdenken*, 9–10.

55. Diels, *Fall John*, 15; on the now largely forgotten uncertainty of the early Federal Republic, see Conze, *Suche*, 10 ff., 109.

56. Peter Fritzsche, *Life and Death in the Third Reich* (Cambridge, Mass.: Harvard University Press, 2008), 291. Rüdiger Overmans has authoritatively estimated German military casualties in the Second World War at 5.3 million: Rüdiger Overmans, *Deutsche militärische Verlüste im zweiten Weltkrieg* (Munich: Oldenbourg Verlag, 1999). For myriad reasons civilian casualties are much harder to calculate, but most estimates range between 1 and 2 million.

57. Conze, *Suche*, 181; Vollnhals, *Entnazifizierung*, 60; Eric A. Johnson, *Nazi Terror: The Gestapo, Jews, and Ordinary Germans* (New York: Basic Books, 2000), 463–87.

58. Peter Merseburger, *Rudolf Augstein: Biographie* (Munich: Deutsche Verlags-Anstalt, 2007), 65–80.

59. Merseburger, *Augstein*, 81, 154, 158.

60. Lutz Hachmeister, *Der Gegnerforscher: Die Karriere des SS Führers Franz Alfred Six* (Munich: C.H. Beck, 1998); Lutz Hachmeister, "Mein Führer, es ist ein Wunder!" *Tageszeitung* December 27, 1996; Alexander Bahar and Wilfried Kugel, "Augstein und die Gestapo-Connection," *Taz Magazin*, February 28, 1998; Merseburger, *Augstein*, 158.

61. Augstein to Presseausschuss, June 22, 1949, SpA, Öffentliche Personen C-E; Merseburger, *Augstein*, 120–22; Wallbaum, *Diels*, 286.

62. Diels to Augstein, October 17, 1950, SpA, VIPS A-F 010 1954; Diels, *Fall John*, 14; Merseburger, *Augstein*, 122; Wallbaum, *Diels*, 290.

63. Augstein to Diels, June 15, 1955, SpA, VIPS A-F 010 1954; Rudolf to Josef Augstein, September 9, 1953, SpA, and information from Spiegel archivist Heinz Egleder, e-mails to the Author, February 18 and 21, 2011; SpA, Binder 1314, Öffentliche Personen M-L; Ploeger, *Schmidt*; Hachmeister, *Gegnerforscher*; FOB to Chief, EE, July 10, 1956, NARA RG 263 Box 83, Horst Mahnke; Augstein, Aktenotiz, December 27, 1996, SpA, Binder 1314, Öffentliche Personen M-L.

64. Gisevius to Allen Dulles, March 16, 1946, ETH NL Gisevius, 10 Correspondence, Allen Dulles; Pechel quoted in Tobias, *Reichstagsbrand*, 531–32; Rudolf Augstein, "Lieber Spiegel-Leser," *Der Spiegel*, April 27, 1960; "Propaganda: Der Abzug," *Der Spiegel*, February 13, 1957.

65. Diels to Daluege, May 23, 1933, BA-BL BDC DS08180 Ordnungspolizei Zirpins, Film Sig. B0017.

66. Zirpins Testimony, July 6, 1961, LNRW-D Rep. 372/992, Bl. 35; Zirpins's Lebenslauf, NHH Nds. 132 Hannover Acc. 80/86, Nr. 9/4, Bl. 92.

67. Staatsanwaltschaft Hannover, Vermerk, March 18, 1961, BA-L B 162/21252; Zirpins Statement, January 4, 1961, NHH Nds. 132 Hannover Acc. 80/86, Nr. 9/2, Bl. 4; Richard J. Evans, "How Willing Were They?" *New York Review of Books*, June 11, 2008.

68. Walter Zirpins, "Das Getto in Litzmannstadt, kriminalpolizeilich gesehen," *Kriminalistik: Monatshefte für die gesamte kriminalistische Wissenschaft u. Praxis*, Bd. 15 Heft 9, September 1941: 97–98.

69. Staatsanwaltschaft Hannover, Vermerk, March 18, 1961, BA-Ludwigsburg B 162/21252; Lucjan Dobroszyckia, ed., *Chronicle of the Lodz Ghetto 1941–1944* (New Haven and London: Yale University Press, 1984), xxxix; Walter Zirpins, "Das Getto in Litzmannstadt, kriminalpolizeilich gesehen," *Kriminalistik: Monatshefte für die gesamte kriminalistische Wissenschaft u. Praxis*, Bd. 15 Heft 10, Oktober 1941: 111–12.

70. Staatsanwaltschaft Hannover, Vermerk, March 18, 1961, BA-Ludwigsburg B 162/21252; Zirpins, "Litzmannstadt," Kriminalistik, Bd. 15 Heft 9, September 1941: 98, Heft 10, October 1941: 112.

71. Niedersachen MdI to Polizeidirektion Hannover, December 8, 1960, NHH Nds. 132 Hannover Acc. 80/86, Nr. 9/2, Bl. 1–2; Zirpins Statement, January 4, 1961, ibid., Bl. 8.

72. Zirpins to NS MdI, September 3, 1951, NHH Nds. 132 Hannover Acc. 80/86, Nr. 9/4, Bl. 90; Zirpins, Lebenslauf, ibid., Bl. 93; Zirpins to Polizeirat Saupe, April 13, 1951, ibid, Bl. 84; "Bescheidigung" January 6, 1949, ibid., Bl. 103; LKA Niedersachsen to NS MdI January 26, 1951, ibid., Bl. 72.

73. Patrick Wagner, *Hitlers Kriminalisten: Die deutsche Kriminalpolizei und die Nationalsozialismus* (Munich: C.H. Beck, 2002), 10; "Revolver Harry für Bonn," *Der Spiegel*, March 14, 1951.

74. Wagner, *Hitlers Kriminalisten*, 164; Dieter Schenk, *Auf dem rechten Auge blind: Die braunen Wurzeln des BKA* (Cologne: Verlag Kiepenhauer & Witsch, 2001), 18; Vermerk, October 27, 1951, Zirpins to NS MdI, September 3, 1951, NHH Nds. 132 Hannover Acc. 80/86, Nr. 9/4, Bl. 77, Bl. 90.

75. NS MdI to Zirpins, January 8, 1952, ibid, Bl. 4; Walter Zirpins, "Wir fanden Halacz," *Der Spiegel*, December 19, 1951.

76. Wehner to Tobias, December 21, 1951, SpA, Tobias Papers, Bd. 1, "Dr. Wehner."

77. Zirpins to Bayerischer Rundfunk, February 4, 1952, IfZ ZS/A 7 Bd. 7.

78. Tobias to Zirpins, January 16, 1960, IfZ ZS/A 7 Bd. 7; Tobias to Zirpins, February 13, 1960, ibid.

79. Zirpins to Wolff, July 28, 1955, IfZ ZS/A 7 Bd. 2.

80. Diels to Zirpins, no date, late October or Early November 1957, Diels to Zirpins, November 8, 1957, Zirpins to Diels, November 11, 1957, NHH VVP 46, NL Diels, Bd. 19.

9: "THE FEARED ONE"

1. Fritz Tobias, interview with the Author, Hannover, July 4, 2009.

2. Fritz Tobias, "Kurzer Rückblick auf die ersten fünfzig Jahre meines Lebens," July 1, 1962, TA.

3. Ibid.; Tobias, interview with the Author, Hannover, July 4, 2009; Bahar and Kugel, *Reichstagsbrand*, 782.

4. Wehner to Tobias, January 18, 1951, SpA, Tobias Papers, Bd. 1, "Dr Wehner."

5. Wagner, *Hitlers Kriminalisten*, 170–71.

6. Wehner to Tobias, July 21, 1951, Vermerk, undated, Wehner to Tobias, December 21, 1951, SpA, Tobias Papers, Bd. 1, "Dr Wehner"; Bernhard Wehner, "Das Spiel ist aus—Arthur Nebe," *Der Spiegel*, March 23, 1950.

7. Tobias to Wiltruf Wehner-Davin, April 13, 1996, Wehner, "Presserecherchen zu einem ursprünglichen geplanten Artikel über die Polizei Hannover," January 14, 1951, Wehner to Tobias, December 21, 1951, SpA, Tobias papers, Bd. 1, "Dr. Wehner."

8. Tobias to Dobbert, December 30, 1957, JA; Arthur Brandt, interview with Südwest Rundfunk, November 4, 1979, JA.

9. Arthur Brandt, interview with Südwest Rundfunk, November 4, 1979, JA; Andreas Pretzel, "Ansprüche auf strafrechtliche Rehabilitierung," in Pretzel, ed., *NS-Opfer unter Vorbehalt: Homosexuelle Männer in Berlin nach 1945* (Münster: Lit Verlag, 2002), 90.

10. Brandt to LG Berlin Strafkammer, April 1, 1957, JA.

11. Pretzel, "Ansprüche," 91.

12. Brandt to the LG Berlin Strafkammer, September 29, 1955, JA.

13. Den Haag an Auswärtiges Amt Bonn, October 1, 1955, BA-L B 141/17511, Bl. 2.

14. Brandt to LG Berlin Strafkammer, April 1, 1957, JA.

15. Arthur Brandt, interview with Südwest Rundfunk, November 4, 1979; Arthur Brandt, "Van der Lubbe ist unschuldig," *Weltwoche*, June 17, 1966; Brandt to LG Berlin Strafkammer, April 1, 1957, JA.

16. Gerhard Jungfer, interview with Helga and Inge Brandt, November 10, 1995, JA; Hans Bernd Gisevius, "Eine Kommission muss aufklären," *Die Zeit*, March 25, 1960.

17. Ruth-Hanna Kuhne, Geschäftsleiterin, Amtsgericht Bremerhaven, to the Author, August 30, 2010.

18. Dobbert to Tobias, November 5, 1957, JA.

19. Vogt to GSTA Berlin, January 1, 1957, JA; Becker Statement, December 5, 1956, LAB B Rep 058/1293, Bl. 69–70.

20. Diels Statement, January 15, 1957, JA.

21. Tobias to Dobbert, November 18, 1957, JA; Peter Brandes (Curt Riess) "Feuer über Deutschland," *Der Stern*, November 9, 1957, November 16, 1957, November 30, 1957.

22. Dobbert to Tobias, September 3, 1959, Judgment, December 15, 1980, Senator for Justice Berlin, Memo, June 24, 1966, GSTA KG to GSTA LG Berlin, July 20, 1966, LG Berlin, Beschluss, April 21, 1967, JA.

23. BGH Beschluss, April 25, 1974, Strafkammer LG Berlin December 15, 1980, Beschluss KG Berlin April 21, 1981, JA.

24. Rudolf Augstein, "Lieber Spiegel-Leser," *Der Spiegel*, October 21, 1959.

25. Tobias to Augstein, March 14, 1956, Hans-Dieter Jaene to Tobias, November 6, 1957, SpA, Tobias Papers, Bd. 8 "Zacharias"; Tobias, interview with the Author, Hannover, July 20, 2008.

26. Tobias deposition, July 6, 1961, ETH NL Gisevius 16.19; Tobias, "Kurzer Rückblick"; *Der Spiegel* to Tobias, February 25, 1958, Tobias to Becker, February 26, 1958, Becker to Tobias, February 28, 1958, SpA, Augstein NL, Bd. 38, 1958 Allgemeine M-Z; Tobias to Dobbert, date unclear, June 1958, Tobias to Dobbert, November 29, 1957, JA.

27. Tobias to Augstein, November 4, 1958, Augstein to Tobias, November 27, 1958, Becker to Tobias, February 28, 1958, SpA, Augstein NL, Bd. 38, 1958 Allgemeine M-Z.

28. Christian Plöger, *Von Ribbentrop zu Springer: Zu Leben und Wirken von Paul Karl Schmidt alias Paul Carell* (Marburg: Tectum Verlag, 2009), 15; Bahar and Kugel, *Reichstagsbrand*, 765; Christina von Hodenberg, "Die Journalisten und der Aufbruch zur kritischen Öffentlichkeit," in Ulrich Herbert, ed., *Wandlungsprozesse in Westdeutschland: Belastung, Integration, Liberalisierung 1945–1980* (Göttingen: Wallstein Verlag, 2002), 289. "Under-cover Nazi" was an American assessment of the paper *Christ und Welt*, which employed several of Schmidt's former colleagues, including Winfried Martini, a friend of both Diels and Tobias.

29. Tobias Deposition, July 6, 1961, ETH NL Gisevius 16.19.

30. Tobias to Jürgen Warner, April 24, 1958, "Auszug aus einer Aktennotiz vom 6. März 1958 von J.F. Warner an Dr. Heine," SpA, Tobias Papers, Bd. 9, "Schmidt-Carell"; Tobias to Schmidt, March 29, 1958, SpA, Tobias Papers, Band 8 "Zacharias"; SpA, Tobias Papers, Bd. 9, "Schmidt-Carell."

31. Tobias to Jürgen Warner, April 24, 1958, Tobias to Willi Peters, March 14, 1958, SpA, Tobias Papers, Bd. 9, "Schmidt-Carell"; Tobias, *Reichstagsbrand*, 516; Tobias to Augstein, November 12, 1969, SpA, Tobias Papers, Bd. 20 "Augstein."

32. Annette Weinke, *Eine Gesellschaft ermittelt gegen sich selbst: Die Geschichte der Zentralstelle Ludwigsburg 1958–2008* (Darmstadt: WBG, 2008), 16–17; Mallmann, *Gestapo nach 1945*, 23–24.

33. Constantin Goschler, "Disputed Victims: The West German Discourse on Restitution for the Victims of Nazism," in Manfred Berg and Bernd Schaefer, eds., *Historical Justice in International Perspective: How Societies Are Trying to Right the Wrongs of the Past* (New York: GHI and Cambridge University Press, 2009); Zentralstelle, Informationsblatt, Gen IV–215, Stand Dezember 2010, 9; Conze, *Suche*, 263–65.

34. See the essays in Mallmann and Angrick, *Die Gestapo nach 1945*; Undated memo, probably summer 1960, NARA RG 263 CIA Name Files Second Release, Box 24, Dickopf, Paul, Vol 1 folder 1 of 2; Wildt, *Generation der Unbedingten*, 770.

35. Braschwitz Statement, BStU MfS HA-IX/11 FV 6170 Bd. 1 Teil 2 von 2, Bl. 328–30.
36. "Überprüfung des ehemaligen Reg. und Kriminalrats Rudolf Braschwitz auf Grund der Vorwürfe der ÖTV Düsseldorf," January 25, 1957, LNRW-W, Personalakten (neue Verzeichnung) Nr. 2688 *Rudolf Braschwitz*, Bd. 1; Schlussbericht, October 5, 1959, ibid., Bl. 65, 69; Braschwitz to NRW Interior Minister, February 14, 1957, ibid.
37. Belz to Staatsanwaltschaft Dortmund, January 2, 1959, BA-L B 162/2973, Bl. 5a; Belz Statement, January 21, 1959, ibid., Bl. 7–10; Schüle to Landeskriminalamt Hessen, ibid., Bl. 2; Oberstaatsanwalt Dortmund to Polizeipräsidenten Dortmund, October 30, 1959, LNRW-W Personalakten (neue Verzeichnung) Nr. 2688 *Rudolf Braschwitz*, Bd. 1., Bl. 93. That the case against Braschwitz for beating the young Communist was stayed is another sign of how hard it was for victims of the Nazis to get justice in postwar Germany. As early as November 1934 Ernst Fraenkel had written, on the basis of his experience acting as lawyer in political cases, that it was an "undeniable fact" that the Gestapo's prisoners were beaten "before, during and after" their interrogations, even if the interrogating officer strategically left the room to allow the beatings to occur. Fraenkel, "In der Maschine der politischen Strafjustiz des III. Reiches," *Sozialistische Warte*, November 1934, 172–73.
38. Siegfried Koehrer Statement, November 25, 1959, Vorläufiger Abschlussbericht, April 5, 1960, BA-L B 162/5302, Bl. 12–14, Bl. 40–43; Schüle, Aktenvermerk April 9, 1959, BA-L B 162/2973, Bl. 22a, Vfg Sachstandsvermerk, April 13, 1963 BA-L B 162/5303, Bl. 489, 542; Adrian Weale, *Army of Evil: A History of the SS* (New York: NAL, 2012), 323–24.
39. OSTA to Polizeipräs. Dortmund, July 26, 1961, OSTA to Polizeipräs. Dortmund, March 30, 1962, LNRW-W Personalakten (neue Verzeichnung) Nr. 2688, Bd. 1., Bl. 108, 112; Braschwitz to NRW MdI, February 14, 1957, ibid.
40. Gisevius to Holste, undated, ETH NL Gisevius 16.2 Gewehr gegen Gisevius; Schulze-Wilde, draft of evidence, undated, ETH Nachlass Gisevius, 10 Correspondence: Schulze-Wilde, Harry.
41. Patrick Wagner, "Die Resozialisierung der NS-Kriminalisten," in Herbert, ed., *Wandlungsprozesse*, 197; "Die Angeglichenen," *Der Spiegel*, October 28, 1959; Tobias to Zacharias, January 5, 1959 [date must be incorrect, probably 1960 or 1961], SpA, Tobias Papers, Bd. 8 "Zacharias."
42. Staatsanwaltschaft Hannover, Vermerk, March 18, 1961, BA-L B 162/21252.
43. Zirpins, "Litzmannstadt," Bd. 15 Heft 10, October 1941: 109; Staatsanwaltschaft Hannover, Vermerk, March 18, 1961, BA-L B 162/21252.
44. "Anmerkungen zum Hefter 11," Tobias to Schmidt, November 11, 1958, Tobias to Schmidt, August 28, 1958, SpA, Tobias Papers, Binder 8 "Zacharias"; Zirpins Testimony, July 6, 1961, LNRW-D Rep. 372/992, Bl. 34, 37.

45. Tobias to Augstein, November 4, 1958, SpA, 1958 Allgemeine M-Z.

46. "Stehen Sie auf, van der Lubbe!" *Der Spiegel*, October 21, 1959; Tobias, *Reichstagsbrand*, 90; Heisig to Diels, October 12, 1948, TA; VT 2, 55.

47. "Stehen Sie auf, van der Lubbe!" *Der Spiegel*, November 4, 1959, November 18, 1959.

48. "Stehen Sie auf, van der Lubbe!" *Der Spiegel*, October 28, 1959; "Stehen Sie auf, van der Lubbe!" *Der Spiegel*, November 25, 1959.

49. 6 VT 62; Tobias, *Reichstagsbrand*, 77.

50. Flöter to IfZ, March 21, 1956, IfZ ZS A7/01.

51. Tobias, *Reichstagsbrand*, 12, 15, 565–66.

52. Thaler Statement, February 28, 1933, BA-BL R. 3003/1, Bl. 17; Statement, March 22, 1933, BA-BL R. 3003/2, Bl. 176–79; Buwert Statement, March 16, 1933 BA-BL R. 3003/2, Bl. 51–52.

53. Tobias, *Reichstagsbrand*, 15; 14 VT 93–94; Tobias, "Der angebliche 'positive Beweis' für die NS-Brandstifterschaft durch die 'wissenschaftliche Dokumentation,' Bd. 2," in Backes, *Reichstagsbrand*, 140–41.

54. Fritz Tobias, *The Reichstag Fire* (New York: G.P. Putnam's Sons, 1964); Tobias, *Reichstagsbrand*, 76–77, 530–50; see the above section on Gisevius.

55. Tobias, *Reichstagsbrand*, 592–93; Judt, *Reappraisals*, 189.

56. Fritz Tobias, "Anmerkungen zum Hefter 11"; Tobias to Schmidt, November 11, 1958; Tobias to Schmidt, August 28, 1958, SpA, Tobias Papers, Bd. 8 "Zacharias."

57. Tobias to Puhle, November 11, 1957, Puhle to Tobias November 29, 1957, Tobias to Puhle, December 9, 1957, Puhle to Tobias, December 21, 1957, IfZ ZS/A 7 Bd. 7; Polchow Statement, March 3, 1933, BA-BL R. 3003/53, Bl. 15–16.

58. Tobias to Zirpins, November 14, 1957, Tobias to Zirpins, January 16, 1960, Zirpins to Tobias, February 9, 1960, Tobias to Zirpins, February 13, 1960, IfZ ZS/A 7 Bd. 7.

59. Tobias, interview with the Author, Hannover, July 20, 2008. It is apparent from a letter from Harry Schulze-Wilde to Gisevius dated April 27, 1962, that they had just learned of this aspect of Zirpins's career from recent magazine accounts. Schulze-Wilde to Gisevius, April 27, 1962, ETH NL Gisevius, IV.16.25.

60. See, e.g., Tobias, *Reichstagsbrand*, 76–77; Tobias, interview with the Author, Hannover, July 4, 2009.

61. Vermerk, February 27, 1952, NHH Nds. 132 Hannover Acc. 80/86, Nr. 9/4, Bl. 98; Heinrich L. Bode to Gisevius, December 1, 1960, ETH NL Gisevius, III.10.

62. Fritz Tobias, interview with the Author, Hannover, July 20, 2008; Diels to Zirpins, October/November 1957, NHH VVP 46 NL Diels, Bd. 19; Reg. Dir. Dr. Zorn, "Veröffentlichung," October 22, 1958, BA-K B 141/17511, Bl. 43–44.

63. Bahar and Kugel, *Reichstagsbrand*, 780–81; Fritz Tobias, interview with the Author, Hannover, July 20, 2008; Bahar and Kugel, *Reichstagsbrand: Provocation*, 301; Friedrich Winterhager, email to the Author, May 10, 2013.

64. Fritz Tobias, interview with the Author, Hannover, July 4, 2009; Augstein to Curt Riess, April 25, 1962, BA-K N 1385 NL Riess, Bd. 74; Fritz Tobias, interview with the Author, Hannover, July 20, 2008.

65. Fritz Tobias, "Auch Fälschungen haben lange Beine," in Reinhard Uhle-Wettler, ed.,*Wagnis Wahrheit: Historiker in Handschellen?* (Kiel: Arndt Verlag, 1998); http://www.fpp.co.uk/docs/Irving/RadDi/2010/120610.html, accessed May 17, 2011; Anton Maegerle, "Zweifelhafter Reichstagsbrandforscher Verstorben," *Vorwärts*, January 11, 2011; for Grabert Verlag see www.grabert-verlag.de.

66. Fritz Tobias, interview with the Author, Hannover, July 4, 2009.

67. Tobias to Braschwitz, December 11, 1968, LAB B Rep 058/10792, Bl. 128–29; Tobias to Krausnick, August 30, 1960, IfZ ID 103/79 Hausarchiv.

68. Conze, *Suche*, 154.

69. Westarp to Diels, July 18, 1952, NHH VVP 46 NL Diels, Bd. 13; NARA RG 263 (CIA) Personal Files, Second Release, Diels, Rudolf, RC Box No 25 Location RC 230/86/22/04; "Contacts with Rudolf Diels," September 10, 1950, and Agent's Monthly Reports, September and October 1948, NARA Army/IRR Files D001018 Diels, Rudolf; Dorls to BIM Schroeder, July 26, 1954, BA-K B 362/4610, Bl. 402–4; Diels to John, January 15, 1953, IWM John Papers, Box 3.

70. NARA RG 263 (CIA) Personal Files, Second Release, Diels, Rudolf, RC Box No 25 Location RC 230/86/22/04; Diels to John, January 15, 1953, IWM John Papers, Box 3.

71. Schnitzler to Diels, March 20, 1948, NL Schnitzler II. The "legendary castle" probably refers to the *Jagdhaus*, a hunting lodge in the Taunus mountains, which in fact was one of the early bases of what became the Gehlen Organization. See James H. Critchfield, *Partners at the Creation: The Men Behind Postwar Germany's Defense and Intelligence Establishments* (Annapolis, Md. Naval Institute Press, 2003), 33.

72. Thomas Polgar, e-mail to the Author, September 7, 2011; G.J. Mitchell to W.L. Burmester, "Subject: Diels, Rudolf (Former Gestapo Chief), December 22, 1949, NARA Army/IRR Files, Diels, Rudolf, XE523844; "Contacts with Rudolf Diels," September 10, 1950, NARA Army/IRR Files, D001018 Diels, Rudolf; Headquarters European Command, Memo, April 20, 1950, ibid.

73. G.J. Mitchell to W.L. Burmester, "Subject: Diels, Rudolf (Former Gestapo Chief), December 22, 1949, NARA Army/IRR Files, Diels, Rudolf, XE523844; Thomas Polgar, e-mail to the Author, September 7, 2011.

74. Bernd Stöver, "Der Fall Otto John," *VfZ* vol. 47 (1999): 103–36; Diels, *Fall John*, 19, 15.

75. Memo, Headquarters Region IV, 66th CIC Group, November 3, 1954, NARA Army/IRR Files, D001018 Diels, Rudolf.

76. Tobias Testimony, July 6, 1961, ETH NL Gisevius, IV.16.9. As an example of Tobias's use of his official position to get documents, he requested the prosecutor's file in the van der Lubbe case by letter written on the letterhead of the Lower Saxon Office for Constitutional Protection, September 23, 1959, without giving any reason. LAB B Rep 058/1293, Bl. 172.

77. Director FBI to SAC Dallas, July 30, 1954, NARA RG 65 230/86/04/05 Box 16, Folder 62–85289 Sec. 1 2 of 2; Memo No. 19 Re: Dr. Hans Bernd Gisevius, May 21, 1953, ibid. The bureau got many things wrong, but this was right: Gisevius considered Niemöller one of his best friends, and he was an advocate of German neutrality. See typed notes dated March 12, 1946, in Mudd Manuscript Library Allen Dulles Papers, Box 29, Folder 2, "Gisevius"; "Propaganda: Der Abzug," *Der Spiegel*, February 13, 1957. The Lower Saxon State Archives advised me by letter dated August 10, 2012, that "in den zur Verfügung stehenden Karteien der vom Niedersächsichen Landesamt für Verfassungsschutz abgegebenen Verschlußsachen keine Hinwiese auf [Gisevius] . . . zu ermitteln [ist]." See also Schwarz, *Adenauer*, vol. 1, 772.

78. Tobias Testimony, July 6, 1961, ETH NL Gisevius, IV.16.9; Tobias to Krausnick, July 31, 1963, IfZ ID 103/108 Hausarchiv; "Gutachten," May 3, 1962, ETH NL Gisevius, IV Prozesse, 15.15; Anne Nelson, *Red Orchestra: The Story of the Berlin Underground and the Circle of Friends Who Resisted Hitler* (New York: Random House, 2009), 275, 287, 294; Heinrich Grosse, "Ankläger von Widerstandskämpfern und Apologet des NS-Regimes nach 1945—Kriegsgerichtsrat Manfred Roeder," *Kritische Justiz* 2005 Heft 1: 36, 39–43, 47.

79. Tobias Testimony, July 6, 1961, ETH NL Gisevius, IV.16.9; Borowski to Hoffmann, July 25, 1954, BA-K VS B 362/10929, Bundesanwaltschaft, Bd. 1, Bl. 25; Reg. Dir. Dr. Zorn, "Veröffentlichung," October 22, 1958, BA-K B 141/17511, Bl. 43–44.

80. Peter-Ferdinand Koch, e-mail to the Author, September 17, 2011; Tobias to Augstein, February 26, 1958, SpA 1958 Allgemeine M-Z 038; Reg. Dir. Dr. Zorn, "Veröffentlichung," October 22, 1958, BA-K B 141/17511, Bl. 44–46. The credibility of Herr Koch's information is enhanced by the fact that he and the publication for which he used to work are sympathetic to Tobias and to his position on the Reichstag fire.

81. Weinke, *Ludwigsburg*, 17; "Mitschrift des Vortrages," November 29, 1961, BA-K N 1415/1, NL Just-Dahlmann; Tobias to Augstein, November 4, 1958, in SpA, 1958 Allgemeine M-Z; Teresa Nentwig, *Hinrich Wilhelm Kopf (1893–1961): Ein konservativer Sozialdemokrat* (Hannover: Hansche Buchhandlung, 2013).

82. "Der Spiegel berichtete," *Der Spiegel*, November 25, 1959; Tobias, Vermerk, August 20, 1959, SpA, Tobias Papers, Bd. 8, "Zacharias."

83. Fritz Tobias, interview with the Author, Hannover, July 20, 2008.

10: "SNOW FROM YESTERDAY"

1. Professor Hans Mommsen, interview with the Author, Feldafing, April 20, 2010.

2. Professor Hans Mommsen, interview with the Author, Feldafing, April 20, 2010; Hermann Graml, "Die fünfziger Jahre," in Horst Möller and Udo Wengst, eds., *50 Jahre Institut für Zeitgeschichte: Eine Bilanz* (Munich: R. Oldenbourg Verlag, 1999), 79.

3. Protokoll der konstituierenden Sitzung des "Deutschen Instituts für Geschichte der nationalsozialistischen Zeit," September 11, 1950, IfZ Archive IF 8/1 Wissenschaftlicher Beirat Protokolle 1949–1950; Krausnick to GSTA Landgericht Berlin, May 5, 1960, LAB B Rep 058/6401, Bl. 1–2; Ergebnisprotokoll, July 30, 1962, IfZ ID 8/14, Wissenschaftlicher Beirat Protokolle, 1962–1963.

4. Tobias to Krausnick, August 22, 1957, Krausnick to Tobias, September 9, 1957, Tobias to Krausnick, October 24, 1957, Hoch to Tobias, November 8, 1957, Tobias to Hoch, November 9, 1957, IfZ ID 103/79.

5. Tobias to Krausnick, March 26, 1960, Krausnick to Tobias, April 2, 1960, Tobias to Krausnick, April 20, 1960, IfZ ID 103/79.

6. Krausnick to Tobias, September 2, 1963, IfZ ID 103/108.

7. Tobias to Krausnick, July 27, 1963, Krausnick to Tobias, September 2, 1963, Tobias to Krausnick, October 6, 1963, IfZ ID 103/108.

8. Tobias to Zacharias, May 27, 1962, SpA, Tobias Papers, Bd. 8 "Zacharias"; Tobias to Robert Spiering, May 19 1962, Spiering to Tobias, May 23, 1962, SpA, Tobias Papers, Bd. 49 B "Redaktion."

9. Tobias to Zacharias, July 29, 1962, SpA, Tobias Papers, Bd. 8 "Zacharias."

10. Tobias to Zacharias, August 11, 1962, SpA, Tobias Papers, Bd. 8, "Zacharias."

11. Tobias to Zacharias, August 25, 1962, SpA, Tobias Papers, Bd. 8, "Zacharias"; Hoch to Gisevius, September 12, 1962, ETH NL Gisevius 10 Correspondence; Tobias to Krausnick, July 27, 1963, IfZ ID 103/108; Krausnick to Mommsen, August 19, 1963, September 30, 1963, IfZ ID 103/100; Tobias to Zacharias, October 14, 1962, SpA, Tobias Papers, Bd. 8, "Zacharias."

12. Krausnick to Mommsen, September 30, 1963, in IfZ ID 103/100.

13. Professor von Aretin to the Author, October 17, 2011.

14. Ian Kershaw, "Beware the Moral High Ground," *Times Literary Supplement*, October 10, 2003.

15. Hans Schneider, *Neues vom Reichstagsbrand? Eine Dokumentation: Ein Versäumnis der deutschen Geschichtsschreibung* (Berlin: Berliner Wissenschafts-Verlag, 2004), 193.

16. Krausnick to Schneider, February 27, 1960, IfZ ZS/A7 Bd. 3/I; Hans Mommsen, Aktennotiz, November, 1962 (no date), ibid.; Krausnick, Tätigkeitsbericht von April 1959–September 1960, IfZ ID 8/12.

17. Krausnick, Tätigkeitsbericht von April 1959–September 1960, IfZ ID 8/12; Hoch, Aktennotiz, July 24, 1961, IfZ ZS/A7 Bd. 3/I.

18. Jürgen Westerhoff (Paul Karl Schmidt), "Lügen haben lange Beinen: Eine Auseinandersetzung mit Bewältigern und Vergewältigern unserer Zeitgeschichte," *Kristall*, 9/1962, 19–24.

19. Krausnick to Rothfels, July 6, 1962, IfZ ID 90/73; Krausnick, Aktennotiz, November 9 and 10, 1962, IfZ ZS/A7 Bd. 3/II.

20. Min. Dir. Keim to Krausnick, April 6, 1962, IfZ ID 6/1, 1962. This case involved a book by one Georg Franz on the early years of the Nazi Party, which itself put forward a number of more or less Nazi views.

21. Hans Mommsen, Aktennotiz, November, 1962 (no date), IfZ ZS/A7 Bd. 3/I.

22. Schneider to the *Monat*, February 10, 1963, quoted in Schneider, *Reichstagsbrand*, 39.

23. Krausnick to Schneider, November 30, 1962, IfZ Reichstag ZS/A7 Bd. 3/II.

24. Hersch Fischler, "Die verflixte Aktennotiz," *Tageszeitung*, November 4, 2000.

25. Hans Mommsen, "Nichts von Manipulation," *Tageszeitung*, November 25, 2000.

26. "Neues vom Reichstagsbrand: Ein Film von Gerhard Brack and Tina Mendelsohn," YouTube, accessed October 13, 2010.

27. "Zur Kontroverse über den Reichstagsbrand," *VfZ* vol. 49 (2001), 553; "Neues vom Reichstagsbrand: Ein Film von Gerhard Brack and Tina Mendelsohn," YouTube, visited October 13, 2010.

28. Professor Hans Mommsen, interview with the Author, April 20, 2010, Feldafing. Unfortunately Professor Graml did not reply to my query about this event.

29. Mommsen to Krausnick, August 12, 1963, Krausnick to Mommsen, April 7, 1964, Mommsen to Krausnick, April 11, 1964, Krausnick to Mommsen, May 13, 1964, IfZ ID 103/100.

30. Wolfgang Benz, "Vorrede—zugleich ein Versuch über Helmut Krausnick," in Wolfgang Benz, ed., *Miscellanea: Festschrift für Helmut Krausnick* (Stuttgart: DVA, 1980); Ergebnisprotokoll, October 21,1960, IfZ ID 8/12.

31. Ergebnisprotokoll, January 13, 1959, IfZ ID 8/11; Ergebnisprotokoll, October 21,1960, IfZ ID 8/12; Min. Dir. Hagelberg to Krausnick, August 12, 1963, IfZ ID 6/3.

32. Jesse in *Recht und Politik*, 1986; Berg, *Holocaust*, 273, 309, 294.

33. Krausnick to Mommsen, September 30, 1963, IfZ ID 100–103.

34. Krausnick to Gisevius, October 20, 1963, ETH NL Gisevius Correspondence 10; Kurt Ziesel, *Der deutsche Selbstmord: Diktatur der Meinungsmacher* (Velbert: Blick + Bild Verlag für politische Bildung, 1963), 313, 314, 317–18.

35. Erich Schmidt-Eenboom, *Undercover: Der BND und die deutschen Journalisten* (Cologne: Kiepenhauer & Witsch, 1998), 245–46.

36. Deborah Lipstadt, *Denying the Holocaust: The Growing Assault on Truth and Memory* (New York: The Free Press, 1993), 73; Ziesel to Krausnick, September 18, 1963, ETH NL Gisevius Correspondence 10.

37. Ergebnisprotokoll, August 2, 1963, IfZ ID 8/15; Tätigkeitsbericht, June 1964, IfZ ID 8/14.

38. Professor Hans Mommsen, interview with the Author, April 20, 2010, Feldafing; Mommsen, "Reichstagsbrand," 356.

39. Professor Hans Mommsen, interview with the Author, April 20, 2010, Feldafing.

40. Mommsen, "Reichstagsbrand," 353 and 353 note 3, 365 and 365 note 48, 380; BA-BL R.3003/56, Bl. 17 ff; Mommsen, "Reichstagsbrand," 385 and 385 note 143.

41. Mommsen, "Reichstagsbrand," 372–82, 407, 412.

42. Mommsen, "Reichstagsbrand," 352, 404–5.

43. "Tätigkeitsbericht vom Dezember 1957–Dezember 1958," IfZ Archive ID 8/11; *Gutachten des Instituts für Zeitgeschichte Bd. II* (Stuttgart: Deutsche Verlags-Anstalt, 1966), 9.

44. Hans Bernd Gisevius, "Reichstagsbrand im Zerrspiegel," *Die Zeit*, March 25, 1960.

45. Krausnick to GSTA Landgericht Berlin, May 5, 1960, LAB B Rep 058/6401, Bl. 1–2; Gisevius, Bemerkungen, July 14, 1960, ETH NL Gisevius 16.27; Gisevius to Schneider, March 31, 1960, ETH NL Gisevius 10 Correspondence, Schneider, Hans.

46. Gisevius to Oberloskamp, November 12, 1960, ETH NL Gisevius, 16.4; Schneider, *Reichstagsbrand*, 56; Schriftsatz from Oberloskamp, Brandt, Ortschig, August 28, 1961, in ETH NL Gisevius 16.21; Gisevius to Otto Grotewohl, March 28, 1960, in ETH NL Gisevius 10 Correspondence, Grotewohl, Otto.

47. Roesen, Schriftsatz, December 3, 1960, ETH NL Gisevius 16.6.

48. Harry Schulze-Wilde to Amtsgericht München, July 28 1961, TA.

49. Einstellung, IfZ ZS/A 7 Bd. 6; Harry Schulze-Wilde to Amtsgericht München, July 28 1961, TA.

50. Strindberg Statement, November 15, 1960, LNRW-D Rep. 372/990, Bl. 109–15; Strindberg, written statement, June 10, 1961, LNRW-D Rep. 372/992, Bl. 28.

51. Tobias to Dobbert, November 18, 1957, JA; Peter Brandes (Curt Riess) "Feuer über Deutschland," *Stern*, November 9, 1957, November 16, 1957, November 30, 1957.

52. "Contacts with Rudolf Diels," September 10, 1950, NARA Army/IRR Files D001018 Diels, Rudolf; Harry Wilde, "Rudolf Diels—Porträt eines verkannten

Mannes," *Politische Studien*, Bd. 9 Heft 99, July 1958: 475–81; Vermerk, October 14, 1983, TA.

53. Graml to Schneider, April 25, 1960, IfZ ZS/A7 Bd. 3/I; Justus Koch to Helmut Krausnick, May 6, 1960, IfZ ID 103/60; Krausnick to Gewehr, May 2, 1960, IfZ ID 103/60; Bahar and Kugel, *Reichstagsbrand*, 577.

54. Krausnick to Mommsen, September 30, 1963, in IfZ ID 103/100.

55. Tobias to Kraunsick, July 27, 1963, in IfZ ID 103/108.

56. Einstellung, IfZ ZS/A 7 Bd. 6.

57. Judgment, February 20, 1962, in ETH NL Gisevius 16.24, Gewehr gegen Gisevius. Weirdly enough, the copy of the judgment in Gisevius's papers obviously came from Tobias—the copy has Tobias's stamp on it with his address, "In den Sieben Stücken" Hannover. The judgment is marked by many red pencil underlinings that look like Tobias's; it is at any rate a document that came from Tobias, not a photocopy.

58. Oberloskamp to Gisevius and Holste, March 19, 1962, ETH NL Gisevius 16.24 Gewehr gegen Gisevius; Gisevius to Sommer, February 24, 1962, ETH NL Gisevius 16.27, Gewehr gegen Gisevius; OLG Düsseldorf, Judgment, August 6, 1963, ETH NL Gisevius 17.14 Gewehr gegen Gisevius Berufung. Again, curiously, Gisevius's copy bears one of Tobias's stamps.

59. OLG Düsseldorf, Judgment, August 6, 1963, in ETH NL Gisevius 17.14 Gewehr gegen Gisevius Berufung.

60. Carl to Gisevius, Holste and Oberloskamp, August 26, 1963, ETH NL Gisevius 17.14; Mommsen, "Reichstagsbrand," 358.

61. NJW 1966, 647; Bahar and Kugel, *Reichstagsbrand*, 791–92.

CONCLUSION

1. Karl-Heinz Janßen, "Calics Erzählungen," in Backes, *Reichstagsbrand*, 216–37, 216; Judgment, November 27, 1982, LAB B Rep. 039 Nr. 128 Bd. 3, Bl. 100 ff, Bl. 10.

2. Uwe Backes, "Das Internationale Kommitee zur wissenschaftlichen Erforschung der Ursachen und Folgen des Zweiten Weltkrieges," in Backes, *Reichstagsbrand*, 92–93; Tobias to Roesen, August 23, 1961, TA. It should be noted that politically there is one important exception on each side: Walther Hofer was a conservative, Hans Mommsen is a Social Democrat.

3. Schmidt Statement, December 19, 1968, Calic to Polizeipräs. Berlin, December 27, 1968. Tobias to GSTA, June 28, 1969, Tobias to Braschwitz, December 11, 1968, LAB B Rep 058/10792.

4. Walther Hofer et al., eds., *Der Reichstagsbrand: Eine wissenschaftliche Dokumentation* (Berlin: arani Verlag, 1972).

5. Walther Hofer et al., eds., *Der Reichstagsbrand: Eine wissenschaftliche Dokumentation* Bd. 2 (Berlin: arani Verlag, 1978); Köhler in Backes, *Reichstagsbrand*, 171, 187–92 and note 7, 283.

6. Karl-Heinz Janßen, "Geschichte aus der Dunkelkammer," *Die Zeit*, September 14, 1979; Tony Judt, *Postwar* (New York: Penguin, 2005), 472; Karl-Heinz Janßen, "Unter falscher Flagge," *Die Zeit*, October 5, 1979. In the 1950s Janßen had been a graduate student under the dean of conservative German historians, Gerhard Ritter; this may help explain his outlook. Broszat and Friedländer: "A Controversy About the Historicization of National Socialism," *New German Critique* 44, Spring–Summer 1988, 90–91, 94–96; Moeller, *War Stories*, 61.

7. Karl-Heinz Janßen, "Geschichte aus der Dunkelkammer," *Die Zeit*, September 14, 1979.

8. Judgment, November 27, 1982, LAB B Rep. 039/128 Bd. 3, Bl. 100ff, 126, 131, 133–35; Uwe Backes, "Das Internationale Komitee zur wissenschaftlichen Erforschung der Ursachen und Folgen des Zweiten Weltkrieges," in Backes, *Reichstagsbrand*, 92.

9. Marcus Giebeler, *Die Kontroverse um den Reichstagsbrand: Quellenprobleme und historiographische Paradigmen* (Munich: Martin Meidenbauer Verlagsbuchhandlung, 2010), 89–91.

10. Giebeler, *Kontroverse*, 91–94.

11. *Die Zeit*, September 21, 1979; Hersch Fischler, "Reichstagsbrand, Osthilfeskandal und das Ende von Weimar: Plädoyer für ein Quellenstudium jenseits verhärteter Polarisierungen," www.zlb.de/projekte/kulturbox-archiv/brand/, accessed June 13, 2013; Bericht, April 18, 1971, BStU MfS Allg. P 6117/74, Bl. 14–16; Handwritten note, February 20, 1974, BStU HA XX AP Nr. 22.217/92, Bl. 1.

12. Giebeler, *Kontroverse*, 98.

13. Alexander Bahar, "Tektonische Platten in Bewegung versetzt," *Junge Welt*, September 25, 2003; Bahar and Kugel, *Reichstagsbrand*, 660–63.

14. Ian Kershaw, *Hitler 1889–1936: Hubris* (New York: W.W. Norton, 1998), 456–60 and notes 111–28, 731–33. On historians' mistakes: Anson Rabinbach, for instance, adopts Tobias's position on the fire in his article on the *Brown Books* (though without citing *either* the English or German language version of Tobias's book). He makes a number of minor, and therefore forgivable, factual errors, although his statement "Göring had been president of the Reichstag since the *Nazi* takeover of the *Prussian* government in *1932*" indicates that he is not exactly at home in the history of these events. More significantly, he reverses an important observation by *Times* reporter Douglas Reed. Rabinbach writes that Reed "remarked at the time that there was only a 'pigeonhole of credulity' for a (Nazi) conspiracy." What Reed actually wrote was "The weight of probability and evidence against this theory [that van der Lubbe set fire to the Reichstag

alone] . . . is overwhelming, but in a world which every day produces proof that nothing is impossible a tiny pigeon hole of credulity must be reserved for it": Anson Rabinbach, "Staging Antifascism: The *Brown Book* of the Reichstag Fire and Hitler Terror," *New German Critique* 103 vol. 35 No. 1, Spring 2008: 97 ff, 100, 102; Reed, *Reichstag*, 9. In accounts of the fire in two of his books, Richard J. Evans also makes many minor factual errors. A graver error, however, is his mis-citation and/or mischaracterization of one source: He writes that "A recent attempt to suggest that the Nazis planned the fire rests on an exaggeration of similarities between earlier discussion papers on emergency powers, and the Reichstag fire decree." Here he claims to be speaking of a 1995 article by Bahar and Kugel, stressing the documentary evidence that became available in the 1990s. But that article actually makes no mention of the connection between the Reichstag Fire Decree and earlier emergency decrees. Professor Evans may have confused it with a later and much longer article co-written by Bahar, Kugel, and Jürgen Schmädeke. However, this article, nearly fifty pages long, devotes just over one page to the emergency decree and its precedents; the rest of the text deals, again, with the newly available empirical evidence about the fire and its putative perpetrators. Therefore it is hardly legitimate to say that the article "rests" on this matter. It is also possible that Evans was thinking of the article by Thomas Raithel and Irene Streng on the Reichstag Fire Decree, which *does* stress the relationship between the Reichstag Fire Decree and its Weimar precedents (though on the real decrees themselves, not "discussion papers" on them), but which does *not* take a position on the Reichstag fire controversy (though it is critical of Mommsen's argument): Evans, *Coming*, 519 note 58; Alexander Bahar and Wilfried Kugel, "Der Reichstagsbrand: Neue Aktenfunde entlarven die NS-Täter," *Zeitschrift für Geschichtswissenschaft*, vol. 43(9) 1995: 823–32; Jurgen Schmädeke, Alexander Bahar, and Wilfried Kugel, "Der Reichstagsbrand in neuem Licht," *Historische Zeitschrift* vol. 269 (3) 1999: 603–51; Thomas Raithel and Irene Streng, "Die Reichstagsbrandverordnung: Grundlegung der Diktatur mit den Instrumenten des Weimarer Ausnahmezustands," *VfZ* vol. 48(3), July 200: 413–60.

15. 27 VT [page number unclear, BStU 324].

16. TBJG Teil 1 Bd. 9, 237.

17. Hermann Graml, "Zur Debatte über den Reichstagsbrand," in Deiseroth, *Reichstagsbrand*, 32, 34 note 15; Friedländer, *Years of Persecution*, 268–74; Friedländer, *Years of Extermination*, 276.

18. Cornelis van der Lubbe quoted in Tobias, *Reichstagbrand*, 14.

19. Conze et al., *Das Amt*, although much of this argument had appeared over thirty years earlier in Christopher Browning, *The Final Solution and the German Foreign Office: A Study of Referat D III of Abteilung Deutschland 1940–1943* (New York: Holmes & Maier Publishers, Inc., 1978); Ulrich Herbert, *Best:*

Biographische Studien über Radikalismus, Weltanschauung und Vernunft 1903–1989 (Bonn: Verlag J.H.W. Dietz Nachfolger, 1996) 501, 641; Michael Wildt, *Generation der Unbedingten: Das Führungskorps des Reichssicherheitshauptamtes* (Hamburg: Hamburger Editions, 2003), 239, 746 ff; Klaus-Michael Mallmann and Andrej Angrick, "Die Mörder sind unter uns: Gestapo Bedienstete in den Nachfolgegesellschaften des Dritten Reiches," in Mallmann and Angrick, eds., *Die Gestapo nach 1945: Karrieren, Konflikte, Konstructionen* (Darmstadt: Wissenschaftliche Buchgesellschaft, 2009), 21–22.

20. Wigbert Benz, *Paul Carell: Ribbentrops Pressechef Paul Karl Schmidt vor und nach 1945* (Berlin: Wissenschaftlicher Verlag Berlin, 2005); Christian Plöger, *Von Ribbentrop zu Springer: Zu Leben und Wirken von Paul Karl Schmidt alias Paul Carell* (Marburg: Tectum Verlag, 2009); Lutz Hachmeister, *Der Gegnerforscher: Die Karriere des SS-Führers Franz Alfred Six* (Munich: C.H. Beck, 1998); Raithel and Strenge, "Die Reichstagsbrandverordnung;" Giebeler, *Kontroverse*, 225.

21. Graml, "Debatte," in Deiseroth, *Reichstagsbrand*, 28; Swett, *Neighbors and Enemies*.

22. Tony Judt with Timothy Snyder, *Thinking the Twentieth Century* (New York: The Penguin Press, 2012), Kindle ed. Loc 5518; Snyder, *Bloodlands*, 197.

23. Markus Henneke, e-mail to the Author, January 10, 2011.

24. Cullen, *Reichstag*, 242–44.

25. Cullen, *Reichstag*, 245–46; Beevor, *Fall of Berlin*, 388–96; Anne Applebaum, *Iron Curtain: The Crushing of Eastern Europe 1944–1956* (New York: Doubleday, 2012), 26.

26. Cullen, *Reichstag*, 264–70.

27. Cullen, *Reichstag*, 267–89; http://www.christojeanneclaude.net/major_reichstag .shtml, accessed March 25, 2012.

28. Cullen, *Reichstag*, 284–85.

29. http://www.generalbundesanwalt.de/prnt/showpress.php?newsid=298, visited February 12, 2012; "75 Years On, Executed Reichstag Arsonist Finally Wins Pardon," *Guardian*, January 11, 2008, http://www.guardian.co.uk/world/2008/ jan/12/secondworldwar.germany visited February 12, 2012; Giebeler, *Kontroverse*, 44–45.

EPILOGUE

1. All Tobias quotes in this section unless otherwise noted are from interviews with Fritz Tobias, Hannover, July 20, 2008, and July 4, 2009.

2. The comment about the interest of the Federal Archives is from Tobias to the Author, March 12, 2009.

ARCHIVAL SOURCES

. . . .

PUBLIC ARCHIVES, GERMANY

POLITISCHES ARCHIV DES AUSWÄRTIGEN AMTS, BERLIN (PA-AA)

R. 98304 Reichstagswahl 1933

R. 98307 Komm. Partei

R. 98417 Reichstagsbrandstiftung

R. 98422–28 Lügenpropaganda, Boykottbewegung

R. 98444–98445 Allgem. Bekämpfung der Hetz und Greuelpropaganda

R. 99488 Hetze seitens deutscher Emigranten

R. 99489 Die schwarze Front (Otto Strasser)

R. 99493 Kommunistische und marxistische Zersetzungsarbeit

R. 99505 Kurt Torgler

R. 99606 Dr. Hermann Rauschning

BAYERISCHES STAATSARCHIV MÜNCHEN (BSM)

Spruchkammer Akten Karton 666, Heisig, Helmut

BAYERISCHES STAATSARCHIV NÜRNBERG (BSN)

Rep 502, KV Anklage Interrogations, various volumes

BAYERISCHES STAATSARCHIV WÜRZBURG (BSW)

Staatsanwaltschaft Würzburg 407, Helmut Heisig
Staatsanwaltschaft Würzburg 2446, Helmut Heisig

BERLINER FEUERWEHR ARCHIV, BERLIN (BFA)

Materials on the Reichstag fire, Oberbranddirektor Gempp and
Oberbranddirektor Wagner.

LANDESARCHIV BERLIN (LAB)

A Rep 358–01 Staatsanwaltschaft Berlin, various volumes
B Rep 39/128 Calic c/a Dönhoff
B Rep 58, Staatsanwaltschaft Berlin, various volumes
C Rep 300/22–27 Köpenicker Blutwoche
C Rep 375-01-13/1525/A1 Braschwitz
A Pr.Br.Rep. 030-Polizeipräsidium Berlin 7505 Schutzpolizei

BUNDESARCHIV BERLIN-LICHTERFELDE (BA-BL)

NS 23
R. 43/II Reichskanzlei
R. 58 RSHA
R. 84 III Reichslandbund Pressearchiv, various volumes
R. 1501 Reichsministerium des Innern
R. 3001 Justizministerium Personalakten
R. 3002 Reichsgericht Personalakten
R. 3003 Oberreichsanwalt beim Reichsgericht Bde. 1–313
R. 3901 Reichsarbeitsministerium Personalakten
Ehemal. BDC-Akten
ZA II 10156
ZA VI/372
ZB 1049
ZM 772
ZR 699 A

BUNDESARCHIV KOBLENZ (BA-K)

B 141/17511, 427513 van der Lubbe Wiederaufnahme
B 362 Bundesanwaltschaft
N 1211 Nachlass Otto Schmidt-Hannover
N 1231 Nachlass Alfred Hugenberg
N 1274 Nachlass Ernst Fraenkel
N 1385 Nachlass Curt Riess
N 1415 Nachlass Barbara Just-Dahlmann
Z/42/IV/1960 Ermittlungssache gegen Rudolf Diels
ZSg.1-44/7 (375) *Wie die Nazi regieren*

BUNDESARCHIV LUDWIGSBURG (BA-L)

B 162/2470 Tagebuch des Reichsjustizminister Dr. Gürtner
B 162/2973 Dr. Rudolf Braschwitz wegen Aussageerpressung u.a.
B 162/5302 Massenerschießungen in Luzk und Umgebung
B 162/21252 Dr. Zirpins wegen Verdachts der Beihilfe zum vielfachen
    Morde (Ghetto Lodz)
B 162/43086 Gegen Gewehr, Hans Georg, Schmidt, Willi
    (Schweinebacke)

DER BUNDESBEAUFTRAGTE FÜR DIE UNTERLAGEN DES
STAATSSICHERHEITSDIENSTES DER EHEMALIGEN DEUTSCHEN
DEMOKRATISCHEN REPUBLIK, BERLIN (BSTU)

MfS Allg. P 2601/76
MfS Allg. P 6117/74
MfS ASt 35 Js 164/48 GA Bd 1
MfS ASt Ic 41/53
MfS HA IX/11 FV 6170 Bd. 1–7
MfS HA IX/11 SV 1/81 Bd. 35
MfS HA IX/11 SV 9/74
MfS HA IX Nr. 20809
MfS HA IX/11 AB 1163
MfS HA VIII/RF/1764/46
MfS HA IX/11 PA 711

MfS HA XX AP Nr. 22.217/92
MfS HA-IX Nr. 21312
MfS ZAIG Nr. 10187

GEHEIMES STAATSARCHIV PREUSSISCHER KULTURBESITZ, BERLIN (GSTA)

I HA R. 77 Innenministerium
I HA R. 84a Justizministerium
I HA R. 90 P Geheimes Staatspolizeiamt
XX HA R. 10 Regierung Königsberg

INSTITUT FÜR ZEITGESCHICHTE, MÜNCHEN (IFZ)

ED 82 Hans Bernd Gisevius
ED 129/1 Joachim Friedrich von Alt-Stutterheim
Fa 74 Gewehr, Hans Georg
ID 4 Kuratorium Protokolle
ID 6 Stiftungsrat Protokolle
ID 8 Wissenschaftlicher Beirat Protokolle
ID 90, 102, 103 Hausarchiv
MA 198/2 Preußisches Innenministerium
ZS/A7 Reichstagsbrand
ZS/A42 Paul Löbe
ZS 20 Heinrich Brüning
ZS 199 Walter Zirpins
ZS 428 Hermann Göring

NIEDERSÄCHSISCHES HAUPTSTAATSARCHIV HANNOVER (NHH)

Nds. 100 (01) Acc. 134/97 Nr. 63, Diels, Rudolf
Nds. 132 Hannover Acc. 80/86, Personalakten Dr. Walter
  Zirpins
Nds. 171 Hannover Nr. 28640, Rudolf Diels
  Entnazifizierungsakten
VVP 46, Nachlaß Rudolf Diels

ARCHIVAL SOURCES

LANDESARCHIV NORDRHEIN-WESTFALEN, ABTEILUNG RHEINLAND,
HAUPTSTAATSARCHIV DÜSSELDORF (LNRW-D)

NW 377/4362 Gegen Rudolf Braschwitz wegen Körperverletzung
NW Pe Nr. 118 Dr. Heinrich Schnitzler Personal-Akten
NW 130 Nr. 168 Innenministerium NRW Beamtenrechte
NW 30 Nr. 456 Kabinettsvorgang
NW 1000 Nr. 20256 Rudolf Braschwitz, Entnazifizierungsakten
NW 1023 Nr. 1865 Heinrich Schnitzler, Entnazifizierungsakten
NW-O Nr. 5042 Heinrich Schnitzler, Verleihung Bundesverdienstkreuz
Rep 372/278 Verfahren gegen Diels
Rep 372/990–992 Verfahren gegen Gewehr

LANDESARCHIV NORDRHEIN-WESTFALEN, ABTEILUNG WESTFALEN,
MÜNSTER (LNRW-M)

Personalakten (neue Verzeichnung) Nr. 2688 Bde. 1–3, Rudolf Braschwitz

LANDESARCHIV SCHLESWIG-HOLSTEIN, SCHLESWIG (LSH)

Abt. 301 Akten des Ober-Präsidiums der Provinz Schleswig-Holstein
Abt. 309 Akten der Regierung zu Schleswig

PUBLIC ARCHIVES IN OTHER COUNTRIES

ZEITGESCHICHTLICHES ARCHIV, EIDGENÖSSISCHE TECHNISCHE
HOCHSCHULE, ZÜRICH, SWITZERLAND (ETH)

Hans Bernd Gisevius, Nachlass

BRITISH NATIONAL ARCHIVES, LONDON, UK (BNA)

FO 1019/94 Evidence by Dr. Rudolf Diels
KV 4/11 Visit of Captain Liddell to Berlin
WO 309/294 Interrogation of Dr. Rudolf Diels
WO 309/768 Report on SS Standartenführer Dr. R Diels

ARCHIVAL SOURCES

IMPERIAL WAR MUSEUM ARCHIVES, DUXFORD, UK (IWM)

Otto John Papers
Sefton Delmer Papers

MANCHESTER GUARDIAN ARCHIVE, LONDON, UK (MGA)

Correspondence and Memos of Frederick Voigt and
W. P. Crozier

BUTLER LIBRARY, COLUMBIA UNIVERSITY, NEW YORK, USA (BL)

H. R. Knickerbocker Papers

LIBRARY OF CONGRESS, WASHINGTON, D.C., USA (LOC)

Martha Dodd Papers
Edgar Ansell Mowrer Papers

NATIONAL ARCHIVES AND RECORDS ADMINISTRATION, COLLEGE PARK,
MARYLAND, USA (NARA)

BDC Collections
RG 65 230/86/04/05, Records of the FBI, Hans Bernd
    Gisevius
RG 238 War Crimes Records Collection
RG 319 Records of the Army Staff, Rudolf Diels, Otto Strasser
RG 263 Records of the CIA, Horst Mahnke, Paul Dickopf, Hubert
    Schrübbers

ARCHIVE OF THE UNITED STATES HOLOCAUST MEMORIAL MUSEUM,
WASHINGTON, D.C. (USHMM)

RG 71 Robert M.W. Kempner Papers

MATERIALS IN PRIVATE COLLECTIONS

LIBRARY AND ARCHIVE OF HERRN RECHTSANWALT GERHARD JUNGFER, BERLIN (JA)

Documents from the van der Lubbe *Wiederaufnahme*; materials on Arthur Brandt

COLLECTION OF HERRN POLIZEIPRÄSIDENT A.D. DIERK SCHNITZLER, BONN, AND HERRN KLAUS-MICHAEL SCHNITZLER, DÜSSELDORF

Heinrich Schnitzler, Nachlass

Note on the Schnitzler Nachlass: in the endnotes, references to Schnitzler's papers are given as "NL Schnitzler I" and "NL Schnitzler II." Material cited as "NL Schnitzler I" was in the possession of Schnitzler's sons when they generously gave me the chance to see it in January, 2012; I saw original documents and took photographs of them. Material cited as "NL Schnitzler II" was kindly sent to me by Dr. Alexander Bahar in the form of a pdf of photocopies in August 2009. My efforts to learn something of the provenance of the "NL Schnitzler II" documents yielded an unclear result. Dr. Bahar advised me that the copies came from the Swiss Bundesarchiv, and that they had been made by Professor Christoph Graf. Professor Graf, however, although he remembered visiting Schnitzler's brother and son in September 1976 and seeing the papers, by 2009 no longer possessed any copies of them and also denied that they were deposited in the Swiss Bundesarchiv. Herr Dierk and Herr Klaus-Michael Schnitzler, for their part, say that Professor Graf took documents from them and never returned them. Putting all of this together, I strongly suspect that the copies which Dr. Bahar sent me were those gathered by Professor Graf in 1976. I sent these copies in turn to Herrn Dierk and Herrn Klaus-Michael Schnitzler. After very careful comparisons of the "NL Schnitzler II" documents with those from "NL Schnitzler I" and other sources, looking at typefaces, typing style, and handwriting and signatures, as well as content, I have no doubts whatsoever regarding the authenticity of the "NL Schnitzler II" documents. Indeed copies of some of these documents can be found in publicly accessible archives. But given the issues that have arisen in the Reichstag fire controversy, the reader is entitled to know of these issues and so I have preserved the distinction.

ARCHIVAL SOURCES

ARCHIVE OF THE *SPIEGEL*, HAMBURG (SPA)

Materials from the Augstein Nachlass, Tobias Papers, VIPS Collection

LIBRARY AND ARCHIVE OF HERRN MINISTERIALRAT A.D. FRITZ TOBIAS, HANNOVER (TA)

Materials from his collection on Rudolf Diels

CORRESPONDENCE

Correspondence and conversations with Karl Otmar von Aretin, Alexander Bahar, Heinz Egleder, Hersch Fischler, Markus Henneke, Gerhard Jungfer, Peter-Ferdinand Koch, Hans Mommsen, Thomas Polgar, Peter Schildhauer, Dierk and Klaus-Michael Schnitzler, Peter Sichel, Karl Stephan, Fritz Tobias, Lothar Weber, and Friedrich Winterhager

INDEX

....

Abegg, Wilhelm, 29–33, 78, 180
Adenauer, Konrad, 26, 77, 236–39, 241, 276, 278–79, 295
Adermann, Paul, 149–50
Adler, H. G., 222, 296
Albada, Piet van, 89–90, 110–11, 146
Albrecht, Herbert, 111–12, 151, 319
Algemeen Handelsblad, 103
Angriff, 48–49, 51, 55, 58, 65, 68, 312
Apfel, Alfred, 48, 53
Arbeiter Illustrierte Zeitung, 127
Arendt, Hannah, 17, 25
Aretin, Karl Otmar von, 288, 310
Arndt, Adolf, 49, 57, 193–94, 302, 307, 350n44
Arnim, Achim von, 154
Association of Persecutees of the Nazi Regime, 173
Augstein, Josef, 240
Augstein, Rudolf, 238–41, 256, 258, 264, 272, 279–81, 292
August Wilhelm (Hohenzollern), 203

Bach-Zelewski, Erich von dem, 200, 261
Bahar, Alexander, 170, 206, 231, 257, 315, 323, 355n10

Bartov, Omer, 200
Baumgarten, Paul, 326–27
Beck, Hermann, 133
Becker, Alois Eugen, 106, 254, 323
Becker, Hans Detlev, 281
Becker, Rudolf, 27
Bennemann, Otto, 281
Berlin am Morgen, 127
Berlin Document Center, 206, 258, 269, 286
Berliner Tageblatt, 40, 53, 71–72
Bernhard, Georg, 190
Best, Werner, 24–25, 67–68, 322
BKA. *See* Federal Criminal Police Office
Blomberg, Werner von, 62
Blum, Leon, 173, 313
Bode, Heinrich L., 271
Boxheimer Documents, 67–68, 320
Bracht, Franz, 32–34, 36, 83
Brandt, Arthur, 251–56, 301, 307, 327, 329
Brandt, Willy, 235, 310
Braschwitz, Rudolf, 70, 81, 106–110, 148, 204, 219, 226, 251, 260–63, 272–73, 289–90, 298–99, 322, 325, 376n10, 384n37

Braun, Otto, 30–32, 63, 77
Breimer, Lisa, 190–91, 305
Breiting, Richard, 310–11, 314
Brömme, Albrecht, 120
Bross, Werner, 201
Broszat, Martin, 284, 288, 290, 312–13
Brown Book, 126–32, 134, 139, 149, 152, 158, 164, 175, 188, 205, 253, 255, 266
Brüning, August, 120, 153
Brüning, Heinrich, 30, 50, 57, 60, 184
Bülow-Schwante, Vicco von, 225
Bunge (Commissar), 12–13, 107, 147, 319
Bünger, Wilhelm, 140, 142–47, 154, 157–162, 167–169, 264
Buske, Alfred, 42–43
Buwert, Karl, 3, 8–10, 94, 150, 165, 267–8
BZ am Mittag, 17

Cabromal (potassium bromide), 171
Calic, Edouard, 173, 309–16, 324, 365n9
Center Party, 30, 71, 77
Central Office of the State Justice Ministries for the Investigation of National Socialist Crimes (Ludwigsburg), 24, 259–60, 263, 280–81, 300
Christo, 326–27
CIA (Central Intelligence Agency), 240, 260, 276
CIC (Counter Intelligence Corps), 275–77
Chicago Tribune, 135
Coenders, Hermann, 153, 167–68

Combat League against Fascism (Kampfbund gegen Faschismus), 22, 36
Comintern (Communist International), 23, 109, 127, 172
Communist Party of Germany, 29–32, 34–36, 68–70, 73–75, 81

Daluege, Kurt, 46, 87, 100, 135–37, 175, 177–78, 241
"Decree Against Betrayal of the German People," 76
"Decree in the Drawer" (Schubkastenordnung), 70–71
Deh, Karl, 42–43
Dell, Robert, 139
Delp, Ludwig, 291–94
Delmer, Sefton (Tom), 15
denazification, 23–24, 214–18, 220–21, 223, 225–30, 233, 235, 238–9, 244, 246–47, 249–50, 259–60, 274, 295
Department IA (Berlin Political Police) 15, 29, 35, 51, 55, 70, 81–82, 106–7
Deutsche Allgemeine Zeitung, 99–100, 103, 124
Deutsche Rundschau, 240
Dickopf, Paul, 260
Diels, Hildegard (Mannesmann), 179
Diels, Ilse (Göring), 28, 178–79
Diels, Rudolf, 15–18, 24, 26–37, 41–43, 51, 65, 69, 73–74, 79, 83–87, 97, 100, 104, 106–9, 123–26, 136–39, 144–45, 147, 155, 162–64, 171–72, 174–180, 181–196, 201–6, 208–14, 218–22, 224–241, 246–49, 254–55, 262, 264–66, 271, 274–77, 280, 284, 298–99, 302–8, 318, 323, 332–33, 355n1, 372n29, 372n35, 383n28

Dimitrov, Georgi, 23, 109–10, 129, 141–44, 148, 151, 154–59, 162, 164, 166, 171–75, 180, 219, 232, 235, 258, 326, 329
Dobbert (Berlin prosecutor), 256, 301
Döblin, Alfred, 99
Dodd, Martha, 26, 142, 155–57, 176–77
Dodd, William E., 26, 73, 125, 176
Donovan, William, 276
Dorls, Fritz, 305–6
DNVP, 8, 22, 31, 52, 62–6, 72–75, 78–79, 81–82, 99–100, 135–36, 184, 300, 315
Dulles, Allen, 179, 185–86, 240, 274, 276

Ebbutt, Norman, 125, 129
Ebermayer, Erich, 43, 62, 67, 77, 98
Ebermayer, Ludwig, 62–63, 98
Eden Dance Palace trial, 50
Ehrhardt, Hermann, 45
Eichmann, Adolf, 18, 24, 218, 259
Einsatzgruppen, 23, 184, 204, 240, 258, 289–90, 321
Enabling Law, 166
Ernst, Karl, 34, 46, 53–58, 84, 130–31, 144, 171, 174–76, 179, 186, 188–89, 193, 195–98, 200, 202–5, 210–14, 224, 255, 266, 302, 304, 306, 319
Erzberger, Matthias, 45, 81
Evans, Richard J., 21, 393n14

Faber-Castell, Countess Nina von, 182–83, 231, 233, 302
Faber-Castell, Count Roland von, 182–83, 302
FBI, 15, 278–79, 288
Federal Criminal Police Office (BKA), 244, 260, 275

Feistel, Wendelin, 55–57
Felseneck, SA attack on, 48–49
Fememord trials, 56
Fest, Joachim, 68, 74
Fiedler, Richard, 131, 203
Fighting Ring (Kampfring), 22, 184, 204
Fischer (Schweder), Bernhard, 204, 258
Fischer, Ruth, 184
Fischler, Hersch, 293, 314–15, 323
Flöter, Hans, 8, 267–68
Foster, Norman, 326
Fraenkel, Ernst, 19–21, 142, 324, 384n37
François-Poncet, André, 98
Frank, Hans, 54, 57, 72–73, 83, 163, 218
Frankfurter Hefte, 236
Frankfurter Rundschau, 254, 302
Frankfurter Zeitung, 124
Fraser, Geoffrey, 135
Frei, Norbert, 235
Freikorps, 45–46, 53, 111
Freisler, Roland, 54, 56, 179, 202, 208, 210
Frick, Wilhelm (Nazi interior minister), 16, 62, 72, 76, 96, 185, 201
Frick, Wilhelm (Swiss lawyer and publisher), 231
Friedländer, Saul, 58–59, 312, 320
Friedrich, Jörg, 218
Frischauer, Willi, 122, 129
Frontbann, 46, 54, 196
Fürst, Max, 62

Galle, Reinhold, 14, 149
Gayl, Baron Wilhelm von, 70
Geheime Feldpolizei, 272, 331
Gehlen, Reinhard, 275, 297, 386n71
Gempp, Walter, 116, 131–34, 138, 151–53, 168

German National People's Party. *See* DNVP

Germania (newspaper), 72

Germania (planned city), 325

Gestapa. *See* Gestapo

Gestapo, 20, 24, 27, 34–35, 42, 67, 78, 80, 106–7, 110, 124, 126, 128–29, 137–39, 145, 147, 163–64, 168, 174–79, 181–83, 185–87, 189–90, 192–94, 198, 201–9, 210–13, 216–24, 226–29, 231, 233–34, 241, 244, 246, 254, 260–62, 264–65, 272–74, 279–80, 296, 302–5, 310–11, 317, 322, 331

Gewehr, Hans Georg, 53–54, 56–57, 84, 115, 179, 188–89, 191–92, 194, 196–201, 206, 210, 213–14, 235, 255, 266, 285, 287–90, 300–8, 319, 325, 332

Gisevius, Hans Bernd, 17–19, 25, 29, 65, 94, 163–64, 175–77, 179, 183–95, 197, 201–3, 205–6, 210–13, 221, 224, 228–29, 231, 240–41, 253, 262, 266, 269, 272, 274, 276–79, 285–87, 300–8, 318, 330, 332, 387n77

Globke, Hans, 26, 295

Goebbels, Joseph, 15–16, 22, 38–59, 61–62, 65–69, 72, 74–76, 81–83, 86, 104, 125–26, 130, 140, 158–59, 181, 188, 193, 213, 255, 319–21

Goerdeler, Carl, 65, 145, 226

Göring, Hermann, 15–16, 27–28, 33–36, 51, 53, 62, 64, 69–71, 73, 75, 78–80, 85–86, 96–100, 102, 107–8, 115–16, 122, 125, 129–30, 132, 134–35, 138, 145, 150, 152, 154–59, 162–64, 166, 168, 171–72, 175–180, 181, 185, 188,

192–93, 195–96, 201, 204, 208–10, 212–14, 225, 233–35, 254, 258, 261, 264–65, 298, 304, 319–20, 323, 355n1, 392n14

Graf, Christoph, 314–15

Gräfe, Heinz, 99

Graml, Hermann, 284–86, 288, 290, 300–301, 305–6, 318, 320, 323–24, 389n28

Grauert, Ludwig, 128, 175–76, 183, 204, 265

"Greater Berlin Decree," 97

Gross, Babette, 127, 129

Grossmann, Kurt, 79

Grothe, Otto, 110, 148–49, 223

Gundolf, Friedrich, 39–40

Gürtner, Franz, 76, 163, 169

Haffner, Sebastian, 35, 62, 98

Halacz, Erich von, 244–45, 251

Hancock, Eleanor, 58

Hanfstaengl, Ernst, 51, 124, 145

Hanussen, Jan Erik, 131–32

Harden, Maximilian, 40–41

Harzburg Front, 52, 65

Hassell, Ulrich von, 178

Haubach, Josef, 222, 230–31

Hays, Arthur Garfield, 126, 141, 145

Heartfield, John, 127, 155

Heinemann, Gustav, 279

Heines, Edmund, 130–31, 135–36, 144

Heinz, Friedrich Wilhelm, 81

Heisig, Helmut, 87–88, 102–11, 144, 146–49, 163–65, 219–223, 229–30, 232–33, 235, 238, 260, 262–66, 270–73, 289–90, 298–99, 308, 316, 322, 325, 355n10

Helldorff, Wolf Heinrich Count von, 33–34, 46, 53–57, 68, 84, 87, 106–7, 130–31, 154–56, 179, 196–97, 199–200, 226, 319, 347n19
Heller, Reinhold, 70, 109, 162–63, 171–72, 262, 298, 311
Helmer, Johann, 109, 148, 166, 223
Herzfelde, Wieland, 78
Hess, Rudolf, 59, 313
Het Vaderland, 103
Heuss, Theodor, 41, 244, 276
Heydrich, Reinhard, 24–25, 27–28, 67, 177–78, 183, 210, 227–28, 231, 241–42, 311
Himmler, Heinrich, 24, 128, 172, 175, 177–79, 181, 198, 200, 204, 227, 231, 273, 306
Hindenburg, Paul von, 19, 30, 32, 60–62, 64–65, 69, 71, 76, 78–79, 169
Hinkler, Paul, 163, 175–76
Hintze, Willi, 92, 321
Hitler, Adolf, 15–20, 22, 28, 31, 34, 40, 43–47, 50–51, 54, 58–59, 60–63, 66–68, 71–72, 74–77, 79, 81, 96, 130, 134, 145, 155–56, 158, 169, 172, 176–78, 192–93, 198, 202, 232, 234–35, 250, 265, 269, 272–73, 297–99, 320, 325, 330
Hoch, Anton, 287, 290
Hodenberg, Christina von, 257
Hoesch, Leopold von, 158
Hofer, Walther, 311, 313–15, 325, 391n2
Hoffmann, Heinrich, 182
Hoggan, David, 285, 297, 324
Höhler, Albrecht (Ali), 48, 58, 174, 186–87, 192–94, 201–4, 206–7, 210, 213, 224, 305

Holocaust (miniseries), 312
Hugenberg, Alfred, 31, 33, 61–62, 64–66, 78–79, 100, 126, 135, 184

Institut für Zeitgeschichte (Institute for Contemporary History), 206, 259, 267, 283–98, 300–301, 305–6, 314–17, 322, 324
Iron Front (*Eiserne Front*), 22
Irving, David, 21, 218, 273, 317–18

Jahnecke, Walter, 91–92, 147, 321
Janßen, Karl-Heinz, 311–15, 324, 392n6
Jeanne-Claude, 326–27
John, Otto, 275–79
Josse, Emil, 112–15, 151, 299
Judt, Tony, 173, 269
Jungfer, Gerhard, 253, 329
Just-Dahlmann, Barbara, 280–81

Kalnoky, Countess Ingeborg, 28, 182–83, 185–86, 194
Kasper, Wilhelm, 31–32, 232
Katyn shootings, 222, 325, 329
Katz, Otto, 127, 137
Kellerhoff, Sven Felix, 107, 361–62n110
Kempner, Robert M. W., 26, 28, 35–36, 79, 183, 193–96, 201, 214, 220, 255, 295, 329
Kerrl, Hans, 205, 211–12
Kershaw, Ian, 21, 289, 316
Kessel, Eugen von, 311, 314
Kessler, Count Harry, 78
Kiaulehn, Walter, 17, 25
Kisch, Egon Erwin, 172
Klemm, Audrey von, 175
Klotz, Waldemar, 11–13, 113–14
Klotz, Helmut, 177

Knickerbocker, H. R., 123–25
Knospe, Franz, 310
Koch, Erich, 83
Koch, Peter-Ferdinand, 280
Koestler, Arthur, 126–27, 130
Kogon, Eugen, 236, 278
Königsberg, SA arson attacks in, 82–84
Königsberger Hartungsche Zeitung, 83
Kopf, Hinrich Wilhelm, 281
KPD. *See* Communist Party of Germany
Krausnick, Helmut, 205–6, 213, 273,
 279, 284–97, 300–301, 305–6, 310,
 317, 324
Kristall, 240, 290
Kristallnacht, 58–59, 75, 320–21
Kristen, Theodor, 112–13, 116
Krüger, Hans-Georg, 199
Kugel, Wilfried, 170, 206, 231, 257,
 315, 323, 355n10
Kugler, Ferdinand, 112, 142, 148
Kurfürstendamm riot, 52–57, 70,
 83–84, 110, 155, 193–94, 197, 218,
 319–21

Landvolk, 81
Lateit, Emil, 9–11, 14, 114, 153, 268
Law for Restitution for National
 Socialist Injustice (Berlin), 251–52,
 254
Lemmer, Ernst, 140, 143–45, 151–52,
 160
Lessenthin, Fritz, 82
Levetzow, Magnus von, 87
Levi, Pierre, 127
lex van der Lubbe (van der Lubbe's Law),
 166, 327
Liddell, Guy, 74, 108, 123
Lipstadt, Deborah, 218
Litten, Hans, 62, 128, 328
Löbe, Paul, 225, 238, 311

Lochner, Louis P., 125, 205
Lodz, 241–44, 247, 270–71, 281
Lodz (Ghetto), 23, 242–45, 263
Loevy, S. A. (firm), 4
Lohse, Hinrich, 63
Longerich, Peter, 45, 83
Losigkeit (Constable), 9–11, 14
Ludecke, Kurt, 99, 124
Lutze, Viktor, 272
Luxembourg Committee, 173, 310–11,
 313–15, 324

Maasbode, 103
Mahnke, Horst, 240, 290
Maikowski, Hans, 42, 46, 64, 106,
 111
Manchester Guardian, 73, 78, 125, 136,
 138–39, 142, 146–47, 153, 157–60,
 162
Marowsky, Kurt, 147, 165, 172
Martini, Winfried, 27
Meissner, Otto, 196
Menzel, Walter, 227
Merseburger, Peter, 239
Meusser, Fritz, 111
Meyer–Collings (interpreter), 159
MI5, 15, 74, 108, 123
Mohrenschildt, Walter von, 131, 203
Möller, Horst, 294
Mommsen, Hans, 21, 73–74, 91,
 120, 232, 283–84, 287, 289–94,
 296, 298–300, 302, 305, 308, 313,
 315–18, 323, 331, 391n2, 393n14
Münzenberg, Willi, 22, 126–30, 135,
 137, 172–75, 266, 324, 326

National Socialist Germany Workers'
 Party (Nazi Party), 19, 30–31, 33,
 40–41, 44–46, 48–54, 60–61,
 63–69, 71–76, 81–84, 99

Nebe, Arthur, 86, 136, 174–75, 177, 183–84, 186–89, 194, 201, 212, 244, 261–62
Neue Politik, 229, 231, 233
Neue Zürcher Zeitung, 140, 151
Neuer Vorwärts, 136–38, 171
"Neumann" (mysterious witness), 9, 267–68
Neurath, Constantin von, 62, 64, 123, 169
New York Times, 171, 353n46
Niemöller, Martin, 278–79, 295, 387n77
Niethammer, Lutz, 217
Nieuwe Rotterdamsche Courant, 103
"Night of the Long Knives" (Röhm purge), 18, 130–31, 58, 187, 193, 196, 198, 202, 224, 226, 228, 234, 240, 272, 303–4, 314, 330
NKVD (People's Commissariat for Internal affairs), 51, 325
nulla poena sine lege, 166
Nuremberg Laws, 26, 295, 302
Nuremberg Trials, 26, 97, 174–76, 181–214, 218, 220–22, 224, 230–31, 235, 258

Oberfohren, Ernst, 8, 63–64, 66, 79, 131, 134–39, 237, 261, 266
Office for Constitutional Protection (Federal) (Bundesamt für Verfassungsschutz), 15, 275–77, 278–79, 281–82
Office for Constitutional Protection (Lower Saxony), 20, 250, 272, 277–82, 286–88, 387n77
Organization Consul, 45, 81
Orwell, George, 125
OSS (Office of Strategic Services), 179, 185, 274

Papen, Franz von, 30–34, 60–65, 70, 78, 97, 100, 136, 180, 218, 313
Pariser Tageblatt, 190
Parrisius, Felix, 140–41, 162, 169
Pechel, Rudolf, 240
Petkov, Nikola, 173
Pfundtner, Hans, 172
Pieck, Wilhelm, 127
Poeschel, Hermann, 10, 11, 14
Pohlenz, Walter, 106, 174, 203, 224
Polchow, Fritz, 12–14, 270, 285, 311
Polgar, Thomas, 276
Popitz, Johannes, 7
Popov, Blagoi, 109–10, 141, 148, 164, 172, 232, 329
Popular Front, 23, 172–73, 310
"Potempa murderers," 69
protective custody (Schutzhaft), 37, 70, 97, 124
Prussian Council of State, 77–78
Prussian Interior Ministry, 26, 28–29, 31, 33, 35–36, 55, 69–70, 82, 86, 100, 154, 175, 183, 195, 323
Public Enlightenment and Propaganda, Ministry of, 42, 139–40, 159
Puhle, Emil, 11–13, 270, 311

Quaatz, Reinhold, 64, 73, 79, 184

Raben (Criminal Secretary), 110, 150–51, 172
Rall, Adolf, 174, 187–90, 192–94, 201, 205–13, 269, 285, 301–4, 306–8, 318
Rathenau, Walther, 45, 81
Red Frontfighters' League (Roter Frontkämpferbund), 22, 36, 54, 110

Reed, Douglas, 104–5, 116, 125,
140, 143–44, 148, 150–53, 158–59,
162
Reese, Maria, 137
Reich Security Main Office (RSHA),
183, 216, 241, 244
Reich Supreme Court, 141, 167–68
Reichbanner Black-Red-Gold
(*Reichsbanner Schwarz-Rot-Gold*), 22,
72, 211
Reichstag (building), layout of, 4–7;
plenary chamber of, 5, 9–15, 95–96,
10–12, 112–21, 133, 145, 153,
161, 165, 229, 233, 326, 361; work
routine of, 3–4; history after 1933,
325–27
Reichstag (institution), deputies of,
5, 8; elections to, 60–61, 65, 71
Reichstag fire, scientific details of, 12,
112–121
Reichstag Fire Decree, 19–21, 96–98,
254, 323, 327, 393n14
Reichstag fire trial, 19–10, 22–3, 102,
114–15, 140–171
Reineking, Karl, 187–90,
205–6, 210–13, 269, 301–4, 306
Reineking, Kurt, 206, 210
Ribbentrop, Joachim von, 53, 181,
214, 218, 257, 272
Riefenstahl, Leni, 28
Riess, Curt, 220, 255, 301,
304
Ritter, Franz, 112, 116, 299
Roeder, Manfred, 279
Roesen, Anton, 227–28, 302
Rohan, Karl Anton von, 78
Röhm, Ernst, 34, 40, 46, 58, 68, 79,
130–32, 144, 176–77, 202, 272,
330
Rosenberg, Alfred, 99, 123–24

Rote Fahne, 31, 50, 81, 124, 127
Roth, Joseph, 80
Rothfels, Hans, 283–84, 289–90,
296–97, 300
Röver, Karl, 63, 65
Rumbold, Horace, 64
Rust, Bernhard, 75

SA (*Sturmabteilungen*), 16, 33–34, 37,
41–59, 65–69, 72, 74–79, 82–84,
87, 99–100, 106–7, 111, 115,
122–23, 129–32, 135, 138, 144–45,
152, 154–55, 166, 171, 174–76,
179, 182, 186–98, 201–6, 209–14,
224, 232–33, 253–5, 272, 301–7,
318–20
Sachs, Hans, 224
Sack, Alfons, 54, 110, 141, 144–46,
150, 152, 163–64, 176, 263
Sackett, Frederic M., 73, 78
Salomon, Ernst von, 81
Schacht, Hjalmar, 27, 185, 218,
221
Schatz, Wilhelm, 112, 114–15,
120–21, 151–53, 165, 205, 207,
269, 299
Scheer, Jonny, 174, 204, 210, 224
Scheidemann, Philipp, 81
Schildhauer, Peter, 117–18,
361n110
Schleicher, Kurt von, 33, 60–62, 68,
70, 176
Schmidt, Paul Karl, 256–58,
263–64, 270, 280, 289–90, 297,
323–24
Schmidt, Willi (*Schweinebacke*), 34,
174–75, 187, 202–4, 206, 210,
212–13, 224, 310
Schmidt-Hannover, Otto, 66, 79, 137,
237

Schneider, Hans, 289–94, 305, 314–15
Schnitzler, Heinrich, 18–19, 25, 33, 117, 144, 183, 219–20, 222, 225–34, 237, 240, 244–45, 262, 264–65, 274–6, 299, 302, 308, 316–17, 401
Schönhaar, Eugen, 174
Schrübbers, Hubert, 276
Schüle, Erwin, 258–59
Schulze-Wilde, Harry, 210–11, 262, 301–4, 306–7
Schwartz, Rudolf, 174
schwarze Reichswehr, 47
Scranowitz, Alexander, 10–12, 14, 95, 101, 114, 120, 149, 153
Seuffert, Philipp, 141, 166, 169
Severing, Carl, 30–32, 63, 77, 225, 227, 231–32, 238
SD (*Sicherheitsdienst*), 183, 222, 224, 243–44
Shirer, William, 177, 285
"Shooting Decree," 71–72
Snyder, Timothy, 173, 200, 325
Social Democratic Party of Germany, 30
Söderman, Harry, 143
Soldatenzeitung, 288
Solmitz, Luise, 98
Sommerfeldt, Martin, 34, 69, 85–86, 88, 105, 134, 145, 196, 214, 218, 229, 319–20, 355n1
Spengler, Oswald, 40
SPD. *See* Social Democratic Party of Germany
Spiegel, 20–21, 120, 205, 234–35, 238–41, 243–44, 250–51, 256–58, 262–70, 272, 280–81, 285–86, 290, 301, 305, 315, 317, 323

Sprecher, Drexel, 182–83
SS (*Schutzstaffel*) 18, 25, 27–28, 33, 72, 128, 175, 177–79, 182–83, 198–200, 204–6, 216–17, 224–25, 228, 233, 240, 249, 261, 305, 326
Stalin, Joseph, 23, 73, 129, 172–3, 258
Stampfer, Friedrich, 62, 73, 78, 353n46
Starker, Kurt, 91–92
Starker, Margarete, 92
Steel Helmet (*Stahlhelm*), 22, 46, 53, 56, 61, 72, 106
Stegerwald, Adam, 71
Steinfurth, Erich, 128, 174
Steinle, Rudolf, 131
Stenig, Paul, 55–56
Stennes, Walter, 51–54, 75, 158
Stephan, Karl, 113, 118–19, 311, 360–62n110
Stern, 255, 304
Strasser, Gregor, 40, 61, 176
Strasser, Otto, 136, 320
Strindberg, Friedrich, 210, 301, 303–4, 306–7

Tanev, Vasil, 109, 141, 148–49, 164, 172, 232, 329
Taylor, A.J.P., 21, 215, 330
Teichert, Paul, 141, 148, 173
Tejessy, Fritz, 26–27, 228
Telegraaf (Amsterdam), 171
Thadden, Adolf von, 191, 305
Thaler, Werner, 8–9, 94, 267–68
Thälmann, Ernst, 110, 124, 175
Thimme, Annelise, 98–99
Thimme, Friedrich, 98–99
Times (London), 104, 116, 125, 129, 140

Tobias, Fritz, 20–21, 24–25, 34, 73, 79, 91, 93, 101–3, 107, 112, 116, 119–20, 128, 131–33, 135, 143–44, 146, 151, 158, 174–76, 189–93, 205, 213, 245–47, 248–82, 285–92, 294, 296–302, 305–6, 308, 310–11, 313–18, 322–25, 328–33, 387n76, 391n57, 391n58

Torgler, Ernst, 8, 31–34, 64, 77–78, 109–11, 120, 129–30, 136–37, 141, 144–46, 148–51, 154, 156, 159, 163–64, 171, 174, 184, 225, 234, 320, 329

Treviranus, Gottfried, 62

Turnerschaft Ulrich von Hutten, 46–47

Ulbricht, Walter, 127

Ulm *Einsatzgruppen* trial, 204, 258–59

Unger, Helmuth, 204

Unit for Special Missions (SA *Sondereinheit zur besonderen Verwendung*), 84, 115, 152, 211, 303

"Valkyrie" resistance, 18, 54, 64–65, 183, 184–86, 188, 194, 226, 235, 277, 295

van der Lubbe, Johannes Marcus (J.M.), 251–52, 255

van der Lubbe, Marinus, 7, 14, 19–20, 87–96, 98–121, 123, 130, 133–34, 140–48, 150–53, 156, 159–66, 168–71, 188, 195–96, 214, 219, 223, 227, 232–35, 245, 252–55, 264, 266, 270, 273, 282, 307–8, 315–19, 321, 327

Victory Column (*Siegessäule*), 80

Vierteljahrshefte für Zeitgeschichte, 284, 289, 294, 298

Viking League, 45, 47

Vink, Jacobus, 111, 146

Vogt, Paul, 92, 95, 109–10, 112, 164–65, 251, 254, 264, 271

Voigt, Frederick, 126, 136–39

Volk, Hans, 108

Völkischer Beobachter 8, 46, 104, 111, 134, 152, 267–68, 297

Vorwärts, 62, 71, 98, 136

Vossische Zeitung, 50, 190

VVN. *See* Association of Persecutees of the Nazi Regime

Wäckerle, Hilmar, 128

Wagner, Gustav, 112–15, 132, 151, 299, 361n110

Waldberg, Max von, 39

Wallot, Paul, 3, 4, 149, 326

Weber, Lothar, 121

Wecke, Walther, 53, 68, 70

Wehner, Bernhard, 244–45, 247, 250–51, 260, 262, 271

Wehner, Herbert, 34

Weimar Republic, 4, 5, 22, 29–30, 45, 53, 56–57, 62–63, 82, 96–97, 107, 178, 251, 269, 307, 323

Weinke, Annette, 281

Weiss, Eduard, 49–50

Welt am Abend, 127

Weltbild, 256, 303

Wendt, Albert, 111, 151

Werner, Karl, 108, 140, 146, 148, 151, 153, 159, 162–63, 169–70, 235

Wessel, Horst, 35, 41, 47–48, 203

WGG. *See* Law for Restitution for National Socialist Injustice

White Book, 130–31, 255, 311

Wiener Allgemeine Zeitung, 122

Wildt, Michael, 24, 322

Wilhelm I, 5, 77

Wilhelm II, 4, 203

Wippermann, Wolfgang, 133

Wolff, Richard, 13, 196, 246, 266, 284–85, 287, 290, 301

Wolff, Theodor, 313

Young, Owen D., 81

Young Plan, 81–82

Zauritz, Josef, 42–43, 106

Zeit, 21, 285, 297, 301, 308, 311–15

Ziesel, Kurt, 287, 296–97, 324

Zirpins, Walter, 87–88, 93, 95, 100–102, 104–7, 116–18, 146–48, 164–65, 219–21, 226, 229–30, 232–33, 241–47, 250–51, 260, 262–65, 267–73, 280–81, 289–90, 298, 308, 316, 322, 324–25, 385n59

Zörgiebel, Karl, 82